Culture, Nation, and Identity: The Ukrainian-Russian Encounter (1600–1945)

Culture, Nation, and Identity
The Ukrainian-Russian Encounter
(1600–1945)

Edited by

Andreas Kappeler, Zenon E. Kohut, Frank E. Sysyn, and Mark von Hagen

КІУС
CIUS

Canadian Institute of Ukrainian Studies Press
Edmonton 2003 Toronto

Canadian Institute of Ukrainian Studies Press

University of Alberta
Edmonton, Alberta
T6G 2E8 CANADA

University of Toronto
Toronto, Ontario
M5S 2J5 CANADA

ISBN 1-895571-46-4 (bound); ISBN 1-895571-47-2 (pbk.)

National Library of Canada Cataloguing in Publication Data

Culture, nation, and identity: the Ukrainian-Russian encounter, 1600–1945
edited by Andreas Kappeler, Zenon E. Kohut, Frank E. Sysyn ... [et al.].

Includes bibliographical references.
ISBN 1–895571–46–4 (bound). —ISBN 1–895571–47–2 (pbk.)

1. Ukraine—Relations—Russia. 2. Russia—Relations—Ukraine.
3. Ukraine—Relations—Soviet Union. 4. Soviet Union— Relations—Ukraine.
5. Nationalism—Ukraine—History. 6. Ukrainians—Ethnic identity—History.
I. Kappeler, Andreas II. Kohut, Zenon E. III. Sysyn, Frank E.

DK508.57.R9C84 2003 303.48'2477047 2003-900667–0

Publication of this book has been generously supported by the Ukrainian Studies Fund, Inc., New York, NY.

Cover: fragments of antiquarian maps of Ukraine reproduced, by permission, from Bohdan S. Kordan, *Land of the Cossacks*, Winnipeg, 1987.

Printed in Canada

Table of Contents

Preface

The series of sessions on the Russian-Ukrainian encounter held alternately in New York and Cologne, Germany, between June 1994 and September 1995 had their origin in both the macro world of great political events and the micro world of scholarly discussions. Ukraine's declaration of independence following the August 1991 coup in Moscow, ratified by the referendum of 1 December 1991 and subsequent international recognition, was followed by the dissolution of the Soviet Union on 25 December 1991. These developments made Ukrainian-Russian relations an international issue of cardinal importance. A new, difficult, and uncertain phase of these relations opened with the establishment of two independent neighboring states. Since Russia was clearly to remain a major world power, while Ukraine was the largest and one of the most populous states of Europe, those relations took on more than binational significance. The future of the post-Soviet order depended largely on how these two largely Slavic countries would work out their relations. The fact that both possessed nuclear weapons compelled world leaders to take an interest in the course of those relations.

While these dramatic international events made broader scholarly and political circles newly aware of the importance of Russian-Ukrainian relations, the content of the sessions in New York and Cologne was shaped more directly by the scholarly interests of the four members of the organizing committee, Andreas Kappeler, Mark von Hagen, Zenon Kohut, and Frank Sysyn. Andreas Kappeler's work on the peoples of the Volga and the multinational character of the Russian Empire had made him aware of the importance of the Ukrainians, the largest non-Russian people in tsarist Russia and the Soviet Union. Mark von Hagen's work on the Red Army provoked his interest in the importance of nationality issues in both the Russian Empire and the Soviet Union, which were being explored by numerous specialists in Ukrainian and other non-Russian nationality studies in North America. Zenon Kohut had long devoted his primary research to Ukrainian-Russian relations in the late eighteenth and early nineteenth centuries. While Frank Sysyn had primarily worked on Ukraine as part of the Polish-Lithuanian Commonwealth, his seventeenth-century specialization led him to focus on the first phase of the Russian-Ukrainian encounter. The first two colleagues might be considered typical post-World War II historians of Russia, typical also by virtue of their non-Slavic descent, whose research had awakened them to the importance of Russian-Ukrainian relations. The latter two were more typical Western specialists in Ukrainian studies, a profile that included sharing Ukrainian descent and having worked in the two major North American institutes of Ukrainian studies. The organizers were united in their belief that the current situation presented an opportunity to attract scholarly interest to this important problem, to explore new paradigms and methods, and to promote further discussion by historians in Ukraine and Russia.

The term "encounter" was borrowed from the title of a volume of conference papers published by the Canadian Institute of Ukrainian Studies in 1992. As a definition of the subject that the organizers wished to explore, this term was more suitable than "relations," which assumed the existence of two fully autonomous polities or cultures. "Encounter" allowed for an examination of all the ambiguities of national, international, transnational, and subnational issues that had developed in the course of three centuries of Russian and Ukrainian interaction. While we sought to make the examination interdisciplinary and comparative, our historical approach was apparent in the chronological organization of the sessions and in the dominance of historians among participants in all sessions except the last, which focused on the post-1991 period.

We embarked upon our project with a certain set of assumptions. We believed that aside from specialists in the early modern period, few scholars in Russian studies had pondered, much less studied, Russian-Ukrainian questions. By contrast, we presumed that most Western specialists in Ukrainian studies were well acquainted with these questions, but had often had to frame their research in such a way as to defend the very validity of Ukrainian studies and their significance for understanding Russian-Ukrainian relations. Consequently, our goal was to encourage scholars in traditional Russian studies to pose questions rather than to present ready-made answers if they had not previously worked on these issues, and to urge specialists in Ukrainian studies to shift their focus from the impact of Russia on Ukraine in order to consider the significance of Ukrainian issues for Russian identity, the tsarist empire, and the Soviet state. Hoping to invite colleagues from Russia and Ukraine to participate in our sessions, we expected that the mindset prevailing among colleagues in the West would be replicated in Ukraine and Russia. We anticipated greater reluctance on the part of Russian scholars to address these questions, which had become so politically charged in the early 1990s.

Essential to our quest was to understand the construction, destruction, and reformulation of identities among Russians and Ukrainians of all social origins. This entailed an examination of the emergence of national identity, a question much studied with reference to the Ukrainians and less so with reference to the Russians. The question is fundamentally important because of historical efforts to create common "all-Russian" and East Slavic identities and because of the implications of Ukrainian independence for the redefinition of Russian identity. But the identities to be explored within the Russian and Ukrainian contexts also impinged on other basic concerns, from religion (*Slavia Orthodoxa,* Uniatism) to social status (Cossack identity, rural and urban speech) to the Soviet internationalist experiment. Central to the subject was the role of states and state formations: Muscovy, the Polish-Lithuanian Commonwealth, the Cossack Hetmanate, the Russian Empire, the Habsburg Monarchy, independent Ukraine (1917–20), the Soviet Union, including the RFSFR and the Ukrainian SSR, interwar Poland, Romania, and Czechoslovakia, and Ukraine and Russia since 1991 (as well as the Commonwealth of Independent States). The fact that from the sixteenth century to 1991 almost all Russians lived within a single state (a Russian state for those who view the Soviet Union as such), while from the seventeenth century at least until World War II Ukrainians were divided among various states, was seen as essential for understanding the evolution of their encounter. The extent of Russia's self-perception as a successor state to the USSR and of Ukraine's acceptance or rejection of its Soviet legacy was seen as crucial in defining the two states' current relations and the nature of the present-day Russian-Ukrainian encounter.

Aside from having shared political boundaries, Ukrainians and Russians professing various identities participated jointly in numerous organizations, institutions, and endeavors, such as Orthodox monasteries, the tsarist army, the Soviet space program, and the colonization of Siberia and Kazakhstan. Without assuming a priori that the Russian-Ukrainian factor is important for all areas of Russian-Ukrainian interaction, the organizers hoped that the question would be addressed in relation to these and many other endeavors and structures. At the same time, they sought to promote comparative studies of segments of society and institutions, whether on a global Russian-Ukrainian basis or, more manageably, on a regional basis. It was hoped that specialists in imperial Russia and the Soviet Union who have usually based their conclusions on evidence originating in Moscow, St. Petersburg, or the Russian heartland would come to examine Ukrainian cases, while specialists on Ukraine would place their research in a new comparative context.

The agenda was large and could not be exhausted in forty, much less four, sessions. The organizers were grateful that so many of their colleagues took up the challenge. As expected, specialists in Ukrainian studies proved much more likely to accept our invitations than those in Russian studies. We also found that even among Russian specialists, North American colleagues were much more likely to respond positively than German colleagues. This may have been due to the North American think-piece format and our peculiar conference culture, but it may also reflect the greater development of nationality studies and research on the non-Russian peoples in North America. The organizers had particular difficulty in finding colleagues from Russia willing to participate in the project.

As might be expected, each session had its own dynamic. The first, which focused on the early modern period and was held in Cologne (15–17 June 1994), assembled a group of scholars most of whom were personally acquainted and knew one another's work. If their papers seemed arcane to the non-specialist, they often fit into a well-developed context of cultural and religious studies. To some extent, the early modern topics were addressed more easily than those of later periods, as there is a consensus on the considerable differences between Russians and Ukrainians in this period and on the importance of the Ukrainian role in cultural transfer to Russia. Nevertheless, the comments of Professor Mikhail Dmitriev of Moscow, who argued for the uniformity of the Eastern Slavs at the time, added greatly to the debate.

The second session, which was held in New York (13–15 November 1994), elicited considerable interest among specialists in imperial Russia. It also broadened the range of fields, adding specialists in anthropology and social history to the literary and cultural fields of the first session, and addressed current interdisciplinary debates, such as the degree to which the Russian-Ukrainian relationship was colonial.

The third session, held in Cologne (15–17 June 1995), dealt with the twentieth century—a period of manifest significance in Russian-Ukrainian relations, since it began with an attempt to establish an independent Ukrainian state and was followed by the formation of the Soviet Union, which comprised both Ukrainian and Russian entities. It involved the very prickly question of whether the Soviet state was Russian and the degree to which communist and Soviet policies were rooted in Russian-Ukrainian relations, especially during the famine of 1932–33 and World War II. The presence of Professor Ronald Suny, who has argued for the positive role of the Soviet period in the nation-building of non-Russian peoples, helped ensure a productive discussion.

The fourth session, held in New York (21–23 September 1995) with the participation of the Russian and Ukrainian ambassadors to the United Nations, reflected the acute interest in Russian-Ukrainian relations on the part of current-affairs specialists. Political scientists, sociologists, and scholars of international affairs overshadowed historians and literary specialists at this session. Given the need to make these observations and analyses immediately available, the papers were published immediately after the session in the *Harriman Review*.

While a primary goal of the organizers was to spark discussion among participants, they also sought to identify scholars who might expand their presentations into research papers. The papers assembled here, culled from the first three sessions of the Russian-Ukrainian encounter series, represent only a fraction of the questions addressed at the sessions. In addition to their individual contributions to scholarship, they serve collectively as a contribution to the study of the Russian-Ukrainian encounter, indicating topics worthy of future research and discussion.

The Early Modern Period

In his article, "The Question of Russo-Ukrainian Unity and Ukrainian Distinctiveness in Early Modern Ukrainian Thought and Culture," Zenon Kohut traces the Ukrainian role in constructing Great Russia and Little Russia as components of an all-Russian unity, as well as the evolution of Little Russian identity until the emergence of the modern Ukrainian national movement. In examining the concept of Ukrainian-Russian unity as an intellectual construct that took shape before the political, social, religious, and cultural merging of Ukraine and Russia in the seventeenth century, Kohut offers an analysis that permits comparison with other early modern supranational constructs (the Polish-Lithuanian Commonwealth, Illyrianism, British identity) and shows how divergent have been the interpretations of the early modern period in subsequent Russian and Ukrainian traditions. In "Lazar Baranovych, 1680: The Union of Lech and Rus," David Frick recreates the political and spiritual world of a prominent Ukrainian intellectual to demonstrate how long Poland remained important in defining Ruthenians and their relations with Muscovy. Frank E. Sysyn analyzes the terminology and content of early modern Ukrainian historical works that formed the image of Muscovy. The increasing importance of Ukrainians and their culture in Muscovy is demonstrated in the late Hans-Joachim Torke's "Moscow and Its West: On the 'Ruthenization' of Russian Culture in the Seventeenth Century." This process occurred largely because of the blurring of the distinction between Ukraine and Russia, which was greatly advanced by the amalgamation of the Orthodox churches, here examined by Viktor Zhivov.

The Imperial Period

Paul Bushkovitch calls into question the long-term impact for Russian national identity of the concepts of nation and society that reached Russia from Ukraine, as well as of the construct of Little and Great Russian unity. He sees the dynasty and state as essential in defining Russian identity and describes the period of Ukrainian influence, which he terms baroque Slavicism, as relatively short. With the annexation of non-East Slavic territories to the Russian state and the increasing influence of Western imperial thought, Russia, according to Buskovitch, adopted a non-ethnic definition of nationality that lasted almost until the end of the empire. For him, the unity of the Great and Little Russians was another example of non-ethnic conceptualization. Andreas Kappeler expands the comparative approach to all the peoples of the empire in his discussion of the imperial ethnic hierarchy. His article, "*Mazepintsy, Malorossy, Khokhly*: Ukrainians in the Ethnic Hierarchy of the Russian Empire," designates various types of Ukrainians, paying special attention to the role of social estates in determining the status of each ethnic group. He also discusses the applicability to Russian-Ukrainian relations of such terms as "Russification" and "colonialism."

Olga Andriewsky's contribution emphasizes that, despite the loss of Ukrainian autonomy in the late eighteenth and early nineteenth centuries, a Russian-Ukrainian intellectual discourse subsequently developed. In addition to showing how everything "Little Russian" became devalued in Russian eyes, so that "all-Russian" became in practice "Great Russian," she examines assertions of Russian identity as ethno-national (or East Slavic) and shows how a Russian state and dynastic identity could assert claims to "Subjugated Rus'" (Western Ukraine) under the Habsburgs. George Grabowicz examines the role of *kotliarevshchyna* in order to develop the question of Russian perception of Ukrainians and the forms chosen by Ukrainians in Russian-Ukrainian literary discourse. Serhy Yekelchyk discusses the presentation of the official scheme of "all-Russian" history in textbooks and how it came to be rejected by leaders of the Ukrainian national revival. Christine Worobec turns our attention to social history per se and the comparative study of the Ukrainian and Russian peasantry. In this discussion, she questions such generally held views as the deleterious nature of the bans on the Ukrainian language for the education of the Ukrainian peasantry.

The Twentieth Century

Social groups and class-based ideologies, as well as a broadly focused treatment of nationality questions in the Russian Empire and the Soviet Union, are featured in Mark von Hagen's contribution. He stresses the importance of the First World War in bringing national issues to the fore and examines how imperial and earlier Russian-Ukrainian relations were recast in the Soviet period under the aegis of Bolshevik ideology. The deconstruction and reformulation of the Russian imperial model under the impact of rising national consciousness, treated from the political viewpoint by von Hagen, is undertaken for cultural affairs by Oleh Ilnytzkyj. Locating the deconstruction of the "all-Russian" paradigm in the decade preceding the Revolution, Ilnytzkyj sees the Ukrainian cultural renaissance of the 1920s as the establishment of a fully autonomous Ukrainian culture, an event never fully accepted in Russian intellectual circles.

Stanislav Kulchytsky examines how the Moscow center came to accept a form of Soviet statehood that gave equal status to the Russian and Ukrainian republics. He demonstrates the importance of this arrangement for Russian-Ukrainian relations despite the centralized nature of the Soviet state. In his article on the GPU-NKVD as an instrument of counter-Ukrainization, Yuri Shapoval illustrates how the creation of a Ukrainian SSR with a Ukrainian face in the 1920s was undone by the organs of political terror. In so doing, he shows how in practice the Soviet state came to promote Russification by attacking Ukrainian autonomy as "bourgeois nationalism." The mass loss of life during the famine and terror of the 1930s and in the course of World War II had a tremendous impact on the demographic, cultural, and political balance between Ukraine and Russia. While this topic has been given considerable attention for the 1930s, especially in discussions of the famine, less attention has been paid to World War II. Dieter Pohl comprehensively examines the policies of the German occupation authorities and their influence on Ukrainians and Russians. He concludes that in the long run the war hastened the Russification of Ukraine.

The contributions to this volume deal only with select aspects of the Russian-Ukrainian encounter. At the third session, relatively few speakers addressed developments between World War II and the break-up of the Soviet Union, perhaps reflecting the limited amount of work done on this period. Economics, anthropology, sociology, and sociolinguistics are sorely missing. The history of women, the professions, religious institutions, and so on has rarely integrated the Russian-Ukrainian aspect. The opening of archives, the training of a new generation of scholars in Russia, Ukraine, and the West, and the greater prominence of the field should serve to promote the development of research on the Russian-Ukrainian encounter and diffuse it to the whole gamut of research on the states and societies in which Russians and Ukrainians lived.

Andreas Kappeler, Zenon Kohut, Frank Sysyn, Mark von Hagen

Note on Transliteration

The names of Ukrainian, Russian, and Belarusian people and places are transliterated in the text according to the simplified Library of Congress system, i.e., without diacritics. The full Library of Congress system, indicating soft signs and other diacritics, is used to transliterate all Cyrillic titles in the footnotes.

Viktor Zhivov

The Question of Ecclesiastical Jurisdiction in Russian-Ukrainian Relations (Seventeenth and Early Eighteenth Centuries)

I

Events at the turn of the seventeenth century that brought about conflict between Russia and Ukraine confronted Russian and Ukrainian elites with the task of constructing anew the conceptual foundations that defined their perceptions of one another. Such events were, first and foremost, the establishment of the Moscow patriarchate in 1589, which gave the Russian church a status different in principle from that of the Ukrainian church; the Union of Brest, which divided Ukrainian society and presented Moscow with the problem of taking a position with regard to those who had renounced the Union; and the Time of Troubles, which brought Russians and Ukrainians face to face for the first time and ended the continuity of Muscovite traditions, including those in the ecclesiastical and religious sphere. The question of ethnic relations is closely associated with religious issues, including the question of ecclesiastical jurisdiction.

As it developed a new view of itself and its milieu following the Time of Troubles, Muscovite Rus' perceived itself above all as an Orthodox power that had been subjected to attack by adherents of alien faiths, but had managed to defend its status as the sole Orthodox realm (an autocratic tsar and a sovereign patriarch proved to be the most important parameters of this conceptualization). This definition of the outside world as one professing alien faiths also applied to Ukraine, with reference to its Orthodox and non-Orthodox populations alike. This is manifest, for example, in the decision of the Council of 1620 concerning the obligatory rebaptism of emigrants from Lithuanian Rus', no matter whether they were Catholics, Uniates or Orthodox.[1] No less typical was the suspicion evidenced toward church books printed in Lithuania, which subjects of the Muscovite state were forbidden to import, buy, or even have in their homes, for

---

1. K. V. Kharlampovich, *Malorossiiskoe vliianie na velikorusskuiu tserkovnuiu zhizn'*, vol. 1 (Kazan, 1914, repr. The Hague and Paris, 1968), pp. 21–24.

according to a decree of 1627, "various books published in Lithuania [contain] many Latin heresies."[2] Facts such as these speak of a prevailing conviction that the faith of Muscovy's Orthodox neighbors had become tainted. This religious perception was transformed into an ethnic one as well.

Lavrentii Zyzanii's debates with Moscow scribes in 1627 are revealing in this regard. Accusing Zyzanii of dogmatic errors—that is, ascribing to him some sort of different faith—the Moscow scribes regarded even his language as alien, as is apparent from their question, "How do you say *sobra* ["gathered"] in Lithuanian? And Lavrentii answered that in Lithuanian the word is also *sobra*."[3] Although this was a mere matter of different versions of Church Slavonic, which was mutually comprehensible to the disputing parties, a difference in language was being postulated here, presupposing an ethnic difference. As a result, a difference in faith became a difference in nationality.

A new attitude took shape gradually, beginning in the 1640s. The original stimulus for it came from attempts at the religious reform of Russian society, especially those associated with the circle of Lovers of God (or Zealots of Piety), but initiated even earlier. At this time, the need for religious instruction prompted them to profit from the achievements of the Ukrainian church. As a result, editions of the *Book of Kirill* (1644), *Book of Faith* (1648), and Meletii Smotrytsky's grammar of Church Slavonic (1648) were published in Moscow. These developments bore no relation either to ethnic consciousness or to canonical issues, but they did reinforce the perception of the Ukrainian church as a church of the same faith, without eliminating all suspicion in this regard. This perception made it possible to consider ethnic differences (national identity) as something separate from religious differences (religious identity)—a potentially important innovation.

The concept of the Muscovite empire as a new Byzantium, evidently adopted by Tsar Aleksei Mikhailovich during the early years of his reign, introduced a fundamentally new idea. The concept of a Christian empire in its Russian version presupposed the rule of the monarch over a variety of Christian peoples united under his

---

2. *Akty Moskovskogo gosudarstva, izdannye Imp. Akademiei nauk,* ed. N. A. Popov (St. Petersburg, 1890–94), vol. 1, no. 201.

3. "Prenie litovskogo protopopa Lavrentiia Zizaniia s igumenom Il'eiu i spravshchikom Grigoriem po voprosu ispravleniia sostavlennogo Lavrentiem katekhizisa," in *Letopisi russkoi literatury i drevnosti,* ed. N. S. Tikhonravov, vol. 2 (Moscow, 1859), p. 81.

authority into a new Orthodox *oikoumenē*. This concept did not require ethnic uniformity. On the contrary, it even presupposed ethnic heterogeneity, although it naturally elicited political actions that were significant for ethnic consciousness. It induced Moscow to resolve on the annexation of Ukraine, which would hardly have been possible under the previous isolationist stance. One of the premises of this decision was the conception of Ukrainians as a people of the same faith, a conception prepared by previous developments.

The imperial model posed questions of a canonical nature, but offered no consistent solution to them. The model of Byzantium, which Aleksei Mikhailovich took as his point of departure, could be interpreted in a variety of ways. In seventeenth-century Russia, it was refracted through innumerable conceptualizations of a political reality that no longer existed. The tsar, taking the Byzantine *basileus* as his model, could head an empire composed of several regions, each enjoying religious autonomy. This imparted to the tsar a uniting (and consequently, to a certain degree, ruling) authority. Generally speaking, such a model could be applied to Russia. For example, in conversations with the Greeks, Arsenii Sukhanov announced that "instead of a pope, the tsar has established a patriarch in the imperial city of Moscow, and instead of your four patriarchs he has four metropolitans."[4] No attempt was made, however, at a full-scale implementation of this model. For Russian-Ukrainian relations, this meant that Kyiv could remain outside the jurisdiction of the Moscow patriarch even after the annexation of Ukraine.

Another interpretation of the Byzantine model treated the tsar and the patriarch as a "sacred dyarchy" or a "divinely elected twofold entity."[5] This interpretation was supported by the teachings of the *Epanagoga* concerning the symphonic relations between emperor and patriarch: they presupposed a parallelism between the authority of the tsar in the secular sphere and that of the patriarch in the religious sphere. In this instance, the treatment of the Byzantine precedent singled out the special relationship between the *basileus* and the patriarch of Constantinople, and was historically associated with the claims of the latter to head the whole Eastern church. In general terms, the implementation of this model should have brought regions newly annexed to the empire under the jurisdiction of the Moscow

---

4. N. F. Kapterev, *Kharakter otnoshenii Rossii k Pravoslavnomu Vostoku v XVI i XVII stoletiiakh* (Sergiev Posad, 1914), p. 391.

5. See Nikon's *Sluzhebnik* (1656), pp. 21, 22, 34, 40.

patriarch. During the reign of Aleksei Mikhailovich, this model also was not consistently applied.

It might nevertheless appear that at the beginning of Aleksei Mikhailovich's reign, when Nikon held the patriarch's throne, the second model was the point of departure. That model is consistent with Nikon's liturgical reforms and the correction of liturgical books, which were carried out concurrently. One of the consequences of this reform (to what extent it was a fundamental goal is open to debate) was to bring about a rapprochement of Muscovite and Ukrainian liturgical observance, while the correction of liturgical books led to the development of a single (in N. S. Trubetskoi's terminology, "pan-Russian"[6]) recension of the Church Slavonic language, which synthesized elements of the Muscovite and Ukrainian recensions. It was also Nikon, first and foremost, who introduced Ukrainian observances into the ritual of the Russian church (an attempt to exert influence in the opposite direction would have exceeded the limits of his authority). In developing his scheme of religious enlightenment, Nikon enlisted the services of Ukrainian scribes for his reforms, evidently intending to create in Moscow an ecclesiastical culture not inferior to that of Kyiv and capable of claiming universal significance in the Orthodox realm. These experiments in "equalization" may be regarded as establishing preconditions for canonical union, that is, the implementation of the second "imperial" model.

The developments just mentioned are all related to ecclesiastical jurisdiction. Although Moscow made no overt move toward the subordination of the Kyivan metropolitan see, Nikon could style himself Patriarch of Great, Little and White Russia, which corresponded to the tsar's new imperial title and raised the prospect of uniting all the eparchies of the expanding empire under the jurisdiction of the Moscow patriarch. Moreover, once the authority of the Muscovite monarch had been established in the Belarusian sees—those of Polatsk, Mahilioŭ, and Smolensk—they were removed from the authority of the Kyivan metropolitan (and the patriarch of Constantinople) in 1654–67 and transferred to Nikon's jurisdiction.[7]

---

6. N. S. Trubetskoi, *Istoriia. Kul'tura. Iazyk,* ed. V. M. Zhivov (Moscow, 1995), pp. 173–74.

7. Kharlampovich, *Malorossiiskoe vliianie*, pp. 179–71. It is significant in this connection that the newly appointed bishop of Smolensk, Filaret, "entered into conflict with church observances there and began to crush the 'liberties' of the clergy and called the priests 'adherents of different creeds'" (ibid., p. 172). These actions were perceived as a potential threat by the Ukrainian clergy (specifically by locum tenens Metodii Fylymonovych), who supposed that in

This may be regarded as a partial implementation of the model of the "divinely elected twofold entity."

Whether full implementation was contemplated remains unclear. At the Pereiaslav Council of 1659, the Muscovite voevoda Prince A. N. Trubetskoi proposed a treaty clause whereby "the Kyivan metropolitan ... is to be under the benediction of the holy patriarch of Moscow and of all Great, Little and White Russia."[8] Nevertheless, the Muscovite government made no sustained effort to put this clause into practice. Although a number of reasons may be suggested for this official reticence (unwillingness to strain relations with the patriarch of Constantinople during the Nikon affair; fears for the eparchies in Right-Bank Ukraine), it seems likely that the most important underlying factor was a shift in conceptualization from the second imperial model to the first. In his struggle with Patriarch Nikon, Aleksei Mikhailovich clearly had no desire to enhance Nikon's patriarchal authority by endowing the latter with a status comparable to his own (indeed, one of the accusations against Nikon was that he had assumed the title "grand sovereign"). Moreover, given that the model of the "sacred dyarchy" was discredited, not only with regard to Patriarch Nikon, but also to his successors, the subordination of the Kyivan metropolitan to the Moscow patriarch ceased to be a pressing question. In particular, the secular authorities did not support Bishop Aleksandr of Viatka, who gave a speech at the Great Council of Moscow (1666–67) proposing further measures to unify the churches within the imperial boundaries. Nor was there any response to Hetman Ivan Briukhovetsky's appeals to Moscow to install a Kyivan metropolitan.

This official reserve on the issue of jurisdiction may have been associated with the deliberate ambiguity, at times even inconsistency, that characterized the policy of Aleksei Mikhailovich toward the Old Believers. They attributed the corruption of the native tradition to the Ukrainian influence, which made them perceive Ukrainians as foreigners and adherents of a different creed. In his petition of the 1660s to Aleksei Mikhailovich, the monk Savvatii writes of "newly arrived *nekhai* (a derisive sobriquet meaning, one must think, emigrants from Kyiv) as those responsible for the heretical emenda-

---

the event of canonical subordination to Moscow, they could expect the same fate (*Arkhiv Iugo-Zapadnoi Rossii, izdavaemyi vremennoi komissiei,* vols. 5–12 [1872–1904], vol. 6, no. 30, p. 70). Thus the Ukrainian clergy fully acknowledged the possibility of the implementation of the second imperial model.

8. *Akty, otnosiashchiesia k istorii Iuzhnoi i Zapadnoi Rossii,* vol. 4, no. 114, p. 264.

tion of liturgical books.[9] At the same time, he introduced a note of ethnic confrontation into the religious polemic. The annexation to Moscow of the Kyivan metropolitan see, "belonging to a different creed," would have been regarded by the Old Believers as reinforcing a hateful order. By adopting a noncommittal attitude on the issue of jurisdiction, the tsar retained a certain freedom of action in relations with the Old Believer party (especially as regards the exertion of pressure on the ecclesiastical hierarchs in the event of their less than full compliance).

The situation changed only after the accession of Ioakim (Savelov) to the patriarch's throne and the death of Aleksei Mikhailovich. A natural weakening of the tsar's absolute power—particularly after the death of Fedor Alekseevich and the succession of the minors Petr and Ioann—strengthened the patriarch's influence in the administration. This was accompanied by a revival of the second imperial model, although there was no explicit reference to the "sacred dyarchy." In 1685 Ioakim ordained Hedeon Chetvertynsky, who was elected in Kyiv, as Kyivan metropolitan, thereby subordinating the Kyivan metropolitan see to himself. He also enlisted the support of Hetman Ivan Samoilovych, who considered that the patriarch of Moscow would not interfere directly in the affairs of the Ukrainian church and change the practices that had become established there. Ioakim obtained the approval of the patriarch of Constantinople with no particular difficulty; thus, in 1686, when Constantinople's assent was secured, the issue of jurisdiction seemed finally resolved.

This canonical act may be viewed as part of Ioakim's policy of religious unification. That policy applied both to the Old Believers, whose most severe persecutor was Ioakim, and to the Ukrainian eparchies. The ethnic component was completely removed from religious policy; in the eyes of the Muscovite authorities, religious identity overrode ethnic identity. The striving for doctrinal and ritual uniformity rendered irrelevant the Old Believers' view of Ukrainians as foreigners, since Ioakim and his associates stressed religious differences without associating them with ethnic differences. Ioakim's interference in Ukrainian affairs began immediately after the investiture of the Kyivan metropolitan and grew more intense with each passing year. Once again, as at the beginning of the century, Ukrainian books were subjected to church censorship, though with conse-

---

9. State Historical Museum, Moscow (henceforth GIM), Uvar. 497/102, 80^{v}; elements of a similar approach may be found in the declarations of Archpriest Avvakum.

quences materially different from those obtaining under Patriarch Filaret. In his time, Ukraine had been a foreign land, and the church could do no more than forbid the distribution in Moscow of Ukrainian books, which had resulted in the isolation of Muscovite learning. Now, since Kyiv was subject to Moscow, Muscovite practices were introduced in Ukraine. If earlier the Ukrainian recension of the Church Slavonic language could be termed a "foreign" language, now it was perceived as a deviation from the Muscovite norm that could be tolerated only to a limited degree. Indeed, in 1693 Patriarch Adrian allowed only the printing of brief works in the "local dialect," forbidding their distribution outside Ukrainian eparchies.[10] The well-known controversy between the Grecophiles and the Latinizers about the moment when the Eucharist was transubstantiated into flesh and blood may be viewed as an element of imperial church policy. Upon discovering a dangerous nonconformity in a newly established congregation (the so-called "bread-worshiping heresy"), Ioakim seized the opportunity to introduce an obligatory doctrine, thereby representing any local peculiarity as a sign of religious corruption and demanding as uncompromising a struggle with it, as with any foreign faith.[11] Thus the change of jurisdiction brought about a change in Moscow's whole approach to the ethnic and religious identity of Ukraine, just as the Ukrainian clergy had feared.

Under Patriarch Adrian there was no substantial change in these attitudes, although the new policy was not carried out as consistently or as harshly as under his predecessor. This mitigation was probably due to the gradual diminution of the patriarch's authority. Gaining ground with every step and moving the patriarch increasingly into the

---

10. *Arkhiv Iugo-Zapadnoi Rossii,* vol. 5, p. cxvii.

11. Patriarch Ioakim's attitude to foreign faiths was clearly apparent in his testament, in which he warned the tsars against relations between Orthodox and non-Orthodox (see M. M. Bogoslovskii, *Petr I: Materialy dlia biografii,* 5 vols. [Moscow, 1940–48], 1: 107; N. G. Ustrialov, *Istoriia tsarstvovaniia Petra Velikogo,* 4 vols. [St. Petersburg, 1858–59], 2: 472). Given Ioakim's approach, the Ukrainian clergy inevitably fell into the category of "church blasphemers," since they conducted the liturgy differently than in Moscow. It is instructive that the condemnation of the "bread-worshiping heresy" was introduced under Ioakim as a separate article of the hierarchal vows, which were also to be read at the installation of Ukrainian bishops: "Furthermore, I believe and hold true that the transubstantiation of Christ's body and blood takes place during the divine liturgy, as our ancient Eastern and Russian teachers have taught us, through the descent and action of the Holy Spirit, and through the summons of the hierarch, in the words of the prayer to God Our Father: make this bread the precious body of Thy Christ" (GIM, Sin. 344, f. 28^{v}).

background, Peter I, the creator of the new empire and a new imperial conception, advanced to center stage to force his autocracy, encompassing both the secular and the religious spheres, upon his subjects.

II

The death of Patriarch Adrian in 1700 gave Peter an opportunity to review the alignment of secular and spiritual authorities. It is unlikely, as some historians have argued, that the concept of collegial rule of the church occurred to Peter immediately following the death of Adrian and that he merely awaited an opportune moment for its implementation, while taking into account the possibility of clerical opposition. It was apparent, however, that Peter was not prepared to tolerate ecclesiastical independence even to the severely restricted extent to which it had existed under Adrian. Striving to extend his authority to the spiritual sphere, he would not permit the election of a new patriarch. Peter, however, could not (and apparently did not intend) immediately to destroy all the canonical foundations of ecclesiastical administration, and therefore found himself obliged to identify some form of canonical organization that would not be in glaring opposition to church tradition. From 1721, that form would be the Synod, but in order to establish this uncanonical institution, Peter had to reform the state as a whole and secure a degree of control over church and society that he did not yet possess in 1700. It is generally accepted that no new form of church administration came into being in 1700 and that ecclesiastical reorganization came to a halt after the adoption of the traditional inter-patriarchal regime. Such a development presupposes the presence of a locum tenens of the patriarchal throne, a role ascribed by historians to the metropolitan of Riazan, Stefan Iavorsky. However, as James Cracraft has correctly observed,[12] Stefan was not accorded that status in any contemporary document, which makes highly unlikely both the assertion of his status as locum tenens and the thesis that the years 1700–21 were indeed a period of inter-patriarchate.

Nevertheless, it may be argued that canonical practice changed after 1700 and that this change was significantly reflected in the conceptualization of relations between the Muscovite and Ukrainian ecclesiastical traditions. Changes in the ceremony of episcopal investiture, which established the responsibilities of the newly

---

12. James Cracraft, *The Church Reform of Peter the Great* (London, 1971), p. 111, note 3.

installed bishop and can therefore be regarded as a normative canonical document, attest to the new canonical practice. A new version of the vows compiled after the death of Patriarch Adrian remained in force until the establishment of the Synod. This version leaves no doubt that the Russian church, at least ostensibly, had come under the authority of the Eastern patriarchs. Thus, in the vows of Dionisii of Viatka and Great Perm, the last hierarch to be installed under Adrian (4 August 1700), we read: "I promise to follow in everything and always to obey my father, the great and most holy Adrian, Archbishop of Moscow and All Russia and Patriarch of all the northern lands. And [I promise] to be in complete agreement and unity with the future most holy patriarch of Moscow and All Russia (when he happens to be installed by the benevolence of God) and with all the holy Russian Council, with the most holy metropolitans, archbishops, and bishops, my fraternity."[13] In the vow of St. Dymytrii of Rostov (Tuptalo), the first hierarch ordained after Adrian's death (23 March 1701), we find a significant change in the phrase: "...to follow in everything and always to obey the universal, most holy four-throned patriarchs and the holy Russian Council."[14] Accordingly, at his installation every new hierarch vowed to submit to the Eastern patriarchs, which indicates that the Russian church, if only pro forma, was canonically subject precisely to them. This peculiar canonical fiction—peculiar because primacy in the church was simultaneously attributed to the four Eastern patriarchs, who were represented as an artificial unit of some kind—was maintained in the Russian church right up to 1721, that is, for more than two decades.[15]

---

13. GIM, Sin. 344, f. 23-23^{v}; cf. A. V. Gorskii and K. I. Nevostruev, *Opisanie slavianskikh rukopisei Moskovskoi Sinodal'noi biblioteki*, vol. 3, pt. 2 (Moscow, 1917), pp. 441-44.

14. GIM, Sin. 430, f. 85^{v}.

15. The perception of the four Eastern patriarchs as a single entity is attested by the fact that all of them in the aggregate may be called *universal*, although in reality the epithet in question belongs exclusively to the patriarch of Constantinople. Prokopovych touches upon this point: "There are also those who, out of ignorance, call all our four patriarchs universal patriarchs: for there is only one Universal Patriarch—the Patriarch of Constantinople" ([Feofan] Prokopovich, "O voznoshenii Imene patriarshago v tserkovnykh molitvakh: Cheso radi onoe nyne v tserkvakh rossiiskikh otstavleno" [St. Petersburg, 1721], pp. l, 8). Be that as it may, the designation of the four Eastern patriarchs as universal was common in Russian texts of the seventeenth century (e.g., *Patriarch Nikon on Church and State. Nikon's "Refutation,"* ed. V. A. Tumins and G. Vernadsky [Berlin, Amsterdam, and New York, 1982], p. 127; Ignatii Rimskii-Korsakov, *Tri poslaniia Blazhennogo Ignatiia,*

A number of circumstances attest to this canonical practice. These circumstances have long been known, but have been regarded only as curiosities with no institutional significance. Neither historians nor church scholars, as far as I know, have paid attention to the ceremony of the installation of hierarchs. In 1715, Peter sent two letters to Kosmas, the patriarch of Constantinople. In the first, Peter asks to be exempted from fasting, while in the second he asks that troops on the march be allowed to eat meat during all fasts. In the first letter it was explained that he was appealing to the patriarch of Constantinople "as the supreme and universal authority [of the Eastern church]."[16] After receiving letters in response, Peter issued them along with his decree[17] as binding on the whole Russian church, which indicates the subordination of the Russian church to the patriarch of Constantinople. That patriarch played a similar role as supreme authority when Peter petitioned him to decree that the baptism of Lutherans and Calvinists was not mandatory, and then enjoined Russian bishops to carry out that decision.[18] Thomas Consett speaks of the same canonical practice. In his description of the Synod, he states that Peter

---

Mitropolita Sibirskogo i Tobol'skogo: Tret'ie poslanie, in *Pravoslavnyi sobesednik*, bk. 2 [1855], p. 103) and may be viewed as established tradition. Characteristically, in announcing its recognition by the Eastern patriarchs, the Synod speaks of a "letter [received] from the Holy Universal Patriarchs" in which the Synod is acknowledged to be equal "to the throne of the four Universal Patriarchs" (*Polnoe sobranie postanovlenii i rasporiazhenii po vedomstvu pravoslavnogo ispovedaniia*, 10 vols. [St. Petersburg-Petrograd, 1869–1916], vol. 4, no. 1331, 22 July 1724, and no. 137, 3 August 1724). Given such an understanding of the situation, the Eastern patriarchs become almost interchangeable in status. It should be noted in this connection that the documents concerning the transfer of the Kyivan metropolitan see from the jurisdiction of the patriarch of Constantinople to that of the patriarch of Moscow were given by the patriarchs of Constantinople and Jerusalem (Kapterev, *Kharakter otnoshenii*, pp. 462–67), although the involvement of the patriarch of Jerusalem in this act had no canonical validity. Mention should also be made of the peculiar appeal of General Anikita Repnin to Dositheos, the patriarch of Jerusalem, with the request to permit him to marry a fourth time: "because no one other than you can grant permission and gracious indulgence, as our pastors do not have the power that you command" (*Pis'ma i bumagi imperatora Petra Velikogo*, 12 vols. [St. Petersburg and Moscow, 1887–1977], 3: 983). The patriarch of Jerusalem was apparently regarded as a supreme authority whose decisions were just as valid in the Russian church as those of the patriarch of Constantinople.

16. Kapterev, *Kharakter otnoshenii*, p. 550.

17. *Polnoe sobranie zakonov Rossiiskoi imperii* [collection 1], 45 vols. (St. Petersburg, 1830), vol. 5, no. 3020 and no. 3178.

18. Ibid., no. 3225, 31 August 1718.

"formed [his bishops...] into a Synod, and set himself as President at the Head of it; the Reasons of which Establishment are declar'd in the Book itself [i.e., the Spiritual Regulation]: but probably one Reason is conceal'd which may be apprehended, that he design'd to exempt himself and his Country from a Dependence on the Patriarchs of *Constantinople*."[19] Finally, it was precisely the question of canonical subordination to the Eastern patriarchs that served as the subtext for the bitter polemic about prayers for the "universal patriarchs" in which Teofan Prokopovych (Feofan Prokopovich) and Stefan Iavorsky engaged immediately after the establishment of the Synod.[20] In justifying the abolition of the prayers for the Eastern patriarchs, Prokopovych wrote in 1721 that such prayers were "nothing more than the profession of a previous subordination." Despite the evidence just cited, P. V. Verkhovskoi confidently asserts in his commentary on this passage : "From this one must draw the conclusion that prayers for the patriarchs in Russia could only be explained by the subordination of the Russian church, which *contradicts reality*."[21] Nevertheless, this peculiar canonical practice did not contradict reality, although it introduced an ambiguity and vagueness that was hardly in keeping with administrative efficiency.

---

19. James Cracraft, ed., *For God and Peter the Great: The Works of Thomas Consett, 1723–1729* (New York, 1982), p. xvi.

20. Prokopovych's text "O voznoshenii Imene patriarshago v tserkovnykh molitvakh: Cheso radi onoe nyne v tserkvakh rossiiskikh otstavleno" was published in 1721. Iavorsky's polemical question-and-answer "Apologiia ili slovesnaia oborona o voznoshenii iavstvennom, i vospominanii v molitvakh tserkovnykh, sviateishikh pravoslavnykh patriarkhov" has come down to us in manuscript (GIM, Uvar. 1728/378/588). In that same year of 1721, Iavorsky's text was banned by the Synod as "highly offensive and antagonistic to church peace, harmful to the government's tranquillity, arousing unease in the salutary peace of the people, and ignorant of the power of the Scriptures, alarming and guilty of much confusion"; it was ruled that these writings be kept "under strict guard so that they not only do not become public, but also not be shown to anyone" (*Polnoe sobranie postanovlenii i rasporiazhenii*, vol. 1, no. 118, p. 165; *Opisanie dokumentov i del, khraniashchikhsia v arkhive Sviateishego Pravitel'stvuiushchego Sinoda*, 49 vols. [St. Petersburg, 1869–1914], vol. 1, no. 325). For some reason this very important text has remained completely unknown to historians of the Russian church. Verkhovskoi confuses it with Iavorsky's cover letter to the Synod (see P. V. Verkhovskoi, *Uchrezhdenie Dukhovnoi kollegii i Dukhovnyi reglament*, 2 vols. [Rostov na Donu, 1916], 1: 668), and Cracraft does not mention it all, perhaps because he accepts Verkhovskoi's inaccurate identification (Cracraft, *The Church Reform of Peter the Great*, p. 163).

21. Verkhovskoi, *Uchrezhdenie*, 1: 665 (emphasis added).

It must be borne in mind that Peter's policies in many areas, including the church, were marked by a deliberate and far-reaching ambiguity that gave him considerable scope for manipulation. The false signals that Peter sent were often associated with malleable interpretations of historical precedent, since Peter was aware that his own projection of the present onto the past diverged from the one that he could expect of his subjects. Beginning in the mid-1690s, for example, various panegyrists praised Peter as the "new Constantine," having in mind Constantine the Great.[22] This archetypal identification clearly arose with the consent and conformed to the wishes of the tsar himself. For most of the intended audience, this parallel merely indicated the piety of the tsar, who had purportedly chosen the first Christian emperor as his model and was following in the footsteps of St. Vladimir, the Equal of the Apostles.[23] For the Ukrainian clergy, the parallel could signify that Peter was assuming the mission of a religious enlightener and taking as his point of departure the imperial model that (as in Byzantium) did not require the subordination of all eparchies to a single patriarch. For Peter, however, the archetype of Constantine most probably corresponded to an entirely different paradigm—that of the emperor as "external bishop" exercising power over both the civil and the spiritual realms. For a time, the paradigm remained vague. Its meaning did not become apparent until the establishment of the Synod in 1721: according to the oath of allegiance taken by the members the Synod, the emperor was the "judge of last resort." Moreover, Prokopovych's "Inquiry into the Pontifex" (*Rozysk o pontifekse*) explained the new paradigm in every detail. Thus Peter's cultural references initially seemed to reproduce or develop familiar paradigms: only later, when the addressee of these false stimuli had been fully engaged, were the tsar's altogether untraditional aims and intentions disclosed. The Ukrainian clergy was undoubtedly one addressee of these ambiguous messages.

Evidently a deception of this sort was carried out with the summons of Ukrainian monks to Moscow and their installation as bishops in Russian dioceses. It must be supposed that the Ukrainian side viewed this as a renewal of the policy of religious enlightenment conducted by Patriarch Nikon and Aleksei Mikhailovich, who had

---

22. Cf. Viktor Zhivov, "Kul'turnye reformy v sisteme preobrazovanii Petra I," in *Iz istorii russkoi kul'tury*, vol. 3, *XVII—nachalo XVIII veka* (Moscow, 1996), pp. 528-83.

23. Especially as portrayed in the *Lives*. See A. A. Zimin, "Pamiat' i pokhvala Iakova mnikha i Zhitie kniazia Vladimira po drevneishemu spisku," *Kratkie soobshcheniia Instituta slavianovedeniia*, vyp. 37 (Moscow, 1963), pp. 66–75.

brought Iepifanii Slavynetsky, Simeon Polotsky and others to Moscow, charging them with the preparation and explanation of ecclesiastical reform. Peter's shift of cultural orientation seemed perfectly natural, given his known dislike of Patriarch Adrian and his hostile relations with Patriarch Ioakim, who had conducted a very rigid policy of religious unification and warned the tsar particularly against relations with the non-Orthodox. Peter's policy of greater openness, especially apparent in his relations with foreigners,[24] was in keeping with his evident regard for Ukrainian learning. The reorganization of the Moscow Academy on the Kyivan model, with Latin as the primary language, was another indication of the tsar's educational intentions that prompted such openness.

We need not consider how vital were Peter's educational purposes, although the ambiguity of his policy misled not only his contemporaries, but also later historians.[25] More than instructive on this point is the ukase of 31 January 1701, which forbade monks to keep pens and paper in their cells.[26] Regardless of the Enlightenment

---

24. The change in the formula of the hierarchal vows is pertinent here as well. A comparison of the vows of Evfimii of Sarsk and the Don region, who was installed on 22 August 1688, with those of Ilarion of Pskov and Izborsk, installed on 1 February 1691, shows that after the death of Patriarch Ioakim the article concerning relations with heretics and the recognition of marriages between Orthodox and non-Orthodox was removed from the hierarchal vows. Before Patriarch Adrian's death, this article read as follows: "In addition, I vow not to communicate with Latins, Lutherans, Calvinists, or other heretics who may come to the capital city of Moscow and not to allow any of our Orthodox to marry them or invite them to be godparents or fraternize with them until they embrace the Orthodox Christian faith of the Eastern Church. And if any priest secretly commits any of these transgressions, I must punish him in accordance with the sacred rules of the Holy Fathers" (GIM, Sin. 1044, l. 2^{v}). This vow was eliminated after Adrian's ascension to the patriarchal throne (see the standard text of the vows compiled under the last patriarch: GIM, Sin. 344, l. 27^{v}-28^{v}). It appears that this change was made not on ecclesiastical initiative, but at the insistence of the secular authorities, who made these particular requirements of the new patriarch a condition of his appointment. There is scarcely any doubt that this insistence came from Peter himself and represented his personal response to the above-cited testament of Ioakim. This was a clear change of religious policy, and the Ukrainian clergy, who were undoubtedly familiar with it, were fully justified in expecting support and cooperation from the tsar.

25. Even Cracraft repeats the commonplace about Peter's attempts to "educate" the Muscovite clergy by compelling it to become learned (*The Church Reform of Peter the Great*, pp. 24–26, 262–70).

26. *Polnoe sobranie zakonov*, vol. 4, no. 1834, p. 140.

discourse that was promoted by Peter, the primary reason that prompted him to appoint Ukrainian monks to positions in Russia was unquestionably the circumstance that, in George Shevelov's words, they did not have "and could not have any firm ground in Russia."[27] On the one hand, this rendered harmless their possible opposition to reform, and on the other it introduced cultural and ethnic confrontation into church affairs, providing the authorities with additional means of controlling the clergy. As far as the educational enticements were concerned, swift disenchantment awaited the Ukrainian hierarchs. "Impoverished in everything, learning, too, became impoverished," wrote Dymytrii of Rostov, who established a school in Rostov for which he no longer had means of support, in the mid-1700s.[28]

A similar ambiguity was created with regard to ecclesiastical jurisdiction. The transfer of authority over the Russian church, now nominally headed by the Eastern patriarchs, was entirely in keeping with Peter's attempts to extend his authority to the sphere of church administration. The Eastern patriarchs did not possess any real power, while the Russian church, bereft of a supreme shepherd, became disorganized and could offer no effective resistance to the tsar's policies. Moreover, the patriarch of Constantinople, who was receiving a significant Muscovite subsidy, could easily be manipulated to render a positive decision with regard to issues on which the Russian and Ukrainian clergies might become unyielding (such as the question of baptizing the non-Orthodox, which Peter referred to Constantinople).[29] If the transfer of the Russian church to the nominal jurisdiction of the Eastern patriarchs had not created a legal instrument that subordinated the church to the tsar (as subsequently was the case with the Spiritual Collegium, i.e., the Synod), then his actual control of church administration and church property completely guaranteed such subordination. At the same time, the canonical vagueness of the situation (the principle of patriarchal leadership had been abolished de facto, but remained in effect as a fiction) concealed the radical nature of this thoroughgoing reorganization and gave grounds for differing interpretations, which made it possible to manipulate and mislead potential opponents.

---

27. J. Sherech [Shevelov], "Stefan Yavorsky and the Conflict of Ideologies in the Age of Peter I," *Slavonic and East European Review* 30, no. 74 (1951): 45.

28. I. A. Shliapkin, *Dmitrii Rostovskii i ego vremia, 1651–1709 gg.* (St. Petersburg, 1891), 339.

29. See *Polnoe sobranie zakonov,* vol. 5, no. 3225, 31 August 1718.

Ukrainian clergymen, who were appointed to many bishoprics in Russia, were quite susceptible to such misleading tactics, since the canonical fiction could have a special appeal to them. It signified an ostensible shift from the second imperial model back to the first, as the transfer of the church to the jurisdiction of the Eastern patriarchs appeared to give Kyiv equal status with Moscow. The concept of the Orthodox empire remained intact, and Peter frequently exploited it (particularly in dealings with the Orthodox East), but the canonical subordination of the Kyivan metropolitan see to the Moscow patriarch no longer applied, since the Muscovite patriarchate no longer existed. This could be interpreted as restoring a situation in which several canonically equal churches existed within the boundaries of a single empire. Such an interpretation was entirely in keeping with Peter's actions in the ecclesiastical sphere, which sprang from his rejection of Patriarch Ioakim's legacy and his partial return to the political ideas of Aleksei Mikhailovich.

Stefan Iavorsky, appointed to fulfill a number of patriarchal functions, acted exactly according to such a plan. He naturally undertook no initiatives to coordinate Ukrainian and Muscovite ecclesiastical practices, of which Dositheos, the patriarch of Jerusalem, had been so apprehensive at the beginning of Iavorsky's tenure. Indeed, Dositheos had written to Peter that "a Greek or any such person, that is to say, from Little or White Russia ... should not be elected patriarch, but only a person from Great Russia."[30] Such coexistence of national ecclesiastical traditions within one polity could be regarded as a natural outcome of the "first imperial model" and interpreted as a good omen with regard to the tsar's intentions in other spheres (the preservation of particular legal status for Ukraine, special requirements concerning military service, etc.). At the same time, Iavorsky's patience with local traditions might be explained by his fairly easy intimacy with local church leaders (the so-called "old Muscovite party," whatever that slipshod term may mean).

Moreover, the situation that arose in Moscow after Patriarch Adrian's death could plausibly strike the Ukrainian clergy as quite usual, if not entirely normal, from the canonical point of view. It did not have to be interpreted as a step toward the abolition of the church administration and the eradication of ecclesiastical independence, but could be compared to known historical precedents and dismissed as an irrelevant interlude with respect to the church canon. Indeed, the

---

30. See Dositheos's message to Iavorsky (1703) in Kapterev, *Kharakter otnoshenii*, p. 545.

situation in Moscow very closely resembled the one that had arisen in Kyiv after the death of Metropolitan Dionisii Balaban (1663), or even that of Sylvestr Kosiv (1657), when Kyiv was ruled by various *locum tenentes,* but canonicity was assured by the supreme direction of the patriarch of Constantinople (this precedent was undoubtedly known to Peter as well). Until Peter's plans were shown to have radical implications for the canonical structure of the church, these ecclesiastical irregularities—given the Ukrainian precedents—could be regarded as temporary oppressions to be endured with patience.

In such a conflict, the issue is decided not by an evaluation of the present, but by the way in which the present projects into the future. Actors in a transitional period isolate various elements of the present that correspond to their view of the future, associate that future with their own survival and prospects, and, on the strength of this assessment, contend with one another to achieve various goals, some of them highly personal, seeing them as tokens of future success. That the future as it unfolds may deprive many of these expectations of all significance in no way lessens their importance to the historian: conflicting expectations determine both the actual politics of the transition and the attitudes of individual historical personages. As each of these viewpoints strives to assert itself, it finds sustenance in the present, resulting in a struggle to determine which interpretation will prevail. In the course of this struggle, symbolic acts become arguments of ultimate significance: money and property are much more readily sacrificed than the least symbolic act, which contemporaries regard as decisive in determining the future.

The canonical subordination of the Russian church to the Eastern patriarchs is an example of such a symbolic act. While it remained in force, the Russian hierarchs could await the restoration of the patriarchate, while the Ukrainians could hope to preserve the relative autonomy of the Kyivan metropolitan see. The death of Peter, for which many nourished hopes,[31] might have put a natural end to this

---

31. In a sermon of 1712, Stefan Iavorsky decried the appointment of financial inspectors (*fiskaly*) and referred to Tsarevich Aleksei as "our only hope" (Ustrialov, *Istoriia,* 6: 31). When Tsarevich Aleksei admitted to his confessor, Iakov Ignatiev, that he wished for the death of his father, the confessor replied: "We all wish for his death, because there is much suffering among the people" (on the deposition of the tsarevich; see ibid., 6: 525, 269, 272; on the deposition of Ignatiev, see ibid., 6: 526, 273). At the assembly of 27 February 1718 that stripped the Rostov hierarch Dosifei of his office (he had wished for the death of the tsar and during church services had referred to Peter's first wife, Evdokiia, then confined to a nunnery, as the tsaritsa), Dosifei appealed to the hierarchs: "Only I have been caught in this affair.

long-drawn-out interlude, establishing the order potentially inherent in the interpretation of each interested party. This is precisely what explains the bitter polemic waged by Prokopovych and Iavorsky after the establishment of the Synod about prayers for the Eastern patriarchs. In defending the principle that the Eastern patriarchs should be recognized as the supreme heads of the Russian church—even if only nominally, in prayers offered on their behalf (i.e., a purely symbolic act)—Iavorsky sought to preserve his vision of the future. It is revealing that in this connection he could make direct reference to the subordination of the Ukrainian church to Constantinople. In affirming the appropriateness of that subordination, Iavorsky wrote that "the metropolitans of all Rus' were ordained by the patriarch of Constantinople and sent to the first capital of all Rus', first to Kyiv and then to Moscow; hence, in our time, the metropolitan of Rus', Petro Mohyla, is called the exarch of the patriarchal throne of Constantinople."[32]

Thus Iavorsky draws on the history of the Ukrainian church for a precedent to illuminate the current situation. He also projects a future structure for the Russian church by analyzing the state of affairs that followed the disorders of the 1660s. Iavorsky even attempts to treat the establishment of the Synod as a development that does not violate the supreme authority of the Eastern patriarchs, i.e., as a transitional expedient with no lasting significance. From such a perspective, Petrine church policy would be merely a temporary disaster and therefore bearable, as it did not impinge on canonical autonomy or national traditions. It was as if the idea of the empire had been purged of ecclesiastical or ethnic aspects and reduced to a matter of personal loyalty to the monarch, regardless of religious denomination, ecclesiastical practices, or ethnic consciousness.

However, according to the thinking of Peter and Teofan Prokopovych, the establishment of the Synod was intended precisely to put an end to the expectations of Iavorsky and his ilk. The Synod represented another imperial paradigm, that of the police state, with all its attendant consequences in the religious and ethnic spheres. In the scheme of ecclesiastical policy it may be regarded as a unique extension of the "second imperial model." Indeed, the only institution

---

Look: what is in your hearts? Be so good as to listen to the people and what is being said among them" (ibid., 6: 213). Such testimonies could easily be multiplied. Among the clergy, hopes for the death of Peter as a relief from oppression were commonplace.

32. GIM, Uvar. 1728/378/588, f. 4^{v}.

of Ioakim's time to be eliminated was the patriarchate, so detested by Peter. It was replaced by the Synod, which reported to the tsar, simultaneously resolving the problems of a single jurisdiction and religious unification. Like any eparchy in the empire, the Kyivan metropolitan see had to submit to the Spiritual Collegium. As under Ioakim, a single jurisdiction entailed religious unification. In organizing the Synod, Peter and Teofan were preoccupied with establishing this model and making precise adjustments that left no room for alternative interpretations. For that very reason, the prayers for the Eastern patriarchs were eliminated from the liturgy immediately after the establishment of the Synod, and Prokopovych wrote the abovementioned work "On Prayers." No less telling was the ukase issued by Peter requiring the complete conformity of Ukrainian liturgical books with Muscovite books.[33] A year later, the Synod issued an analogous directive that required the legal deposit of all church books, "so that there be no disagreement or particular dialect."[34]

The resolution of the questions of church jurisdiction and national ecclesiastical traditions entailed the resolution of ethnic questions: bereft of a religious identity, Ukraine was to lose its national identity as well. The policy of ethnic unification and the establishment of Russian institutions in Ukraine developed in tandem with the policy of religious unification. This close association emphasizes the significance of questions of ecclesiastical jurisdiction for the discussion of Russian-Ukrainian ethnic relations.

---

33. *Polnoe sobranie postanovlenii,* vol. 1, no. 173; Kharlampovich, *Malorossiiskoe vliianie,* p. 787; ukase of 5 October 1720.

34. *Polnoe sobranie postanovlenii,* vol. 1, no. 173; *Opisanie dokumentov i del,* vol. 1, no. 402.

David A. Frick

Lazar Baranovych, 1680: The Union of Lech and Rus

In 1680 the Treaty of Andrusovo between Poland-Lithuania and Muscovy was to be renegotiated. It had first been signed in 1667, marking an end to hostilities between the two powers. Its provisions had called for, among other things, recognition of a new border dividing Ukraine along the Dnipro River into a Right Bank under Polish-Lithuanian rule and a Left Bank under Muscovite rule; for a common Muscovite-Polish front against Turkish incursions; and for the eventual reversion of the city of Kyiv to Polish-Lithuanian control.[1] In that same year Lazar Baranovych, the archbishop of Chernihiv and Novhorod-Siverskyi in Left-Bank Ukraine, published two curious works of unfixed genre, language, and alphabets that he dedicated to Tsar Fedor Alekseevich. In comments scattered throughout these tracts he developed further one of the underlying themes of his earlier books—that of a peculiar kind of Polish-Ruthenian bond.[2]

There were possible conflicts here between Baranovych's acknowledgment of Muscovite authority and his vision of a Ruthenian identity defined in terms of association with Poland. The year 1680 was to have marked a progression in the redrawing of borders whereby

---

1. On relations between Poland-Lithuania and Muscovy in the period between 1667 and 1680, see Zbigniew Wójcik, *Między Traktatem andruszowskim a Wojną turecką: Stosunki polsko-rosyjskie 1667–1672* (Warsaw, 1968); idem, *Rzeczpospolita wobec Turcji i Rosji 1674–1679: Studium z dziejów polskiej polityki zagranicznej* (Wrocław, 1976); and E. Zamyslovskii, "Snosheniia Rossii s Pol'shei v tsarstvovanie Feodora Alekseevicha," *Zhurnal Ministerstva narodnogo prosveshcheniia* 261 (1888): 161–97.

2. Since this paper was completed, an insightful article has appeared on this topic. See Teresa Chynczewska-Hennel, "Pojednanie polsko-ukraińskie w wierszach Łazarza Baranowicza," in *Kultura staropolska—kultura europejska: Prace ofiarowane Januszowi Tazbirowi w siedemdziesiątą rocznicę urodzin* (Warsaw, 1997), pp. 325–29. The present article focuses on two large works not included in Chynczewska-Hennel's study, and thus on prose as well as poetry; it also makes some further arguments about the origins and significance of Baranovych's worldview.

Baranovych's world would become more thoroughly divided from that of Poland-Lithuania, while old differences with Muscovy were to be further effaced. And yet, in 1680 Baranovych chose to develop further his exploration of the relationship between Poland and Rus'. In this essay I wish to examine this paradox by investigating aspects of Baranovych's version of Ruthenian identity as it was shaped in the fields of tension between East and West, Greek and Latin, Muscovite and Pole, Orthodoxy and Catholicism. My goal will be to shed light on some aspects of the ways in which, at least for some of the Ruthenian elite, mental geographies changed more slowly than, and at times in directions somewhat different from, political realities. I begin with a brief biographical sketch of Baranovych, followed by an assessment of his sense of the limits that defined his world. I then turn my attention to the images and arguments that Baranovych employed in representing the unities that crossed some of these divisions. I conclude with a discussion of Baranovych's vision of Ruthenian identity in the context of the international politics of 1680.

A Life in the Borderlands

Baranovych died in 1693—at the age of seventy-three in one account; at one hundred, according to other evidence—as archbishop of Chernihiv and Novhorod-Siverskyi, an office he had held for some thirty-five years.[3] He was born Luka—whether in 1593, 1620, or sometime in between—a citizen of the Polish-Lithuanian Commonwealth, perhaps to Uniate parents.[4] His studies took him to Vilnius

---

3. On Baranovych, see N. F. Sumtsov, *K istorii iuzhnorusskoi literatury semnadtsatogo stoletiia,* vyp. 1, *Lazar' Baranovich* (Kharkiv, 1885); K. V. Kharlampovich, *Malorossiiskoe vliianie na velikorusskuiu tserkovnuiu zhizn',* vol. 1 (Kazan, 1914); R. P. Radyshevs'kyi, "Lazar Baranovych—ukraïns'kyi pys'mennyk i suspil'no-politychnyi diiach XVII st. v otsintsi suchasnykiv," in *Rol' Kyievo-Mohylians'koï akademiï v kul'turnomu iednanni slov'ians'kykh narodiv* (Kyiv, 1988), pp. 93–102; idem, "Davn'orus'ki motyvy v poeziï Lazaria Baranovycha," in *Pys'mennist' Kyïvs'koï Rusi i stanovlennia ukraïns'koï literatury* (Kyiv, 1988), pp. 244–70; idem, "Barokkovyi kontseptyzm poeziï Lazaria Baranovycha," in *Ukraïns'ke literaturne barokko* (Kyiv, 1987), pp. 156–77; and Peter Rolland, "'Nieskoro' prawi 'monsztuk do tych trąb otrzymacie': On Lazar Baranovyč's *Truby sloves propovidnyx* and their Non-Publication in Moscow," *Journal of Ukrainian Studies* 17, nos. 1–2 (1992): 205–16. On the conflicting evidence for Baranovych's year of birth, see Sumtsov, pp. 4–6.

4. For Baranovych's given name, see Radyshevs'kyi, "Lazar Baranovych," p. 96. Michał Wiszniewski thought the Baranovyches were Uniate (*Historia literatury polskiej,* vol. 8 [Cracow, 1851], p. 4). Sumtsov doubted it (p. 4). Neither adduced any evidence.

and eventually to Kyiv, where he drew the attention of Petro Mohyla. Baranovych was among the Ruthenians sent "abroad" for further education at the expense of the metropolitan.[5] After finishing his studies at the Jesuit school in Kalisz in Great Poland, he returned to Rus' and took monastic orders with the name Lazar. By the early 1640s, under the rectorship of Inokentii Gizel, Baranovych had become an instructor for the lower grades at the Kyivan Academy, where Ioanikii Galiatovsky and Antonii Radyvylovsky were among his students. By 1650, two years into the Khmelnytsky Uprising, Baranovych had become rector of the academy and hegumen of the Brotherhood Monastery.[6] From the end of the Khmelnytsky Uprising in 1654 until his death in 1693, he was a subject of the tsar.

In 1657, armed with charters from Hetman Bohdan Khmelnytsky, Secretary Ivan Vyhovsky, and Metropolitan Sylvestr Kosiv, Baranovych made his way to Iaşi in Moldavia, where on 8 March he was consecrated bishop of Chernihiv and Novhorod-Siverskyi.[7] The aged Zosyma Prokopovych still held that office, however, and Baranovych took up residence for the time being in the Transfiguration Monastery of Novhorod-Siverskyi. Prokopovych, who had been consecrated bishop in the late 1640s, was the first Orthodox bishop of Chernihiv since the Union of Brest, although he was not immediately able to reside there. In the late sixteenth century the diocese of Chernihiv and Novhorod-Siverskyi had been divided into two episcopal sees, the former occupied by Inokentii Borkovsky, who became a Uniate in 1596, and the latter by Ioann Lezhaisky, who remained Orthodox. The Union of Brest marked the beginning of a strong Uniate and Catholic presence in the area, represented above all by Basilians, Dominicans, and Franciscans. In 1638 a Jesuit college offering free education to local sons was founded in Novhorod-Siverskyi. Prokopovych took up residence in his see only after the Uniates and Dominicans moved from the area in the wake of the Khmelnytsky Uprising. He died in 1659.

With the deaths of Khmelnytsky and Kosiv in 1657, Baranovych was called upon to serve as administrator of the Kyiv metropolitan

---

5. Sumtsov (p. 7) doubted that Mohyla had financed Baranovych's trip, but Radyshevsky has found convincing evidence ("Lazar Baranovych," p. 96).

6. Our best source of information on Baranovych's studies, early career as a teacher, and later cultural work in Chernihiv is the dedicatory epistle to Galiatovsky. See Ioanikii Galiatovs'kyi, *Stary kościół zachodni nowemu kościołowi rzymskiemu* (Novhorod-Siverskyi, 1678), [1]1^r–3^r.

7. For these events, see Sumtsov, *K istorii iuzhnorusskoi literatury*, pp. 13–15.

see and to make arrangements for the election of a new head of the church.[8] Muscovite demands for the subordination of Kyiv to the patriarch of Moscow would effectively have split the ecclesiastical jurisdiction of the Left and Right Banks. Baranovych neither opposed nor supported such plans openly, but his general goal seems to have been to block Muscovite policy on this issue. His choice, Dionisii Balaban, was among those who sought autonomies for Rus' ecclesiastical structures. The new metropolitan placed under Baranovych's control three archpriests who had formerly belonged to the Kyiv metropolitanate and acknowledged the independence of the Chernihiv bishopric from Kyiv. This put Baranovych directly under the rule of the patriarch of Constantinople.

Baranovych became a major figure in Ruthenian ecclesiastical and political life in the 1660s and 1670s. It was he who was called upon to consecrate the hetman's symbols of office and pass them on to Khmelnytsky's successor, Ivan Vyhovsky, on 17 October 1657. When Balaban followed Vyhovsky in submitting to Polish sovereignty in 1658, Baranovych was again put temporarily in charge of the Kyivan church to guide the choice of a new metropolitan. In 1666 he took part in the church council in Moscow that removed Nikon from office and condemned the Old Believers. One result of the council was the elevation of Chernihiv to an archepiscopal see.[9]

Baranovych oversaw the reunification and re-orthodoxization of the see of Chernihiv. Under his energetic rule, monasteries and churches were renovated and built de novo; archpriests were established in larger towns and their representatives in smaller ones. He opened a printing office in Novhorod-Siverskyi in the early 1670s and had it moved to Chernihiv in 1679. The two works of 1680 under consideration here were among his first new projects after the move.[10]

Baranovych's politics were not straightforward. He expressed his subservience to Moscow at the appropriate moments and in the required places. He urged—and made certain it was known in Moscow that he had urged—Cossack leaders to choose Muscovite tsar

---

8. Ibid., pp. 15–17.

9. On these events, see ibid., pp. 17–19, 63–64, 70–75.

10. For Baranovych's own account of the difficulties he encountered in establishing and controlling his printing house in the late 1670s, see Baranovych, *Pis'ma preosviashchennogo Lazaria Baranovicha: S primechaniiami*, 2d ed. (Chernihiv, 1865), pp. 242–46. Baranovych had become frustrated in his attempts to publish his works in timely fashion in Moscow and Kyiv.

over Polish king, "to cease internal discord and be under the high hand of the great sovereign, and, both on this side of the Dnipro and on the other ... not to wish to listen to calls that they be subject to the Polish king."[11] Baranovych repeatedly urged the tsar not to return Kyiv to the Commonwealth (as stipulated by the Treaty of Andrusovo):

> it has been made known here that it [Kyiv] was surrendered to the Lachs at the commission, and that on the last day of November in the current year it was to be surrendered, about which all most glorious citizens of Kyiv lament, and the whole Orthodox Little Russian nation is in commotion. Yea, most merciful Orthodox tsar, have pity upon your blood and your eternal patrimony from of old. For this is the true blood of Your Most Illustrious Imperial Highness, those Orthodox grand princes and tsars of Kyiv, such as, among others, Grand Prince Volodymyr, who was equal to the apostles. Do not give up your acquisition and the royal crown of that holy great city of Kyiv from your sovereign Orthodox hand into the heterodox one, unto eternal (God forfend) defamation and pain of the whole one Orthodox Christian people."[12]

Muscovite authorities, however, seem to have had doubts about the archbishop's reliability, and there were distances and tensions in their

---

11. See Iakov Khapchinsky's report of December 1668 to the Ambassadorial Office (*Posol'skii prikaz*). This was Baranovych's own account of his actions, related by Khapchinsky in the third person (*Akty, otnosiashchiesia k istorii Iuzhnoi i Zapadnoi Rossii,* vol. 7 [St. Petersburg, 1872], pp. 153–54): "А епископъ де Баранович безпрестани во всѣ полки пишет и утвержаетъ ихъ, чтоб онѣ отъ междоусобия отстали и были бъ подъ высокою рукою государя. А какъ де на сей, такъ и на той сторонѣ Днѣпра всѣ, старшина и чернь, и слушать того не хотятъ, что быть в подданствѣ у Полского короля ..."

12. See the letters of 1669 from Baranovych to Tsar Aleksei Mikhailovich in Baranovych, *Pis'ma*, p. 61; and *Akty*, vol. 9 (St. Petersburg, 1878), pp. 170–71 (dated 12 July): "вѣсно здѣ учинилось, что онъ на комисіи отданъ Ляхомъ и послѣдняго числа ноября въ нынѣшнемъ году отдан имѣетъ быть; о чем всѣ преславные кіевскіе обители плачютъ и весь православный малоросійскій народъ во смятеній. Ей, премилосердый православный царю, возжалѣейся надъ кровію своею и искони вѣчнымъ отечествомъ! Понеже сущая то вашего царского пресвѣтлого величества кровь, правовѣрные оные великія князи и царіе кіевскіе, яко равноапостолный великій князь Владимеръ и протчіе; не отпущай же своего присвоенія и вѣнца царского того святаго великого града Кіева отъ своея государскія руки правовѣрныя во иновѣрную, въ вѣчное (не даждь Боже) поношеніе и жалость всего православного христіянского народа."

relationship. One such cause of doubt was the allegation that Baranovych, in his struggle to have the Muscovite voivodes or palatines removed, had once declared a desire that "not a single Muscovite foot" remain in Rus'.[13] Still others were the "Catholic" and "Polish" elements in his religion and politics—a pronounced Mariolatry and a longing for Polish-Ruthenian brotherhood—there for any to see who read his printed works, especially those of 1680.[14]

Baranovych's position seems to have become more difficult toward the end of his life. From the 1660s to 1680, he had dedicated to the tsar and to the patriarch a series of works of questionable political and theological correctness from the Muscovite point of view. In the late 1680s, Patriarch Ioakim initiated a correspondance with Baranovych, allegedly seeking illumination on two main issues: the nature of the Council of Florence and the time of the transubstantiation during the liturgy. It seems more likely, however, that the patriarch already knew the "answers" to his questions and was actually interested in allowing Baranovych to establish—if he could—his Orthodoxy on these issues. Baranovych was reluctant to become involved in the discussion and had to be threatened with ecclesiastical censure; by then, however, his responses revealed a desire to fall into line with the patriarch. Ioakim soon condemned the theology of a variety of Ruthenian works, including Baranovych's large collections of sermons from 1666 and 1674.[15]

Distinctions

Baranovych's works of 1680 stood out in a long career of writing long books. They were not exactly homiletics, a genre to which the archbishop had devoted much of his life's work and published in two large collections in the Slavonic-language *Mech' dukhovnyi* (*Spiritual Sword*, 1666) and *Truby* (*Trumpets*, 1674); not exactly apologetics, to

---

13. See the denunciation submitted by the archpriest of Nizhyn, Symeon Adamovych, dated January 1669 (*Akty*, vol. 8 [St. Petersburg, 1875], p. 10), where Baranovych is alleged to have said: "надобно намъ того, чтобъ у насъ въ Малой Росіи и нога Московская не постояла...."

14. Baranovych's Mariolatry was one of the reasons why it proved impossible to publish his *Truba* in Moscow. On this issue, see Rolland.

15. On this exchange, see Sumtsov, *K istorii iuzhnorusskoi literatury*, pp. 175–78. The letters are printed in *Akty*, 7: 262–68 and Baranovych, *Pis'ma*, pp. 230–36. For Ioakim's letter threatening Baranovych with ecclesiastical trial, see A. V. Gorskii and K. I. Nevostruev, *Opisanie slavianskikh rukopisei Moskovskoi sinodal'noi biblioteki*, vol. 3 (Moscow, 1862), p. 512.

which he turned his attention in the Polish-language *Nowa miara* (*New Measure*, 1675); not exactly verse, which he seems to have made sleeping and waking and collected in the massive Polish-language *Lutnia apollinowa* (*Apollo's Lute*, 1671); nor, finally, were they quite hagiography, a large collection of which he had also produced in Polish verse under the title *Żywoty Świętych* (*Lives of the Saints*, 1670). Baranovych's works of 1680 fit none of these genres, although they contained aspects of all of them. One of their peculiarities lay in their programmatic avoidance of any one genre—or even language—and in their attempt to bring the languages and cultures of East and West into a sort of mystical union and harmony.

Although both works bore Polish-language title pages and could be described as largely Polish books, Baranovych shifted languages and alphabets frequently enough and in contexts important enough to call into question at times the "real" language of the narration. Lengthy quotations appeared in both Latin and Cyrillic-letter Church Slavonic. But Church Slavonic passages also appeared in Latin-letter transliteration, as did Ruthenian proverbs. Baranovych also mixed languages and alphabets mid-sentence and mid-poem, causing Church Slavonic phrases to agree grammatically with Polish contexts and matching Polish distychs to Slavonic ones. This was a special kind of Ukrainian baroque macaronism in which the alphabets and languages of the Latin-Greek borderlands mixed and competed with each other, producing cross-cultural and cross-linguistic rhymes and conceits.

Baranovych extended this macaronic approach from the level of languages to that of genre. His first book of 1680, *W Wieniec Bożey Matki ŚŚ. Ocyów kwiatki* (*Flowers from the Holy Fathers for the Wreath of the Mother of God*), was part dictionary florilegium and part original prose and poetry in praise of the Virgin Mary. Baranovych drew programmatically from church authorities of both East and West. In fact, he relied most heavily on two authors from the Polish Counter-Reformation. The first was Franciszek Rychłowski (ca. 1611–1673), provincial of the Franciscans, who was active in Red Ruthenia and had issued several collections of sermons in the 1660s and 1670s.[16] The other was the arch-Catholic chancellor of Lithuania, Albrycht Stanisław Radziwiłł (1593–1656), whose writings included a memoir as well as hagiographic publications that contributed to popularizing

16. Rychłowski published several collections of sermons for the entire church calendar (Cracow, 1664, 1672, 1667), as well as *Sermons for the Feasts of the Most Holy Virgin* (*Kazania na Święta Panny Przenaświętszey*, Cracow, 1667).

the cult of the Virgin in Poland-Lithuania.[17] Baranovych's second work of 1680, *Notiy pięć: Ran Chrystusowych pięć* (*Five Marks: The Five Wounds of Christ*), was a loosely organized disquisition in prose and verse, presenting a Christ-centered vision of Ruthenian religion, culture, and politics. Both works were dedicated (repeatedly in the course of the narration) to tsar, patriarch, and hetman, but especially to Tsar Fedor Alekseevich.

In between the heterogeneous—not to mention heterodox—praise of Christ and the Virgin, Baranovych presented a vision of a mystical reunion of East and West and of Ruthenians and Poles. Before I proceed to mystical unions, however, I will devote some attention to Baranovych's sense of the limits that defined his world. Although my ultimate focus will be on the events of 1680, the themes, images, and arguments I will be examining in the archbishop's works of that year have a history in his writings of the 1660s and 1670s, and I will also look to them for evidence. All these works, it is important to bear in mind, were published in Left-Bank Ukraine after 1654 by a subject of the tsar, and dedicated to him.

1. Patria

In the time and milieu in which Baranovych was educated and had his first experiences as a teacher (i.e., before the Khmelnytsky Uprising of 1648), Polish terminology concerning states and peoples was largely uniform, whether used by Poles or Ruthenians. (Recall that Baranovych wrote much of his work in Polish; moreover, his Ruthenian usage reflected Polish norms.) *Ojczyzna* (*patria*, "fatherland") usually meant the Polish-Lithuanian Commonwealth as a whole, although it could occasionally refer to something more limited and local. *Polak, polski, Polska* (Pole, Polish, Poland), especially if opposed to terms referring to other ethnicities of Poland-Lithuania, referred to the Polish Crown lands alone and came more and more—especially in Orthodox usage—to imply Catholicism. (When used in isolation, these terms often referred more broadly to the Commonwealth as a whole.) *Litwin, litewski, Litwa* (Lithuanian, Lithuania) referred to the citizens—again, in Orthodox usage, the Catholic citizens—of the Grand Duchy of Lithuania. *Rusin* (also *Rusak), ruski* (also *rosyiski), Rus'* (also *Rossiia)* generally referred to the Orthodox populace of Poland and Lithuania (i.e., Ruthenian and Ruthenia);

17. Radziwiłł published a *Life of the Virgin Mary* (*Żywot Panny Maryi* [Warsaw, 1650]) in addition to Baranovych's frequent source here, his edition of the *Lives of the Saints* (*Żywoty Świętych* [Cracow, 1653]).

these terms were regularly opposed to "Muscovites" and "Muscovy" *(Moskwicin, moskiewski, Moskwa).* In this period, Protestants were more and more frequently challenged to defend their "Polishness," and Orthodox usage tended to speak of Poles (i.e., Catholics) in opposition to Ruthenians (i.e., Orthodox), and of Poles and Ruthenians in opposition to "heretics."

Ukraina, ukrainny (sometimes *ukraiński)* usually referred to a territory, a region, or a palatinate, not to a people. In 1677, the Polish envoy to the Porte, Jan Gniński, would declare: "Ukraine is nothing other than a border, *limes et fimbria* [a boundary and an edge] .... This word Ukraine is not found in any of our Polish laws."[18] And the Porte's secretary (*reis effendi*) Mustafa—although the Porte had long been dealing with representatives of the peoples of those territories—found common ground with his interlocutor: "Ukraine is a province ..."[19]

Ruthenian usage began to shift as Ruthenians sought contact with and support from Muscovy; it was bound to undergo a more thorough restructuring as Rus' recognized Muscovite sovereignty. In official usage, lines of distinction between Rus' and Muscovy were gradually blurred, and barriers were erected between Rus' and Poland-Lithuania. These changes did not come overnight, however, and the new meaning of these old terms in the usage of what we might call "former Ruthenians" offers some insight into the gradual reconfiguration of the borderlands in the minds of those who lived there.

Baranovych's usage was inconsistent or, perhaps more to the point, it consistently avoided settling exclusively into either Muscovite or Polish schemes. Ample evidence could be found that Baranovych adhered fully to both the new Muscovite usage or the old Polish usage (although such lines of investigation would be forced to ignore the other part of the evidence).

In his dedications and apostrophes to tsars and tsareviches, Baranovych came close to erasing all distinction between Rus' and Muscovy. Tsar Fedor Alekseevich was the autocrat of "All Great and Little and White Rossiia"[20] or of "Great, Little, and White Rus'."[21] The tsar

18. Wójcik, *Rzeczpospolita wobec,* p. 119: "Ukraina nie jest nic inszego tylko granica, limes et fimbria ... słowa tego Ukraina w żadnych naszych polskich prawach ... nie masz."

19. Ibid., pp. 119–20: "Ukraina prowincyja jest ..."

20. Baranovych, *Notiy pięć: Ran Chrystvsowych pięć* (Chernihiv, 1680), C1^r, C4^v.

21. Ibid., CC2^v.

covered Rus' with his three crowns.[22] In such passages, when Baranovych spoke of the *narod Rosski*,[23] it would seem that he had made the shift to a new, Moscow-oriented way of thinking.

But such passages, although on prominent display, were extremely few, limited to direct addresses to the books' immediate recipients, the tsars and tsareviches. And even there, subdivisions still played a role: by referring to "Great, Little, and White Rus'," Baranovych maintained some articulation between them: Rus' may have been singular, but it was covered by *three* crowns. One could argue that, even here, Baranovych's frame of reference was a Polish-style federation under an elected king, not a Muscovite-style autocracy.

Most striking, however, are the passages that adhered unequivocally to the old Polish-Lithuanian usage, as if no borders had been redrawn. Consider, for example, the long poem found toward the end of *Lutnia apollinowa* (1671), in which Baranovych waxed etymological on the names associated with the peoples of the Polish-Lithuanian Commonwealth. The Lithuanian nobleman's name ended in *-icz* because "he prepares his *bicz* (scourge) for every enemy." The Pole's name ended in *-ski* "because he prepares a *kij* (club) against all enemies." To the *-iczes* and the *-skis*, Baranovych added the Ruthenian, "the one who fights on land and water, a dashing lad who can take all misfortunes in stride." His name ended in *-ko* "because he can easily hit the enemy in the *oko* (eye) with his firearm." Baranovych joined these three peoples in one *patria:* "Rejoice, O Fatherland *(ojczyzna)*, that you have glorious men who carry arms not for show, but are ready to die for the Fatherland. Let them be at best readiness."[24]

This was the Ruthenian version of the old Polish-Lithuanian *ojczyzna*, or Fatherland—and an optimistic version at that. The dominant parties had long thought in terms of a *Rzecz Pospolita Obojga Narodów*, a Commonwealth of the Two—Polish and Lithuanian—Nations. In Baranovych's poetry we find the image of a *Rzecz Pospolita Trojga Narodów*, a Commonwealth of Three Nations—Poland, Lithuania, and Rus'—as Ruthenian polemicists had long been asserting for their own purposes, and as the architects of the Treaty of Hadiach

22. Ibid., C4^{v}.

23. Baranovych, *W Wieniec Bożey Matki ŚŚ. Oyców Kwiatki* (Chernihiv, 1680), p. 113.

24. Baranovych, *Lutnia apollinowa* (Kyiv, 1671), p. 533: "Ciesz się Oyczyzno, że masz sławne męze,/Co nie dla kształtu naszaią oręże,/Lecz za Oyczyznę vmierać gotowi,/Niechayże będą naylepiey gotowi."

had planned.[25] In past usage, Muscovy had had no usual place within this scheme. It was certainly beyond the borders, possibly an external enemy. Note that even the implied criticism of effeminate noblemen who carry arms only for show was in keeping with the cultural rhetoric of seventeenth-century Poland-Lithuania, which yearned for a golden age of true knights.

Elsewhere, Baranovych drew less militarized borders between Rus' and Muscovy, but still they were borders: "Greece, Rus', Muscovy, the nation that uses the Slavonic language";[26] "every nation has its own patrons ... Muscovy, too, has many of its own saints."[27] And Baranovych still cited—and tacitly accepted—the taxonomy found in Maciej Stryjkowski's *Kronika:* "Ruthenians, Muscovy, Bulgarians or 'Volgarians,' so called from the Volga River, as also other Slavs, began to write before we Poles did."[28]

Baranovych's mental world would seem to have remained largely that of his training in the Polish-Lithuanian Commonwealth. When he looked for images to employ in his poetry, they were largely those with associations for Polish-Lithuanian culture and society. When he wrote of "circles" as images of divine perfection, his thoughts naturally brought him to the *koła*, the circles of Polish-Lithuanian parliamentary politics.[29] His fund of proverbs was held largely in common with Poles. Both Pole and Ruthenian were "wise after the harm": "As the Pole, so also the Ruthenian becomes wise after the harm. So let the one not scoff at the other."[30] This was a version of the still current saying, "Polak mądry po szkodzie," which, in the

---

25. On the Treaty of Hadiach, see Andrzej Sulima Kamiński, "The Cossack Experiment in *Szlachta* Democracy in the Polish-Lithuanian Commonwealth: The Hadiach (*Hadziacz*) Union," *Harvard Ukrainian Studies* 1, no. 2 (1977): 178–97.

26. Baranovych, *Nowa miara* (Novhorod-Siverskyi, 1675), p. 74: "Grecya, Ruś, Moskwa, Naród Słowieńskiego ięzyka vżywaiący ..."

27. Ibid., p. 59: "każda Nacya ma swoie osobliwe Patrony ... ma y Moskwa wiele swoich świętych."

28. Ibid., p. 92: "Rusacy, Moskwa, Bułgarowie albo Wołgarowie od Wołgi rzeki nazwani, także y insi Słowacy, pierwey niż my Polacy pisać poczęli."

29. Baranovych (*W Wieniec*, p. 116) wrote of the Senators', Delegates', and Knights' circles. On this political institution, see Zygmunt Gloger, *Encyklopedia staropolska ilustrowana*, vols. 3–4 (Warsaw, 1978), 3: 62.

30. Baranovych, *Lutnia apollinowa*, p. 527: "Iak Lach tak Rusin po szkodzie mędrzeie,/Niechże się ieden z drugiego nie śmieie."

seventeenth century, was used by Ruthenians as well as Poles.[31] Even the negative aspects of relations between Pole and Ruthenian came from a parlance shared with the Poles: "As long as the world is the world, the Ruthenian will not be brother to the Pole."[32] Baranovych, it should be noted, cited this proverb not as a simple fact, but as a piece of "wisdom" to be questioned and overcome. More typical was his lament: "God have pity upon the unhappy hour in which Sarmatian sons did battle with each other."[33]

A frequently told story—one that we find in the *Annales* of Jan Długosz[34]—had it that in days of old the knights of Poland-Lithuania customarily bared their swords in church during the reading of the Gospel as a sign of their willingness to die for the true faith. In the controversies of the sixteenth century both Catholic and Protestant polemicists had attempted to claim these swashbuckling defenders of the Gospel as their own confessional ancestors. We find this not only in works of the Polish Jesuits, but also in those of a leader of the Czech Brethren, Symon Teofil Turnowski, who claimed that "true Evangelicals ... especially of the knightly estate" were identified precisely by their readiness to draw their swords during the reading of the Evangels.[35] With Baranovych, the Orthodox joined this Polish-Lithuanian debate. "What Were Rus' and the Poles of Yore?" Baranovych asked in the title of a poem:

> When the Gospel was read, naked arms were drawn. That was in the Crown. Poles made it clear in this way during the Lord's

---

31. In a letter of 1669 to the archimandrite of the Kyivan Caves Monastery, Inokentii Gizel, Baranovych wrote: "after the harm, both Lach and Ruthenian are wise" (Baranovych, *Pis'ma*, p. 45).

32. Baranovych, *Lutnia apollinowa*, p. 427: "Nie będzie, iako świat światem,/ Rusin Polakowi bratem." On the origins of the saying, see G. Labuda, "Geneza przysłowia: 'Jak świat światem, nie będzie Niemiec Polakowi bratem,'" in *Zeszyty Naukowe Uniwersytetu im. Adama Mickiewicza*, Historia, z. 8 (Poznań, 1968), pp. 17–32.

33. Ibid., p. 428: "Pożal się Boże nieszczęsney godziny/Że się sarmackie z sobą tłukli syny."

34. The heading of the entry for AD 979 read: "On the custom of drawing the sword from the scabbard during the Mass while the Holy Gospel is sung." See Gloger, *Encyklopedia*, 4: 297.

35. Symon Teofil Turnowski, *Źwierciadło nabożeństwa chrześciańskiego w Polszcze* (Vilnius, 1594), B3^{r-v}: "Tych tam wieków za Ś. Woyciecha y Ś. Stanisława (według vstawy podaney od Mieczysława Książęcia) y potym przez niemały wiek Polacy zwłaszcza stanu Rycerskiego powstaiąc ku słuchaniu Ewangeliey, mieczów do połowy dobywali, przy Ewangeliey się iako prawdziwi Ewangelicy, wierni Chrześcianie, popisuiąc ...."

> words that they were ready to be in the grave. The Ruthenian does not yield to the Pole in this regard, for he is ready to die for his good faith.[36]

Here again Baranovych picked up the theme of nostalgia for the Polish-Lithuanian heroic past (and pointed out that Ruthenians were no less heroic than Poles).

What I am attempting to establish here is the general tonality of Baranovych's use of terms referring to confessions, peoples, and states. My argument is that, for Baranovych and, by extension, for some readership of his works, although Rus' (or, at least, much of Rus') was now obedient to the "Orthodox tsar," its identity was still largely defined by its relationship to Poland and Lithuania. Muscovy was strangely lacking as a source of associations and images for Baranovych. It was as if—in Baranovych's mind—Muscovy was now a part of Rus', not Rus' a part of Muscovy; as if the political might of the tsar would finally allow Rus' to play the game successfully by the old Polish-Lithuanian rules, not that it had radically changed the rules of the game for Rus'.

Thus Baranovych was still seeking answers to the old problems caused by Polish-Lithuanian-Ruthenian cohabitation of one Commonwealth. Focusing his attention on the discrepancies between the two calendars, for instance, he asked, "Why Does the Roman Precede the Ruthenian Birth of the Lord":

> Is it that Lech flies ahead with his Crown Eagle, and the Lithuanian prepares his chase, that the Ruthenian takes the lazy ass from the stable, that his way is not quick in this regard? ... Rus' rises in the morning. Why did they oversleep the Lord's birth? Lech ran on ahead. That the last are sometimes first [Matthew 19:30, 20:16; Mark 10:31; Luke 13:30], Rus' lends an ear to these words. Those who came to the vineyard in the eleventh hour also received a penny [Matthew 20:1–16].[37]

---

36. Baranovych, *Lutnia apollinowa*, p. 527: "Ewangelią gdy czytano, bronie/ Gołe dobyto, było to w Koronie./Polacy dali znać z tego po sobie,/Przy słowach Pańskich gotowi być w grobie./Rusin Polaka nie wyda w tey mierze/Bo gotów vmrzeć przy swey dobrey wierze."

37. Baranovych, *Zodyak, Księgi śmierci abo Krzyż Chrystusów* (Chernihiv, 1676), B1^r: "Czy Lech Koronnym Orłem dolatuie/Wprzód? a swą Litwin Pogonię gotuie./Że leniwego osła z stayni bierze/Rusin, nie spieszna droga mu w tey mierze. [...] Ruś rano wstaie, Narodzenie czemu/Pańskie zaspali? Lech zabiegł dobremu/Wprzód. Że posledni, pierwszemu bywaią,/Ruś na te słowa vcha nakłaniaią./Co iedynastey godziny przybyli/Do winogradu, y ci grosz zdobyli."

Here we have a new trio of coats of arms: to the eagle of the Polish Crown and the chase of the Lithuanian Grand Duchy, Baranovych has added the Ruthenian ass, with all its biblical associations.

The plots of Baranovych's stories implied a continuing coexistence, even a marriage, of Lech and Rus. A poem on Easter imagined precisely the *domestic* blessings to be gained from a reunification of the calendars. The bells would be rung at the same time in Catholic and Orthodox churches. Husband-Pole and wife-Ruthenian would fast at the same time and eat at the same time. In short, "when the Resurrection occurs in common, it engenders also the dearer pleasure for Pole and Ruthenian."[38]

Such passages created a tonality in which all the many other, less specific conjunctions of Lech and Rusin (usually in the context of calls for an anti-Turkish and anti-Tatar coalition) sounded like the old usage: "Lamb of God, who takes away sins, cause that Rus' fight the Tatars together with the Poles. Amen, God grant it, pray to God for it, that the Tatar be trod upon like mud."[39]

And yet, on one or two occasions only, Baranovych spoke of a specifically *Muscovite*-Polish alliance against the Infidel: "The Author wishes every good thing to the Muscovite and the Polish eagles";[40] "when the Muscovite eagle flies with the Polish, fathers and children will fly with them. We trust in God that the eagles of those two monarchs will land upon the Turks with their claws."[41] These passages do not, however, necessarily call into question the argument I have been making here. Notice that Baranovych addressed these powers—Pole and Muscovite—as "them." "We" remained in some contested position in the middle. It had been the

38. Baranovych, *W Wieniec*, p. 44: "Wstęp by był do iedności pewnie znamienity;/Gdyby ieden Kalendarz obom był odkryty./Do Kościołów y Cerkwi dzwonionob iednako,/Mąż Lech Żenie Rusce nie mowił ladako./Ten ie, a ta zaś pości; iaka ma bydź zgoda?/Z kalendarza różnego pewna niepogoda./Z martwych wstanie pospołu kiedy się przygodzi,/w Lechu, w Rusinie, milszą y vciechę rodzi./W Kościołach, w Cerkwiach społem w dzwony biją;/Iednakich potraw v stołu zażyią."

39. Baranovych, *Lutnia apollinowa*, p. 422: "Baranku Boży, który gładzisz grzechi,/Spraw niech Tatarów Ruś woiuie z Lechi,/Amen, day Boże, prosić Boga o to/By Tatarzyna zdeptano iak błoto."

40. Baranovych, *Notiy pięć*, [::]2^{v}: "Do Orłów Moskiewskiego y Polskiego/Author im życzy wszystkiego dobrego."

41. Baranovych, *Lutnia apollinowa*, p. 424: "Moskiewski z Polskim Orłem gdy poleci,/Z nimi polecą y Oycy y dzieci,/Vfamy Bogu Orły z pazurami/Tych dwóch Monarchów siędą nad Turkami."

lot of Rus' to recognize the sovereignty of one or the other of those eagles.

2. North, South, East, West, and In Between

Baranovych's world was a Europe one-fourth of which had been taken from the "monarchs" by the Turk.[42] Here we find an equation of Europe with Christendom and a division between Christendom and the Islamic world, but no internal division within Europe. More often, however, Baranovych saw his world in terms of a split between East and West within Christendom, and he saw the reconciliation of Ruthenian and Pole as the foundation for overcoming that divide.

Baranovych's East was not the same as Eastern Europe in our sense of the term. In his world one spoke of a north that included Poland-Lithuania and Muscovy. He and his contemporaries thought in terms of an opposition recodified in the Renaissance between a civilized South and a barbaric North. Eastern Europe was an invention of the Enlightenment, and even in the late eighteenth century one still spoke of Russia as Europe's North.[43] It is worth considering, however, to what extent the North-South opposition formed the prehistory of the division of Europe into East and West; to what extent the barbarians of the North were to become the barbarians of the East. Further, to what extent did the East-West opposition used in Baranovych's time—that between Eastern and Western Christendom—become implicated in divisions between civilization and barbarity and thus help prepare a way for the later division into Eastern and Western Europe?

However we answer these larger questions, it is important to note that Baranovych saw himself occupying the borderlands between the Latin West and the Greek East, as well as those where civilization (Baranovych might have called it *polityczność)* shaded into barbarity. Baranovych was formed in a world that regularly made use of both sets of oppositions. This world was, moreover, the scene of attempts by Poles to draw boundaries that placed themselves firmly on the civilized side of the North and on the Latin side of the East. These attempts revealed both the formation of early modern Polish cultural and confessional identities and the presence of insecurities about those allegiances. Put very simply, the Polish elite was secure in its

42. Baranovych, *W Wieniec*, p. 45: "Europę, czwartą część, Monarchom bierze."

43. See Larry Wolff, *Inventing Eastern Europe: The Map of Civilization on the Mind of the Enlightenment* (Stanford, 1994), pp. 4–5.

identities when it faced North and East; insecure when it faced South and West.

A few examples will stand for the many. Early Jesuits often longed for the heroic careers of missions to India, the Far East, or the New World. The Polish Jesuit Piotr Skarga was among those who reminded the Order that an equally exotic land in need of conversion lay considerably closer at hand: "We do not need the East and West Indies. Lithuania and the North are a true India."[44] Skarga had in mind the Orthodox Christians of Poland-Lithuania, toward whom he had directed so much of his effort, but perhaps also those of Muscovy. Whether, with this statement, he placed the boundary of the North in Lithuania or just beyond it, he thereby placed Poles (i.e., Catholics) this side of barbarity. The Antitrinitarian polemicist and biblical philologist Szymon Budny, who had also lived, worked, and proselytized among the Ruthenians, represented the Orthodox Christians of Poland-Lithuania (in a letter to the Calvinist leader Heinrich Bullinger in Zürich, dated 18 April 1563) as "the admirer and most diligent imitator, or rather, the most superstitious ape, of all Greek superstitions."[45] A Polish envoy named Paweł Palczowski, who spent several years in captivity in Moscow during the Time of Troubles, wrote of fantastic barbarity among "Muscovite cannibals" and set up a definition by analogy: Muscovy was to Poland-Lithuania as the East and West Indies were to Spain and Portugal. It was the mission of Poland-Lithuania to bring Christianity and civilization to a barbarous and—according to Palczowski—un-Christian people and to enjoy the economic benefits from the exploitation of the land's resources.[46]

But Poles who were self-sufficient when they looked North and East betrayed insecurities toward the civilization of the South and West. The Catholic polemicist Stanisław Orzechowski wrote (in the

---

44. Cited according to Jan Sygański, ed., *Listy ks. Piotra Skargi T. J. z lat 1566–1610* (Cracow, 1912), p. 55. A Czech Jesuit by the name of Baltazar Hostounský (who had arrived in Poland-Lithuania in 1563) was of like mind: "Let those who get the urge to wander even unto India come here. They will experience here the same difficulties as in India, and they will learn the Polish language just as easily as they would the Hindu" (cited in Marceli Kosman, *Reformacja i kontrreformacja w Wielkim Księstwie Litewskim w świetle propagandy wyznaniowej* [Wrocław, 1978], p. 112).

45. Theodor Wotschke, *Der Briefwechsel der Schweizer mit den Polen: Archiv für Reformationsgeschichte*, Ergänzungsband 3 (Leipzig, 1908), p. 174: "Est enim Russia omnium graecanicarum superstitionum admiratrix imitatrixque diligentissima vel potius simia superstitiosissima."

46. See Paweł Palczowski, *Kolęda moskiewska* (Cracow, 1609), E4^{r-v}, H3^{v}.

1560s) with some pain that in "the world" (i.e., in his German and Italian universities) one found people who supposed that *Polonia* was a city like the Italian city *Bononia*.[47] The Antitrinitarian historian Stanisław Lubieniecki wrote (in the 1610s) that before the election of Henri Valois to the Polish throne one encountered "rather outstanding people who believed that *Polonia* is a certain region of Germany."[48] Łukasz Górnicki's Polish adaptation of Castiglione's *Il Cortegiano* betrayed a similar ambivalence toward the Polish courtier's relationship to Italian civilization: it showed both pride through its assertion that a Pole could be a courtier and diffidence in its acknowledgment that Polish society was not ready for Castiglione unadulterated.[49]

Baranovych, like others of the Ruthenian elite, seems to have accepted and internalized these "Polish" oppositions. This was one of the causes of tensions within the identities of the elite of the Orthodox-Catholic borderlands. Some, like the convert to Roman Catholicism Kasiian Sakovych, seem to have found these tensions a burden.[50] What makes Baranovych interesting to me here is that he seems to have had little difficulty in reconciling his allegiances to Orthodoxy and to Muscovy with his "Polish" views of civilization.

Baranovych accepted, for example, the Polish usage that made of the Italian the equally admired and despised repository of wordly polish:

> We live in such a land where quite a few die from an arrow. The *concepta* have to become confused when the winds of Mars move .... When Mars covers him with dust, you will change your concept, *even if you were an Italian*.[51]

---

47. See Stanisław Orzechowski, *Wybór pism*, ed. Jerzy Starnawski (Wrocław, 1972), pp. 417–18.

48. See Andrzej Lubieniecki, *Poloneutychia*, ed. Alina Linga, Maria Maciejewska, Janusz Tazbir, and Zdzisław Zawadzki (Warsaw, 1982), p. 63.

49. For an assessment of the changes required in order to polonize the Courtier, see Riccardo Picchio, "Le Courtisan selon Górnicki," *Etudes littéraires slavo-romanes* (Florence, 1978), pp. 69–91.

50. For an investigation of the relationship between Polish civilization and Ruthenian self-hatred, see David A. Frick, "'Foolish Rus'': On Polish Civilization, Ruthenian Self-Hatred, and Kasijan Sakovyč," *Harvard Ukrainian Studies* 18, nos. 3–4 (December 1994): 210–48.

51. Baranovych, *Lutnia apollinowa*, 1671: ***1^r: "W takiey mieszkamy krainie/Gdzie nie ieden strzałą ginie./concepta się mieszać muszą,/Gdy Marsa wiatry ruszą. [...] Gdy mars zakurzy mu prochem,/Zmienisz koncept *byś był Włochem*" (emphasis added).

And *even* Italians were human and suffered from their mortality: "Whether a Ruthenian or an Italian, if you wash yourself, know that you will certainly not wash yourself of your dust."[52] Here Baranovych echoed a series of Polish writers who were defensively humble toward Italian civilization. Szymon Budny, for example, had written in the preface to his *O urzędzie miecza używającem* (*On the Office of the Sword*, Łosk, 1583): "I acknowledge that, in addressing this person, a writer with a better wit and a more polished Pole was required, but where were we to find such Italians?"[53]

Baranovych's sense of an opposition between civilization and its lack extended to his relationship as a Ruthenian writer of Polish to Polish writing in general and to the poet who had already become *the* model of Polish verse, Jan Kochanowski.[54] Here the Ruthenian donkey again made its appearance and was contrasted to the Polish Pegasus:

> Although it is not Kochanowski who bears these verses, may you nonetheless take delight in them. These are verses of God; they recall God's Mother and the Saints, in whom they take delight. We did not run with a poetic Pegasus; what wonder is it that we did not catch up with Kochanowski, who ran with a flying Pegasus? We lazily rode a simple ass here. Respect the fact that the Lord rode on an ass, thus receive the ass as a guest as well. The ass entered where the Lamb was born, and there that ass was also rewarded.[55]

---

52. Ibid.: "Lub się rusinie lub się myjesz Włochu,/Wiedz z twego pewnie nie wymyiesz prochu."

53. Szymon Budny, *O urzędzie miecza używającem (1583). Zabytki literatury z doby Reformacji*, ed. Stanisław Kot (Warsaw, 1932), p. 15: "Znam sie do tego, że było trzeba z lepszym do tej osoby obrotem skrybenta i polerowaniejszego Polaka, ale gdzież nam ty Wlochy brać?"

54. On the seventeenth-century cult of Jan Kochanowski, see Janusz Pelc, *Jan Kochanowski w tradycjach literatury polskiej: Od XVI do połowy XVIII w.* (Warsaw, 1965), p. 15. On Kochanowski as a model in courses of rhetoric and poetics in Rus', see Ryszard Łużny, *Pisarze kręgu Akademii Kijowsko-Mohylańskiej a literatura polska: Z dziejów związków kulturnych polskowschodnio-słowiańskich w XVII–XVIII w.* (Cracow, 1966).

55. Baranovych, *Żywoty Świętych* (Kyiv, 1670), *3r: "Nie Kochanowski lub te Rythmy noszę/Byście się przecie w nich Kochali proszę./Boga te Rythmy, Bożą wspominaią/Matkę, y Świętych, w tych się zaś Kochaią./Nie Poetyckim Pegazem biegano,/Kochanowskiego w tym nie doiachano./Osłem tu prostym iachano leniwo,/Kto biegł Pegazem lotnym co za dziwo?/Że Pan na Ośle ieździł respektuycie,/Y Osła iako Gościa w dom przyimuycie./Osieł wszedł tam gdzie Baranek się rodził:/Y tu się Osieł ten także nagrodził."

Baranovych's continuing apologies for his style focused on the physical aspects of Rus' rusticality: "The Ruthenian cackles something at the Pole in Polish."[56] His invitations to Poles to speak as equals were modest, and they remained defensive with regard to the civilization of Rus' vis-à-vis the more polished "brothers":

> Please forgive me, O Pole, if you find things not to your taste here. If you were to greet us in Ruthenian, I, a Ruthenian, would gladly read it. For the Ruthenian, Polish and Latin are the same sort of beast. If the beast has horns, O worthy Pole, do not be harsh.[57]

In Baranovych's world, relations in the realm of spiritual culture were reflected by those of material culture. Medical care, for example, was—as far as Baranovych was concerned—less sophisticated where he lived than it was on the other side of the border. Baranovych complained all his life—in prose and in verse—of, among other infirmities, his *kołtuny* (which, at one point, he wished upon the Tatar).[58] This was a disease known as *plica polonica,* or "Polish plait," a condition characterized by a painful matting of the hair.[59] He saw himself as living in a place where remedies known elsewhere were simply unavailable. He wrote on 13 January 1670 to Father Vasylevych, an archimandrite in Slutsk, "I live in places where the only medicine is suffering." And he told his correspondent from the other side of the Polish-Muscovite border, "I would be glad to receive medicine from your parts against my suffering; against my decay."[60] Even his ironic acknowledgment of a Muscovite "cure" for *kołtuny* was based on an opposition of barbarity to civilization: "The *kołtun* digs quite a lot at a man's shoulders. It does not exist in Muscovy; there it retreats before the knout. May the *kołtuny* always fear the knout and not cause us any more ill from now on."[61]

---

56. Baranovych, *Lutnia apollinowa,* pp. 549–50: "Rusin do Polaka/Coś po Polsku gdaka."

57. Ibid., p. 550: "Proszę przebacz mnie Polaku,/Ieżeli tu ni masz smaku,/Byś ty po Rusku nas witał,/Ia bym Rusin chętnie czytał:/Rusinowi to zwierzyna,/Iak polszczyzna tak łacina./Ta zwierzyna gdy ma rogi,/Cny Polaku nie bądź srogi."

58. See Baranovych, *Pis'ma,* pp. 152, 180, 203.

59. On *kołtuny,* see Gloger, *Encyklopedia,* 3: 63–64.

60. Baranovych, *Pis'ma,* pp. 105–6.

61. Baranovych, *Lutnia apollinowa,* p. 454: "Kołtun człowieku barziey w plecy maca,/Niemasz go w Moskwie od knuta odwraca./Niechay się knuta wżdy kołtuny boią/A nam tam złego iuż odtąd nie stroią."

Or consider an example from the world of print culture. Baranovych had devoted several years and much energy to establishing a printing house under his direct control in Chernihiv. He addressed his printings to a reading pubic that reached across political boundaries and included the urban centers of Vilnius, Lviv, Kyiv, and Moscow. He complained of the quality of the books printed for him by one Symeon Ialynsky: that "no one would even wish to look at such unclear print"; that the ink was poorly made and rubbed off on the reader's hands.[62] Here, too, Baranovych seems to have thought that centers on the Polish side of the border provided the standard by which printing quality was to be judged; he seems to have despaired of competing in that market and to have looked to Moscow as the place where he could "unload" these inferior products.[63]

3. Ukraina

Where, then, was Rus' in Baranovych's world? Was it part of a Commonwealth of Three Nations, or was it one of the Three Ruses covered by the tsar's crown? Was Baranovych worried that the tsar *would* remove his power from Kyiv? Or that he would *not* remove his palatines from Ukraine? One solution to this problem may involve questioning the "or" of the formulations given above. The same Baranovych who wrote of the equal status of Rus' with the Poles and Lithuanians in the fatherland that was the Commonwealth also urged acknowledging the tsar's rule in his "Pastor's Advice to His Flock":

> Who like the Orthodox TSAR is the leader of the sheep? He was ready to receive the gathering sheep. Let the little sheep hold *kripko* [fast] here to the head, for it is very *chibko* [shaky] for them to be under the wolf's head .... Serve the tsar faithfully, for you have liberties. And you will increase them further through your faithful service. May God strengthen you under the Orthodox tsar; never be led astray by the Crooked-odox tsar.[64]

Notice, however, that this was a call, a plea that assumed that the "little sheep" might not see the wisdom of following the Orthodox

---

62. See Baranovych, *Pis'ma*, p. 244.

63. See Sumtsov, *K istorii*, p. 29.

64. Baranovych, *W Wieniec*, [i]2^v: "Któż iak Prawosławny CAR iest owczey głowy?/On garnące owieczki przyiąć był gotowy./Tu się niechay owieczki Głowy dzierżą *kripko;*/Bo im pod wilczą głową być iest wielce *chibko*. [...] Wiernie Carowi służcie wszak wolności macie,/Wierną waszą vsługą ieszcze pomnażacie. [...] Niechay was Bóg pod Carem zmacnia prawosławnym,/Nie vwodźcie się nigdy Carem krzywosławnym."

shepherd/tsar. Further, that Baranovych inserted in his Polish verse—and in italics—a folksy "Ukrainian" rhyme (*kripko—chibko*) in his attempt to persuade the flock. This was an element of his rhetoric; an attempt to speak directly to his own people in "their" language. The "crooked-odox tsar," moreover, was the Turkish sultan, not the Polish king. Note further that Baranovych promised his sheep the granting of "liberties" in exchange for allegiance to the tsar. That is, Baranovych seems to have been looking to Moscow to make good on Polish promises.

One aspect of Baranovych's sense of place and allegiance was a more local Rus'. Baranovych's Rus' was defined by associations with Poland-Lithuania and by allegiance to Muscovy. It was further defined by the Muscovite-Polish border, which divided it. Baranovych lamented that his access to compatriots in Lviv in Right-Bank Ukraine had now become difficult. To Arsenii Zhelyborsky, bishop of Lviv, he wrote in 1657: "A great abyss has become established between you and us. Neither do we have safe access to you, nor you to us."[65] Although Baranovych would probably still have spoken, as did his predecessors a generation earlier, of the Rus' of Vilnius, there are signs that his Rus' was becoming a more and more locally Ukrainian Rus'. Ukraine was the scene of his work, the place whose division he regretted, and where discord had caused strife:

> As a ship is heavily rocked on the water, so it is with our poor Ukraine. Nay, even worse: the ship sails on water, but Ukraine on blood, because it is in discord. O Lord, you rule the winds, you the waters—cause there to be peace among us.[66]

And elsewhere he wrote: "Let Ukraine become different .... God grant holy harmony in Ukraine .... Enough blood has already been spilled in Ukraine."[67]

Mystical Harmonies, Unions, and Identities

For Baranovych, the foundation of peace in Ukraine lay in the realization of a brotherhood between Lech and Rus. Although Baranovych always portrayed this brotherhood as having a very

---

65. Baranovych, *Pis'ma*, p. 6.

66. Baranovych, *Lutnia apollinowa*, p. 413: "Iak łódź na wodzie wałami się chwieie,/Toż z Vkrainą naszą biedną dzieie,/Y gorzey ieszcze, łódź płynie na wodzie,/A Vkraina we krwi, że w niezgodzie./Panie Ty wiatry Ty władniesz wodami,/Spraw niechay cicho będzie miedzy nami."

67. Ibid., p. 410: "Niech Vkraina,/Zostaie inna,/.../Day Boże świętą zgodę w Vkrainie,/.../Dość w Vkrainie iuż się krwie wylało."

practical goal—an anti-Turkish and anti-Tatar crusade—its foundation was in the realm of the mystical. One of the underlying themes of his work was the search for a way across the "abyss"; for spiritual harmony between East and West, Orthodox and Catholic, Ruthenian and Pole.

Baranovych saw a particular urgency for realizing the brotherhood of Lech and Rus in 1680, and he devoted many passages scattered throughout the two works of that year to an investigation of the spiritual unities underlying that fraternity. He called for a non-confessionalized religion and for an end to the confessional polemics between Pole and Ruthenian; he prophesied the imminent realization of that fraternity in etymologies, numerologies, and divine alchemies; he represented the relationship of Lech and Rus in images of mutually formed crosses and flowers.

1. Anti-apologetics

Although Baranovych was a poor controversialist, he seems to have perceived a pressing need that someone answer a Polish Jesuit from Lviv named Benedykt Paweł Boym (1630–70). Boym's more famous brother, Michał Piotr (1612–59), likewise a Jesuit, had made a career as a missionary in China and had become a noted Sinologist—an expert, among other things, in Chinese medicine.[68] Benedykt Paweł seems also to have felt a strong calling to missionary work and to have agreed with those, such as Piotr Skarga, who drew analogies between the Jesuits' presence in the East and West Indies and their activities in the Polish-Lithuanian East. In 1668, Boym published in Vilnius one of the more interesting Catholic treatments of Orthodoxy, a work based on a knowledge of Orthodox authorities more thorough than was usual among Catholic controversialists and that cited many testimonies in Church Slavonic. It was entitled *Stara wiara abo jasne pokazanie, iż ci co w dizuniey trwaią wiary nie mają* (*The Old Faith, or a Clear Demonstration that Those Who Remain in the Dis-Union Do Not Have the Faith*). Ruthenian churchmen under Muscovite rule seem to have felt that, even though Boym had written from the other side of the border, they could not afford to ignore this attack; indeed, that

68. Among other things, a *Clavis medica a Chinarum doctrinam de pulsibus* was published in 1686 and a *Specimen medicinae sinicae* in 1682. His work was translated in the seventeenth century into French, Italian, and German. On Boym, see Bolesław Szcześniak, "The Writing of Michael Boym," *Monumenta Serica: Journal of Oriental Studies* 14 (1949–55): 481–538.

Kyiv—the "Ruthenian Paris"[69]—had now become the only center able to respond, and that it was a matter almost of honor to demonstrate to Polish society that "there are Polish letters in Rus'."[70] In fact, both responses to Boym came from the lands under Muscovite rule. Ioanikii Galiatovsky also published an answer to Boym in his *Stary kościół zachodni* (*The Old Western Church*) of 1678. Here, too, in the area of writing and readership, the events of 1654 had only partially redrawn the old borders.

Baranovych's own response, *Nowa miara*, belongs to the weaker of his literary efforts. One of the reasons for this—in addition to a possible lack of the training required of successful controversialists—was lack of the requisite interest: although Baranovych seems not to have doubted that Orthodox Christianity was the True Church, and that attacks like those from Boym had to be met, he had little interest in defining what Orthodoxy was in relation to those challenges. Baranovych's Orthodoxy sounded sometimes like Catholic Mariolatry; sometimes like a humanist *religio Christi*. It was, in any case, fundamentally anti-apologetic, and he devoted some of his most impassioned prose (and worst poetry) to calling for an end to confessional controversy.

While the anti-apologetic stance was never far from the surface in all of Baranovych's many passages devoted to the relation of Lech and Rus, it was a constant and overt theme in a large portion of *Notiy pięć*. Here Baranovych developed, in the context of a defense of Orthodox doctrine on the procession of the Holy Spirit, an apology for an anti-apologetics. He argued in verse that:

> An unneeded curiosity to discourse boldly about God will not pass here, as one can pass off sham brilliance elsewhere. God's school teaches us to bow our forehead to God. It is entirely unnecessary to make a discourse about God... [and so on, for eight more couplets].[71]

And he also argued in prose that:

> Great things are spoken best by not speaking. He speaks best about God who adds wonder to his discourse. It is safer to believe in God than to investigate. Silence is the treasury of great

69. Baranovych, *Pis'ma*, p. 117.

70. Ibid., p. 180.

71. Baranovych, *Notiy pięć*, p. 53: "Niepotrzebna ciekawość śmiele dyszkurować/o Bogu, nie vydzie tu, iako gdzieś bliktrować./Bogu nachylać czoła, Boża vczy szkoła;/o Bogu dyszkurs czynić, nie potrzebna zgoła..."

> social polish (*polityka*). By being silent, you do not cause offense; by being silent you answer [an opponent]; by being silent you gain understanding; by being silent you offer proof.[72]

Baranovych cited in testimony for his apophatic theology authorities ranging from Scripture (Psalms 36:6; 2 Timothy 3:7; 1 Corinthians 3:18)[73] to St. Augustine ("Understand if you are able; if you are unable, believe")[74] to Erasmus.[75] The goal of this anti-argumental argument was, as always, the formation of a Ruthenian-Polish anti-Turkish league. Here Baranovych's prose again faded into verse:

> It would be more fitting for the Ruthenian together with the Pole, and for all who boast of the Holy Cross, together to pull out their weapons (*dobyć kurka*), and not to reach for their pens (*dobywać piórka*) against each other *de Processione Spiritus Sancti* [concerning the procession of the Holy Spirit].[76]

Some polemicists of the Age of Reform were sensitive to the notion that theological arguments were often used in what were at least partly political and social arguments. Only the weaker parties, however, saw a strategic benefit in commenting on this aspect of the debate. For example, a leader of the Czech Brethren, Symon Teofil Turnowski, revealed the rhetorical rules of the polemic (and sought thereby a polemical advantage) when he wrote that "in compliance with the will of the adversaries of the Lord's church, we ourselves also sing that *little ditty* [emphasis added]: 'Whatever is older and more original is also better and more genuine.'"[77] In similar fashion, Baranovych brought to the surface the political and social subtext of the Polish-

---

72. Ibid., p. 75: "Wielkie rzeczy nie mówiąc naylepiey się mówią. Naylepiey o Bogu mówi, kto podziwieniem dokłada. O bogu bespiecznieysza wierzyć, niżeli się badać. Milczenie skarb wielkiey polityki; milcząc nie vrazisz, milcząc zbędziesz, milcząc wyrozumiesz, milcząc dokażesz."

73. Ibid., pp. 53, 54, 77.

74. Ibid., p. 48.

75. Ibid., p. 58.

76. Ibid., p. 47: "Raczey by Rusinowi z Polakiem, y kożdemu kto się tylko Krzyżem Świętym chwali, na Turka spólnie dobyć kurka, a nie z sobą de Processione Spiritus Sancti dobywać piórka."

77. Turnowski, *Żwierciadło*, A4^{v}: "Przetosz dogadzaiąc woley Adwersarzów Zboru Pańskiego Śpiewamy też y sami tę piosneczkę: Co iest dawnieyszego y pierwszego, to też iest lepsze y prawdziwsze."

Ruthenian confessional debate and argued that his opponents were not acting in good faith when they sang their own little ditties:

> The issue between Rus' and the Romans is not so much *de religione* [about religion] as *de regione* [about rule]. They do not want Rus' to have *rus* [land]. The issue is not so much whether the Holy Spirit proceeds *a patre solo* [from the Father alone] as *de paterno solo* [only about the paternal country].[78]

Rus', according to Baranovych, was left holding the horns (i.e., the privileges granted by the kings of Poland), but "someone else" was doing the milking.[79] (Notice again that in characterizing the Polish-Ruthenian relationship Baranovych reached for images from the realm of the physical aspects of rural life.)

2. Etymologies

Baranovych, like so many of his age, believed in etymologies. Secret connections between words revealed hidden truths. Part of Baranovych's function as a writer was to bring these covert concordances to the surface; to make them the foundation and the goal of his theology, poetics, and politics. Etymologies revealed the mystical fraternity of Lech and Rus that had not yet been realized in the temporal world. The word *mater*, for example, "foreordains that Rus' will make peace with the Latins, because they all call the Mother of God by the same word, Rus' *mater*, and the Latins *mater*." The Mother of God was able to "reconcile virginity with motherhood, and these things are never reconciled to one another"; therefore, she would be able to reconcile East and West. The core of this secret harmony resided in a cross-lingual, Slavic-Latin pun/etymology: *ma ter* means *ma trzy*: "she has (Polish[80] *ma*) three (Latin *ter*)," that is, she has the Father, to Whom she is a daughter; the Son, to Whom she is mother; and the Holy Ghost, to Whom she is betrothed (*oblubienica*).[81]

Musings on linguistic correspondences led to a series of messianic prophecies for Rus'. *RVS* was an acronym for *Radix* (Root), *Verbum*

78. Baranovych, *Nowa miara*, [] [2] []$^{r-v}$: "Rusi z Rzymiany nie tak idzie *de Religione* iak *de Regione*, nie chcą aby Ruś miała *Rus*, nie tak im o to idzie, ieśli pochodzi Duch Ś. *a Patre solo*, iako *de paterno solo* ..."

79. Baranovych, *Żywoty Świętych*, p. 108.

80. Note that Baranovych made the Polish verb form stand for the "Eastern" element here. For Baranovych, Polish could function as a "Ruthenian language."

81. Baranovych, *W Wieniec*, p. 128.

(Word), and *Spiritus Sanctus* (Holy Spirit).[82] Letter counts of three and five revealed further mysterious correspondences: *IESVS—RVSIN* (JESUS —RUTHENIAN);[83] *BOG—RVS* (GOD—Rus');[84] MARIA—RVSIN (MARY—RUTHENIAN);[85] *BOG—CAR—RVS* (GOD—TSAR—Rus').[86]

Harmonies extended from words and morphemes to letters. Baranovych cited Luke 1:39: "Въставши МАРІАМ иде вгорняя" (And Mary arose in those days, and went into the hill country). Why, he asked, does Scripture read "Mariam" and not "Maria"? Because, he argued, "Mariam" has the Cyrillic letter called *myslite* (i.e., "think") at the beginning and *myslite* at the end; and it has the Latin letter *em* beginning and end, which is an anagram for the Latin *me*. Thereby did the Alpha and Omega (i.e., Beginning and End) before the ages "*think* about *me*, Mary, about *me*, the Mother of God."[87]

3. Numerologies

With letters came also numbers. Baranovych's *Wieniec* and *Notiy pięć* were, to a large extent, prophecies for Rus' for the year 1680, often accompanied by imagery from the Apocalypse of St. John. There were, of course, the expected numbers: 6666 plagues; 666, the number of the Antichrist; 999, the number of the Virgin.[88] But the ruling numbers for AD 1680 were 8 and 0. 0 was the shape of Baranovych's *Wieniec* (i.e., "wreath") to the Virgin. Circles abounded. "The Wreath (*Wieniec*) knows nothing (*wie nic*): 0";[89] "0, our beginning is nothing (*nic*), our middle a spider's web (*nić*), our end to decay (*gnić*)."[90] Baranovych made of the circles of Polish parliamentary politics an image of the Turk's defeat in 1680: "The Senators' Circle, the Representatives' Circle, and the Knights' Circle intone thus to the Turks together with David [Psalms 82]: 'O my God, make them like a wheel (i.e., 'circle').'"[91]

---

82. Ibid.
83. Baranovych, *Notiy pięć*, p. 335.
84. Ibid., pp. 335, 340.
85. Ibid., p. 336.
86. Ibid., p. 338.
87. Baranovych, *W Wieniec*, p. 108–9.
88. Ibid., p. 14.
89. Ibid., p. 25.
90. Ibid., p. 107.
91. Ibid., p. 116: "Koło Senatorskie, Poselskie, Rycerskie, tak Turkom z Dawidem intonuie: Boże móy połóż ich iako koło."

A collocation of two 0s formed the number 8, which was the sign of infinity and perfection. In a poem simply entitled "8," Baranovych wrote:

> Eight has within it two wreaths; in my eighth book I offer two wreaths, O Virgin, to Your adornment. East and West gave birth to such flowers for You, carrying the Eastern and Western Fathers for adornment.[92]

The most important circle was Christ Himself, the Alpha and Omega. Baranovych called upon Christ—"who has thrice 8 in his name"—to come to the aid of Rus' in 1680 against the Antichrist Turk.[93]

Here, too, the numerologies crossed the boundaries of alphabets, revealing the mystic unity of East and West. (But note that time was reckoned here solely in Western style, i.e., since the birth of Christ, never Eastern style, since the creation of the world.) Baranovych wrote: "The year axп [1680] from the birth of the Lord ends on the letter п called *pokój* [peace]."[94] But peace for Rus' required war against the Turk: "A gallows for the Turk П."[95] In other words, the Cyrillic letter П (*pokój*, 'peace') was a gallows (*furca*) for the Turk. Here, the East-West fraternity was again identified as specifically Ruthenian-Polish: "Lech will make a derision of the Turk. That haughty viper will come to know the manly Ruthenian. In Ruthenian П, a gallows for the Turk. In Polish 0, a bullet against the Turk, that one must hold him as a cipher."[96] Thus, under certain conditions, the 0 of perfection could be reinterpreted as a bullet or a cipher, a zero, and the П of peace could serve as a gallows.

4. Divine Alchemies

For Baranovych, the elements formed a kind of divine chemistry. He wrote: "Let the *elementatum* composed of the four elements thus take Divinity from Fire, from Air, from Water, from Earth."[97] And in one

---

92. Ibid., p. 24: "Ośm ma w sobie dwa wieńca, w książce ósmey moiey,/Dwa wieńca Panno daię, ku ozdobie twoiey./Wschód y Zachód, zrodzili iakie kwiatki tobie,/Wschodnich Zachodnich Oyców niosąc ku ozdobie."

93. Ibid., pp. 75–76.

94. Ibid., p. 122.

95. Ibid., p. 123: "Na Turka *furca* П."

96. Ibid., p. 136: "Lech, z Turka vczyni śmiech. Ta harda gadzina pozna mężnego Rusina, po Rusku П. na Turka *furca*, po Polsku O, kula na Turka; za cyfrę go mieć trzeba."

97. Baranovych, *Notiy pięć*, pp. 185–87: "*Elementatum* z czterech Elementow złożony niech bierze stąd Bóstwo z Ognia, z Powietrza, z wody, z Ziemi."

of the emblematic poems on the cross in his *Lutnia apollinowa* of 1671 he gave the elements a role in the divine mystery of death and resurrection: "The four *elementa* gathered here. They came to love the four sides of Christ's cross. The earth, into which the wood of the crosses was inserted, WATER, AIR, where the hands were laid, fire where a candle burned on the top of the cross and sought the lost drachma."[98] Musings on the theology of the elements led Baranovych to thoughts of gold. Baranovych consistently linked—often, in fact, rhymed—gold and mud (*złoto-błoto*) and turned one into the other: "As gold, so mud";[99] "Golden mud will reward you with heavenly gold; will liberate you from all the suffering that afflicts you."[100]

Similarly, silk was the costly cloth produced by a worm. Together, silk and gold were part of an alchemy that united Lech and Rus in one mystical body, as it united the divine and the human in Christ:

> Rus' and the Lachs are a golden bobbin. One must not unwind on it the gold from the silk, for they are both to go together. With gold alone one could not make a thread, since it is stiff. It cannot be used for sewing; one needs silk in addition. And that is why gold and silk must be held in equal regard. Just as in Christ the gold is of the Divine person, and the silk is of the human nature, which the little worm made. God joined both of them together in His one person, as if He had braided them into one. He did not use divinity alone as the gold, for it to be required for our salvation; in it alone the Lord could not suffer and die, whereas in the human nature joined with the divine He could do all of that. It is not fitting to unwind that; to separate the one nature from the other. So Rus' must not be separated from the Lachs, or the Lachs from Rus'. In the original Church it was one. Rus' and the Lachs commemorate twelve popes. They will not sew themselves wedding garments from gold alone, unwound from the silk. Although we are the East, and thus gold ought to belong to us, and silk to the West, nonetheless we will relinquish the gold to you, the elder brethren; we will take the silk for ourselves. But we do not wish to be *divisi* (divided), for that way we shall accomplish nothing.[101]

---

98. Baranovych, *Lutnia apollinowa*, p. 159: "*Elementa* się tu cztery skupili/Rogi Krzyżowe sobie vlubili,/Ziemia gdzie drzewo Krzyżowe wetknione/WODA, POWIETRZE, gdzie Ręce złożone,/Ogień na wierzchu Krzyża gdzie gorzała/Świeca, a drachmy zgubioney szukała."

99. Ibid., p. 187: "Iak złoto, tak błoto."

100. Baranovych, *W Wieniec*, p. 89: "Żółte błoto niebieskim wam złotem nagrodzi/Od wszelakich bid, ktore was trapią, wyswobodzi."

101. Baranovych, *Notiy pięć*, pp. 315–16: "Ruś a Lachi, cewka złota, nie trzeba w niey rozwijać złota od iedwabiu, bo to pospołu chodzić ma oboie; samym

Thus the gold and silk threads of fine cloth, the divine and human natures in Christ, became figures of Lech and Rus: they were indivisible, hypostatically united; worthless individually, priceless together.

5. Crosses and Clubs

Together, Lech and Rus were to slay the Antichrist with two clubs. When united, these two clubs formed a cross with equal arms: "The Turk is made stupid with the moon. + The Cross, two clubs, from Ruthenian and Lech, will beat the Turk."[102] The edges of the cross were *rogi* or "horns." Lech and Rus occupied the cross's opposing "horns": "If those two horns would agree, Ukraine would be eating *pirogi* [i.e., pi-rogi] right away. Today the Tatar eats the *pirogi*—hunger for the Christians; for the Christians suffering."[103]

The Cross was also like the Ruthenian letter T, *twerdo* (Ruthenian "hard"), a sign that it was *twardo* (Polish for the same thing) for the Lord on the Cross.[104] Arguing against apologetics, Baranovych etymologized: "That (*ten*) argument, that (*ta*) reason, that (*to*) dilemma. Try this one, that one, the other one, thus does the snake in Paradise advise. *Tentato* [i.e., Polish *ten-ta-to*, or the masculine, feminine, and neuter singular nominative forms of the demonstrative pronoun "that"; but also the Latin *tentato* (from *tento*, "to try")] try it; and thus does he tempt you; lead you into temptation."[105] In this context, Baranovych

---

złotem nie mógłby nić zrobić, bo tęgie, nie da się vżyć na szycie, trzeba do niego iedwabiu. Y dla tego iedwab y złoto pospołu ważyć trzeba z sobą. Iak w Chrystusie y złoto iest Boskiey osoby, y iedwab natury ludzkiey, ktorą robaczek vczynił, pospołu to oboie w iedney osobie iego Bóg z sobą złączył, iakoby w iedno skręcił; samego Bóstwa iako złota nie vżył by potrzebno do zbawienia naszego, nie mogł by w nim samym Pan cierpieć, vmrzeć: w człowieczey zasię naturze z Boską złączoney to wszystko odprawować mógł, nie godzi się tego odkręcać iedney od drugiey natury oddzielać. Tak się Ruś nie ma oddzielać od Lechów, Lechi od Rusi. s Pierworodney Cerkwi, iedno to było. 12. Papieżów y Ruś y Lachi święcą: szaty sobie nie vszyią weselney z iednego złota od iedwabiu odkręconego. Chociaśmy Wschód, nam by złoto należało, Zachodowi iedwab; iednak my wam starszey Braci złota vstępuiemy, iedwab sobie bierzemy, ale *diuisi* bydż nie chcemy, bo tak nic nie zrobiemy."

102. Ibid., b3^{r}: "Z Luną Turek głupi. + Krzyż dwa kije, od Rusina y Lecha, zbiją Turczyna."

103. Baranovych, *Lutnia apollinowa*, p. 421: "Gdyby się oba te zgodzili Rogi,/ Vkraina by wnet iadła pirogi,/Dzisia Tatarzyn pirogi poiada,/Głód Chrześcianom, Chrześcianom biada."

104. Baranovych, *Notiy pięć*, [ii]1^{v}.

105. Ibid., p. 106: "Ten Argument, ta racya, to dilemma. Na ten, na ta, na to, tak Rayski wąż radzi: *tentato*, próbuy; a tak cię *tentat*, vwodzi w *tentatią*."

referred to Revelations 20:4, bringing together several of the themes I have been developing here: etymological proofs, arguments against confessional polemics, the cross, a Ruthenian-Polish mystical confraternity, and an anti-Turkish crusade: "Against this one (*ten*), against that one (*ta*), place a T. a *tau* on the forehead. He tempts you. You have recourse to the Cross against the enemy of the Cross."[106]

6. Flowers of the Field

Christ was the *flos campi*, the flower of the field (Song of Solomon 2:1). Lech and Rus were wheat; the heretics were tares.[107] Lech and Rus were linked with the flowers of the field (*flores campi; kwiatki polne*). This was standard usage and not particularly surprising. What was unusual was the etymological connection that Baranovych made in this particular context between "Poles," "Polish," "Poland," and their relation to the "field" (*pole*). Thus *kwiatki polne* ("flowers of the field") were also *kwiatki polskie* ("Polish flowers"). And the field or *pole* was the place to which the Polish-Ruthenian confraternity had to take in order to defeat the infidel. The field leader, Christ, was the "Polish (i.e., 'field') tsar," the "flower of the field," the king of pain (Polish *ból*) and glory (Polish *sława*), that is, King *Bolesław:*

> The King of pain is crowned not with gold but with pain, not with diamonds but with wounds. Truly a King Bolesław on account of more and more pains (*bóle*). The Tsar of the Field [or, "Polish Tsar"], the Flower of the Field, go into the field to Him, Ruthenian, Pole, Cossack.[108]

Christ was also the "Polish—i.e., 'field'—representative," the heavenly envoy sent by God: "Casting the treasure, a golden ring, into the emperor's golden treasures, the field representative *auro addidit aurum* (added gold to gold). Our heavenly representative. *As the Father sent me* [John 20:21]."[109] Baranovych cited the Song of Solomon (7:11)—"Come, my beloved, let us go forth into the field"—in preface to his exhortation to a crusade: "O Ruthenian, Pole, Cossack, the flower of

---

106. Ibid., p. 125: "Na ten, na ta, połóż T. tau na czele. On cię *tentat*, ty do Krzyża na nieprzyiaciela Krzyżowego."

107. Baranovych, *W Wieniec*, p. 44.

108. Baranovych, *Notiy pięć*, p. [..]1^{v}: "Król boleści nie złotem ale bólem, nie dyamentami ale ranami vkoronowany. Król prawie Bolesław od bólów nowych a nowych. Car Polski, kwiat polny, w Pole do niego Rusaku, Polaku, Kozaku."

109. Ibid., p. [..]3^{v}: "Polski Poseł skarbek złoty pierścień do skarbów złotych Cesarskich rzucaiąc *Auro addidit aurum*. Poseł nasz Niebieski. *Iako mię posłal Ociec*."

the field—into the field against the Turk."[110] Baranovych's addresses to the Poles urged them to live up to their etymological promise: "If, O Pole, you take delight in this Flower of the Field, then I acknowledge that you are a wise child. It is fitting for the Pole to delight in the Flower of the Field. The Flower is the generous Lord; you will be treated generously by him."[111]

Rara Concordia Fratrum

In 1680 the Treaty of Andrusovo was to be renegotiated. Much of the international politics between Poland and Muscovy had been based on a northern triangle that included Sweden and a southern triangle that included the Ottoman Empire (plus, on occasion, the Tatar Khanate). Thus diplomacy at home and abroad, for all powers involved, especially for the weakening Polish-Lithuanian Commonwealth, often consisted in establishing support for a coalition of two against one. This was, in most cases, a question of identifying the lesser evil. As the royal envoy Kazimierz Bieniewski put it in a report to King Jan Sobieski sometime before 1675: "none of these sides can turn against the other two in war, neither the Porte against us and Moscow, nor Moscow against us and the Turk, nor we against both these monarchs."[112] On 16 April 1675, Khan Selim Giray wrote suggesting such a coalition to Jan Sobieski: "That Fatherland knew, and will now come to know, much good when we turn our three sabers [Polish, Tatar, and Turkish] against someone else .... Whatever harm it has suffered, with God's help, we will together recompense."[113]

Poland's politics of the 1670s had been marked by shifts between the Muscovite and the Turkish-Tatar alternative. These shifts informed both Sobieski's policy and *szlachta* approval (and disapproval) of the king's moves; thus the question of the lesser evil was also an important part of the domestic political scene in Poland-Lithuania. As a result of the Turkish War, which began in 1672, Poland-Lithuania suffered large losses in Ukraine. Most notably, Kamianets-Podilskyi now came under Turkish rule. Sobieski worked in the 1670s, through military campaigns and diplomacy, toward recouping these losses.

---

110. Ibid., p. b3^{v}: "Rusaku, Polaku, Kozaku, kwiat polny w pole na Turka."

111. Baranovych, *Żywoty Świętych*, p. 122: "Ieśli Polaku w tym Polnym Kwiecie/Kochasz: to przyznam żeś iest mędre Dziecię./Polaku w Polnym Kwiatku kochać stroyno,/Kwiat to Pan hoyny, będzie mu z nim hoyno."

112. Cited in Wójcik, *Rzeczpospolita*, p. 39.

113. Cited in ibid., p. 31.

After a major encounter on 17 October 1676, Poland-Lithuania and the Porte signed the Truce of Żurawno (Zhuravno), causing a marked deterioration in already bad relations between Poland and Muscovy. Sobieski wrote to Tsar Fedor Alekseevich on 21 October 1676, explaining the necessity for the treaty with the Porte on the basis of Muscovite non-involvement in the Polish-Turkish struggle, in spite of the stipulations of the Treaty of Andrusovo:

> It is known to the Lord God with what patience and harm to our domains, loss of Christian people, especially of the Ruthenian religion, and ruin of castles, for nearly five years, when the Turkish and Tatar might fought us, and especially since we did not receive your forces, Great Sovereign, Our Brother, Your Imperial Majesty, so often reminding you both through letters and through our personal envoys, finally through the Commission of Andrusovo we renewed our demands, trusting that the promises made would sometime be realized.[114]

(Note that both sides—Poland-Lithuania and Muscovy—could pose as protectors of Ruthenian Christians in their attempts to stake out strategically advantageous positions in their diplomatic encounters.) The papal nuncio Francesco Martelli wrote to Rome in those days of an impending Polish-Tatar war against Muscovy, the truce with which was to expire in 1680.[115]

The years 1676 to 1680 thus marked a crisis in Polish-Muscovite relations. At the Sejm of 1677 a decision was reached to send embassies to both Moscow and Istanbul. The palatine of Chełm, Jan Gniński, set off for the Porte in 1677. Meanwhile, Sobieski was assuring the nuncio that he could foresee no collaboration "with the infidel against the Christians." The failure of Gniński's embassy to Istanbul, along with the disrespectful treatment he received there, helped to turn gentry opinion away from the Turkish alternative. In the spring of 1678, Poland-Lithuania sent as envoys to Moscow the palatine of Volhynia, Michał Czartoryski, and the palatine of Polatsk, Kazimierz Jan Sapieha.[116]

Although the Polish side continued to complain about Muscovite behavior in Ukraine—that Ivan Samoilovych was calling himself "Hetman of Both Sides of the Dnipro" and that the tsar was making claims to all of Ukraine—a perceived weakness in the Porte encouraged thoughts at this juncture of a Muscovite-Polish alliance. The

---

114. Cited in ibid., p. 80.

115. Ibid.

116. On these events, see Wójcik, pp. 105, 110–42, 108, 142–91.

Polish resident in Istanbul, Samuel Proski, reported to Gniński in January 1679: "there has long not been, and I suppose there will not be a better opportunity to eradicate the Turks from Europe than now."[117] Proski wrote to Sobieski in July 1679: "The Porte is weak as never before. They have not enough people or counsel .... With Muscovy at the fore and us from behind, I do not know how they would wiggle away."[118] On 17 August 1678, both sides had signed an agreement temporarily prolonging the Treaty of Andrusovo. Further talks were scheduled for 30 June 1680 in Andrusovo.[119]

The Lithuanian referendary Cyprian Paweł Brzostowski and the starosta of Radzyń, Jan Gniński (the younger), were directed to Moscow by the Hrodna Sejm of 15 April 1679 for secret talks intended to lead to an anti-Turkish league and to prepare for the Andrusovo talks of 1680.[120] Sobieski's instructions for Brzostowski's audience with the tsar verged on the apocalyptic: "there is nothing more certain than the fact that the Turkish power has taken it into its head not only to possess all of Christendom, but to reign over the entire world."[121] In 1679, however, Moscow seems to have been more interested in peace with the Porte and with the Khanate. Brzostowski was received by the tsar—with much delay—on 17 August 1679.[122] The Polish envoys negotiated throughout the fall of 1679, with no apparent success. The Muscovite side was largely (with the exception of Patriarch Ioakim) in favor of peace with the Porte; all on the Muscovite side were opposed to the Polish terms.[123]

This "serious defeat" and "diplomatic disaster"[124] gave rise to a new pendulum swing in Polish-Lithuanian opinion, and voices now called for peace with the Porte. The palatine of Łęczyca, Władysław Leszczyński, now wrote:

> Whoever will reflect upon all the behavior of the Muscovite nation whereby they have proceeded with us, in older ages as in our times, must acknowledge their *lubriciam fidem* [slippery faithfulness], and

117. Cited in ibid., pp. 167–68.
118. Cited in ibid., pp. 194–95.
119. Ibid., p. 189.
120. Ibid., p. 197 (193–229).
121. Cited in ibid., p. 200.
122. Ibid., p. 202.
123. Ibid., p. 212.
124. These are Wójcik's terms (p. 226).

> thence that the counsels were cautious and sagacious of those who wished that, not relying on the vain promises of that nation, we not enter upon a war with the Turks or announce to the entire world that we are preparing for it .... I would wish *omnibus modis* [by all means] to repair our credit with the Porte and demonstrate that we sincerely wish to maintain peace with them.[125]

Nonetheless, Sobieski continued to send envoys to Moscow. In 1680 the embassy was led by the castellan of Wieluń, Konstantyn Tomicki, who declaimed in his speech before the tsar on 3 September "that these two nations, in whose brave arms Europe has placed all its hopes for wholeness; that these great monarchs, among whom the hand of God by its fate has divided the greatest Sarmatian domains, might make bold to humble the common enemy through their confederated forces."[126] Another Polish embassy sent to Moscow in 1681 failed again to bring about a rapprochement. These defeats led Sobieski to shift his thoughts westward in his search for alliances. In 1681 Muscovy signed a peace treaty with the Porte, and in 1683 Sobieski led his Polish forces to the "Relief of Vienna." It was not until 1686 that the Poles and Muscovites signed an "eternal peace," and thoughts agains turned to a "Sarmatian" anti-Turkish campaign.

Once Baranovych had control of his own printing house, first in Novhorod-Siverskyi and then in Chernihiv, he was in a position to see his works through the press in timely fashion, and his books began to take on some qualities of "occasional literature." He wrote, for instance, as Sobieski's Polish armies were headed toward Żurawno in 1676: "Why, O Pole, do you not hasten to take such fertile land? And why, O Ruthenian, do you not help him?"[127] The works of 1680, and especially the *Wieniec*, were couched as apocalyptic prophecies for that year. What did Baranovych intend by them? Was he taking a position on the issues of international politics in those days?

Given Baranovych's long-standing interest in the Treaty of Andrusovo and the terms of its repeated renegotiations, it would seem likely that the "occasion" for him in the works of 1680 was at least partially the pending Polish-Muscovite talks. If this was the case, then Baranovych was, at the very least, somewhat out of step with the international political movements of 1680. His appeals for an anti-Turkish crusade were more in tune with what had been Polish

---

125. Cited in ibid., p. 228.

126. Cited in ibid., p. 302.

127. Baranovych, *Zodyak*, M1^{r}: "Na tak żyzną czemu się nie kwapisz Polaku/ Ziemię? y nie pomagasz czemu mu Rusaku?"

diplomacy than with Muscovite, although by now even the Poles were looking elsewhere for alliances. But were subjects of the tsar supposed to be helping Poland-Lithuania make good its losses in Ukraine? What did Baranovych mean by such statements?

One partial answer is that Baranovych's vision was couched in mystical terms and was not specifically, or at least not only, a program for direct political action. It may have owed something—at whatever remove—to the rhetoric of what Frances Yates called a "Rosicrucian enlightenment."[128] Yates saw in the Rosicrucian manifestoes of the early seventeenth century and in the interest they generated throughout the century an expression of the hopes of irenicists of various confessions for a supraconfessional reformation of religion and society. This reformation was opposed to the confessional polemics through which the Christian confessions of the early seventeenth century had been drawing ever stricter lines of demarcation among themselves. It reasoned with the language of alchemy and made the rose at the center of the cross its symbol. It told its stories in terms of mystical, "chemical" weddings.

Baranovych's arguments against a confessionalized religion, his use of images of roses, crosses, rosy crosses, dew, mud, gold,[129] especially their concentration in passages exploring the relationship of Lech and Rus, make me wonder whether the archbishop had perhaps come into contact with the hermetic manifestoes of the Rosicrucian movement.[130] When he wrote of the *Rara concordia fratrum*[131]—the "rare

---

128. Frances A. Yates, *The Rosicrucian Enlightenment* (London, 1972).

129. A brief sampling must suffice here. Baranovych's *Wieniec* for the Virgin was composed of "red and white roses" (pp. 25–26). Tsar Fedor Alekseevich was to "destroy the Turk and glorify the name of God in the East," where he would "burn the thorns and plant roses" (*Notiy pięć,* [,,]3^r). The East itself—Latin *Ortus*—was an anagram for *Tu Ros*, "Thou [i.e., Christ] are Dew": "Dew is Christ, and that East bedews the sons of the East" (*Notiy pięć*:[**]3^v). Dew was one of the alchemistic images employed by the fellow travelers of the Rosicrucian movement, which gave rise to speculation as to whether these mysterious people were followers of the Rosy (*rosa*) Cross or of the Dewy (*ros*) Cross. Was Baranovych making a mystical cross-linguistic pun when he wrote that the "east bedews the sons of the East"—"Wschod wschodnie syny Rosi?" Finally, I would note that Rosy Crosses had been the subject of two of Baranovych's sixty emblematic poems on the cross (*Lutnia apollinowa*, 149, 159).

130. Baranovych was not a hermetic poet. He could at times, however, write like one. Consider the following poem: "Niechay w dół ślepy nie padnie day Boże,/Ciernie namorzey ziemi zarodź Roże,/Plewy na ziarno złoto w błoto przemień,/Niech z siebie ogień wyda vderz w krzemień" (*Lutnia apollinowa*, p. 173).

131. Baranovych, *W Wieniec*, p. 42.

harmony of brothers"—was he playing a game in the spirit of Johann Valentin Andreae's manifestoes, which had made a talisman of these same initials, *RCF: Rosae Crucis Fraternitatis* (or *Fratres* or *Familia*); *Rosicrucis Confessio et Fama; Confessio Fraternitatis Rosicrucis?*[132]

Baranovych's mystical vision may, nonetheless, have owed nothing to Rosicrucianism. It may have been his own creation, drawing on less specifically defined baroque rhetoric and poetics, along with the imagery of Revelation. Whatever its origins, it remains remarkable. The statement that the two Polish and Ruthenian natures were united in one Sarmatian hypostasis verged on sacrilege. The vision of a Polish-Ruthenian anti-Turkish crusade cannot have had only spiritual implications for readers of 1680. Statements that Lech and Rus inhabited one Fatherland must have been politically risky in Muscovy.

To which parties was Baranovych directing these messages? His immediate readership seems to have been Rus'. The works of 1680 particularly assumed an audience of the intellectual borderlands, ready to switch among rhetorical and linguistic systems. Two points come to mind here. First, part of Baranovych's audience remained on the other side of the border between the Commonwealth and Muscovy. He had answered the Jesuit Boym in defense of Ruthenians on both sides of the border. He clearly hoped for a Polish-reading audience for his Polish works. Second, part of his audience were those Ruthenians who had been tempted by the Turkish-Tatar alternative. To this extent, his message was not only yes to an alliance with the Commonwealth, but no to the Turks and Tatars as political allies for Rus', and—above all—peace among Ruthenians.

Baranovych's vision of a mystical Sarmatian brotherhood should be read not only against the background of Polish-Muscovite international relations, but also with an eye to internal Ukrainian-Ruthenian affairs, including those that crossed the border partitioning Rus'. The third dedicatee of his works—after tsar and patriarch—was always the hetman.[133] Baranovych's vision was a reaction to the period of Ukrainian history known as the *Ruïna*, which often saw two and at times three competing hetmans leading Ukrainians into battle against one another, allied in turn with Poland-Lithuania, Muscovy, and the Porte. A brief survey will give a sense of the turmoil. After the partition of Rus'

132. For English translations of the texts and a bibliography, see Yates, *The Rosicrucian Enlightenment*, pp. 235–60.

133. The copy of the *Wieniec* now found in the Library of the Jagiellonian University in Cracow (St. Dr. 311004 II) bears Baranovych's own handwritten dedication of the book to Hetman Ivan Mazepa.

under the terms of the Treaty of Andrusovo, Petro Doroshenko, hetman of Right-Bank Ukraine, abandoned his former pro-Polish policy and looked to Ottoman support for his project of reunification. He invaded Left-Bank Ukraine, deposed Hetman Ivan Briukhovetsky, and, in 1668, declared himself Hetman of All Ukraine. Challenged by rival hetmans, Doroshenko was forced to turn his attention back to Right-Bank Ukraine and to appoint Damian Mnohohrishny acting hetman on the Left Bank. Muscovy forced Mnohohrishny to renounce his ties to Doroshenko, and in 1675–76 Muscovy and Left-Bank Cossacks attacked the Porte at Chyhyryn. Doroshenko now surrendered his office to Ivan Samoilovych, the new hetman of Left-Bank Ukraine, who began to style himself "Hetman of Both Sides of the Dnipro." Meanwhile, the Porte had brought Iurii Khmelnytsky out of his monastic retirement, appointing him "Prince of Sarmatia and Ukraine, Lord of the Zaporozhian Host." In 1677–78 Khmelnytsky led his troops, with Ottoman backing, against Left-Bank forces at Chyhyryn. Thus Baranovych's message was not only harmony between Lech and Rus', but harmony within Rus'.

But Rus' clearly was not Baranovych's only audience. Moreover, it was one thing for an envoy of the Polish-Lithuanian Commonwealth to play the "Sarmatian Brotherhood" card in his orations before the tsar in an attempt to persuade the Muscovite side to join forces with the Poles. It was quite another thing for a Polish-speaking, Jesuit-educated spiritual leader of a people of suspect allegiance to write of the mysteries that joined Lech and Rus. It would almost seem at times that Baranovych expected the tsar and patriarch to read no more of his work than the portions dedicated directly to them (which, in fact, were often in Cyrillic-letter Slavonic, and thus set somewhat apart from the rest of the book). But that cannot have been the entire explanation here. Baranovych was clearly interested in the tsar's literary patronage for his works, as well as in his political patronage for his flock. He dedicated his works to the tsar and tsarevich, wrote letters bringing the authorities' attention to his works, and had them sent by courier to their Muscovite addressees. They were, in this sense, his first audience.[134] There is no reason to think he was insincere in urging his countrymen to acknowledge the sovereignty of the tsar.

Part of the answer may be that there was no immediate paradox here *for Baranovych*. I find no evidence that he was hiding this

134. In 1681 Patriarch Ioakim thanked Baranovych for sending him a copy of *Notiy pięć*. See *Arkhiv Iugo-Zapadnoi Rossii* (Kyiv), pt. 1, vol. 5 (1872): 208–9.

particular message of Polish-Ruthenian brotherhood from Muscovite authorities. In fact, he seems to have thought such ideas would be acceptable in Moscow. Although he did not argue in a public forum—if this indeed was his opinion and not only Adamovych's slander—that "no Muscovite foot" should remain in Rus', he felt that he *could* write publicly of Polish-Ruthenian brotherhood. Perhaps he was aided here by certain ambiguities on the border between Rus' and Muscovy. Although his usage was shaped by the Polish usage of the first half of the century, he himself blurred certain distinctions at times (mostly on those infrequent occasions when he addressed himself directly to the tsar). Thus he was in a position to claim, if challenged, that his vision of Polish-Ruthenian union did not necessarily exclude Muscovy. Perhaps Baranovych's political imagination could be compared to that of the Polish nobles who, in the late sixteenth century, had supported the election of Muscovite tsars as Polish kings.[135] Perhaps he thought in terms of a new, strong, Moscow-backed Rus' that was still in some way federated with Poland-Lithuania—whether "only" spiritually or also politically was a question he did not directly address. And yet, if Baranovych felt that he—like the Blessed Virgin Mary—could reconcile the irreconcilable, it is not clear that his view was widely shared. Perhaps it was only in the course of his correspondence with Patriarch Ioakim in the 1680s that he began to realize the extent to which spiritual and political borders were being redrawn and the extent of the discrepancy between his understanding of those borders and that of his superiors in Moscow.

135. For an investigation of the mentality that allowed Polish nobles seriously to consider electing Ivan the Terrible as king of Poland, see Wiktor Weintraub, "Ivan the Terrible as the Gentry's Candidate for the Polish Throne: A Study in Political Mentality," *Cross Currents* (1982): 45–54.

Zenon E. Kohut

The Question of Russo-Ukrainian Unity and Ukrainian Distinctiveness in Early Modern Ukrainian Thought and Culture

Introduction

Many present-day Russians still consider Ukraine to be part of Russia in historical, cultural, and even spiritual terms. So pervasive has been the myth of Russo-Ukrainian unity that any attempt at asserting a Ukrainian identity has been viewed by many Russians as treason or foreign intrigue. Despite the persecution of Ukrainian culture in both imperial Russia and the Soviet Union, Ukrainians have developed the idea of a distinct Ukrainian nationhood. Many current misunderstandings between Russia and Ukraine are based on fundamental disagreements about the historical role of Ukraine. Are Ukrainians and Russians the same people? Were Ukrainians somewhat distinct only because their "Russianness" was corrupted by Polish practices? Were Ukrainians really a distinct people in the past, and are they still distinct today?[1]

In this clash, both sides refer to the same historical experience but reach diametrically opposed conclusions. In large measure, each side selects examples that corroborate its own interpretation and ignores or explains away evidence to the contrary. But the problem goes deeper than this, for there has been an ambiguity in the Russo-Ukrainian encounter from its very inception in the seventeenth century. Much of the ambiguity comes from posturing; from what Kliuchevsky observed when writing about the 1654 Pereiaslav Agreement, in which both sides "did not say what they thought and did what they did not wish to do."[2] In their early encounters, both

---

1. For a discussion of current Russo-Ukrainian disputes on history and relevant literature, see my article "History as a Battleground: Russian-Ukrainian Relations and Historical Consciousness in Contemporary Ukraine," in S. Frederick Starr, ed., *The Legacy of History in Russia and the New States of Eurasia* (Armonk, N.Y., 1994), pp. 123–46.

2. V. O. Kliuchevskii, *Kurs russkoi istorii,* in his *Sochineniia,* 8 vols. (Moscow, 1956–59), 3: 118.

sides found it convenient to overlook differences and concentrate on areas of real or imagined unity. But how did Ukrainian elites view the relationship with Russia? In which areas did they seek links with Russia, and in which ones did they hold on to what they considered essential differences? In order to get at the root of these questions, it is necessary at least to touch upon the Ukrainian outlook prior to the encounter with Russia.

The Polish-Lithuanian Experience

When in 1654 Hetman Bohdan Khmelnytsky placed Ukraine under the protection of the Muscovite tsar, the country had experienced more than half a century of political, religious, cultural, and social turmoil. Up to the 1654 Pereiaslav Agreement, and even after it, Ukrainian elites were trying to find a place for themselves within the Polish-Lithuanian Commonwealth. Only after the failure to reach an accommodation within Poland-Lithuania did Ukrainian elites begin looking toward Muscovy and involving it in Ukrainian affairs. In their encounter with Russia in the seventeenth century, Ukrainian elites were primarily focusing on and reacting to political, social, religious, and cultural issues within the Polish-Lithuanian Commonwealth.

By the sixteenth century, the Commonwealth was, in theory, a "republic of nobles" of two territories, the Kingdom of Poland and the Grand Duchy of Lithuania. The nobles who constituted the political nation could be of diverse ethnic origins—Polish, Lithuanian, Ruthenian (Ukrainians and Belarusians), or German—and diverse faiths—Roman Catholic, Protestant, or Eastern Orthodox—but enjoyed individual liberties and equal rights. Reality differed greatly from theory, particularly in the territories of the Commonwealth inhabited by Ruthenians. There was no equality among the nobles: political leadership was exercised by the princely houses of the Riurikides and the Gediminids, while the nobles, who were descended from the boyars of Kyivan Rus', acted as subordinates and retainers. Although the Union of Lublin, which transferred Volhynia and the Kyiv land from the Grand Duchy to Poland, did not create a third Rus' entity, it did guarantee the rights of the Ruthenian language and recognized the laws of Rus' as the official code in the annexed territories. The Rus' faith—Eastern Orthodoxy—provided another link to ancient Kyiv. Thus, despite Lithuanian and, after 1569, Polish rule, Ukrainian society preserved the social structure, religious faith, language, and law code of Kyivan Rus'.[3]

---

3. The literature on the history of the Lithuanian-Ruthenian state and the Polish-Lithuanian Commonwealth is voluminous. The works most relevant to

Ukrainians conceived of unity within the Commonwealth primarily as a political matter. They were part of the Polish political nation because they belonged to the *szlachta* (Ukr. *shliakhta*, nobility). There were ethnic, religious, and cultural differences between the Ruthenian *shliakhta* and the Polish, Lithuanian, and German nobilities, but these were not significant for the unity of the state. Thus a Ukrainian nobleman could be designated as *gente ruthenus, natione polonus*. Since the political nation encompassed religious and cultural differences, such differences were also tolerated in other orders of society.[4] Because some members of the *szlachta* were Orthodox, townsfolk or even peasants could also be Orthodox. While this is a highly idealized and theoretical picture, it does reflect to some degree the tolerance and cultural heterogeneity of the Polish-Lithuanian Commonwealth up to the mid-sixteenth century.

In the latter half of the sixteenth century, Ruthenian Orthodox society was challenged intellectually by both the Catholic Counter-Reformation and the Protestant reforms. In the programmatic vision of the Jesuit ideologue Piotr Skarga, confessional unity was essential for political unity, and Eastern Orthodoxy was considered not only erroneous, but also subversive of the state.[5] Owing to increasing political pressure, accompanied by a Polish cultural flowering, Ruthenian nobles began converting to Roman Catholicism and adopting the Polish language and culture. As the Ruthenian political nation declined because of these defections, the remaining Ruthenian elites—both nobles and clergymen—began looking for ways of defining a Ruthenian

---

our analysis include M. K. Liubavskii, *Ocherk istorii Litovsko-russkogo gosudarstva do Liublinskoi unii vkliuchitel'no* (Moscow, 1910); and F. M. Shabul'do, *Zemli Iugo-Zapadnoi Rusi v sostave Velikogo Kniazhestva Litovskogo* (Kyiv, 1987). For a discussion of the nobility in the Ukrainian lands after 1569, with extensive bibliographic notes, see Frank E. Sysyn, "The Problem of Nobilities in the Ukrainian Past: The Polish Period, 1569–1648," in Ivan L. Rudnytsky, ed., *Rethinking Ukrainian History* (Edmonton, 1987), pp. 29–102. The most recent, and extremely valuable, addition to the literature of the subject is N. M. Iakovenko, *Ukraïns'ka shliakhta z kintsia XIV do seredyny XVII st. (Volyn' i Tsentral'na Ukraina)* (Kyiv, 1993).

4. Natalia Iakovenko has noted the significant presence of a nobility of Tatar background in the Ukrainian lands of the Lithuanian-Ruthenian state in the fourteenth and fifteenth centuries, as well as an influx of nobles from Muscovy in the sixteenth. See Iakovenko, *Ukraïns'ka shliakhta*, pp. 170–74, 242.

5. See Janusz Tazbir, *A State without Stakes: Polish Religious Toleration in the Sixteenth and Seventeenth Centuries* (New York, 1973); and Wiktor Weintraub, "Tolerance and Intolerance in Old Poland," *Canadian Slavonic Papers* 13, no. 1 (1971): 21–44.

identity that would find acceptance in the political, social, and cultural structure of the Commonwealth. One such attempt was the ecclesiastical Union of Brest (1596), whereby the Ruthenian Orthodox Church recognized the pope but retained its Eastern Christian traditions. Another response was a vigorous Orthodox Slavic reform that attempted to counter the Catholic offensive on theological, intellectual, and even cultural grounds. In the end, these efforts failed. By the seventeenth century, the Commonwealth was increasingly becoming an association of culturally Polish Roman Catholic nobles. Others were considered politically unreliable, heretical, or simply uncivilized and unsuited to be part of the political nation. Thus the areas that Ukrainians had defined as distinct—religion and culture—were no longer legitimate. Unity in the Commonwealth had to pertain to all spheres: the political *szlachta* nation had to be Roman Catholic in religion and Polish in language and culture.[6]

In attempting to find a place for a reformed Eastern Orthodoxy and Ruthenian culture in the Polish-Lithuanian Commonwealth, the Ruthenian clerical and cultural elites entered a larger struggle between Eastern and Western churches; between Greco-Slavonic and Latin-Polish culture—in essence, a struggle between West and East. It was hardly an equal struggle, for the Western side simply viewed the East as heretical, ignorant, and backward, while the Eastern side, using Western models, strove to affirm its doctrinal correctness and revitalize humanistic learning among the Ruthenian Orthodox. Although the Ruthenian side could never bridge the gap of perceived inferiority within the Polish-Lithuanian Commonwealth, it was certain of having established the most enlightened Orthodox Church—one that could and should play a leading role in the renovation of Eastern Orthodox Christianity.[7]

The new learning and polemics over the church union sparked a keen interest in history, particularly that of Kyivan Rus'. Not only were the old Kyivan chronicles recopied in the early seventeenth

---

6. See David A. Frick, *Meletij Smotryc'kyj* (Cambridge, Mass., 1995), pp. 232–34.

7. For definitive works on the Ukrainian ecclesiastical elite of the time, see S. T. Golubev, *Kievskii mitropolit Petr Mogila i ego spodvizhniki*, 2 vols. (Kyiv, 1883–98); V. O. Ėingorn, *O snosheniiakh malorosiiskogo dukhovenstva s moskovskim pravitel'stvom v tsarstvovanie Alekseia Mikhailovicha* (Moscow, 1894); *The Kiev Mohyla Academy*, special issue, *Harvard Ukrainian Studies* 8, nos. 1–2 (June 1984); Frank E. Sysyn, "The Formation of Modern Ukrainian Religious Culture: The Sixteenth and Seventeenth Centuries," in *Church, Nation, and State in Russia and Ukraine*, ed. Geoffrey A. Hosking (Edmonton, 1990), pp. 1–22.

century, but new historical writing brought them up to more contemporary times. The polemical literature debating the Union of Brest drew on the Rus' past. Moreover, inspired by Polish historical writings, Ukrainian authors introduced new concepts and terminology into history writing, such as a Rus' "fatherland" and a Ruthenian or Rus' people. These writings went beyond the Polish-Lithuanian concept of a *szlachta* nation, implying the existence of a Rus' nation that included Orthodox Ruthenians of various social estates.[8]

The religious and social picture in Ukraine was further complicated by the emergence of a new social group—the Cossacks. Recruited primarily from non-noble elements of the population, the Cossacks organized themselves into a military host that defended the southern frontier against the Tatars and Turks. The Cossacks saw themselves as frontier knights, a military order that possessed certain "rights and liberties." Although at times the Commonwealth recognized these rights for some of the Cossacks, the idea of a non-noble brotherhood of Cossack warriors enjoying political liberties clashed fundamentally with the concept of a Commonwealth of free nobles. The non-recognition of Cossack estate rights led to a series of Cossack revolts, including the fateful one of 1648.[9]

Up to the end of the sixteenth century, political leadership in Rus' was held by the princely households and exercised through a system of subordinate noble retainers.[10] For example, the princes of Ostrih led the Orthodox revival by printing the Orthodox Bible and founding the Ostrih Academy, which generated cadres for the cultural revival of the late sixteenth and early seventeenth centuries. However, owing to the extinction of some princely households and the conversion to Roman Catholicism and Polish culture of others, princely leadership began to wane, and the subordinate Ukrainian nobility became disoriented. By the time of the Khmelnytsky Uprising, the lesser Ukrainian nobles had either become Polish or joined the Cossacks, but

---

8. See Frank E. Sysyn, "The Cultural, Social, and Political Context of Ukrainian History Writing, 1620–1690," *Europa Orientalis* 5 (1986): 285–310; idem, "Concepts of Nationhood in Ukrainian History Writing, 1620–1690," in *Concepts of Nationhood in Early Modern Eastern Europe* (=*Harvard Ukrainian Studies* 10, nos. 3–4 [December 1986]), pp. 393–423.

9. The history of the Cossacks from the fifteenth to the seventeenth century is well summarized in V. A. Golobutskii, *Zaporozhskoe kazachestvo* (Kyiv, 1957) and Günther Stökl, *Die Entstehung des Kosakentums* (Munich, 1953). The topic is treated in much greater detail in volumes 6–10 of Mykhailo Hrushevsky's *Istoriia Ukraïny-Rusy*, 10 vols. (Lviv and Kyiv, 1898–1937).

10. This notion is developed in Iakovenko, *Ukraïns'ka shliakhta*, pp. 268–69.

had ceased to act on behalf of a Ruthenian noble order. A new leadership role was assumed, rather hesitantly, by the Cossacks. In 1620, the entire hierarchy of the then outlawed Orthodox Church was consecrated in Kyiv under Cossack protection. From that time on, the Cossacks fought not only for their estate rights, but also for the Rus' faith.[11]

Despite increasing intolerance, the Ruthenian elites, including the remaining *shliakhta*, the Orthodox clergy, and the Cossack officers, remained loyal to the Polish-Lithuanian Commonwealth and continued to identify themselves with it. The revival of the Rus' faith, the resurgence of interest in Rus' history and culture, and the assertion of a distinct Ruthenian or Rus' identity called for some degree of political acceptance of Rus' within the Commonwealth. But finding a place for Ukraine or Rus' within Poland-Lithuania would require a fundamental restructuring of the Commonwealth. Such an attempt was made in 1658, after Ukraine's break with the Commonwealth and the Pereiaslav Agreement (1654) with Muscovy. The Treaty of Hadiach (1658) transformed the dual Commonwealth into a confederation of three states: the Polish Crown, the Grand Duchy of Lithuania, and the Grand Duchy of Rus'. The latter had its own administration, treasury, army, and judiciary, while the rights of the Orthodox Church were to be guaranteed throughout the Commonwealth.[12] But the arrangement could not succeed, for it required that Ukraine, in the form of the Grand Duchy of Rus', return to *szlachta* rule, while in fact it was governed by the Cossacks. The attempted ennoblement of Cossack officers was accepted neither by the Polish and Lithuanian *szlachta* nor by the Cossack rank and file. Thus the most fundamental definition of the Commonwealth as a political expression of the *szlachta* nation could not be maintained. Muscovy, moreover, now deeply involved in Ukrainian affairs, would not permit the existence of a Rus' state within the Commonwealth. Nevertheless, the notion of Rus' as part of the Commonwealth continued to linger. In the early eighteenth century a popular poem described Poland as the mother of three children: Liakh, Rus', and Lytva. Liakh and Lytva killed their brother

---

11. Cossack intervention in the religious conflict is best treated in volume 7 of Hrushevsky's *Istoriia Ukraïny-Rusy*. See also Teresa Chynczewska-Hennel, "The National Consciousness of Ukrainian Nobles and Cossacks from the End of the Sixteenth to the Mid-Seventeenth Century" in *Concepts of Nationhood in Early Modern Eastern Europe*, pp. 377–92.

12. Andrzej Kamiński, "The Cossack Experiment in *Szlachta* Democracy in the Polish-Lithuanian Commonwealth: The Hadiach (*Hadziacz*) Union," *Harvard Ukrainian Studies* 1, no. 2 (June 1977): 178–97.

Rus' against the will of Poland. The poem seeks to show that Poland (or the Commonwealth) is the true mother of Rus' who grieves over the injustice done to Rus' by his brothers.[13]

The fundamental outlook of the Ukrainian elites had been shaped by the Polish-Lithuanian experience. The Orthodox clerical elite strongly identified itself with an enlightened Orthodoxy in competition with Catholicism and the West. Both the secular and the clerical elites had a concept of a Commonwealth or a state composed of several political entities—Poland, Lithuania, and possibly Rus'. Historical writings had propagated the idea of a Rus' people and of ancient Rus' as a direct historical predecessor. And parts of Ukrainian society believed in the political "rights and liberties" of estates and lands, particularly of the Cossack estate. These beliefs and perceptions would color the behavior of Ukrainians as they encountered Muscovy and the Russians.

The Search for Links with Muscovy/Russia

The Ukrainian elites, striving for inclusion in the *szlachta* nation of the Commonwealth, generally avoided any overt links with Muscovy. If in Polish eyes Rus' was backward and schismatic, then Muscovy was nothing less than barbaric. Moreover, Muscovy was frequently an enemy of the Commonwealth, and ties with it could be viewed as treasonous. Nevertheless, the Ukrainian elites were aware that Muscovy was the only independent and powerful Orthodox polity. Some elements of the Ukrainian clergy began looking to Muscovy for religious, political, and financial support.[14]

---

13. See Serhii Plokhy, "The Symbol of Little Russia: The Pokrova Icon and Early Modern Ukrainian Political Ideology," *Journal of Ukrainian Studies* 17, nos. 1–2 (Summer-Winter 1992): 173. The poem, "Hlaholet Pol'shcha..." is reprinted in *Ukraïns'ka literatura XVII stolittia: Synkretychna pysemnist'. Poeziia. Dramaturhiia. Beletrystyka*, ed. O. V. Myshanych (Kyiv, 1987), pp. 284–85, 564–65.

14. The state of the Ukrainian Orthodox Church in the seventeenth century is described in V. O. Ėingorn, *O snosheniiakh malorossiiskogo dukhovenstva s moskovskim pravitel'stvom v tsarstvovanie Alekseia Mikhailovicha* (Moscow, 1894); Metropolitan Makarii (Bulgakov), *Istoriia russkoi tserkvi*, 12 vols. (St. Petersburg, 1889–1903), vol. 12; and Ivan Vlasovs'kyi, *Narys istoriï Ukraïns'koï Pravoslavnoï Tserkvy*, 4 vols. (New York, 1956–66), vol. 2. The subordination of the Kyiv metropolitan to the Moscow patriarch has been exhaustively treated in S. A. Ternovskii, *Issledovanie o podchinenii Kievskoi metropolii Moskovskomu patriarkhatu* (Kyiv, 1912). The church in the eighteenth century is treated in I. A. Chistovich, *Ocherki istorii zapadno-russkoi Tserkvi*, 2 vols. (St. Petersburg, 1882–84), vol. 2; Konstantin Kharlampovich (Kostiantyn Kharlampovych),

As the Ukrainians began coming to Muscovy, seeking alms for monasteries or subsidies for publications, they were treated with considerable hostility. The Muscovites doubted the Ukrainians' Orthodoxy and viewed the "Lithuanians" or "Cherkasy," as they called them, as foreign and dangerous. The Ukrainians persisted nevertheless. It was they who developed the terminology and concepts that would bring Rus' and Muscovy closer together.

Given their renewed interest in the Rus' past, the Ukrainian clerics of the 1620s and 1640s turned not only to their own historical tradition, but also to Polish and Muscovite sources. From Polish historians, particularly Stryjkowski, they learned about Slavic unity and the joint claim of Muscovites and Ruthenians to ancient Rus'. More importantly, in seeking to differentiate Rus' from Lithuania and Poland within the Commonwealth, these writers began looking more closely at Muscovite chronicles. From such sources, Ukrainian writers created an image of the Rus' past that transcended contemporary political boundaries. In fact, they somewhat mechanically incorporated a number of contradictory views of Rus'—Polish, Ukrainian, and Russian—into their writings. By assembling these varied traditions, some of these writers were able to link Ukraine and Muscovy through religion, dynasty, land, and even people.[15]

The work that went farthest in establishing such links was the *Synopsis*, frequently described as the first history of the Eastern Slavs. Attributed to Inokentii Gizel, the archimandrite of the Kyivan Caves Monastery, the *Synopsis* first appeared in Kyiv between 1670 and 1674.[16] While attempting to enlist the help of the tsar, the author

---

Malorossiiskoe vliianie na velikorusskuiu tserkovnuiu zhizn' (Kazan, 1914); and Vlasovs'kyi, *Narys*, 3: 5–30.

15. See O. P. Tolochko, "Mizh Russiu i Pol'shcheiu: Ukraïns'ka istoriohrafiia XVII st. v katehoriiakh pohranychnosti." Paper presented at the conference "Peoples, Nations, Identities: The Ukrainian-Russian Encounter," Cologne University, 23–25 June 1994.

16. The scholarly literature on the *Synopsis* is examined in the introduction to Hans Rothe, ed., *Sinopsis, Kiev 1681: Facsimile mit einer Einleitung* (Cologne and Vienna, 1983). Of particular note are S. I. Maslov, "K istorii izdanii kievskogo Sinopsisa," in *Stat'i po slavianskoi filologii i russkoi slovesnosti: Sobranie statei v chest' akademika A. I. Sobolevskogo* (Leningrad, 1928), pp. 341–48; I. P. Eremin, "K istorii obshchestvennoi mysli na Ukraine vtoroi poloviny XVII v.," *Trudy otdela drevnerusskoi literatury* (henceforth *TODRL*), vol. 10 (1954): 212–22; and S. L. Peshtich, "*Sinopsis* kak istoricheskoe proizvedenie," *TODRL*, vol. 15 (1958): 284–98. An interesting recent addition to the literature is Gianfranco Giraudo, "'Russkoe' nastoiashchee i proshedshee v tvorchestve Innokentiia Gizelia," *Mediaevalia Ucrainica: Mental'nist' ta istoriia idei* (Kyiv) 1 (1992): 92–103.

fiercely maintained the autonomy of the Caves Monastery vis-à-vis the Kyiv metropolitan and the Moscow patriarch. For Gizel, it was vital that the monastery retain its stauropigial status, subordinated directly to the patriarch of Constantinople.

The main thesis of the work is encapsulated in its title, *The Synopsis, or short compilation from various chronicles about the origin of the Slavic-Rus' nation and the first princes of the divinely preserved city of Kyiv and the life of the holy, pious grand prince of Kyiv and all Rossiia, the first autocrat, Volodymyr, and about the inheritors of his virtous Rus' domain, even unto our illustrious and virtuous sovereign, tsar, and grand prince Aleksei Mikhailovich, autocrat of all Great, Little, and White Rossiia.* The author intertwines the concepts of people, dynasty, and state. He begins in pre-Kyivan times with the *slaveno-rossiiskii narod* (Slavo-Rossian nation, meaning, more or less, the Orthodox Eastern Slavs), which is subsequently ruled by "Varangian princes," beginning with Ihor Riurikovich. For subsequent periods of history, the author uses the terms *rossy*, *rusy*, and *rossiiane* to denote a people inhabiting a historical territory north of the Black Sea, between the Volga-Don and Danube-Dnister-Dnipro river systems. Although no northern boundary is given, Novgorod the Great is included.[17] The author of the *Synopsis* states that the Riurikide princely family established the Russian state. This *gosudarstvo Rossiiskoe* emerges fully with Volodymyr's conversion to Christianity and encompasses Muscovy, as well as the lands of the Polish-Lithuanian Commonwealth.[18] The story of the Russian state is, in fact, the story of the Riurikides, which allows the author to include in the chronicle various fragments of Russian and Ukrainian history (including a lengthy episode involving Dmitrii Donskoi) and link various territories, time frames, and centers of power. For example, the princely seat of Rus' is moved from Kyiv to Vladimir on the Kliazma, and from there to Moscow, because this is in keeping with princely desires.[19] Two metropolitanates (those of Kyiv and Moscow) are established because one part of Rus' (Kyiv) comes under the rule of a foreign prince, the

17. *Sinopsis, Kiev 1681*, pp. 149–51. The author continues to use the terms *russkie* and *Rossiia* to denote both Vladimir-Moscow and Ukrainian lands from the thirteenth to the fifteenth century (pp. 328, 335, 349, 351, 354), and his *pravoslavnorossiiskii narod* designates both Ukrainians and Muscovites under the rule of Aleksei Mikhailovich (pp. 278, 364–65).

18. For the first use of the term *gosudarstvo Ruskoe*, see ibid., p. 167. Volodymyr is called *Velikii Samoderzhets Rossiiskii* (p. 216).

19. Ibid., p. 208.

Lithuanian Vytautas.[20] And, most importantly, when Kyiv comes under Muscovy, this is lauded because "the first-born of all the cities of *Rossiia*, the *tsarstvennyi* [tsar's] city of Kyiv," has come under the rule of the *pravoslavnyi samoderzhets* (Orthodox autocrat).[21] Orthodoxy is also identified with the tsar, land, and people. Thus the wars fought by the Zaporozhian Cossacks against the Turks are waged in the interests of the *pravoslavnyi rossiiskii narod* (Orthodox Rus' nation). Rus' is called *pravoslavnyi krai* (Orthodox land), and the tsar is referred to as the *pravoslavnyi samoderzhets*.[22]

Despite considerable confusion in its account of history and ethnography, the *Synopsis* brought together a number of ideas that had been reverberating in Ukraine during the second half of the seventeenth century: (1) Rus', or, as it was beginning to be called in the 1670s and 1680s, "Little Russia," belonged within a larger, all-Russian context on account of its historical ties to the house of Riurik and its Orthodox faith; (2) in spite of ethnic multiplicity, there was a larger *pravoslavnyi rossiiskii narod* that inhabited the territory ruled by the house of Riurik; (3) *Rossiia*, which included Muscovy and Little Russia, and the entire *rossiiskii narod* were to be ruled by the Orthodox autocrat, whose ancestry derived from the house of Riurik; (4) the Muscovite tsar represented the continuation of the house of Riurik (the fact that the tsars were no longer Riurikides was never mentioned).

The extreme Russocentrism of the *Synopsis* was one of several orientations among the members of the Ukrainian clerical elite. In the 1670s, Feodosii Sofonovych, the archimandrite of St. Michael's Golden-Domed Monastery, wrote another major historical work, *Krojnika*. Sofonovych traces the history of Rus' during the period of Kyivan Rus', then describes how Lithuania absorbed Rus', and finally focuses on Poland's entry into Rus' history. He shows little concern for the Russian territories of Rus'. Like Gizel in the *Synopsis*, Sofonovych concentrates on rulers, but the Russian Riurikides are of no interest to him. Instead, he lavishes attention on Prince Danylo of Galicia-Volhynia. He sees the Muscovites and Ruthenians as separate peoples. In describing Hetman Khmelnytsky's decision to place Ukraine under the suzerainty of the Muscovite tsar, Sofonovych simply reports the event without expressing any opinion about it.[23]

---

20. Ibid., p. 353.

21. Ibid., p. 360.

22. Ibid., p. 364.

23. See Feodosii Sofonovych, *Khronika z litopystsiv starodavnikh*, ed. Iu. A. Mytsyk and V. M. Kravchenko (Kyiv, 1992), pp. 231, 255; and Sysyn, "The

It must be remembered that the search for Rus' identity, whether within the Polish-Lithuanian Commonwealth or under the rule of the Muscovite tsar, occurred against the background of unceasing crisis and turmoil in Ukraine: the renewal of the Orthodox hierarchy (1620), the Khmelnytsky Uprising (1648), the Pereiaslav Agreement with Muscovy (1654), and a period of continuous struggle for control of Ukraine known as the Ruin (1660s-80s). After three decades of conflict, the Ukrainian elite was decimated, and Right-Bank Ukraine (west of the Dnipro River) devastated and depopulated. For some members of the elite, the protection of the Muscovite tsar and the powerful Muscovite state seemed the only guarantee of a measure of stability.

In turning to the Muscovite tsar, the author of the *Synopsis* and numerous other Ukrainian petitioners were seeking the help of Muscovy in promoting and protecting *Slavia Orthodoxa*. This Slavic Orthodox world, based on the Orthodox faith, the Slavonic language, Byzantine and post-Byzantine culture, the literature and art of Rus', and South Slavic cultural influence included Ukraine, Belarus, Muscovy, Bulgaria and non-Slavic Moldavia. It was this culture of *Slavia Orthodoxa* that was threatened by the Counter-Reformation in the Polish-Lithuanian Commonwealth.[24]

In responding to the Polish, Catholic, and Western challenge, the Ukrainian prelates transformed the culture of *Slavia Orthodoxa* to some extent. They combined post-Byzantine and Western cultural models, introducing the "Greek-Latin-Slavonic" school (the Ostrih Academy and the Kyiv Mohyla Collegium). They attempted to provide Orthodox answers to theological questions never before posed in the Orthodox world. Perhaps the most lasting Ukrainian contribution to the revitalized *Slavia Orthodoxa* was the recodification of Church Slavonic so that it could equal Latin as a sacred language. The "Meletian" (named after Meletii Smotrytsky, compiler of the grammar) norm of Church Slavonic became the standard not only in Ukraine, but throughout *Slavia Orthodoxa*.[25]

Cultural, Social, and Political Context of Ukrainian History Writing, 1620–1690," p. 306.

24. See Harvey Goldblatt, "Orthodox Slavic Heritage and National Consciousness: Aspects of the East Slavic and South Slavic National Revivals," in *Concepts of Nationhood in Early Modern Eastern Europe*, pp. 337–38.

25. Goldblatt, "Orthodox Slavic Heritage and National Consciousness," p. 342; and Bohdan Strumins'kyj, "The Language Question in the Ukrainian Lands before the Nineteenth Century," in *Aspects of the Slavic Language Question*, vol. 2, ed. Riccardo Picchio and Harvey Goldblatt (New Haven, Conn., 1984), pp. 13–14.

In fact, a spiritual and cultural revitalization of *Slavia Orthodoxa* through Ukrainian learning was the vision of such Ukrainian clerics as Smotrytsky. As he contemplated the Orthodox world, he saw it in chains, except in Muscovy, where it was free but ignorant, and in Ukraine, where Orthodoxy was both free and learned.[26] It was this learning that the Ukrainian clerics wanted to bring to Muscovy. In going there, they were not only obtaining protection, alms, or a good office, but also attempting to create a united revitalized Orthodoxy capable of meeting the Roman Catholic and Protestant challenges.

The Insistence on Distinctiveness from Muscovy/Russia

Even as some Ukrainians were attempting to find affinity with Muscovy/Russia in religion, dynasty, high culture, and even ethnos, they insisted on their own distinctiveness within the existing political, ecclesiastical, and social structures. For the most part, the proponents of Ukrainian political and social distinctiveness belonged to the secular political elite. The clergy, however, were also adamant defenders of Ukrainian privileges, particularly their own.

The secular political elite was represented by the Cossack officers and administrators who in fact ruled Ukraine. This elite performed two political roles, acting as representatives of their own corporate estates and, in some fashion, as representatives of Ukraine. This dual function was in effect a continuation of the role assumed by the Cossack elite after the Khmelnytsky Uprising of 1648. Two important documents, the Treaty of Zboriv and the Pereiaslav Agreement, defined the political status accorded to the Cossacks in seventeenth-century Ukraine.[27] The Treaty of Zboriv, concluded with Poland in 1649, affirmed that relations between the king of Poland and the Cossack elite constituted a contractual bond between the sovereign and the Zaporozhian Host. The Host, in turn, had almost complete control over a good part of Ukraine. The Pereiaslav Agreement concluded with Muscovy in 1654 was modeled on the Treaty of Zboriv.[28] From the Cossack viewpoint, the Pereiaslav Agreement

26. Frick, *Meletij Smotryc'kyj*, p. 238.

27. The ever-expanding contractual relationship between the Cossacks and the king of Poland is very well traced in volumes 7 and 8 of Mykhailo Hrushevsky's *Istoriia Ukraïny-Rusy*; the Treaty of Zboriv is discussed in vol. 8, pt. 3, pp. 193–288.

28. On the Pereiaslav Agreement, see *Vossoedinenie Ukrainy s Rossiei: dokumenty i materialy v 3–kh tomakh*, vol. 3 (Moscow, 1954); *Akty, otnosiashchiesia*

maintained the same contractual relations between the Zaporozhian Host and the monarch: the Muscovite tsar was merely substituted for the Polish king. The idea of contractual relations between tsar and subject was, however, incompatible with the Muscovites' sense of authority. They regarded the Pereiaslav Agreement as an instrument of unilateral submission of the Cossacks and Ukraine to the tsar.[29]

Whatever the legal interpretation, the tsar did confirm certain "Little Russian rights and liberties" at Pereiaslav. He reconfirmed them—sometimes in radically altered form—each time a new leader of Ukraine, or hetman, assumed office (1657, 1659, 1663, 1665, 1669, 1672, 1674, and 1687). Thus the tsar and the Muscovite state formally acknowledged that Ukraine was a distinct political entity and that Ukrainians were privileged subjects. Indeed, there was hardly any doubt about Ukraine's political distinctiveness, since it acted as a semi-independent Cossack polity. Despite the Pereiaslav Agreement with the Muscovite tsar, the Ukrainian Cossack elite pursued alliances with various states that were in fact Moscow's enemies: Poland-Lithuania (the politics of the Hadiach Union and the Right-Bank Ukrainian hetmans), the Ottoman Empire (Hetman Petro Doroshenko), and Sweden (Hetman Ivan Mazepa).

It was only after the Battle of Poltava (1709) that Russian control over the Ukrainian Cossack polity, known as the Hetmanate, was consolidated. In the post-Poltava period the secular political elite—the Cossack officer stratum—gradually transformed itself into a *shliakhta* or gentry. Its members developed a more consistent political outlook that attempted to blend the presumed unity of the emerging Orthodox Slavo-Russian empire with the political and social distinctiveness of Ukraine.

The concept of Little Russia emerged gradually throughout the eighteenth century.[30] Its basic elements were the acceptance of the

---

k istorii Iuzhnoi i Zapadnoi Rossii, 15 vols. (St. Petersburg, 1863–92), vol. 10; and John Basarab, *Pereiaslav 1654: A Historiographical Study* (Edmonton, 1982). The articles of the agreement are analyzed in Andrii Iakovliv, *Ukraïns'ko-moskovs'ki dohovory v XVII-XVIII vikakh*, Pratsi Ukraïns'koho naukovoho instytutu, vol. 19 (Warsaw, 1934).

29. The conflicting Ukrainian and Muscovite interpretations of the Pereiaslav Agreement are analyzed in B. E. Nol'de, *Ocherki russkogo gosudarstvennogo prava* (St. Petersburg, 1911). The section dealing with Ukraine has been translated into English: "Essays in Russian State Law," *Annals of the Ukrainian Academy of Arts and Sciences in the United States* 4, no. 3 (Winter–Spring 1955): 873–903.

30. For a more detailed discussion of the concept of Little Russia, see Zenon E. Kohut, "The Development of a Little Russian Identity and Ukrainian Nation-building," in *Concepts of Nationhood in Early Modern Eastern Europe*, pp. 559–76.

term "Little Russia" for Ukraine or part of Ukraine, the emergence of a specific Ukrainian historical consciousness, the conceptualization of a distinct "Little Russia" that was nevertheless part of a larger Russian imperial order, and the further refinement of the idea of "Little Russian rights and liberties."

The term "Little Russia" won acceptance because of its historical precedence in ecclesiastical usage, official status in Russia, and terminological linkage with Russia. This term first appeared in fourteenth-century ecclesiastical usage: the patriarchate of Constantinople used the term *mikra Rosia* to identify Ukraine, while the term *makra Rosia* identified the territory of Muscovy. Prior to the Pereiaslav Agreement, the Muscovite tsar styled himself *tsar' vseia Rusi* (tsar of all Rus'); after the agreement, Aleksei Mikhailovich adopted the title *tsar' vseia Velikiia i Malyia Rossii* (tsar of all Great and Little Russia). Bohdan Khmelnytsky referred to Ukraine as "Little Russia" in his dealings with the Muscovites. Nevertheless, a number of terms—"Ukraine," "Little Russia," "Rus'"—continued to be utilized in designating Ukraine.[31]

The gradual acceptance of the term "Little Russia," the emergence of a historical consciousness, the idea of loyalty to a Ukrainian political entity, and its relationship to Russia were all elaborated in a new historical/literary genre, the Cossack chronicle. In fact, this genre was partly inspired by the indignation felt by the Ukrainian Cossack elite over the clergy's inattention to the Cossack polity. In 1718, Stefan Savytsky, a clerk in the Lubny regiment, lamented that none of his countrymen had written a history, "particularly from the spiritual rank, who since the time of emancipation from Poland lacked neither people capable of the task nor the necessary typographical means."[32] In response, the Cossack elite produced its own history. Two of the most influential Cossack chronicles were those of Hryhorii Hrabianka (1710) and Samuil Velychko (1720).[33]

---

31. The transformation of the term "Rus'" into "Rossiia" and then "Malorossiia" is best summarized in M. A. Maksimovich, "Ob upotreblenii nazvanii Rossiia i Malorossiia v Zapadnoi Rusi," in his *Sobranie sochinenii*, 2 vols. (Kyiv, 1877), 2: 307–11. See also the discussion of the terms "Rus'" and "Little Russia" by Mykhailo Hrushevsky in "Velyka, Mala i Bila Rus'," *Ukraïns'kyi istorychnyi zhurnal*, 1991, no. 2: 77–85 (originally published in *Ukraïna*, 1917, nos. 1–2: 7–19); and A. Solov'ev, "Velikaia, Malaia i Belaia Rus'," *Voprosy istorii*, 1947, no. 7: 24–38.

32. Mykhailo Hrushevs'kyi, "Some Reflections on Ukrainian Historiography of the XVIII Century," in *The Eyewitness Chronicle*, Harvard Series in Ukrainian Studies, vol. 7, pt. 1 (Munich, 1972), p. 12.

33. Hrabianka's chronicle was published under the title *Deistviia prezel'noi i ot nachala poliakov krvavshoi nebyvaloi brani Bogdana Khmelnitskogo…roku 1710*

The two works are not really chronicles but histories that attempt to document and explain how the new Ukrainian Cossack polity came into existence. For both works, the central event was the great uprising under the leadership of Bohdan Khmelnytsky, who is presented as the hero and founder of the Cossack state. At the same time, both chronicles connect the Cossack polity with an ancient lineage. In Hrabianka's work, the Ukrainian Cossacks are linked to the Khazars and to Rus'. Velychko asserts that the Sarmatian Cossack Rus' provinces had been the "Ukrainian Little Russian fatherland" since the time of Volodymyr, who baptized Rus'.[34] Both chronicles attempt to demonstrate the historical continuity and legitimacy of the current political and social order by establishing this lineage.

In referring to Ukraine, both chronicles exhibit a great deal of terminological fluidity.[35] In Hrabianka, "Rus'," "Ros'," "Rossiia," "Mala Rossiia," "Malaia Rossiia," "Malorussiia," "Malorossiiskaia Ukraina," and "Ukraïna" are all used to denote Ukraine or Ukrainian territory. Velychko uses the terms "Rus'," "Malaia Rus'," "Ukraïna," and "Malaia Rossiia" when referring to Cossack Ukraine. Both chronicles distinguish Ukraine from Muscovy and Ukrainians from Russians. Hrabianka presents the Pereiaslav Agreement as a pact necessitated by political and military circumstances.[36] Because of the

---

(Kyiv, 1854) (*Dîjstvija prezîl"noj y ot" načala poljakov" krvavšoj nebyvaloj brany Bohdana Xmelnyckoho*); and Velychko's under the title *Letopis' sobytii v Iugo-Zapadnoi Rossii v XVII veke: Sostavil Samoil Velichko byvshii kantseliarist Voiska Zaporozhskogo, 1720* (Kyiv), vol. 1 (1848), vol. 2 (1851), vol. 3 (1885), vol. 4 (1864). My references are to the facsimile edition of Hryhorii Hrabianka, *The Great War of Bohdan Xmel'nyc'kyj* (=Harvard Library of Early Ukrainian Literature, Texts, vol. 9) (Cambridge, Mass., 1990); and Valerii Shevchuk's translation of Velychko in Samiilo Velychko, *Litopys*, 2 vols. (Kyiv, 1991).

34. See, for example, "A tsia zemlia—predkovichna vitchyzna nasha, iaka siiaie pravdeshnim i neskhytnym blahochestiam vid sviatoho i ravnoapostol'noho kniazia Volodymyra Kyivs'koho, shcho prosvityv Rus' khreshcheniam" (Velychko, vol. 1, p. 79). The quotation is from the text of Bohdan Khmelnytsky's proclamation as reproduced in Velychko. According to Mykola Kostomarov and Vladimir Ikonnikov, Velychko edited the text of the actual document. According to Ivan Franko, Mykhailo Hrushevsky, Orest Levytsky, and Mykola Petrovsky, the entire text is a creation of Velychko's (see Valerii Shevchuk's footnote on the same page). For references to the fatherland as *kozats'ko-rus'ka malorosiis'ka Ukraina* (Cossack-Ruthenian Little Russian Ukraine), see vol. 2, pp. 200–202 and elsewhere.

35. For a discussion of names used in the Cossack histories, see Serhii Shelukhin, *Ukraïna—nazva nashoï zemli z naidavniishykh chasiv* (Prague, 1936), pp. 145–50.

36. Hrabianka, *The Great War of Bohdan Xmel'nyc'kyj*, pp. 359–60.

common Orthodox faith, Khmelnytsky was able to obtain the tsar's protection for Ukraine, as well as a guarantee of Cossack rights. Velychko develops further than Hrabianka the idea of contractual relations between Little Russia and its people on the one hand and the tsar on the other hand. In Velychko's version, the tsarist envoys at Pereiaslav swear in the name of the tsar that all Ukrainian rights will be respected in perpetuity.[37]

Unlike the *Synopsis*, the Cossack chronicles developed no general scheme of East European history, nor did they present justifications for tsarist protection based on dynastic claims, or even link Ukraine with Russia on the basis of religion or ethnicity. They strove instead to present the story of Ukraine from the Ukrainian Cossack point of view. For them, the Kyivan Rus' period is the murky past: their primary interest is in Cossack Ukraine under Poland, the great liberator Hetman Bohdan Khmelnytsky, and Cossack and *szlachta* rights and liberties. At the same time, these post-Poltava authors wanted to show their loyalty to the tsar.

The Cossack chronicles demonstrate and imply a number of crucial components of the emerging Little Russian concept: (1) that Little Russia and Great Russia were separate lands and peoples; (2) that the two lands were linked by a common tsar; (3) that the Zaporozhian Host, the Little Russian people, and Little Russia itself entered into voluntary agreements first with the Polish king and later with the Muscovite tsar; and (4) that Little Russia and its people always retained their "rights and liberties."

In the second half of the eighteenth century, the Little Russian concept appears as a fully developed viewpoint in two important sources, *Razgovor Velikorossii s Malorossiei* (Conversation of Great Russia with Little Russia) and the works of Hryhorii Poletyka. However, there are two significant departures from the views of the Cossack chronicles. Although the chronicles had shown little precision with regard to the territorial extent of Little Russia, they presumed that at the very least Little Russia encompassed Ukraine on both sides of the Dnieper. Later authors still used the term in this larger sense when speaking of historical Little Russia, but to late eighteenth-century contemporaries, "Little Russia" meant only the Hetmanate, the truncated Left-Bank polity ruled by the tsar on the basis of the Pereiaslav Agreement. They regarded this Little Russia, not the much larger seventeenth-century entity, as their "fatherland."

---

37. Velychko, *Litopys*, 1: 137. Velychko's treatment of the Pereiaslav Agreement stands in contradiction to the actual events, for the Russian envoys refused to swear an oath on behalf of the tsar.

The second major transformation was the emergence of a Ukrainian gentry or *shliakhta* as Little Russia's leading social class. The differentiation between the Cossack rank and file and the officers was clearly apparent in the chronicles. However, the early eighteenth-century chronicles still identified the Zaporozhian Host and the Cossacks as the major contracting parties with the tsar. Without excluding the Zaporozhian Host or the Cossacks, the late eighteenth-century authors depicted the gentry or *shliakhta* as the corporate representative of Little Russia and the main contracting party with the tsar.

Razgovor Velikorossii s Malorossiei reflects the thinking of this newly established Ukrainian gentry. Dedicated to the "honor, glory and defense of all Little Russia," it includes a panegyric to Bohdan Khmelnytsky.[38] The poem ascribes the paramount role in liberating Little Russia from the Polish yoke to the Ukrainian gentry and laments that Ukrainian nobiliary and military ranks have not been recognized by the imperial authorities. Most importantly, the poem flatly rejects the notion of Little Russia as a constituent of a uniform Russian Empire. The personified Little Russia bluntly tells Great Russia that it swore allegiance to the tsar, not to Russia. It goes on to state that Little Russia and Great Russia are in fact separate lands bound only by a common monarch, and that Little Russia has its own rights, guaranteed by all the tsars.

In his writings, Hryhorii Poletyka insisted that Little Russia had always possessed certain rights guaranteed by the Muscovite tsar. He wrote a treatise entitled "Historical Information on What Basis Little Russia Was under the Polish Republic and by What Treaties It Came under Russian Sovereigns, and a Patriotic Opinion as to How It Could Be Ordered So That It Would Be Useful to the Russian State without Violations of Its Rights and Freedoms."[39] Poletyka, who identified the rights of the Little Russian gentry with the Polish nobility's "golden liberties," wanted to revive the administrative, judicial and social systems of Ukraine as they had existed under the Polish-Lithuanian

---

38. The poem was published by Nikolai (Mykola) Petrov: "Razgovor Velikorossii s Malorossiei (literaturnyi pamiatnik vtoroi poloviny XVIII veka)," *Kievskaia starina*, 1882, no. 2: 313–65, and "Dopolneniia razgovora Velikorossii s Malorossiei," *Kievskaia starina*, 1882, no. 7: 137. A slightly abridged version appears in O. I. Bilets'kyi, ed., *Khrestomatiia davn'oï ukraïns'koï literatury* (Kyiv, 1967), pp. 165–83.

39. "Istoricheskoe izvestie na kakom osnovanii Malaia Rossiia byla pod respublikoiu Pol'skoiu, i na kakikh dogovorakh otdalas' Rossiiskim Gdriam, i patrioticheskoe rassuzhdenie, kakim obrazom mozhno by onuiu nyne uchredit' chtob ona polezna mogla byt' Rossiiskomu Gosudarstvu bez narusheniia prav ee i vol'nostei," *Ukraïns'kyi arkheohrafichnyi zbirnyk* 1 (1926): 147–161.

Commonwealth prior to the Khmelnytsky Uprising.[40] At that time, according to Poletyka, regular diets of the *shliakhta* had acted as legislative bodies, consulting with other corporate estates on important matters, while courts of the nobility and town magistrates had adjudicated civilian cases. According to Poletyka, Ukraine's misfortunes were the consequence of the Cossacks' usurpation of these powers from the nobility following the Khmelnytsky Uprising.

While Poletyka's concept of gentry democracy may have been extreme, his views on Ukrainian autonomy and Ukraine's relationship with Russia reflected the thinking of the Ukrainian gentry. Similar views were presented at an Officers' Council of 1763 attended by 100 delegates from all parts of Little Russia. Moreover, the various petitions to the Legislative Commission of 1767, signed by more than 950 members of the gentry, indicate a widespread acceptance of the Little Russian concept by the Ukrainian gentry.[41]

By the end of the eighteenth century, the Little Russian concept encompassed historical consciousness of Little Russia and political loyalty to that entity and its particular constitutional and administrative prerogatives. At the same time, the Ukrainian gentry viewed Little Russia as linked through the tsar to a larger Russian state or empire. Such a conceptualization of relations between Ukraine and Russia allowed members of the Ukrainian gentry to maintain their political and social order in Little Russia, affirm loyalty to the tsar and even the empire, and take part in the political and social life of that empire, if they so desired.

Ukraine and the Evolution of Imperial Russia

When Ukrainians first encountered Muscovy, in the seventeenth century, it was an increasingly powerful but remote country on the

---

40. See "Vozrazhenie deputata Grigoriia Poletiki na nastavleniia Malorossiiskoi kollegii gospodinu zhe deputatu Dimitriiu Natal"inu," *Chteniia v Imperatorskom obshchestve istorii i drevnostei rossiiskikh pri Moskovskom universitete* 3 (1858): 72; "Proshenie malorossiiskikh deputatov vo vremia sostavleniia Ulozheniia," *Nakazy malorossiiskim deputatam 1767 g. i akty o vyborakh deputatov v Komissiiu sochineniia ulozheniia* (Kyiv, 1890), pp. 178; and "Istoricheskoe izvestie," pp. 154–61. For a discussion of Poletyka's political views, see my article, "A Gentry Democracy within an Autocracy: The Politics of Hryhorii Poletyka (1723/25–1784)," in *Eucharisterion: Essays Presented to Omeljan Pritsak by His Students and Colleagues on His Sixtieth Birthday* (=*Harvard Ukrainian Studies*, vols. 3–4) (Cambridge, Mass., 1980), pp. 507–19.

41. On the Officers' Council of 1763 and the participation of the Ukrainian elite in the Legislative Commission, see Zenon E. Kohut, *Russian Centralism and Ukrainian Autonomy: Imperial Absorption of the Hetmanate, 1760s–1830s* (Cambridge, Mass., 1988), pp. 86–95, 125–90.

fringe of Europe. By the late eighteenth century, Russia was a huge multinational empire and a major European power. The evolution of Muscovy into imperial Russia involved not only territorial expansion, but also a fundamental administrative, military, and cultural transformation. Ukrainians played an important role in this transformation and, at the same time, were profoundly affected by it.

Ukrainian clerics began coming to Muscovy in search of alms and support for publications well before the Pereiaslav Agreement of 1654. These contacts proved very difficult because of the insularity of Muscovite Orthodoxy. In essence, the Muscovite church did not regard the Orthodox population of the Polish-Lithuanian Commonwealth as truly Orthodox. It placed the Ukrainian Orthodox in the same category as Roman Catholics, Protestants, and Uniates, requiring that they be rebaptized before being accepted into the Muscovite Orthodox Church. This attitude grew even stronger when the liturgical reforms instituted by Metropolitan Petro Mohyla of Kyiv in the 1630s further distanced the Ukrainian church from Muscovite practices.

Official Muscovite attitudes changed at the time of the Pereiaslav Agreement. Since the main justification for bringing Ukraine under the suzerainty of the tsar was the protection of Orthodoxy (as asserted by the *Zemskii sobor* of 1653), it could hardly be maintained that Ukrainians were not truly Orthodox. Muscovite expansion into Ukraine had also whetted the appetite of Patriarch Nikon for establishing a universal Eastern Orthodox Church subordinate to him. Moreover, the Muscovite church could not avoid the Western challenge. The Roman Catholic king of Poland had been a serious contender for the Muscovite throne, and coalition politics made Muscovy an ally of Protestant states. If the Muscovite church were to play a leadership role for Eastern Orthodoxy, then it also needed to assume, at least partially, the mission of the Ukrainian Orthodox clergy, that is, to develop an Orthodoxy capable of withstanding the Catholic and Protestant challenge. For Patriarch Nikon, reform of the Muscovite church was necessary not in order to bring it closer to the West, but rather to consolidate Orthodox forces against the West. This could be done only by unifying the Greek, Kyivan, and Muscovite traditions, and the Ukrainian Orthodox clergy was particularly well placed to accomplish such a task.[42]

Patriarch Nikon's political ambitions notwithstanding, the Muscovite church was hardly prepared for a blending of various Orthodox traditions. Muscovite Orthodoxy was grounded in the belief that it

42. See Tetiana Oparina, "Spryiniattia uniï v Rosiï XVII stolittia," in Borys Gudziak, ed., *Derzhava, suspil'stvo i Tserkva v Ukraïni u XVII stolitti*, Materiialy Druhykh "Beresteis'kykh chytan'" (Lviv, 1996), pp. 131–63.

possessed the one true faith, in its fullness, in the only Orthodox—i.e., truly Christian—realm. It emphasized simplicity as the virtue most pleasing to God and was fundamentally opposed to Ukrainian influences, Latin, and the "study of philosophy." Thus, Muscovy had a well-developed autarkic cultural tradition that could only view the Ukrainian presence as alien.

The Ukrainian clerics were able to penetrate and have an impact on Russian religious and cultural life because they received support from the tsar and the court. As Muscovy began its westward expansion, the Ukrainian clerics provided an important vehicle for Muscovy's acquisition of Western ideas and intellectual techniques. Although the Kyiv Mohyla Academy and its Russian copy, the Greco-Slavonic-Latin Academy, were hardly at the cutting edge of Western learning, they were nevertheless firmly planted within the Western intellectual tradition. The curriculum of rhetoric, logic, neoscholasticism, Latin and Greek taught by the Kyivan clerics established the intellectual foundations for natural philosophy and political theories drawn from other sources. Most importantly, the Ukrainian elites provided a large number of educated cadres without whom the early drive toward empire could hardly have been sustained.

Thus, from the mid-seventeenth century, several waves of Ukrainian clerics moved or were summoned to Muscovy, where they assumed prominent roles in religious, educational, cultural, and intellectual life. Among the Ukrainians who dominated Muscovite high culture during this period were Arsenii Satanovsky, Iepifanii Slavynetsky, Dymytrii Tuptalo, Stefan Iavorsky, Lazar Baranovych, and Teofan Prokopovych. The Belarusian Simiaon Polatski (Simeon Polotsky) should also be noted.[43] Considering the different worldviews of the Muscovite and Ukrainian clergy, it is hardly surprising that they clashed over the doctrines of transubstantiation and the immaculate conception of the Virgin Mary.[44] In theory, Kyivan theology yielded to the authority of Muscovite tradition on these questions, but in practice Western and Kyivan iconography, literature, music, and intellectual currents poured into Muscovy thanks to the influence of the Ukrainians.

---

43. The influence of these Ukrainian clerics on Muscovite church life is the subject of Kharlampovich, *Malorossiskoe vliianie na velikorusskuiu tserkovnuiu zhizn'*.

44. On the conflict between Kyivan and Muscovite clerics concerning transubstantiation, see Grigorii Mirkovich, *O vremeni presushchestvleniia sv. darov, spor, byvshei v Moskve, vo vtoroi polovine XVII-go veka* (Vilnius, 1886), pp. 31–82, appendix, pp. i-xxvi.

This attempted Ukrainization of Muscovite Orthodoxy helped trigger the Old Believer schism in Russia. Patriarch Nikon's attempt to reform Muscovite Orthodoxy according to Ukrainian and Greek models, which, during the sixteenth and seventeenth centuries, had also been Westernized by Greek scholars educated at Italian universities, resulted in the *raskol* (schism) that divides the Russian church to this day.

Despite the *raskol* (against which the Muscovite church engaged the efforts of Ukrainian scholars and preachers), the Ukrainian presence in Muscovy brought Ukrainian and some Russian clerics (the younger generation of whom were being educated by émigré Ukrainians) closer together intellectually. The Ukrainian clerics were attempting to bring the two traditions together so as to create a coherent *Slavia Orthodoxa*. Their vision linked "enlightened" Orthodoxy with the tsar, ancient Rus', and the Slavonic language and culture. In essence, they were proponents of a unified "Slavo-Rossian" (*slaveno-rossiiska*) high culture based partly on the post-Mohyla Jesuit school version of Ukrainian Orthodoxy and on the Ukrainian version of Church Slavonic.

The impact of Ukrainian clerics on Russian intellectual and cultural life has been the subject of considerable debate. Traditional historiography has represented the Ukrainian influence as a major transformation of Muscovite culture. Some scholars, among them Georges Florovsky, saw that transformation as a tragedy, a corruption of Orthodoxy and Russian culture by Latin, Catholic, and Protestant elements.[45] Others, such as Prince Nikolai Trubetskoi and Dmitrii Likhachev, welcomed the Ukrainian influx as a beneficial "Ukrainianization" of Muscovite culture that greatly enriched Russia.[46] Most scholars credit Ukrainian human-

---

45. Georges Florovsky, *Ways of Russian Theology*, 2 vols. (Belmont, Mass., 1979–87), esp. 1: 59–60, 65, 85, 121, 131–32. For a scholarly critique of Florovsky, see Frank E. Sysyn, "Peter Mohyla and the Kyiv Academy in Recent Western Works: Divergent Views on Seventeenth-Century Ukrainian Culture," *The Kiev Mohyla Academy* (=*Harvard Ukrainian Studies* 8, nos. 1–2 [June 1984]), pp. 160–70; and Francis J. Thomson, "Peter Mogila's Ecclesiastical Reforms and the Ukrainian Contribution to Russian Culture: A Critique of Georges Florovsky's Theory of the Pseudomorphosis of Orthodoxy," *Belgian Contributions to the 11th International Congress of Slavists, Bratislava, 30 Aug.-8 Sept. 1993* (=*Slavica Gandensia* 20 [1993]), pp. 67–119.

46. Nikolai Sergeevich Trubetzkoy, *The Legacy of Genghis Khan and Other Essays on Russia's Identity*, ed. and with a postscript by Anatoly Liberman, preface by Viacheslav V. Ivanov (Ann Arbor, 1991), pp. 245–68; and Dmitrii S. Likhachev, *Reflections on Russia*, trans. Christina Sever, ed. Nikolai N. Petro (Boulder, Colo., 1991), pp. 74–75 (Likhachev asserts that for centuries Russia and Ukraine "have formed not only a political, but also a culturally dualistic unity").

ism with preparing the Petrine "revolution" and aiding in the transformation of Muscovy into modern Russia.[47]

Recently, Max Okenfuss has advanced a revisionist view, arguing that the large influx of Ukrainians had a minimal impact on Russian culture. On the basis of a careful study of both book and manuscript libraries in Russia, Okenfuss concludes that the combination of Orthodoxy with humanism was limited to Ukrainians and other foreigners. He argues for the fundamental cultural autarky of the Muscovite nobility and most of the clergy. Okenfuss claims that the "Ukrainian-Lithuanian-Belarusian community was small, isolated, and alien" and that "the growth of humane secular learning was not an organic development within Muscovite society, but the struggle of Kyivans—the struggle of Ukrainian humanists to make themselves heard above the din raised by an avalanche of psalters and liturgical books."[48] At most, Ukrainian humanism created "the 'Russian Levites,' a caste with educations alien to those of nobles, most of the middle estates, and the peasantry."[49]

Despite the resistance to Slavo-Rossian humanistic culture in Muscovy, this culture of the Ukrainian clerics was subsequently viewed as a point of unity between Russia and Ukraine and as an important step in the evolution of modern Russian culture. Moreover, these Ukrainian clerics did in fact help to "jump-start" Muscovy's transformation into imperial Russia. Other ideas and developments soon made that process more European and, paradoxically, more Russian as well. Cameralism and the concept of the well-ordered police state, imported from the Germanies, formed the intellectual underpinnings of the new state activism. The cameralists had the political goal of maximizing society's productive potential through the agency of the state, which assumed the role of policing and developing society. From the time of Peter I, the Russian Empire pursued the goals of increasing the power and wealth of the state not only through annexation and conquest, but also by attempting to rationalize government, extract greater state revenues, and increase productivity.[50]

---

47. See Marc Raeff, "The Enlightenment in Russia and Russian Thought in the Enlightenment," in *The Eighteenth Century in Russia*, ed. John G. Garrard (Oxford, 1973), pp. 25–47, here 25; and Donald W. Treadgold, *The West in Russia and China*, vol. 1, *Russia 1472–1917* (Cambridge, 1973), p. 115.

48. Max J. Okenfuss, *The Rise and Fall of Latin Humanism in Early-Modern Russia: Pagan Authors, Ukrainians, and the Resiliency of Muscovy* (Leiden, 1995), pp. 70, 57.

49. Ibid., p. 109.

50. See V. I. Syromiatnikov, *"Reguliarnoe gosudarstvo" Petra Pervogo i ego ideologiia* (Moscow, 1943); and Marc Raeff, *The Well-Ordered Police State: Social*

In its activism, Westernization, and pursuit of reforms, imperial Russia began developing a more secular, cosmopolitan and, at the same time, more Russian imperial culture that initially supplemented and then began to displace Slavo-Rossian culture. Paramount in this process was the development of a modern literary Russian language and a secular Russian literature. The imperial Russian state introduced the civil script, which sharpened distinctions between ecclesiastical and civil linguistic forms; published grammars and dictionaries; and produced works dealing with all aspects of the secular world, from practical manuals to translations of foreign literature.[51] The linguistic medium that began to emerge was a middle style incorporating elements of the "high" style of Slavo-Rossian and the "low" style of colloquial Russian. By the nineteenth century, the new literary Russian had become the linguistic medium of the empire. At the same time, the imperial elites had an increasing knowledge of German and, by the end of the eighteenth century, French. Although elements of Slavo-Rossian culture survived well into the nineteenth century, it was gradually being relegated to Orthodox Church services and spiritual literature.

For the Ukrainian elites, the evolving Russian Empire presented both opportunities and dangers. A strong Orthodox state based largely on Slavo-Rossian culture and challenging both Poland-Lithuania and the Tatar-Ottoman world certainly fulfilled the aspirations of at least a part of the Ukrainian clerical elite. The evolution of the Little Russian concept allowed the clerical and non-clerical elites to express political loyalty to the tsar and to a greater Russia, even as they insisted on specific "Little Russian rights and liberties." The cameralist police-state concepts were not hostile to such regional autonomy and corporate traditions. In fact, cameralist practice was to subordinate the corporate bodies to the new purposes of the state rather than to curtail or abolish them. Nor was the evolving Russian imperial culture considered a threat by the Ukrainian elite, which continued to share the empire's high culture, whether Slavo-Rossian or a mixture of imperial Russian and Slavo-Rossian. The Ukrainian elite of the late eighteenth century readily accepted the fact that it shared a monarch, some aspects of history, and a high culture with Russia. At the same time, this elite continued to insist on the special juridical and social

---

and Institutional Change through Law in the Germanies and Russia, 1600–1800 (New Haven, Conn., 1983).

51. V. V. Vinogradov, *Ocherki po istorii russkogo literaturnogo iazyka XVII–XIX vv.* (repr. Leiden, 1949), pp. 72–84.

arrangements and distinct historical development of Ukraine (i.e., the Hetmanate of the Left Bank).

While the Little Russian concept provided sufficient intellectual space for the Ukrainian elite to participate in imperial Russia and, at the same time, to remain distinct within it, it had a number of basic flaws. First, it could not accommodate the prevailing concept of tsarist authority and power. From the time at Pereiaslav when tsarist envoys refused to take an oath on behalf of the tsar because such an act was an unthinkable encroachment on autocratic rule, Ukrainian "rights and liberties" had been at the mercy of tsarist wishes and even whims. It is true that in the seventeenth century the tsar had issued charters upon each election of a Ukrainian hetman, thereby effectively confirming traditional "rights and liberties." Moreover, every break with Muscovy/Russia by Hetmans Vyhovsky, Doroshenko, and Mazepa was justified by the Ukrainians with the argument that the tsar had violated his solemn obligations toward Ukraine.[52] But obligations to subjects were antithetical both to traditional autocracy and to the more modern absolutism of the eighteenth century. In the final analysis, the Ukrainian elite had no legal or moral recourse when its "rights" were violated; it could only appeal to tradition and the tsar's sense of justice.

The Little Russian concept also clashed with Enlightenment ideas that became dominant in mid-eighteenth-century Russia. While cameralism recognized regional, historic, and cultural differences, the Enlightenment insisted that there was a basic uniformity in nature and society. What was important to "enlightened thought" was the discovery of these basic rules or laws, not concentration on superficial differences. For good government, it was crucial to discover the laws of governance and apply them. It was very difficult for the Ukrainian elite to defend the historical and legal traditions of their "homeland" against the argument that the introduction of the "best of all possible laws" would bring greater development and progress.

Catherine II's introduction of what she conceived to be the "best of all orders"[53] resulted in administrative uniformity for the empire, including Ukraine. The Hetmanate was divided into three provinces; the Ukrainian administrative, military, and fiscal institutions were dis-

52. See Iakovliv, *Ukraïns'ko-moskovs'ki dohovory v XVII–XVIII vikakh.*

53. This expression was used by Catherine in 1765 in her instructions to the newly appointed governor-general and president of the Little Russian College, Count Petr Rumiantsev. The instructions were published in *Sbornik Imperatorskogo russkogo istoricheskogo obshchestva*, vol. 7 (St. Petersburg, 1871), pp. 376–91.

mantled; and a new Russian imperial provincial and district administration was installed. Similarly, the Orthodox Church in Ukraine was reorganized along imperial lines. By the beginning of the nineteenth century, little remained of the legal institutions, historical legacy, and corporate "rights and liberties" that, in the eyes of Ukrainians, distinguished them from Russians.

The Remnants of Distinctiveness: The Little Russian Concept in the Early Nineteenth Century

The abolition of the Hetmanate's institutions and the introduction of an imperial administration effected a gradual fusion of Ukrainian and Russian social structures. Yet alongside this absorption of the Ukrainian elite into the Russian imperial system, the Little Russian identity continued to exist as a subset either of an all-Russian identity or of one centered on the notion of empire. The Little Russian identity continued to exist because of a number of factors: (1) the Ukrainian gentry's dominant role in the imperial administration of Little Russia; (2) the survival of Ukrainian customary law; (3) the occasional restitution of certain legal and military formations traditional to Little Russia; and (4) an interest in the history and folklore of Ukraine that helped nurture the idea of a Little Russian fatherland.

The first factor, the gentry's role in the administration of this territory, was due to the Little Russian gentry's acceptance into the imperial ruling class. In 1785 Catherine II permitted the Little Russian gentry to be recognized as part of the imperial *dvorianstvo*.[54] Previously, the Little Russian gentry had attempted to claim the rights enjoyed by the *szlachta* under Polish-Lithuanian rule.[55] This, of course, was unacceptable to Catherine, as the Polish *szlachta* enjoyed much greater privileges than did the Russian *dvoriane*. The abolition of all Ukrainian institutions and the introduction of the provincial regulations of 1775, however, finally forced the imperial Russian

---

54. The provisions of the charter are discussed at length in Robert E. Jones, *The Emancipation of the Russian Nobility, 1762–1785* (Princeton, N.J., 1973), pp. 272–99.

55. The Ukrainian gentry's claims are outlined in a preliminary draft (1784) of the charter. For a good summary of these, see D. Miller, "Ocherki iz istorii i iuridicheskogo byta staroi Malorossii: Prevrashchenie kozatskoi starshiny v dvorianstvo," *Kievskaia starina*, 1897, no. 2: 194–96. A detailed listing is to be found in the law code of 1786: Nikolai Vasilenko (Mykola Vasylenko), ed., *Ėkstrakt iz ukazov instruktsii i uchrezhdenii s razdeleniem po materialam na deviatnadtsat' chastei (=Materialy dlia istorii ėkonomicheskogo, iuridicheskogo i obshchestvennogo byta Staroi Malorossii*, vol. 2) (Chernihiv, 1902), pp. 216–31.

authorities to recognize the Little Russian gentry.[56] Since nobles were to play an essential role in the new provincial administration, the former claim that there were "no nobles in Little Russia" had to be dropped, and a Little Russian *dvorianstvo* had to be created out of the old Ukrainian gentry. The Ukrainian elite's integration into the Russian nobility, along with the complete enserfment of the Ukrainian peasantry in 1783, provided the Ukrainian gentry with unprecedented opportunities to pursue imperial careers and acquire immense wealth.[57] Consequently, as a nobiliary class they absolutely dominated the local administration of Little Russia.

The second factor that ensured the continuation of the Little Russian concept was the survival of Ukrainian common law. In 1801, Ukrainian courts on the territory of Little Russia were abolished and replaced with imperial Russian courts.[58] Ukrainian common law, however, was appended to the Russian law code in these courts, thereby ensuring that the legal system would continue to operate somewhat differently in Little Russia than in the rest of the Russian Empire.[59] These legal peculiarities survived until the 1917 Revolution as the last vestige of the Hetmanate's former autonomous status.

The third factor that sustained a sense of Little Russian identity was the occasional revival of certain legal and military institutions that had previously been abolished. For example, Ukrainian traditionalists were able to convince the imperial authorities partially to restore one of the most important elements of Cossack Ukraine—the Cossack Host. During the Napoleonic invasion, fifteen Cossack regiments were reestablished and then disbanded after the Russian victory.[60] During

---

56. For the Basic Statute for the Administration of the Provinces of the Russian Empire (1775), see *Polnoe sobranie zakonov Rossiiskoi imperii* (henceforth *PSZ*) (St. Petersburg, 1830–1916), no. 14392 (7 November 1775), 20: 229–304.

57. For Catherine's decree forbidding the movement of Ukrainian peasants and extending the poll tax to Ukraine, see *PSZ*, no. 15724 (3 May 1783), 21: 908.

58. Described in "Dnevnik Akima Semenovicha Sulimy," *Russkii biograficheskii slovar'* (St. Petersburg, 1896–1918), vol. 20 (Suvorova-Tkachev), pp. 141–42.

59. Mykola Vasylenko enumerates the local legal practices retained with the introduction of the imperial code in his article "Iak skasovano Lytovs'koho statuta," *Zapysky Sotsiial'no-ekonomichnoho viddilu VUAN*, vol. 2–3 (1923–25), pp. 288–316.

60. The organization, activities, and disbandment of the 1812–16 Cossack formations have been studied in numerous works. The most important are I. Pavlovskii, "Malorossiiskoe kozach'e opolchenie v 1812 godu," *Kievskaia*

the Polish uprising of 1830, Tsar Nicholas authorized the reactivation of eight Cossack regiments consisting of 1,200 men each.[61] Again, once the uprising was crushed, the Cossack units were no longer needed and subsequently disbanded. Any attempt to revitalize the Cossacks as free warriors of old Ukraine, however, was forestalled by imperial opposition and by the Cossacks' own economic decline. By 1837 the Cossacks were under the jurisdiction of the Ministry of State Properties (*Ministerstvo gosudarstvennykh imushchestv*), an agency intended primarily for state peasants.[62] However, the Cossacks retained certain privileges with regard to land ownership, taxes, and military service.

The fourth development that encouraged the survival of the Little Russian concept was literary—the unprecedented body of writing concerning the history of the Little Russian fatherland and nostalgia for it. The most influential work of this type was the anonymous *Istoriia Rusov*.[63] This early nineteenth-century work presents a long, elaborate, and largely fictitious history extending from Kyivan times to the Turkish war of 1760. Perhaps its most interesting claim is that the Kyivan Rus' period properly belonged to the Ukrainians and had been inappropriately included in Russian history. The *Istoriia Rusov* was enormously popular among the nobility of the former Hetmanate and circulated widely in manuscript. While recognizing Ukrainian history as a special branch of a greater "all-Russian" entity, the work simultaneously stresses Ukrainian distinctiveness and is an eloquent apology for the Hetmanate and Cossack rights and privileges. Its tone is at times quite anti-Russian, and it insists that Ukraine has certain inalienable and guaranteed rights that must be upheld. However, the *Istoriia Rusov* never questions the tsar's claim to sovereignty over Little Russia—indeed, it looks to the tsar in the hope that he will maintain

---

starina, 1906, no. 9: 1–20 and no. 10: 137–54; N. Storozhenko, "K istorii malorossiiskikh kozakov v kontse XVIII i v nachale XIX veka," *Kievskaia starina*, 1897, no. 6: 460–83; P. Klepats'kyi, "Dvorians'ke zems'ke opolchennia (kozaky)," *Za sto lit* 31 (1930): 6–21; V. I. Strel'skii, *Uchastie ukrainskogo naroda v Otechestvennoi voine 1812 goda* (Kiev, 1953); and B. S. Abolikhin, "Ukrainskoe opolchenie 1812 g.," *Istoricheskie zapiski* 72 (Moscow, 1962).

61. For a detailed discussion of the 1830–31 Cossack project, see N. Storozhenko, "K istorii malorossiiskikh kozakov v kontse XVIII i v nachale XIX veka," *Kievskaia starina*, 1897, no. 10: 115–31.

62. *Istoricheskoe obozrenie piatidesiatiletnei deiatel'nosti Ministerstva gosudarstvennykh imushchestv, 1837–1887*, pt. 2 (St. Petersburg, 1888), p. 18.

63. See *Istoriia Rusov ili Maloi Rossii: Sochinenie Georgiia Koniskago Arkhiepiskopa Beloruskago* (Moscow, 1846).

the last remnants of Ukrainian autonomy and even restore the traditional rights of the Ukrainian elite.

But no restoration was possible. On the contrary, the imperial authorities continued to pursue a policy of administrative uniformity. The loss of any semblance of political distinctiveness convinced some of the more reflective members of the Ukrainian gentry that they were epigones of a country and a nation that had ceased to exist. Oleksa Martos captured this mood in a diary entry written at the grave of Hetman Mazepa in 1812:

> Mazepa died far away from his country, whose independence he defended. He was a friend of liberty and therefore deserves to be honored by posterity. After his expulsion from Little Russia, its inhabitants lost their sacred rights, which Mazepa had defended for so long with great enthusiasm and patriotic ardor. He is no more, and the name of Little Russia and its brave Cossacks have [*sic*] disappeared from the list of nations who, although small in numbers, are yet famous for their way of life and their constitution. Now rich Little Russia is reduced to two or three provinces. That this is the common destiny of states and republics, we can see from the history of other nations.[64]

After one and a half centuries, the balancing by the Ukrainian elite between assertions of Russo-Ukrainian unity and insistence on Ukrainian political distinctiveness seemed to be at an end. Russians and Ukrainians shared an all-Russian tsar, an all-Russian Orthodox faith and church, an empire, and an imperial Russian high culture. Russians and Ukrainians were administered in a similar manner and were part of one imperial social structure. The only factor that distinguished the Ukrainian elite lay in Ukraine's distinct past. The Ukrainian elite was certainly aware that Ukrainians spoke a different "vulgar" language than Russians and had different songs and folk customs, but in the pre-Romantic era such distinctions in popular culture were of little significance. For the elite, Little Russia was long dead. What lingered for some was a nostalgia for the distinctiveness of the past.

Concepts of Russo-Ukrainian Unity and Ukrainian Distinctiveness: Epilogue and Conclusions

For most of the early modern period, Ukrainians were part of two large states: Poland-Lithuania and Muscovy/Russia. In both instances,

---

64. Dmytro Doroshenko, *A Survey of Ukrainian Historiography*, Annals of the Ukrainian Academy of Arts and Sciences in the U.S., vols. 5–6 (New York, 1957), p. 112.

Ukrainians accepted some form of unity, while at the same time insisting on maintaining essential differences. In the case of Poland-Lithuania, Ukrainians subscribed to political unity as part of the *szlachta* nation, yet insisted on religious and cultural differences. As these and other attempted arrangements within Poland-Lithuania proved unworkable, some Ukrainians began looking for succor to Muscovy. In their pro-Muscovite orientation, Ukrainians claimed affinity with Muscovy in religion, dynasty, high culture, and even ethnicity. However, they insisted on maintaining their distinctiveness in political, social, and, on occasion, ecclesiastical structures. The claim to distinctiveness proved so strong that it even survived the abolition of separate Ukrainian political and juridical institutions.

That Ukrainians could claim unity with Russia and at the same time insist on their own distinctiveness was not surprising. Before the advent of nationalism, multiple identities and loyalties were the norm, particularly in large multinational states. Thus it was possible to be a political Pole, a devout Orthodox Christian, and an advocate of Rus' culture. It was normal to be loyal to the tsar, Orthodoxy, and imperial Russia, yet at the same time to be a fervent defender of Little Russia. In fact, the whole Little Russian concept was nothing more than an intellectual justification of such multiple loyalties and identities.

From the first quarter of the nineteenth century, Ukrainians began discovering other areas of distinctiveness from Russians. Under the influence of Herder and Romanticism, a new generation discovered the Ukrainian folk and its vernacular language. Until its prohibition in the 1860s and 1870s, literature written in vernacular Ukrainian evolved slowly under the cover of a mere local variant of a larger all-Russian literature. In this respect, Ukrainians were still employing the old Little Russian concept but applying it to vernacular language and literature. In the late nineteenth century, Ukrainian intellectuals emancipated themselves from the Russian connection, positing that Ukraine was different from Russia in all respects: language, literature, culture, history, and politics. This marked the birth of modern Ukrainian nationalism, which no longer permitted multiple identities. By identifying themselves as Ukrainian, the nationalists excluded the possibility of being Russian.

Concomitantly, Russians began identifying the imperial Russian state primarily with the Great Russian people and culture. This was a rejection of a meta-Russian nationality made up of distinct and legitimate Little Russian and Great Russian components. The imperial and even the Slavo-Rossian culture began to be treated as narrowly Russian. Thus what had been shared in the past by Ukrainians, Belarusians, Moldavians, and Russians was appropriated to a Russian or Great Russian nationality. For some, the identification of the entire *Slavia Orthodoxa* with Russia and Russians made the Moldavian-Ukrainian prelate Petro Mohyla, who had never been to Russia and remained a patriot of the Polish-Lithuanian Commonwealth until his death, a defender of "Russian" religion, culture, and values. Such a view also sanctioned the banning of the Ukrainian language on the grounds that there "never has been, is not, and cannot be a Ukrainian language."

By the late nineteenth century, Ukrainians and Russians were interpreting their history on the basis of two completely opposed paradigms. In discussing the early modern period, Ukrainians emphasized those areas that were distinct from Russia and saw in them evidence of Ukraine's autochthonous development. Russians emphasized those aspects that Ukrainians held in common with Russia and saw in them proof that Ukraine had been and always would be Russian. These two fundamentally opposed views still cast their shadow on current debates concerning the question of Russo-Ukrainian unity and Ukrainian distinctiveness in the early modern period.

Hans-Joachim Torke

Moscow and Its West: On the "Ruthenization" of Russian Culture in the Seventeenth Century*

Moskva z Ross'iu nasheiu, na Moskvu pryiezhdchaiucheiu, iak' i poslove moskovskiie v Litvie i v Koronie byvaiuchii, spolech'nost' tserkovnuiu z soboiu mievali.[1]

Zakhariia Kopystensky, Palinodiia (1619)

The yoking together of Polish and Russian history not only since the eighteenth century, but also in the context of the "Jagiellonian variant of old Rus' history from the fourteenth to the sixteenth century," has recently been examined in a monumental work by Klaus Zernack.[2] The glossing over of the seventeenth century in this connection can undoubtedly be attributed to the many confrontations between the two states, beginning with the Polish invasion of Muscovy and the occupation of the Kremlin during the Time of Troubles. These conflicts were not settled until the armistice of Andrusovo (1667) and the "eternal peace" of Moscow (1686). It is not surprising that during this period Western influences did not traverse the West-East cultural gradient to Russia directly from Poland: the religious barrier represented an insuperable obstacle to closer contacts as long as the Orthodox Church monopolized intellectual life in Muscovy. That "Pole" and "Catholic" became synonymous for Russians is a historical tragedy with far-reaching consequences.

One result of this situation was that during the period of secularization in the eighteenth century, Western influences sought

---

* The German version of this article appeared under the title "Moskau und sein Westen: Zur 'Ruthenisierung' der russischen Kultur" in *Berliner Jahrbuch für osteuropäische Geschichte*, 1996, no. 1: 101–20.

1. "...the Muscovites had ecclesiastic communion with our Ruthenians both when our people came to Moscow and when their envoys visited Lithuania and the Crown Land" (Lev Krevza's A Defense of Church Unity and *Zaxarija Kopystens'kyj's* Palinodia, trans. Bohdan Strumiński [Cambridge, Mass., 1995], p. 775).

2. Klaus Zernack, Polen und Rußland. Zwei Wege in der europäischen Geschichte (Berlin, 1994).

different routes: state-driven Europeanization[3] brought material goods, including weapons, from Sweden, Germany, the Netherlands, and England. The church, however, guided the flow of ideas by admitting religious and moral influences, initially from Byzantium. In the seventeenth century, it showed increased tolerance for cultural innovations from the West (=White) Russian regions and Ukraine (and only through this filter from Poland) in fields ranging from philosophy to the arts. With Muscovy's gradual adoption of Western absolutism in the last quarter of the seventeenth century, the government had to tolerate more and more infiltration of this kind. It began to pay attention to culture and abandoned the previous division of functions between church and state. The Orthodox belief that predominated in the southwest, or the "intermediate confessional empire," as it was termed by Albert Ammann, facilitated (though not without difficulty, given the Uniate "aberration") the Muscovites' adoption of Western ideas, with which historical fate had brought the immediate neighbors of the Great Russians into close contact.

For the inhabitants of the Tsardom of Muscovy, the terms "White Russian" (or, rather, White Ruthenian), "Ukrainian," and, for the most part, "Lithuanian" were still generally interchangeable in the seventeenth century. "Ukraine" gained a specific meaning only with the gradual decline of the term "Rus'," which referred to the whole East Slavic region. Oddly, "Litva" was understood around 1600 to refer to both Poles and Orthodox, and only later were Poles and Lithuanians perceived as a unit, while the Orthodox inhabitants of the region between Poland and Muscovy were called "Ruthenians" (*rusiny*) and their language "White Ruthenian." For example, whenever Bohdan Khmelnytsky, the hetman of the Zaporozhian Cossacks, wrote to Tsar Aleksei Mikhailovich, his letters were translated in Moscow "from the White Ruthenian script" (*s beloruskogo pis'ma*).[4] Within the context of a White Ruthenian-Ukrainian cultural community, these terms referred to the East Slavic inhabitants of the Grand Duchy of Lithuania, the southern part of which had fallen to Poland with the Union of Lublin (1569). Consequently, following the initial territorial gains in the Second Northern War of 1654, Aleksei Mikhailovich replaced the title "Tsar of all Rus'" with "Tsar of all Great, Little, and White Russia."

---

3. This term is only a stopgap, faute de mieux, for it assumes that Russia did not previously belong to Europe and that Byzantine culture was non-European. The actual meaning is West Europeanization.

4. See, e.g., the letter of 8 January 1654 in *Vossoedinenie Ukrainy s Rossiei: Dokumenty i materialy v trekh tomakh*, vol. 3 (Moscow, 1954), no. 225, p. 516.

The struggle over this region that began in the fourteenth century between Lithuania and Muscovy is, of course, only one aspect of its history. Of at least equal importance is the mediating role of this borderland, which was already apparent in political terms in the fifteenth century.[5] From a cultural viewpoint, however, this role actually pertains only to the period after the ecclesiastical Union of Brest (1596) and the subsequent exacerbation of differences between Orthodox and Catholics. While the modern political distinction between Russia and Poland originated here,[6] in 1649 Muscovy had no qualms whatever about using the third edition of the Lithuanian Statute (1588), written in the "White Ruthenian" chancery language, in which Polish (and perhaps also Czech) law was merged with Rus' law, as one of the sources for its new law code, the *Ulozhenie*. In particular, ordinances for the protection of the person of the tsar and the court were adopted in the process.[7] Contrary to earlier belief, the Lithuanian Statute was not first translated into "Great Russian" in the mid-1640s, but had already been partly translated in 1606, when the False Dmitrii had a codex prepared.[8]

More numerous and significant than the legal adaptations, however, were the religious/philosophical and cultural/pedagogical impulses from Moscow's immediate West. Before 1914, when Kharlampovich published his detailed study of "Little Russian" influence on the Great Russian church,[9] Russian research took a

---

5. See Horst Jablonowski, *Westrußland zwischen Wilna und Moskau: Die politische Stellung und die politischen Tendenzen der russischen Bevölkerung des Großfürstentums Litauen im 15. Jahrhundert* (Leiden, 1955).

6. Ibid., p. 155.

7. See articles 2 and 3 of the *Ulozhenie* in the new annotated edition by A. G. Man'kov, *Rossiiskoe zakonodatel'stvo X-XX vekov v deviati tomakh*, vol. 3, *Akty Zemskikh soborov* (Moscow, 1985), pp. 86–91. On the third Lithuanian Statute, see the anthology *1588 metų trečiasis Lietuvos Statutas—Tretii Litovskii statut 1588 goda* (Vilnius, 1989). Still indispensable for the statute's influence on the *Ulozhenie* is M. F. Vladimirskii-Budanov, "Otnosheniia mezhdu Litovskim statutom i ulozheniem tsaria Alekseia Mikhailovicha," in *Sbornik gosudarstvennykh znanii*, vol. 4 (St. Petersburg, 1877).

8. See V. D. Nazarov, "O pervom perevode tekstov Litovskogo statuta 1588 g. v Rossii," in *1588 metų*, pp. 230–40.

9. See K. V. Kharlampovich, *Malorossiiskoe vliianie na velikorusskuiu tserkovnuiu zhizn'*, vol. 1 (Kazan, 1914). The book is very comprehensive, although it is only the first, rather empirical, volume of an intended trilogy of which, according to the author, "only the final volume will explain what the Little Russians gave to the Great Russians" (p. v). After more than eight

reticent or negative view of these foreign influences. In that regard, it was a loyal successor to seventeenth-century Muscovite Orthodoxy, whose synod of 16 December 1620 resolved to subject settlers from Ruthenia to a second baptism, as they had not been immersed three times but only sprinkled with water (*oblivantsy*) in the Uniate-Catholic manner.[10] The Muscovite attitude toward Ukraine was at first astoundingly passive and even somewhat defensive, despite the readily available memory of a common history and the greatness of the Kyivan Empire. Edward Keenan has noted that no feeling of East Slavic unity developed between the mid-sixteenth and mid-seventeenth century.[11] Indeed, the initial impulses came from immigrants and writings from the southwest.

Alms seekers who came to Muscovy not only from the Orthodox lands in general, including Ukraine and White Ruthenia, do not, of course, belong to this group, nor do the individual wandering monks who made their first appearance in the fourteenth century. On the other hand, Archdeacon Isaia of Kamianets-Podilskyi may be identified as the first learned cleric to make this journey. He came to Moscow in 1561 to obtain a copy of the Slavic Bible and other writings, which were to be reprinted in Ukraine "for our Rus' Lithuanian people and the Rus' Muscovite people and for all Orthodox Christians everywhere."[12] His fate, however, is somewhat emblematic of relations between Moscow and its West, which were fragile even before the Union of Brest: Isaia was charged with slander and imprisoned for five years. True, during a second visit in 1582 he was able to debate questions of the faith with Ivan the Terrible,[13] but it is well known that many contemporary Ruthenian clerics complained of "Muscovite boorishness."

---

decades, a deeper analysis that goes beyond the present work is urgently needed, especially as Lewitter's study is also outdated (L. R. Lewitter, "Poland, the Ukraine and Russia in the 17th Century," *Slavonic Review* 27 [1948–49]: 157–71, 414–29).

10. Mentioned in the *Euchologion* of 1639. See A. Grenkov, "Sobor byvshii v Rossii pri Patriarkhe Filarete v 1620 godu i ego opredeleniia," *Pravoslavnyi sobesednik*, 1864, no. 1: 153–80.

11. See Edward L. Keenan, "Muscovite Perceptions of Other East Slavs before 1654—An Agenda for Historians," in *Ukraine and Russia in Their Historical Encounter*, ed. Peter J. Potichnyj et al. (Edmonton, 1992), pp. 20–38.

12. E. V. Barsov, ed., *Iz rukopisei E. V. Barsova*; "Puteshestvie kievskogo ierodiakona Iakoma v Moskvu za knigami i predstavlenie ego tsariu Groznomu v prisutstvii boiarskoi dumy v 1582 g," in *Chteniia v Moskovskom obshchestve istorii i drevnostei*, 1883, no. 1: 1–3.

13. See Kharlampovich, *Malorossiiskoe vliianie*, p. 7ff.

Something of a prelude to the "Ruthenization"[14] of Muscovite culture was the activity of East Slavic printers in the sixteenth century. Ivan Fedorov and Petr Mstsislavets, who came from Mstsislaŭ in Belarus, were cultural mediators of a particular type, as they produced the first books in Muscovy and then went on to Lithuania and Ukraine. Of the few Ukrainian and Lithuanian magnates who avoided Polonization, several held fast to their Orthodox faith and brought about its "rebirth" by providing the two printers with employment. The Belarusian hetman Ryhor Khadkevich set up a printshop for them in Zabludiv (Zabłudów). Their paths later separated. While Mstsislavets reprinted his work in Vilnius, where Frantsysk Skaryna of Polatsk had already established a printshop shortly after 1520,[15] Fedorov went to Lviv in 1570. After 1578 he had the opportunity to publish, among other works, his most famous book, the "Ostrih Bible" (1581), the first printed Slavic Bible, at the printshop of Prince Kostiantyn Ostrozky in Ostrih (Ostroh, Ostrog). In the present context, it is important to note that the works of these men also found their way into the churches and monasteries of Muscovy. While Isaia still wanted to obtain church writings in Muscovy, the direction was reversed in the seventeenth century: owing to the progress of education in the southwest, it was Muscovy that needed the literature appearing there. This was not, of course, unproblematic, for the Muscovite church had long since maneuvered itself into a fundamentalist dead end.

As early as the fourteenth century, Metopolitan Aleksii had complained that the liturgical texts in use often differed from one another, and in the first half of the sixteenth century, after comparing the Russian texts with the Greek ones, Maksim Grek had even suspected the Russians with heresy because of these deviations (which he lived to regret). The lack of uniformity was a matter of concern to the *Stoglav* Synod of 1551, as a result of which the first printshop in Moscow was established two years later to eliminate the variant readings caused by sloppy copying. Yet Fedorov, who had worked there since 1563, and Mstsislavets were finally banished for "many heresies."[16] It proved impossible to reach agreement on a uniform printed version.

---

14. In place of the word "Ruthenian," the traditionally Russocentric literature tends to use "South Russian."

15. See W. Heller, "Franciscus Skaryna (1486–1541)—der 'Erstdrucker' der Ostslaven," in *Horizonte der Christenheit: Festschrift für Friedrich Heyer zu seinem 85. Geburtstag*, ed. M. Kohlbacher and M. Lesinski (Erlangen, 1995), pp. 320–26.

16. This is apparent from the afterword to the *Apostol* of 1574 printed in Lviv, even though the literature consistently refers to the "unexplained circumstances" of the banishment.

In the seventeenth century, efforts to overcome the problem were also initially unsuccessful. In 1617, a Commission for the Correction of Books was established; in addition to Archimandrite Dionisii of the Trinity-Sergius Monastery, it included the monks Arsenii (Glukhoi) and Antonii (Krylov) and the priest Ivan Nasedka. Dionisii had distinguished himself after 1610 in the struggle against the Poles. In 1618–19 he found himself imprisoned, together with his colleagues, because of the correction of the Euchologion (*sluzhebnik, trebnik*), which had been undertaken on the basis of Greek sources. He was released only after Patriarch Theophanes of Jerusalem interceded with Patriarch Filaret of Moscow, who had returned from Polish captivity in mid-1619. The dilemma became intractable: there were no scholars in Muscovy to deal with the tasks at hand, and yet there was no desire to bring in Ukrainian monks. Lavrentii Zyzanii, for example, who had been instructed to write a catechism, was accused of various errors. On 1 December 1627, Mikhail Fedorovich and Filaret sent a joint circular to all voevodas prohibiting the ownership or purchase of the writings of the Chernihiv archimandrite Kyrylo Stavrovetsky-Tranquillon, because they were allegedly "full of heretical teachings." The names of those who possessed these books were to be written down and the books themselves collected and burned. The opportunity was taken to issue a general decree that subsequent purchasers of books of "Lithuanian printing" would be subject to "great" secular and religious penalties.[17] The primary goal here was to ward off the influence of the Kyiv Academy.

The emergence of Ukrainian schools, like the establishment of the printshops, was due in part to initiatives of the magnates. Probably as early as the 1570s, Prince Iurii Slutsky founded a school on his estate, and Prince Ostrozky did the same in Turaŭ and Volodymyr. The latter gave rise in 1580 to the Ostrih Academy, where Greek preceptors and the Ukrainian Meletii Smotrytsky taught, in addition to Greek, Latin, and Church Slavonic, the seven liberal arts (grammar, rhetoric, dialectics, arithmetic, geometry, music, and astronomy).[18] Also active here, along with several Poles, were Herasym Smotrytsky (as rector), the priest Damian Nalyvaiko, the monk Vasyl Ostrozky (Surazky), who had attended Italian universities, and the future patriarch of Constantinople, Cyril Lucaris, who was then seeking a connection

---

17. *Sobranie gosudarstvennykh gramot i dogovorov*, 5 vols. (Moscow, 1813–94), vol. 3, no. 77 (letter to the voevoda of Verkhoturie).

18. On the influence of Greek culture in Ukraine, see Iaroslav Isaievych, "Greek Culture in the Ukraine: 1550–1650," *Modern Greek Studies Yearbook* 6 (1990): 97–122.

between Protestant theology and Orthodoxy. After the death of the prince, his daughter handed the academy over to the Jesuits.

In addition to the princes' schools, there were religious confraternities, a type of organization that came to Ruthenia via Byzantium in the fifteenth century. Their membership consisted mainly of burghers. The first school emerged at the end of the sixteenth century in Lviv, where the confraternity had already helped establish the aforementioned printshop; among the teachers was the future metropolitan Iov (Ivan) Boretsky. Other towns followed suit, including Kyiv (1615), whose confraternity school was closely associated with the Zaporozhian Cossacks. Although these schools became centers of intellectual resistance to Roman Catholicism, many clerics who could not withstand the pressure went to Moscow.

The greatest influence on the Russians was, of course, that of the Kyiv Collegium (after 1701, an academy). It was founded in 1632 on the model of the Jesuit schools by Metropolitan Petro Mohyla, who came from Moldavia and had studied at the Lviv Confraternity School and in Paris. He consolidated his school, established the previous year in the Kyivan Caves Monastery, with the confraternity school. Following a Jesuit-influenced reform, the curriculum neglected Greek in favor of Latin. Moreover, Mohyla's still strictly Orthodox *Euchologion* (1629) contained Roman teachings in the editions of 1639 and 1646. It is not surprising that in 1640 Tsar Mikhail Fedorovich rejected Mohyla's proposal to establish a similar school in Moscow, but five years later a similar proposal from the Greek patriarch again fell on deaf ears. Nothing had changed in Muscovy since the patriarch of Alexandria, Meletios Pēgas, proposed a similar plan in connection with the establishment of the Moscow Patriarchate (1589).

Greek books were not usually trusted by the Orthodox Church, because the Greeks published their works in Italy after the fall of Constantinople. Those, like Dionisii, who corrected the Russian texts by substituting the "original" Greek text for the particular national developments that came in with the beginning of the autocephaly of the Muscovite church in the mid-fifteenth century were reproached for deviating from sacred tradition (*starina*). At that time, Greek Orthodoxy was considered tantamount to heresy. A re-Hellenization of the kind managed by Patriarch Nikon, beginning in 1652, was only possible if it could be proved that the Greeks had also retained the pure faith. A piquant aspect of this dilemma was that such proof could be produced only by the Ukrainians, owing to their erudition. In Ukraine, there had emerged a learned monkhood that, having no connection with monastery life, represented a wholly new phenomenon in the Orthodox world. Its members usually came from the nobility and lived accordingly.

A new policy—initially, at least, toward Ukrainian coreligionists—required a new tsar in Muscovy. In May 1649, Aleksei Mikhailovich asked Metropolitan Sylvestr Kosiv (Kosov) of Kyiv, also newly appointed, "to send teachers well versed in Holy Scripture and the Greek language to Moscow for a time in order to improve [i.e., translate] the Bible." Three monks were sent: Arsenii Satanovsky, Iepifanii Slavynetsky, and, a year later, Damaskyn Ptytsky. A fourth was sent by Hegumen Inokentii Gizel (Giesel of Königsberg) of the Epiphany Confraternity Monastery for the express purpose of receiving the traditional alms from Moscow, now requested as a quid pro quo.[19] The twenty-five-year tenure of Slavynetsky proved most significant.

There were historical, ideological, political, and material reasons for the involvement of Ukrainian clerics with Moscow, an early example of which was Metropolitan Boretsky's proposal of 1625 to subordinate Ukraine to the tsar. The Ukrainians knew—and still know today—that the idea of Holy Rus' had originated in Kyiv, and were convinced that with the metropolitan's move to the northeast in 1299, it had been transmitted to Muscovite Orthodoxy. Ideologically, the Byzantine doctrine of symphony—the unity of secular and religious authority—was the deciding factor. Associated with it was the Ukrainian Orthodox perception of the tsar as a powerful protector who would support his coreligionists, not least financially. These mutually reinforcing factors ensured the unity of *Slavia Orthodoxa.*

However, the subordination of Ukrainians to Muscovites in contentious questions of faith could not obscure the fact that in certain philosophical views, and most particularly in liturgical practice (music, iconography, homiletics), they were indeed deeply under Western influence. Beyond the religious and liturgical issues, the Ruthenization of Muscovite culture manifested itself, for example, through the baroque style in art. This was ultimately a consequence of the Slavic Renaissance, which had penetrated numerous Polish cultural centers in Ukraine. Not only the Polish Sarmatians, whose worldview exhibited certain Ukrainian influences as a result of the eastward expansion of the *Rzeczpospolita*, but also Croats (Mauro Orbini in Dubrovnik) had gone back to antiquity and made a place for the Slavs in ancient culture by means of invented genealogies, identifying them with the Sarmatians.[20] On the basis of Church

---

19. Letter of 8 June 1649 to the tsar in *Akty, otnosiashchiesia k istorii Iuzhnoi i Zapadnoi Rossii* (St. Petersburg, 1863–92; henceforth *Akty IuZR*), vol. 3, no. 259.

20. See Tadeusz Ulewicz, *Sarmacja: Studium z problematyki słowiańskiej XV i XVI w.* (Cracow, 1950).

Slavonic, it was easy enough to promote a commonality into which the Great Russians were now drawn. The first to attempt this, as early as 1659, was the Croat Juraj Križanić, who advocated a close connection between Ukraine and Moscow in two works ("Description of a Journey from Lviv to Moscow" and "Conversation with a Cossack"). He concocted an artificial language from various Slavic elements and called for Slavic unity, especially in view of the Turkish threat. As a member of the Congregation for the Propagation of the Faith, he inevitably fell victim to Muscovite mistrust of the Romans and spent the years from 1661 to 1676 in Siberian exile. On the other hand, in his Easter address of 1655 Aleksei Mikhailovich himself spoke of liberating coreligionists in the Balkans. The idea was also popular in the Kyiv Academy, where in his *Łabędź* (Swan) Ioanikii Galiatovsky propagated an alliance of Orthodox Slavs against the Ottomans.

Križanić's works, including his famous "Politika," did not reach the public, whoever may have constituted it at the time. More effective was Gizel's famous *Synopsis,* which first appeared in Kyiv in 1674 and was reprinted in 1678 and 1680. Regarded as the first textbook of Rus' history, it is a reworking of the *Vyklad o Tserkvi sviatoi* (Tract on the Holy Church, 1667), translated into Russian by the monk Feodosii (Teodosii) Sofonovych, who, for his part, used Polish sources. The *Synopsis* asserted for the first time that the East Slavs were really one Slavic-"Russian" people (*slaveno-rossiiskii narod*). Its main source was certainly the work of the Polish chronicler Maciej Stryjkowski (1582), but probably only the foreign-born Gizel could have written so unselfconsciously that the "patrimony" of Kyiv, to which he naturally ascribed a special place on account of its history, belonged to the Romanovs in their capacity as successors to the Riurikides.[21]

Thus, in the context of the Slavic Renaissance (though not without an eye on material interests), the Ukrainian scholars and the Belarusian Simiaon Polatski (Polatsky; Simeon Polotsky) turned to Muscovy. It is hard to know what conclusions to draw about East Slavic culture on the basis of the notion of a "Slavic-Russian people," especially as Muscovite clerics initially put up vehement resistance to Jesuit-tinged Ruthenian influences. The clearest sign of intellectual ferment was Avvakum's Old Believer movement, for the re-Hellenization of the Muscovite church by Patriarch Nikon after 1652 was wholly in keeping with the Ruthenization of Muscovite culture. Even the Greek church was reformed by clerics who had studied in Italy.

---

21. A facsimile of the 1681 edition was published by Hans Rothe as *Sinopsis, Kiev 1681: Facsimile mit einer Einleitung* (Cologne, 1983).

Moreover, Nikon made use of Ruthenian scholars and even of a Pole (Mikołaj Olszewski), whose authority rested on their knowledge of Latin. These people, disparaged as "gapers" by the Muscovites, made fun of the ignorant Russian priests.[22] The spreading Latinophobia can largely be traced to the Old Believers, whose anti-intellectualism was manifested in the *Domostroi* (House Manager). This work prescribed the Christian way of life as understood in mid-sixteenth-century Muscovy.

The influence of Ukrainian theology, on the other hand, could no longer be overlooked. In early 1644, for example, after long hesitation, Prince Waldemar of Denmark came to Moscow, because Mikhail Fedorovich wanted him to marry his daughter Irina. At the tsar's bidding, the entrepreneur Peter Marselis had assured Waldemar that he would be permitted to remain Protestant, but the Russians did not keep their promise, insisted on conversion, and detained him for a year and a half. In the course of the polemic against Protestantism attendant on this affair, one of the tsarist censors was again pressed into service. This was Ivan Nasedka, who had fallen into disfavor in 1618, as mentioned earlier. For his *Izlozhenie na liutory* (Treatise against the Lutherans), completed in 1623, Nasedka made use of the book *On the Orthodox Faith,* written by the Ukrainian priest Vasyl Ostrozky (Roman Catholicism was, of course, the main target). The services of the Kyivan monk Isaia (Isaakii) were also employed in this dispute, as Muscovite Orthodoxy had produced no scholarly advocates, with the exception of Zinovii Otensky (mid-sixteenth century). From this point on, Ukrainian works had an easier time in Muscovy. The anthology of St. John Chrysostom's writings printed in Ostrih in 1595 was issued in Muscovy in 1641 under the title *Margarit dukhovnyi* (Spiritual Pearls). Mikhail Rogov's *Kirillova kniga* (Book of Cyril, 1644), of which more than a thousand copies were sold within four weeks, contained excerpts from the writings of Vasyl Ostrozky, the Belarusian Stefan Zyzanii, Zakhariia Kopystensky, and other Ukrainian scholars, along with excerpts from Nasedka's *Izlozhenie.* The year 1648 saw the anonymous appearance in Muscovy of the *Slavonic Grammar* written in 1619 by the Podolian author Meletii Smotrytsky, who later taught in Vilnius, as well as the *Kniga o vere edinoi istinoi pravoslavnoi* (Book of the One True Orthodox Faith), which consisted of compilations by the Kyiv hegumen Natanail.[23] A year later, Mohyla's *Small Catechism* was

22. See V. O. Kliuchevskii, *Kurs russkoi istorii*, vol. 3 (Moscow, 1957), pp. 309–10.

23. See H. P. Niess, *Kirche in Rußland zwischen Tradition und Glaube? Eine Untersuchung der Kirillova kniga und der Kniga o vere aus der 1. Hälfte des 17. Jahrhunderts* (Göttingen, 1977).

published in translation, and, as already mentioned, in the same year Iepifanii Slavynetsky, among others, finally came to Muscovy at the request of the tsar. Even the 1650 edition of the *Kormchaia kniga* (Book of the Helmsman) was supplemented with extracts from Mohyla's writings. In 1653, Pamva Berynda's *Leksikon slavenorosskyi* (Slavonic Lexicon), which had appeared twenty-six years previously in Kyiv, was published in Muscovy.

As a result of the ever more frequent appearance of Protestant foreigners (*nemtsy*)—although in 1652 they were restricted by Patriarch Nikon to the (new) "German suburb," like the Poles in their special residential areas—Russian Orthodoxy found itself in a situation like the one experienced long before by Ruthenian Orthodoxy in its conflict with the Roman Catholics. Unlike Kyiv, Moscow still had no school to provide instruction in apologetics to clerics who had adequately familiarized themselves with non-Orthodox teachings. The humble Slavynetsky, who probably came from Pinsk in Belarus, preferred to work in the background. He translated Vesalius (*De humani corporis fabrica, epitome*, 1542) and Blaeu (*Theatrum orbis terrarum, sive Atlas novus*, 1653), introducing the Copernican worldview to Moscow in the latter work. And it was probably Slavynetsky who prepared the translation of Erasmus's *De civilitate morum puerilium*, which was issued in a large number of copies. It is disputed whether he ran an actual school in the Moscow Chudov Monastery in the course of his work on correcting books, but "pupils" is surely the correct term for his colleagues, the "Rtishchev Brotherhood," who translated many books in addition to the Greek Bible, primarily scientific ones obtained from Poland.

The first precursor of a religious academy, however, goes back rather to the "tsar's favorite" (according to Pavel Miliukov) Fedor Rtishchev, a rich boyar who had the St. Andrew Monastery built in 1648–49 and staffed it with about thirty Ruthenian scholars. He himself was one of the pupils who were now able to learn Slavonic and Greek grammar, rhetoric, and philosophy. Two of them even received permission to travel to Kyiv in order to learn Latin. This was astounding, given the conventional wisdom: "He who learns Latin has strayed from the true path."[24] Rtishchev brought in other innovations as well. With the aid of a choir invited from Kyiv, Rtishchev introduced polyphonic music, based on the five-line system known as "Kyivan signs" (*kievskie znamena*). In Ukraine, polyphony had emerged

24. "Kto po-latyni nauchitsia, tot s pravogo puti sovratilsia," cited in S. M. Solov'ev, *Istoriia Rossii s drevneishikh vremen*, vol. 5 (Moscow, 1961), p. 492.

at the beginning of the century as a result of competition with the sumptuous Roman Catholic services. Admittedly, the Muscovite church officially restored the traditional chant in 1667, but polyphony (*partesnoe penie*) could no longer be suppressed, and in 1681 the *Musiiskaia grammatika* (Music Grammar) by the Kyiv composer Mykola Dyletsky appeared in a translation from the Polish.[25] Since Rtishchev also founded the first hospital, a field hospital, a poorhouse and a house of reform, his actions may be regarded as early evidence of the adoption of social tasks by the state, modeled on the Western idea of absolutist paternalism.

The conviction that educated clerics were needed in Muscovy grew from mid-century on and became stronger with the impending church schism, which came about in 1667. Now even Greek clerics, such as Metropolitan Paisios Ligarides of Gaza and the Eastern patriarchs, advised learning Latin. It was not Iepifanii Slavynetsky but Simeon Polotsky (Samuil Petrovsky-Sitnianovich, to give him his secular name), who became their mouthpiece. He had lived in Moscow since 1663 and had only an incomplete command of Greek. Polotsky had studied with the scholar Lazar Baranovych at the Kyiv Collegium after the Latinizing reform and apparently adopted the Roman view of transubstantiation from Baranovych. Aleksei Mikhailovich took note of Polotsky in May 1656, during the Second Northern War, when he visited Polatsk and was greeted by Simeon with a panegyric. When Polotsky first visited Moscow in 1660, on the occasion of the Nikon affair, he brought sixteen pupils with him who recited verse at court. Subsequently, this admirer of Jan Kochanowski was active as a court poet in Moscow and introduced Ukrainian syllabic verse into Russian poetry, which he embellished with Roman classical forms and citations from Western poets. His poem "Orel rossiiskii" (The Russian Eagle), composed on New Year's Day 1667, marks the beginning of modern Russian literature.[26] This poem established a positive attitude toward a common Slavic antiquity: "Rejoice, Russia, Sarmatian tribe" ("Likui, Rossio, sarmatskoe plemia").

Polotsky also engaged in polemics against the Old Believers, especially Nikita Dobrynin (Pustosviat), and wrote the scholarly work *Zhezl pravleniia* (The Scepter of Government), which was not free of

---

25. See Karl Laux, *Die Musik in Rußland und in der Sowjetunion* (Berlin, 1958), pp. 21ff. and 25.

26. See A. S. Demin, *Russkaia literatura vtoroi poloviny XVII—nachala XVIII veka. Novye khudozhestvennye predstavleniia o mire, prirode, cheloveke* (Moscow, 1977), p. 6.

invective. The work was used by the Synod in 1666 in its arguments against Avvakum and was published in the following year. Twice Polotsky tried in vain, at the tsar's request, to change Avvakum's mind. At the Dormition Cathedral, Polotsky self-confidently announced that wisdom (Holy Sophia) had not yet found a resting place in Muscovy[27] and went on to condemn ignorance. Influenced by Jan Amos Komenský (Comenius), among others, he developed a veritable cult of education, promoted libraries and schools, and tried to persuade the Muscovites to show tolerance for books printed in Rome, Venice, and Paris.[28] In 1666 he opened a school at the Zaikonospasskii Monastery, for which a special building had been erected the year before. In its absolutist way, the government now took control of education for the first time, after numerous attempts to establish Greek-oriented schools had failed, and designated four young scribes from the Office of Secret Affairs (Prikaz tainykh del) as the first pupils to learn Latin (!) and grammar. In that course, which lasted only two years, Polotsky taught them much more, for his ideal was the dissemination of knowledge for the education of a "modern man" (*sovremennyi chelovek*), that is, one who loved both the tsar and Christ. This experiment was also short-lived, expiring with Polotsky's two-year course.

Polotsky's influence did not stop there. In 1678 he founded the court printshop, the sixth in Muscovy (there were already thirteen in Ukraine at the time). Polotsky's most lasting influence was exercised through one of the four pupils already mentioned, who later became a monk—Silvestr Medvedev, his worthy successor, who continued the campaign for Latin. Moreover, Polotsky, who evidently also taught various noble children, became the educator of the tsar's sons Aleksei and Fedor. He supervised the education of their sister Sofiia and even advised Nikita Zotov, the teacher of Peter I. In this way, after the early death of their older brother, both Tsar Fedor Alekseevich and the Regent Sofiia had their share of Ruthenian culture and Thomistic ideas. They learned Polish from Polotsky, and Fedor learned Latin as well; later they occasionally wore Western dress. Under Sofiia, an attempt was made to send young nobles to be educated in Poland, and Polish tutors were tolerated in Moscow.

The progress of intellectual "Europeanization" after 1676 is therefore attributable in no small measure to the influence of Simeon

27. See Kliuchevskii, *Kurs*, p. 310.

28. See A. S. Eleonskaia, *Russkaia publitsistika vtoroi poloviny XVII veka* (Moscow, 1978), pp. 137–85.

Polotsky. He also provided the decisive impulse for the founding of the first Muscovite academy on the model of the Kyiv Academy, an endeavor in which he was in agreement with his Ukrainian adversary Slavynetsky. It may be assumed that his ideas were the basis of the first draft of the "Privileges" of 1682, in which the ruler, as absolutist paterfamilias, was charged on the basis of natural law with caring for the general welfare. The academy, known as the Slavic-Greek-Latin School or the Helleno-Greek Academy, came into being only after his death (1680) under Sofiia's regency (in 1687) on the basis of the statute as revised by Medvedev. The founding of the academy occurred in the midst of the dispute between the Latin and Greek camps and the "first truly theological controversy within Russian Orthodoxy"[29] over the question of whether the transformation of the Eucharist (transubstantiation) occurred during the words of institution ("Take, eat") or, as in Byzantine practice, during the subsequent prayer (*epiclesis*). The Roman interpretation was represented in Ukraine not only by the aforementioned Sofonovych, but also, as early as the first decade of the seventeenth century, in the Euchologion of Hedeon Balaban (1604) and in the Vilnius edition of the Euchologion (1610).[30]

There are several reasons why the Ruthenian interpretation of transubstantiation and Roman ideas could persist so long in the Orthodox stronghold of Muscovy, championed by Polotsky and other "bread-worshippers" (*khlebopoklonniki*), as they were derisively called at the time, that is, those who knelt during the words of institution. At one time, knowledge of the Byzantine interpretation had been lost in Muscovy. Before Evfimii set him right, Patriarch Ioakim himself considered that transubstantiation was effected by the words of institution; the synods of 1675 and 1681 confirmed it, and the Old Believers, too, considered themselves to be following a traditional interpretation. At the time of Polotsky's influence, the church as a whole was weakened by the schism (*raskol*), from which it never recovered. An outward sign of this was the elimination of the second christening for Catholics by the synod of 1667. Polotsky enjoyed the greatest respect and supreme protection of Aleksei Mikhailovich. Moreover, he understood the need to offset his opinion on this question with the strict repudiation of what the Orthodox considered another Roman heresy, the "filioque," whereby the Holy Spirit

29. Konrad Onasch, *Grundzüge der russischen Kirchengeschichte* (Göttingen, 1967), p. 78ff.

30. See I. K. Smolitsch, *Russisches Mönchtum: Entstehung, Entwicklung und Wesen, 988–1917* (Würzburg, 1953), p. 346.

proceeds from God the Father "and from the Son." Polotsky's pupil Fedor Alekseevich also watched over him. Finally, though, his only protector was the Regent Sofiia. Ultimately, her insecure position made it impossible for her to sponsor Medvedev, who propagated Polotsky's views in his *Khleb zhivotnyi* (Bread of Life) and other works. If Sofiia had continued to support Medvedev, she would have incurred a charge of heresy. She had been educated by Karion Istomin, who was inclined toward the Greek party.

Since these disputes delayed the opening of the academy, Medvedev was allowed to revive the school in the Zaikonospasskii Monastery in 1682. Medvedev taught Latin, while the Greek party under Slavynetsky's pupil, Evfimii, opened its school in the printshop two years later. Evfimii and Patriarch Ioakim,[31] who was intellectually dependent on him, then prevented the employment of Kyivan teachers in the academy, contrary to Medvedev's wishes. The statute of the academy, in fact, expressly forbade this and left the selection of teachers up to the patriarch of Constantinople! Since Medvedev was allowed to prepare the final revision of the statute, instruction in Latin (as well as in Polish) was half-heartedly permitted and later even practiced as necessary by Padua-trained Greek teachers, the Leichudes brothers. The struggle against the Kyivan teachings intensified, however, until 1689, ending a year later with Medvedev's execution. Even the Leichudes were dismissed for their linguistic sins in 1694 at the instigation of the ecumenical patriarch and the patriarch of Jerusalem. The academy led a shadow existence until the beginning of the eighteenth century, when Stefan Iavorsky's reform made Latin the sole language of learning.

Stefan Iavorsky (whose secular name was Symeon) was not only rector of the Moscow Academy at this time, but also administrator of the patriarchal chair. Twenty years earlier, as a student at the Kyiv Academy (of which he later became prefect), he had been one of the Ukrainian theologians who wanted to place "Slavic-Russian" culture on a firmer administrative footing by supporting the subordination of the Kyivan metropolitan to the patriarch of Moscow.[32] This group included Archbishop Lazar Baranovych of Chernihiv, who had been

---

31. This is not to deny Ekkehard Kraft's point that Ioakim was not so uneducated as he was made out to be by his adversary, Medvedev. See E. Kraft, *Moskaus griechisches Jahrhundert: Russisch-griechische Beziehungen und metabyzantinischer Einfluß, 1619–1694* (Stuttgart, 1995), p. 156.

32. See S. A. Ternovskii, *Issledovanie o podchinenii Kievskoi metropolii Moskovskomu patriarkhatu* (Kiev, 1912).

appointed "provisional" metropolitan of Left-Bank Ukraine by Aleksei Mikhailovich in 1658, because the incumbent metropolitan, Dionisii Balaban, had defected to Poland as a supporter of Hetman Ivan Vyhovsky. It also included Hedeon Sviatopolk-Chetvertynsky, a candidate for the post of Kyivan metropolitan who had been supported in 1685 by the Left-Bank hetman Ivan Samoilovych, a relative.[33] Those who opposed relinquishing Kyiv's autonomy, which had been won in 1458 after the demise of Byzantium, were initially more numerous (among them were Balaban, Gizel, and Kosiv) than those who favored subordination to Moscow, as Mohyla had won great respect for the metropolitan's office through his activity. Moreover, the metropolitanate had been materially strengthened by the return of property appropriated by the Uniate Church, a development associated with the emergence of the Hetmanate.[34] Even earlier, however, indigenous tradition had carried such political weight that in 1589 consideration had even been given to establishing a patriarchate in Kyiv as a counterweight to the new patriarchate of Muscovy, or to moving the seat of the ecumenical patriarch to Kyiv.[35]

Now, however, the desires of those who supported annexation to Muscovy corresponded to the view of the Muscovite hierarchy that political unification with Left-Bank Ukraine should be followed by ecclesiastical union. If it is true that the initiative for the Pereiaslav Agreement of 1654 came from Nikon,[36] then there was a connection from the very beginning between the subordination of the Zaporozhian Cossacks to the "high hand" of the tsar and the installation of Prince Chetvertynsky by Muscovy, i.e., the transition of the metropolitanate from the jurisdiction of the ecumenical patriarch to that of the patriarch of Moscow in November 1685. In fact, Nikon had first

33. On Muscophile tendencies in the Ukrainian clergy, see V. O. Ėingorn, *O snosheniiakh malorossiiskogo dukhovenstva s moskovskim pravitel'stvom v tsarstvovanie Alekseia Mikhailovicha* (Moscow, 1894).

34. See Zenon E. Kohut, "The Problem of Ukrainian Orthodox Church Autonomy in the Hetmanate (1654–1780s)," *Harvard Ukrainian Studies* 14, nos. 3–4 (December 1990): 364–76.

35. To be sure, there also appears to have been a desire at the time to unite the "Lithuanian" and Muscovite churches. A remark made by Prince Ostrozky on 21 June 1593 can at least be interpreted in this way. See "Antiritsis ili Apologiia protiv Khristofora Filareta v dvukh tekstakh," *Russkaia istoricheskaia biblioteka* 19 (1903), p. 581.

36. See Hans-Joachim Torke, "The Unloved Alliance: Political Relations between Muscovy and Ukraine in the Seventeenth Century," in *Ukraine and Russia in Their Historical Encounter*, p. 45.

proposed this plan after the taking of Smolensk and Polatsk (1654–55).[37] The interval of thirty years between the two events can be explained, on the one hand, by the resistance of the Ukrainians concerning this matter, which had been discussed repeatedly since 1657,[38] and, on the other, by the generally cautious attitude of the tsar toward Ukraine as long as relations with Poland-Lithuania remained uncertain.

This changed after the armistice of Andrusovo (1667), when even Afanasii Ordin-Nashchokin, head of the Foreign Office and occasionally, therefore, of the Office for Little Russia, who had hitherto regarded the incorporation of Ukraine as detrimental to his policy toward Poland, supported a union of churches in 1669–70.[39] He hoped to strengthen Muscovy's weak administrative presence on the Left Bank through the appointment of voevodas and to deflect the Cossack charge that at Andrusovo he had surrendered the Right Bank too quickly. He even attempted (unsuccessfully) to make his idea palatable to the Poles by explaining that after the union of churches the Ukrainians would be less inclined to ally themselves with the sultan.[40] The "chancellor" clearly lost the tsar's confidence in the matter and failed in an attempt at administrative reform. He retired in early 1671. Muscovy's position in Ukraine did, however, become more secure with the signing of the "eternal peace" of Moscow in 1686 and the incorporation of the Kyiv metropolitanate half a year later. Chertvertynsky, elected by a synod in Kyiv whose canonical legitimacy was evidently in question, traveled to Moscow for the installation. He retained all his rights except the title "Exarch of the Patriarch of Constantinople," which is to say that Ukrainian Orthodoxy remained relatively autonomous. Admittedly, the title "Metropolitan of Kyiv, Halych and all Rus'" had to be changed to "Metropolitan of Kyiv, Halych and Little Russia." Finally, in May 1686, under pressure from the grand vizier, who hoped to prevent the Russians

37. See Robert Stupperich, "Der Anteil der Kirche beim Anschluß der Ukraine an Moskau (1654)," *Kirche im Osten* 14 (1971): 81.

38. See O. M. Shevchenko, "Pro pidporiadkuvaniia Kyïvs'koï mytropoliï Moskovs'komu patriarkhatu naprykintsi XVII st.," *Ukraïns'kyi istorychnyi zhurnal*, 1994, no. 1: 54–61.

39. See *Akty IuZR*, vol. 9, no. 2, I and II.

40. See V. O. Ėingorn, "Otstavka A. L. Ordina-Nashchokina i ego otnoshenie k malorossiiskomu voprosu," *Zhurnal Ministerstva narodnogo prosveshcheniia*, 1897, no. 11: 92–176, here 147–51.

from joining the Holy League by means of this favor, the patriarch of Constantinople consented to the transfer of authority.[41]

It is striking that the jurisdictional and administrative separation of the Kyiv metropolitanate from Muscovy for more than two centuries did not lead to religious alienation. This had as much to do with the political power of Muscovy as with the religious situation in Rus', where the Orthodox had to stand up to the Roman Catholics and the Uniates. That circumstance, however, also helped promote the Ruthenization of Muscovite culture. Even such thinkers as Simeon Polotsky, who accepted the Roman interpretation on *one* question, transubstantiation, never considered church union (with the Catholics), and even Iavorsky—and many others like him—went over to the Union only temporarily so as to be able to study in Poland. Moreover, Ukraine was Muscovy's source of anti-Roman polemical literature.

Now, of course, the official church no longer yielded even on the question of transubstantiation. Perhaps Medvedev's punishment was so severe because it was intended to serve as a warning to the bishops from the southwest who had recently come under the patriarch's jurisdiction. In 1690, Patriarch Ioakim exacted a declaration of subordination to Muscovite teaching from the Kyiv metropolitan and clergy and placed fifteen books on the Index, including works by Mohyla, Gizel, Baranovych, Polotsky, Tranquillon, and Kosiv. Yet the dispute over transubstantiation was an important event in Russian intellectual history, for after centuries of Orthodox dogmatism, individual clerics were now theoretically free to consider a question carefully and choose between two "truths." Medvedev therefore stands at the threshold of the modern age, i.e., of critical thinking, because for him religion was less a matter of dogma than of scientific inquiry.[42] The controversy over the Eucharist was a struggle for or against enlightenment, which for Medvedev came directly from God through prayer. The short-lived reaction of the 1690s was defeated under Peter the Great by the forces of autonomous reason and Western rationalism.

If Ukrainian scholars also exerted an influence in Peter's Russia, this was no longer anything extraordinary. It is more noteworthy

---

41. See the note in *Polnoe sobranie zakonov Rossiiskoi imperii* (St. Petersburg, 1830–1916), series 1, vol. 2: 792ff. See also Natala Carynnyk-Sinclair, *Die Unterstellung der Kiever Metropolie unter das Moskauer Patriarchat* (Munich, 1970), pp. 157ff.

42. Smolitsch, *Russisches Mönchtum*, p. 355ff.

that Ruthenian influence in the Russian church grew as a direct result of the subordination of the Kyivan metropolitanate to the patriarchate of Moscow. Individual bishops even broke away from Kyiv and subordinated themselves directly to the patriarch, as did Lazar Baranovych of Chernihiv in 1688. Peter deliberately brought the so-called "wanderers," who studied in Poland or Western Europe and then taught at the Kyiv Academy, to Moscow and St. Petersburg, because he needed them for his reform work. Besides Iavorsky, they included Teofan Prokopovych, Dymytrii Rostovsky (Danylo Tuptalo), and Feodosii Ianovsky, whose father had been a noble (*szlachcic*) in Smolensk. More than seventy Ukrainians and Belarusians, i.e., 55 percent, with 37 percent Russians, held high office in the Russian church between 1700 and 1762.[43] The significant role of Ukrainian clerics in Muscovite Orthodoxy and their strong influence on theology helps account for the fact that Ukrainians did not regard the church leadership as foreign and largely subordinated themselves to St. Petersburg in political terms as well. Despite their considerable numbers, however, Ukrainians and Belarusians no longer played a dominant role in Europeanization across the whole cultural spectrum, as they had in earlier times. First of all, as is well known, Peter's interest was directed from the beginning toward Protestant, northwestern Europe, and, second, after the settlement with Poland the direct route to the West opened up as the significance of confessional distinctions receded during the early Enlightenment. As noted earlier, there were already attempts during Sofiia's reign to send young nobles to Poland, and Polish tutors were active in Muscovy.

We can agree with Kliuchevsky that despite its brevity, Fedor Alekseevich's six-year reign was crucial to Russia's cultural development. Had Fedor, who was educated by Simeon Polotsky, reigned for ten years or more and produced a son, Western culture would have come to Russia from Rome, not from Amsterdam.[44] One might add that this would also have been the case had Sofiia been able to realize her plans.[45] Patriarch Ioakim, who was fundamentally opposed to rule by a woman, supported Peter during the transition of power and

43. See Kharlampovich, *Malorossiiskoe vliianie*, p. 459.

44. Diary entry of 23 April 1909 about a conversation with A. S. Lappo-Danilevskii, in V. O. Kliuchevskii, *Pis'ma—dnevniki—aforizmy i mysli ob istorii* (Moscow, 1968), p. 303.

45. See Lindsey Hughes, *Sophia, Regent of Russia, 1657–1704* (New Haven, Conn., 1990).

opposed Sofiia partly because he was aware of her inclination toward Latinity and her sympathy for Medvedev, as well as of the openness of her favorite, Vasilii Golitsyn, to the West (e.g., the Jesuits). (Golitsyn conversed with foreigners in Latin.) In 1689, Ioakim did not yet know in which direction Peter would develop. The fact that "baroque Europeanization" was not yet a fait accompli upon Peter's assumption of power is shown by the epilogue of the Aleksei affair, for the tsar's conflict with his son may be understood as a continuation of the dispute between the Latinists and Grecophile Ruthenians.[46]

Despite the different thrust of Petrine Europeanization, for which there had been precursors in the seventeenth century, the importance of cultural Ruthenization before Peter should not be underestimated. It brought Polish humanism into a country that had printed only seven books of purely secular content in the course of the whole seventeenth century,[47] although many others circulated in manuscript form. Along with the originally editorial and later increasingly pedagogical activity of the Ruthenian churchmen came the introduction of the baroque into Russian literature, painting, architecture, and music. This drew Russia for the first time into a pan-European cultural movement, a development banned by the Orthodox Church since the Renaissance, with the exception of certain influences ca. 1500.[48] Now an emotional prose style and the Kyivan verses (*virshi*) could no more be suppressed than the Kyivan style of singing, allegorical icon painting, and realist portraiture (usually the work of Polish painters), or three-dimensional figures of saints and the "Cossack baroque" in architecture (e.g., in the Znamenskaia Church, built by a Ukrainian architect in the village of Dubrovitsy near Moscow). One may justifiably assert that the Ruthenians brought the modern age to Russia.

On several occasions in the seventeenth century (1648–49, 1656–58, 1667–69 and 1674), the tsars entertained the illusory prospect of donning the Polish king's crown (as Ivan IV had once done for his son Fedor). Whether the Polish diplomats were serious about the Muscovite offers or merely making skillful chess moves is impossible to say. Even though the boyar negotiators impressed upon the Poles that

46. This opinion was expressed by Paul Bushkovitch in an unpublished essay.

47. See S. P. Luppov, *Kniga v Rossii v XVII veke* (Leningrad, 1970), p. 29.

48. See Günther Stökl, "Das Echo von Renaissance und Reformation im Moskauer Rußland," *Jahrbücher für Geschichte Osteuropas*, n.s., 7 (1959): 413–30.

their tsar, Aleksei Mikhailovich, was "at the height of all proprieties in Europe" (*vsiakimi godnost'mi vo Evrope tsvetushchii*), the Poles were well aware in 1656 that "Ducem Moschoviae hic et nunc impossibile ad fidem catholicam inducere."[49] One final speculation: the chances of a personal union were better for the tsar's sons, who had been educated by Simeon Polotsky, and, thanks to Ruthenian mediation, the prematurely deceased Aleksei Alekseevich or his brother Fedor would also have been intellectually and culturally equipped for the prospect "ut in perpetuum respublica Polona cum Domino Moschorum sit una respublica in aevum."[50] Only at the beginning of the nineteenth century, however, did Alexander I assume this task under entirely different circumstances: Muscovite and Ukrainian culture had long since merged into a joint "Russian-Western" culture.

49. From a letter dated 25 September 1656 (N.S.), written by a Polish negotiator from Niemiża near Vilnius to the Grand Duke of Lithuania (Augustin Theiner, *Monuments historiques relatifs aux règnes d'Alexis Michaélo-witch, Féodor III et Pierre le Grand, czars de Russie, extraits des Archives du Vatican et de Naples* [Rome, 1859], p. 10). For the Russian citation, see "Diplomaticheskoe prilozhenie" in *Trudy i letopisi Obschestva istorii i drevnostei rossiiskikh, uchrezhdennogo pri Imperatorskom Moskovskom universitete*, pt. 6 (1833), p. 274.

50. Theiner, *Monuments historiques*, p. 10.

Frank E. Sysyn

The Image of Russia and Russian-Ukrainian Relations in Ukrainian Historiography of the Late Seventeenth and Early Eighteenth Centuries*

From the mid-seventeenth century, contacts between Ukrainians and Russians markedly intensified. Ukrainians of all social groups came into daily contact with Russian troops and officials stationed in Ukraine. Ukrainian Cossack units served together with Russian units from the Baltic to the Black Sea. Delegations of Cossack officers, burghers, and clergymen traveled to the imperial capitals. Ukrainian clergymen filled the monasteries and ecclesiastical posts of the huge empire. The territories along the present-day Russian-Ukrainian border were settled by a Ukrainian population moving east and a Russian population moving south.

Except for tracing the role of the Ukrainian clergy in Russia, little has been done to examine the significance of this intensified Ukrainian-Russian contact.[1] Even the study of how the two peoples viewed

---

* I thank the Alexander von Humboldt Stiftung for its support of my research for this article and my project on Ukrainian historiography and political culture. In this article, I have used the Library of Congress system of transliteration employed in the rest of this volume, except for the transliteration of pre-nineteenth-century titles and words or passages from the chronicles, which are best rendered in International Scholarly Transliteration adapted for Middle Ukrainian and the Ukrainian redaction of Slavonic. I have not attempted to correct the orthography of the later publications, which is frequently modernized, and have generally adhered to a system whereby every Cyrillic letter is given a uniform transliteration, regardless of historical changes in pronunciation.

1. See the studies of K. V. Kharlampovich (Kharlampovych), *Malorossiiskoe vliianie na velikorusskuiu tserkovnuiu zhizn'*, vol. 1 (Kazan, 1914, repr. The Hague and Paris, 1968); Hans Rothe, "Zur Kiever Literatur in Moskau I," *Studien zu Literatur und Kultur in Osteuropa: Bonner Beiträge zum 9. Internationalen Slavistenkongress in Kiew* (Cologne and Vienna, 1983), pp. 232–60; Hans Rothe, "Zur Kiever Literatur in Moskau II," *Slavistische Studien zum IX Internationalen Slavistenkongress in Kiew* (Cologne and Vienna, 1983), pp. 417–34; and V. O. Ėingorn, *O snosheniiakh malorossiiskogo dukhovenstva s moskovskim pravitel'stvom v tsarstvovanie Alekseia Mikhailovicha* (Moscow, 1894).

each other has not gone beyond the anecdotal stage. Obviously, early modern Ukrainians penetrated Russian life as no other outsiders did. They managed to do so because their Orthodox faith, Slavonic culture, and East Slavic vernacular also made them insiders. Consequently, Ukrainian accounts should be a rich source for understanding Muscovy-Russia as it entered the phase of rapid Europeanization. Ukrainians were catalysts for this change, and their integration into Muscovite society served to transform Muscovy into imperial Russia.[2] At the same time, the Muscovite political and religious system profoundly influenced Ukraine. With the Petrine reforms of the early eighteenth century, the imperial capitals came to play a major role in shaping Ukrainian culture and intellectual life.

One of the source bases useful for understanding how Ukrainians perceived Russians and their relations with them is the series of Ukrainian historical works written between the 1670s and the 1720s.[3] They are a complex source, as they frequently contain composites of texts from different periods, and earlier works were often used as sources for passages in later works, diminishing the consistency and chronological coherence of the texts. In addition, they were written in a variety of styles ranging from Slavonic to almost vernacular

---

Political relations are well summarized in Hans-Joachim Torke, "The Unloved Alliance: Political Relations between Muscovy and Ukraine in the Seventeenth Century," in *Ukraine and Russia in Their Historical Encounter*, ed. Peter J. Potichnyj et al. (Edmonton, 1992), pp. 39–66.

2. See Hans Torke, "Moskau und sein Westen. Zur 'Ruthenisierung' der russischen Kultur," *Berliner Jahrbuch für osteuropäische Geschichte*, 1996, no. 1: 101–20 (translated in the present volume). For a new interpretation suggesting that Muscovites were more resistant to Western influences transmitted through Ukraine than has hitherto been supposed, see Max J. Okenfuss, *The Rise and Fall of Latin Humanism in Early-Modern Russia: Pagan Authors, Ukrainians, and the Resiliency of Muscovy* (Leiden, 1995).

3. I have excluded the chronograph of 1699 by Leontii Bobylynsky, as well as the *Khronograf* (1681) and *Obšyrnyi synopsis* (1681–82) of Petro Kokhanovsky, which have not been published and were largely compilations. The Hustynia Chronicle is usually dated to the 1620s, and I have dealt with it, as well as Sofonovych's *Krojnika* and the *Synopsis*, in "Concepts of Nationhood in Ukrainian History Writing, 1620–1690," *Harvard Ukrainian Studies* 10, nos. 3–4 (December, 1986): 393–423; and in "The Cultural, Social and Political Context of Ukrainian History-Writing, 1620–1690," *Europa Orientalis* 5 (1986): 285–310. When writing those articles, I had access only to fragments of Sofonovych's work (which was not published until 1992) and some of Iurii Mytsyk's studies. The copying of the Hustynia Chronicle in the 1670s inspired the patriotic preface by Mykhailo Losytsky, which should be placed in the context of the writings discussed in this article.

Ukrainian, with the choice of language influencing the mode of expression and terminology of the works.

The accounts examined here were not histories of Russia and Russians, if one does not view the recounting of the Kyivan Rus' past in the *Synopsis* and Feodosii (Teodosii) Sofonovych's *Krojnika* as Russian history per se. Indeed, until the publication of Vasilii Tatishchev's history, Ukrainian readers would primarily have had to turn to Polish narratives, above all Maciej Stryjkowski's work, or to Western and Central European accounts such as that of Sigmund von Herberstein in order to find out about the history and character of Muscovy. Sofonovych's *Krojnika*, the *Synopsis*, the Eyewitness Chronicle, Hryhorii Hrabianka's *Dîjstvija* (Events), and Samiilo Velychko's *Skazanie* (Tale) recounted actions taken by Russians and the Muscovite state without providing a coherent discussion of them. The first two works are the culmination of Ukrainian monastic history writing, while the latter three represent the formation of a new historiography written by the secular elite of the Cossack Hetmanate.

Two difficulties complicate the study of views of Russia and Russians. First, there is a certain tendency to assume that modern concepts—be they the state, the nation, or the terms "Russia" or "Russians"—were meaningful to the early modern Ukrainian chronicler or historian. Shifts in meaning also make it difficult to interpret texts: when, for example, does *hosudarstvo/gosudarstvo* take on the meaning of "state"? The second issue is the relation of Russians and Russia to the definition of Ukrainian self-awareness, above all the evolution of terms, especially *Rossija* (Rossia), *Malaja Rossija* or *Malorossija* (Little Rossia), and *Malorossijane* (Little Rossians)[4] and the development of national identity and political culture in Ukraine. This pertains especially to relations between the hetman and the Cossack Host on the one hand and the tsar and the Russian state on the other.

---

4. Terms derived from *Rosija* or *Rossija* in early modern Ukraine had many meanings for various East Slavic polities and societies. Considerable attention is devoted to these meanings in the present article. "Rossia" has been used in preference to "Russia," which would lead most readers to think in terms of the modern Russian people or the Russian state. On the evolution of these terms, see N. Maksimovich [Mykola Maksymovych], "Ob upotreblenii nazvanii Rossiia i Malorossiia v Zapadnoi Rusi," in his *Sobranie sochinenii*, vol. 2 (Kyiv, 1877), pp. 307–11; Serhii Sheliukhyn, *Ukraïna—nazva nashoï zemli z naidavniishykh chasiv* (Prague, 1936); and Hans Rothe, "What Is the Meaning of 'Rossijski' and 'Rossija' in the Polish and Russian Conception of the State in the 17th Century?" *Ricerche slavistiche* 37 (1990): 111–21. Petro Tolochko, "Rus'—Mala Rus'—rus'kyi narod u druhii polovyni XIII-XVII st.," *Kyïvs'ka starovyna*, 1993, no. 3: 3–14, adds little to the discussion.

Certainly the chronicles are a more important source for the development of Ukrainian self-awareness than for Ukrainian views of Muscovy/Russia and Ukrainian-Russian relations, but they also offer material on the latter subject.

Two Traditions of Monastic Historiography: Ukrainian and Russian History

Just as the church and clergy led the cultural revival in late sixteenth- and early seventeenth-century Ukraine, so the monasteries became centers for collecting sources and writing historical accounts. Interest in the past developed partly under the influence of Polish Renaissance historiography, but more directly as a result of debates over the Union of Brest and the nature of Volodymyr's conversion. Centered in Kyiv, which took on a leading cultural role in the Ukrainian and Belarusian territories from the second decade of the seventeenth century, monastic history writing concentrated on the period of the conversion and Kyivan Rus'. The revival of historical consciousness that began in the late sixteenth century reached its culmination in the monastic historiography of the 1670s, two decades after the Pereiaslav Agreement recognized the suzerainty of the Russian tsar, involving Russia and Russians more directly in Ukrainian affairs.

This rewriting of the history of Kyivan Rus' eventually stimulated Russian historical consciousness through the copying of texts in Russia in the late seventeenth and early eighteenth centuries, and particularly through the publication of the *Synopsis*. The Kyivan legacy resurrected in early seventeenth-century Ukraine could always be adapted to serve the purposes of rulers and polities claiming descent from the world of Volodymyr/Vladimir/Volodimer. In the same way, concepts of Slavic and Rus' origins worked out by Polish and Ukrainian historians could be applied to the Muscovite ruler and state. Terms and concepts such as "monarch" (*monarxa*), "fatherland" (*otčyzna*), "state" (*panstvo*, later *hosudarstvo* and *deržava*), "nation" or "people" (*narod*) and "Rossia," "Great Rossia," and "Little Rossia" that had been elaborated in Ukraine during the seventeenth century could easily be transferred to the north. Indeed, it has been posited that it was the Ukrainian side that first inserted the appellations "Great Rossia" and "Little Rossia" into the tsar's title in the negotiations of the 1650s.[5]

---

5. Mykhailo Hrushevs'kyi, "Velyka, Mala i Bila Rus'," *Ukraïna*, 1917, nos. 1–2: 7–19. See also A. Solov'ev, "Velikaia, Malaia i Belaia Rus'," *Voprosy istorii*, 1947, no. 7: 24–38.

Frequently, the Ukrainian monastic tradition has been seen as the direct predecessor of the *Synopsis* and the postulation of some sort of East Slavic unity. The search for the roots of "all-Russian," "Little Russian," and "Great Russian" concepts has tended to oversimplify the complex Ukrainian monastic and clerical legacy of the seventeenth century. In addition, emphasis on clerics such as Teofan Prokopovych who formulated political thought in Russia has overshadowed other trends among the Ukrainian clergy, including those that influenced Russia. In the general literature, the complexity and diversity of views presented in the *Synopsis* have often been simplified. An examination of the two major works of the 1670s and 1680s, Feodosii Sofonovych's *Krojnika* and the *Synopsis*, usually attributed to Inokentii Gizel, reveals the variety of Ukrainian monastic history writing in its depiction of Russia.

Sofonovych's *Krojnika* of 1672–73, presumably the earlier of these works, remained almost entirely in manuscript form (barring the destroyed edition of 1917) until it was published in 1992.[6] Through its manuscript copies, however, it influenced subsequent history writing in Ukraine and Russia. The three parts of the *Krojnika* deal with Rus' in the "*Krojnika* about Rus'," Lithuania in the "*Krojnika* and Name of Lithuania," and Poland in the "Annals or *Krojnika* about the Polish Land."[7] Written in middle Ukrainian, the *Krojnika* forms an account of the history of the Ukrainian lands from the origin of the Slavs to the late seventeenth century. It is prefaced with a statement to the effect that the archimandrite of St. Michael's Monastery in Kyiv wished to ensure that the sons of Rus' would know the origins of the Rus' state or domain (*panstvo Ruskoe*) and its history down to the present, since it is necessary to know about one's fatherland (*o svoe otčyznî*). Sofonovych then explains the origins of the Rus' nation/people (*Ruskyj narod*). Applying the term "fatherland" to Rus'—for all practical purposes, Ukraine—the *Krojnika* represents the culmination of the rebirth of historical consciousness that took place in late sixteenth-century Ukraine and Belarus. It examines the accounts of Polish historians and early Rus' chronicles, relating them to contemporary Ukraine, which had emerged as a nascent polity after

6. Almost two decades after having written a candidate thesis on the Sofonovych chronicle, Iurii Mytsyk was able to publish the text with an extensive introduction: Feodosii Sofonovych, *Khronika z litopystsiv starodavnikh* (Kyiv, 1992).

7. I employ Mytsyk's shortened titles, which are based on headings in the manuscript copies.

the Khmelnytsky Uprising. The Hustynia Chronicle, written in Slavonic and extant in a copy of the 1670s (though usually dated to the 1620s), constitutes the other major historical account, though it ends with the Union of Brest (1596). While the Hustynia Chronicle is significant for developing the chronicle form into a narrative account of historical events and for its discussion of the origins of the Cossacks and their role in Ukrainian history, Sofonovych's *Krojnika* stands out for its presentation of a continuous history of the Ukrainian lands within the parameters of traditional dynastic and political historiography. Sofonovych's account of the history of Lithuania and Lithuanian rulers, which precedes his narrative of events in the Ukrainian lands and is followed by a similar treatment of Polish rulers, provides a framework for his account of Ukrainian history.[8]

Like all works that revived interest in Kyivan Rus', the *Krojnika* deals with a period in which the northern and southern lands of the Eastern Slavs were closely related, and the polity or territory called the Rus' lands, Rus', or Rossia encompassed Suzdal and Novgorod as well as Kyiv and Halych. In the "*Krojnika* about Rus'," which is based on a chronicle of the Hypatian tradition as well as accounts by Polish historians, Sofonovych prefers the traditional designation "Rus'" or "Rus' lands" to "Rossia" (*Rosija* in his usual spelling, more seldom *Rossija*), and in citing the titles of rulers (usually termed *samoderžec'* and, in one instance, *monarxa*),[9] uses *Rusija* as well as *Rosija*.[10] Sofonovych uses *Rossija* in discussing the origins of Rus', deriving the name of the land from the wide dispersion of its peoples.[11] He frequently points out that the Rus' also lived in the north and even employs the phrase "Rus' lying in the south" in order to distinguish those territories from the northern ones. He also describes Danylo of Galicia-Volhynia as king of all Rus' lying in the south.[12] But in

8. Mytsyk points out that similar divisions exist in the second Ukrainian redaction of the Rus' Chronograph, but that the unpublished chronograph differs from the *Krojnika* in not being primarily devoted to East Slavic or Ukrainian history (p. 29).

9. This word is used with reference to Oleh, whom Sofonovych terms "monarch of Kyiv and all Rus'" (p. 60).

10. Sofonovych uses various forms of the word "Rus'" to denote the territory, people, and language. On two occasions he employs "Rus' state" or "domain" (*panstvo Ruskoe*). In the ruler's title he uses both *Rosija* and *Rusija*.

11. "Ot šyrokoho yx" po svîtu rozsyjanyja" (p. 56).

12. He uses the phrase "nad Rusyju, na poludne ležačeju" in discussing Askold and Dyr (p. 59) and again, together with "all Rus'," in describing

several instances, dealing with periods as late as the twelfth century, he refers to north-south travel as "going to Rus'" (p. 114). He links the Kyivan period with later Muscovite history when he mentions that Volodymyr built a city beyond Moscow named Vladimir ("Volodymer"). It became the capital of the Muscovite princes until the time of "Ivan the Great, Prince Danilovich," who made Moscow the capital of the Rus' grand princes (p. 64). In this passage, as elsewhere (p. 114), he anachronistically interjects Moscow into the early history of Kyivan Rus'. Nevertheless, while events in Russian territories are mentioned in the Rus' section of the *Krojnika*, it is the Ukrainian land, especially the Galician-Volhynian principality, that receives most attention.

The reader of the Lithuanian and Polish sections of the *Krojnika* would find it difficult to place Muscovy and Russian history into the context of the "*Krojnika* about Rus'." Only one note links Muscovite rulers with those of Kyiv. Ivan Vasilievich is described as "the most fortunate monarch after Volodymyr Monomakh" for having thrown off Tatar overlordship and subjugated the Tatars (p. 185). Most significantly, Sofonovych did not write a fourth component, a "*Krojnika* about the Grand Princes of Moscow," etc., which would have served to present Muscovite rulers like the Lithuanian and Polish ones, thereby introducing a Muscovite period into Ukrainian history. Presumably, the Muscovite link was too new and the political situation too uncertain for Sofonovych to undertake such an innovative project. One also wonders how many sources were available to him in Kyiv in the 1670s for such an undertaking.

There is considerable material about Muscovy, its rulers and inhabitants in the *Krojnika*. In particular, the *Krojnika* recounts wars between the Lithuanian and Polish rulers and the country to which it refers as Muscovy (*Moskva*) and its ruler, the Muscovite grand prince (*Moskovskyj Velykyj Knjaz'*), never employing "Rossia" (*Rosija*) even in the titles of grand princes and tsars. The seventeenth-century use of *Moskva* for both place and people is equivalent to the use of *Rus'* for Ukraine and Belarus and their inhabitants. Its development in Polish and Ukrainian writings should be examined more closely. In the Lithuanian section of the *Krojnika*, *Moskva* is not, strictly speaking, the only Russian polity mentioned, since attention is also paid to Tver and to Novgorod. Tver is described as a principality having a Rus' army,[13] and Moscow's conquest of Novgorod is noted (1479, p. 185).

Danylo as king (p. 153). This may be the first use of "south" to modify "Rus'," prefiguring nineteenth-century nomenclature for Ukraine.

13. "Voysko ruskoe," 1432 (p. 183).

There is little about customs and culture, except for the assertion that the Caspian Sea is called "Xvalynskoe, in Muscovite" (p. 185) and that "Ivan Vasilievich was terrifying to all the people and banned drunkenness in Muscovy" (p. 185).

It is in the Polish section that Muscovy enters the work more directly. Under the year 1558, the title of the ruler becomes "Muscovite tsar" (*C[a]r moskovskyy*, p. 218). Indeed, the account of the wars between Ivan IV and Poland and Lithuania entails more discussion of Muscovy, including the statement that "a certain Muscovite" (*nîjakyi moskal"*) reported that the "Muscovite lords" (*panove moskovskyji*) wished to give the "Tsardom of Muscovy" (*C[a]rstvo Moskovskoe*) to King Zygmunt August (p. 219).[14] On encountering these ambiguous terms, one senses an attempt to speak of Muscovy in ways then current in the Polish-Lithuanian state, with *Rusyn* (Ruthenian), *panove lytovskyji čy polskiji* (Lithuanian or Polish lords), and *Korona Polska* (the Polish Crown or Kingdom) serving as linguistic and conceptual models. The amount of information and frequency of terms pertaining to Muscovy increase considerably in the account of the Time of Troubles. It is in this context that Moscow is called the ruling city (*carstvujuščy horod*, p. 225).

Following the account of the Khmelnytsky Uprising, Russians figure more frequently in the *Krojnika*. Such references become particularly frequent after the assertion that in the presence of the boyar Vasilii Vasilievich Buturlin, "Bohdan Khmelnytsky with all Ukraine on both sides of the Dnipro, subjecting himself to the Orthodox tsar and grand prince Aleksei Mikhailovich, took an oath with all his officers at the church in Pereiaslav" (p. 231). This laconic passage mentions that the Cossacks and burghers also took the oath, but makes no comment on the reasons for it or the public reaction to it. In general, the tsar is thereafter referred to primarily as Orthodox, only once as Muscovite, and never as Rossian.[15] This relatively casual formulation of the tsar's title is in marked contrast to its treatment in the Eyewitness Chronicle, which parallels Sofonovych's work in the presentation of events and may have drawn on the same source for its

---

14. For a discussion of the use of *car* and *carstvo* in the Russian context, see Gianfranco Giraudo, "Car, Carstvo et termes correlants dans les textes russes de la deuxième moitié du XVI siècle," *Popoli e spazio romano tra diritto e profezia* (Naples, 1986), pp. 1566–67.

15. On the evolution of the tsar's title, see Marc Szeftel, "The Title of the Muscovite Monarch up to the End of the Seventeenth Century," *Canadian-American Slavic Studies* 13, nos. 1–2 (Spring–Summer 1979): 59–81.

account of those years.[16] We also find no mention of "Great Rossia" or "Great Rus'" either as a territorial designation or as part of the tsar's title anywhere in the work. Correspondingly, "Little Rossia" does not occur in the text.[17] From Khmelnytsky's time on, the Russian figures mentioned most frequently are military commanders and troops. The troops are variously called the "Muscovite army" (*Vojsko moskovskoe*), the "tsar's army" (*Carske vojsko*), "Muscovites" or "Muscovy" (*Moskva*), and the "tsar's people" (*Carski Ljudy*).

The constant references to joint campaigns of the "Muscovite troops" (*Moskovskiji vojska*) and the "Cossack troops" (*kazac'kiji vojska*) bear witness to the development of ever closer relations. Indeed, the account of the miracles of St. Barbara written by Sofonovych and published in Mytsyk's volume reveals a number of incidents of Russian officials' and troops' interaction with the Ukrainian population. Yet in Sofonovych's *Krojnika*, there is little discussion of the Russians and their world. The most interesting remark on the subject is that in 1665 Aleksei Mikhailovich made Hetman Ivan Briukhovetsky a boyar, with the explanation that this means a senator. Obviously, Sofonovych knew that these terms were not exact equivalents, but it is significant that he thought he should add an explanation (p. 239).

Using silence as evidence is always risky, but it is useful to consider what is not discussed in the *Krojnika* and what terms do not appear. The evolution of the Muscovite grand prince into an Orthodox tsar in Sofonovych's text illustrates the importance of religion in justifying the tsar's status in Ukraine. It is significant, however, that there is no mention of the proclamation of the Moscow patriarchate or of the seventeenth-century Russian church and clergy. We also search in vain for any mention of what might be termed the tsar's hereditary rights to the Ukrainian territories. The tsar's right to rule Ukraine is based entirely on Khmelnytsky's submission.

The publication of the *Synopsis*, traditionally attributed to Inokentii Gizel (Giesel), is seen as a major development in the process of cultural transfer from Ukraine to Russia, as well as in the formation of a Russian ideology and identity incorporating Ukraine.[18] It also

---

16. Mytsyk postulates that an Uman Chronicle was used for both later works.

17. A late seventeenth-century copy of Sofonovych's section on Poland containing entries up to 1690 describes Ivan Samoilovych as the Little Rossian hetman in an entry for 1679 (p. 259).

18. A facsimile of the edition of 1681, together with some pages of the 1674 edition, was published by Hans Rothe, *Sinopsis, Kiev 1681. Facsimile mit einer*

represents a very different view of the Ukrainian and Russian past than Sofonovych's work. Written in Slavonic, the *Synopsis* was published in Kyiv in 1674, though there is speculation that it appeared earlier. Greatly enlarged in its third edition of 1680–81, the *Synopsis* became the major source for the history of the Russian state; Peter I ordered its translation into Greek and Latin. Unlike Sofonovych, who had declared it his goal to teach the sons of the Ukrainian fatherland their history, the author of the *Synopsis, or short compilation from various chronicles about the origins of the Slavic-Rossian nation* [o načalî Slavjano-Rossijskaho naroda] *and the first princes of the divinely preserved city of Kyiv and the life of the holy, pious grand prince of Kyiv and all Rossia* [Vseja Rossiy], *the first autocrat* [Samoderžavca], *Volodymyr, and about the inheritors of his virtuous Rossian domain* [Bl(a)hočestyvvyja deržavy eho Rossijskija], *even unto our illustrious and pious sovereign, tsar, and grand prince Aleksei Mikhailovich, autocrat of all Great, Little, and White Rossia* [Rossiy] manifestly caters to the need of the Russian ruler to demonstrate his claim to Ukraine, while emphasizing the importance of Kyiv and its monasteries and churches. The *Synopsis* did more, however, than argue for the dynastic rights of the Muscovite tsar. It also provided a historical basis for seeing the Ukrainians and Russians as part of a "Slaveno-Rossian nation/people" of Kyivan times and reinforcing that conceptualization for its time. In its preference for *Rossija* instead of *Rus'* for both the Kyivan Rus' period and later times, the *Synopsis* firmly established a new nomenclature for the Russian state, the East Slavic peoples, and the Russians, though not all of its usages proved lasting.[19] The Hellenistic *Rossija* had come into use in

---

Einleitung (= Bausteine zur Geschichte der Literatur bei den Slaven, 17) (Cologne and Vienna, 1983). The volume contains an extensive discussion of the pertinent literature, text, cultural context, and political thought of the work by Rothe, who accepts the probable authorship of Inokentii Gizel (Giesel), a German convert to Orthodoxy. Iurii Mytsyk argues for the authorship of Petro Kokhanovsky in his introduction to Sofonovych, *Khronika* (p. 36). Comparing the two works as representing different strains of thought in Kyivan church circles should be a corrective to the tendency to treat the *Synopsis* as solely representative of Kyivan clerical views. Indeed, those who accept Gizel as the author should at least consider how much his thinking was still that of an outsider. His German and Western Christian origins should also be taken into account in discussions of the use of the concept of nation in the *Synopsis*.

19. For a discussion of these terms in the *Synopsis*, see Gianfranco Giraudo, "Passé et présent 'Russes' dans l'oeuvre d'Innokentij Gizel'," *Ricerche slavistiche* 37 (1990): 333–51; Russian version: "'Russkoe' nastoiashchee i proshedshee v tvorchestve Innokentiia Gizelia," *Mediaevalia Ucrainica: Mental'nist' ta istoriia idei* (Kyiv) 1 (1992): 92–103.

Russia in the sixteenth century, presumably under the influence of Constantinople, though it may have had a Western origin and certainly was used by late sixteenth-century Polish historians.[20] In Ukraine, it made a rapid career in ecclesiastical circles from the second decade of the seventeenth century and was used with reference to Kyivan Rus', the Eastern Slavs, and the Ukrainian and Belarusians and their institutions. Indeed, used in adjectival forms with *narod* (nation, people) and in nominative forms (*Rossijane, Rossove, Rosŷ*) as the equivalent of *Rus', Rusyny* (Ruthenians), it came to define what was usually called the Ruthenian nation in the Polish-Lithuanian Commonwealth.[21] It was this usage, with some new nominal forms and etymological explanations, that the *Synopsis* brought to Russia and utilized in describing an East Slavic people and its past.[22] Thus the author described two metropolitan sees as emerging in "Rossia" in the fifteenth century, and while his description of how the "whole Orthodox Rossian nation" (*Ves' Pravoslavno Rossijskii Narod*) greeted the return of Kyiv to tsarist rule may have been intended primarily for Ukrainian readers, the term was certainly ambivalent and could serve as a model for conceptualizing Ukrainians and Russians as one East Slavic people.

The *Synopsis* was, however, by no means a comprehensive history of the Eastern Slavs. It was rather a study of their origins and the Kyivan Rus' realm. In the first edition of 1674, the history of Kyivan Rus' is followed by a list of rulers of the Kyivan Principality, which the *Synopsis* describes as having been transformed into a palatinate, down to the "return" of the city of Kyiv during the rule of Aleksei Mikhailovich.[23] How the return occurred is unclear, since there is no

20. For a discussion of the evolution of the term "Rossija," see Rothe, "What Is the Meaning of 'Rossijski' and 'Rossija'?"

21. See Rothe, "What is the Meaning of 'Rossijski' and 'Rossija,'" pp. 117–18. Various forms of *Rossija* are used to refer to Kyivan Rus' and seventeenth-century Ukrainians in Losytsky's preface to the Hustynia Chronicle, *Polnoe sobranie russkikh letopisei*, vol. 2 (St. Petersburg, 1908), p. 233 (English translation in Sysyn, "Concepts of Nationhood," p. 419). Losytsky's introduction is interesting for its use of both "fatherland" (*otčyzna*) and "Rus'/Rossian nation" (*narodovy Rossijskomu*, oblique case, henceforth obl. c.). The title contains the phrase "Slaveno-Rossian nation" (*Slavenskoho Rossijskoho narodu*, obl. c.).

22. See Giraudo, "'Russkoe,'" p. 98, n. 37.

23. See Rothe, *Sinopsis*, pp. 360–61. Both the palatinate and the city are mentioned on p. 360, but only the city is mentioned in the section on the "return" (p. 361). For a discussion of the *Synopsis* and the Pereiaslav

mention of the Cossack revolt against the Polish-Lithuanian Commonwealth or of Bohdan Khmelnytsky. In the 1681 edition, the author interpolated a long account of an episode from Russian history—that of Dmitrii Ivanovich's struggle against Mamai in the fourteenth century. This episode paralleled the contemporary description of the East Slavic and Orthodox struggle against the Muslim foe, i.e., the Chyhyryn campaign against the Ottomans, which was added to the second edition of 1678 and expanded in the edition of 1681. While the first edition contained an account of the establishment of the separate metropolitan sees of Moscow and Kyiv in the fifteenth century, the later edition included a section on the creation of the Moscow patriarchate in the sixteenth century.

The nomenclature of the *Synopsis* largely reflects the chapter entitled "About the Rus' or, more properly, Rossian nation" (*O narodî ruskom yly svojstvenîe rossijskom"*), but the author does not hold consistently to this conception and preferred terminology. Terms derived from *Rus'* still occur, especially in the interpolated text on the campaign against Mamai in the later edition. The usual seventeenth-century distinction between Russians and Ukrainians emerges in the description of Sarmatia as inhabited by Muscovites (*Moskva*), Ruthenians (*Rus'*), Poles (*Poljaky*), Lithuanians (*Lytva*), Prussians (*Prusy*), and others. The need to distinguish Russians from Ukrainians also emerges in the account of the Chyhyryn campaign, in which the forces of the Cossack Hetmanate are usually referred to as "Zaporozhian" and occasionally as "Little Rossian," while the Russian forces are called the "armed forces of his tsarist majesty," as well as "Muscovite" and "Great Rossian." Frequently, however, the combined troops are termed Orthodox or Christian, reflecting a major ideological premise of the work and echoing the account of the campaign against Mamai. "Great Rossian" is also used to refer to the metropolitan of Moscow and the church council called to elevate him to the status of patriarch. The same adjective is employed to denote the Russian state, otherwise called "Muscovite" in the text. Except for the tsar's title, "Great Rossia" and "Little Rossia" are not used (in one case, Fedor Alekseevich has only "Great Rossia" added to his title, in an apparent omission of "Little Rossia" and "White Rossia," p. 354). This may have been due in part to the text's concentration on the Kyivan Rus' period, but it may also have reflected the author's desire not to stress distinctions, as well as his emphasis on the tsar and the unity of the

---

Agreement, see John Basarab, *Pereiaslav 1654: A Historiographical Study* (Edmonton, 1982), pp. 60–62.

Rossian people rather than on the two separate polities that existed in the 1670s.

The *Krojnika* and the *Synopsis* marked the high point of monastic history writing in Ukraine. Sofonovych, who addressed his text to a Ukrainian audience, continued the seventeenth-century historiographic tradition of recounting the history of Kyivan Rus' and recording contemporary Ukrainian affairs. His account of the Khmelnytsky revolt and its consequences constituted a transition to the new period in Ukrainian historiography. Sofonovych also reproduced earlier attitudes toward Muscovy and used established terminology pertaining to Russians, while at the same time responding to the new situation created by the Pereiaslav Agreement. Through copies of his text that reached other Ukrainian and Russian chroniclers, certain parts of Sofonovych's work influenced Russian historiography, but his impact cannot compare with that of the *Synopsis*. His successors were the Cossack chroniclers, who dealt more thoroughly with the new relationship between Ukraine and Russia and developed the concepts of Little and Great Rossia.

In contrast to Sofonovych, the *Synopsis* did not integrate the Kyivan Rus' legacy with subsequent Ukrainian history. It ignored the Khmelnytsky revolt and the Pereiaslav Agreement. It was not Rus', Ukraine, Little Rossia, or the Cossack Hetmanate that the *Synopsis* related to the situation after the Pereiaslav Agreement, but the city of Kyiv. The author of the *Synopsis* used the Kyivan Rus' past to serve the needs of the Muscovite/Russian ruler, even though he recounted only a few episodes of Muscovite history. In providing the basis for a dynastic history of the Eastern Slavs, the *Synopsis* not only prepared the way for the political history of the Russian state. It also brought the concept of the Slaveno-Rossian nation/people into the discussion of Russian history, thereby nationalizing Russian historiography and making it impossible to reduce Russian identity to mere identification with the dynasty or the state. While the *Synopsis* gave short shrift to a separate Ukrainian national and political experience, its fusion of Ukrainian and Russian history was far from seamless. It was the Cossack chroniclers who would turn to a discussion of relations between the two histories and traditions in the post-Pereiaslav situation.

The Eyewitness Chronicle and the Recording of Late Seventeenth-Century Ukrainian-Russian Contacts

History writing in Ukraine after the *Krojnika* and *Synopsis* dealt little with the Kyivan Rus' past, but concentrated instead on the results of the Khmelnytsky Uprising and the history of the Hetmanate. These works were produced by the Cossack officer stratum rather than the monastic clergy.[24] By the early eighteenth century, Ukrainian history had become closely intertwined with the newly established Russian Empire. The major Cossack chronicles, the Eyewitness Chronicle and the works of Hryhorii Hrabianka and Samiilo Velychko, were completed or written at that time. Their traditional designation as chronicles is only partly appropriate, since their basic sections on the Khmelnytsky Uprising and its consequences were full-fledged historical treatises, especially in the case of the latter two works. The designation "Cossack" is more apt, because their central theme was the history of the Cossacks and/or the Cossack Hetmanate, and their authors, though in one case unknown, reflected the interests of the new Ukrainian Cossack elite.

In contrast to the works of Hrabianka and Velychko, the Eyewitness Chronicle has stood the test of time as a primary source for the second half of the seventeenth century.[25] Most scholars believe that

---

24. Even though Roman Rakushka-Romanovsky, considered by most scholars to have been the author of the Eyewitness Chronicle, became the archpriest of Bratslav later in his career, he was primarily a Cossack officer. In contrast to the monastic clergy, the married secular clergy of the Hetmanate was in any event more closely linked with the officer stratum. On this stratum and the writing of Ukrainian history, see M. Grushevskii [Mykhailo Hrushevs'kyi], "Ob ukrainskoi istoriografii XVIII veka: Neskol'ko soobrazhenii," *Bulletin de l'Académie des Sciences de l'URSS: Classe des sciences sociales* (1934): 215–33, translated by Zenon Kohut as "Some Reflections on Ukrainian Historiography of the XVIII Century" in *The Eyewitness Chronicle*, pt. 1 (=Harvard Series in Ukrainian Studies 7, pt. 1) (Munich, 1972), pp. 9–16; and Omelian Pritsak, "Doba viis'kovykh kantseliarystiv," *Kyïvs'ka starovyna*, 1993, no. 4: 62–66.

25. It was first published in 1846 by Osyp Bodiansky in the Moscow *Chteniia* and separately as *Letopis' Samovidtsa o voinakh Bogdana Khmel'nitskogo i o mezhdousobiiakh byvshikh v Maloi Rossii po ego smerti* (Moscow, 1846). Thirty years later a more authoritative edition appeared, with an introduction by Orest Levytsky: *Letopis' Samovidtsa po novootkrytym spiskam* (Kyiv, 1878). It was reprinted in the Harvard Series in Ukrainian Studies, vol. 7, pt.1, as *The Eyewitness Chronicle*, pt. 1 (Munich, 1972). The second part, intended to reprint scholarly works on the Eyewitness Chronicle, never appeared. A year before the Harvard reprint was issued, Iaroslav Dzyra published a new edition, *Litopys Samovydtsia* (Kyiv, 1971), which was intended to be the first volume in a series of source publications including the Cossack chronicles. The series never appeared because of the crackdown on Ukrainian scholarship and culture in 1972, involving repressive measures against a number of historians, including Dzyra. For a criticism of some of the archaeographical methodology of this edition, see Omeljan Pritsak's review in *Recenzija* 2, no. 1 (1971): 27–58. Page references in the present article are to the 1971 Kyiv edition.

the first half of the work, covering the years from 1648 to 1672 or 1677, which begins with the title "About the Beginning of Khmelnytsky's War" (*O načalî vojny Xmelnyckoho*), represents the writing of a participant in the events, probably on the basis of notes, while the rest of the work down to 1702 is a chronicle in the traditional sense. Scholars have generally suggested that Roman Rakushka-Romanovsky, treasurer (*pidskarbii*) of the Zaporozhian Host and later archpriest of Bratslav, is the most likely author.[26] The work reflects the changing political situation in Ukraine: while Russia rarely appears in the first part of the chronicle, it comes to occupy an important place by the time of Peter I and Hetman Ivan Mazepa. Throughout, the text reflects the terminology current in seventeenth-century Ukraine and the Polish-Lithuanian Commonwealth rather than ecclesiastical usage. For example, it refers to Russia and Russians as *Moskva* (in one case *Moskovščyna*; 1661, p. 84), the Russian armies as "Muscovite troops," and the Russian ruler as the "Muscovite tsar" (*car moskovkij*). In eschewing the high-style clerical derivatives of *Rossija* (except for two instances in the tsar's title; 1654, p. 66; 1682, p. 135), the Eyewitness Chronicle seems to approach popular usage, frequently employing "Ukraine" (*Ukrajina*) in various territorial meanings for the Ukrainian lands and avoiding "Little Rossia."[27]

After the Pereiaslav Agreement, the Russian tsars are frequently mentioned, almost always with the title "His Tsarist Majesty" (*joho carske velyčestvo*), or "Their Tsarist Majesties" during the dyarchy of Peter and Ivan. It is this titulature that caused the chronicle's nineteenth-century editor, Orest Levytsky, to describe it as pro-Russian, though in disputing this view in 1930 Mykola Petrovsky pointed out that the chronicler was careful to use almost all current titles of sovereigns.[28] Petrovsky also discerned a negative attitude toward Peter in the accounts of his cruelties and defeats. Even taking into account that such criticisms would have had to be veiled, since the early eighteenth century was a dangerous time for Ukraine, one finds it difficult to accept his argument on the basis of the scanty opinions

26. For a discussion of the debate on the author and argumentation in favor of Rakushka, see Mykola Petrovs'kyi, *Narysy istoriï Ukraïny XVII-pochatku XVIII stolit'*, vol. 1 (*Doslidy nad litopysom Samovydtsia*) (Kharkiv, 1930), pp. 134–84.

27. Interestingly, Belarus is mentioned as a toponymic *Bîlaja Rus'* and an addition to the tsar's title in 1654: "y Bîlaja Rossiji" (1654, p. 69).

28. See Petrovs'kyi, *Narysy*, pp. 123–31, for a discussion of attitudes toward Muscovy/Russia and Peter I.

offered in the Chronicle.[29] Yet instances of cruel treatment and sentencing by Peter, at times in conjunction with Ivan Alekseevich, appear frequently in the chronicle (for the sons of Hetman Ivan Samoilovych, 1687, pp. 144–45; against the revolt of the *strel'tsy*, 1682, pp. 137–38; punishment of a revolt against Peter in 1699 [p. 162]). In the reign of Aleksei Mikhailovich, the suppression of the Solovets Islands monastery (1676, p. 123) also is presented negatively. Indeed, the most frequently mentioned Russian toponym, other than Moscow and the border town of Putyvl, is Siberia, which appears four times as a place of exile for Ukrainians (1663, p. 93; 1665, p. 98; 1672, p. 113; 1687, p. 147). The only tsar for whom there is a positive evaluation is Fedor Alekseevich, whose death is described as follows: "In the month of May the sovereign tsar of Muscovy and all Rossiia, Fedor Alekseevich, who had great love for our nation, for he ordered all services in Muscovy [or Moscow] in churches and monasteries to be conducted in our chant, and Muscovite dress was abolished [*otmineno*], but he permitted wearing our style, died at a young age, to the grief of all Christendom" (1682, p. 135).[30]

Whatever the attitude toward the tsar and his officials, in the chronicle they come to have a considerable influence on life in Ukraine. From the Pereiaslav Agreement on, issues in Ukraine, including the removal of hetmans, are more and more decided by the tsarist government (see, for example, the order of the boyar Prince Vasilii Golitsyn to call a new council to select a hetman after the deposition of Ivan Samoilovych; 1687, p. 146). As early as 1665, Hetman Ivan Briukhovetsky was given the title of boyar and a Russian wife as a sign of favor in an attempt to ensure his loyalty. After the Azov campaign, the tsar showed his graciousness by dining with Hetman Mazepa and spending the day with him (1696, p. 158). Gaining the ear of tsarist officials became an important means of accumulating power, as in the case of Simeon, the archpriest of Nizhyn ("who was in great repute in Muscovy [Moscow]" and "to whom the voevoda listened [questioned]," 1677, p. 124).

A good part of the story that the Eyewitness Chronicle tells about the late seventeenth century concerns revolts against Russian influence

---

29. For a discussion of self-censorship in the Cossack chronicles, see Petrovs'kyi, *Narysy*, pp. 81–84.

30. "Mîsjacja maja hosudar moskovskij j vseja Rossiji Feodor Aleksîevyč pomer c žalem useho xrystyjanstva v molodyx lîtax, kotorij velykuju ljubov do našoho narodu mîl, bo y naboženstva na Moskvî našym napîvom po cerkvax y po manastyrax otpravovaty prykazal, y odežu moskovskuju otmîneno, ale po našomu nosyty pozvolyl."

in Ukraine and attempts to make arrangements with other powers, including the great revolt against the tsarist census and the installation of new voevodas in 1666. While the author of the chronicle outlines the grievances of the populace in 1666, he is ever the monarchist and shows little sympathy for rebellion, especially on the part of the Cossacks of the Zaporizhzhia, of whom he is quite critical (see his description of the conflict between the Cossacks of the Zaporozhian Sich and the Russians; 1667, p. 101). His royalism extends to the Polish king as regards the Ukrainian lands under the latter's scepter, and in one instance he puts aside his anti-Muslim feelings, citing a response to a Cossack overture by the Turkish sultan, who condemns "Cossack inconstancy" and states that "I am no Polish king, Muscovite tsar, or Hungarian king, whom you swindled, betraying your own faith."[31] It is difficult to ascertain to what extent the chronicler's respectful attitude toward the Russian tsar was also motivated by his realization of whose power had triumphed and by the need to ensure that the manuscript contain nothing compromising. At times, however, there are oblique indications of his dissatisfaction at this turn of events, as in his description of the capitulation of Hetman Petro Doroshenko in 1676: "And thus his hetmancy ended with the great decline of Ukraine, and from that time the Muscovites remained in Chyhyryn by order of his tsarist majesty."[32]

The basis for Ukraine's relations with the Russian tsar and Russia is the Pereiaslav Agreement, which the Eyewitness Chronicle describes somewhat more fully than Sofonovych's *Krojnika*. The latter describes Khmelnytsky and his officers as no longer wishing to be subjects of the king of Poland and not wishing to submit to the Tatars. The Cossack council accordingly decides to submit to the tsar. A short passage recounts the oath of the hetman and officers, after which they receive presents, as well as the administration of the oath of eternal submission in the regiments, which "the whole people throughout Ukraine did with enthusiasm."[33] The Russian tsar is generally treated as sovereign over all or part of the Ukrainian territories, but there is only one instance of the attribution "our" (in the attack on Hetman

31. "nestatečnost' kozackuju," obl. c., and "ja ne korol' polskij, anî car moskovskij, anî korol' vengerskij, kotoryx vy oshukyvaly y yzdradyly svoju ž vîru" (1669, p. 107).

32. "Y tak hetmanstvo eho skončylosja pry upadku velykom Ukrajiny: a ot toho času Moskva stala u Čyhrynî po ukazu eho carskoho velyčestva" (1676, p. 122).

33. 1654, pp. 66–67. See the discussion in Basarab, *Pereiaslav 1654*, pp. 62–65.

Ivan Samoilovych after his downfall, he is described as plotting something "against our Muscovite monarchs").[34] There is even less indication that this relationship with the Russian tsar extended to a communality with Russia and Russians (or, to use the chronicler's terminology, *Moskva*). The constant military campaigns are always depicted as being fought by the Muscovite army or troops and the Cossack army or troops, with the Cossack troops frequently referred to as "ours."[35] The two lands are seen as quite separate, as is apparent when the colonel of Starodub, Petro Rostyslavets, is depicted as not wishing to be "in obedience to his hetman" and attempting to turn Starodub, Sumy and Rybne into Muscovite border towns. His act is described as treasonous, and he is turned over to the hetman's emissaries in Moscow and taken back to Ukraine to face a military court (1676, p. 123). The Old Believers, who are depicted as fiercely persecuted "in the Muscovite land," go to Ukraine (*na Ukrajinu*) for refuge (1676, p. 123). There is little discussion of the political structure and relationship of the two lands, though in one somewhat corrupt passage Muscovy is described as having states or dominions (*panstva*): Ukraine's place in this arrangement is not clear.[36] Despite the considerable material on religious issues, one finds relatively little mention of relations between the Russian and Ukrainian churches. When the tsar "returns" (*pryvernul*) Svinskii Monastery near Briansk to the Kyivan Caves Monastery, the Kyivan monks are reported to have gone there, and it is mentioned that a year earlier, when the Trubchevsk Monastery was given over, the Russian monks departed. But the transfer of the Kyiv metropolitanate from the jurisdiction of the patriarchate of Constantinople to that of the Moscow patriarchate is dealt with only in passing: the chronicle states that Prince Hedeon Chetvertynsky, bishop of Lutsk, was elected metropolitan of Kyiv in 1685 and returned from Moscow in 1686 (p. 141).

Despite its extensive treatment of events in Russia and the activities of Russians in Ukraine, the Eyewitness Chronicle gives little

---

34. "protyvko monarxov našyx moskovskyx" (1687, p. 145).

35. I find only one case in which the two armies are mentioned and then referred to collectively as "ours": "but ours beat many Swedes that time" (*ale naši švedov toho ž času mnoho pobyly*) (1700, p. 163). The Ukrainian Cossacks, whether of the settled area, the Hetmanate, or the Zaporozhian Sich, are called Cossacks (*kozaky*), while the Cossacks of the Don are usually called "Donites" (*donci*) (1678, p. 129).

36. The passage reads differently in different manuscripts: "vojska velykie jix carskyx velyčectv zo vsej Moskvy i panstv prynaležnyx do nas [k tsarstvu; do neji]" (1687, p. 143)

indication of broader perspectives on the political, cultural and historical relations of the two lands and peoples. It does, however, reflect the increasing contacts between Ukraine and Russia and the political change that came with recognition of the sovereignty of the Muscovite/Russian tsar. Broader questions emerge more substantially in the two later Cossack chronicles, which are also more important for Ukrainian political theory. The two major histories of the Cossack Hetmanate by Hryhorii Hrabianka and Samiilo Velychko were written soon after the Battle of Poltava, which sealed the fate of the Hetmanate. The crisis after Poltava may have hastened the crystallization of political thought, including assessments of the Ukrainian-Russian relationship.

Hryhorii Hrabianka: The Depiction of the Cossack Nation, the Ideal Hetman, and the Proper Relationship with the Russian Tsar

Hrabianka's history, a paean to Bohdan Khmelnytsky, circulated in many copies in eighteenth-century Ukraine.[37] Written or completed by the Hadiach regimental judge Hryhorii Hrabianka ca. 1710, the *Dîjstvija* is for the most part not a chronicle, as it is conventionally called, but a historical work with more than forty principal topics. Dates in chronicle style are only inserted in the last third of the work, starting with 1664.[38] The relatively short text (257 pages in the 1854

37. For a discussion of Ukrainian manuscript book culture of the eighteenth century and the number of copies of Hrabianka's work, as well as other historical works, see E. M. Apanovich (Olena Apanovych), *Rukopisnaia svetskaia kniga XVIII v. na Ukraine: Istoricheskie sborniki* (Kyiv, 1983).

38. Dîjstvija prezîl"noj y ot" načala poljakov" krvavšoj nebyvaloj brany Bohdana Xmelnyckoho, hetmana zaporožskoho, s" poliaky [The events of the greatest, bloodiest, and, from the beginning of the Poles, unprecedented war of Bohdan Khmelnytsky, Zaporozhian hetman, against the Poles] (Kyiv, 1854). A fragment deleted by censors from the 1854 edition was published in 1894 in Aleksandr Lazarevskii [Oleksander Lazarevs'kyi], "Opushchennaia v pechati stranitsa iz letopisi Grabianki," *Kievskaia starina*, 1894, no. 11: 297–300. The 1854 edition, as well as a partial publication of 1793 unknown to the editors of that edition, have been reprinted, together with facsimiles of two manuscripts, in the Harvard Library of Early Ukrainian Literature, no. 9: *Hryhorij Hrabjanka's* The Great War of Bohdan Xmel'nyc'kyj ([Cambridge, Mass.], 1990). We still lack an adequate scholarly edition, which is particularly important in view of the large number of texts. A modern Ukrainian translation of the text appeared as *Litopys hadiats'koho polkovnyka Hryhoriia Hrabianky* (Kyiv, 1992). Page references in the present article are to the 1854 edition. The major study of the chronicle by Mykola Zerov and Iurii

edition) was written in an elevated Slavonic style rather than in the Ukrainian vernacular of the Eyewitness Chronicle. While much of the material in the *Dîjstvija* cannot withstand historical scrutiny as an accurate reflection of seventeenth-century reality, the work should be studied, as Mykhailo Hrushevsky suggested sixty years ago, as a fundamental text of early eighteenth-century political thought.[39]

The *Dîjstvija* argues that the Cossacks of Ukraine, whom it identifies with the Little Rossian nation, were descended from the Khazars.[40] Alhough its discussion of origins is complex and not always consistent, it effectively places the Cossacks/Ukrainians at the center of the emergence of the Slavs and of Rus'. It presents an account of the genesis of the Cossack-Little Rossian nation that in practice distinguishes it from the Russians by noting its Khazar origins and the Cossack element. It then traces the decline of Volodymyr's state under Tatar, Lithuanian and Polish rule, resulting in the division of Little Rossia (*Malaja Rossija*) into Polish counties. Echoing a phrase in the *Synopsis*, the *Dîjstvija* laments that this process continued until the "Rossian scepter so declined that a tsardom was transformed into a principality and a principality into a palatinate."[41] From that point, the work returns to the history of the Cossacks, with the Khmelnytsky revolt as its centerpiece.

In practice, the early history of Muscovy/Russia is ignored, even though the introduction asserts that Khmelnytsky brought "Little Rossia" into subjection to the "Rossian monarch."[42] It is Ukraine's relations with the Russian ruler that dominate the latter half of the

---

Lutsenko's dissertation on the subject remain unpublished. Lutsenko wrote the introduction to the Harvard edition and compiled a bibliography of the literature on Hrabianka's chronicle.

39. Hrushevsky, "Some Reflections on Ukrainian Historiography of the XVIII Century," pp. 9–16.

40. The initial section, a discussion of the origins of the Cossacks, begins with a reference to "the people/nation of the Little Rossian land, called Cossacks" (*Narod'' Malorossijskoj strany, narycaemij Kozaky*, p. 3), and follows with a discussion of the two as synonymous.

41. "Ednako že vo unyčtoženie Rossijkij skypter'' tako pryšel'', jako ot'' carstija vo knjaženie, a ot'' knjaženija v'' voevodstvo premînysja" (p. 18). See Lutsenko, "Introduction," p. xxxv.

42. "Rossijskomu Monarsî," obl. c., p. iii. How the Muscovite ruler became the Rossian monarch is unclear, since the work describes Lithuania as having occupied the Rossian throne: "y obladaša Lytva Rosijskym'' prestolom''" (p. 17). The preface also mentions the Muscovite prince Dmitrii's victory over Mamai (p. iii).

historical narrative. Writing after the defeat of Hetman Mazepa at Poltava, Hrabianka sought to delineate the historic rights and privileges enjoyed by Little Rossia and the Cossacks, which were endangered by the Petrine government.[43] In postulating ancient origins for the Cossacks and exalting their martial virtues as badges of high social status, Hrabianka's history provided a justification for keeping Ukraine's political and social order in place even as it came under the more direct rule of the tsar.[44] Hrabianka proclaims it his goal to prove to all peoples that not only the Slaveno-Rossian monarchs, but also their subjects consistently defended their patrimony (*otčestvie*).[45] He asserts that the Ukrainians came freely under the scepter of the Russian tsar and rendered many loyal services to him. Hrabianka makes this point mainly by depicting Bohdan Khmelnytsky as a heroic figure and his hetmancy as a model of appropriate relations between the tsar and his Ukrainian subjects.[46]

---

43. Indeed, the preface even mentions the Petrine historical translation project as a reason for undertaking the work (p. i).

44. This justification is particularly manifest in the reaction that Hrabianka reports among the Polish nobility after the Hadiach negotiations. The Cossacks are described as having won their freedom through valor. The Polish nobility, which contemptuously regards the Cossacks as peasants, is enjoined to remember that the Macedonians were initially farmers and the Romans shepherds, while the Turks came to power through banditry. The Polish nobles are described as recalling that their own ancestors were not nobles at first, but attained that status by shedding blood and demonstrating valor. The Polish nobles repeat a prophecy attributed to King Stefan Batory that "someday these [Cossack] younkers will establish a free Commonwealth of their own," and Hrabianka asserts that this has come to pass (p. 164).

45. The preface to the 1854 edition uses *raby* (servants or slaves) for "subjects" (p. 126), but the Tumansky edition of 1793 uses *podannye* (*Hryhorij Hrabjanka's* The Great War, p. 440). It also contains a statement to the effect that the "subjects" had also responded to insults to the Rossians. In this case, "Rossians" seems to refer to Eastern Slavs in general. This very Slavonic preface seems to have been intended specifically for a Russian audience. Its mention of Peter's title of "all-Rossian Emperor" and of the translation of Pufendorf, which appeared in 1718, indicates that it was written after 1710, the year given in the text (pp. i-iv). Peter began using the title "emperor" only in 1710: see James Cracraft, "Empire versus Nation: Russian Political Theory under Peter I," *Harvard Ukrainian Studies* 10, nos. 3–4 (December 1986): 536.

46. See Serhii Plokhy, "The Symbol of Little Russia: The Pokrova Icon and Early Modern Ukrainian Political Ideology," *Journal of Ukrainian Studies* 17, nos. 1–2 (Summer-Winter 1992): 171–88. Even if one does not accept his hypothesis that the Khmelnytsky cult was created after the Battle of Poltava to meet the needs of Ukrainian autonomists and represented an "anti-Mazepa

The account of the Pereiaslav Agreement is replete with descriptions of the ancient liberties and freedoms of the Little Rossians and Cossacks. The tsar is described as guaranteeing the Pereiaslav Articles forever and affixing seals to them. On the other hand, the account has Khmelnytsky pledging in a letter to the tsar never to commit treason. Hrabianka has Khmelnytsky writing to Tsar Aleksei Mikhailovich about the confirmation of "rights, statutes, privileges and all manner of freedoms and possessions of the clergy and laity of every estate." He describes these freedoms as deriving from ancient times, from the pious Rus' princes and lords and from the Polish kings. The Cossacks had held fast to these freedoms since the days of their grandfathers and great-grandfathers and had shed their blood to preserve them. Khmelnytsky declares that the Cossacks fall before his tsarist majesty and most humbly beg him to confirm these rights with charters forever. He says this was promised by his tsarist majesty's boyar and his comrades, who declared that the tsar would make better grants than the Polish kings and the ancient princes, as long as the Ukrainians made obeisance and rendered loyal service.[47] Relations between the tsar and Ukraine are based on oaths sworn by the Ukrainians and rights and liberties granted in perpetuity at Pereiaslav; in the description of that act, no mention is made of any hereditary rights of the tsar.

Covering more than fifty years of rapid change, the text reflects the changing designations of Russia in titles and descriptions of the tsar. In general, as time goes on, "Muscovite" and "Muscovy" are augmented by forms derived from "Rossia." In recounting the early years of the Khmelnytsky revolt, the tsar is described as the "monarch, the great Muscovite sovereign of the same faith"; the term "Muscovite monarch" also appears.[48] In discussing the tsar with the khan, Khmelnytsky describes him as a "believer of the same faith, our Muscovite monarch." But even in the account of this period, one finds Khmelnytsky using the formula "sovereign, tsar and all-Rossian great prince"[49] in a purported letter to the tsar. The phrase "all-Rossian" clearly belongs to eighteenth-century political vocabulary and is used on only one other occasion in the work, with reference to Peter I.

cult," one can see how Hrabianka and Velychko made use of that cult in the new situation.

47. Pp. 125–26. See the account in Basarab, *Pereiaslav 1654*, pp. 65–70.

48. "do edynovîrnoho sebî Monarxa Velykoho Hosudarja Moskovskoho" (p. 83); "na Edynovîrnoho nam" Monarxa Moskovskoho," obl. c., p. 142.

49. "Hosudarju, Carju i Velykomu Knjazju Vserossijskomu" (p. 123).

Indeed, the expression "to the autocrat of all Rossia,"[50] which occurs in the same letter, rings truer to seventeenth-century usage. The political change after Pereiaslav is noted by the mention of "Great, Little and White Rossia" as an element of the tsar's title (p. 131). In other passages, "Orthodox" is used, reflecting the emphasis that Hrabianka placed on the religious link between Ukraine and Russia and the significance of religion in bringing about the Pereiaslav Agreement.

The names of political and geographic entities that correspond to Muscovy, Russia, the Russian Empire, and the lands of the tsar vary both in accordance with the time period discussed and the context of the discussion. The change in nomenclature for these entities does not proceed as rapidly as changes in the designation of the tsar or the nomenclature for Russians. The traditional Ukrainian term "Muscovy" or "Moscow" (*Moskva*) is employed frequently, and on a few occasions "Muscovite lands" (*moskovskie zemli*) and "Muscovite state" (*Moskovskoe Hosudarstvo*) are used. As early as Khmelnytsky's time there is an occurrence of "Rossian tsardom" (p. 127), and in Peter's time the Baltic provinces are annexed to the "Rossian Crown" (p. 255). For later periods, "Rossia" for Russia appears seldom, and its meaning is not certain.[51] The term "Rossians" occurs without qualification in reference to the Russian polity.[52] In contrast to "Little Rossia" (which in the latter part of the work gradually replaces "Rus'," "Rossia," and the frequently used "Ukraine" as a designation for Ukraine), "Great Rossia" appears only a few times in the chronicle.[53]

---

50. "Vseja Rossiy Samoderžavcu" (p. 125).

51. The two instances are somewhat obscure, since they refer to Tatar attacks on Poland and *Rossija* in the 1690s and may refer to Ukrainian lands (pp. 238–39). The variety of the meanings of *Rossia* in Hrabianka's text shows how difficult it was to use the term consistently, since forms of *Rossia* appear in Prince Volodymyr's title (p. 17) and as a synonym for *Rus'* (Ruthenians or Ukraine, p. 125) in the account of seventeenth-century developments. The latter meaning would seem appropriate in the panegyrical "Praise in Verse to Khmelnytsky from the Little Rossian Nation" (p. v), but given the forms derived from *Rossija* in the rest of the text, one can see how ambiguous the term had become by Hrabianka's time.

52. Khmelnytsky is described as having submitted to the Rossians ("Xmelnyckij poddaesja Rossijanam"" (p. 120). See also p. 165. This use of *Rossijane* may be seen as analogous to the use of *Moskva* for both the country and the people.

53. Migrations in Khmelnytsky's time are said to occur in the direction of Great Rossia (p. 112). A discussion of freedom of movement contrasts "Great Rossia" with "Little Rossia" (p. 171). See also p. 244.

Hrabianka's work is particularly interesting for its changing use of the terms "Muscovite," "Great Rossian," and "Rossian" in relation to "Cossack" and "Little Rossian," especially in discussing military affairs. In the early period, preference is given to "Moscow" or "Muscovites" (*Moskva*) and "Muscovite forces" (*Moskovskie sily*), which are contrasted with the Cossacks. There are, however, also instances of "Rossian regiments" (*rosijskie polky*), and "Rossian armed forces" (*rossijskoe voinstvo*). But as the chronicle reaches the 1670s, instances of "Great Rossian army" and "Great Rossians" (*Velikorossijane*) appear more frequently. This usage is especially important for the Chyhyryn campaigns of 1678 and 1679, in his account of which Hrabianka incorporates whole passages of the *Synopsis*, substituting "Great Rossian" and "Great Rossians" for "the armed forces of his tsarist majesty" used in the *Synopsis* and frequently employing "Little Rossian" where the *Synopsis* has "Zaporozhian" and "Cossack."[54] Instances of "Great Rossians" do not entirely supplant the earlier use of *Moskva* (Muscovites), nor do they appear more frequently than the newer *Rossijane* (Rossians) and adjectives pertaining to them. They do, however, reflect the terminological change for the Ukrainian forces, for which "Little Rossian" comes to replace "Cossack" in the frequent mentions of joint military operations, partly reflecting increased attention to the Hetmanate ("Little Rossia").

In contrast to the Eyewitness Chronicle, which provides an increasing amount of information on Muscovy/Russia as Russia comes to control events in Ukraine more fully, Hrabianka's more thematically constructed work has a greater focus on Ukraine. Hrabianka comments on internal affairs in Russia, but usually only insofar as they affect developments in Ukraine. For example, he discusses the Smolensk War (1632–34) in a passage on the tsar's reasons for siding with Khmelnytsky against the Poles (pp. 83–84).[55] Khmelnytsky is quoted as pointing out that the Tatars of the East are under the yoke of the "Muscovite autocracy."[56] Hrabianka identifies loyalty to the tsar as the principal criterion for judging Ukrainian political leaders, but devotes little direct attention to the tsars, except as they affected events in Ukraine. Despite this loyalist stance, the

---

54. See Rothe, *Sinopsis*, pp. 365–76 and Hrabianka, pp. 222–30.

55. He deals with the Cossack role in fighting the Russians by stating that Khmelnytsky, together with the Cossacks, had been with the Polish king at Smolensk, where he sympathized with the defeated Russians and realized that oppression of the Ukrainians would follow.

56. "Pod" ygom" raboty Moskovskoho Samoderžavstija" (p. 143).

work relates arguments against Russian attempts to take away Cossack liberties, install Russian voivodes, and collect taxes (pp. 190–92). Indeed, the criticism of tsarist policy in the speech of Hetman Ivan Briukhovetsky was strong enough to be censored in the 1854 edition of the chronicle.[57]

Although Hrabianka wrote relatively little about Russia, his history at times reflects a perception that the Ukrainian-Russian relationship involved not only Little Rossia and the tsar, but also two countries and two peoples.[58] In the Pereiaslav negotiations, the tsar is said to be pleased that the Cossacks are seeking to join the Muscovite state "with their populous lands and principalities."[59] In the discussion of Khmelnytsky's reasons for this decision, there is an account of the Poles' attempt to force Muscovy and Ukraine into conflict, placing the two countries on a similar footing (in this case, as part of the linguistic pairing with "Muscovy," the term "Ukraine" is used rather than "Little Rossia" [p. 117]). There is discussion of such questions as the boundaries between Russia and Ukraine (pp. 111–12, 171, 210–11).

That the Ukrainian-Russian relationship involved more than the sovereign is shown by the statement that Khmelnytsky subordinated himself "to the Rossians" (*Rossijanam*") in 1654. This reference to a whole people (p. 120) prefigures modern usage and departs from seventeenth-century Ukrainian usage, which employed the term to refer to all East Slavic territories or to Ukraine.[60]

---

57. It was only published in 1895 by Lazarevsky in "Opushchennaia v pechati stranitsa iz letopisi Grabianki."

58. There is a mention of "belonging to the same tribe" (*edinopleminost'*), which may be interpreted as referring to Russians and Ukrainians, in Khmelnytsky's letter to the tsar (p. 124).

59. "Y Velykij Hosudar' rad" bjaše Kozakom", jako pryklonytysja k" Moskovskomu Hosudarstvu z" tak" mnoho narodnymy zemljamy y knjažemij xoščut"" (p. 98).

60. On another occasion, someone caught on Ukrainian territory is described as having been sent to the Rossians ("do Rosijan," p. 165). This use of *Rossijane* also reveals the process whereby the term came to refer to Russians alone, although in the same section *Rossijane* is used to refer to Ukrainians as well. In seventeenth-century ecclesiastical literature, *Rossijane* could mean Eastern Slavs or Ukrainians alone. In *Dîjstvija*, Khmelnytsky is described as acting "with the whole Rossian nation," meaning the Ukrainians ("so vsîm" narodom" Rossijskym," p. 125). The term is used by Khmelnytsky in a document addressed to the tsar and may therefore reflect archaic usage, most likely a rendering of the "Rus'kyi narod" used to denote Ruthenians in the Commonwealth. The document is preceded by Hrabianka's discussion of the importance of Khmelnytsky's actions on behalf of the "Little Rossian nation."

Hrabianka outlines his vision of Ukrainian-Russian relations in stating that at Azov in 1696 a Ukrainian delegation wished to serve His Tsarist Majesty "and their mother, Little Rossia" (p. 248). Thus the sovereign who commanded the loyalty of Little Rossia, its hetman and people also ruled over the Muscovites and Muscovy, to whom Hrabianka occasionally refers in his work as Great Rossia and Great Rossians, or as Rossia and Rossians. In establishing the history, rights and privileges of the Cossacks and Little Russia, Hrabianka creates an image of appropriate relations between the tsar and Ukraine. He defines Muscovy as the land of the Rossians or Great Rossians, who are subject to the same ruler as the Little Rossians, although they live under a different political and social order. The very preface to his work, partly intended to document his people's services to the Rossian monarch in defense of his patrimony, shows that Hrabianka was well aware how different were the political culture and mores of Muscovy, now transforming itself into the Russian Empire, from those prevailing in Ukraine.

The Velychko Chronicle: The Vindication of the Rights of the Little Rossian Nation in the Imperial Russian Context

A fuller elaboration of Ukrainian autonomist views and the creation of the Khmelnytsky cult came with the writing of Samiilo Velychko's *Skazanie* in the 1720s.[61] Describing himself as a "true son of Little Rossia" and addressing himself to the "reader of that fatherland" in

61. The *Skazanie o vojnî kazackoj z poljakamy* (The Tale of the Cossack War against the Poles) was published in the *Letopis' sobytii v Iugo-Zapadnoi Rossii v XVII veke*, 4 vols. (Kyiv, 1848–64). The first volume was published in a new edition in Kyiv in 1926: *Samiila Velychka Skazanie o voinî kozatskoj z poliakamy*, ed. Kateryna Lazarevs'ka (=Monumenta Litterarum Ucrainicarum 16). This volume, which corrected the tendency of the first edition to impose modern Russian orthography on the work, was the first in a series of historical sources issued by a newly formed Archaeographic Commission that intended to publish a new edition of Velychko and the other Cossack chronicles. Its work was halted by the onset of Stalinism, just as the Archaeographic Commission of the early 1970s was disbanded during the assault on Ukrainian culture in 1972. There is a modern Ukrainian translation by Valerii Shevchuk: Samiilo Velychko, *Litopys*, 2 vols. (Kyiv, 1991), with an introduction by the translator. The scholarly work on Velychko is very limited. Most of the literature is mentioned in Iaroslav Dzyra, "Samiilo Velychko ta ioho litopys," *Istoriohrafichni doslidzhennia v URSR* 6 (1971): 198–223. In the present article, section, chapter and page numbers are given according to the 1926 edition for volume 1 and according to the nineteenth-century edition for volumes 2 and 3.

the preface, Velychko set out with patriotic fervor to document the history of his country from the perspective and in the language of his people ("the Cossack language").[62] The massive work (more than 1,500 printed pages, even without the missing section for 1649 to 1652) contains a history of the Khmelnytsky period based on and framed as a response to Samuel Twardowski's *Wojna domowa*, as well as a compendium of commentaries and documents on events in Ukraine down to 1700.[63] Written primarily in Middle Ukrainian, with some segments Slavonicized and many documents reproduced in the original Polish and Russian, the bulky *Skazanie* never attained the popularity of Hrabianka's work and has come down to us only in the original and one manuscript copy. It has not been carefully examined in modern scholarship, and most scholarly commentary has centered on the veracity of documents for the Khmelnytsky period that Velychko attributes to the diary of the purported secretary of the Cossack Host, Samiilo Zorka, leading to speculation that they were actually penned by Velychko.[64] The style, content and terminology of the documents are more in keeping with early eighteenth-century Ukrainian political culture than with that of the mid-seventeenth century. They are an invaluable source on the way in which early eighteenth-century society wished to perceive its origins. Through his frequent citation or creation of letters from the Zaporozhian Sich to the Hetmanate, Velychko emphasized the particular role of the Cossacks as a warrior society embodying the Little Rossian nation. Regrettably, no full analysis has been undertaken of the documents for the post-Khmelnytsky period to ascertain how authentic they are and to what extent they constitute Velychko's reworking or even creation.

Velychko's work, with its copious use of "Cossack," "Rus'," "Ukrainian," "Little Rus'," and "Little Rossian" in various combinations to describe the Ukrainians and their language and culture, as well as to characterize the "fatherland," his oft-repeated characterization of

---

62. For a discussion of Ukrainian national consciousness in this period, see Ihor Ševčenko, "The Rise of National Identity to 1700," in his *Ukraine between East and West: Essays on Cultural History to the Early Eighteenth Century* (Edmonton and Toronto, 1996), pp. 187–96.

63. Samuel Twardowski, *Wojna domowa z Kozaki i Tatary, Moskwą potym Szwedami i z Węgry ...* (Kalisz, 1681). The relationship between the two works is discussed in V. Petrykevych, *Litopys S. Velychka a* Wojna domowa *S. Tvardovs'koho* (Ternopil, 1910).

64. Mykola Petrovs'kyi, "Psevdo-diariush Samiila Zorki," *Zapysky Istorychno-filolohichnoho viddilu VUAN* 17 (1928): 168–204.

Ukraine, also deploys a rich vocabulary to describe Russia and Russians.[65] The country is called "Muscovy,"[66] "Rossia,"[67] and "Great Rossia."[68] The state is referred to as the "Muscovite state,"[69] the "Rossian tsardom,"[70] the "Rossian state,"[71] and the "Great Rossian state or domain,"[72] with national designations for Russians ("Rossians"[73] and "Muscovites"[74]) standing in at times for the polity. Its rulers are variously called "Muscovite monarchs,"[75] "Muscovite great sovereigns,"[76] the "Orthodox Muscovite monarch,"[77] "Their majesties the Muscovite tsars,"[78] "Muscovite and all Great Rossia,"[79] "great sovereign tsar and grand prince, autocrat of all Great and Little Rossia,"[80] the "Rossian monarch,"[81] "our Orthodox Rossian monarchs,"[82] the "most greatly powerful and most illustrious monarch

65. For many of the adjectives referring to Ukraine and its people, see the preface to volume 2, pp. 7–9.

66. "Moskva," 1: 6: 3, p. 79.

67. "V" Rossiy," 2: 22, p. 502. This chapter heading, which deals with the death of Tsar Fedor Alekseevich, is placed next to a heading that pertains to the introduction of the Union by King Jan Sobieski "into Rus' remaining under the Polish Crown," which retains the traditional, pre-seventeenth-century name for the Ukrainian and Belarusian territories.

68. "Na Velykuju Rosiju," obl. c., 2: 1, p. 10.

69. "Ot" hosudarstva Moskovskoho," 2: 5, pp. 79–80.

70. "Carstvija Rosijskoho," obl. c., 2: 22, p. 503, and "Carstvo ... Rossijskoe," 2: 23, p. 515.

71. "Rosijskoj deržavî," obl. c., 1: 10: 13, p. 172; "z" Hosudarstvom" Rosijskym"," obl. c., 2: 8, p. 102.

72. "Deržavu Velykorossijskuju," obl. c., 1: 11: 3, p. 186.

73. "Z Rosijany," 1: 12, p. 199.

74. "Moskva, Moskalî," 3: 31, p. 112.

75. "Monarxov" Moskovskyx"," obl. c., 3: 35, p. 211.

76. "Velykie Hosudary Moskovskie," 3: 36, p. 272.

77. "Pravoslavnomu Monarxu Moskovskomu," obl. c., 2: 172: 12, p. 396.

78. "Carem" Yx" Moscom" Moskovskym"," obl. c., 3: 35, p. 211.

79. "Moskovskoho y zo vsej Velykoj Rosiy," obl. c., 2: 27, p. 590.

80. "Velykyj h[osu]d[a]r" tsar" y velykyj knjaz', Aleksij Myxajlovyč, vseja Velykija y Malija Rosyỳ samoderžec," 1: 7: 5, p. 100, later adding White Rossia (1: 12: 4, p. 208).

81. "Ot" Monarxa Rosijskoho," obl. c., 2: 1, p. 12.

82. "Pravoslavnyx" Monarxov" našyx" Rosijskyx"," 2: 32, p. 509.

and Rossian autocrat,"[83] the "autocrat of all Rossia,"[84] "His tsarist illustrious majesty and all-Rossian autocrat,"[85] "Illustrious all-Rossian monarch,"[86] "all-Rossian tsar,"[87] "all-Rossian autocrats,"[88] "your illustrious tsarist majesty, the only illustrious zealot and defender of Eastern Orthodoxy under the sun,"[89] the "Christian sovereign,"[90] and, after the change in Peter I's title, "all-Rossian emperor."[91] Frequently, armies are referred to as the Muscovite army or armies,[92] the Great Rossian army or armies,[93] and the Rossian army or armies.[94] The people or their armed forces in Ukraine are known as Great Rossians,[95] Rossians,[96] in one case the Muscovite nation,[97] and in another the Great Rossian nation.[98]

The frequent appearance of these names in official Ukrainian, Russian, and Polish documents, which Velychko may merely have copied, makes it relatively difficult to speak of a tendency for the period covered in the work. It is clear that names derived from

---

83. "Velykoderžavnîjšyj y presvîtlîšyj monarx" y samoderžec" rosyjskyj," 1: 7: 2, p. 94.

84. "Vseja Rossiy samoderžec," 2: 4, p. 37.

85. "Jeho carskoho presvîtloho velyčestva iy samoderžca vserosijskoho," 1: 7: 2, p. 93.

86. "Presvîtlîšoho Monarxy Vserosijskoho," obl. c., 3: 31, p. 90.

87. "Carja Vserosijskoho," obl. c., 2: 10, p. 179.

88. "Samoderžcy Vserossijskiy," 3: 36, p. 272.

89. "Vašemu Carskomu Presvîtlomu Velyčestvu, edynym" pod" solncem" presvîtlosylnym Pravoslavija Vostočnoho revnytelem" y oboroncem"," obl. c., 3: 33, p. 117.

90. "Hosudar' Xrystijanskij," 2: 10, p. 188.

91. "Ymperatorom" Vserosijskym"," obl. c., 2: 23, p. 518.

92. "Vojska Moskovskie," 3: 28, p. 13.

93. "Vojsko velykorosijskoe," 3: 38, p. 436.

94. "Ekspedycijax" voenyx" Rosijskyx," 2: 27, p. 561.

95. "Velykorosyjanov," obl. c., 1: 12: 3, p. 206.

96. "Ot Rosyjan, z Rossyjanamy," 1: 11: 4, p. 190.

97. "Moskovskoho narodu," 1: 12: 7, p. 233.

98. "O soedynenij naroda Malorossijskoho z Velykorossijskym," obl. c., 3: 38, pp. 48–49. Adjectival forms of "Rus'" are used only in the discussion of cultural change and sending Russians abroad at the time of Peter I ("Ruskym" ljudem"," obl. c., 2: 23, p. 516, 518), though "Great Rossians" appear in the same passages.

Moskva decrease in frequency, while those derived from *Rossija* and *Velykaja Rossija* increase. But there is no full-scale development of a consistent terminology for Russians equivalent to the growing concentration on "Little Rossia," which replaces "Ukraine" in descriptions of the later seventeenth century and is projected backward into descriptions of the mid-seventeenth century and the "Little Rossian nation," the possessor of rights, privileges, and freedoms.

In many appellations of the Russian ruler, Velychko mentions his Orthodox faith. In this emphasis on religious commonality between Ukrainians and Russians, as well as on joint struggles against Muslim and Catholic foes, Velychko follows the tradition of the monastic and Cossack chronicles. Given his encyclopedic range of documents and his attention to the Right Bank and the spread of the Union there, his coverage of seventeenth-century religious affairs is quite extensive. Nevertheless, he records the election of Hedeon Sviatopolk Chetvertynsky as metropolitan of Kyiv (2: 26, p. 552) and his confirmation in Moscow in 1685 (2: 27, pp. 602–12) without mentioning the significance of the transfer of the Kyiv metropolitanate to the jurisdiction of the Moscow patriarchate.[99] Later in his work, the significance of this event becomes clear as Velychko chronicles the increasing influence of the patriarchate in Ukrainian church affairs, including its insistence that the patriarch of Moscow, not the metropolitan of Kyiv, consecrate the bishop of Pereiaslav (3: 36, pp. 295–97).

Velychko describes the Pereiaslav Agreement as an acceptance of the protection of the Russian tsar, and letters from the Zaporozhian Cossacks to Khmelnytsky around that time speak of pacts, alliance, and protection.[100] In asserting that at Pereiaslav the tsar's emissaries bound him by an oath to preserve the rights and liberties of Little Rossia and the Zaporozhian Host, Velychko rewrites the facts of 1654 and recasts Russian political practices to fit the needs of the Cossack Hetmanate.[101] Khmelnytsky had demanded such an oath at Pereiaslav, but the tsarist emissaries had firmly rejected that demand as an affront to the autocratic tsar. In the rest of his work, Velychko generally follows Hrabianka in emphasizing the positive aspects of

---

99. In Patriarch Ioakim's encyclical on this matter one finds the beginning of the tendency to limit the term "Little Rossia" to the territories of the Cossack Hetmanate under the tsar's jurisdiction, since he describes the appointment as pertaining to "Little Rossia" and "Rossians" living under other rulers (i.e., in the Commonwealth).

100. 1: 7: 2, p. 94.

101. See 1: 1: 3, p. 95, and Basarab, *Pereiaslav 1654*, pp. 70–74.

loyalty to the tsar and Ukraine's adherence to the Pereiaslav Agreement. As Velychko spent some years in prison after the Battle of Poltava (the reasons for this are murky, given that he was an official of Mazepa's enemy Vasyl Kochubei), he had considerable reason to know the actual power of the tsar in Ukraine. To this were added his anti-Catholic and anti-Muslim views, which made him support an Orthodox ruler. But to some degree he was merely acknowledging the political reality resulting from the late seventeenth-century struggles and the Battle of Poltava, as well as advocating the only strategy whereby Ukraine could maintain some measure of autonomy within a Russian political structure.

One finds in Velychko, however, even more evidence than in Hrabianka that the policies of the tsar and the Russian authorities were often baneful and encountered resistance from many groups in Ukrainian society. At times, Velychko provides such evidence even when he later cites opinions countervailing those voices that speak out most forcefully against the Russians. Thus, in a letter of 1692 to the Zaporozhian Host, Ivan Petryk calls for a struggle against the Russians, arguing that "this war against the Muscovites began for no other reason than your liberties and the common good" and that it was being conducted so that they might emerge "from under the Muscovite yoke and constitute among yourselves the kind of order you desire so as to live according to the liberties that your ancestors enjoyed under Khmelnytsky" (3: 31, p. 112). An opposing letter from the Poltava regiment argues that the Cossacks are not doomed to depredations and servitude: if wrongs are done in Little Rossia, redress should be sought by wise and worthy leaders, not by Petryk (3: 31, p. 115).[102] But the emphasis in the material presented is on the defense of liberties, and the justification of Russian actions is rather lame. At times, Velychko's voice is direct rather than mediated through documents. This is particularly true in his discussion of resistance to the stationing of Russian voevodas in Ukraine in 1666 (2: 7, p. 96). He describes the universal outcry against Hetman Ivan Briukhovetsky "for the destruction of ancient Little Rossian rights and liberties and for accepting voevodas and Muscovite troops into Little Rossia" (2: 8, p. 136). The partition of Ukraine at Andrusovo in 1667 is a similar case (2: 12, pp. 295–302). It is described, in conjunction with the election of Hetman Ivan Samoilovych, as having been

102. This document also contains a mention of "our Rossian nation." While the phrase may refer to Ukraine alone, it may also reflect the concept of an East Slavic nation.

"concluded injuriously with the Poles without the Cossacks, with the division of the unity of Little Rossia" (2: 13, p. 329).

Velychko provides considerable material on relations between Ukraine and Russia and between Russians and Ukrainians. In many ways, he expresses his view of the proper nature of this relationship when he describes his patron, Vasyl Leontiiovych Kochubei, as having served "God, the great sovereign the Rossian tsar, his Little Rossian fatherland, and the Zaporozhian Host" (3: 41, p. 553). Inevitably, however, the Little Rossian fatherland was involved in a relationship not only with the tsar but also with Russia and Russians. This comes out in comments to the effect that books were being issued not only by "our" printing presses but also "Great Rossian" ones (3: 37, p. 418), that the "Rossian" and "Cossack" armies had won victories (3: 38, p. 483), and that the damage done by the Tatars in "Great Rossia" and "Little Rossia" had led the "Great Rossian and Little Rossian Mars" to launch a campaign (3: 28, pp. 5–6, 8). This point is also apparent in Velychko's citation of the Kolomak articles of 1687, which were proclaimed at the election of Hetman Mazepa: in them, the Russian tsar called for measures to unite the "Little Rossian nation" with the "Great Rossian" one by all possible means, including intermarriage (3: 28, pp. 48–49).

Velychko describes such Russian developments as the Razin revolt and changes of rulers, but most of his forays into Russian affairs were occasioned by ramifications of his vision of Ukraine. Thus an essential moment in Russian history, the Pereiaslav negotiations, was rewritten to fit the needs of Ukrainian political thought. The image of Muscovy was recast so that the tsar and his delegates could be described as having entered into a contractual relationship with Hetman Bohdan Khmelnytsky and "Little Rossia." The articles received by the tsar in 1659 are referred to as "constitutions," recalling the old order of the Commonwealth.[103] But this need to advance a particular vision of the Khmelnytsky era sprang from the overriding issue of Velychko's time—how to deal with the Petrine reaction to the "treason" of Hetman Mazepa and the Zaporozhian Cossacks. That imperative shapes Velychko's lengthy description of Peter and his deeds. Velychko enumerates his battles and reforms in a generally favorable manner, including the point that by sending Russians to study in the German lands, Peter turned them from ignoramuses into learned men. Nevertheless, on the negative side, Velychko points out that Peter gave the Right Bank of Ukraine to Poland, after which it became

103. The heading of the Pereiaslav articles of 1659 is *Sta[t]"y al"bo kon"stytucŷ* (1: 12: 7, p. 221).

Uniate. On concluding an account of Peter's deeds in Russia, Velychko penned what can only be seen as an indictment of the tsar's actions in Ukraine. He declared that during the struggle with the Swedes, Peter had promised the "Little Rossians" liberties enjoyed by no other nation under the sun if they served loyally. But he did not fulfill that promise, and after the death of Skoropadsky in 1722, disregarding the rights of the Zaporozhian Host, Peter did not permit the election of a hetman. Instead, he established a college to rule Little Rossia, yoking together Little Rossians of the Cossack nobiliary estate and commoners (2: 23, pp. 519–20).

Ardent though Velychko was in defending Little Rossian autonomy and distinguishing Russia from Ukraine, his own text reveals the difficulties of maintaining this position, given the changing nature of Ukrainian-Russian relations and the emergence of imperial Russia. The new cultural and intellectual relationship that developed between Russia and Ukraine after the onset of the Petrine reforms was illustrated by Velychko's availing himself of a work by Samuel Pufendorf in Russian translation, one of the first cases of a Western work entering Ukraine not directly or through Polish intermediacy but through Russia.[104] In a few instances toward the end of his work, Velychko even used "Rossian" in joint references to Russians and Ukrainians and referred to Russian forces as "ours" (3: 38, p. 429). These were but a few slips of the pen in a work that consistently defended the rights and privileges of the Little Rossian nation, but they revealed other realities of eighteenth-century Ukraine. Certainly the documents that Velychko took from Russian sources showed how greatly the Russian view of Ukrainian-Russian relations differed from his own. Documents issued by the tsar defined Ukraine as a patrimony on the basis of claims to the Kyiv and Chernihiv principalities.[105] As early as 1695, Patriarch Adrian wrote to Hetman Mazepa about the need to extend the borders of the "Rossian fatherland and autocracy" (*otečestva i samoderžavstva Rosijskogo*, obl. c., 3: 36, p. 266), meaning the Russian state including Ukraine.

Velychko wrote long after the Petrine political and ideological reforms. He provided ample evidence of Russia's integration of Ukraine and its infringement of Ukrainian political and religious autonomy, culminating in the establishment of the Little Rossian

104. *Vvedenie v gistoriju evropejskuju črez Samuila Pufendorfija, na nemeckom" jazўce složennoe: Taže črez Ioanna Friderika na latinskii preložennoe ...* (St. Petersburg, 1718).

105. 1: 7: 5, p. 99; 1: 7: 8, p. 107.

College. Yet he maintained that Little Rossia and the Little Rossian nation were involved in a relationship with a sovereign who was bound by his oath at Pereiaslav to respect their liberties. In Velychko's view, Russia and the Great Rossians remained a separate land and people. With the decline of differences in culture and nomenclature that had once so sharply divided Ukraine and Russia, political theory and history writing came to the fore to distinguish the two peoples.

The Image of Russia as a Gauge of Ukraine's Transformation

The Ukrainian historical works under discussion do not contain extensive material on Russia's internal affairs. They are indeed relatively laconic in discussing Ukraine's northern neighbor, except as it affected Ukraine. They do, however, provide information on some of the major transfers of terms and concepts between Ukraine and Russia in the early modern period.

Through the Ukrainians, the Russians came into contact with a historiography that dealt with the history of a people or nation rather than a dynasty or a state. Polish Renaissance historiography had inspired the Ruthenians to think of themselves as a nation (*narod, gens, natio*), and the pressure of Western Christianity on Orthodoxy had challenged the Ruthenians to examine their historical and religious roots. That search had particular significance for Russia because it led to Kyivan Rus', which the Ruthenian clergy in the early seventeenth century increasingly called "Rossia," as they did Rus' and its people in their own time. In the 1620s the search for identity, as well as the need for support against the Catholic Commonwealth, led some of the clergy to turn to the Muscovite tsar, who claimed the Riurikide legacy. With this appeal to the tsar came the increasing use of the terms "Little Rossia" and "Great Rossia" to describe two lands that could be seen as deriving from ancient Rossia. After the political changes of the mid-seventeenth century and the assertion of tsarist claims to Ukraine, these notions took on a new meaning and developed into the concept of an East Slavic nation/people. The Ukrainians thus introduced both the concept of a people or nation and that of East Slavic commonality into Russian political and historical thought in its formative stage. The rediscovery of Kyivan Rus' that occurred in early seventeenth-century Ukraine was certainly transmitted by the Sofonovych *Krojnika* and the *Synopsis*; indeed, the latter work even strengthened convictions about the hereditary claim of the Russian tsar to Ukraine.

If the *Synopsis* presented the tsar's proclamation of sovereignty over Ukraine in 1654 as a culminating event, the actual establishment of Muscovite rule in Ukraine proved a lengthy process in the course of which the Cossack Hetmanate developed as an autonomous political and social entity. That development occurred in the context of close relations and contacts with the Russian tsar and Muscovy. As a result, Rus' of the early seventeenth century, part of which emerged by the mid-seventeenth century as Cossack Ukraine, was gradually transformed into Little Rossia, the fatherland of the Little Rossian nation that claimed distinct rights and privileges.[106]

In this process, the Ukrainians developed numerous names and concepts of themselves and of the Russians, thereby contributing to analogous processes in Russia. Ultimately, the Ukrainians evolved concepts of "Great Rossia," "Great Rossians," "Rossians," and an "all-Rossian" ruler that were essential to the development of the concepts of "Little Rossia" and the "Little Rossian nation."

While it is certain that mid-seventeenth-century Ukrainian ideas and views pertaining to religious, cultural, and political affairs had a great impact on Russia, we know little about the influence of later Ukrainian political thought. The political views reflected in the works of Hrabianka and Velychko, with their concepts of rights, liberties, and estates, surely must have become known in Russia because of its extensive contacts with Ukraine, just as their concepts of "Little Rossia" and "Great Rossia" must have been current. While these authors may not have had a major influence on the thought of Petrine Russia, they did create an image of the Ukrainian-Russian relationship that informed eighteenth-century Ukrainian thought and historical consciousness.[107] Through their influence on later Ukrainian histori-

---

106. The development of the view that the palatinates of Volhynia, Bratslav, Kyiv, and Chernihiv were a Rus' land or *patria* with its own rights and privileges preceded the Khmelnytsky revolt and served as a foundation for the emergence of the Cossack Ukrainian polity. See Frank E. Sysyn, "Regionalism and Political Thought in Seventeenth-Century Ukraine: The Nobility's Grievances at the Diet of 1641," *Harvard Ukrainian Studies* 6, no. 2 (June 1982): 167–90.

107. James Cracraft points out that while Peter used Ukrainian terminology before and just after the Battle of Poltava, "given what we know already of Petrine political theory, we can see that Peter's promises in these same documents to respect the Cossack 'liberties, rights, and privileges' guaranteed by his father were largely—one might say necessarily—meaningless." While Cracraft may be correct in his assessment of the role of Ukrainian political thought in influencing Petrine ideology, his assertion that Petrine notions of undivided sovereignty and unlimited monarchy began to take hold in Left-Bank Ukraine after Poltava leaves out of account the continuing importance of the rights and liberties of the Little Rossian nation (Cracraft, "Empire

cal and political texts, including *Istorija Rusov*, and the rediscovery and publication of their works in the early nineteenth century, these writers helped determine the course of modern Ukrainian-Russian relations.[108]

---

versus Nation," pp. 533–34). On Ukrainian identity and political thought in the eighteenth century, see Zenon Kohut, "The Development of a Little Russian Identity and Ukrainian Nationbuilding," *Harvard Ukrainian Studies* 10, nos. 3–4 (December 1986): 559–76.

108. See Volodymyr Kravchenko, *Narysy z ukraïns'koï istoriohrafiï epokhy natsional'noho vidrodzhennia (druha polovyna XVIII–seredyna XIX st.)* (Kharkiv, 1996); and Frank E. Sysyn, "The Cossack Chronicles and the Development of Modern Ukrainian Culture and National Identity," *Harvard Ukrainian Studies* 14, nos. 3–4 (December 1990): 593–607.

Paul Bushkovitch

What Is Russia? Russian National Identity and the State, 1500–1917

In Western historical literature, national consciousness is understood to be a product of history that changes and develops over time. National identities are not established once and for all at the beginning of time, and they are not necessarily based on a common language. Any number of national identities may share a language; indeed, the very concept of language, as opposed to dialect, is mutable. Dutch is a language; Bavarian is a dialect. There is no great law defining one form of speech as a language and the other as a dialect, only a historic evolution. Further, identities can be ambiguous, or multilayered. They are not necessarily exclusive. A Frenchman can also see himself as an Alsatian; a Finland Swede as both a Swede and a Finlander. By and large, historians and other scholars studying Russia and Eastern Europe in the West have taken this approach, which often differentiates them sharply from their colleagues in the East. This does not mean that Western historians have solved all the relevant problems, for there has been relatively little interest until recent years in problems of nationality. Those historians in the West who have dealt with such issues in Russian history (Rogger, Kappeler, Thaden) have been primarily interested in nationality relations and nationality policy, not in perceptions or in fundamental issues of identity.[1] Furthermore, until recently most Western historians lumped

1. Hans Rogger, *National Consciousness in Eighteenth-Century Russia* (Cambridge, Mass., 1960); Edward C. Thaden, ed., *Russification in the Baltic Provinces and Finland, 1855–1914* (Princeton, N.J., 1981); Edward C. Thaden and Marianna Forster Thaden, *Russia's Western Borderlands, 1710–1870* (Princeton, N.J., 1984); Andreas Kappeler, *Rußlands erste Nationalitäten: das Zarenreich und die Völker der Mittleren Wolga vom 16. bis 19. Jahrhundert* (Cologne and Vienna, 1982); and *Rußland als Vielvölkerreich: Entstehung, Geschichte, Zerfall* (Munich, 1992); Theodore Weeks, *Nation and State in Late Imperial Russia* (DeKalb, Ill., 1996); Geoffrey Hosking, *Empire and Nation in Russian History* (Waco, Texas, 1993); and idem, *Russia: People and Empire 1552–1917* (London, 1997). Hosking differs from most Western historians in positing that Russian national consciousness ought in some way to be ethnolinguistic, the Russians being "unable" to decide for empire or a small ethnic Russia.

together national identity, national consciousness, and nationalism, which are distinct phenonomena. Nationalism is a political movement, the product of modern (after about 1800) society. National consciousness is the complex of ideas about a nation, while national identity is much more basic. The subject of this essay is Russian national identity, and by that term I mean the very basic significance of the words "Russia" and "Russian," not the various ideas attached to those words. Naturally, the latter will affect ideas of identity, as does nationalism, but below both remains the fundamental layer of identity—which populations and lands the word for a given nation includes and which it excludes.

In the Soviet era, "Russia" came to mean largely an ethnic unit populated by Russians, but was this always the case? Pre-1917 Russia was a multinational state. It certainly had a Russification policy, but the Western historians who have studied it have been primarily struck by the failure and even half-hearted nature of the policy. Furthermore, it was a society with a strikingly cosmopolitan elite. In 1914, at a time of supposedly universal chauvinism, Minister of War B. V. Stürmer sent General P. K. Rennenkampf to fight Germany, Baron Gustav Mannerheim (the future president of Finland) commanded the Twelfth Cavalry Division, and the Chief of the Naval General Staff was Prince A. A. Lieven. Clearly, Stürmer and Rennenkampf saw themselves as "Russians" in some sense, but were Russians of a special kind. Russian was higher in their hierarchy of identities than German. I would suggest that these men were neither unusual nor exceptional.[2] Their conception of Russia, like that of their more "Russian" colleagues, was of a state that stood above even the dominant nationality, not that of an ethnic state. It is the purpose of this paper to propose that their conception of the state was typical, not exceptional. Before 1917, the term "Russia" held the place in the hierarchy of national identities corresponding to the place later occupied by the "Soviet Union," not the RSFSR or the Russian Federation. To take another example, Russia was equivalent to Spain, not Castile.

If I am right, then the identity found in the term "Russia" was of a type that could be called statist or even dynastic. The older Western literature on nationalism normally asserted that national consciousness in Western Europe emphasized statehood and, later,

---

2. D. C. B. Lieven, *Russia and the Origins of the First World War* (New York, 1983), p. 40. According to Lieven, 28 percent of the members of the Council of State at the turn of the century were non-Russian: idem, *Russia's Rulers under the Old Regime* (New Haven, Conn., 1989).

citizenship over "ethnicity," that is, common language and origins, real or imagined. The emphasis on ethnicity was allegedly characteristic of Central and Eastern Europe. More recent scholarship has not altered this picture, save to point out that at various times some East European societies have also stressed statehood over ethnicity. Walicki has noted that Poland's national consciousness was statist for the whole period from the sixteenth to the nineteenth century, and I shall argue that Russia was also an exception to this putative East-West division.[3]

It needs stressing at the outset that much of what follows is hypothetical. For most periods of Russian history, the meaning of "Russia" as a term has not been examined. What scholars have examined is certain (by no means all) manifestations of nationalism, a different if related question. Thus the account that follows, though necessarily presented in declarative form, remains a proposition, not a carefully weighed conclusion based on a massive accumulation of evidence. It relies heavily on texts produced by the better-educated members of the elite and, later, by the intelligentsia, and thus necessarily slights even the "average" nobleman, to say nothing of the peasantry. In the process, I hope not merely to propound a more or less plausible hypothesis, but to suggest how really ignorant we remain of the relevant factors of national identity in Russia, and thus to stimulate further empirical investigation.

---

3. The distinction between Western and Eastern Europe on this issue was most fully articulated in Hans Kohn, *The Idea of Nationalism* (New York, 1944), and other of his writings. More recent studies of national identity and nationalism include William Hagen, *Germans, Poles, and Jews: The Nationality Conflict in the Prussian East, 1772–1914* (Chicago, 1980); Harold James, *A German Identity, 1770 to the Present Day* (London, 1994); Hagen Schulze, *Der Weg zum Nationalstaat* (Munich, 1985); Linda Colley, *Britons: Forging the Nation, 1707–1837* (New Haven, Conn., 1992); E. J. Hobsbawm, *Nations and Nationalism since 1780* (Cambridge, 1990); Ernest Gellner, *Nations and Nationalism* (Oxford, 1983); Benedict Anderson, *Imagined Communities: Reflections on the Origins of Nationalism* (London, 1983); Andrzej Walicki, *Philosophy and Romantic Nationalism: The Case of Poland* (Oxford, 1982); Ole Feldbaek, ed., *Dansk identitetshistorie*, 4 vols. (Copenhagen, 1991–92); and Hagen Schultze, *Staat und Nation in der europäischen Geschichte* (Munich, 1994). The titles of most of these works reflect the primary concern of most Western scholars with nationalism rather than national identity. James, for example, writes of national identity in the title, but in fact describes only nationalism (as does Rogger; see n. 1 above). The basic German debate about the meaning of "Germany" in the nineteenth century was the debate over *Klein-* and *Großdeutschland*, which James ignores. Only Colley and the Danes look at identity rather than just nationalism, trying to see what characteristics made up that identity.

Russia from the Fifteenth Century to the Crimean War

From the formation of the modern Russian state at the end of the fifteenth century until (roughly) the reign of Aleksei Mikhailovich, "Russia" meant the territories under the control of the Riurikovich and, later, the Romanov dynasty. This form of identity did not mean that it was a concept like that of the Habsburg *Erblande*, without national focus, for its basic population consisted of Russians (*russkie, rus'*). As the term *Rossiia* came to replace the older *Rus'* in the fifteenth century, it still included non-Russians, such as Karelians, Mordovians and, later, Tatars. ("Great" and "Little" Russia were church terms not found in official documents or secular sources until the seventeenth century.) The dominance of the dynastic definition may be seen in the conceptions of Russia's history. Already implicit in the Primary Chronicle, the dynastic conception reached full flower in the sixteenth-century *Stepennaia kniga* (Book of Degrees), where Russian history was converted explicitly into the deeds of the Riurikovich dynasty. The foundation legends of the Russian state, such as the *Skazanie o kniaziakh vladimirskikh* (Relation about the Princes of Vladimir), were about the dynasty, not about the land or the people.[4]

The Russian conception of neighboring states was also essentially dynastic. Russian sources of the fifteenth and sixteenth centuries did not understand other East Slavic territories claimed by the Russian tsars to be populated by Russians. The Moscow princes and Russian tsars claimed the Grand Duchy of Lithuania and Livonia as a patrimony (*votchina*)—a dynastic claim. The people who lived in Lithuania were normally called *litva* by Russians, even if they were Orthodox East Slavs. Only the Cossacks, called *cherkasy* (Cherkasians), were distinct. "Russia" was defined by the dynasty, not the people, as was Lithuania in the minds of the Russians. The Russians did not define themselves by Orthodoxy. However central to the consciousness of the dynasty and the nation in other ways, religion was not a defining element, for there were plenty of other Orthodox peoples,

---

4. A. V. Soloviev, *Le nom byzantin de la Russie*, Musagetes 3 (The Hague, 1957); idem, "Velikaia, Malaia i Belaia Rus'," *Voprosy istorii*, 1947, no. 7: 24–38; idem, "Der Begriff 'Rußland' im Mittelalter," *Studien zur älteren Geschichte Osteuropas. Wiener Archiv für Geschichte des Slaventums und Osteuropas*, vol. 2, pt. 1 (1958): 143–68; and Paul Bushkovitch, "The Formation of a National Consciousness in Early Modern Russia," *Harvard Ukrainian Studies* 10, nos. 3–4 (1980): 355–76.

East Slavs and Greeks. Some Russians may have considered the Greeks and Ukrainians imperfectly Orthodox, but that was not a universal view and, in any case, belongs to the realm of national consciousness, not of basic national identity. "Russia" remained a dynastic, that is to say, a statist concept.

Into this relatively simple picture came the war of 1653–67 against Poland and the addition of the eastern Ukrainian lands to Russia. With these events Russia became a composite state rather like Britain, Spain or the Habsburg lands, a fairly common form of state in early modern Europe.[5] For the first time, this development created a potential difference between the dynastic and ethnic meanings of "Russia." The Russians of the 1650s, like their ancestors, knew that the Zaporozhian Cossacks who had asked to come under the tsar's "high hand" were not Russians: they were *cherkasy*, as the Russian internal documents call them. The Russians referred to the Ukrainian territory that they controlled as *cherkasskie goroda* (Cherkasian towns). Very soon the Russian administrators, while continuing to call the Cossacks *cherkasy*, began to refer to the land as *Ukraina*; indeed, this became the norm. *Malorossiia* (Little Russia) was extremely rare, confined to the title of the tsar, the name of the administrative unit in Moscow that dealt with the area, and people like Afanasii Ordin-Nashchokin, who employed a rather arcane and very literary vocabulary in his memoranda.[6]

The effect of the change was to broaden the meaning of "Russia" to include at least one non-Russian unit, one that was understood in the seventeenth century to have the same religion and a related culture, but whose people were not identical with the Russians.

---

5. By composite state I mean one that was both multinational and admitted some form of political or at least administrative autonomy. In Russia, the Ukrainian Hetmanate and, later, the Baltic provinces were the main autonomous units. It should be noted that the conquest of Kazan did not have this effect, for its administration was the same as that of the rest of the state. The status of Tatars as *iasachnye liudi* (people who paid tax in kind) was personal, not regional. Like the Karelians, they became people of a particular status within the dynastic unit of Russia.

6. See, for example, *Akty, otnosiashchiesia k istorii Iuzhnoi i Zapadnoi Rossii*, vol. 9 (St. Petersburg, 1877), pp. 7–22 (Ordin-Nashchokin, 1669). Compare *Akty*, 9: 222–26 (1670, memorandum to the tsar from the Little Russian Chancellery, then under Artamon Matveev, speaks of "Kiev i vsia Ukraina" [Kyiv and all Ukraine]); *Akty*, 10 (1878): 157 (on the way to the Pereiaslav council in October 1653, Buturlin speaks of "educhi dorogoiu do Kieva v cherkaskikh gorodekh" [proceeding along the road to Kyiv in the Cherkasian towns]).

Perhaps, if no more territory had been added, "Russia" would have come to mean only the Great and Little Russia of the terminology used in the church and in the tsar's title, but that was not to be.[7] With the annexation by Peter I of the Baltic provinces in the Northern War, recognized in the Treaty of Nystadt (1721), the Romanov dynasty came to rule yet more lands populated by non-Russians who were more than just a subject rural people. The Romanovs came to rule over two non-Russian elites, the Ukrainian Cossack gentry and the Livonian German nobility, both with autonomous rights recognized by the tsar. Russian elite culture had to accommodate them to the conception of Russia. At the same time, the impact of European political thought in Peter's time meant that the notion of the state began to grow alongside that of the dynasty. It was this cultural change, not any proto-imperialism of the modern kind, that was Peter's contribution to Russian national consciousness.[8]

These changes are apparent in the correspondence and memoranda of Peter the Great and the writings of his contemporaries. Fundamentally, they evince a statist conception, with some influence of church terminology ("Great and Little Russia"). In these sources, the East European plain was divided between Russia and Poland, each with a semi-autonomous political unit, Lithuania and the Hetmanate, the latter normally called simply *Ukraina*. Peter's more learned diplomats had recourse to both usages. In his draft for a history of Peter's rule, Prince Boris Kurakin spoke of a *Vserossiiskaia imperiia* (all-Russian empire) going back to Kyivan times. In his account of Peter's early years (1682–99), Matveev describes them as occuring in the *Velikorossiiskaia imperiia*. In an internal memorandum on Russian

---

7. The use of Great and Little Russia was a result of the Pereiaslav Agreement of 1654. Earlier the tsar was the ruler of *vseia Rusi*; after 1654, of *vseia velikiia i malyia Rusi*.

8. The adoption of the title "Imperator" by Peter I in 1721 had nothing to do with later conceptions of empire, as sometimes asserted in post-Soviet polemics. It reflected rather the desire to give the tsar a title recognizably equal in rank to that of the Holy Roman Emperor, not to found a colonial empire. The act itself gives three reasons for the title: that Peter had advanced Russia's glory, that he had made peace with Sweden, and that Emperor Maximilian had given the title to Russia's rulers (*Polnoe sobranie zakonov Rossiiskoi imperii* [St. Petersburg, 1830–1916], 6: 444–46). Conquest was not mentioned. Wittram saw this correctly: Reinhard Wittram, *Peter I: Czar und Kaiser*, 2 vols. (Göttingen, 1964), 2: 461–67. Peter's Persian campaigns of 1722–23 are the closest to European imperial practice of the time, if they are to be interpreted as commercial in aim, for which see Evgenii Anisimov, *Vremia petrovskikh reform* (Leningrad, 1989), pp. 408–32.

politics of 1720, however, Boris Kurakin's terminology is much less elevated: the army and fleet are simply *rossiiskaia*, and Russia turns out to be made up of various *natsii* besides the Russians, the *cherkasy* or *kazaki ukrainskie*, the Don Cossacks, the Iaik and Grebnia (Terek) Cossacks, the Kalmyks, and the Bashkirs, all of them inclined to rebel in order to recover lost privileges.[9]

Kurakin and Matveev occasionally also reveal the influence of baroque Slavism. This was a learned conception familiar to such well-educated aristocrats, but with few implications for practical affairs and terminology. It affected historical scholarship, not daily life, and derived from Renaissance Slavism, which entered Russia in baroque form in the reign of Tsar Aleksei. Renaissance Slavism arose in Poland, Croatia, and other Slavic lands in an attempt to defend the antiquity and dignity of the Slavs in the context of West European civilization. The Polish Sarmatianists and Mauro Orbini of Dubrovnik (d. 1611) found fanciful genealogies for the Slavs, placing them among the Sarmatian tribes of classical antiquity. In baroque dress, Renaissance Slavism entered Russia from the Kyiv Academy, beginning with Simeon Polotsky, who came to the Russian court in 1669. In his "Orel vserossiiskii" (All-Russian Eagle), Polotsky appropriated Polish Sarmatianism for Russia: "Likui, Rossio, sarmatskoe plemia" (Rejoice, Russia, Sarmatian tribe). Similarly, the Kyiv *Synopsis* of 1681, a history of Russia that included all the Eastern Slavs, located them among the ancient Sarmatians.[10] The *Synopsis* was widely published in eight-

---

9. *Pis'ma i bumagi Petra Velikogo*, 13 vols. (St. Petersburg and Moscow, 1887–1992). See, for example, vol. 3 (St. Petersburg, 1893), p. 84 (F. A. Golovin to Peter, *Ukraina*); vol. 4 (St. Petersburg, 1900), p. 860 (Mazepa to Peter, *Malorossiiskie granitsy*); vol. 5 (St. Petersburg, 1907), p. 248 (Peter I to Prince D. M. Golitsyn, *Ukraina*); A. A. Matveev, "Zapiski" in *Zapiski russkikh liudei: Sobytiia vremen Petra Velikogo* (St. Petersburg, 1841, reprint ed. Hans-Joachim Torke, Newtonville, Mass., 1980), p. 3; and Prince B. I. Kurakin, "*Gistoriia o tsare Petre Alekseeviche*," "*Zapiska o voine i mire s Shvetsiei*," in *Arkhiv kniazia F. A. Kurakina*, vol. 1, pp. 39–78, esp. 39–43, and pp. 340–49, esp. 345–48. In his note of 1707 on the provinces of the *Rossiiskoe* (or *Moskovskoe*) *gosudarstvo*, Kurakin listed the Little Russian towns and Kyiv as being under the "protection" of the tsar, a category in which he also placed the Don Cossacks and the Kalmyks: *Arkhiv ... Kurakina*, vol. 3 (St. Petersburg, 1892), pp. 175–76.

10. Simeon Polotskii, *Orel rossiiskii*, ed. N. A. Smirnov, Obshchestvo liubitelei drevnei pis'mennosti 133 (St. Petersburg, 1915), p. 23; and Hans Rothe, ed., *Sinopsis, Kiev 1681*, Bausteine zur Geschichte der Literatur bei den Slaven 17 (Cologne and Vienna, 1983). The main source of the *Synopsis* was Maciej Stryjkowski's *Kronika polska, litewska, żmodźka i wszystkiey Rusi* (1582), which described the Sarmatian origins of Poland in great detail. See Tadeusz Ulewicz, *Sarmacja: Studium z problematyki słowiańskiej XV i XVI w.*, Biblioteka

eenth-century Russia and went farther than other texts in claiming the essential identity of the Eastern Slavs, but that claim still rested on a dynastic foundation. The influence of such ideas was limited, for the *Synopsis* was soon challenged.

Vasilii Tatishchev already rejected the identification of Slavs with Sarmatians. To be sure, he defended the antiquity and dignity of the Slavs, but he and Mikhail Lomonosov simply added these notions to a political history of Russia that equated it with the ruling dynasty.[11] Both saw the history of the state (virtually identified with the ruling dynasties) as central, but also wished to embellish that history with learned theories demonstrating the antiquity of the Slavs. By the end of the eighteenth century, baroque Slavism and Sarmatianism were dead, killed by changes in historical scholarship and by their irrelevance to the actual ethnic structure of the empire.[12]

Ultimately, baroque Slavism proved an episode in the history of

---

Studium Słowiańskiego Uniwersytetu Jagiellońskiego, series A, no. 7 (Cracow, 1950). For discussions of a similar Renaissance concern with origins in Western Europe, see Claude-Gilbert Dubois, *Celtes et gaulois au XVIe siècle: Le développement littéraire d'un mythe nationaliste* (Paris, 1972); Jacques Ridé, *L'image du germain dans la pensée et la littérature allemandes de la redécouverte de Tacite à la fin du XVIe siècle*, 3 vols. (Lille and Paris, 1977); Ludwig Krapf, *Germanenmythus und Reichsideologie: Frühhumanistische Rezeptionsweisen der taciteischen "Germania"* (Tübingen, 1979); and Richard Helgerson, *Forms of Nationhood: The Elizabethan Writing of England* (Chicago and London, 1992).

The *Synopsis* also proclaimed for the first time that the three East Slavic peoples were really one, the *slaveno-rossiiskii narod*.

11. S. M. Solov'ev, "Pisateli russkoi istorii XVIII veka," in *Sobranie sochinenii* (St. Petersburg, n.d.), pp. 1317–88; V. N. Tatishchev, *Istoriia rrossiiskaia*, 7 vols. (Moscow and Leningrad, 1962–68); M. V. Lomonosov, "Drevniaia rossiiskaia istoriia" [1766], in *Polnoe sobranie sochinenii*, 10 vols. (Moscow and Leningrad, 1950–57), vol. 6 (1952).

Peter (or at least his ministers) was also unsatisfied with existing knowledge on Slavic origins, for he deputed Johann Christoph von Urbich, then the tsar's ambassador to Vienna, to inquire for literature on the origins of the Slavs. The answer from Leibniz merely repeated the Sarmatian theory: V. Ger'e, *Sbornik pisem i memorialov Leibnitsa, otnosiashchikhsia k Rossii i Petru Velikomu* (St. Petersburg, 1873), pp. 209–13 (Urbich to Golovkin, 5 March 1712).

12. Mikhail Shcherbatov's history (1770), conservative in all respects, continued the Sarmatianist tradition. Ivan Boltin broke with this decisively. See M. M. Shcherbatov, *Istoriia Rossiiskaia ot drevneishikh vremen* (St. Petersburg, 1770); I. N. Boltin, *Kriticheskie zamechaniia na pervyi tom Istorii kn. Shcherbatova* (St. Petersburg, 1793). The final blow was undoubtedly the work of August Ludwig Schlözer, which appeared only in 1802. He destroyed the intellectual basis of baroque Slavism by placing the Primary Chronicle (which says nothing of Sarmatians) at the center of the history of Kyivan Rus'.

Russian national consciousness that had no effect on national identity. Eighteenth-century culture in Russia was more significant, for it reinforced the statist element of national identity without eliminating the dynastic conception of the state. Enlightenment thought, in Russia as elsewhere, focused attention on the political structure of the state to the virtual exclusion of other issues. This can be seen not only in political writings (Denis Fonvizin, Aleksandr Radishchev), but also in Russian literature: Aleksandr Sumarokov and Iakov Kniazhnin were concerned with the morality of politics in an absolute monarchy, not with ethnohistory.

Another aspect of eighteenth-century culture that influenced concepts of national identity was modern European ideas of empire, which entered Russia against the background of the victorious wars of Catherine the Great. Insofar as the Russian state was an empire, European ideas of empire in the modern sense referred to a metropolitan state ruling over subject races. The imperial idea expressed more clearly the dominance of the Russian element, but did not succeed in defining that element in ethnic terms. Imperial consciousness largely revolved around Russia's expansion against the Turks and into Transcaucasia, not around European conquests. The new mood was visible in Russian literature. Mikhail Kheraskov devoted his longest efforts to the victory at Chesme ("Chesmenskii boi," 1770) and the conquest of Kazan ("Rossiada," 1779). Gavriil Derzhavin celebrated the later Turkish wars ("Na vziatie Izmaila," 1790–91) and the Caucasian campaign of 1796 ("Na pokorenie Derbenta"). The success of Russia in the Turkish wars, which gave it an international significance it had previously lacked, strengthened the imperial idea. Success also placed Russia in more direct competition with the West European empires, those of Britain and France, over the Ottoman Empire, one of the classic imperial rivalries of the next century. Russian officials even began to advance commercial justifications for expansionist policies, though it is difficult to believe that such justifications were the main reasons for Russian decisions.[13] More likely, Valerian Zubov or even Catherine herself were demonstrating that they saw Russia as similar to Britain or France in its colonial aims.

The imperial idea had its limits, however, for reality did not allow the emergence of a Russian empire similar to those of France or Britain. Georgia and the Crimea did not become Canada or India, and Russia pursued its traditional policy of trying to integrate the elite, with some success in Georgia and almost none in the Crimea. The lands of the old

---

13. Muriel Atkin, *Russia and Iran, 1780–1828* (Minneapolis, 1980), p. 32.

Crimean Khanate became the site of Russian and Ukrainian peasant migration, while Georgia remained a small and distant, if strategically valuable, appendage. The lack of a European-style colonial empire before the 1860s (and the relative insignificance of Central Asia thereafter) meant that the old structures of identity could stay in place, merely adding a few new peoples to those subject to Russia and constituting part of Russian conceptions of Russian identity. "Russia" continued to mean a state, not the land of an ethnic group.[14]

An excellent example of the power of the statist view of Russian identity is one of Pushkin's poems (inspired by Horace, Odes III, 30: "Exegi monumentum aere perennius").

> Слух обо мне пройдет по всей Руси великой,
> И назовет меня всяк сущий в ней язык,
> И гордый внук славян, и финн, и ныне дикий
> Тунгус, и друг степей калмык.

When Pushkin's fame spreads through Russia, it will necessarily include the Slav, the Finn, the Tungus and the Kalmyk. Pushkin implies that each will name him in his own tongue, not necessarily in Russian.[15]

The statist form of identity, including the imperial idea, facilitated the inclusion of various non-Russians in the elite, and their presence in turn strengthened the dynastic, statist conception of Russia. The Russian German general Schubert wrote of his participation in the wars of 1812–15, speaking of Russians as "we" and Germans as "they." In later years, Karl Nesselrode directed Russian foreign policy, and Aleksandr Benckendorf the Third Section. The "official" publicists of the regime of Nicholas I, Faddei Bulgarin, Nikolai Grech, and Osip Senkovsky, included no actual Russians by ethnicity. In reality they

---

14. The focus on the state, with the state understood as an empire, is most clearly apparent in Nikolai Karamzin's history of Russia. He titled his work the history of the Russian *state*, not just of Russia. Karamzin celebrated Ivan the Terrible's conquest of Kazan, whatever his reservations about the rest of the reign. His early chapters on the Slavs naturally present them as the main inhabitants of early Russia, but he also devoted space to the ethnography of the early Finns and other peoples of the empire. N. M. Karamzin, *Istoriia gosudarstva rossiiskogo* (St. Petersburg, 1816–29), esp. book 1.

15. The mention of non-Russians does not come from the imitation of Horace. Horace only speaks of his fame enduring as long as Rome:

> ...Dum Capitolium
> scandet cum tacita virgine pontifex...

He goes on to assert that his fame will rest on his achievement in bringing the Aetolian meters to Rome. Horace makes no mention of other nations, as one would expect of a Roman citizen, for whom they were simply barbarians.

were Tadeusz Bułharyn, a veteran of the Polish cavalry in Napoleon's Grande Armée of 1812, Grech, a Russian German, and Józef-Julian Sękowski, a Polish orientalist from Vilnius (Wilno). Intelligentsia tradition has maintained that the official ideology of the period of Nicholas I was "official nationality," but that was only the ideology of Sergei Uvarov and the Ministry of Education. The cosmopolitan monarchism of Bulgarin, Grech, and Senkovsky was far more important and more official. Furthermore, their conception of "Russian" was not exclusively Great Russian. In his writings on language, Grech maintained that East Slavic was a *iazyk* called Russian, which consisted of three *narechiia*. This terminology may be strange to the modern reader, but it does not signify that Great Russian is a language and Ukrainian merely a dialect.[16] The ideology of these true spokemen of the government of Nicholas I was a sort of cosmopolitan legitimism, appropriate to a multinational empire whose sense of identity was dynastic and statist rather than ethnic.

1855–1905

The identification of Russia with the state in the form of the monarchy persisted long after the monarchy ceased to command universal assent. Russian liberalism did not replace statist identity with an ethnic conception of Russia: it merely formulated an alternative statism. Conservative nationalism also failed to challenge the monarchy effectively on this issue, and its influence remained limited in any case. The liberal attitude was especially important, for some form of liberalism was the dominant ideology of the intelligentsia in this period and attracted some support among the gentry. The result was that these

16. Friedrich von Schubert, *Unter dem Doppeladler* (Stuttgart, 1962); Paul Bushkovitch, "Orthodoxy and Old Rus' in the Thought of S. P. Shevyrev," *Forschungen zur osteuropäischen Geschichte* 46 (1992): 203–20; and Cynthia Whittaker, *The Origins of Modern Russian Education: An Intellectual Biography of Count Sergei Uvarov, 1786–1855* (DeKalb, Ill., 1984). Paradoxically (to the modern reader), in this generation the imperial and statist conception implied a more favorable view of the non-Russians than those that preceded or followed it. Ukraine and even Poland (until 1830) appeared in a favorable light in Russian literature, and writers celebrated Finland (Baratynsky) and Livonia (Lazhechnikov, Bestuzhev-Marlinsky). On the positive view of the non-Russians up to the Crimean War, see Vasyl' Sypovs'kyi, *Ukraïna v rosiis'komu pys'menstvi. Ch. 1 (1801–1850 rr.)*, Zbirnyk Istorychno-filolohichnoho viddilu Vseukraïns'koi akademiï nauk 58 (Kyiv, 1928); and Paul Bushkovitch, "The Ukraine in Russian Culture, 1790–1860: The Evidence of the Journals," *Jahrbücher für Geschichte Osteuropas* 39, no. 3 (1991): 339–63. (On Grech's linguistic theories, see Bushkovitch, "Ukraine," p. 348, n. 20.)

changes in national consciousness either reinforced statism or were not strong enough to formulate an ethnic conception of Russia.

The liberals, to be sure, paid little attention to issues of national identity.[17] Like the intelligentsia as a whole, they concerned themselves with general social issues and Russia's political structure. Serfdom and autocracy were debated endlessly; nationality was not. As the Ukrainian publicist Mykhailo Drahomanov put it in 1873: "Russian society is wholly indifferent to nationalism, placing (like almost all societies of the great political units that long ago attained extensive state boundaries, such as England or France) at the forefront socio-cultural questions and the matter of the development and order of one's own house. For this reason, Pan-Slavism, Russophilism, and Ukrainophilism ... are all little valued in Russia."[18]

The major liberal journals, *Russkii vestnik* (to 1863), Chicherin's short-lived *Atenei*, and even *Vestnik Evropy* (at first) barely touched on the question. By 1868, however, the latter had to say something, and a clear statement appeared: "In our Russia...the Russian state is greater than the national (*natsional'nyi*) principle." The author went on to say that all sorts of nationalities could exist side by side in Russia, and the nation was Russian only in the political sense, that is, it constituted a Russian state. Indeed, it would be deleterious to the unity of the state if the Poles or Tatars were to cease to be nationalities and become nations. The term "nation" was here reserved for state-nations such as France or Russia. The article was both a political program and a conception of national identity. Its author was one Leonid Polonsky, that is, the Pole Leon Połoński, who remained one of *Vestnik Evropy*'s principal political writers for several decades. That a Pole should express the journal's view on national questions was no accident. Most of the articles on Ukrainian affairs came from Mykola Kostomarov, and on Slavic matters Drahomanov was a principal spokesman. The Slavist A. N. Pypin was one of the few actual Russians to write on such matters in the journal, and he naturally shared its perspective.[19]

---

17. On mid-century liberalism see, most recently, Gary M. Hamburg, *Boris Chicherin and Early Russian Liberalism, 1828–1866* (Stanford, 1992). Typical liberal writings ignore national issues: see, e.g., Boris Chicherin, *Neskol'ko sovremennykh voprosov* (Moscow, 1862); or P. V. Dolgorukov, *Des réformes en Russie* (Paris, Brussels, and Leipzig, 1862).

18. M. P. Drahomanov, "Literatura rosiis'ka, velykorus'ka, ukraïns'ka i halyts'ka," in his *Literaturno-publitsystychni pratsi*, 2 vols. (Kyiv, 1970), 1: 86.

19. [L. A. Polonskii], "Ezhemesiachnaia khronika," *Vestnik Evropy*, 1869, no. 1: 389–400; *Ėntsiklopedicheskii slovar' Brokgauz-Efron* (St. Petersburg, 1891–1904), 14: 649, s.v. *Vestnik Evropy* and 47: 360–61, s.v. Polonskii, Leonid Aleksandro-

Such radicals as Nikolai Chernyshevsky and Dmitrii Pisarev were, if anything, even less interested in the subject than the liberals.[20]

Movement toward an ethnic definition of Russia came from the conservatives. The most famous in this respect are the Slavophiles, though their transition to Russian ethnic identity was hardly complete. Fundamentally they were interested more in the greater problem of Russia and Europe than in the specifics of identity, but they did have views on that subject. Before the Crimean War the Slavophiles preferred a terminology that stressed Slavs rather than just Russians. After the war, some of them (for example, Ivan Aksakov) began to speak more of Russia, and tended to mean Russian culture when they spoke of Slavic culture. For most Slavophiles, Russians themselves were a sort of meta-people whose language, Russian, was made up of the "dialects" of Great Russian and Ukrainian. Thus the Slavophiles, for all their nationalism, did not see their country as an ethnic state of the Great Russians. Even if they had developed such a vision, their limited influence would have prevented the adoption of their notions.[21]

---

vich; Zygmunt Łukasiński, "Połoński, Leon," *Polski Słownik Biograficzny* (Cracow, 1935ff.), 27: 352. See also Pypin's articles on Pan-Slavism reprinted in A. N. Pypin, *Panslavizm v proshlom i nastoiashchem* (St. Petersburg, 1913); M. T-ov [M. Drahomanov], "Vostochnaia politika Germanii i obrusenie," *Vestnik Evropy*, 1872, February: 640–94, March: 183–241, April: 644–79, May: 210–53 (reprinted in M. P. Drahomanov, *Politicheskie sochineniia*, vol. 1 [Moscow, 1908], ed. I. M. Grevs and B. A. Kistiakovskii); N. I. Kostomarov, "Malorusskoe slovo," *Vestnik Evropy* (January 1881): 401–7; "Po povodu malorusskogo slova 'Sovremennym Izvestiiam,'" ibid. (March 1881): 359–65; "Esche po povodu malorusskogo slova 'Moskovskim Vedomost'iam,'" ibid. (April 1881): 764–71; "Po povodu stat'i g. de-Pule v 'Russkom Vestnike,'" ibid. (May 1882): 434–37; A. N. Pypin, "K sporam ob ukrainofil'stve," ibid. (May 1882): 438–42.

20. The radicals of the 1860s and the populist generation as a whole saw Russian life as a great conflict of State and People, both rather nebulous abstractions that excluded national concerns. They believed that the area of settlement of the Russian people (however defined) needed to be broken up into smaller units, albeit with the same language and culture.

Bakunin's *Gosudarstvennost' i anarkhiia* (1873) was the only work of a radical of that era to evince national concerns. It depicted the Russian state as the result of an entirely alien, German (and Jewish) principle of statehood. The Slavs, by contrast, were natural anarchists: Michael Bakunin, *Gosdarstvennost' i anarkhiia*, in *Archives Bakounine*, ed. A. Lehning, 7 vols. (Leiden, 1963–81), vol. 6: *Etatisme et anarchie* (1967).

21. Khomiakov saw the three East Slavic peoples as branches of the "Russian" people: A. S. Khomiakov, *Polnoe sobranie sochinenii*, 7 vols. (Moscow, 1900), 3: 285–88. The Slavist A. N. Pypin, though basically a liberal, shared this view: A. N. Pypin, *Moi zametki* (Moscow, 1910), pp. 36–39. The Slavophile press was small in circulation and, as early as the 1860s, required various forms of subsidy from Moscow

Mikhail Katkov was much more of a true nationalist. For him, Russian nationalism was, together with autocracy, a central idea and value. His Russia was not only a state but a nation (*narod*) and a nationality (*natsional'nost'*). It possessed a definable spirit and had distinct national, not just state, interests that needed to be defended. Katkov did not see Russia as, first and foremost, part of the larger Slavic community, and by "Russians" he meant Great Russians, not a higher unity of three distinct "tribes." The state was to be understood as the emanation of a narrowly conceived ethnic consciousness, secondary to the nation (ethnos). In policy it was to be assimilationist and in culture intolerant of national minorities. This analogy is no mere accident. The American historian Martin Katz has called Katkov a "conservative Westernizer," and this label is in many ways accurate.[22] For Katkov, imperial Germany was the great enemy, but also the great model.

But how representative was Katkov of the conservative camp? In many ways, Dostoevsky or N. N. Strakhov were similar in their views of Russia, though they lacked Katkov's desire to emulate Germany. The government, however, was another matter. On the cultural level (church-building, court festivals) it paid a certain tribute to "Russianness," but its policies were couched in terms that held to the statist and dynastic concept of Russia. This was true even in some of the more famous cases of Russification, such as the policies of General N. I. Bobrikov in Finland. In a memorandum to the tsar proposing a new policy, Bobrikov complained that in Finland "Russian views and Russian feelings are not taken into account" and promised more Russian officials and the use of Russian in the administration and in the Finnish Senate. His notorious programmatic speech in Helsingfors on 30 September 1898 presented the ideal of unity (*edinenie*) with Russia—hardly a call for assimilation, whatever it meant. The conservative newspaper *Novoe vremia* praised the speech for its defense of Russian state interests; for Bobrikov's political sagacity (*gosudarstvennyi smysl*).[23] The views of conservatives among the

---

industrialists in order to survive: Thomas C. Owen, "The Moscow Merchants and the Public Press," *Jahrbücher für Geschichte Osteuropas* 23, no. 1 (March 1975): 26–38.

22. Martin Katz, *Mikhail N. Katkov: A Political Biography, 1818–1887* (The Hague and Paris, 1966); [M. N. Katkov], *Sobranie peredovykh statei "Moskovskikh vedomostei"*, 24 vols. (Moscow, 1897–98), vol. 4, *1865* (16 June), pp. 351–54, noting the predominance of one nationality in Western European states; and vol. 6, *1867* (19 September), pp. 523–27, denying the existence of a Ukrainian nationality.

23. M[ikhail] Borodkin, *Iz noveishei istorii Finliandii* (St. Petersburg, 1905), pp. 66–71 (with text of the speech); "Rech' finliandskogo general-gubernatora," *Novoe vremia*, 2/14 October 1898, pp. 1–2. *Novoe vremia*'s other comments

gentry and at court remain to be investigated, but until 1905 we should probably start from the hypothesis that their conceptions of Russia remained dynastic and thus "statist," not Katkovian.

1905–1917

The 1905 Revolution, as is widely recognized, moved Russia sharply in the direction of a more modern political structure and more contemporary forms of political thought. One little-noticed effect of this process was the sharp rise of nationalism, both Russian and non-Russian.[24] Nevertheless, among Russians at least, a purely ethnic conception of Russia was to be found only in the views of certain conservatives, not in the government or among liberals and the left.

The most striking symptom of the new atmosphere was the appearance of a nationalist and even imperialist stream within liberalism. In politics this meant primarily the Struve group among the Constitutional Democrats (Kadets). The were joined in this by the Riabushinsky-Trubetskoi circle, represented both by the *Progressisty* party and the publication of *Velikaia Rossiia*.[25] The collection *Vekhi* barely touched on national issues, but its opponents (including Ukrainian and Jewish spokesmen) understood its editorial line to imply espousal or at least collaboration with Russian nationalism. If *Vekhi* offered little on national issues, some of its authors elaborated on them elsewhere. In Petr Struve's journalism of the time, he saw Russia as a "national Russian state," albeit with two unassimilable

---

about the speech were that Russia must have a single throne and administration (i.e., not merely a personal union with Finland), that autonomy was perfectly fine as long as it did not violate the organic unity of the empire (*organicheskoe edinstvo imperii*), and that the Finnish and Russian peoples should have the same aims of unity and culture (*edinenie i kul'tura*), whatever that meant. None of this, unpleasant as it was for the Finnish national movement, sounds like ethnic assimilation.

For the larger context, see Tuomo Polvinen, *Imperial Borderland: Bobrikov and the Attempted Russification of Finland* (1995); and George C. Schoolfield, *Helsinki of the Czars: Finland's Capital, 1808–1918* (Columbia, S. C., 1995), p. 205.

24. On Russian nationalist currents, see Caspar Ferenczi, "Nationalismus und Neoslawismus im Rußland vor dem ersten Weltkrieg," *Forschungen zur osteuropäischen Geschichte* (Berlin) 34 (1984): 1–128.

25. The avowed imperialism of Struve and the *Progressisty* came in part from European liberal traditions, for their explicit models were French and, particularly, British imperialism, both the reality and the theory (J. R. Seeley). See Martyna Agata Fox, "The Eastern Question in Russian Politics: The Interplay of Diplomacy, Opinion, and Interest, 1905–1917," Ph.D. dissertation, Yale University, 1993.

appendages—Poland and Finland. Struve was a great admirer of the British Empire, whose core in the British Isles he regarded as a "national state" like Germany. In the view of the Ukrainian Maksym Slavinsky (1868–1945), *Vekhi* represented a change from the traditional "full neutralization of nationalist characteristics" on the part of the Russian intelligentsia, signaling a new move by Struve and others toward chauvinism. Slavinsky also rejected Struve's admiration of Western Europe. He agreed with Struve that England, France, and the United States were ethnic states like Germany, exemplifying the dominance of one nation over others within the state and the destruction of minority cultures, but he did not approve.[26] Struve and the *Progressisty* were harbingers of the future, but until 1917 most Kadets, and the liberal intelligentsia generally, held to the older statist conception of Russian identity. The violent response to *Vekhi* demonstrated the isolation of Struve on this issue, as on others.

The clearest shift away from statism toward a sort of ethnic nationalism seems to have taken place among the Nationalists, both Duma politicians and their journalistic spokesmen. Unfortunately, work on the political activity of the Nationalists has not been matched by similar studies of their ideology. As far as can be made out from existing studies, the Nationalists quite definitely had a strictly ethnic conception of Russia, owing perhaps in part to the influence of the Kyiv Right (Vasilii Shulgin and others). The Octobrists seem to have supported the government on this issue, as on most others, which meant the avoidance of ethnic nationalism.[27] The government held to the idea of Russia as a state. In 1910, the issue of Finland came up before the Duma, and Stolypin's government proposed a new legal framework for Finland that was essentially Bobrikov's old program of

---

26. See *Vekhi* (Moscow, 1909); P. B. Struve, "Velikaia Rossiia" (1908) and "Politika vnutrennaia i politika vneshnaia" (1910), in *Patriotica* (St. Petersburg, 1911), pp. 73–96, 274–88. "Polnaia neitralizatsiia natsionalisticheskikh ochertanii": M. Slavinskii, "Russkaia intelligentsiia i natsional'nyi vopros," in *Intelligentsiia v Rossii* (St. Petersburg, 1910), pp. 220–34, quotation 232, a collection of liberal replies to *Vekhi*. See also *Po vekham: Sbornik statei ob intelligentsii i natsional'nom litse*, 2d ed. (Moscow, 1909), especially the contributions by Maksim Vinaver, Vladimir Zh[abotinsky?], and M. Slavinsky. On the controversy, see Gisela Oberländer, *Die Vechi-Diskussion (1909–1912)* (Cologne, 1965); and Richard Pipes, *Struve: Liberal on the Right* (Cambridge, Mass., 1980), pp. 90–97, 106–14.

27. Ben-Cion Pinchuk, *The Octobrists in the Third Duma, 1907–1912* (Seattle, 1974); and Robert Edelman, *Gentry Politics on the Eve of the Russian Revolution: The Nationalist Party, 1907–1917* (New Brunswick, N.J., 1980). On nationality issues, see A. Ia. Avrekh, *Stolypin i tret'ia duma* (Moscow, 1968), pp. 44–91.

1898: Russians were to be allowed to serve in the Finnish administration; Russian was to be the administrative language (at least at higher levels); military service was to be introduced; and other similar enactments. V. F. Deitrikh, once Bobrikov's assistant, introduced the bill, stating that "Russia is a single and indivisible state, and Finland is an integral part of it that is guaranteed extensive self-administration and legislation only in internal affairs." Stolypin defended the bill, adding nothing to Deitrikh's assertions.[28] The government saw Russia as a state, not as an ethnic unit.

Conclusion

Historians of Russia, at least in the West, are used to noting the time lag in the appearance of common ideas and phenomena in Russia. Issues of national identity, I would propose, are no different.

The existence of a fairly pure dynastic conception of Russia was beginning to be anachronistic even in the sixteenth century. By then, the Renaissance had had its effect in the West, adding learned fantasies of national origin to existing conceptions of dynasty and state. National ideas continued to develop, in some cases in association with a statist conception of nationhood, in other cases inclining more toward ethnic identity. Russia remained in the dynastic statist world. Only after the Crimean War did a liberal non-dynastic statist conception arise, and it remained an oppositional ideology. Ethnic conceptions of Russia similar to that of Germany after 1871 remained a fringe phenomenon, even among conservatives, until at least 1905.

The persistence into the early twentieth century of dynastic statism is without precedent in Europe, save in the anomalous case of Austria-Hungary. The dynastic statism that dominated conceptions of the Russian state had real roots in archaic features of Russian life, mainly in the persistence of autocracy and the structures that supported it. The adoption of liberal statism, as in France, or the more strictly ethnic model of Germany was not possible in Russia as long as the old regime persisted.

The liberal statism of the Russian intelligentsia was also partly out of phase with its European counterparts. In asserting a statist conception of Russian identity, they showed no originality, but merely

---

28. E. V. [Ekaterina Verpakhovskaia], *Gosudarstvennaia deiatel'nost' predsedatelia Soveta ministrov stats-sekretaria Petra Arkad'evicha Stolypina*, 3 vols. (St. Petersburg, 1911), 1: 148–63: "Rossiia—edinoe i nerazdel'noe gosudarstvo, a Finliandiia—ee integral'naia chast', kotoroi obezpechivaetsia shirokoe samoupravlenie i zakonodatel'stvo lish' vo vnutrennikh delakh."

followed the traditions of liberalism more typical of France or Western Europe than of Central and Eastern Europe. At the same time, until 1905 Russian liberals lagged behind their European counterparts in many ways. Indeed, before 1917 they did not generally espouse the shrill chauvinism that was common currency farther west, even in France and Britain. However, the presence of Struve and his friends demonstrates that the time was coming when Russian liberals would move in that direction. The First World War pushed many toward chauvinism, as did the Revolution and emigration after 1917.

Given this history, it is perhaps not so surprising that the Bolsheviks tried to build a sort of transnational political identity in the Soviet Union. In the process, however, they began to reduce Russia to something of an ethnic state like present-day Croatia or Serbia. Whether statist or ethnic conceptions will ultimately prevail in Russia is a matter for the future.

Andreas Kappeler

Mazepintsy, Malorossy, Khokhly: Ukrainians in the Ethnic Hierarchy of the Russian Empire

Every national historiography tends to treat its nation as *sui generis*. Rare is the comparison with other nations or the measured consideration of the overarching context of the multiethnic empire. This holds true for the history of the Ukrainians in the tsarist and Soviet states. In the present article, I propose to examine some of the structural elements of the Russian Empire and determine the status of the Ukrainians within its "ethnic hierarchy."

In the Russian Empire, as in other premodern polyethnic empires, ethnic factors such as language, culture and, frequently, religion played a subordinate role.[1] The decisive elements of legitimation and organization were the ruler and the dynasty, the estate system of society, and the imperial mindset. Showing loyalty to ruler and empire and belonging to an estate were more important than belonging to an ethnic or confessional group.

Nevertheless, the more than one hundred ethnic groups counted in the national census of the tsarist empire in 1897 were not regarded by the imperial center as having equal status, but were arranged in an informal hierarchy that was very important to tsarist policy and perception.

I have identified three hierarchies, one based on the criterion of political loyalty, a second on estate and social criteria, and a third on

---

1. See Marc Raeff, "Patterns of Russian Imperial Policy toward the Nationalities," in Edward Allworth, ed., *Soviet Nationality Problems* (New York, 1971), pp. 22–42; S. Frederick Starr, "Tsarist Government: The Imperial Dimension," in Jeremy R. Azrael, ed., *Soviet Nationality Policies and Practices* (New York, 1978), pp. 3–38; Edward C. Thaden and Marianna Forster Thaden, *Russia's Western Borderlands, 1710–1870* (Princeton, N.J., 1984); N. I. Tsimbaev, "Rossiia i russkie (natsional'nyi vopros v Rossiiskoi imperii)," in *Russkii narod: istoricheskaia sud'ba v XX veke* (Moscow, 1993), pp. 39–50; Dominic Lieven, "The Russian Empire and the Soviet Union as Imperial Polities," *Journal of Contemporary History* 30, no. 4 (1995): 607–36; and my book, *Rußland als Vielvölkerreich: Entstehung, Geschichte, Zerfall* (Munich, 1992); English ed.: *The Russian Empire: A Multiethnic History* (Harlow, 2001). The most important sources and works that appeared up to 1991 are listed in the latter work.

cultural criteria, such as religion, way of life, or language. These three hierarchies interacted. They were not static: the classification of individual ethnic groups and the relative importance of the three hierarchies changed over the centuries. This model of three hierarchies considered as ideal types has never been explicitly formulated. It could feasibly be applied to other multiethnic empires, such as the Habsburg or Ottoman empires.

The Hierarchy of Political Loyalty

The loyalty of subjects to the ruler and the dynasty was a linchpin of the Russian Empire. The center's first priority was to secure power and sociopolitical stability; hence the loyalty of the non-Russians in the peripheral regions was of prime importance. From the viewpoint of the tsarist government, the ethnic groups of the empire were arranged in an (unofficial) hierarchy according to the degree of their (actual or suspected) loyalty. Most of the nomads and, later, the Poles and Jews were regarded as unreliable subjects, while the German Balts, Finns, and Armenians, until the mid-nineteenth century, were regarded as faithful servants of the tsar.

In the seventeenth century, the Ukrainians were perceived by the imperial center as unreliable Cossacks (*cherkasy*). The Cossacks were seen, to some extent, as inhabitants of the steppe and consequently regarded, like the Kalmyks, Crimean Tatars and other mounted nomads, as rebels and potential traitors.[2] The frequent political vacillations of Bohdan Khmelnytsky and his followers among Russia, Poland-Lithuania, the Crimean Khanate, and the Ottoman Empire increased this mistrust. It reached its climax with the defection of Ivan Mazepa, who was subsequently regarded in Russia as a prototypical traitor. From the eighteenth century, the center viewed at least some Ukrainians as disloyal separatists or Mazepists (*mazepintsy*).

The gradual integration of the Cossack upper stratum of the Hetmanate into the Russian nobility reduced the center's mistrust of the Ukrainian elite. Beginning in the mid-eighteenth century, many of its representatives, such as Kyrylo Rozumovsky, Oleksander Bezborodko, Petro Zavadovsky, and Viktor Kochubei, entered the service of the rulers of Russia. The restive Cossacks and Mazepists gradually

---

2. See Hans-Joachim Torke, "The Unloved Alliance: Political Relations between Muscovy and Ukraine in the Seventeenth Century," in *Ukraine and Russia in their Historical Encounter*, ed. Peter J. Potichnyj et al. (Edmonton, 1992), pp. 39–66; Andreas Kappeler, "Das Moskauer Reich des 17. Jahrhunderts und seine nichtrussischen Untertanen," *Forschungen zur osteuropäischen Geschichte* 50 (1995): 185–98.

turned into "Little Russians" (*malorossy*) and loyal servants of the dynasty. Accordingly, in the first half of the nineteenth century, a positive image of the "Little Russians" as a picturesque variant of the Russian people was dominant in official circles and in Russian society generally.[3] Although the elite of the Hetmanate rose in the hierarchy of loyalty as a result of its steady integration into the Russian elite, the stereotype of the traitorous "Mazepists" was revived at the end of the nineteenth century in order to delegitimize representatives of the Ukrainian national movement and associate them with the Poles and with Austria-Hungary.

In the mid-nineteenth century, the Poles, Jews, Crimean Tatars, and North Caucasians were at the bottom of the hierarchy of political loyalty, while the German Balts, Armenians, and Finns were at the top. In the last quarter of the century, these last three ethnic groups lost their reputation one after another as faithful servants of the tsar and slid down the pyramid of loyalty. This was associated with the rise of national consciousness and the concomitant cultural hierarchization of the empire's ethnic groups. The Ukrainians, too, descended the hierarchy once again. This was a result of the Ukrainian national movement's presentation of its first political demands and of the belief that the Ukrainians were in close association with the Poles, who had become the very embodiment of traitors after the uprising of 1863. It is no accident that the modest demands of the Ukrainian national movement were referred to as "Polish" or "Jesuit" intrigues. The reason for this association with the Poles may be found in the estate hierarchy.

The Estate Hierarchy

From the sixteenth century, the central principle guaranteeing the coherence of the Russian Empire was the cooptation of non-Russian elites into the imperial upper stratum.[4] This corresponded to the

---

3. See David Saunders, *The Ukrainian Impact on Russian Culture, 1750–1850* (Edmonton, 1985); Paul Bushkovitch, "The Ukraine in Russian Culture, 1790–1860: The Evidence of the Journals," *Jährbücher für Geschichte Osteuropas* 39 (1991): 339–63; and Marc Raeff, "Ukraine and Imperial Russia: Intellectual and Political Encounters from the Seventeenth to the Nineteenth Century," in *Ukraine and Russia in Their Historical Encounter*, pp. 69–85.

4. See the literature cited in note 1. For a short summary, see Andreas Kappeler, "Vkliuchenie nerusskikh elit v rossiiskoe dvorianstvo XVI-XIX vv. Kratkii obzor problemy," in *Sosloviia i gosudarstvennaia vlast' v Rossii: XVI–seredina XIX vv. Mezhdunarodnaia konferentsiia. Chteniia pamiati akad. L. V. Cherepnina. Tezisy dokladov* (Moscow, 1994), pp. 215–25.

estate structure of the tsarist empire and its most important political element, the alliance of the ruler with the nobility. The model for this elite was the Russian nobility as it had emerged in Muscovy and consolidated its position in the eighteenth-century empire.

In determining the hierarchical status of the non-Russian ethnic groups, which were constantly changing in number, it was therefore critically important whether they possessed their own elites, whether those elites were loyal to the tsar, and whether they conformed to the model of the Russian nobility. If they owned landed property with dependent peasants and had an advanced culture recognized as autonomous, they were recognized as equals of the Russian nobility and, along with the Russians, were assigned a place at the top of the hierarchy.

As early as the sixteenth century, those members of the loyal Muslim Volga Tatar elite who had not been killed or put to flight were coopted into the imperial nobility and even provided with Russian Christian peasants. They were followed in the seventeenth century by the Polonized *szlachta* of Smolensk; in the eighteenth century by the German Baltic and Polish nobility; and in the nineteenth century by the Finnish-Swedish, Romanian-Bessarabian, and Georgian nobility, as well as (with some restrictions) the Muslim aristocracy of the Crimea, Transcaucasia, and several ethnic groups of the North Caucasus. By the last third of the nineteenth century, however, the Muslim aristocrats of Central Asia were no longer being coopted into the imperial nobility. In principle, the Russian nobles enjoyed no special estate privileges vis-à-vis the coopted non-Russians, just as Russian city dwellers and peasants found themselves in an even worse legal and social position than many non-Russians.

The non-Russian elites received a guarantee of their privileges and their landed property (with dependent peasants), as well as freedom of religion. In time, their position came to approximate that of the Russian nobility. In return, like the Russian nobles, they were required to serve the tsar in the army and bureaucracy and to guarantee sociopolitical stability in their regions. This principle of cooperation remained in force until the mid-nineteenth century. The fact that the coopted elites included non-Orthodox and even non-Christian groups shows that the autocracy set greater store by the estate principle than by Orthodoxy (*pravoslavie*) and nationality (*narodnost'*).

If the coopted elites withdrew or appeared to withdraw their loyalty to the tsar, the government revoked some of their privileges. The first to experience this, after the uprisings of 1830–31 and 1863, were the Poles. Since loyalty to the ruler and the dynasty was a precondition of the official alliance with the elites, this was a predictable reaction. The estate hierarchy and the hierarchy of loyalty were thus closely interrelated.

At the next level of the social hierarchy were ethnic groups with elites that did not conform to the model of the Russian nobility. Privileges and certain rights of self-government were also guaranteed to these elites, although they were not regarded as equals of the Russian nobles, and, with the exception of individual dignitaries, were not coopted into the nobility of the empire. This group consisted mainly of inhabitants of peripheral regions in the East and South of the empire, nomads such as the Bashkirs, Kalmyks, and Buriats in the seventeenth and eighteenth centuries and the Kazakhs in the nineteenth.

The Ukrainians of the Hetmanate with their Cossack elite were also regarded by Moscow as belonging to the steppe population; in the seventeenth century, they could be assigned to the second level of the hierarchy.[5] Basically, the elites of the ethnic groups belonging to this category had two prospects: either they achieved recognition as nobles or they were demoted to the status of state peasants or aliens (*inorodtsy*). While the Ukrainian Cossack aristocracy took the first path and its members gradually became "Little Russians," in the course of the nineteenth century the imperial center became steadily less willing to recognize the nomadic elites as equal partners. Thus the second level of the hierarchy gradually disappeared.

As a rule, ethnic groups with no indigenous elites could not become partners of the tsarist empire. Incidentally, this applied in part to mobilized diaspora groups of Jews, Armenians, and Greeks, and in the nineteenth century to the Volga Tatars as well, all of whom had an urban middle stratum and an independent church.[6] The tsarist state had long depended on particular complementary skills of these groups and therefore worked together with them, coopting their elites into the upper urban strata. Rich merchants and religious dignitaries were in part able to assume the role of the noble elite as partners with the empire. These diaspora groups may therefore be assigned to the third level of the estate pyramid.

On the fourth level were several ethnic groups living in the eastern part of the empire. While they possessed no indigenous nobility and were made up mostly of peasants, they were not dependent on foreign landowners. This applies to the Chuvash,

---

5. See Kappeler, "Das Moskauer Reich."

6. On this concept, see John A. Armstrong, "Mobilized and Proletarian Diasporas," *American Political Science Review* 70, no. 2 (1976): 393–406.

Mordvinians, Mari, Udmurts, Votiaks, Komi, Iakuts, and other ethnic groups of Siberia, as well as several mountain peoples of the Caucasus, such as the Chechens.

At the bottom of the imperial hierarchy were ethnic groups consisting predominantly of peasants and dependent on the elites of other ethnic groups. Together with the aforementioned ethnic groups assigned to the fourth level, they are referred to in comparative research on nationalism as "small" or "young" peoples, possessing neither an indigenous elite nor a continuous tradition of statehood, a standard language or an advanced culture.[7] In the Russian Empire, this category included the Finns, Estonians, Latvians, Lithuanians, Belarusians, and the Ukrainians who had been ruled by the Polish-Lithuanian Commonwealth until the partitions. For a long time, the center did not regard these peasant peoples as independent ethnic groups or political subjects, acknowledging them only in connection with the superordinate nobles. Consequently, the imperial center long associated the Estonians and Latvians with the German Balts and the Lithuanians, Belarusians, and (Right-Bank) Ukrainians with the Poles.

The estate hierarchy, ranging from ethnic groups possessing a landowning nobility down to the peasant peoples with no medium or upper stratum, was an important structural element of the tsarist empire. It also determined the hierarchy of cultures and languages. Only those ethnic groups with their own elites could possess advanced cultures and standard languages; namely, in addition to the Russians, the Poles, Swedish Finns, German Balts, and Tatars, and, within limits, the Jews, Armenians, and Georgians. The languages of the other ethnic groups, which generally lacked a literary standard (the Ukrainian language included), were not officially acknowledged.

It was characteristic of the Ukrainians that they were originally assigned to two different levels of the ethnic hierarchy: the Ukrainians of the Cossack Hetmanate to the second level and those Ukrainians

---

7. Miroslav Hroch, *Social Preconditions of National Revival in Europe: A Comparative Analysis of the Social Composition of Patriotic Groups among the Smaller European Nations* (Cambridge, 1985); and Józef Chlebowczyk, *On Small and Young Nations in Europe* (Wrocław, 1980). On the Ukrainians, see Ivan L. Rudnytsky, "Observations on the Problem of 'Historical' and 'Non-Historical' Nations," *Harvard Ukrainian Studies* 5, no. 3 (1981): 358–68; George G. Grabowicz, "Some Further Observations on 'Non-Historical' Nations and 'Incomplete' Literatures: A Reply," ibid., 369–88; and Andreas Kappeler, "Ein 'kleines Volk' von 25 Millionen: Die Ukrainer um 1900," in M. Alexander et al., ed., *Kleine Völker in der Geschichte Osteuropas: Festschrift für Günther Stökl zum 75. Geburtstag* (Stuttgart, 1991), pp. 33–42; abridged translation in *Journal of Ukrainian Studies* 18, nos. 1–2 (1993): 85–92.

who came under Russian rule only at the end of the eighteenth century to the lowest level. It is true that by the end of the eighteenth century the Cossack elite of the Hetmanate had been coopted into the nobility of the empire and thus in theory met the preconditions for advancement to the first level of the pyramid.[8] The simultaneous gradual acculturation of the Cossack nobility to the Russian nobility meant, however, that the *malorossy* were no longer regarded by the center as an independent ethnic group. Since the "Little Russian" nobility was equal in status to the Russian nobility and increasingly perceived as Russian, all Ukrainians of the former Hetmanate were regarded as a regional variant of the Russians and dropped out of the ethnic hierarchy entirely. If they were accepted as an indigenous ethnic group, they descended to the lowest level, that of a peasant people ruled by a foreign (Russian) elite. Furthermore, the partitions of Poland brought a large number of Ukrainians under Russian rule, most of whom were dependent on the Polish nobility and therefore assigned to the level of peasant peoples. Thus, in the course of the nineteenth century, the mass of the Ukrainian people became *khokhly*—prototypes of uncivilized peasants—in the eyes of the Russians.[9] The Ukrainians were no longer direct objects of tsarist policy, but were regarded as a function of the Polish and Russian or Russified elite dominant in their region.

The government's view of the Ukrainians as closely connected with the Poles continued to influence tsarist policy in the second half of the nineteenth century. At the same time, however, the tsarist government began to move away from the principle of cooperation with the non-Russian nobles and tried, through the agrarian reforms of 1863 and 1864, to play off the Polish, Lithuanian, Belarusian, and Ukrainian peasants against their Polish masters. This policy was by no means consistently applied, at least in Right-Bank Ukraine.[10] By the time of the Revolution of 1905, if not earlier, the government

---

8. Zenon E. Kohut, *Russian Centralism and Ukrainian Autonomy: Imperial Absorption of the Hetmanate, 1760s-1830s* (Cambridge, Mass., 1988); Saunders, *The Ukrainian Impact*; and Marc Raeff, "Some Observations on Russo-Ukrainian Relations in the 18th and Early 19th Centuries (Primarily Cultural from a Russian Perspective)," in Teresa Chynczewska-Hennel et al., eds., *Między Wschodem a Zachodem: Rzeczpospolita XVI-XVIII w. Studia ofiarowane Zbigniewowi Wójcikowi w siedemdziesiątą rocznicę urodzin* (Warsaw, 1993), pp. 179–86.

9. See Serhy Yekelchyk, "The Grand Narrative and Its Discontents," in the present volume.

10. Daniel Beauvois, *La bataille de la terre en Ukraine 1863–1914: Les Polonais et les conflits socio-ethniques* (Lille, 1993).

realized that this course of action was undermining the basis of the autocracy.

Cultural Circles

Estate categories were dominant in defining the hierarchy of ethnic groups in the Russian Empire. Admittedly, from the eighteenth century on they were challenged and partially eclipsed by cultural factors. The first of these factors was confession/religion, which had always been an official criterion of demarcation, but had remained subordinate to the estate principle. In the first half of the eighteenth century, non-Christians were briefly segregated as adherents of different faiths (*inovertsy*). The enlightened absolutism of Catherine II lessened the importance of religion and brought the evolutionist criterion to the fore, distinguishing (progressive) settled people from (backward) nomads (*inorodtsy*). Under Nicholas I and again under Alexander III, Orthodoxy regained its status as a pillar of state policy.

With the rise of the concept of the nation—that is to say, the secular political community and the ethnic cultural community that transcended estate boundaries—Russian ethno-national elements gradually emerged in the course of the nineteenth century. They mingled with the dynastic, estate, cultural, and religious principles without completely prevailing over the traditional factors of integration and demarcation in tsarist policy. These new elements exerted less influence over government policy than over Russian society, in which the national movement became increasingly dominant.[11]

The cultural hierarchy of ethnic groups with its mutable categories of way of life, religion, and language/culture determined the degree of otherness (*altérité*) in the Russian Empire. In its nineteenth-century form, this hierarchy may be represented as a system of concentric circles extending from the innermost circle of "true" Russians outward to ever more alien peoples. The whole range of subjects of the empire was defined by opposition to foreigners (*inostrannye poddannye*).

---

11. On this, see Edward C. Thaden, ed., *Russification in the Baltic Provinces and Finland, 1855–1914* (Princeton, N.J., 1981); Andreas Kappeler, ed., *Die Russen: Ihr Nationalbewußtsein in Geschichte und Gegenwart* (Cologne, 1990); Theodore R. Weeks, *Nation and State in Late Imperial Russia: Nationalism and Russification on the Western Frontier, 1863–1914* (DeKalb, Ill., 1996); V. S. Diakin, "Natsional'nyi vopros vo vnutrennei politike tsarizma (XIX v.)," *Voprosy istorii*, 1995, no. 9: 130–42; and Andreas Renner, *Russischer Nationalismus und Öffentlichkeit im Zarenreich 1855–1875* (Cologne, 2000).

1. The subjects of the tsar were legally divided, first and foremost, into *prirodnye* ("natural") inhabitants and *inorodtsy* (aliens, allogens).[12] As a result of the Speransky reforms, the *inorodtsy* included the unsettled population of the empire, such as the nomadic Kalmyks, Kazakhs, Buriats, and other ethnic groups of Siberia. The criterion of definition here was their way of life. The nomadic *inorodtsy* were not equal citizens of the Russian Empire, as their rights were restricted; on the other hand, they had few obligations and enjoyed limited rights of self-government.

This principle was later violated by official policy toward the Jews, who were legally *inorodtsy* but still required to render contributions and service, such as providing recruits. If not in principle, then in practice the settled Muslims of Turkestan were also declared *inorodtsy*; their status as indigenous inhabitants (*tuzemtsy*) was largely equivalent to that of the nomads of Central Asia. Thus, in the second half of the nineteenth century, the prevailing view of the nomadic way of life as backward was no longer the decisive criterion for allocation to the *inorodtsy*; in essence, the decisive criterion was that of foreign race. The *inorodtsy*, who formed the outermost circle of the empire's cultural hierarchy, were those ethnic groups whose cultural and racial characteristics were deemed so alien as to preclude their integration into the empire. They were therefore isolated from the mass of "natural" citizens and discriminated against; on the other hand, they experienced only slight pressure to integrate.

2. Moving inward, the next circle was defined by the Christian/non-Christian opposition. The religious criterion had long played a certain role in establishing the hierarchy of ethnic groups. In the first half of the eighteenth century, there were indeed forced conversions to Christianity, but from the time of Catherine II the non-Christians of the Russian Empire (with the exception of Jews) remained unmolested. The practice of non-Christian faiths was permitted, although the non-Orthodox were forbidden to engage in missionary activities. By establishing official institutions, the state sought to keep tabs on those of other faiths. The category of settled non-Christians not designated as *inorodtsy* included several Muslim ethnic groups, the Volga Tatars, Bashkirs, Crimean Tatars, and the Muslims of the

---

12. Henning Bauer et al., ed., *Die Nationalitäten des Russischen Reiches in der Volkszählung von 1897*, vol. A (Stuttgart, 1991), pp. 416–28; and John W. Slocum, "Who, and When, Were the *Inorodtsy*? The Evolution of the Category of 'Aliens' in Imperial Russia," *Russian Review* 57, no. 2 (1998): 173-90. The term *inorodtsy* was also used pejoratively in the nineteenth century to denote other non-Russian and non-Orthodox ethnic groups in the empire.

Caucasus region, while the remnants of the Animist population in the north and in Siberia, as well as the Lamaists and Jews, belonged to the outer circle of *inorodtsy*. The second circle was thus made up predominantly of those ethnic groups whose upper stratum had been partially coopted into the nobility of the Russian Empire. Even in the second half of the nineteenth century, the tsarist state made scarcely any effort to convert Muslims to Christianity or Russify them linguistically.

3. The next circle inward consisted of non-Orthodox Christians. Westernized official Russia guaranteed the practice of other Christian faiths and recognized their religious organizations, but the ban on missionary activity applied to them as well. The Orthodox Church undertook only sporadic efforts to conduct missionary activity among non-Orthodox Christians, mainly among ethnic groups with indigenous landowning or urban elites: the Gregorian Armenians, the Catholic Poles, the Lutheran Finns, and Baltic Germans. On the other hand, in the nineteenth century the Orthodox Church repeatedly conducted missionary work among ethnic groups consisting mainly of peasants: the Estonians, Latvians, Lithuanians, and Catholic Belarusians. Belarusian and Ukrainian Uniates were not considered Catholics at all, but were regarded as heretics who had fallen away from Orthodoxy. Their church was therefore dissolved in 1839 and completely abolished in 1875.

Beginning in the 1860s, the tsarist government steadily imposed restrictions on the churches and clergies of several non-Orthodox Christian ethnic groups, and then switched to a policy of partial linguistic assimilation. This policy was first applied to the Poles (and the Lithuanians along with them) as a reaction to the uprising of January 1863. Only in the nineteenth and early twentieth centuries were restrictive measures taken against the Lutheran Church and the German language in the Baltic provinces and against the Armenian Church and its schools. Such measures, intended to impose Orthodoxy and promote Russification, were not motivated by cultural and religious considerations alone. Concerns about the allegedly inadequate loyalty of several non-Russian ethnic groups, which were also generally suspected of subversive contacts with foreign powers, combined with the nationalist urge to ward off all foreign elements.

4. The three innermost circles encompassed the Orthodox ethnic groups of the empire. Their confession bound them more closely than the other ethnic groups to ruler, dynasty and empire, and *pravoslavie* was officially proclaimed one of Russia's three basic principles. The Orthodox Church was regarded as the "leading and ruling" church in the Russian Empire. It alone had the right to conduct missionary

activity, and until 1905 apostasy from Orthodox belief was strictly prohibited under threat of criminal prosecution.

The outer circle of Orthodox believers included Orthodox non-Slavs, namely the Georgians, the Romanians of Bessarabia, and the Christianized Animists of the Middle Volga, the Urals, the Far North, and Siberia. Orthodoxy was often equated with Russian identity, and in the nineteenth century Orthodox ethnic groups were exposed to stronger pressure to Russify than were the non-Orthodox of the empire. Even before the mid-nineteenth century, Russian schools were established for Orthodox non-Slavs, such as the Georgians and Romanians, and in the final third of the century, the policy of linguistic Russification was intensified vis-à-vis both these ethnic groups. In the case of the Christianized Animists, however, native-language schools were encouraged in order to strengthen them in their own faith before any attempt at Russification. The policy of assimilation had no lasting success with the Georgians, while the Romanian elite of Bessarabia was partially Russified, with the so-called Moldavians joining the edge of the inner circle of Eastern Slavs.

5. At the center of this system of concentric rings were the Orthodox Eastern Slavs. Officially, the Russian people included all Eastern Slavs, while the Great Russians, Little Russians, and Belarusians were conceded only the status of tribes (*plemia*). Ukrainian and Belarusian were regarded as dialects (*narechiia*), not languages (*iazyki*) on a par with Russian.[13] Consequently, the written languages and high cultures of the Ukrainians and Belarusians, like their elites, were not considered independent.

Relations between Russians and Ukrainians became a problem with the beginnings of the Ukrainian national movement and the emergence of modern Russian nationalism in the second half of the nineteenth century. If the Russian nation included all Eastern Slavs, then nation-building among the Ukrainians (the largest ethnic group in the empire after the Russians) directly threatened the unity of the Russian nation.[14] This explains the particularly intense persecution of Ukrainian linguistic and cultural activity embodied in the two language bans of 1863 and 1876. The first decree had an overt anti-

---

13. *Die Nationälitaten*, vol. A, pp. 166–71.

14. A. I. Miller, *"Ukrainskii vopros" v politike vlastei i russkom obshchestvennom mnenii (vtoraia polovina XIX v.)* (St. Petersburg, 2000); Olga Andriewsky, "The Politics of National Identity: The Ukrainian Question in Russia, 1904–1912," Ph.D. dissertation, Harvard University, 1991; and, generally, Roman Szporluk, "The Ukraine and Russia," in Robert Conquest, ed., *The Last Empire: Nationality and the Soviet Future* (Stanford, 1986), pp. 151–82.

Polish focus. As noted above, the Right-Bank Ukrainians, Belarusians and Lithuanians had long been considered functionally linked with the Polish elite; their cultural aspirations were termed "Polish intrigues," and the language bans were also directed against the restive Poles. The anti-Polish thrust was underlined by the imposition of restrictions not only on the Ukrainian and Belarusian languages, but also on Lithuanian-language writings in "Latin-Polish characters."

Despite the repressive language policy, the Ukrainians did not become the center of attention until the early twentieth century. The government and the public generally regarded them as loyal "Little Russians" or as harmless peasants (*khokhly*). The Russian government did not believe that the Ukrainians were capable of becoming a nation through their own efforts, but feared that they might be exploited by more dangerous enemies of Russia. These included the Poles and, later, Austria, which was believed to be pursuing the goal of turning the "Little Russians" into Mazepists.[15]

While the Ukrainians and Belarusians were subjected to harsh repression as ethnic groups, as individuals they were discriminated against less than those occupying the outer circles. Since Ukrainians and Belarusians were officially regarded as Russians, all careers were open to them in principle, provided that they used the Russian language. There was no impediment to mixed marriages between Russians and Ukrainians. As Orthodox Eastern Slavs, Ukrainians were neither isolated nor disadvantaged on the basis of confessional or racial criteria. This did not mean, however, that the Ukrainian language and culture and the Ukrainian ethnos were held in high regard. On the contrary, they were not accorded independent status, and their protagonists were either derided as *khokhly* or combated as *mazepintsy*.

The dividing line between the innermost circle of Great Russians and the second circle of other Orthodox Eastern Slavs was thus blurred in the nineteenth century. In the official view, as noted earlier, distinctions were made between "tribes" and "dialects"—distinctions significant enough for the census of 1897 to inquire about them.

The system of concentric circles had, therefore, a dual effect. The further the ethnic group was from the Orthodox Russian center, the greater the legal, social, and political discrimination against its members, but the lesser the danger to its ethnic identity. The

---

15. See, for example, S. N. Shchegolev, *Ukrainskoe dvizhenie kak sovremennyi ètap iuzhnorusskogo separatizma* (Kyiv, 1912); and John S. Reshetar, Jr., "Ukrainian and Russian Perceptions of the Ukrainian Revolution," in *Ukraine and Russia in Their Historical Encounter*, pp. 140–64.

assimilating effect of the Russian language and culture was weakest among the *inorodtsy* (who, like the Jews, did not serve in the army) and the other non-Christian ethnic groups. It was somewhat stronger among the non-Orthodox Christians, especially if they lived in the center of the empire, stronger still among Orthodox non-Slavs like the Karelians, Mordvinians, and Romanians, and strongest among the Orthodox Eastern Slavs. This applies both to the Russification policy promoted by the government and to the "natural assimilation" of those who migrated to Russian areas or Russian-dominated towns.

The Ukrainians and Belarusians, who were very close to the center, were not regarded as separate ethnic groups and were put under pressure to assimilate, although as individuals they experienced scarcely any discrimination. That Ukrainians, in contrast to members of the mostly non-East Slavic and non-Orthodox ethnic groups (namely, Poles or Jews), were accepted by both government and society as members of the Russian elite increased the attractiveness of a policy of assimilation through advancement. A contributing factor was that, considered as ethnic Ukrainians in the nineteenth century, they were on the lowest rung of the estate hierarchy and were regarded as *khokhly*. The image of an uncultivated, inferior peasant people was adopted and internalized by many Ukrainians. Their inferiority complex could be overcome only by joining the Russian community and its advanced culture.

This is the background to the phenomenon of the social climbers, disrespectfully termed *malorossy* on the Ukrainian national side as well, who made their careers in Russia. They combined their loyalty to emperor and state and their allegiance to Russian high culture with loyalty to Ukraine and its traditions. Members of this important group of more or less Russified Ukrainians, who are difficult to locate in the sources and therefore have not been systematically examined, are regarded anachronistically by Ukrainian nationalists as collaborators. This ignores the fact that the tsarist empire, even in the final decades of its existence, was by no means a national state, and that the traditional criteria of the dynastic-estate polyethnic empire were still in force. Under such conditions, multiple identities and loyalties were not unusual. It was not necessary to opt for an exclusively Russian, Polish, or Ukrainian identity; loyalty to the state was enough, though admittedly it entailed renunciation of illegal activities, such as Ukrainophile agitation. Another possible route of social advancement was membership in the "counter-elite" of the revolutionary movement, which also led to partial Russification.

Not all of these partially Russified social climbers became Russians. Their identity may be termed situational: the state of the late tsarist empire demanded adaptation to the Russian language and culture. When the situation changed in 1917, numerous *malorossy* remembered their Ukrainian identity, dormant beneath the Russified surface, and became supporters or even ministers of the Ukrainian People's Republic and, later, of the linguistically Ukrainized Ukrainian Soviet Republic.

By the beginning of the twentieth century, the criteria of political loyalty and culture were converging. Based on the model of the European national states, the view gained ground in Russia that allegiance to the state must be congruent with allegiance to the ethnic nation. Non-Orthodox and non-Russian inhabitants of the empire, not only Poles and Jews but also, increasingly, Armenians and Russian Germans, were now regarded a priori as unreliable. Some Russians used the term *inorodtsy* (no longer a legal term but a political and ideological one) to differentiate them from "natural" inhabitants of the empire. The government exploited these nationalist stirrings, which were reinforced by foreign-policy tensions, to stabilize its authority. It did not do so consistently, however, and achieved its aims only in part, further alienating large sections of the non-Russian population, which in 1897 comprised at least 57 percent of the total population of the empire.

Conclusions

The situation of the Ukrainians in the sociopolitical system of the nineteenth-century Russian Empire was complex. The tsarist government and the Russian public regarded them as *khokhly*, *malorossy* or *mazepintsy*. The Ukrainian peasant masses, who continued to live in their traditional Ukrainian-language world, were considered charming, harmless, and even picturesque with their songs and dances, but on the whole they were despised as stupid, uncultivated *khokhly*.

The *malorossy*—those Ukrainians who had chosen the path of social advancement and achieved some degree of integration into Russian society—were regarded as part of the Russian people, despite certain linguistic and cultural peculiarities. The few Ukrainians who wanted to create an autonomous Ukrainian high culture and established national associations and parties to that end were met with incomprehension in Russian society: why would they want to exchange the great Russian culture for a provincial peasant one? Ukrainians were regarded as dangerous, disloyal *mazepintsy* only by those who saw them as tools of the Polish national movement or of Austrian foreign policy. In the final years before the First World War, the opinion was occasionally expressed—by Petr Struve, for example—that the "Ukrainophiles" might represent a danger to the unity of the empire and the Russian nation.[16]

What general conclusions can be drawn about the significance of the tsarist empire for the Russian-Ukrainian encounter?

The hierarchies of political loyalty and social estate were defining structural elements of the Russian Empire and remained in place until its demise. They were supplemented and partially eclipsed by the cultural hierarchy of ethnic groups, which gained importance in the second half of the nineteenth century. The interaction of these three constantly changing hierarchies shows that the complex structure of the multiethnic empire and the traditional, far from uniform government policy, which combined with new nationalist elements, cannot be reduced to one-dimensional terms. The tsarist empire was not merely a prison-house of peoples, as Lenin and a variety of national historians have asserted. The term "Russification" does not adequately describe the uneven and complex nationalities policy. The Russian Empire was not a classical colonial empire, as is often maintained. The Ukrainians were neither a people bound to the Russians by eternal friendship nor a colonial people discriminated against and exploited at every turn. Nor were the Russians a typical imperial "ruling nation."

For some time, researchers have questioned the aptness of the term "Russification" to describe tsarist nationalities policy.[17] A long-term effort on the part of the Russian government to bring about administrative, economic, social and, in part, cultural integration of the non-Russian ethnic groups can indeed be established. In my view, however, the term "Russification" should be limited to the cultural and linguistic realm and employed to denote a purposeful, high-priority policy to promote the linguistic and cultural assimilation of the non-Russian ethnic groups to the Russians.[18] Russification in this sense did not exist before the emergence of Russian nationalism in the mid-nineteenth century. Within the context of modernization, the

---

16. See Andriewsky, "The Politics of National Identity."

17. Thaden, ed., *Russification*; Weeks, *Nation and State*; and Gert von Pistohlkors, "'Russifizierung' in den baltischen Provinzen und in Finnland im 19. und beginnenden 20. Jahrhundert," *Zeitschrift für Ostforschung* 33, no. 4 (1984): 592–606.

18. On the other hand, Eli Weinerman argues for a definition that differentiates political, linguistic, religious, cultural, and ethnic Russification and stresses that in the long run all variants served the purpose of assimilation ("Russification in Imperial Russia: The Search for Ethnic Homogeneity in the Multinational State," unpublished manuscript).

repeated efforts initiated in the eighteenth century to achieve administrative and legal uniformity in the empire, including the establishment of Russian as the official language and *lingua franca,* cannot be regarded as constituting Russification in the narrower sense of the term. Whenever the sources refer to Russification, care must be taken to determine whether the term *russkii* is being used in the ethnic sense or whether it stands for the empire and its values and standards.

A specific policy of cultural and linguistic Russification can be discerned only from the 1860s. At that time, it was not an overarching concept that suppressed the basic, traditional, supranational model. Most ethnic groups in the Asian part of the Russian Empire, which we have assigned to the outer circles of the cultural hierarchy, were scarcely affected by Russification. On the other hand, agressive linguistic Russification was undertaken against non-Orthodox ethnic groups in the West whose nobilities and standard languages had traditionally enjoyed equal rights. The most important reason for this was the emergence of national movements among Russians and non-Russians alike, which undermined the traditional legitimacy of the tsarist empire and caused the government to play the national card for the first time. Its goal was to integrate Russian society, which was riven by the deepening political and social crisis. Admittedly, this policy, too, was implemented only gradually and inconsistently, first of all against the rebellious Poles, later and less vigorously against the German Balts and Armenians, and only rudimentarily in Finland. The results were counter-productive, for aggressive Russification only strengthened the national movements of the nationally mobilized ethnic groups.

Among the Orthodox ethnic groups of the inner circles, cultural and linguistic Russification was implemented somewhat earlier and with some success, particularly if no elites were present or if they had assimilated to Russian society. For the innermost circle of Eastern Slavs, however, the center saw no need for Russification, since it already regarded the Ukrainians and Belarusians as Russians. From this perspective, the language bans were directed against a few intellectuals, allegedly incited by Poland and later by Austria to create written languages and advanced cultures artificially out of Russian dialects and regional cultures so as to split the Russian nation and destabilize the tsarist empire. Nationally minded Ukrainians, however, interpreted these measures as aggressive Russification. The policy was considerably more successful among the Eastern Slavs and several Orthodox non-Slavic ethnic groups than among peoples more distant from the Russians and more strongly consolidated as ethnic communities.

In my view, the application of the term "colonialism" to the tsarist empire must also be refined. Most Asiatic regions of the empire were indisputably colonies, either economic colonies like Turkestan or settlement colonies like Siberia. The ethnic groups that lived there occupied the lower rungs of the estate and cultural hierarchy; in territorial, social, cultural, and racial terms, they were distant from the Russian imperial center. On the other hand, the northwestern regions of the empire—Finland, the Baltic provinces, and Poland—were indeed peripheries ruled by the center and at least partially foreign-controlled, but they were considerably more developed economically and culturally than the Russian center and cannot therefore be regarded as colonies.[19]

An important distinction vis-à-vis the colonial empires of the West was the absence in the estate-structured Russian Empire of a bifurcation into an imperial Russian ruling stratum and non-Russian subject strata. It is true that most of the political and military elite of the empire was Russian or Russified, but Russians as a people were not systematically favored; on the contrary, they were quite often disadvantaged in comparison with non-Russians. The legal, economic, and social situation of Russian serfs and their descendants was worse than that of non-Russian state peasants in the East or of Finnish, Estonian, and Polish peasants in the West of the empire. In 1897 the Russians were still average among the ethnic groups of the empire in terms of urbanization and level of education. Unlike in Western colonial empires, therefore, the dominant nation was not legally, economically, or socially privileged.

Even Ukraine was not a classical colony of the Russian Empire. It lacked geographic, cultural, and racial distance, nor were Ukrainians legally disadvantaged as compared with the Russians. Nonetheless, Ukrainian historians have repeatedly asked whether Ukraine was a European-type colony or an *internal* colony of the tsarist empire. The term "internal colony," employed by Lenin, was adopted by Ukrainian economists of the 1920s, such as Mykhailo Volobuiev, Mykhailo Slabchenko, and Matvii Iavorsky, and was taken up in the 1970s by the social scientist Michael Hechter.[20] All of them made a primarily

19. See Robert J. Hind, "The Internal Colonial Concept," *Comparative Studies in Society and History* 26, no. 3 (July 1984): 543–68, esp. 554–60; Jürgen Osterhammel (*Kolonialismus: Geschichte—Formen—Folgen* [Munich, 1995], p. 122) rightly objects that concepts of colonialism "have not yet been discussed with sufficient care" in the case of Russia and the Soviet Union.

20. Mykhailo Volobuiev, "Do problemy ukraïns'koï ekonomiky," *Bil'shovyk Ukraïny*, 1928, nos. 2–3, cited in *Dokumenty ukraïns'koho komunizmu* (New York,

economic argument and stressed the economic dependency of ethnic groups on the periphery, as well as their exploitation and instrumentalization by the politically dominant center.

In my view, the term "internal colony" does not adequately describe Russian-Ukrainian relations in the Russian Empire.[21] While the relationship between the Russian center and the Ukrainian periphery undoubtedly involved elements of economic dependency, exploitation, and cultural discrimination, too many factors militate against the use of the term "colony." The tsarist center regarded Ukraine as part of the Russian motherland and, as noted above, did not discriminate against Ukrainians as citizens in favor of Russians. To prevent the devaluation of such terms as colonialism, colonial, and colony, their use should be restricted to the analysis of classical colonialism, which is not applicable to Ukraine.

The model of social-estate and cultural hierarchies of ethnic groups can also be applied to the territory of Ukraine and its ethnic groups. In the estate hierarchy of Ukraine, Russians and Poles stood close together, in social contrast to the other ethnic groups, particularly the Ukrainian peasant stratum at the bottom of the pyramid. As Daniel Beauvois has shown, this coalition remained largely intact, despite numerous political conflicts in Right-Bank Ukraine, until the demise of the tsarist empire.[22] The fact that the Orthodox "Little Russians" remained, with the approval of the tsarist government, under the social, economic and, in part, cultural hegemony of the Polish nobility is further testimony to the lasting effect of the estate hierarchy.

In the hierarchy of cultures and loyalties, on the other hand, Russians and Ukrainians were natural allies against foreigners, namely, in the final decades of the tsarist empire, the Jews, Poles, and Germans. Russian nationalists, abetted to some extent by the Russian state, tried through anti-Semitism, as well as anti-Polish and

---

1962), pp. 132–230; Michael Hechter, *Internal Colonialism: The Celtic Fringe in British National Development, 1536–1966* (Berkeley, 1975); James E. Mace, *Communism and the Dilemmas of National Liberation: National Communism in Soviet Ukraine, 1918–1933* (Cambridge, Mass., 1983), pp. 161–90; and Hind, "The Internal Colonial Concept."

21. A similar argument was made by Ivan L. Rudnytsky, "The Role of the Ukraine in Modern History," *Slavic Review* 22, no. 2 (1963): 204–5. A brief argument for the application of the colonial paradigm to the history of Ukraine has been made by George G. Grabowicz, "Framing the Contexts," *Slavic Review* 54, no. 3 (1995): 676–79.

22. Beauvois, *La bataille de la terre*.

anti-German campaigns, to exploit this constellation (not always without success) in order to integrate all Orthodox Eastern Slavs into the "one and indivisible Russia."[23] Of course, cultural proximity could also engender conflicts, as happened when nationally mobilized Ukrainians began to resist the Russian language and culture. For the Ukrainian national movement, which was directed primarily against the Russian state, Jews, Poles, and Germans could become allies in this situation.

This rough model can perhaps provide pointers for the Russian-Ukrainian encounter not only in the tsarist empire, but also in the Soviet Union. The three social hierarchies described very schematically here continued to exert their influence after the revolution. It is true that social hierarchies in the Soviet Union were turned upside down, and that the categories of estate and nobility disappeared. Nevertheless, the principle of coopting non-Russian elites remained in force, as did the premises of political loyalty. The strength of the industrial proletariat and the consolidation of the Communist Party played an important role in establishing a new social hierarchy of ethnic groups. The system of concentric cultural circles was somewhat altered, allowing the (secularized and linguistically Russified) Jews to shake off segregation in the 1920s. However, the center kept its distance from the Asiatic ethnic groups. Under Stalin, the Russians regained their prominent place in the cultural hierarchy, which had been put into question in the 1920s. The condition of political loyalty remained crucially important, and in the hierarchy based upon it the Stalinist empire, which built upon tsarist models, maintained many rankings from prerevolutionary times. This was apparent in the forced deportations of the Second World War.

In the social hierarchy, the Ukrainians, with their deep agrarian stamp, ranked far below the Russians and other more industrialized and urbanized ethnic groups even in the interwar period. The cultural distinction between Ukrainians and Russians first became more pronounced as a result of the national mobilization of the revolutionary period and the Ukrainization of the twenties. With the industrialization and urbanization of Ukraine, the position of Ukrainians in the

---

23. See Charters Wynn, *Workers, Strikes and Pogroms: The Donbass-Dnepr Bend in Late Imperial Russia, 1870–1905* (Princeton, N.J., 1992); Theodore Weeks, "Ukrainians and Official Russia: A Deafening Silence," discussion paper, conference in New York, November 1994; and Andreas Kappeler, "Ukrainians and Germans in Southern Ukraine, 1870s to 1914," in Hans-Joachim Torke and John-Paul Himka, ed., *German-Ukrainian Relations in Historical Perspective* (Edmonton, 1994), pp. 60–61.

social hierarchy improved, while cultural differences from the Russians were again effaced.

The traditionally ambivalent status of the Ukrainians again became apparent when Russian national and imperial elements came to the fore under Stalin. On the one hand, Ukrainian proximity to the Russian core produced particularly sensitive reactions against (suspected) disloyalty and nationalism. This found expression in the particularly repressive Soviet policy toward Ukraine in the 1930s and again in the seventies. The political center and Russian society regarded the Ukrainian *petliurovtsy* and *banderovtsy* as successors to the *mazepintsy*. The "stab in the back" delivered to the Soviet Union by the Ukrainian leadership in December 1991 reinforced the image of treacherous *mazepintsy*. On the other hand, loyal Ukrainians who adjusted to Russian culture had good opportunities for advancement in the Soviet Union. Khrushchev even temporarily made Ukrainian *malorossy* the junior partners of the Russians in the government and party; the political leadership was perceived by non-Slavs at this time as Russian-Ukrainian. In Russia today, Belarusians and Ukrainians are still regarded among the ethnic groups of the "near abroad" as particularly close relatives, with whom one gladly cooperates and to whom one is ready to make certain concessions, but whom one does not recognize as socially and culturally equal or accept as independent nations with national states. Most Russians still see the Ukrainians as *malorossy*, a part of the Russian nation, and cannot conceive why the Ukrainians strive for their own language, culture, and state. Despite urbanization and industrialization, the Ukrainians are still regarded as an uncultivated peasant people, *khokhly*. It is true that linguistic, cultural, and historical proximity has ensured that ethnic antagonisms barely exist between Russians and Ukrainians. A true "friendship of peoples," however, can develop only if Russians accept Ukrainians as equals.

Olga Andriewsky

The Russian-Ukrainian Discourse and the Failure of the "Little Russian Solution," 1782–1917*

To the historian, modern Russian-Ukrainian relations are something of an enigma. In the strictly formal sense of the term, Russian-Ukrainian relations ceased to exist after 1782, when Ukrainian autonomy was abolished and the Cossack territories were integrated into the Russian administrative system. Subsequently, over the course of the next 120 years, Russian-Ukrainian relations came to be dominated by a peculiar kind of silence. The relative absence of overt friction and conflict—indeed, of any kind of candid political interaction—greatly diminished the public profile of the "Little Russians," creating an impression of harmony and agreement that ultimately led many foreign observers to doubt the very existence of a distinct Ukrainian people. As Nevin O. Winter noted in *The National Geographic* in 1918, "In recent years the Ukraine has quieted down, so that the casual students of today hardly realized that there was such a distinctive section left, living in the belief that the Slavs of the Ukraine or Little Russia, as it is better known, had become thoroughly amalgamated with the Great Russians of the Petrograd and Moscow sections."[1] To be sure, much of this silence was officially imposed, as demonstrated by the rapid emergence of a Ukrainian national movement after 1905 and the almost immediate breakdown of Russian-Ukrainian political relations in 1917. Yet it is precisely the curious instability of modern Russian-Ukrainian relations—the sudden revival of the long-dormant "Ukrainian question" during moments of general political crisis (1905, 1917, 1991)—that continues to perplex Russian and Ukrainian specialists alike.

What I propose to do in this essay is to shift the focus of discussion away from these more dramatic moments of political crisis—which, in any event, have been comparatively well documented by other

---

*. Research for this article was made possible by a grant from the Social Sciences and Humanities Research Council of Canada.

1. Nevin O. Winter, "The Ukraine, Past and Present," *National Geographic* (August 1918), p. 114.

authors—and to explore, at least in some preliminary fashion, the discourse that lay behind the "silence," that is, the patterns, rhetoric, and myths that defined the territory and boundaries of Russian-Ukrainian relations between 1782 and 1917.[2] The nature of this discourse, I shall argue, changed rather profoundly in the course of the nineteenth century in a way that precluded the formation of a modern and stable "Little Russian" identity. In the long run, it was the "silence" itself and, specifically, the increasingly constricted ways in which issues of "Russianness" and identity came to be understood and redefined that, I believe, lay at the root of the modern political crisis.

Narrowing Horizons

One of the more striking characteristics of the history of Russian-Ukrainian relations is how limited that discourse actually became in the nineteenth century; how narrow was the scope of interaction; how few points of intellectual and cultural contact really existed.[3] Indeed, it can be argued that much of what Russians learned about Ukraine

---

2. This discourse can be traced in imaginative literature, journalism, travel writing, ethnographic description, historiography, political speeches, administrative documents, and statutes of law. The present essay does not pretend to offer an exhaustive treatment of these sources. For a more specialized approach that deals exclusively with historiography, see Stephen Velychenko, *National History as Cultural Process: A Survey of the Interpretations of Ukraine's Past in Polish, Russian and Ukrainian Historical Writing from the Earliest Times to 1914* (Edmonton, 1992).

3. As Edward Keenan has observed, a large part of what eventually became "common" to Russians and Ukrainians was the result of modern processes—large-scale migration, urbanization, the development of railways and communications, universal military conscription, and universal education—processes that, I would add, took on significant momentum among Ukrainians only in the twentieth century. In this respect, it may be more useful to think about Russian-Ukrainian relations in the nineteenth century in terms of "separate spheres." The noted Russian archeologist and ethnographer D. N. Anuchin made much the same point in 1902. Commenting on the insularity of Ukrainian peasant culture, he observed that "even in their faraway Siberian colonies [the Little Russians] preserve their distinctiveness." By 1902, however, he believed that "the introduction of railways, the development of urban life, the growth of factories and plants, conscription and schools, etc., are exerting their influence little by little and beginning to lead to the loss of many unique and original traits." See Edward L. Keenan, "Muscovite Perceptions of Other East Slavs before 1654—An Agenda for Historians," in *Ukraine and Russia in Their Historical Encounter*, ed. Peter J. Potichnyj et al. (Edmonton, 1992), p. 23; and D. A. [D. N. Anuchin] "Malorussy," *Éntsiklopedicheskii slovar'*, vol. 18 (St. Petersburg, 1896), p. 485.

and Ukrainian culture after the end of Ukrainian autonomy was acquired through the medium of a Russian-speaking and Russian-writing Ukrainian gentry, that is, by way of the most acculturated segment of Ukrainian society. The Russian image of Ukraine was substantially shaped and refined by men like Vasilii (Vasyl) Ruban (1742–95), Fedor (Fedir) Tumansky (1756–1810), Dmitrii (Dmytro) Bantysh-Kamensky, (1788–1850), Vasilii Narezhny (Vasyl Narizhny, 1780–1825), Orest Somov (1793–1833), and Nikolai Gogol (Mykola Hohol, 1809–1852)—those Ukrainians who sought their fame and fortune in the Russian capitals and made their careers by serving as cultural mediators between Ukraine and educated Russian society.[4] Through their publications, these authors did much to capture the imagination of the Russian reading public with colorful tales of Cossacks and good-natured country rubes and to bring the "northerners" closer to their "southern provinces."[5] Implicitly if not explicitly, their work tended to minimize or aestheticize differences between Russia and Ukraine and thus to discount the inherent autonomy or "otherness" of the Ukrainian historical and cultural experience. In fact, it was the ability of these Ukrainian writers to interpret and order—and ultimately tame—the Ukrainian experience so as to make it accessible to a Russian audience that became a key to their literary success. As the reviewer for *Severnaia pchela* (Northern Bee), Russia's most widely read newspaper, remarked on reading Gogol's *Vechera na khutore bliz Dikan'ki* (Evenings at a Farmstead near Dykanka, 1831), the "Little Russian school" of writers was to be applauded for abandoning its efforts "to preserve in all their purity

---

4. For a fuller discussion of the literary careers of these men and their influence on the Russian image of Ukraine, see David Saunders, *The Ukrainian Impact on Russian Culture* (Edmonton, 1985), chapters 5–7.

5. A measure of their success in this regard was the "Ukrainian theme" in the writings of such Russian writers as Kondratii Ryleev, Fedor Glinka, and Aleksandr Pushkin in the 1820s and early 1830s. See, for example, Ryleev's *Dumy* (1821–23), *Voinarovskii* (1824), and *Nalivaiko* (1824–25); Pushkin's *Poltava* (1827); and Faddei Bulgarin's *Dmitrii Samozvanets* (1830) and *Mazepa* (1833–34). *Severnye tsvety* (Northern Flowers) also frequently published works on Ukrainian themes and appeared through the efforts of Orest Somov and the Pushkin circle (1827–31). In later Russian literature, as Jeffrey Brooks has noted (*When Russia Learned to Read* [Princeton, N.J., 1985], p. 228), Ukrainians came to be represented by the stock image of the Cossack frontiersman or the easy-going country bumpkin. For more on the image of Ukraine in Russian publications, see Paul Bushkovitch, "The Ukraine in Russian Culture, 1790–1860: The Evidence of the Journals," *Jahrbücher für Geschichte Osteuropas* 39, no. 3 (1991): 339–63.

the peculiarities of their dialect and the originality of a long-past life-style" and for leaving behind "this ... too local goal, and turn[ing] to deeper thought ..."[6]

The progressive insubstantialization of the image of Ukraine is a fair indication of just how narrow the points of cultural contact actually were. Because Russian ideas about Ukraine were so closely associated with a gentry culture and the extinct political order from which it came,[7] the Ukrainian literary revival of the 1830s came to be regarded by many as the last echo of a dying world. Much of the discussion surrounding this revival, in fact, centered on the question of the value and necessity of resuscitating a "dead" language and culture.[8] "Is a Little Russian literature possible today?" asked one literary critic in his review of Hryhorii Kvitka-Osnovianenko's short

---

6. *Severnaia pchela*, no. 219 (29 September 1831), quoted in Saunders, *Ukrainian Impact*, p. 167. The reception of Gogol's Ukrainian stories revealed an interesting Ukrainian-Russian divide. Russian critics such as Vissarion Belinsky praised Gogol as a genius for finding the "universal and human" in Little Russian life. By contrast, the Ukrainian literary critic Andrii Storozhenko criticized the short stories for their many ethnographic, historical, and linguistic inaccuracies. Storozhenko believed that the Russian reviewers had praised Gogol's stories because "in all likelihood they were unfamiliar with the ordinary way of life of the inhabitants of Little Russia." This view was echoed years later by Panteleimon Kulish. "If the Russian reading public were educated in its native Slavic culture so as to be able to read Kvitka and Shevchenko freely, as familiar Slavic poets, then in those perfected mirrors of national sensibility, custom and tradition they would recognize the scandalous errors of Gogol's stories and would regret all the words that were wasted on shining ghosts from an inauthentic world." See Andrei Tsarinnyi [Andrii Storozhenko], "Mysli malorossiianina po prochtenii povestei Pasichnika Rudogo-Pan'ka, izdannykh im pod zaglaviem: *Vechera na khutore bliz Dikan'ki*, i retsenzii na onye," *Syn otechestva* 147 (1832): 41–49, 101–15, 159–64, 223–42, 288–312; and P. Kulish, "Gogol', kak avtor povestei iz ukrainskoi zhizni," *Osnova*, 1861, no. 4, cited in Nikolai Barsukov, *Zhizn' i trudy M. P. Pogodina*, 22 vols. (St. Petersburg, 1888–1910), 16: 129–30. See also Belinsky's review of the Ukrainian almanac *Lastivka* and Kvitka-Osnovianenko's *Svatannia* in *Otechestvennye zapiski*, 1841, no. 16: 32–34, reprinted in *Polnoe sobranie sochinenii V. G. Belinskogo* [henceforth *PSS*], ed. S. A. Vengerov, vol. 6 (St. Petersburg, 1903), pp. 199–202; and D. B. Saunders, "Contemporary Critics of Gogol's *Vechera* and the Debate about Russian *Narodnost'* (1831–1832)," *Harvard Ukrainian Studies* 5, no. 1 (March 1981): 66–82.

7. Bushkovitch, "The Ukraine in Russian Culture," p. 344.

8. This debate was summarized by A. N. Pypin in his "Spor mezhdu iuzhanami i severianami," *Vestnik Evropy*, 1886, no. 4: 736–76; see also his *Istoriia russkoi ėtnografii* (St. Petersburg, 1890–92), vol. 3, *Ėtnografiia malorusskaia*, pp. 301–25.

stories. "Look at Little Russia in its present state and you will obtain a negative answer ... the past, the former language, and the bygone way of life have been preserved only among the lower classes of the people; everything else is Russified [*obruselo*]. Why produce a literature for a people who have lost their individuality, their personal physiognomy?"[9] Little Russian culture, like the Hetmanate itself, belonged to the past. Increasingly, in the view of many Russian intellectuals, it no longer had any reason to exist. (For his part, an exasperated Kvitka-Osnovianenko tried to remind Russian publishers, editors, and critics that Ukrainian was, after all, a language still spoken by ten million people.)[10]

Asymmetry

The other notable feature of the modern Russian-Ukrainian discourse was its imbalance, its asymmetry. While for the better part of three centuries Ukrainians have been obsessed with their neighbors to the north and their own relationship to them, Russians, by contrast, have given relatively little thought to the "south." "For the majority of Russian society, the Little Russian people are *terra incognita*," observed

---

9. The reviewer was, in fact, very favorably disposed toward Kvitka-Osnovianenko's work and lamented that Russian readers "were deprived of this delight." See the review of Kvitka-Osnovianenko's *Malorossiiskiia povesti razskazyvaemyia Gryts'kom Osnov'ianenkom* in *Severnaia pchela*, 1834, no. 248: 1–2. On Ukrainian as a "dying" language and culture, see also the review of *Zaporozhskaia starina* in *Biblioteka dlia chteniia* 2 (1834): 13–19; the review of Kirill Topolia's *Chary, ili neskol'ko stsen iz narodnykh bylei i rasskazov ukrainskikh* in *Biblioteka dlia chteniia*, no. 25 (1837): 51–72; the review of Amvrosii Mohyla's *Dumki i pesni* in *Severnaia pchela*, 1839, no. 110: 438; the review of Taras Shevchenko's *Kobzar* in *Severnaia pchela*, 1840, no. 101: 403; the review of *Lastivka* by L. L. in *Severnaia pchela*, 1841, no. 143: 571; and Vissarion Belinsky's review of Kvitka-Osnovianenko's *Svatannia* in *Otechestvennye zapiski* (1841), reprinted in Belinskii, *PSS*, 6: 200–201.

10. As Kvitka wrote to the editor of *Utrenniaia zvezda* in 1833, Russian critics "do not understand our language and hence they growl and say about our books: 'there is no need to print them when nobody understands them'.... Wait, gentlemen, don't be so contemptuous. There are some Orthodox Christians left in the world who know and like our language. Not everything is for the Russians. Perhaps we deserve to have something too .... Let our writers try as they can to write our language. I believe that we should write as we speak." See H. Kvitka-Osnov'ianenko, "Suplika do pana izdatelia," in his *Tvory*, vol. 4 (Kyiv, 1957), pp. 41–43; and V. Tarnavs'kyi, "Dva lysty H. F. Kvitky do A. O. Kraievs'koho," *Literatura* (Kyiv, 1928); and George S. N. Luckyj, *Between Gogol' and Ševčenko: Polarity in the Literary Ukraine, 1798–1847* (Munich, 1971), p. 47.

Aleksandr Pypin, the nineteenth-century Russian Slavist and cultural historian.[11] For the Ukrainian elite—Gogol no less than Shevchenko, and Viktor Kochubei no less than Mykhailo Hrushevsky—their place within the larger framework of the Russian Empire and their identity vis-à-vis Russian culture were fundamental issues. Russians seem to have been far less troubled by their relationship to the "south." Russians like Nikolai Repnin[12] and Izmail Sreznevsky[13] who had

11. A. N. Pypin, *Istoriia russkoi ėtnografii*, vol. 2, *Ėtnografiia malorusskaia* (St. Petersburg, 1892), p. 309. Similar observations were made many times by Ukrainian intellectuals. See, for example, N. Vasilenko [Mykola Vasylenko], "O. M. Bodianskii i ego zaslugi dlia izucheniia Malorossii," *Kievskaia starina* 80 (December 1903): 715.

12. Nikolai Repnin (1778–1845) served as governor of Little Russia (Malorossiia) between 1816 and 1834 and was married to the granddaughter of Kyrylo Rozumovsky, the last hetman of Ukraine. His memorandum of 1821 urging the tsar to honor the terms of the Treaty of Pereiaslav and arguing that autonomy was compatible with autocracy stands out as an exception in Russian writings about Ukraine. See N. Repnin, "Zapiska o malorossiiskikh kozakakh," *Chteniia v Imperatorskom obshchestve istorii i drevnostei rossiiskikh pri Moskovskom universitete*, April–June 1864, no. 5: 85–130. Velychenko, *National History*, p. 112; and Saunders, *Ukrainian Impact*, 23–25 and passim.

13. Izmail Sreznevsky (1812–80), the renowned Russian philologist and Slavist, grew up in Kharkiv and spent a large part of his career at Kharkiv University, where he emerged as a central figure of the Kharkiv Romantic school. As a young scholar, he published *Zaporozhskaia starina* (1833–38), a collection of historical Ukrainian stories, legends, songs and *dumy*, as well as excerpts from the Cossack chronicles, including a selection from the yet unpublished *Istoriia Rusov*. He also tried his hand at Ukrainian verse (*Ukrainskii al'manakh*, 1831) and energetically defended the integrity and independence of the Ukrainian language, calling it "one of the richest of the Slavic languages" ("Vzgliad na pamiatniki ukrainskoi narodnoi slovesnosti," *Uchenye zapiski Imperatorskogo Moskovskogo universiteta* 6 [Moscow, 1834], no. 4). His circle of colleagues and friends included Amvrosii Metlynsky, Gogol, Hryhorii Kvitka-Osnovianenko, Vasyl Karazyn, Ivan Kotliarevsky, Panteleimon Kulish, Levko Borovykovsky, and Mykola Kostomarov, his student at Kharkiv University. In 1847, shortly before the arrest of Kulish and Kostomarov and the other members of the Brotherhood of SS. Cyril and Methodius, Sreznevsky moved to St. Petersburg. When the Third Section, in its efforts to combat the "revolutionary" ideas of the pan-Slavists, turned its attention to the field of Slavic studies as a whole, Sreznevsky began to distance himself from Ukrainian circles, and his views and attitudes toward the Ukrainian language and culture also began to change. In 1849 he published *Mysli ob istorii russkogo iazyka*, in which he argued that Ukrainian was the southern vernacular of Old Russian and arose only in the thirteenth and fourteenth centuries. As we shall see, this work had a profound effect not only on the subsequent development of Russian linguistics, but also on the Russian-

lived in Ukraine constituted a notable exception, although by the late 1850s even Sreznevsky had repudiated his earlier views on the separate existence of a Ukrainian language.[14]

Thus, when the Ukrainian cultural revival caught the attention of educated Russian society in the 1830s, it did so largely because it was perceived as a *native* phenomenon, a vital aid to understanding "Russian" (in the sense of *russkii*) antiquity and "Russian" national character, and as a reaffirmation of Russian (as opposed to Polish) claims to Right-Bank Ukraine.[15] Indeed, among the staunchest

---

Ukrainian discourse in the second half of the nineteenth century. Sreznevsky's theory remained current in Russia for decades, but was later successfully challenged by the work of such linguists as Oleksander Potebnia (1835–91) and Aleksei Shakhmatov (1864–1920), who posited the much earlier and autochthonous development of Ukrainian. "Izmail Ivanovich Sreznevskii," *Russkii biograficheskii slovar'*, vol. 19 (1909), pp. 276–98; N. I. Kostomarov, *Istoricheskie issledovaniia. Avtobiografiia* (Kyiv, 1989), pp. 460–61, 560; Pypin, *Istoriia russkoi ėtnografii*, 2: 312–25; Barsukov, *Zhizn' i trudy*, vol. 15 (St. Petersburg, 1901), pp. 366–77; Luckyj, *Between Gogol' and Ševčenko*, pp. 60–62.

14. The list of "philo-Ukrainians"—to use Paul Bushkovitch's term—who had lived in Ukraine or were themselves partly Ukrainian includes M. T. Kachenovsky, the editor of *Vestnik Evropy*; A. A. Kraevsky, the editor of *Otechestvennye zapiski*; and S. A. Burachek, the publisher of *Maiak* (1840–45), the most consistently pro-Ukrainian periodical in nineteenth-century Russia. Indeed, many of the *Maiak* staff and contributors had personal connections to Ukraine (Sementovsky, Kalaidensky, Korsun, Tikhorsky, Korsakov).

15. See, for example, M. Pogodin, "Istoricheskie razmyshleniia ob otnosheniiakh Pol'shi i Rossii," *Teleskop*, 1831, no. 2: 295–311.

Both Luckyj (*Between Gogol' and Ševčenko)* and Bushkovitch ("The Ukraine in Russian Culture") have framed the discussion of Russian attitudes toward Ukrainian cultural efforts in terms of political camps—liberal, conservative, reactionary—and have convincingly demonstrated that such attitudes transcended political orientation and ideology. Indeed, Bushkovitch regards Vissarion Belinsky, the Russian literary critic and Westernizer, and Osip Senkovsky, the conservative editor of *Biblioteka dlia chteniia*, as exceptions to the general "philo-Ukrainian" feelings of the age, which was still largely informed by notions of dynastic statism and a certain old-world cosmopolitanism. The difficulty with this general approach is that it overlooks the *nature* of the discourse and how it changed in the 1830s and 1840s, i.e., the way in which Russian intellectuals actually thought and wrote about the Ukrainian movement—and the degree to which Belinsky's and Senkovsky's "exceptional" views on the "provincialism" and "plebeianism" of Ukrainian culture eventually came to dominate the discourse on Ukraine after 1850. This approach also makes it difficult to explain why it was the least "cosmopolitan" and most nationally minded circles in Russia that embraced the Ukrainian movement with such great enthusiasm—or why most of these same individuals (Mikhail Pogodin, Nikolai Polevoi, etc.) later turned hostile to it defenders of the Ukrainian literary experiment were the proponents of "official nationality," especially intellectuals like Stepan Shevyrev

---

in the 1850s and 1860s. The common denominator among the "philo-Ukrainians" of the 1830s and 1840s was not, in fact, their "cosmopolitanism," but rather their Romantic interest in national character (*narodnost'*). For them, Slavic history and culture were a way of understanding Russian history and culture, especially of the early period. (And not all Russians who shared this fascination were necessarily "conservative" or "reactionary"—witness the enthusiasm of the "dangerous liberal" Nikolai Polevoi in the early 1830s.) Indeed, many of the "philo-Ukrainians," such as Pogodin, Shevyrev, Khomiakov, Polevoi, and Nadezhdin, were associated with the Moscow intellectual milieu—Moscow University was the first to introduce Slavic history and literature into its curriculum and long remained the leading center of Slavic studies in Russia. The key figures in stimulating and sustaining their interest in Ukrainian matters were Mykhailo Maksymovych (1804–73), the Ukrainian cultural historian and paterfamilias of the early Ukrainian movement, and Osyp Bodiansky (1808–78), professor of Slavic "dialectics" and editor of the prestigious *Chteniia v Imperatorskom obshchestve istorii i drevnostei rossiiskikh*. Both studied and taught at Moscow University (Maksymovych moved to Kyiv in 1832), were active in Moscow intellectual circles, and played a crucial role in bringing together Russian and Ukrainian scholars and writers.

Tellingly, the government investigation of the secret Brotherhood of SS. Cyril and Methodius in 1847 focused on the activities of the Russian as well as the Ukrainian "Slavophiles," as they were referred to in the official documents. ("Slavist" or "Pan-Slavist" are perhaps better terms, so as to avoid confusion with the "Slavophiles," though even these terms are problematic and misleading, because they conceal the degree to which the first Russian "Pan-Slavs" were intellectually preoccupied with their own culture and history and how distant they still were before 1848 from any political program.) The Russian Slavists were "for the most part Moscow writers" who were "concerned with affirming a real Russian language and philosophy, with purifying our nationality [*narodnost'*] of superfluous foreign accretions," noted Count Orlov, who headed the investigation, in his report to the tsar in May 1847. Orlov believed that this preoccupation with *narodnost'* on the part of the Russian Slavists could be a positive force in Russian society, whereas the interest of the "Little Russians" in their language, literature, and customs, on the other hand, could lead to dreams of restoring the Hetmanate and their former rights. Even so, the Third Section continued to monitor closely the publications and activities of the Moscow Slavists, and the Ministry of Education greatly tightened its control over the teaching of "Slavic studies" in schools and universities. See *Kyrylo-Mefodiïvs'ke tovarystvo*, ed. P. S. Sokhan', vol. 3 (Kyiv, 1990), pp. 306–24. On the links between Moscow intellectuals and the Ukrainian movement, see *Pis'ma M. P. Pogodina k M. A. Maksimovichu* (St. Petersburg, 1882); Barsukov, *Zhizn' i trudy*, esp. 4: 113–18; 5: 107, 216–17, 457–62; 7: 3–4, 141–47; 12: 54; Vasilenko, "O. M. Bodianskii i ego zaslugi dlia izucheniia Malorossii," *Kievskaia starina* 80 (1903): 1–50, 295–322, 462–91; 81 (1903): 315–46; 83 (1903): 140–52; 389–430, 701–35; and Pypin, *Istoriia russkoi ètnografii*, 1: 31–49.

(1806–64) and Mikhail Pogodin (1800–75), who had an abiding interest, both scholarly and philosophical, in issues of "Russianness" and *narodnost'*.[16] For them, as for many of the early Russian champions of Ukrainian literature, Ukraine and the Ukrainian language and culture were associated—at least initially—with visions of Kyivan Rus', which they regarded as the spiritual and physical core of ancient Russia.[17] They took an active interest in Ukrainian publications, developed extensive ties with Ukrainian writers and academics and, for more than a decade, supported the Ukrainian cultural revival on the grounds that it was the key to comprehending their *own* past and enriching their *own* language and culture.[18] As Nikolai Nadezhdin, editor of *Teleskop* and member of the Moscow "Ukrainophile" circles, declared in 1831, the Little Russians had a special mission: "to be for us the organs of their poetic land, rich in the priceless remains of *Russian antiquity common to us all*. Let them plow this fertile soil, under which *lie the memories of our own youth*, frozen by the cold northern clime"[19] (emphasis added).

As the wave of enthusiasm for Romanticism waned and Ukrainian "tribal particularism" asserted itself ever more forcefully, Russian interest in the Ukrainian revival began to fade. Ironically, it was the

---

16. On the considerable influence of these two Russian thinkers, see Nicholas V. Riasanovsky, "Pogodin and Ševyrëv in Russian Intellectual History," in *Russian Thought and Politics*, ed. Hugh McLean, Martin E. Malia, and George Fischer (Cambridge, Mass., 1957), pp. 149–67; Paul Bushkovitch, "Orthodoxy and Old Rus' in the Thought of S. P. Shevyrev," *Forschungen zur osteuropäischen Geschichte* 46 (1992): 204–20; Ulrich Picht, *M. P. Pogodin und die Slavische Frage: Ein Beitrag zur Geschichte des Panslavismus* (Stuttgart, 1969); Barsukov, *Zhizn' i trudy*; and Pypin, *Istoriia russkoi ėtnografii*, 1: 32; 2: 319–25.

17. On the Russian Romantic association between Ukraine and Kyivan Rus', see Nikolai Barsukov's monumental biography, *Zhizn' i trudy M. P. Pogodina*, esp. 4: 54–118, 327–30.

18. See, for example, *Moskvitianin*, 1841, no. 10: 444–55; 1842, no. 3: 179; and 1843, no. 7: 126–33. Andrei Aleksandrovich Kraevsky, the editor of *Otechestvennye zapiski*, once confided to Maksymovych: "The sounds of the poetic Ukraine were always pleasant to my heart; they touched something native and close to the ideally Russian" ("Lyst do A. O. Kraievs'koho," in H. F. Kvitka-Osnov'ianenko, *Tvory*, vol. 6 [Kyiv, 1957], p. 635).

19. See Nadezhdin's review of *Ukrainskii al'manakh* in *Teleskop*, 1831, no. 5: 104–6; and his "Evropeizm i narodnost' v otnoshenii k russkoi slovenosti," *Teleskop* 31 (1836): 5–60, 203–64, esp. p. 247. V. Lugansky expressed the same idea even more bluntly in his review of Kvitka's short stories: "We ought to study [Little Russian] as an aid to our language" (*Severnaia pchela*, 1835, no. 17: 2–3).

inaccessibility of the Ukrainian language and experience—its very foreignness—that contributed to the decline in interest. In the end, even well-disposed Russian publishers and literary critics could not escape the fact that the Ukrainian "dialect" was an insurmountable barrier for the Russian reading public.[20] As the reviewer for *Biblioteka dlia chteniia* (Library for Reading) remarked in 1842, on the occasion of the printing of the first full edition of Ivan Kotliarevsky's *Eneïda* (Aeneid), "Humor ... simply cannot be exported from one land to another like pork fat and hemp.... For Russian readers who have not had the opportunity to live in Little Russia or its neighboring lands, Mr. Kotliarevsky's poem is incomprehensible, even with the help of a dictionary."[21] Indeed, the more deeply Ukrainian writers and intellectuals "plowed the fertile soil of their poetic land," the more plainly they exposed a differing cultural sensibility, a singular past, and an "uncommon" historical consciousness. As Mikhail Pogodin himself confessed in 1845, "The Great Russians live side by side with the Little Russians, profess one faith, share one fate and, for many years, one history. But how many differences there are between the Great Russians and the Little Russians! In certain respects, we [the Great Russians] have more in common with the French than with them!" "What is the nature of our similarity?" Pogodin wondered. "That is a very difficult question...."[22]

The turning point was, of course, the publication of Taras Shevchenko's *Kobzar* (1840), undoubtedly the single most important event in modern Ukrainian literature.[23] Shevchenko's work, more than any

---

20. Kvitka-Osnovianenko was repeatedly told by publishers that there was no point in publishing Ukrainian works, as "nobody understands them." See his "Suplika do pana izdatelia," *Tvory*, vol. 4 (Kyiv, 1957), pp. 41–43.

21. *Biblioteka dlia chteniia* 56 (1843): 46–49. The incomprehensibility of the Ukrainian "dialect" became a common complaint among reviewers. See, for example, *Severnaia pchela*, 1834, no. 248: 1–2; *Molva*, 1835, no. 27–30; *Biblioteka dlia chteniia* 48 (1841): 43–46; and Vasilenko, "O. M. Bodianskii," p. 468.

22. *Moskvitianin*, 1845, no. 3, quoted in M. Maksymovych, *Kiev iavilsia gradom velikim* (Kyiv, 1994), p. 351.

23. It is telling that in 1847 Shevchenko was punished *not* for his involvement in the Brotherhood of SS. Cyril and Methodius—the official government reports concluded that there was no evidence of Shevchenko's formal involvement in the secret society—but rather for the "seditious spirit and impertinence" of his Ukrainian poetry and the enormous influence it enjoyed among the Little Russians. In his poetry, according to the report, Shevchenko "expressed a lament for the imaginary enslavement and calamities [suffered] by Ukraine; he proclaimed the glories of hetman rule and the former freedoms [enjoyed by] the Cossacks, and with unbelievable depravity slandered the

other, gave living expression to the collective—and clearly distinctive—myths that served to define Ukrainians. It was, in the words of George Grabowicz, the articulation of an entire cultural language—a language grounded in the Cossack past, its heroic epics (*dumy*) and folklore, as well as a profound sense of loss and victimization—a language that was "stunningly manifest to virtually all Ukrainians" and yet "hardly perceived" by the Russian critics.[24] *Kobzar* met with a mixed reception by Russian reviewers, most of whom acknowledged the young poet's abilities, but failed to discern entire facets of his poetry. "We really do not understand how anyone with talent can waste his time [on Little Russian poetry]," lamented the publicist and erstwhile "Ukrainophile" Nikolai Polevoi in his review of *Kobzar* in *Syn otechestva* (Son of the Fatherland). "It is sad to see Mr. Shevchenko disfigure ideas and the Russian language by surrendering to the *khokhol* manner. He has soul and feeling and his Russian verse would undoubtedly augment the development of contemporary Russian poetry."[25] (This notion of Ukrainian as a "disfigurement" or "corruption" of a "true" and "pure" Russian language and culture soon became, as we shall see, a recurrent—indeed, dominant—motif in the second half of the nineteenth century.)[26]

The Ukrainian cultural revival never again elicited as much interest or sympathy from Russian educated society as it did during

members of the imperial family, forgetting that they were his personal benefactors" (*Kyrylo-Mefodiïvs'ke tovarystvo*, 2: 329–32; 3: 306–10).

24. The problem of Shevchenko's reception does not turn on the issue of "Ukrainophilia" or "Ukrainophobia"—Shevchenko clearly had many Russian admirers, including Turgenev, Chernyshevsky, and Dobroliubov. Rather, as George Grabowicz has argued, it involves the considered response to his poetry. In this respect, "large, indeed defining aspects of his poetry and his thought remained invisible." See George G. Grabowicz, "Insight and Blindness in the Reception of Ševčenko: The Case of Kostomarov," *Harvard Ukrainian Studies* 17, nos. 3–4 (December 1993): 304–5; and idem, "Ukrainian-Russian Literary Relations," in *Ukraine and Russia in Their Historical Encounter*, p. 219.

25. *Syn otechestva*, 1840, no. 2: 836–37. See also *Otechestvennye zapiski*, 1840, no. 6: 23–24; *Severnaia pchela*, 1840, no. 101: 403; *Moskvitianin*, 1844, no. 6: 71–72; *Severnaia pchela*, 1844, no. 140: 558–59; and *Biblioteka dlia chteniia* 65 (1844): 1–7. In all, there were nine reviews of *Kobzar*. See *T. H. Shevchenko: Bibliohrafiia literatury pro zhyttia i tvorchist', 1839–1959*, ed. I. Z. Boiko et al., vol. 1 (Kyiv, 1963), pp. 9–13.

26. For example, in his memorandum of July 1863 banning publications in the Ukrainian language, Petr Valuev (1815–90), the minister of internal affairs, referred to Ukrainian as a "dialect of Russian used by the common folk that has been corrupted by the influence on it of the Polish language" (M. Lemke, *Ėpokha tsenzurnykh reform 1859–1865 godov* [St. Petersburg, 1904], p. 303).

the 1830s and early 1840s.[27] In 1861, when the Ukrainian journal *Osnova* (Foundation) began to appear, the Russian cultural establishment, which had so eagerly welcomed the Ukrainian movement only two decades earlier, opposed this new publishing venture. By this time, former "Ukrainophiles" like Mikhail Pogodin and Ivan Aksakov had become convinced that the further encouragement of the Ukrainian language and culture would only vitiate the development of an "all-Russian" culture and nation (*obshcherusskoe razvitie*).[28]

Enduring Myths and Identities

The third notable feature of the modern Russian-Ukrainian discourse has been the tenacity and stability of certain historical and cultural myths. Russians and Ukrainians alike have tended to view themselves and each other through the prism of their own respective historical narratives, cultural constructs, and identities. For Russians, that identity was rooted in the dynasty, the church, and the state—for much of its history a monolithic, unitary, and centralized state. To be

27. Bushkovitch has argued ("The Ukraine in Russian Culture," p. 361) that "the general turn" against the Ukrainian cultural movement came only after the Crimean War. If we look at the frequency with which Ukrainian publications (i.e., books in Ukrainian and/or books about Ukraine) were reviewed in the major journals of the period, there is a noticeable decline in interest in the 1840s, particularly after the arrest of the members of the Brotherhood of SS. Cyril and Methodius in 1847. (*Maiak*, the most unabashedly pro-Ukrainian periodical, ceased publication in 1845.) Moreover, the tone of the increasingly rare reviews themselves changed, becoming more dismissive and clearly less enthusiastic. Indeed, the first hints of Mikhail Pogodin's own disillusionment with the Ukrainian movement can be found in his review of *Istoriia Rusov* (*Moskvitianin*, 1849, no. 20: 55–74). See also Vasyl' Sypovs'kyi, *Ukraïna v rosiis'komu pys'menstvi. Ch. 1 (1801–1850 rr.)*, Zbirnyk Istorychno-filolohichnoho viddilu Vseukraïns'koï akademiï nauk 58 (Kyiv, 1928); and A. I. Komarov, "Ukrainskii iazyk, fol'klor i literatura v russkom obshchestve nachala XIX veka," *Uchenye zapiski Leningradskogo universiteta: Seriia filologicheskikh nauk*, 1939, no. 4: 124–58.

28. Barsukov, *Zhizn' i trudy*, 16: 124. By the 1860s, as Paul Bushkovitch has observed, "philo-Ukrainian" sentiments could be found only in radical circles (Chernyshevsky, Dobroliubov, etc.) ("The Ukraine in Russian Culture," p. 363). But here, too, the nature of the Russian radical discourse on Ukraine needs to be fully examined. The radicals of the 1860s sympathized with Ukrainians not because they were interested in Ukrainian culture per se, but rather because the Ukrainian question had social relevance. Indeed, in the language of Russian radical politics, Ukrainian cultural and national concerns came to be regarded as an obstacle to social emancipation and progress—a position that ultimately put the Ukrainian movement at odds with the Russian political opposition.

sure, Russian identity underwent a complex evolution and produced a number of significant variations—dynastic statism, official nationality, Slavophilism—but the Russian myth, I would nonetheless argue, rested to a large degree on the uninterrupted history of these three institutions.[29] The Ukrainian myth, by contrast, has been constructed, since at least the seventeenth century, around the concept of a Ukrainian people apart from the state (a Ruthenian or Rus' *narod*) and the idea of a distinct historical experience and culture.[30] Ukrainian identity also underwent considerable change in the course of two centuries after the Treaty of Pereiaslav, evolving from an association with the distinct legal order of the Hetmanate to an association with a distinct culture, a distinct "ethnos." Yet a sense of distinctiveness and individuality, cultivated and reinforced by the traditions of elite and folk culture, remained at the very heart of this identity.[31]

Well into the nineteenth century, travelers to Ukraine—including Russian visitors—continued to remark on the persistence and intensity of these perceived differences.[32] As Iurii Venelin (1802–39), a Moscow

---

29. At the conference at which this paper was presented, Paul Bushkovitch made a similar point at much greater length. Bushkovitch, however, puts greater emphasis on statist conceptions of Russian identity and less emphasis on the importance of Orthodoxy. See his "What is Russia? Russian National Identity and the State, 1500–1917" in this volume.

30. As Frank Sysyn has noted, Ukrainians began using the term *natio* to refer to themselves in the sixteeenth century, while the term *narod* came into use in the seventeenth century. See Frank E. Sysyn, "Concepts of Nationhood in Ukrainian History Writing, 1620–1690," *Concepts of Nationhood in Early Modern Eastern Europe* (=*Harvard Ukrainian Studies* 10, nos. 3–4 [December 1986]), pp. 393–423; idem, "The Cultural, Social and Political Context of Ukrainian History-Writing, 1620–1690," *Europa Orientalis* 5 (1986): 285–310; Ihor Ševčenko, "The Rise of National Identity to 1700," in his *Ukraine between East and West* (Edmonton and Toronto, 1996), pp. 186–96; and Velychenko, *National History*, esp. chapter 8.

31. Despite the existence of a considerable body of nineteenth-century Ukrainian folklore and folklore scholarship, the role of *dumy*, folk songs, folk tales and legends in constructing and transmitting popular notions of identity, geography, and history has been badly neglected by Western scholars. Contrary to the idea that "Ukrainians were far from any sense of belonging to a Ukrainian nation" in the nineteenth century (Geoffrey Hosking, *Russia: People and Empire* [Cambridge, Mass., 1997], p. 27), these songs and stories demonstrate a rather sophisticated sense of identity. See, for example, a song recorded in Kharkiv province in 1886 and recently republished in *Ukraïns'ki narodni dumy ta istorychni pisni* (Kyiv, 1990), p. 151, and in *Heroïchnyi epos ukraïns'koho narodu* (Kyiv, 1993), p. 159.

32. In 1838, the German traveler Johann Georg Kohl observed that "Ukrainians are extremely bad Russian patriots. Love and adoration of the tsar, so

scholar originally from Transcarpathia, lamented in 1832, the "Southerners" or Little Russians still regarded Russians as aliens (*ne svoi*).[33] "The Southerners do not permit the Northerners to participate in their

---

proper to the Muscovites, are to the Ukrainians completely alien and incomprehensible. The Ukrainians obey the tsar because they are forced to, but they consider his authority alien and imposed .... If you do not want to offend a Ukrainian, do not tell him about the conquest of Ukraine by Muscovy, for the Ukrainian is aware of the fact that his country concluded a treaty with Muscovy, only to be deceived by the latter" (J. G. Kohl, *Russia: St. Petersburg, Moscow, Kharkoff, Riga, Odessa, the German Provinces on the Baltic, the Steppes, the Crimea, and the Interior of the Empire* [London, 1842], p. 197). This was not an uncommon observation in travel accounts from the late eighteenth to the mid-nineteenth century. See, for example, V. Zuev, *Puteshestvennye zapiski Vasil'ia Zueva ot S. Peterburga do Khersona v 1781 i 1782 godu* (St. Petersburg, 1787); P. Sumarokov, *Dosugi krymskogo sud'i* (St. Petersburg, 1803); A. Levshin, *Pis'ma iz Malorossii* (Kharkiv, 1816); Charles-Louis Lesur, *Histoire des Kosaques* (Paris, 1812–13); C. Maltebrun, *Tableau de la Pologne ancienne et moderne* (Paris, 1807); A. Pishchevich, "Primechaniia na Novorossiiskii krai," *Kievskaia starina*, 1884, no. 1: 111–34; Freiherr August Franz Ludwig Maria von Haxthausen-Abbenburg, *Studien über die inneren Zustände, das Volksleben und insbesondere die ländlichen Einrichtungen Rußlands* (Hanover, 1847), trans. into English by Robert Faire as *The Russian Empire, Its People, Institutions, and Resources* (London, 1856); Johann Heinrich Blasius, *Reise im europäischen Rußland in den Jahren 1840 und 1841* (Braunschweig, 1844); A. Petzholdt, *Reise im westlichen und südlichen europäischen Rußland im Jahre 1855* (Leipzig, 1864); Ivan Aksakov, *Ivan Sergeevich Aksakov v ego pis'makh*, vol. 1 (Moscow, 1888); Friedrich Bodenstedt, *Die poetische Ukraine* (Stuttgart, 1845); and K. Delamarre, *Un peuple européen de quinze millions oublié devant l'histoire* (Paris, 1869).

For a survey of the travel literature, see D. Doroschenko, "Die Ukraine und ihre Geschichte im Lichte der westeuropäischen Literatur des XVIII. und der ersten Hälfte des XIX. Jahrhunderts," *Abhandlungen des Ukrainischen Wissenschaftlichen Institutes* 1 (Berlin, 1927); Volodymyr Sichynsky, *Ukraine in Foreign Comments and Descriptions from the VIth to XXth Century* (New York, 1953); and Oleksa Vintoniak, *Ukraïna v opysakh zakhidn'oievropeis'kykh podorozhnykiv druhoï polovyny XVIII stolittia* (Lviv and Munich, 1995).

33. Venelin argued, in fact, that these distinctions were just as strong among Russian peasants: "If you say you are a *Malo-ross* (Little Russian), all the same you are not a Russian (*russkii*), because the word *ross* is foreign to the Russian common folk. They care little whether you are a little *ross* or a big one, all the same you are not a Russian, but rather a Pole, a *khokhol*, a *litva*, a Cossack, a Ukrainian, or something similar. In short, you are not one of them...." What is new and remarkable in Venelin's article, I would argue, is the expectation that these distinctions, which had been operative for more than three centuries, should be considered somehow "unnatural." See Iu. Venelin, "O spore mezhdu iuzhanami i severianami na shchet ikh rossizma," *Chteniia Moskovskogo obshchestva istorii i drevnostei*, 1847, no. 4: 4–5. Similarly, A. N. Pypin noted the persistence of these distinctions between Russians and Ukrainians at the end of the century (*Istoriia russkoi ètnografii*, 2: 5–6).

'Russianness' (*v rossizme*); as often as a Russian may call himself a Russian (*russkii*), all the same he will not be deemed a *rusyn*, but a *moskal'*, a *lypovan*, and a *katsap* [derogatory Ukrainian terms for Russians]." As a fervent Pan-Russianist and Pan-Slavist, Venelin considered these popular perceptions "erroneous" and a serious obstacle to the unity of the "Russian nation."[34]

Indeed, much of the instability inherent in the modern Russian-Ukrainian relationship, I would argue, was rooted in two distinct and sometimes competing visions of identity and "Russianness" (or *rossizm*, as Venelin called it), two different cultural paradigms and, ultimately, two different political models. One vision was founded on the idea of an ancient and sovereign Ukrainian-Rus' land and people. It was shaped by the struggle for rights and status—and cultural self-preservation—within the political framework of the Polish-Lithuanian Commonwealth, legitimized by the great uprising of 1648, sustained throughout the eighteenth century by the historical writings of the Cossack elite, and given a modern, Enlightenment form by the *Istoriia Rusov*.[35] Central to this vision was the notion that Ukraine-Rus' had freely and voluntarily submitted to Polish and, later, Russian

---

34. Venelin's article, which circulated for some time before its publication, was important in its own right and exerted an enormous influence on the subsequent "debate between the Southerners and Northerners." It was Venelin who, in 1832, became the first scholar in Russia to pose the problem of Russian-Ukrainian relations in ethnographic, linguistic, and cultural terms and postulate the idea of one Russian nation consisting of a southern (Little Russian) and northern (Great Russian) branch. See Pypin, *Istoriia russkoi ėtnografii*, 2: 301–7; Barsukov, *Zhizn' i trudy*, vol. 4 (1891), p. 54; Saunders, *Ukrainian Impact*, pp. 225–27; and Tamara Baitsura, *Iurii Ivanovych Venelin* (Bratislava, 1968).

35. The most widely read Cossack chronicles were those of Hryhorii Hrabianka, *Deistviia prezel'noi i ot nachala poliakov krvavshoi nebuvaloi brani Bogdana Khmelnitskogo* (1710); Samuil Velychko, *Letopis' sobytii v Iugo-Zapadnoi Rossii v XVII veke* (1720); and the anonymous *Kratkoe opisanie Malorossii* (1734). Of special interest is Semen Divovych's *Razgovor Velikorossii s Malorossieiu* (1762), written in the form of a dialogue in which Little Russia tells Great Russia that she swore fealty to the Russian tsar, not to Great Russia. All these works were reprinted in the nineteenth century. *Istoriia Rusov* was first published in full in Moscow in 1846, after circulating in manuscript for more than twenty years. While relying heavily on the Cossack chronicles and eighteenth-century archival materials, *Istoriia Rusov* nonetheless departs from this tradition with the introduction of unmistakably "modern" Enlightenment themes: life, liberty, and property as the inalienable rights of all individuals and the assumption that each nation has a natural right to independent political development.

monarchs "for all eternity" on the basis of legal covenants that guaranteed its specific corporate rights.[36]

The other vision emphasized the postulate of an all-Russian nation—the idea that Ukrainians and Russians shared a common "Russian" identity based on a common Orthodox heritage, a common Rus' origin, and a common historical destiny. It was a vision that, paradoxically, had also been animated by the religious and political turmoil of the late sixteenth- and seventeenth-century Polish-Lithuanian Commonwealth. Promoted initially by Orthodox clerical circles in Ukraine—by those Ukrainians who built the first intellectual bridges between Ukraine and Muscovy—it was inspired by the concept of *Slavia Orthodoxa*, a larger Slavic Orthodox spiritual and cultural community that extended well beyond the boundaries of the *Rzeczpospolita*.[37] In

---

36. Ukrainian folk culture evinces a number of very interesting counterparts to this idea of a contractual relationship. In a legend about the origins of the Zaporozhian Cossacks recorded in Katerynoslav province in 1894, for example, the tsar sets out—and fails—to conquer the Zaporozhians, is himself captured by them, and agrees to issue a decree granting the Zaporozhians control over their land ("so that our land will be demarcated and whosoever crosses the boundary belongs to us"). See "Pokhodzhennia zaporozhtsiv," *Heroïchnyi epos ukraïns'koho narodu* (Kyiv, 1993), p. 266. See also *Istoriia Rusov* (Moscow, 1846; repr. Kyiv, 1991), p. 6; and Velychenko, *National History*, pp. 148, 156. Many of the nineteenth-century travel accounts (Lesur, Maltebrun, Pishchevich, Kohl, Delamarre) also emphasize the antiquity of the "Little Russian race" and/or the voluntary nature of Ukraine's association with Russia.

37. The idea of an "Eastern" church that united Ukrainians with the Greek East and Muscovite Rus' in the struggle against the "Latin West" strongly influenced the writings of Ivan Vyshensky, Meletii Smotrytsky, Zakhariia Kopystensky, and other anti-Uniate polemicists of the late sixteenth and early seventeenth centuries. One aspect of this was the revival of the Greek-derived ecclesiastical terms "Mala" and "Velika Rosiia" (the metropolitan sees of Little and Great Rosiia) in an attempt to enlist the interest and support of Ukraine's northern neighbor. (The term "Mala Rosiia" had come into use in Ukraine in the fourteenth century with the division of the Kyiv metropolitan see and the creation of the Lviv metropolitanate, but was unknown in Muscovy before 1592.) According to Serhii Plokhy, the first known use of these ecclesiastical terms since the fourteenth century occurred in a letter of 1592 from the Lviv brotherhood to the Russian tsar, in which Metropolitan Dionysios of Tŭrnovo was referred to as the exarch of "Mala and Velyka Rosiia." The terms "Malaia Rossiia" (Little Russia) and "Velikaia Rossiia" (Great Russia) came into civil use in Muscovy only in 1654, when they were added to the tsar's title. See Harvey Goldblatt, "Orthodox Slavic Heritage and National Consciousness: Aspects of the East Slavic and South Slavic National Revivals," *Harvard Ukrainian Studies* 10, nos. 3–4 (December 1986): 336–54; Paul Bushkovitch, "The Formation of National Consciousness in Early Modern Russia," ibid., pp.

fact, the idea of an all-Russian nation found its first full expression in the *Synopsis*,[38] a history of the "origins of the Slaveno-Rossian nation" (*slaveno-rosiiskii narod*) published in Kyiv in 1674 under the patronage of Inokentii Gizel, the archimandrite of the Caves Monastery.[39] By justifying the union with Muscovy on religious and dynastic grounds and casting the tsar in the role of the Orthodox autocrat (*pravoslavnyi samoderzhets*), a successor to Volodymyr and the defender of a Slavic-Rus' Orthodox realm, the *Synopsis* prepared the way for a modern Russian historical narrative in which the Treaty of Pereiaslav came to be regarded as the reaffirmation of an organic, virtually inevitable process—the "reunion of the Russians lands and nation."[40]

355–76; Teresa Chynczewska-Hennel, "The National Consciousness of Ukrainian Nobles and Cossacks from the End of the Sixteenth to the Mid-Seventeenth Century," ibid., pp. 377–92; N. N. [N. Nadezhdin], "Velikaia Rossiia," *Ėntsiklopedicheskii leksikon*, vol. 9 (St. Petersburg, 1837), pp. 261–77; A. Solov'ev, "Velikaia, Malaia i Belaia Rus'," *Voprosy istorii*, 1947, no. 7: 24–38; and Serhii Plokhy, "Beresteis'ka uniia ta novi kontseptsiï Rusi" (unpublished paper presented at the Brest Readings, Session 6, Kyiv, May 1996). On the concept of *Slavia Orthodoxa*, see the seminal work of Riccardo Picchio, "Die historisch-philologische Bedeutung der kirchenslavichen Tradition," *Die Welt der Slaven* 7 (1962): 1–27.

38. The original title was *The Synopsis, or short compilation from various chronicles about the origin of the Slavic-Rus' nation and the first princes of the divinely preserved city of Kyiv and the life of the holy, pious grand prince of Kyiv and all Rossiia, the first autocrat, Volodymyr, and about the inheritors of his virtuous Rus' domain, even unto our illustrious and virtuous sovereign, tsar, and grand prince Aleksei Mikhailovich, autocrat of all Great, Little, and White Rossiia.* The *Synopsis* was published in thirty editions between 1674 and 1881. The edition of 1681 was reprinted as Hans Rothe, ed., *Sinopsis, Kiev 1681: Facsimile mit einer Einleitung* (Cologne and Vienna, 1983). On the importance of the *Synopsis* for later Russian historiography, see Pavel Miliukov, *Glavnye techeniia russkoi istoricheskoi mysli*, vol. 1 (1898), pp. 7–16; Anatole G. Mazour, *Modern Russian Historiography*, rev. ed. (Westport, Conn., and London, 1975), pp. 16–19; N. L. Rubinshtein, *Russkaia istoriografiia* (Moscow, 1941), pp. 45–48; S. I. Maslov, "K istorii izdanii Kievskogo Sinopsisa," in *Stat'i po slavianskoi filologii i russkoi slovesnosti: Sobranie statei v chest' akademika A. I. Sobolevskogo* (Leningrad, 1928), pp. 341–48; and S. A. Peshtich, "Sinopsis kak istoricheskoe proizvedenie," *Trudy Otdela drevne-russkoi literatury* 15 (1958): 284–98.

39. By comparison, as Stephen Velychenko has noted, the Russian chronicles written shortly after the Treaty of Pereiaslav (the *Letopis' o mnogikh miatezhakh*, 1658, and the *Mazurinskii letopisets*, 1681–82) spoke of the "conquest of Lithuania, White Russia, and Little Russia," generally making no connection between Kyivan Rus' and contemporary Kyiv (Velychenko, *National History*, pp. 80–81).

40. The first modern history to characterize the Russian historical process after 1240 as a struggle for "reunion" was N. G. Ustrialov's *Russkaia istoriia*

Devaluation

The existence of two such different constructs of identity and Russianness did not, of course, preclude the possibility of a compromise "Little Russian solution," that is, a larger Russian identity that would allow room for the existence of a distinct Ukrainian "branch." Indeed, such had been the premise of the *Synopsis*, which portrayed the *slaveno-rosiiskii narod* as a kind of "meta-people," a holy alliance of "Moskva" (Muscovy) and "Rus'," each with its own national and spiritual center.[41] (The term *narod*, in this respect, was used in the medieval sense to denote common lineage, that is, descent from a common ancestor.)[42] The subordination of the Ukrainian church and the abolition of Ukrainian political autonomy notwithstanding, this bipartite (later tripartite) notion of Russianness remained operative throughout the eighteenth century, owing in no small measure to the ongoing influence of the *Synopsis* itself.[43] Eventually it became

(St. Petersburg, 1837). In the 1857 edition, Ustrialov added another dimension to the argument, portraying the Eastern Slavs as one people largely motivated by a "desire for union" after the fall of Kyivan Rus'. The text was officially endorsed by Count S. S. Uvarov, the minister of education and ideologue of "official nationality," and provided the interpretative framework for much of nineteenth- and early twentieth-century Russian historiography. See Velychenko, *National History*, pp. 97–100; and Serhy Yekelchyk, "The Grand Narrative and Its Discontents: Ukraine in Russian History Textbooks and Ukrainian Students' Minds, 1830s–1900s," in this volume.

41. As the author(s) of the *Synopsis* emphasized, in 1654 "Kyiv returned to its former condition and ancient imperial dignity." Indeed, even in its most pro-Muscovite edition of 1681, the narrative of the *Synopsis* focused largely on Kyiv, the "ruling" city and "capital of the Rus' nation," and stressed the need for Moscow and Kyiv to recognize their common interests.

42. This is certainly the sense in which the term was used by Ukrainian authors before the nineteenth century (Velychenko, *National History*, p. 144).

43. Until the publication of Lomonosov's *Kratkoi letopisets* in 1760, the *Synopsis* was the only Russian history textbook used in Russian schools, and thus served as the foundation of Russian historiography in the eighteenth century (Mazour, *Modern Russian Historiography*, p. 18; and Miliukov, *Glavnye techeniia*, 1: 7–16.) The degree to which the eighteenth-century Ukrainian secular elite actually accepted the idea of a larger Russian *nation* as opposed to state and identity remains rather unclear. In Divovych's *Razgovor Velikorossii s Malorossieiu*, for example, Little Russia says to Great Russia: "That I am called Little and you [are called] Great is as strange to me as it is to you ..." See *Kievskaia starina*, 1882, no. 2: 313–65; reprinted in *Ukraïns'ka literatura XVIII v.*, ed. V. I. Krekoten' (Kyiv, 1983), pp. 384–414. See also Zenon E. Kohut, "The Development of a Little Russian Identity and Ukrainian Nationbuilding,"

enshrined in the secular foundations of Russian scholarship as the "scientific" doctrine of an all-Russian nation consisting of three "tribes" (*plemena*) or "nationalities" (*narodnosti*): the Great Russians, Little Russians, and White Russians (Belarusians).[44]

In the long run, however, the practical success of the "Little Russian solution" depended on some sort of enduring acceptance and tolerance for the paradoxes of Ukrainian "particularism"—the "foreignness" of Ukrainian culture and experience. Yet viewing Ukrainians through the prism of a new Romantic understanding of the nation as a cultural, linguistic, and ethnic unit was something the Russian elite (including a certain ultra-loyalist segment of the Little Russian elite) found increasingly difficult to do.[45] It accorded poorly with their understanding of the needs of the Russian state, church, and dynasty (especially the need to assert Russia's historical title to Right-Bank Ukraine as a counter to Polish claims).

Concepts of Nationhood in Early Modern Eastern Europe (=*Harvard Ukrainian Studies* 10, nos. 3–4 [December 1986]), pp. 559–76.

44. The influence of the *Synopsis* on Russia's first ethnographers and cultural historians is quite unmistakable. In the *Ėntsiklopedicheskii leksikon*, 9: 263, for example, Nikolai Nadezhdin referred to the Eastern Slavs as a "*Slavianorusskoe plemia*" (tribe) which, as he explained, consisted of the *Velikorossiiskii*, *Belorusskii*, and *Malorusskii narody* (the Great Russian, White Russian, and Little Russian peoples). By the 1850s and 1860s, following the publication of Sreznevsky's *Mysli ob istorii russkogo iazyka* (1849) and several other studies that "demoted" Ukrainian to the status of a vernacular dialect of a proto-Russian language, the term *russkii narod* became the academic norm in discussing the Eastern Slavs, and it became customary to refer to the Little Russians, White Russians, and Great Russians as *plemena* (tribes), rather than *narody* (peoples). This, in fact, was the scheme adopted in the census of 1897, where the Great Russians, Little Russians, and White Russians were listed as subsets of the Russian *narod*. See *Pervaia vseobshchaia perepis' naseleniia Rossiiskoi Imperii 1897 goda* (St. Petersburg, 1897–1905). See also P. Lavrovskii, *O iazykakh severnykh russkikh letopisei* (St. Petersburg, 1852); and M. Pogodin, "Zapiska o drevnem russkom iazyke," *Izvestiia Akademii nauk po [vtorom] Otdeleniiu russkogo iazyka i slovesnosti* 5 (St. Petersburg, 1856): 70–92.

45. One example of this growing impatience with a "foreign" Ukrainian sensibility is Mikhail Pogodin's review of *Istoriia Rusov* (Z. Z., "Ob Istorii rusov Georgiia Konniskogo," *Moskvitianin*, 1849, no. 20, pt. 4: 55–74). In strikingly emotional tones, Pogodin criticized the work for its failure to present a Russian perspective on the history of Ukraine. For example, he accused the alleged eighteenth-century author of misunderstanding the peaceful intentions of Peter the Great to transform Little Russia into a Russian province and of neglecting to discuss all the benefits that had accrued from union with "mighty Great Rus', the heart of the Russian state."

Much of the difficulty, I would argue, was linked to the rather rapid devaluation of Little Russian culture between 1830 and 1860—unquestionably the defining moment in modern Russian-Ukrainian relations. The reasons for this devaluation were complex and diverse: (1) the integration of the Little Russian Cossack officer caste (*starshyna*) into the Russian nobility (1835) and the virtual disappearance of a distinct Ukrainian elite; (2) the introduction of the policy of "official nationality," with its programmatic focus on the "eternal unity of the Russian lands owing to the holy bonds of nationality"; (3) the influence of Hegelian philosophy, with its emphasis on the unilinear, teleological development of history and the distinction between "historical" and "non-historical" nations;[46] (4) the influence of Polish writings, particularly the new messianic historiography, which treated the seventeenth-century Polish-Ukrainian conflict as a struggle between "civilization" and "barbarism";[47] and (5) the Ukrainian movement's gradual shift away from gentry patriotism toward a new focus on populism, which actively identified itself with the Ukrainian peasantry. The cumulative effect of these trends and developments was that by the early 1860s Ukrainian culture had largely been "demoted" in Russian discourse to the status of a plebeian culture. *Maloross*, in effect, became synonymous with "peasant."[48]

---

46. The influence of Hegelian philosophy was particularly evident in Vissarion Belinsky's views on Ukrainian literature. It was not his "fear of a Ukrainian separatist movement" that informed his criticism of the Ukrainian literary experiment, as George Luckyj has argued, but rather his larger conception of historical development—the conviction that the "Little Russians," as a people, had never entered the stage of universal consciousness and were incapable of overcoming their "tribal particularism." His views on the Ukrainian literary revival were best summarized in his reviews of *Lastivka*, Kvitka-Osnovianenko's *Svatannia*, Shevchenko's *Haidamaky*, and Markevych's *Istoriia Malorossii*. See *Otechestvennye zapiski*, 1841, no. 16: 32–34; 1842, no. 22: 54–55; and 1843, no. 28: 1–18. See also Belinskii, *PSS*, vol. 6 (1903), pp. 199–202; vol. 7 (1904), pp. 214–16; and Andrzej Walicki, *The Slavophile Controversy* (Oxford, 1975), pp. 328–34, 369–76, 396–420.

47. See, for example, Bibiana Moraczewska's *Co się działo w Polsce* (Poznań, 1852); and W. Koronowicz [Walerian Wróblewski], *Słowo dziejów polskich*, 2 vols. (Leipzig, 1858). For a discussion of the influence of Polish historiography on Russian scholarship, see Mykola Kostomarov's *Avtobiografiia* (repr. Kyiv, 1992), p. 196; Velychenko, *National History*, pp. 32–34; and Frank Sysyn, "The Changing Image of the Hetman: On the 350th Anniversary of the Khmel'nyts'kyi Uprising," *Jahrbücher für Geschichte Osteuropas* 46 (1998): 531–45.

48. See n. 28 above.

Indeed, it was the *absence* of a distinct and integral history, language and culture that increasingly defined the Russian image of Ukraine and Ukrainians. "Little Russia was never a state," asserted Vissarion Belinsky, Russia's foremost literary critic, in 1843 in his review of Mykola Markevych's *Istoriia Malorossii*, "therefore, in the strict sense of the word, it did not have a history." The Hetmanate was a "parody of a republic," ruled not by law but by ritual, "that cornerstone of the Asiatic system."[49] As a people, he believed, the "Southerners" had never entered the stage of "universal consciousness," were unable to overcome their "tribal particularism," and were therefore incapable of producing a great literature or of making their mark on history. They were a "provincial people," their language a "provincial dialect," their poetry and chronicles a "provincial literature," "dumb and useless to the people of other nations, having meaning only for the people who gave birth to it." (It was on these grounds that Belinsky dismissed Shevchenko's epic poem *Haidamaky* and accused the author of writing solely for his own pleasure.)[50] "The history of Little Russia is nothing more than an episode in the reign of Alexei Mikhailovich," concluded Belinsky. In a different review of the same book, Osip Senkovsky (Józef-Julian Sękowski, 1800–58), the capricious editor of *Biblioteka dlia chteniia*, Russia's most widely read journal of the 1830s, went even further in discounting the Ukrainian phenomenon. Little Russian culture, he believed, was by its very nature a hybrid, a corruption of an original Russian culture, its people runaway Poles and Lithuanians, its language a mish-mash of words "forelocked and bearded, shaven and unshaven, southern taken from northern."[51] Contrary to the Romantic image of the Cossacks as defenders of the Orthodox faith—a view promoted vigorously by Markevych in *Istoriia Malorossii*—the Cossacks, asserted Senkovsky, were little more than lawless bandits who had largely brought their misfortunes on themselves. Markevych, himself the scion of an old Cossack family, was so incensed by this review that he demanded the arrest of the censor who had approved the article for publication. The matter was then referred to Count S. S. Uvarov and the Censorship Committee of the Ministry of Education, who ruled that Senkovsky was merely offering a scholarly opinion and that there was, in fact, much truth in what he said.[52]

---

49. Review of N. Markevich (Mykola Markevych), *Istoriia Malorossii* (Moscow, 1842–43), in Belinskii, *PSS*, vol. 7 (Moscow, 1955), pp. 44–65.

50. *Otechstvennye zapiski*, 1842, no. 22: 54–55; and Belinskii, *PSS*, vol. 7 (1904), pp. 214–16.

51. *Biblioteka dlia chteniia* 6 (1834): 6, 15; 39 (1840): 15; and 57 (1843): 50–64.

52. In the end, the issue was brought before the tsar, who concluded that

This trend toward the depreciation of the Ukrainian past and culture increasingly found expression in the more serious academic literature as well. The Cossack as renegade—one of Senkovsky's favorite themes—became a standard motif in Russian historical scholarship after 1848, particularly with the work of Sergei Soloviev (1820–79).[53] Portraying history as a great struggle between the forces of *gosudarstvennost'* and *antigosudarstvennost'* (state order and disorder), Soloviev cast the Cossacks in the role of an unruly, anarchical element—runaways who had fled the "obligations of productive labor in settled agriculture." (In general, he regarded "South Russia" as a hotbed of sedition, a constant source of trouble for the autocracy.)[54] Alhough ultimately Soloviev—unlike Senkovsky—did not deny the part the Cossacks had played as "defenders of the faith," he argued that it was largely an accident of history—the disappearance of the traditional Rus' elite—that had thrust them into this "unnatural" role.[55] In Soloviev's scheme, Cossack Ukraine thus came to represent a set of *internal* qualities—lack of discipline, egoism, and factiousness—that he considered a threat to the Russian state order. It was the "immaturity" of Little Russian society in the seventeenth and eighteenth centuries, concluded Soloviev in his monumental *Istoriia Rossii s drevneishikh vremen* (History of Russia since Ancient Times), that was its defining feature.[56]

In many ways, however, it was the work of the Russian historian and Pan-Slavist Mikhail Pogodin that most clearly epitomized this trend toward the devaluation and insubstantialization of the Ukrainian past

---

it should be left to scholars themselves to demonstrate the inaccuracy of Senkovsky's views. See A. V. Nikitenko, *Dnevnik*, vol. 1 (Leningrad, 1955), pp. 227–78; A. Nikitenko, *Moia povest' o samom sebe*, vol. 1 (St. Petersburg, 1904), pp. 349–50; E. M. Kosachevskaia, *N. A. Markevich* (Leningrad, 1987), pp. 6–10; Bushkovitch, "Ukraine in Russian Culture," p. 353; and Velychenko, *National History*, p. 233.

53. S. M. Solov'ev, "Ocherk istorii Malorossii do podchineniia ee tsariu Alekseiu Mikhailovichu," *Otechestennye zapiski* 61 (1848): 1–34, 147–60; 62 (1849): 215–70; idem, "Getman Ivan Vygovskii," *Otechestvennye zapiski* 127 (1859): 1–67; idem, "Malorossiiskoe kozachestvo do Bogdana Khmel'nitskogo," *Russkii vestnik* (September 1859), pp. 177–96; and idem, *Istoriia Rossii s drevneishikh vremen*, 26 vols. (St. Petersburg, 1851–79, repr. Moscow, 1959–66), esp. vols. 11–12.

54. Solov'ev, *Istoriia Rossii*, 11–12: 188–89; and Velychenko, *National History*, pp. 100–102.

55. Solov'ev, "Malorossiiskoe kozachestvo," pp. 177–96; Kostomarov, *Avtobiografiia*, p. 196; and Velychenko, *National History*, p. 117.

56. Solov'ev, *Istoriia Rossii*, 11–12: 190–91.

and culture and gave it much of its impetus. During his career at the University of Moscow (1820–44), Pogodin, as we have noted, had been an enthusiastic and outspoken Ukrainophile.[57] He was convinced at the time that "Little Russian" history and literature held the key to an understanding of early Russian history and culture, especially the high culture of Kyivan Rus'. The Primary Chronicle, he argued, was essentially a "Little Russian" document—the descendants of Riurik had "become Little Russians within five and six generations," and even when the dynasty had "moved to the northeast," he believed, it had nonetheless "preserved [its] Little Russian origins."[58] Throughout the 1830s and 1840s, Pogodin took an active interest in the Ukrainian cultural revival. He cultivated friendships with all the leading Ukrainian writers and intellectuals—Mykhailo Maksymovych, Mykola Hohol (Gogol), Hryhorii Kvitka-Osnovianenko, Semen Hulak-Artemovsky, Panteleimon Kulish, and Taras Shevchenko. He encouraged the development of Ukrainian scholarship, as well as the progress of young scholars, such as Osyp Bodiansky. And, beginning in 1835, he made several trips to Ukraine, including two celebrated visits to Lviv, in Austrian Galicia, where he established contact with local "Ruthenian" circles and adamantly insisted that they were *russkie*, in no way different from the "Little Russians in Chernihiv, Poltava, and Kharkiv."[59] Indeed, for a number of years, Pogodin, along with his close friend and colleague Stepan Shevyrev, vigorously promoted and defended the Ukrainian movement in the pages of their journal, *Moskvitianin* (The Muscovite, 1841–56). In the words of Shevyrev, Little Russia was Great Russia's "elder sister," and it would be "ingratitude" on the part of the Great Russians "not to give her her proper due."[60]

After 1847 and the discovery of the secret Brotherhood of SS. Cyril and Methodius—an affair in which the Russian historian was himself very nearly implicated because of his close association with the

57. On Pogodin, see n. 17 above. See especially Barsukov, *Zhizn' i trudy*, 4: 113–18, 425–27; 7: 141–47; and 10: 87, 422–25.

58. *Moskvitianin*, 1845, no. 3, quoted in Maksymovych, *Kiev iavilsia gradom velikim*, pp. 345–46. The Primary Chronicle reflected Little Russia and the Novgorod Chronicles Great Russia (*Issledovaniia*, 1846, 3: 357).

59. The account of his trip through Central and Eastern Europe was published in *Zhurnal Ministerstva Narodnogo Prosveshcheniia* 7 (1835): 544–52; 9 (1836): 218–25; 11 (1836): 203–7. See also Barsukov, *Zhizn' i trudy*, 4: 327–35; 7: 17; and *Pis'ma k M. P. Pogodinu iz slavianskikh zemel'* (Moscow, 1879), esp. pp. 471, 574.

60. *Moskvitianin*, 1843, no. 7: 126; and Barsukov, *Zhizn' i trudy*, 7: 141.

Ukrainian movement—Pogodin's ardor cooled noticeably.[61] Significantly, Pogodin also began to rethink his concept of Rus' and the role and place of the "Little Russians" within it. In 1856, in a rather dramatic reversal of his earlier views, Pogodin published his article "Zapiska o drevnem russkom iazyke" (Note on the Old Russian Language) in the *Izvestiia* of the Imperial Academy of Sciences, in which he asserted the historical primacy of the Great Russians. Invoking Izmail Sreznevsky's *Mysli ob istorii russkago iazyka* (Thoughts on the History of the Russian Language, 1849), which dated the origins of the "southern dialect" (Ukrainian) from the fourteenth century, Pogodin now argued that it was the Great Russians and *not* the Little Russians who were the original inhabitants of ancient Kyiv and the Dnipro (Dnieper) River basin.[62] The Little Russians, he now insisted, were a "migrant population" from Subcarpathia who gradually settled the Dnipro basin following the Mongol invasion and the evacuation of the Great Russians to the north. (The Cossacks, he believed, were a separate Slavic-Turkic tribe.) It was the Great Russians, he concluded, and *not* the Little Russians who had created the high culture of ancient Rus', its ruling dynasty, warrior caste, and

---

61. On 27 May 1847, in a secret report to the police on the reaction in Moscow to the arrest of the members of the brotherhood, M. O. Kashintsov wrote, "[It] has had a clear impact on Pogodin; he has started to talk differently about Slavdom—and he, after all, is the one, it can be said, who was the first to develop the idea." (*Kyrylo-Mefodiïvs'ke tovarystvo*, 3: 302). Remarkably, however, Pogodin's name was not directly mentioned in Count Orlov's report to the tsar, although Shevyrev and virtually all the other members of Pogodin's circle were named. Pogodin was extremely well connected in government circles—he was closely associated with Count Uvarov—and undoubtedly this played a role in the conspicuous omission of his name. In his prodigious biography of Pogodin, Barsukov describes the revulsion that the "Slavophiles" felt when they learned of the existence of the secret society (*Zhizn' i trudy*, 9: 228–38). The abrupt change in Pogodin's attitude toward the Ukrainian movement may be seen in his review of *Istoriia Rusov* in 1849—Pogodin dismissed the work as a mere panegyric to Little Russia and criticized the author for "passing over in silence all the advantages that accrued to [Little Russia] from unification with mighty Great Rus', the heart of the Russian state" (*Moskvitianin*, 1849, no. 20: 55–74). On the investigation of the Pogodin circle in 1847, see "Sprava pro Slov'ianofil'stvo ta ukraïnofil'stvo," *Kyrylo-Mefodiïvs'ke tovarystvo*, 3: 291–324; and Barsukov, *Zhizn' i trudy*, 9: 230–34.

62. M. P. Pogodin, "Zapiska o drevnem russkom iazyke," reprinted in his *Issledovaniia, zamechaniia i lektsii o russkoi istorii*, vol. 7 (St. Petersburg, 1856), pp. 410–42; idem, "Pis'mo," *Russkaia beseda*, 1856, no. 4: 124–41; and idem, *Pis'ma M. P. Pogodina k M. A. Maksimovichu*.

clergy. Pogodin thus deprived Ukrainians of any meaningful share of the Kyivan inheritance—indeed, of any meaningful share of "Russian" history and culture.[63] Ukrainian language and culture, scholars and

---

63. The Pogodin thesis dominated Russian scholarship and the Russian-Ukrainian discourse for more than 50 years. Among its many adherents were Aleksei Sobolovesky (1857–1929), the noted Russian linguist, and Vasilii Kliuchevsky (1841–1911), the historian and author of the monumental *Kurs russkoi istorii* (5 vols., 1904–21). Kliuchevsky in fact endorsed and incorporated Pogodin's theory in the first volume of his *Kurs russkoi istorii* (1904). Beginning with Mykhailo Maksymovych's passionate rejoinder in *Russkaia beseda* in 1856, the Pogodin thesis was challenged by successive generations of Ukrainian historians (Volodymyr Antonovych, Mykola Dashkevych, Mykhailo Hrushevsky) and philologists and linguists (Mykhailo Maksymovych, Pavlo Zhytetsky, Oleksander Potebnia, Ahatanhel Krymsky). The definitive refutation, however, was provided by Aleksei Shakhmatov (1864–1920), Sobolevsky's former student and arguably the most important Russian linguist of the twentieth century. On the basis of his study of Ukrainian and Belarusian dialectal groups, Shakhmatov finally abandoned the Pogodin-Sobolevsky theory in 1899 and concluded that "we have no reason to believe that the present-day Little Russians arrived in the Dnipro basin [after the fall of Kyivan Rus']. We ought to recognize them as original inhabitants of Russia.... From the shores of the Prypiat River to the Black Sea, from the Dnipro to the Carpathian Mountains, the Little Russians speak a dialect that gives clear testimony to their primordial unity" (A. A. Shakhmatov, "K voprosu ob obrazovanii russkikh narechii i russkikh narodnostei," *Zhurnal Ministerstva Narodnogo Prosveshcheniia,* April 1899, no. 322: 324–84).

What is remarkable, however, is how quickly and readily the Russian cultural establishment accepted the Pogodin thesis in 1856. Pogodin himself had offered scant evidence to support his hypothesis and had confessed to Maksymovych that he considered himself a "dilettante" in such matters. Nonetheless, such intellectual luminaries as I. I. Sreznevsky, A. S. Khomiakov, and I. I. Davydov immediately endorsed his hypothesis. As Davydov, the head of the Division of Russian Language and Literature at the Academy of Sciences, wrote to Pogodin, "As concerns the ancient settlement of the Great Russians in Kyiv—no one will dispute that save Maksymovych." Similarly, Ivan Aksakov wrote, "[Your article] almost entirely coincides with my own convictions.... I have thought much the same about the Little Russians for some time, though I trace the origins of the *khokhol*s to Tmutarakan" (Barsukov, *Zhizn' i trudy*, 15: 366–91).

Equally remarkable is how long the myth of Ukrainian as a "corrupt peasant dialect" survived. For years after Shakhmatov disproved this hypothesis, many Russian academics and intellectuals, including Sobolevsky, continued to promote it. Indeed, in 1905, when the Committee of Ministers was considering the elimination of the existing restrictions against publishing in the "Little Russian dialect," the minister of education was able to thwart the repeal by enlisting the support of several Slavists, most notably Professor T. D. Florinsky (1854–1919) and A. S. Budilovich (1846–1908). Notwithstanding a thirty-page brief prepared by the Imperial Academy of Sciences affirming writers now began to argue, were little more than low versions of an "all-Russian" language and culture "corrupted" by Polish and Lithuanian influences.[64]

The progressive devaluation of the Ukrainian past and image profoundly altered the terms of the Russian-Ukrainian discourse. It rendered the "Little Russians" symbolically invisible and, in effect, sanctioned the notion that "there never has been, is not, and cannot be" (*ne bylo, net, i byt' ne mozhet*) a Ukrainian language and culture.[65]

---

the antiquity and integrity of the Ukrainian language (written largely by Shakhmatov and Fedor Korsh), the minister of education restated the view in his report to the Committee of Ministers that Ukrainian was little more than a peasant dialect and, in the words of Professor Florinsky, "ought to rid itself of the pretension of serving as a medium of higher education." The Committee of Ministers, in fact, never repealed the Ems Ukase. Rather, in 1907, the Main Department of Publishing simply ruled that the new publishing regulations of 1905 and 1906 superseded the Ems Ukase and all previous restrictions on the "Little Russian dialect." It was only after the revolution, I would argue, that this myth of Ukrainian as a "corrupt peasant dialect" was eventually supplanted.

See M. Maksymovych, "Filologicheskie pis'ma k M. P. Pogodinu," *Russkaia beseda*, 1856, no. 3: 78–139; idem, "Otvetnye pis'ma M. P. Pogodinu," *Russkaia beseda*, 1857, no. 2: 80–104; idem, "O mnimom zapustenii Ukrainy v nashestvie Batyevo i naselenii ee novoprishlym narodom," *Russkaia beseda*, 1857, no. 4: 22–35; A. I. Sobolevskii, *Ocherki iz istorii russkogo iazyka* (Kyiv, 1884); idem, *Lektsii po istorii russkogo iazyka* (Kyiv, 1888); idem, "K istorii malorusskogo narechiia," *Russkii filologicheskii vestnik* 63 (1910): 106–13; O. Potebnia, "Otzyv o sochinenii A. Sobolevskogo 'Ocherki iz istorii russkogo iazyka,'" *Izvestiia Otdeleniia russkogo iazyka i slovesnosti Imperatorskoi Akademii Nauk* 1 (1896), bk. 4, pp. 804–31; A. Krymskii, "Filologiia i Pogodinskaia gipoteza," *Kievskaia starina*, 1898, no. 6: 347–65; 1898, no. 9: 234–66; 1899, no. 1: 9–29; 1899, no. 6: 307–16; and 1899, no. 9: 277–307; Mykhailo Hrushevs'kyi, *Istoriia Ukraïny-Rusy*, vol. 1, 3d rev. ed. (Lviv, 1913), trans. Marta Skorupsky as *History of Ukraine-Rus'*, vol. 1 (Edmonton, 1997), pp. 423–27; T. D. Florinskii, "Malorusskoe narechie," *Ėntsiklopedicheskii slovar'*, vol. 18 (St. Petersburg, 1896), pp. 486–87; idem, *Neskol'ko slov o malorusskom iazyke (narechii) v noveishikh popytkakh usvoit' emu rol' organa nauki i vysshei obrazovannosti* (Kyiv, 1899); A. S. Budilovich, *K voprosu o literaturnom iazyke Iugo-zapadnoi Rusi* (Iuriev, 1900); and Olga Andriewsky, "The Politics of National Identity: The Ukrainian Question in Russia, 1904–1912" (Ph.D. dissertation, Harvard University, 1991), esp. chapter 4.

64. This argument, energetically advanced by Senkovsky in *Biblioteka dlia chteniia* in the 1830s and 1840s, was revived by V. I. Lamansky in 1861, subsequently popularized by the journalist M. N. Katkov, and officially endorsed by the Russian government in the Valuev Ukase of 1863. See Barsukov, *Zhizn' i trudy*, 18: 124–34; 20: 322–37; and Lemke, *Moia povest'*, pp. 300–309.

65. Petr Valuev did not himself coin the expression ("there never has been, is not, and cannot be" a Ukrainian language). It was first used by the Kyiv

By the early 1860s, as the Ukrainian historian Mykola Kostomarov discovered, much to his chagrin, the very act of discussing in public the idea of two distinct "Russian nationalities" ("Dve russkie narodnosti," *Osnova*, March 1861) could quickly lead to charges of "separatism."[66]

Subversion

By 1863, whatever tolerance Russian authorities may have once had for the Ukrainian cultural revival had clearly given way to a set of larger, more pressing political, cultural, and social concerns.[67] Aroused by the Polish revolt of 1830–31 and heightened by the discovery of the secret Brotherhood of SS. Cyril and Methodius in 1847, the revolt of the Habsburg minorities in 1848,[68] Russia's crushing defeat in the Crimean War, and the Polish uprising of 1863, these anxieties found their expression in the first prohibitions against

---

Censorship Committee in a letter to the minister of internal affairs on 27 June 1863 explaining why the committee felt it necessary to prohibit the publication of a work entitled *The Parables of Our Lord Jesus Christ Related in Ukrainian*. Valuev did, however, quote from the letter and thus incorporated the phrase in his own memorandum to the tsar; hence it is commonly attributed to him. See Lemke, *Moia povest'*, pp. 302–4; Barsukov, *Zhizn' i trudy*, 20: 322–23; and David Saunders, "Russia and Ukraine under Alexander II: The Valuev *ukaz* of 1863," *International History Review* 17, no. 1 (1995): 23–50.

66. Kostomarov, *Avtobiografiia*, pp. 198–99. The larger theme of the essay, as Kostomarov took pains to point out in his autobiography, was that the "two Russian nationalities" complemented each other and that their fraternal unity was thus a necessity for both.

67. Uvarov's statement of 8 August 1835 summarized the anxieties of the age in the following way: "We, that is, people of the nineteenth century, are in a difficult position: we are living in the midst of political storms and political unrest. Nations are changing their way of life; they are experiencing rebirth, are in ferment, and are advancing. No one can prescribe his own rules here. But Russia is young and virgin, and she should not taste these bitter troubles, at least for the time being.... If I can succeed in delaying for fifty years the kind of future that theories are brewing for Russia, I shall have performed my duty and shall die in peace...." (quoted in A. V. Nikitenko, *The Diary of a Russian Censor*, ed. and trans. Helen Saltz Jacobson [Amherst, Mass., 1975], p. 62).

68. In his private notes, Osyp Bodiansky spoke of the profound change in the intellectual atmosphere in 1848; the strict surveillance and persecutions that began in the universities and in the press. Bodiansky himself was dismissed as secretary of the *Chteniia Obshchestva istorii i drevnostei rossiiskikh* in 1848 for publishing Giles Fletcher's account of his sixteenth-century journey to Muscovy. See Vasilenko, "O. M. Bodianskii," pp. 392–400.

the Ukrainian language,[69] as well as in a new and fervent emphasis on the unity, indivisibility, and uniformity of the "Russian nation." Increasingly, it was the myth of the "Russianness" of the Russian Empire, rather than purely dynastic and aristocratic concepts of political legitimacy, that many intellectuals and officials came to regard as the essential bond of stability and order.[70] (As Pogodin declared in 1852, when a colleague "indelicately" reminded him of the multinational character of the Russian state, "Russia is one integral

69. The Valuev Circular (July 1863) banned the publication of all Ukrainian books other than belles-lettres. The Ems Ukase (May 1876) further banned the import of Ukrainian books, the publication of original works, lyrics, and translations, and the use of the Ukrainian language in the theater. It permitted the publication of historical documents and belles-lettres, but only in Russian orthography. The Ems Ukase also prohibited teaching in Ukrainian in elementary schools and instructed the ministry of education to review the political reliability of the teaching personnel in the school districts of Ukraine, especially as concerned possible "Ukrainophile tendencies." For a discussion of the Valuev Circular and the Ems Ukase, see Mikhail Lemke, *Ėpokha tsenzurnykh reform 1859–1865 godov* (St. Petersburg, 1904); and Fedir Savchenko, *Zaborona ukraïnstva 1876 r.* (Kharkiv and Kyiv, 1930, repr. Munich, 1970). For a more recent treatment, see David Saunders, "Russia's Ukrainian Policy (1847–1905): A Demographic Approach" (unpublished paper, 1994); and his "Russia and Ukraine under Alexander II."

70. I do not mean to imply that this shift in political vocabulary took place uniformly. Clearly, even as late as 1914, there were still many individuals within the imperial elite who subscribed to what Paul Bushkovitch has called "dynastic statism," that is, premodern concepts of allegiance and identity in which regional loyalties were not incompatible with fealty to the throne and state. After 1847–48, however, this perspective steadily lost ground to a more modern "national" concept of political legitimacy. This new and dynamic concept of Russia as a nation-state was especially evident in the formulation of the government's Ukrainian policy (discussed below). As the Main Censorship Administration argued in 1861: "The gradual and durable fusion of [the Little Russian nationality] with the Great Russian nationality into a single indissoluble whole ought to be the subject of peaceful but nonetheless constant endeavors on the part of the government ... the emergence of the separation of the two related tribes could well be dangerous from the point of view of the unity of the state" (quoted in F. A. Iastrebov, *Revoliutsionnye demokraty na Ukraine: vtoraia polovina 50–kh—nachalo 60–kh godov XIX st.* [Kyiv, 1960], p. 283). Indeed, the prohibitions against the Ukrainian language were often justified as part of a "unifying movement" that was a "natural" counterpart to German and Italian unification. See, for example, a memorandum of 1876, "O vrede literatunoi deiatel'nosti ukrainofilov i merakh k ego otvrashcheniiu," quoted in Saunders, "Russia's Ukrainian Policy," pp. 9–13; Bushkovitch, "What is Russia?"; and Andriewsky, "Politics of National Identity," chapters 4, 6.

state, one integral people, confessing one faith, speaking one language, and bound to one ruler!")[71] And nowhere was this shift in the Russian political lexicon more apparent than in the evolution of the government's Ukrainian policy.

Indeed, the official documents relating to the investigation of the Brotherhood of SS. Cyril and Methodius in 1847 and the Valuev Circular of 1863 provide compelling evidence of this transformation. In 1847, the focus of Count Orlov's investigation had been the alleged *political* sedition of the Brotherhood circle. Not every "Little Russian filled with love for his native land (*k rodine*)," Orlov readily admitted in his report to the tsar, should be considered a conspirator. As head of the Third Section, he was mainly concerned that "the love [of the Little Russians] for their native land not be permitted to surpass their love for their fatherland (*k otechestvu*)." "Severe measures," Orlov warned, "would only make forbidden ideas even dearer to [the Little Russians] and force the hitherto loyal Little Russians into opposition..."[72] By 1863, however, it was the *cultural* loyalty of the "Little Russians" to the "all-Russian nation," as much as their political loyalty to the empire, that had come to be perceived as a security risk. The immediate pretext for the Valuev Circular was, in fact, the prospect of the publication of a "Little Russian" translation of the New Testament—a possibility that the Kyiv Censorship Committee, the governor-general of Kyiv province and, ultimately, the minister of internal affairs deemed "dangerous and harmful." They concurred that "Ukrainophiles" who were engaged in publishing elementary readers, grammar books, geography texts, and religious materials in the "so-called Ukrainian language" were "striving to realize their own political designs"—to "alienate the people from the 'all-Russian' *language and nationality*" (emphasis added). In light of "present circumstances" (an obvious reference to the Polish uprising), Count Valuev, the minister of internal affairs, recommended introducing general restrictions on publishing in the "Little Russian dialect"—restrictions that remained in force for more than 42 years.[73]

---

71. Barsukov, *Zhizn' i trudy*, 12: 418–22. In 1862 Mikhail Katkov asserted that only Russians lived in Russia and that "from time immemorial the Russian nation has lived in Little Russia; here the Russian state had its origins, here began the Russian faith, and here the Russian language had its beginnings" (*Sovremennaia letopis' Russkogo vestnika* [14 November 1862], quoted in Lemke, *Ėpokha tsenzurnykh reform*, p. 300).

72. *Kyrylo-Mefodiïvs'ke tovarystvo*, 3: 306–8.

73. Valuev's memorandum to the tsar quoted extensively from the minister's correspondence with the Kyiv Censorship Committee and the

The Valuev prescript and the Ems Ukase thus *politicized* issues of language, culture, and identity to an unparalleled—and, ultimately, untenable—degree. After 1863, all cultural and educational work in the Ukrainian language, from the founding of Sunday schools to the preparation of elementary school primers to the translation of the Holy Scriptures, was brought to a halt. Virtually all public expressions of Ukrainian identity—even the most innocent, such as the translation of religious materials—became synonymous with "separatism." Terms like "Ukraine" and "Hetmanate" that invoked the memory of "South Russia's" distinct political past were routinely censored in Russian-language publications. Indeed, in the wake of the Valuev prescript, the boundaries of what constituted *legitimate* expression of "Little Russian" culture and identity, whether public or private, became entirely confused (and thus increasingly subject to the arbitrary whims of local officials). As one anonymous correspondent reported in 1863: "If you think that Ukrainians at least have freedom in private life, then you are mistaken. If you wear Ukrainian clothes, you will be taken to the police or beaten up on the street. If you speak Ukrainian, you will never be taken into service, but instead will be placed under police surveillance.... If you sing Ukrainian songs, you will be thrown into jail. If an officer overhears you on the street, he will take you to the police station and say, 'Stop speaking *khokhol*. Little Russia has not existed since the time of Tsar Aleksei Mikhailovich.'"[74] In numerous instances between 1863 and 1917, Ukrainians (including peasants)

---

governor-general of Kyiv province. The relevant documents are cited and discussed in Saunders, "Russia and Ukraine," pp. 8–10, 13–15, 25–26; and in Iastrebov, *Revoliutsionnye demokraty*, p. 283.

74. Ukraïnets', "Z Ukraïny," *Slovo*, no. 85 (Lviv, 1863), quoted in Vasyl' Lyzanchuk, *Navichno kaidany kuvaly: Fakty, dokumenty, komentari pro rusyfikatsiiu v Ukraïni* (Lviv, 1995), pp. 95–97. It would be naive to suggest that all expressions of Ukrainian culture were systematically suppressed after 1863. The nineteenth-century imperial Russian bureaucracy was notoriously inefficient, arbitrary, and inert—and still included far too many Ukrainians. At the same time, however, it is important not to overlook the degree to which the Valuev Circular and the Ems Ukase created a climate in which Ukrainians were liable to fall under suspicion simply by virtue of being Ukrainian. In a footnote to the Ems Ukase, for example, the ministry of education was advised to assign, as a general rule, Great Russian teachers to Ukrainian school districts and send Little Russian teachers to the St. Petersburg, Kazan or Orenburg (i.e., Great Russian) provinces (Savchenko, *Zaborona ukraïnstva*, pp. 382–83; Lyzanchuk, *Navichno kaidany kuvaly*, pp. 99–102). On the imperial bureaucracy in Ukraine, see Stephen Velychenko, "Identities, Loyalties, and Service in Imperial Russia: Who Administered the Borderlands?" *Russian Review* 54, no. 2 (April 1995): 188–208.

were harassed, detained, and even arrested for what had previously been considered ordinary demonstrations of "affection for their native land."[75]

Perhaps the most fatal consequence of the myth of "one indissoluble Russian nation" (*edinyi, nedelimyi russkii narod*) was that it served to conceal from Russian public view the very existence of a distinct group that by the turn of the century numbered some twenty-one million people, for the most part agrarian, illiterate, and poor, consigned to a particularly insular existence by virtue of the enormous

---

75. In 1863, for example, an eighteen-year-old Ukrainian, Volodymyr Synehub, was imprisoned for six months for teaching old Cossack songs to the boys in his village. Indeed, in his memoirs, Ivan Petrunkevich, the noted zemstvo liberal and former district judge from Chernihiv, remarked that in the 1870s Ukrainian peasants were frequently charged with disturbing the peace and taken to court for singing Ukrainian folk songs. Petrunkevich, himself the scion of an old Cossack family, dismissed the charges as a matter of course. In 1877, to cite another example, Iakiv Novytsky, a Ukrainian schoolteacher in Katerynoslav province, was fired from his job for purchasing six Ukrainian books that had all been legally published in Russia.

The best example of the contradictions and inconsistencies in the application of the government's Ukrainian policy, however, is the dedication of the Ivan Kotliarevsky monument in Poltava in 1903, the single largest public gathering of the Ukrainian intelligentsia before 1905. The monument had been the result of a fifteen-year effort, initiated by the Poltava City Duma, to gain permission to raise funds to honor this native poet and a five-year battle with the ministry of internal affairs to allow a public dedication ceremony. During the official ceremony, when the delegate from the Chernihiv Drama Society began to deliver her address in Ukrainian—which was, technically, not against the law—a local official insisted, on orders from the ministry of internal affairs, that the ceremony be conducted in Russian. The event ended abruptly, and an official complaint was subsequently submitted to the Senate by the Ukrainians. In 1906, the Senate ruled that the ministry of internal affairs had acted incorrectly in issuing the prohibition.

The confusion over what constituted legal Ukrainian activity became especially pronounced after 1905 and the granting of civil liberties in Russia. In fact, it took two years for the Main Department of Publishing to rule that the new publishing regulations of 1905 and 1906 superseded the Ems Ukase and all previous restrictions on the "Little Russian dialect." Even so, many local officials, regarding all Ukrainian-language periodicals as politically subversive, continued to destroy Ukrainian-language publications when they arrived in the village. See A. A. Kizevetter, ed., "Iv. Il. Petrunkevich: Iz zapisok obshchestvennogo deiatelia. Vospominaniia," *Arkhiv russkoi revoliutsii* 21 (1934): 303–5; Lyzanchuk, *Navichno kaidany kuvaly*, pp. 95–149; S. Siropolko, *Istoriia osvity na Ukraïni* (Lviv, 1937), p. 112; Ie. Chykalenko, *Spohady, 1861–1907* (Lviv, 1925), pt. 3, pp. 68–69, 103–9; and Andriewsky, "Politics of National Identity," pp. 6–7, 133–48.

cultural differences between themselves and the ruling imperial elite.[76] The vast majority of Ukrainians had yet to be incorporated into an "all-Russian" culture. Moreover, it remained to be seen whether it was even possible to do so under the strict terms set by the Russian government after 1863—that is, to inculcate in Ukrainians a sense of an "all-Russian" identity without regard for their "Little Russian" linguistic, historical, and cultural particularism. In this respect, the Ukrainian question ultimately became not only an issue of identity and cultural allegiance, but also a problem of development and modernization.

* * *

In the long run, the myth of a "single, indissoluble Russian nation" thus precluded the formation of a loyal *and* modern—and hence stable—"Little Russian" identity. After 1863, the Russian government, in essence, staked its future on this myth, on the notion that "there never has been, does not exist, and cannot exist" a separate Ukrainian language and culture, and on a policy that left little room to be both distinctively Ukrainian and all-Russian. It was a wager that would come back to haunt the old imperial elite in 1917. Indeed, the myth of a "single, indissoluble Russian nation" left educated Russian society entirely unprepared for the sudden reemergence of the Ukrainian movement within the borders of the Russian Empire once the existing

76. For the Ukrainian peasant, as Steven Guthier has argued ("The Roots of Popular Ukrainian Nationalism: A Demographic, Social, and Political Study of the Ukrainian Nationality to 1917," Ph.D. dissertation, University of Michigan, 1990), virtually all social, economic, and administrative relations had an ethnic dimension. Landlords were typically Polish or Russian; merchants, inkeepers, and moneylenders were Jewish or Russian; factory owners and shop stewards were Russian, Polish, or Jewish. The city was Russian and the business of administration, the courts, and schools was conducted exclusively in Russian.

The extent of this cultural gap is evident in the literacy rates (i.e., literacy in the Russian language). As the 1897 census revealed, literacy rates among Ukrainians were significantly lower than those among other segments of the population in European Russia. In Right-Bank Ukraine, for example, the literacy rate among Russians was 38 percent as compared to 10 percent for Ukrainians. In Left-Bank Ukraine, i.e., in the zemstvo provinces, 20 percent of Russians were literate, as compared with 14 percent of Ukrainians. Moreover, literacy rates among Ukrainian peasants were consistently lower than those among Russian peasants. See *Pervaia vseobshchaia perepis'*, table 14, vols. 8, 13, 16, 32, 33, 41, 46, 47, 48; see also Andriewsky, "Politics of National Identity," pp. 185–87; and Lyzanchuk, *Navichno kaidany kuvaly*, pp. 107–11.

restrictions against Ukrainian cultural work and political participation were removed. As General Anton Denikin, the Army commander who led the White movement in Southern Russia under the banner of "Russia, One and Indivisible," continued to wonder more than a decade after his defeat, "Where did all those Ukrainians come from?" («Откуда же появилось столько украинцев?»).[77]

Ultimately, of course, the attempts to establish a sovereign Ukrainian state between 1917 and 1920 also failed. But in other, perhaps less obvious ways, the Revolution marked the triumph of the myth of Ukrainian distinctiveness. Indeed, it was the willingness of the Bolsheviks by 1919 to foster a new kind of "Little Russian" identity—an identity based on an overarching loyalty to the Soviet state and the Communist Party that still left some room for Ukrainian "particularism"—that proved to be an important ingredient in their success. It was an identity that in the wake of the collapse of the Soviet Union could emerge as fully—if still tentatively—Ukrainian.

---

77. Bakhmeteff Archive (Columbia University, New York), Anton and Kseniia Denikin Collection, box 10, A. Denikin, "Natsional'nyi vopros v staroi Russkoi Armii" (unpublished manuscript, 1930), p. 39. On the White movement and the Ukrainian question, see Anna Procyk, *Russian Nationalism and Ukraine: The Nationality Policy of the Volunteer Army during the Civil War* (Edmonton and Toronto, 1995).

George G. Grabowicz

Between Subversion and Self-Assertion: The Role of *Kotliarevshchyna* in Russian-Ukrainian Literary Relations

The present paper is conceived as a brief introduction to a larger historical study of the cultural and literary semantics and the stylistic and ultimately social and cultural metamorphoses of *kotliarevshchyna,* the burlesque style or mode named after Ivan Kotliarevsky (1769–1838), popularly known as the "father" of modern Ukrainian literature.[1] As I will elaborate below, *kotliarevshchyna,* as a critical and historical term, has had and continues to have a decidedly pejorative connotation, and has been traditionally and all but exclusively applied only to Kotliarevsky's epigones. I shall be using it, however, as a generic and non-evaluative term and applying it to the broadly ramified style and mode initiated by Kotliarevsky's travesty of Virgil's *Aeneid,* the *Eneïda,* whose appearance in St. Petersburg (1798), in an unauthorized edition, ushered in the new Ukrainian literature in the vernacular. The wider issues subsumed by my topic are the problems of ethnicity (and, in the political sphere, national identity), populism or *narodnytstvo,* and canon formation. My basic contention is that this style or mode is much deeper and more pervasive than has been assumed, and that it animates not only the pre-Shevchenkian period (up to the 1840s), but (albeit in modified form) much of nineteenth-century Ukrainian literature; its traces are clearly visible in the twentieth century, particularly in Ukrainian socialist-realist literature. Central to my concern is that this mode not only sets the terms or encodes the interrelations of Ukrainian and Russian literature in its initial phase, which I take to be the period between Kotliarevsky's *Eneïda* and the appearance of Shevchenko (the *Kobzar* of 1840), but also affects mutual perceptions, particularly Russian perceptions of Ukrainian culture, to this day.

I take it as a given that literary expression is often a crucial vehicle or hypostasis in the process of forming ethnic and then

---

1. An earlier version of this paper, "Semantyka kotliarevshchyny," appeared in the Kyiv journal *Suchasnist',* 1994, no. 5: 65–73.

national identity. This is all the more true in nineteenth-century Ukrainian as well as Russian history, where literature was the privileged cultural medium, and, in the absence of empowered institutions or forums, *the* surrogate for political discourse. In the Ukrainian case, as I will argue, what appeared to be but a literary style was actually a basic model of self-identification.

The matter is further complicated by the fact that during the period in question Ukrainian literature existed largely if not exclusively as a regional addendum to an imperial all-Russian literature.[2] In effect, just as my discussion of *kotliarevshchyna* entails both a reconsideration of the literary and historical data, the texts, historiographic formulas, and our "theory," so also the larger issue of what is meant by "Ukrainian" and "Russian" presupposes a historiographic reconsideration. At the very least one should guard against ahistorical usage, which applies equally to the Ukrainian and Russian sides of the equation. This issue is, of course, a chapter in itself. For the moment I simply want to stress that some contemporary formulations (and the cultural sensitivity they project), such as, for example, Mykhailo Drahomanov's discussion of "Literatura rosiis'ka, velykorus'ka, ukraïns'ka i halyts'ka" (1873), or Dmitrii Ovsianiko-Kulikovsky's discussion of Gogol/Hohol as "obshcherus na malorusskoi osnove" are frequently more meaningful and offer more insights into the problem than later "nationally crystallized" designations.[3]

A more global formulation of the preceding is that the issue of Russian-Ukrainian relations, whether in the more discrete form of literary relations or, more generally, as cultural and historical relations, has not really had adequate, dispassionate and comprehensive treatment. The issue was held hostage to ideological strictures and national (not to speak of nationalist) passions and biases. The very fact of Ukraine's colonial existence within the Russian and then the Russian-Soviet Empire, however, imposed an even greater distortion, for it affected not only the "internal" (Russian-Ukrainian) context, but also the "external" one, so that the reasoning and perspective of putatively dispassionate critics—for example, scholars

---

2. Cf. also my "Russian-Ukrainian Literary Relations: A Formulation of the Problem," in *Russia and Ukraine in Their Historical Encounter*, ed. Peter J. Potichnyj et al. (Edmonton, 1992), pp. 214–44; and "Teoriia ta istoriia: 'horyzont spodivan'' i rannia retseptsiia novoï ukraïns'koï literatury," in my *Do istoriï ukraïns'koï literatury* (Kyiv, 1997), pp. 46–136.

3. Cf. M. P. Drahomanov, *Literaturno-publitsystychni pratsi*, 2 vols. (Kyiv, 1970), 1: 80–220, and D. N. Ovsianiko-Kulikovskii, *Gogol'* (Moscow and Petrograd, 1923).

from the West—ended up as contorted by the imperial perspective as that of the most orthodox native imperialists. This legacy is especially pervasive, and a major antidote here is a conscious focus on the paradigm.

In this connection the present situation reveals a poignant paradox. With the onset of independence and the demise of old dogmas, Ukrainian history and culture, specifically literature, face the need and the opportunity for a fundamental reconsideration and revision of their canons. (There is, in fact, a fair amount of actual reconfiguration, although largely in a syncretic manner, whereby the old Soviet socialist-realist canon is left in place, but is also fleshed out by that which was censored: works of canonical writers; dissident literature; the whole corpus of émigré and non-Soviet writing.)[4] At the same time, the most basic issue—the fact and the implications of colonial status—is addressed only superficially. Often it is implicitly denied in the guise of national assertiveness, pathos, and various forms of self-aggrandizement. It is highly revealing that the only (and very brief) discussion of Russian and Ukrainian modes of perceiving the other (in fact, the focus is mainly on Russian perceptions of things Ukrainian), with specific reference to historical imprinting, occurred in a small, elitist Russian-Jewish literary magazine, *Novyi krug*, under the telling heading of "Russian-Ukrainian Marginalia."[5] The larger issue this subtends is that there is simply no forum, and little structured discourse, in this area.[6]

Traditional Perceptions: Kotliarevshchyna *as the Work of Epigones and as a "Literary Disease"*

At first glance, the traditional definition of *kotliarevshchyna* is clear and unambiguous. To be sure, the first to use the term was Panteleimon Kulish, who applied it not to the epigones but to Kotliarevsky himself—in an undisguised negative sense.[7] Soon, however, it came to be applied exclusively to the imitators, various third-rate writers—

---

4. Cf. Marko Pavlyshyn, "Kanon ta ikonostas," *Svitovyd* (Kyiv and New York), 1992, no. 3 (8): 69–81.

5. *Novyi krug* (Kyiv), no. 2, pp. 19–24.

6. A telling event in this connection was the first Congress of the Republican (subsequently, National) Association for Ukrainian Studies, held on 20–23 December 1990 in Kyiv and devoted to the topic of "Ukraine and Russia." No scholars from Russia attended; to all appearances, there were also no Russians from Ukraine included as speakers.

7. Cf. Kulish, "Obzor ukrainskoi slovesnosti," *Osnova*, no. 1 (1861).

Pavlo Biletsky-Nosenko, Porfyrii Korynetsky, Stepan Oleksandriv, Kostiantyn Puzyna, and others, some of them anonymous—who according to an earlier and more generous terminology would have been called a "school." As we see from Iefremov's by now classic formulation, the transition from the "school of Kotliarevsky" to *kotliarevshchyna* was predicated on the conclusion that all of them were bad students, or bad "sons":

> Their ties to Kotliarevsky, and to all of Ukrainian literature, are only formal; not having understood the spirit and direction of the *Eneïda*, not having literary talent, but only an itch for writing, they copied only the surface of Kotliarevsky's poem and threw themselves into remarkable excess and mindless caricature. The only thing that these writers achieved through their failed efforts was that there soon came to exist an attitude which saw all Ukrainian writing as crude babble, as half-witted play, as a sanctuary of "Little Russian jokes," and genuine writers had to prove in all earnestness that the Ukrainian language was fit for serious creativity and meaningful works. These heedless imitators ultimately threw a dark shadow on Kotliarevsky himself, although he himself was least responsible for this mindless *kotliarevshchyna* that his self-appointed and witless students let loose under his name.[8]

Leaving aside for the moment the validity of this argument, and noting only that its most profound (i.e., systemic) idea about the broader context, the "opinion of others," in effect the all-Russian critical response, is stated as if in passing, one can only stress that this definition became canonical and came to be utilized by scholars, such as Zerov or Chyzhevsky, who in all other respects were far removed from Iefremov. For the former, *kotliarevshchyna* is subsequently defined as a specifically literary disease; for the latter, it becomes a symptom of a national disorder.[9]

The reasons for this judgment were different in each case. Iefremov, for whom the people (*narod*) and its liberation was the highest value and perhaps the only criterion of literary progress, rejected *kotliarevshchyna* as a kind of betrayal of this ideal. For Zerov and Chyzhevsky, with their implicit esthetic norms, *kotliarevshchyna* was first and foremost the incarnation of bad taste. Both approaches made further

---

8. Serhii Iefremov, *Istoriia ukraïns'koho pys'menstva* (Kyiv and Leipzig, 1924), vol. 1, pp. 374–75.

9. Cf. Mykola Zerov, *Nove ukraïns'ke pys'menstvo* (Munich, 1960), p. 98; and Dmytro Chyzhevs'kyi, *Istoriia ukraïns'koï literatury* (New York, 1956), pp. 370–71.

examination of this phenomenon difficult in that they tended to obscure its essential psychological and structural features and ignored the fact that this was, after all, the first style and model of the newly born Ukrainian literature, and as such could hardly be dismissed by the metaphor of a "disease." For if it could, then, in the manner of a Belinsky, the whole literature could be dismissed in this way.[10]

Ieremiia Aizenshtok's lengthy introduction to the first volume of *Kotliarevshchyna* presents an important corrective to the normativism of his predecessors.[11] While stressing the social role and nature of *kotliarevshchyna*, he treats it as a normal product of popular literature, which he, like Iefremov and Zerov before him, calls a "literature of the middle-class reader." But while Aizenshtok continually emphasizes the formal influence of Kotliarevsky and concretely illustrates how given authors are "readers with pen in hand,"[12] his range of texts—the fact that he still confines himself to Kotliarevsky's imitators—ultimately blurs and underestimates the essence of the phenomenon in question. Despite his professed intent to the contrary, by separating *kotliarevshchyna* from Kotliarevsky and from the important writers who would subsequently modify it, he still marginalizes the phenomenon. In the final analysis he does not see that *kotliarevshchyna* is defined not so much by generic and stylistic features as by deeper socio-cultural moments.

My further analysis will focus on *kotliarevshchyna* as a broad modality. Its narrower core—the various epigones, from Biletsky-Nosenko to Puzyna—will not be an issue here. The paradox, if any, is purely superficial: the epigones are unambiguous, and the essence of the cultural phenomenon is best conveyed through semantic complexity. The narrow understanding of *kotliarevshchyna* epitomized by Iefremov had far-reaching and basically negative conse-

---

10. If one were to continue with the metaphor, one would have to say that it is the kind of disease that leaves its mark on the whole life of the patient, and as such deserves serious examination. As for Belinsky, his hostile and mocking attitude toward Ukrainian literature also needs to be examined, especially as, until recently, he was depicted in the Soviet canon as a friend and teacher of the very literature he found so backward and disreputable. It is significant, however, that his judgments are based precisely on the features of *kotliarevshchyna*, as expressed in both the burlesque and the sentimental keys. Cf. his reviews of Kvitka or the almanac *Lastivka* in his *Polnoe sobranie sochinenii*, vol. 5 (Moscow, 1954), pp. 176–79. Cf. also my "Teoriia ta istoriia."

11. I. Aizenshtok, *Kotliarevshchyna*, Ukraïns'ki propyleï, vol. 1 (Kyiv, 1928), pp. 9–121.

12. Ibid., pp. 108–12.

quences for further study, particularly in literary history. On the one hand, it justified an evaluative, normative approach to a major cultural phenomenon, blurring it and impeding a deeper understanding. The paradigm of a "literary disease" fetishized the issue of "coarseness" and "vulgarity" and in the same degree ignored the underlying cultural and psychological dynamics. On the other hand, this narrow view distorted the literary process as such by making it impossible to establish clearly when style is replaced by stylization. To the extent that the model of *kotliarevshchyna* was based on the production of epigones, it forced the literary historian to deal with something peripheral, so to speak. What was not noticed was that the very mainstream of the new Ukrainian literature was drawing from the deep well of Kotliarevsky's style. The import of this becomes fully apparent when we see the way in which it becomes an inheritance for such writers as Hryhorii Kvitka-Osnovianenko, Taras Shevchenko, Kulish, and others.

The Question of Functions: Kotliarevshchyna *as Ethnic Self-Assertion*

To my mind, *kotliarevshchyna*—as a broadly resonant style and modality—must be defined in terms of its functions, its conscious and "unconscious" roles. The first of these is its historical or, in the broadest sense, "ideological" function, which manifests itself in both internal and external ways. The "external" is precisely the delimitation, the separation from Russian (all-Russian) literature. The basic signal for this is the choice of linguistic code. Having chosen the vernacular Ukrainian language, Ukrainian literature (which at first, of course, is only a limited set of works) becomes to some extent inaccessible to the general all-Russian reader; at the same time it privileges the Ukrainian-speaking—in effect, Ukrainian—reader. (The fact that the first, unauthorized edition of the *Eneïda*, as noted on the title page, includes a small dictionary of "Little Russian words" is as telling as it is ambiguous. It stresses, on the one hand, that some translation is presumably necessary, but supplies only a select number of words, not the whole text. The question, then, of whether this text is "native" [*svii*] or "foreign" [*chuzhyi*] is left open.) The choice of language carries with it other differentiations: of audience, of thematics and voice—in short, of emotional and cultural tonality. The sharpest manifestation of these, especially of tonality—the innermost code or "language"—is found in texts with a heightened metathematical function, such as Petro Hulak-Artemovsky's "Deshcho pro toho Haras'ka" (1819), Kvitka's "Suplika do Pana Izdatelia" (1833), or the foreword ("Tak sobi do zemliakiv") and afterword ("Do zobachennia") to Ievhen Hrebinka's almanac, *Lastivka* (1841).[13]

The internal differentiating function of this style, i.e., *kotliarevshchyna*'s role *within* Ukrainian literature, is no less complex. There is no doubt that it separates—again primarily by linguistic code—the new Ukrainian literature from its earlier period. At the same time, in some aspects (principally the burlesque mode, baroque devices and topoi, and so on), it continues that earlier period. For many critics (in effect, the whole non-Soviet literary and historical tradition, i.e., such scholars as Zerov, Chyzhevsky, George Luckyj, and others) this style also denotes a pre-modern and pre-national mind-set, one that various writers and publicists of the 1920s, such as Mykola Khvylovy, Dmytro Dontsov, or Evhen Malaniuk, were pleased to call "Little Russianism" (*malorosiistvo*).[14] For them, this style reflected a mentality anchored in the national "somnolence" or "semi-consciousness" of the eighteenth century, a state of lethargy that was dispelled by Shevchenko. Thus, from its appearance with *Eneïda* to its hazy dissolution (and it existed until Khvylovy's time, and arguably still exists), it was a style expressing a *sui generis* regression, the immaturity of national consciousness or of the "national idea."

One can hardly agree with these militantly ahistorical premises and conclusions, but the fact that *kotliarevshchyna* was a transitional (and inordinately long) period in Ukrainian literature is also unquestionable.

Most often the definition of *kotliarevshchyna* is argued on the basis of its generic and formal features, in effect, in terms of the burlesque. This is its traditional and canonical designation, and in and of itself it is correct. The humor that underlies this burlesque is largely crude and earthy, but it is organic, and this applies equally to the *Eneïda* and to its epigones.

It was seldom if ever noticed, however, that earthy humor is not an essential feature of the burlesque as such, and that in other literatures burlesque can exist without it. It would follow, therefore, that this is

---

13. A striking instance of this differentiating function, which appears now not as metathematic allusion but as direct terminology, is found in alternative generic names. Although we do not have the full range, the pattern is obvious: instead of "epistle" (*poslanie*) we have "pysul'ka"; instead of "anecdote," "pobrekhen'ka"; "instead of "ode," "pisnia," and so on. The paradigmatic example is Kvitka's "Spyhachky abo po-moskovs'komu Epigramy." Cf. my *Toward a History of Ukrainian Literature* (Cambridge, Mass., 1991), pp. 57–58.

14. Cf., for example, Malaniuk's "Malorosiistvo," in his *Knyha sposterezhen'*, vol. 2 (Toronto, 1966), pp. 229–46.

somehow specific to the Ukrainian case. In fact, the mode of the burlesque plays a central role in Ukrainian literature of the seventeenth and eighteenth centuries. In turn, this also shows that even while the linguistic code (the shift from bookish Ukrainian to the vernacular) introduces a major break with the poetics of the earlier period, voice and tone do provide continuity.

The fact that one of the major functions of this humor is the assertion of life and identity has been frequently noted.[15] Clearly, this could provide the energy and momentum to brave the social and conventional risk of separating oneself from the system of Russian (all-Russian) literature. In some measure, such separation was like slipping anchor and embarking without charts. The sanction for this could be ridicule—and that is precisely what occurred.

The fact that *in relation to the external context of Russian literature* the content of this burlesque was parody and subversion was commented on very gingerly, and most frequently ignored; in Soviet scholarship an unambiguous taboo was placed on this topic. But herein lies the basic function of *kotliarevshchyna*—to mock the inflated, self-important, artificial, cold, and ultimately "inhuman" world of normative imperial society and normative canonical literature. This function informs all of *kotliarevshchyna*, with the basic distinction, however, that for Kotliarevsky and his imitators this was basically implicit and unconscious, while for later writers who drew on his style it was largely conscious and sometimes even programmatic. We see this most clearly in Shevchenko, in various poetic contexts and, in its plainest programmatic form, in the introduction to the unpublished *Kobzar* of 1847. In Kulish, this juxtaposition of the native and human with the foreign and normative assumes systemic and ideological form in his "homestead philosophy."

The parodic/subversive essence of *kotliarevshchyna*, however, also has a double bottom. On the barely concealed or largely visible level this is a mode that mocks imperial reality and canonical poetics. On the deeper and always concealed level it continually reveals that this reality is precisely the measure of all things. In effect, *kotliarevshchyna* is totally dependent on a colonial relationship (actual or spiritual) with the literature of the "center"; otherwise, *kotliarevshchyna* is not functional or relevant (unless as stylization or archaism).

---

15. Cf. M. T. Iatsenko, *Na rubezhi literaturnykh epokh* (Kyiv, 1977), pp. 61–62 and passim; cf. also Ievhen Sverstiuk, "Ivan Kotliarevs'kyi smiiet'sia," *Suchasnist'*, 1972, no. 5: 35–59.

To the extent that *kotliarevshchyna* was the only mode of Ukrainian writing up to the appearance of the pre-Romantics and the programmatic sentimentalism of Kvitka, we are justified in speaking of Ukrainian literature at this stage as monostylistic and monothematic. In itself this is probably not a unique phenomenon, and may be found in other literatures. For Ukrainian literature, however, it is of considerable import that the first and exclusive stage at which both literary and national consciousness were being molded was *kotliarevshchyna*. Consequently, it left a lasting mark (one is tempted to use the metaphor of genetic coding and imprinting) on the entire literary process, particularly on its first stages. The model or the very possibility of a monostylistic and monothematic literature also became fixed and reappeared in later hypostases, from the appeals of Nechui-Levytsky for a monolithic Ukrainian literature to the unificationist postulates of Soviet Ukrainian socialist realists.

The genre and style of *kotliarevshchyna* also provide a practical boon—a ready voice and, with it, a literary persona. As is well known, in the beginning phases of any literature the search for a voice, for an effective narrative strategy, are a first priority as much for the individual writer as for the process in general. The voice and persona of a "simple" narrator (Rudyi Panko, Belkin, Soplica) and the narrative genre of the *skaz* or *gawęda* were sanctioned by Romantic poetics in that they presumably articulated the collective voice of the *narod*. *Kotliarevshchyna* clearly falls within this paradigm. But it also clearly set up a context different from the one in which Gogol, Pushkin and Rzewuski were creating. In the Ukrainian case, as a result of the exclusivity and monostylistic nature of *kotliarevshchyna*, the boundary between the writer and his literary-generic persona was blurred. While in Russian or Polish literature the boundary between the writer's social and literary hypostasis was clear, and such a combination as Pushkin-Belkin or Rzewuski-Soplica would have seemed absurd, the combination of Kvitka-Osnovianenko was not only possible, but actually became canonical. In accordance with the model that *kotliarevshchyna* inscribed into Ukrainian literature, this fusion of the social persona, the true author, and his literary projection, his voice, remained a normal phenomenon in Ukrainian literature long after *kotliarevshchyna* ceased to be a vital presence. Direct evidence of this is to be found in the rich, even hypertrophied, range of canonical literary pseudonyms: Marko Vovchok, Panas Myrny, Ivan Karpenko-Kary, Lesia Ukrainka, Mykola Khvylovy, Vasyl Barka, and so on.

In the formal, linguistic/stylistic sense, *kotliarevshchyna* articulated not only an abstract populism (*narodnist'*) but something much more concrete—in the diction of the time, the voice of the common man, the *prostoliudin.* A concise overview of the features of this voice was recently provided by George Shevelov. While his focus is on the epistolary genre, he is describing the modality as such:

> Stylistically speaking, the epistolary genre (and belletristic narrative prose in general) in Ukrainian in the nineteenth century was born of an imitation of the peasant, or *muzhik*, stylized monologue-narration or dialogue, in its exaggerated literary expression. Features of this narrative *à la moujik* are well known in connection with the prose of Kvitka-Osnovianenko or Hulak-Artemovsky, or Ievhen Hrebinka.... Such features include dialogisms, an excess of vulgarisms or diminutives, a circling around the same word, coordinate syntax and catalogues, avoidance of foreign words and their substitution by descriptive locutions or approximate ad hoc inventions ... or through a folk phonetics and folk etymology, the use of purely local facts as if universally well known, an excess of exclamations, proverbs, interruptions, etc.
>
> All this taken together creates an image-mask of a simple and dim-witted provincial narrator.[16]

The question to what degree these features describe and exhaust this style remains open, however. What is its essence? For if this "essence" is not somehow of a piece, but changes in such or another way, then what allows us to speak about the unity of the phenomenon and not about a plurality of discrete phenomena?

That unity, I submit, is based on the following: along with all of the above functions, *kotliarevshchyna* also performed—indeed primarily, as I see it—an important psychological role, the role of a mask or shield that allows the author to assume a subversive stance, mock the "foreign" and emphasize his own separateness, his "native" emotional and cultural code—*without direct risk*. The author, in short, appears as a masked player. As in a play, the mask enables one to face a truth that cannot be stated directly at the time.

As Franko expressed it in another context,[17] the necessary consequence of this in the social and psychological sense was that the mask would adhere to the face and become part of it. And the issue here is not so much an immanent "adhesion" as the fact that in the perception of "foreigners" there was no difference between the player and

16. Iurii Shevel'ov [George Y. Shevelov], "Kulishevi lysty i Kulish v lystakh," in *Vybrani tvory Panteleimona Kulisha ukraïns'koiu movoiu pysani,* ed. Iurii Luts'kyi [George S. N. Luckyj] (New York, 1984), p. 21.

17. Cf. his "Ivan Vyshens'kyi i ioho tvory," in *Zibrani tvory u 50 tomakh,* vol. 30 (Kyiv, 1981), p. 127.

his mask; in the words of Iefremov, "there soon came to exist an attitude which saw all Ukrainian writing as crude babble, as half-witted play, as a sanctuary of 'Little Russian jokes.'" In this sense *kotliarevshchyna,* as a self-imposed steretotype, came to play an exceedingly important role in the formation of Russian-Ukrainian literary relations.

In this context, too, we can see a peculiar double bottom in *kotliarevshchyna*: its role of separating Ukrainian literature from Russian imperial literature appears to be largely relative, indeed, illusory. At issue is not only the fact that the *Eneïda*, for example, was modeled on the Russian travesty of Virgil's *Aeneid* written by Nikolai Osipov and Aleksandr Kotelnitsky, or that its small dictionary for the Russian speaker suggests an *implicit* orientation on an all-Russian audience. The key moment in this pseudo-separation is the basic paradigm that sees Ukrainian literature as essentially and exclusively of and for the common people; as popular (*narodna*); as a literature that, according to the formula Kostomarov would use with regard to Shevchenko, presumably speaks in the name and in the voice of the *narod* itself, that is, the language the common people (*prostyi narod*) would use if it could so speak.[18] And such a reading—not only from our perspective, but also from the contemporary point of view—clearly did not accord with reality. For at that stage in particular, and throughout the nineteenth century—at least until it was officially proscribed and persecuted—Ukrainian literature in the Russian Empire was inscribed into and was part of imperial, all-Russian literature. All Ukrainian writers took part in the general all-Russian literary process. Indeed, at that stage, functionally Ukrainian literature—the writing that served Ukrainian society—was bilingual, and perhaps more reliant on Russian than on Ukrainian. In that context, the Ukrainian reader of the time surely did not perceive the Russian-language novels of Kvitka or the Russian stories of Hrebinka, or the Russian-language "Oda Safo" of Kotliarevsky, or the Russian-language articles in *Osnova* as something "foreign" or "Russian" in the contemporary sense of the term, that is, as Great Russian.

And what is the role of *kotliarevshchyna* in this context? While projecting subversion and parody it also functions as a mask of sincerity and solidarity, of *narodnist'*, as a modality that covers up the hybrid nature of the Ukrainian literary process (its colonialism) and

---

18. Cf. N. Kostomarov, "Malorusskaia literatura," in *Poeziia slavian*, ed. N. V. Gerbel' (St. Petersburg, 1871), p. 160. Cf. also my "Insight and Blindness in the Reception of Ševčenko: The Case of Kostomarov," *Harvard Ukrainian Studies* 27, nos. 3–4 (December 1993): 278–339.

postulates, or pretends to, a continuity and wholeness to the Ukrainian cultural and incipiently political discourse. In its early stages, *kotliarevshchyna* is a prime measure of Ukrainianness. Within its convention, the writer who writes in this style is eo ipso a Ukrainian writer, that is, a true friend of the *narod,* and his use of this style conceals—for his audience, and for himself, no doubt—the whole social reality, that is, the whole gamut of objective, manifest, hierarchical connections, differentiations, compromises, and so on. In a word, *kotliarevshchyna* creates a magic space, an Eliotic objective correlative of an ideal community or *communitas,* and a foreshadowing of what in the twentieth century would be called the domain of the word (*derzhava slova*).

The Canon of Anticanonicity

In sum, the subversion contained in *kotliarevshchyna* is directed against canonical and normative literature, against authority and authoritarianism, against all that is 'foreign," that is, distant, cold, and somehow not entirely human. We are speaking, of course, not about some abstract "idea of *kotliarevshchyna*" but about concrete texts and the patterns and structures they project. Upon examining these elements in numerous and complex texts we can demonstrate that the phenomenon of *kotliarevshchyna* is much more substantial than we may have assumed, and that in the first decades of the nineteenth century it constitutes one of the two main tendencies of the Ukrainian literary process. If we look at this process dialectically—as an opposition, as it were, between the tendencies of addressing "the world" and addressing the "native soil"—then the latter, exemplified by *kotliarevshchyna,* is clearly dominant. When is its hegemony overcome? As early as the appearance of Shevchenko? The writings of *Osnova?* The activities of Drahomanov, Ivan Franko, and Lesia Ukrainka? The answer clearly requires further investigation. But it is already apparent that in the first stage *kotliarevshchyna* determines the identity and consciousness of Ukrainian literature: it is the first thesis. If we accept the proposition that literature is a subset of the cultural process and that the phenomenon of nativism, as an inevitable response to the *realia* of political history and colonial status, largely characterizes Ukrainian culture of the nineteenth and twentieth centuries, then *kotliarevshchyna* stands revealed as a deep archetype. Its distant echoes may be heard in such disparate phenomena as the *khokhlandiia* that Khvylovy tilted at and that was officially nurtured by Stalinist and post-Stalinist Soviet cultural policy and the search for an "organic national style" that arose in the emigration as a response to the fetishization of "Europe" and "Europeanism."

The most complex function of *kotliarevshchyna*, as I have noted, is its modeling of Russian-Ukrainian literary relations, at the very least, up to the mid-nineteenth century, but surely beyond it as well. The topic is as broad as it is interesting, and here I can only sketch its outline.

From the perspective of Russian literature, *kotliarevshchyna* long becomes synonymous with all of Ukrainian literature. For a long time Russian criticism, following in the footsteps of Belinsky, sees nothing in Ukrainian literature other than burlesque and parody, and, what is more important, loses the ability to distinguish meaning and quality owing to the influence of this paradigm. (For many Russian critics there is simply no difference between a Shevchenko and a Topolia.) At the same time, neither the Ukrainians nor the Russians seem to realize that *kotliarevshchyna* manages a deep penetration into Russian literature in the person and creativity of Gogol/Hohol. He is a powerful projection of this modality onto the literature of the "center": through him a literature of the canon is infected by a literature of the anti-canon. At issue is not only the question of linguistic level that was analyzed by Ėikhenbaum.[19] In fact, a whole gamut of Gogolian features and strategies—parody, subversion, *épatage*, ambiguity, and decentering—have their source in the archetypal model created by Kotliarevsky (which Gogol, among other things, also overtly acknowledges in the epigraphs to his "Sorochinskaia iarmarka"). Like everything in Gogol, however, his introduction of Ukraine into the Russian consciousness has a double or triple bottom. On the one hand, he "discovers" Ukraine, makes it interesting and attractive, and gives rise to a massive (not so much Russian as Ukrainian) emotional involvement with it and with its pathos. But he introduces Ukraine in an exotic key (inevitable in a colonial reality) and in the key of a myth about its death, a myth that did not fully do its work only because it was so quickly "supplanted" (in the Ukrainian collective mind, of course) by Shevchenko's myth. Finally, Gogol introduces his Ukraine with striking notes of parody and burlesque. Suffice it to compare the tonality of his *Taras Bul'ba* with, say, the *Istoriia Rusov*, or Shevchenko's *Haidamaky*. This cardinal difference was already obvious to such contemporaries as Shevchenko and Kulish.

A distant echo and a very specific metamorphosis of *kotliarevshchyna* can be perceived in Soviet Ukrainian literature. Here, too, we can see the underlying strictures of Ukrainian-Russian literary relations (or, as

---

19. Cf. his *Lermontov* (Leningrad, 1924), p. 135; cited in George S. N. Luckyj, *Between Gogol' and Ševčenko: Polarity in the Literary Ukraine, 1798–1847* (Munich, 1971), p. 107.

it was then called, "union," *iednannia*), but now under circumstances of totalitarianism, where the relationship is regulated not only by the hierarchy of "center" and "periphery," but also by rigorous control, and terror as well. In such circumstances the devices of *kotliarevshchyna*, especially the masking of the ego behind the persona of the narrator, flight into seeming simplicity, self-protection by means of intimization and the voice of the collective all become highly motivated and functional. Not only functional, but necessary. It seems clear to me that in the Stalinist period Pavlo Tychyna defended himself precisely with such devices. Such poetic collections as *Chernihiv* or *Partiia vede* reveal the above repertoire, as well as the strategic moment of parody. For the paradigmatic poem "Partiia vede," with its refrain of "...vsikh paniv d'odnoï iamy," functions as both an assertion of a new Stalinist/neo-Kotliarevskian canon and as its parody. Even more revealing of this stance, pushing parody and subversion to the very brink—but successfully masking them precisely with the sanctioned modalities of epos and ideology—is Tychyna's still unacknowledged masterpiece "Shablia Kotovs'koho" (1938). A similar poetics is revealed in Ostap Vyshnia, especially in such works as "Chukhraïntsi." In fact, one can generally hypothesize that the deep poetics (not the official, Marxist-Leninist, "theoretical" poetics, but the actual, structural poetics) of Soviet Ukrainian—and specifically Ukrainian, not Russian—socialist realism draws its sustenance from the traditions and archetypes of *kotliarevshchyna*. The problem deserves further analysis, especially with respect to the overarching legacy of populism (*narodnytstvo*), which I have barely touched upon here.

Serhy Yekelchyk

The Grand Narrative and Its Discontents: Ukraine in Russian History Textbooks and Ukrainian Students' Minds, 1830s–1900s

The starting point of this paper is the disparity between two generally accepted beliefs.[1] On the one hand, it is well known that secondary school history textbooks of the Russian Empire inculcated and fostered Russian patriotism, even chauvinism, as well as loyalty to the tsar. On the other, few would deny that from the 1830s through the 1910s, thousands of Ukrainians graduated from imperial secondary schools holding views on national history that differed significantly from the official scheme of "all-Russian" history.

To explore the validity of this apparent contradiction, I shall proceed in two directions. First, in a search for any notable flaws or internal inconsistencies, I shall consider the representation of Ukraine and Ukrainians in major secondary school textbooks of the Russian Empire. Second, in an effort to discover evidence of the students' apprehension or rejection of those texts and of alternative influences on their view of Ukrainian history, I shall examine the memoirs of a dozen prominent Ukrainian patriots.

Texts and Gaps

The importance of education in the process of socialization and shaping student identity is easily established. The French Marxist philosopher Louis Althusser even went so far as to claim that the school, as the principal ideological apparatus of the bourgeois state, replaced religion as that of the feudal state.[2] While an attempt to apply the categories of feudalism and capitalism to nineteenth-century East European history may create considerable difficulties, education

---

1. For their help and suggestions during the preparation of this article, I would like to thank John-Paul Himka, Zenon E. Kohut, Frank E. Sysyn, and Myroslav Yurkevich. I am grateful to Peter Klovan for correcting errors in my English.

2. Louis Althusser, "Ideology and Ideological State Apparatuses," in his *Lenin and Philosophy and Other Essays* (New York, 1971), pp. 127–85.

certainly *did* play a pivotal role in imbuing the subjects of the tsars with a sense of "citizenship" or, rather, "subjectship."[3]

Most studies single out history teaching as one of the most important tools of socialization and ideological indoctrination in the modern world and regard it as particularly instrumental in developing nationalist sentiments. Examples best studied include the role of primary and secondary education in the development of South Slav, German, and Finnish nationalism, as well as British and French racism.[4]

Although some important research has been done on the representation of non-Russian nationalities in major surveys of Russian history,[5] nothing has been published specifically on nineteenth-century textbooks. Stephen Velychenko's important study of Russian, Polish, and Ukrainian interpretations of Ukrainian history deals with school textbooks only in passing.[6] All in all, the portrayal of the

---

3. Good general surveys of Russian educational policy are Nicholas Hans, *History of Russian Educational Policy* (1701–1917) (New York, 1964); and Patrick L. Alston, *Education and the State in Tsarist Russia* (Stanford, 1969). Specifically for the nineteenth century, see Nicholas V. Riasanovsky, *Nicholas I and Official Nationality in Russia, 1825–1855* (Berkeley, 1969); Allen Sinel, *The Classroom and the Chancellery: State Educational Reform in Russia under Count Dmitry Tolstoi* (Cambridge, Mass., 1973); Alain Besançon, *Éducation et société en Russie dans le second tiers du XIXe siècle* (Paris, 1974); and Cynthia H. Whittaker, *The Origins of Modern Russian Education: An Intellectual Biography of Count Sergei Uvarov, 1786–1855* (DeKalb, Ill., 1984).

4. See Marc Ferro, *The Use and Abuse of History, or, How the Past Is Taught* (London, 1984); Charles Jelavich, *South Slav Nationalisms—Textbooks and Yugoslav Union before 1914* (Columbus, Ohio, 1990); James M. Olson, "Nationalistic Values in Prussian Schoolbooks prior to World War I," *Canadian Review of Studies in Nationalism* 1, no. 1 (1973): 47–59; Katharine D. Kennedy, "Regionalism and Nationalism in South German History Lessons 1871–1914," *German Studies Review* 12, no. 1 (1989): 11–33; and F. J. Glendenning, "Attitude to Colonialism and Race in British and French History Textbooks," *History of Education* 3, no. 2 (1974): 57–72.

5. Seymour Baker, "Contributions to a Nationalist Ideology: Histories of Russia in the First Half of the Nineteenth Century," *Russian History/Histoire russe* 13, no. 4 (Winter 1986): 331–53; Carl W. Reddel, "S. M. Solov'ev and Multi-National History," ibid., 355–66; and Robert Byrnes, "Kliuchevskii on the Multi-National Russian State," ibid., 313–30.

6. Stephen Velychenko, *National History as Cultural Process: A Survey of the Interpretations of Ukraine's Past in Polish, Russian, and Ukrainian Historical Writing from the Earliest Times to 1914* (Edmonton, 1992), pp. 98, 105–7. Velychenko is interested in selected textbooks insofar as they are, in his opinion, important surveys of Russian history in themselves. As a result, the textbooks most widely used in Russian schools are absent from his analysis.

history of the Ukrainian ethnic lands in Russian imperial textbooks has not yet received the treatment it deserves.

As is well known, the foundations of the comprehensive and scholarly "traditional scheme" of Russian history were laid by Nikolai Karamzin's *Istoriia gosudarstva rossiiskogo* (History of the Russian State, 12 vols., 1818–24). The essence of Karamzin's scheme, later developed and strengthened by Nikolai Ustrialov, Sergei Soloviev, Vasilii Kliuchevsky and others, is as follows. Russian history begins with a "Kyivan period," and all Eastern Slavs are termed "Russian Slavs."[7] The political center of the "Russian" state later shifts to Vladimir-Suzdal, then to Moscow, and finally to St. Petersburg. Thus the continuity of Russian history and the unity of the "Russian" people are ensured. In general, Russian history is identified with the history of the autocracy and the state. Karamzin's is the dynastic approach, already outdated by the time of its appearance (though strengthened in Karamzin's interpretation by nineteenth-century progressive historicism).[8]

Karamzin's *magnum opus* began to appear in 1818, just after the Napoleonic wars, when new ideas of liberty and nationhood were circulating in Russia. Karamzin failed to include the new Romantic notions of nationality and state legitimacy in his work,[9] but, as David Saunders has persuasively argued, this *History*, which was insensitive to the national question, prompted a prolonged debate on the definition of Russian "nationality" (*narodnost'*) owing to the very fact of its appearance.[10] One of the consequences of this debate was the

---

7. N. M. Karamzin, *Istoriia gosudarstva rossiiskogo*, 5th ed., 12 vols. (St. Petersburg, 1842–43), 1: 63.

8. On Karamzin's scheme of Russian history, see J. L. Black, "Nicholas Karamzin's Scheme for Russian History," in H. C. Schlieper, ed., *Eastern Europe: Historical Essays Presented to Professor Milos Mladenovic on His Sixty-Fifth Birthday by His Students* (Toronto, 1969), pp. 16–33; and J. L. Black, *Nicholas Karamzin and Russian Society in the Nineteenth Century: A Study of Russian Historical and Political Thought* (Toronto, 1975).

9. For a discussion of the origins and essence of the modern idea of the nation as a community based on a common language and culture, see, for example, E. J. Hobsbawm, *Nations and Nationalism since 1780: Programme, Myth, Reality*, 2d ed. (Cambridge, 1992), ch. 1; and Daniel Chirot, "Herder's Multicultural Theory of Nationalism and Its Consequences," *East European Politics and Societies* 10, no. 1 (Winter 1996): 1–15. Curiously enough, in 1817, Karamzin himself admitted to having read a small book of Herder's three times, without ever having understood it (Black, *Nicholas Karamzin and Russian Society*, p. 127).

10. David B. Saunders, "Historians and Concepts of Nationality in Early Nineteenth-Century Russia," *Slavonic and East European Review* 60, no. 1 (January 1982): 44–62.

appearance in 1839 of the first officially solicited and approved school history textbook in the empire, that by Nikolai Ustrialov.[11] Like all subsequent textbooks, this work already had to take into account and somehow accommodate the new understanding of the nation as a community based on a shared language and culture.

As R. G. Collingwood notes perceptively in his *Idea of History*, "it is not only the results of historical thought that are out of date by the time they get into the text-book. It is also the principles of historical thought."[12] While in Russia a full-fledged debate on nationality and the meaning of national history was taking place by about 1820, its first traces did not appear in the textbooks until ca. 1840, and these issues were not openly discussed in textbooks until the 1860s.

Karamzin himself did not write a textbook based on his best-selling twelve-volume *History*. That task was carried out by Ivan Kaidanov, the author of several school textbooks relying heavily on Karamzin, most notably *Nachertanie istorii gosudarstva rossiiskogo* (Outline History of the Russian State, five editions between 1829 and 1834).[13] Following Karamzin, Kaidanov took the realm of Iaroslav the Wise to be the patrimony of the Russian tsars and thus justified the struggle for its "recovery." Characteristically, notions of linguistic (i.e., ethnic) and even religious ties between the Eastern Slavs were of secondary importance for Kaidanov, as they were for Karamzin. Kaidanov's was the textbook that introduced the history of the Eastern Slavs to such prominent Ukrainian historians as Panteleimon Kulish and, most likely, Mykola Kostomarov in their school years.

Karamzin's failure to acknowledge the existence of other Eastern Slavs and take account of the new understanding of nationality was apparent to his contemporaries. Indeed, the Russian historian Nikolai Ustrialov criticized Karamzin precisely for these weaknesses.[14] Ustrialov's approach to the history of the Ukrainian lands is of great importance for the present analysis, as he wrote the first officially approved textbook of Russian history with the aim of demonstrating the "unity of Polish, Lithuanian, and Russian history" and the

---

11. Ibid., pp. 58–61. Another major impetus was, of course, the Polish rebellion of 1830–31.

12. R. G. Collingwood, *The Idea of History*, edited and with an introduction by Jan Van Der Dussen (Oxford, 1993), p. 8.

13. I. K. Kaidanov, *Nachertanie istorii gosudarstva rossiiskogo* (St. Petersburg, 1829).

14. Velychenko, *National History as Cultural Process*, p. xix.

"Russian character" of the southwestern part of the empire.[15] In his other works, Ustrialov argues that there is a need for a "pragmatic history of Russia" emphasizing the "historical unity" of the Eastern Slavs and refuting Polish claims to the Ukrainian and Belarusian lands.[16]

It is clearly apparent that Ustrialov's approach is already informed by the new understanding of "nationhood" and "sovereignty" as vested in the people and not in their rulers. In fact, his famous textbook, *Nachertanie russkoi istorii dlia uchebnykh zavedenii* (Outline of Russian History for Schools, 1839), employs the Russian term for "nationality" in arguing for the "Russian" character of "Western Rus'" (i.e., Right-Bank Ukraine and Belarus). Thus, he speaks of the "efforts of Polish governments to obliterate nationality [*unichtozhit' narodnost'*] in Western Rus'."[17] According to Ustrialov, "Russia" already existed in Kyivan times as a political nation with a common language. Ustrialov challenges the accepted practice of focusing exclusively on Vladimir-Suzdal and Muscovy after 1169 and claims that the Grand Duchy of Lithuania was also a "Russian" state. Thus the two parts of the Russian nation were alienated only by the establishment of Polish rule over Ukraine and Belarus, and the major trend of Russian history was the "reestablishment of the Russian land within the borders it had under Iaroslav."[18]

In the context of this "joining together of Russia," Ustrialov provides a rather detailed account of sixteenth- and seventeenth-century Ukrainian history. He includes the new notion of nationhood, but does not stress it, sometimes ignoring it in favor of dynastic and territorial substantiations, at other times not expressing it clearly. Consider, for example, Ustrialov's explanation of the reasons for the Pereiaslav Agreement: Tsar Aleksei Mikhailovich "understood the necessity and possibility of reestablishing the Russian land within its ancient borders and terminating the centuries-old conflict between Russia and Poland over the Lithuanian principality by joining all three

15. Saunders, "Historians and Concepts of Nationality," p. 60.

16. Velychenko, *National History as Cultural Process*, pp. xix-xx.

17. N. G. Ustrialov, *Nachertanie russkoi istorii dlia uchebnykh zavedenii* (St. Petersburg, 1839), pp. xix–xx.

18. Ibid., p. xiii. This and all subsequent translations are mine, unless otherwise indicated. Also, unless otherwise noted, the "Russia" of my translation stands for *Rossiia* and "Russian" for *russkii* (*=aia, =oe, =ie*) of the original text.

states into one."[19] The same inconsistency is expressed once again when Ustrialov says that the Bakhchesarai treaty of 1681 "ended the twenty-seven-year-old war for Little Russia."[20]

The main problem with this utilization of the new idea of nationhood was not inconsistency, but rather inattention to national (i.e., linguistic and cultural) distinctions between Russians and Ukrainians. This "correction" of the concept of nationality was characteristic of the so-called "official nationality," that is, the ideology of Russian official nationalism and monarchism put forward from the 1830s under the *name* of the new principle of nationhood.[21] Indeed, Ustrialov thinks mainly in the old dynastic and territorial terms. He knows "Little Russia" as a geographical and historical term from the past, but consistently designates its population as "Russians" or "the Orthodox [people]." Finally, his periodization by "reigns" completes the impression of an old-fashioned narrative. Thus I would conclude that Ustrialov's book was a *reaction* but not a *response* to the new idea of nationality. It was unable to accommodate the interests or still the doubts of schoolchildren of the 1850s such as Mykhailo Drahomanov and Volodymyr Antonovych.

An attempt to account for the presence of the somehow ethnically distinct Little Russians in Russian history was made by Dmitrii Ilovaisky, the author of by far the most influential history textbooks in use from the 1860s to the second decade of the twentieth century. One might, however, judge the success of this attempt from the fact that by the 1870s and 1880s "teaching history according to Ilovaisky" had already become an idiomatic expression denoting primitive loyalism and Russian chauvinism.[22]

---

19. Ibid., p. 210.

20. Ibid., p. 222.

21. On "official nationality," see the works by Nicholas V. Riasanovsky and Cynthia H. Whittaker cited above. Here I am referring to the "new" Romantic idea of nation as a community based on shared language and culture. In fact, the textbooks also ignored the "old" seventeenth- and eighteenth-century concept of the Ukrainian (Cossack, Little Russian) people as represented by the Cossack officer class and a distinct Ukrainian high culture. I am grateful to Dr. Frank Sysyn for this observation. See Frank E. Sysyn, "The Cossack Chronicles and the Development of Modern Ukrainian Culture and National Identity," in *Adelphotes: A Tribute to Omeljan Pritsak by His Students* (=*Harvard Ukrainian Studies* 14, nos. 3–4 [December 1990]), p. 604. See also Zenon E. Kohut, "The Development of a Little Russian Identity and Ukrainian Nationbuilding," in *Concepts of Nationhood in Early Modern Eastern Europe* (=*Harvard Ukrainian Studies* 10, nos. 3–4 [December 1986]), pp. 559–76.

22. A. N. Fuks, "Shkol'nye uchebniki D. I. Ilovaiskogo i ikh reaktsionnaia sushchnost'," *Prepodavanie istorii v shkole* 5 (1982): 75–78; and E. Willis Brooks,

Ilovaisky wrote three major textbooks of Russian history. One, for those of "young [school] age," combined a narrative of Russian history with a general review of world history. The second, written for those of "middle [school] age," provided a slightly expanded version of the previous textbook's account of Russian history. The third, that considered fit for pupils of "senior [school] age," presented an altogether new and different, more detailed and sophisticated treatment of Russian history.[23]

It is extremely interesting to trace changes in the presentation of Ukraine and Ukrainians to schoolchildren of different ages. Ilovaisky's textbooks for youngsters and for the "middle" age do not directly discuss the idea of nationality. All Eastern Slavs are called "Russian Slavs" and, subsequently, "Russians." The terms "Rus'" and "Russia" are used interchangeably. Thus, the Polish-Lithuanian state "included all of Southwestern Russia," but the title of the next chapter reads, "Poland and Southwestern Rus', 1569–1683."[24] "Little Rus'" is located "on both banks of the middle course of the Dnipro" but settled by "Russians" or "Russian people."[25] Since the textbook is not concerned with the ethnic distinction (or relation) between the Russians and Ukrainians, or with ethnicity itself, for that matter, the only explanation for the Ukrainians' metaphysical "desire to reunite with Russia" may be a religious one: "The hetman and all the Cossack officers appealed to the coreligionist Muscovite tsar and asked him to take Little Russia under his high hand."[26] Subsequently, Ilovaisky refers to the same Ukrainian lands interchangeably as "Little Russia" and "Ukraine," with no explanation whatsoever. Thus, in 1654, "the tsar sent an embassy to Ukraine to administer the oath [of allegiance]," and in the early eighteenth century, "Mazepa proposed to return Little Russia once again to Polish servitude."[27] On the whole, the first two

---

"Ilovaiskii, Dmitrii Ivanovich," in *The Modern Encyclopedia of Russian and Soviet History*, vol. 14 (New York, 1979), pp. 149–51, here 151.

23. D. I. Ilovaiskii, *Sokrashchennoe rukovodstvo ko vseobshchei i russkoi istorii: kurs mladshego vozrasta*, 31st ed. (Moscow, 1915); idem, *Rukovodstvo k russkoi istorii: kurs srednego vozrasta*, 40th ed. (Moscow, 1901); and idem, *Kratkie ocherki russkoi istorii: kurs starshego vozrasta*, 36th ed. (Moscow, 1912).

24. Ilovaiskii, *Sokrashchennoe rukovodstvo*, pp. 185, 220. This chapter title is, of course, evidence of the implicit organization of Ilovaisky's history around the notion of nationality (or national territory).

25. Ibid., p. 221.

26. Ibid., p. 247.

27. Ibid., pp. 247, 278.

textbooks provide a rather primitive, mainly dynastic and religious, explanation of East Slavic history.

A much more sophisticated picture is presented in the textbook for the senior grades, *Kratkie ocherki russkoi istorii: kurs starshego vozrasta* (Brief Essays in Russian History: A Course for Those of Senior [School] Age). In the introduction, Ilovaisky already explores the problem of Ukrainian ethnic distinctiveness, which he had thoroughly ignored in the previous two textbooks. This discussion, however, includes an immediate and, for Ukrainians, unflattering connection between national character and state-building:

> The rather warm climate and rich expanses of black earth ... facilitated the development of a predominantly agricultural way of life among the South Russian or Little Russian population; the close proximity of the steppe and of wild hordes prevented the consolidation of a strong state structure and successful civil society there. Meanwhile, the Great Russian tribe, which occupied a land with a rather severe climate ... developed an enterprising, energetic character and talents for a variety of activities. Our state structure grew and gained strength there.[28]

After this tour de force, Ilovaisky *never* returns to the question of the ethnic distinctiveness of the Ukrainians. However, he devotes much more attention to "Little Russia," with a fair amount of confusion in his terminology—and with good reason. The beginning of the chapter "Western Rus' in the Sixteenth and the First Half of the Seventeenth Centuries" informs students that "the southern half of the Russian Dnipro region received the name of Ukraine or Little Russia ([it included the] ancient principalities of Kyiv, Chernihiv, and part of Siversk)."[29] The next one hundred fifty pages give no indication that the terms "Little Russia" and "Ukraine" have different meanings. On p. 276, however, Ilovaisky says that Serbian colonists settled "on the borders of Ukraine (near the upper reaches of the Inhul [river]),"[30] moving the borders of "Ukraine" far to the southeast. Nor do students have long to wait for the westward

---

28. Ilovaiskii, *Kratkie ocherki*, p. 4. Translated by Myroslav Shkandrij for use in his manuscript "The Imperial Imagination and Ukrainian Literature," p. 163. Shkandrij quotes from the text of my unpublished Ukrainian-language paper "Little Russia: The Imperial(ist) Myth of Ukraine in Russian Textbooks, ca. 1860–1917," presented at a conference on "Peoples, Nations, Identities: The Russian-Ukrainian Encounter," Columbia University, New York, 13–15 November 1994.

29. Ilovaiskii, *Kratkie ocherki*, p. 134.

30. Ibid., p. 276.

expansion. Although Ilovaisky proclaims, in the tenor of official rhetoric, that the annexation of the Ukrainian and Belarusian lands from Poland at the end of the eighteenth century constituted "the return of the West Russian regions,"[31] in a more detailed discussion he does not hesitate to refer to the newly acquired territories as "Ukraine." Thus the uprising of 1768 led by Maksym Zalizniak in the Kyiv, Bratslav, and Podilia palatinates took place, according to Ilovaisky, in "Ukraine beyond the Dnipro," and Zalizniak was proclaimed the "Ukrainian hetman" by his followers.[32] And so the "Ukraine" of Ilovaisky's textbook is effectively made to conform with the actual borders of Ukrainian *ethnic* territory in the Russian Empire. Even though the author never recognizes the existence of a territorially coherent country settled by ethnically distinct Ukrainians, his narrative reveals his *implicit* use of the criterion of nationhood based on peasant language and culture. In fact, the major flaw of Ilovaisky's narrative is that his implicit use of the category of nationality undermines the basic principle of his scheme, i.e., the supreme rationality of the imperial structure, which knows only administrative divisions, not ethno-territorial ones.

Ilovaisky does not speak of ethnic affinity as a reason for the "reunion" of Little Russia with Russia. His operative term is, rather, "the Little Russian question," which is resolved by Russia's use of military force against its neighbors; the effective "settlement of the Little Russian question" is, for Ilovaisky, the Treaty of Bakhchesarai (1681) between Muscovy and the Ottoman Empire.[33] Sometime around the end of the eighteenth century, both "Little Russia" and "Ukraine" disappear from the textbook. They are, "together with the other regions of the empire, divided into gubernias"[34] and are not mentioned again. Their exclusion from the text is "natural," for Ilovaisky does not, of course, explicitly recognize the ethnic unity of the Ukrainian lands, and strives to treat them as a number of discrete Russian provinces.

Ilovaisky prefers to use euphemisms such as "southern grain-producing regions of the empire"[35] when referring to Ukraine in the nineteenth century. His discussion of the relatively recent Inventory

---

31. Ibid., p. 285.
32. Ibid., p. 289n.
33. Ibid., pp. 169–76.
34. Ibid., p. 275.
35. Ibid., p. 302.

reform of 1847–48 in Right-Bank Ukraine is quite significant as an exposition of his concept of nationality. In his words, the introduction of the Inventory Regulations in Kyiv, Podilia, and Volhynia gubernias was intended mainly "to protect the villagers, Russian and mostly Orthodox, from oppression by the Polish Catholic nobility (*szlachta*)."[36] In fact, in the nineteenth century the overwhelming majority of villagers on the Right Bank were Ukrainian (and stubbornly Ukrainian-speaking) peasants. While it is difficult to speak of a full-fledged sense of Ukrainian national identity at the time, debates about the membership of these Ukrainian-speaking peasants in the modern Russian, Polish, or Ukrainian nations, with their corresponding "high" cultures and literary languages, were extremely heated in educated society on the Right Bank from at least the 1850s. The tension between the textbook's silence and the intelligentsia's animated discussion of the nationality problem in Ukraine may have encouraged students to read the textbook "against the grain."

This paper's emphasis on Ilovaisky's textbooks is warranted by their predominance in the empire's secondary schools for half a century (1860s-1910s). S. N. Iuzhakov, who studied the problem of school history textbooks in the last years of the nineteenth century, claims that Ilovaisky's status was unchallenged only during the 1870s and 1880s.[37] But recent archival research shows otherwise. According to I. V. Babich, as late as 1894, a survey by the Scholarly Committee of the Ministry of Education showed the "dominant (though not monopolistic) position of D. I. Ilovaisky among authors of textbooks in Russian history."[38] It was not until 1913 that questionnaires distributed among teachers began to show "the transition from

---

36. Ibid., p. 318.

37. S. N. Iuzhakov, "Dnevnik zhurnalista. O gimnazicheskikh uchebnikakh istorii," *Russkoe bogatstvo* 7 (1897): 133–38. See also the anonymous entry on "Ilovaiskii" in *Bol'shaia ėntsiklopediia*, vol. 10 (St. Petersburg, 1902), p. 43.

38. I. V. Babich, "Problema uchebnika otechestvennoi istorii v politike Ministerstva narodnogo prosveshcheniia v kontse XIX-nachale XX v.," *Vestnik Moskovskogo universiteta, seriia 8: Istoriia* 2 (1990): 73–82 (quotations are from pp. 73–74 and 80). The author shows that the Scholarly Committee pursued a relatively liberal policy and tried to limit the influence of the "reactionary monarchist" Ilovaisky. The ministry's official journal published negative reviews of Ilovaisky's textbooks, which were approved for use in the schools only after delays, critiques, and prolonged correspondence with the author. However, beginning in the 1860s, the selection of textbooks from the list of those approved by the ministry was determined by the school councils, which, eager to demonstrate their orthodoxy, opted overwhelmingly for Ilovaisky.

Ilovaisky to Ivanov and Elpatievsky, and from those two to Platonov."[39]

This means, among other things, that Sergei Soloviev's textbook, *Uchebnaia kniga russkoi istorii* (Textbook of Russian History), often mentioned mainly because of its author, who also wrote the monumental 29–volume *History of Russia*, was never widely used in secondary schools. Ilovaisky himself based his narrative on Soloviev's *magnum opus*, and his presentation of the "abridged" Soloviev suited the ideology of the empire better than Soloviev's own synopsis.

Actually, Soloviev's textbook is no more successful than Ilovaisky's in dealing with Ukraine. He assumes the ethnic unity (or even uniformity) of the Eastern Slavs by referring to them interchangeably as "Slavs," "Russian Slavs," "Russians," and "the Russian people."[40] He refers to the Ukrainian lands after the thirteenth century as "southwestern Russia."[41] Moreover, he never acknowledges the ethnic distinctiveness of the "southwesterners," although he does provide some hints of an anecdotal character. Thus, in describing the visit of King Danylo of Halych to the khan of the Golden Horde, Soloviev allows himself a "lyrical digression": "It was difficult for a young prince in whom discretion did not prevail over emotions, as it did in [the personalities] of northern princes ... to abase himself before the steppe barbarian."[42]

Soloviev feels no need to explain the ethnic affinity between Ukrainians and Russians: he simply refers to the inhabitants of the Ukrainian lands as "the Orthodox Russian people."[43] It follows for Soloviev that they "desired" to unite with Russia, for in their conflict with Poland "class hatred combined with religious hatred."[44] Soloviev's is perhaps the best-documented account of the Pereiaslav Agreement of 1654 to be found in any Russian textbook, interspersed with extensive quotations from documents, especially Hetman Bohdan Khmelnytsky's speech and the text of the oath.[45] Otherwise, Soloviev presents Ukrainian history in the same spirit and manner as Ilovaisky,

---

39. Ibid., p. 80.

40. S. M. Solov'ev, *Uchebnaia kniga russkoi istorii*, 9th ed. (Moscow, 1887), pp. 3–5.

41. Ibid., pp. 40–43.

42. Ibid., p. 41.

43. Ibid., p. 197.

44. Ibid., p. 201.

45. Ibid., pp. 201–4.

but in even less detail after the mid-seventeenth century. Finally, Soloviev does not even raise the issue of nationality.

The textbooks mentioned in the survey of 1913 as substitutes for Ilovaisky—those by K. Ivanov and K. V. Elpatievsky[46]—deserve even less mention in this connection, as they completely ignore ethnic distinctions between the Eastern Slavs and follow the traditional scheme in representing Ukrainians at all times as the "Orthodox Russian people."

The third textbook, which, according to the survey, finally replaced Ilovaisky's text, offers a slightly more sophisticated interpretation. Sergei Platonov's *Uchebnik russkoi istorii* (Textbook of Russian History) follows tradition in referring to the Eastern Slavs as "Russian Slavs" and subsequently "Russians."[47] Platonov does not, however, use the term "Russia" in his discussion of pre-eighteenth-century history, but employs the historically correct terms "Rus'," "Kyivan Rus'," and "Southwestern Rus'."[48] The term "Russian" in his account of these times is a derivative of "Rus'" rather than of "Russia"; for example, "two third of all Gediminas's lands were Russian lands."[49]

This historically more sensitive interpretation does not, however, lead Platonov to consider the ethnic distinctiveness of the Ukrainians. Thus, his interpretation of the agreement of 1654 and the Russian-Polish conflict is fairly traditional: "The object of the struggle was Little Russia—Polish possessions on the middle Dnipro where the Russian population separated from Poland and strove to unite with Orthodox Moscow."[50]

It remains to be said that there *were* several unorthodox textbooks of Russian history, mostly published in the early twentieth century,

---

46. K. Ivanov, *Uchebnik russkoi istorii*, 4th ed. (St. Petersburg, 1911); and K. V. Elpat'evskii, *Uchebnik russkoi istorii*, 13th ed. (St. Petersburg, 1912).

47. S. F. Platonov, *Uchebnik russkoi istorii*, 9th ed. (St. Petersburg, 1917), pp. 6, 10.

48. Ibid., pp. 23, 42, 60.

49. Ibid., p. 63.

50. Ibid., p. 153. In fact, Platonov was influenced by Social Darwinism, and his more advanced (i.e., university) course of Russian history, *Lektsii po russkoi istorii* (Lectures in Russian History), interpreted the "reunion" in the light of "our tribe's" need for self-defence. The "tribe" obviously included "Russians" in both Russia proper and "Little Russia." He saw the difference between Russia proper and the Ukrainian lands as one of social structure, not ethnicity, and justified the elimination of this difference by citing the interests of "our historical existence .., the unity of the tribe and its religion" (Velychenko, *National History as Cultural Process*, pp. 105–6).

that presented schoolchildren with a different view of Ukrainian history. Reflecting the liberal and autonomist tendencies of the time, Venedikt Miakotin regards "Little Russia" after 1654 as a de facto independent state in dynastic union with Russia and as the first example of autonomy in modern Russian history.[51] A textbook written by the first female Ukrainian historian, Aleksandra Iefymenko, also develops this autonomist interpretation, which implied the national distinctiveness of the Ukrainians.[52] A Russian Marxist historian, Mikhail Pokrovsky, adopts a totally different view of Russian history by emphasizing the role of socio-economic forces. For him, the Pereiaslav Agreement resulted from the Cossacks' desire to defend their rights as "small landholders" discriminated against by the Polish magnates but, presumably, privileged in seventeenth-century Russia.[53]

All these "unorthodox" textbooks, however, were of almost negligible significance, for they were used by a minuscule number of secondary schools for only a few years before 1917. The typical textbook continued to follow the notorious "traditional scheme" of Russian history.

Teachers and Students

The preceding discussion focuses on the message contained in the textbooks. It is reasonable, however, to suppose that this message was not fully and unconditionally accepted by all students; indeed, many Ukrainian patriots evinced quite a different view of history after they graduated from Russian secondary schools. Moreover, all the scholars who first conceived and then formulated the idea of a separate Ukrainian historical process—Mykola Kostomarov, Volodymyr Antonovych, Mykhailo Hrushevsky, Viacheslav Lypynsky[54]—were

---

51. On Miakotin's textbook, see Velychenko, *National History as Cultural Process*, p. 106.

52. A. Efimenko, *Ėlementarnyi uchebnik russkoi istorii* (St. Petersburg, 1912).

53. M. N. Pokrovskii, *Russkaia istoriia*, in his *Izbrannye proizvedeniia* (Moscow, 1965), vol. 1, esp. pp. 461–79.

54. The discussion of the development of the Ukrainian academic tradition, its subversion of the official narrative of "Russian" history, and its changing understanding of "nation" are outside the scope of this paper. The best surveys of the development of Ukrainian historiography currently available in English are *A Survey of Ukrainian Historiography* by Dmytro Doroshenko (published as a special issue of the *Annals of the Ukrainian Academy of Arts and Sciences in the U.S.*, nos. 5–6 [1957]; the volume also contains an article by Olexander Ohloblyn, "Ukrainian Historiography, 1917–1956"); and Velychenko,

graduates of Russian gymnasiums, the most "indoctrinating" variety of Russian schools, which were designed to provide the empire with cadres for its bureaucracy. A significant number of Ukrainian activists were employed as secondary school teachers, often teaching—of all subjects—Russian history, as we shall see below.

How, then, did they become conscious Ukrainians? How did the Ukrainian intellectual elite emerge, reproduce itself, and transmit the national historical memory to the next generation? A plausible preliminary suggestion is that the linear-process model of communication, in which the message is simply transmitted to its receiver, does not describe the actual situation in the schools of the empire. The students' minds were not *tabulae rasae*, nor was a teacher always a loyal transmitter of officially approved ideas. To reveal what happened to the message of official historiography in the classroom, I shall examine the memoirs of some well-known Ukrainian patriots who were all students at Russian secondary schools between the 1830s and 1900s.

Two of these memoirists, Kulish and Kostomarov, became secondary school teachers in their twenties; both later became prominent historians. Significantly, their autobiographies suggest that studying Russian history at a gymnasium played almost no role in fashioning their worldview. Panteleimon Kulish (1819–97) uses the third person to describe his years at the Chernihiv gymnasium: "He learned all of Kaidanov's *History* (there was none better at the time) by heart, and whatever the teacher asked him, he responded in the same high-flown style that now only sounds ridiculous."[55] Kulish knew how to please his teachers, but his actual vision of Ukrainian history and his general outlook were shaped by a different source: a collection of Ukrainian folk songs published by Mykhailo Maksymovych.[56] After Kulish found this volume by accident at a grocery shop, the collection became "the most important of his books." He even read it aloud to

---

National History as Cultural Process. See also Zenon E. Kohut, "The Development of a Ukrainian National Historiography in Imperial Russia," in *Historiography of Imperial Russia: The Profession and Writing of History in a Multinational State*, ed. Thomas Sanders (Armonk, N.Y., 1999).

55. Panteleimon Kulish, "Avtobiohrafiia" [original title "Zhizn' Kulisha"], in Iurii Luts'kyi, ed., *Sami pro sebe: Avtobiohrafiï vydatnykh ukraïntsiv XIX-ho stolittia* (New York, 1989), p. 30.

56. Ibid., p. 31. Mykhailo Maksymovych published three collections of Ukrainian folk songs: *Malorossiiskie pesni* (Little Russian Songs, 1827), *Ukrainskie narodnye pesni* (Ukrainian Folk Songs, 1834), and *Sbornik narodnykh ukrainskikh pesen* (A Collection of Ukrainian Folk Songs, 1849).

his classmates at the gymnasium, especially those fragments dealing with Ukrainian history: "Somko Mushket," "Konovchenko," "The Azov Brothers," and "Khmelnytsky and Barabash."[57]

In the 1840s, Kulish was working as a secondary teacher in Lutsk, Kyiv, and Rivne while writing his historical novels, *Mykhailo Charnyshenko* and *Chorna Rada* (The Black Council), and collecting materials for his *Zapiski o Iuzhnoi Rusi* (Notes on Southern Rus', 2 vols., 1856–57). During those years, he also wrote *Povest' ob ukrainskom narode* (The Story of the Ukrainian People, 1846), a Romantic populist survey of Ukraine's past intended "for older children" that clearly departed from the official historical scheme.[58] Given his interest in history, it is surprising that Kulish's generally self-laudatory autobiography includes no mention of his teaching, even though the autobiography was not only written at a relatively liberal time, in 1867, but also published abroad, in the Lviv *Pravda*. Did Kulish make any attempt to expose his students to alternative visions of Ukraine and its past?

This puzzling silence continues in the autobiography of another prominent contemporary, Mykola Kostomarov (1817–85). While remembering his stay at the Voronezh gymnasium, he criticizes its teaching of the Russian language and literature, natural history and world history, Greek, French, and German, but says nothing at all about Russian history. The turning point in Kostomarov's life was his initial period of study at Kharkiv University, where he first read Maksymovych's *Malorossiiskie pesni* (Little Russian Songs, 1827) and Izmail Sreznevsky's *Zaporozhskaia starina* (Zaporozhian Antiquity, 1833–38).[59] Here, he was highly influenced by a German-trained professor of world history, Mikhail Lunin, while Petro Hulak-Artemovsky's lectures on Russian history "were notable for idle rhetoric and oratory."[60]

---

57. Ibid., p. 31.

58. The full title of the original publication was *Povest' ob ukrainskom narode. Napisal dlia detei starshego vozrasta P. Kulish* (St. Petersburg, 1846). *Povest'* stressed the ethnic and linguistic distinctiveness of Ukrainians and the continuity of their historical tradition. The book was confiscated after Kulish's arrest in 1847 for participation in the SS. Cyril and Methodius Brotherhood. For a detailed analysis of *Povest'*, see Velychenko, *National History as Cultural Process*, pp. 167–71.

59. N. I. Kostomarov, "Avtobiografiia," in his *Istoricheskie proizvedeniia. Avtobiografiia* (Kyiv, 1989), pp. 446–49.

60. Ibid., pp. 440–41.

In the 1840s, Kostomarov taught history at the Rivne gymnasium and then at the First Kyiv gymnasium when he was already an established professional historian of Ukraine and the author of Romantic poems in Ukrainian. In his *Avtobiografiia*, Kostomarov describes in great detail his research trips in Right-Bank Ukraine, his living quarters, and even his participation in the SS. Cyril and Methodius Brotherhood, but says *nothing* about his teaching.[61]

The first generation of Ukrainian patriots in my sample experienced a revival of national sentiment under the influence of the Romantic concept of nationality. They became acquainted with it through the works of folklorists who also provided them with an alternative (at first merely mythopoetic) version of the Ukrainian past. This generation did not find a ready-made structure of Ukrainian cultural circles or political organizations with which to become affiliated; it had to create them itself. However, given the kind of administrative scrutiny to which Kulish and Kostomarov were subjected, they are unlikely to have been radicals in the classroom. More probably, they followed the official line of the textbook, while striving in their spare time to employ the folk songs that had shaped their own outlook in order to expose their students to a new concept of nationhood and an alternative vision of the Ukrainian past.

The next generation of Ukrainian activists (born around 1840) had different memories of their school years, which coincided with the liberal 1850s. But these activists, too, devoted little or no attention to Russian history in their memoirs. Mykhailo Drahomanov (1841–95), who read Karamzin's twelve volumes (twice) and Dmytro Bantysh-Kamensky's *History of Little Russia* in the lower grades, makes no mention whatever of studying Russian history at the Poltava gymnasium. His memoirs reveal his fondness for the Latin language and Roman history, as well as the formative influence of his history teacher, Oleksander Stronin. It is not clear from the text, however, whether Stronin taught both world and Russian history or just world history. Drahomanov recalls a wealth of details about Stronin's world history class:

---

61. Ibid., pp. 461–76. Kostomarov, in fact, penned the programmatic document of the Brotherhood, *Knyhy buttia ukraïns'koho narodu* (The Books of the Genesis of the Ukrainian People), which condemned Russian oppression of Ukraine and presented a messianic vision of the Ukrainian past and future. Also, in fairness to Kostomarov, I should immediately add that there *exists* a testimony of Kostomarov's efforts to involve students in Rivne in a Romantic populist pursuit. According to one memoirist, Kostomarov once asked his pupils to collect folk songs during their vacations. See Thomas M. Prymak, *Mykola Kostomarov: A Biography* (Toronto, 1996), p. 24.

> I should also render great thanks to the gymnasium where I was lucky enough to encounter...a very good history teacher who taught us the course of modern history to 1859 (until the Italian war), explaining to us, in fact, the essence of the Reformation, the Dutch and English revolutions, eighteenth-century philosophy, the principles of liberalism and nationalism and, finally, socialism (in connection with the year 1848).... He was the one who gave me Herzen to read and instructed me that in order to strengthen one's humane and liberal ideas, one must study a great deal and read historical and political writings in foreign languages, since, as he said, the government might forbid all literature in Russian should it so choose. Together with some friends I began reading the new, just published translations of [Friedrich Christoph] Schlosser's *History of the Eighteenth Century*, Macaulay, Prescott, and Guizot in the original, and began learning the German language. We established the hand-written journal of which I was the editor.[62]

These ideas, while not necessarily Ukrainian-specific, had, of course, little in common with the official Ustrialov/Ilovaisky scheme. It is interesting that Drahomanov, who subsequently became docent of ancient history at Kyiv University, taught Russian history free of charge at the Temporary Pedagogical School in Kyiv in 1862–63. As is well known, the radical and patriotic students of the 1860s tried to make use of this school to propagandize future elementary teachers.[63] Unfortunately, Drahomanov provides no details of his teaching of Russian history there.

His contemporary Volodymyr Antonovych (1834–1908), subsequently a professor of Russian history at Kyiv University, does not mention studying this subject at secondary school.[64] Antonovych recognizes

---

62. Mykhailo Drahomanov, "Avtobiograficheskaia zametka," in his *Literaturno-publitsystychni pratsi*, 2 vols. (Kyiv, 1970), 1: 40. In another article Drahomanov adds that Stronin gave him Marko Vovchok's stories. In fact, Stronin was selling in Poltava the cheap popular Ukrainian editions published in St. Petersburg by Kulish (Mykhailo Drahomanov, "Avstro-rus'ki spomyny," ibid., 2: 153). Thus Stronin popularized among the pupils not only European liberal and democratic ideas, but also Ukrainian Romantic populism (Oleksander Stronin [1826–1889], historian, sociologist, educator and civic leader. Active in the Poltava Hromada. Arrested in 1862 for "disseminating Little Russian propaganda" and exiled to Siberia. See A. Zhukovsky, "Stronin, Oleksander," in *Encyclopedia of Ukraine*, 5 vols. [Toronto, 1984–93], 5: 67–68).

63. R. P. Ivanova, *Mykhailo Drahomanov u suspil'no-politychnomu rusi Rosiï ta Ukraïny (druha polovyna XIX st.)* (Kyiv, 1973), pp. 29–31.

64. He studied at the prestigious Richelieu Lyceum in Odesa.

that the decisive influence on the development of his worldview in his teens was French literature, especially works by Montesquieu, Rousseau, Voltaire, and other encyclopedists. Raised in a Polish cultural milieu, he never heard of Shevchenko's poetry or the SS. Cyril and Methodius Brotherhood, although he was fascinated by Polish Romantic Cossackophile literature (Michał Czajkowski's novels).[65] It was his knowledge of world history and Western democratic ideas that led to his discovery of the Ukrainian nationality:

> I began thinking how to apply the general principles of theoretical democracy to our country. It appeared that the democratic element in our country was the peasantry.... It became clear that the peasants constituted a separate nationality [from the Polish gentry].... Applying my weak knowledge of things Ukrainian to general French democratic theory, I discovered Ukrainianness by myself.[66]

Whatever the textbook from which he learned Russian history, Antonovych became a prominent Ukrainian historian and activist because of other, outside influences he experienced in his school and university years. His reading of Enlightenment authors, combined with the influence of the cultural and political ideology of the mid-nineteenth-century Polish *szlachta*, provided him with the concepts of liberty and nationality, and his application of these notions to Ukraine made him a Ukrainian.

Mykhailo Starytsky (1840–1904), in his memoirs of his and Mykola Lysenko's (1842–1912) youth, does not describe their education. He does mention in passing the historian Stronin as his "unforgettable teacher-enlightener" at the Poltava gymnasium.[67] Starytsky's memoirs, however, afford us a glimpse of the extracurricular reading and activities of this generation. Unlike Drahomanov, who came from a relatively Russified family, and Antonovych, who was raised as a Pole, both Starytsky and Lysenko came from old and relatively well-off Ukrainian-speaking indigenous noble families with Cossack roots. The details that remained in Starytsky's memory include small Cossack cannons and other memorabilia of their ancestors; a portrait

---

65. See, besides Antonovych's own memoirs, O. I. Kyian, "Zhyttievyi ta tvorchyi shliakh V. B. Antonovycha," *Ukraïns'kyi istorychnyi zhurnal*, 1991, no. 2: 64–66.

66. Volodymyr Antonovych, "Avtobiohrafichni zapysky," in Luts'kyi, ed., *Sami pro sebe*, p. 147.

67. Mykhailo Staryts'kyi, "K biografii N. V. Lysenka," in his *Tvory*, 8 vols. (Kyiv, 1965), 8: 397.

of Voltaire and sympathy for Napoleon; a mixture of the French and Ukrainian languages at home; and Lysenko's uncle, who provided the boys with a copy of Shevchenko's forbidden poems.[68]

In grade 5, Starytsky bought his own first copies of *Eneïda* and *Kobzar*. Lysenko's parents subscribed to several "thick journals," including the liberal *Sovremennik* and *Otechestvennye zapiski,* which were at the students' disposal. A future playwright, Starytsky was vividly impressed during his teens by amateur theater in Poltava, which was staging "exclusively [the Ukrainian musicals] *Natalka Poltavka, Moskal'-charivnyk,* and *Svatannia na Honcharivtsi....*"[69] However, Starytsky's and Lysenko's true introduction to Ukrainian history was a historical novel. While in grade 6, Starytsky dropped by the bookstore "by chance" and found there Kulish's famous novel of Cossack times, *Chorna Rada* (The Black Council). In his memoirs, he recalls the "exquisite joy" that he and Lysenko felt while reading this novel.[70]

The "nationalist" genre of the novel[71] provided the young Starytsky and Lysenko with a powerful alternative "Ukrainian" reading of national history. Kulish's *Zapiski o Iuzhnoi Rusi* (Notes on Southern Rus') inspired Lysenko to start collecting Ukrainian folk songs,[72] a step that would eventually lead him to his unique role as founder of modern Ukrainian music.

Another interesting (and quite different) representative of the same generation was the first prominent Ukrainian novelist, Ivan Nechui-Levytsky (1838–1918). Born to a poor clerical family in Right-Bank Ukraine, he was educated at several church institutions, but spent

---

68. Ibid., pp. 335–412; and his "Zo mly mynuloho (Uryvky spohadiv)," in *Tvory*, 8: 364–84.

69. Staryts'kyi, "K biografii N. V. Lysenka," p. 397. Interestingly, Drahomanov, who studied at the Poltava gymnasium in the 1850s as well, also speaks of *Natalka Poltavka* as his first and most impressive theatrical experience. Writing abroad, he adds incidentally that many gymnasium students had Shevchenko's forbidden poems "The Caucasus" and "A Dream" in their notebooks (Drahomanov, "Avstro-rus'ki spomyny," 2: 153).

70. Staryts'kyi, "K biografii N. V. Lysenka," pp. 398–99. Only the limitations of space prevent me from reproducing here in full this long description of the delight and sense of discovering the past that they experienced while reading *Chorna Rada*.

71. On the importance of the novel as a genre for modern nationalism, see Benedict Anderson, *Imagined Communities: Reflections on the Origins and Spread of Nationalism*, rev. ed. (London, 1991), pp. 28–40.

72. Staryts'kyi, "K biografii N. V. Lysenka," p. 399.

most of his life teaching the Russian language, history, and geography at various gymnasiums. His autobiography was published abroad, in the Lviv journal *Svit*, and is quite frank. Unlike most Ukrainian patriots of his time, Nechui did not have to "discover" Ukraine. He came from a different social milieu, that of the impoverished Right-Bank clergy, which lived among the peasantry and was close to it in language and culture. In fact, Nechui did not speak Russian at all, and for some time was not able to understand his teachers when he started school. He gives no account of studying Russian history as part of his curriculum, but speaks about the influence of his father's views on history:

> My father loved our native country; he used to tell us that Ukraine was being oppressed by the Polish landlords and the Jews; that Muscovy was abusing our language and nationality; [he] narrated Ukrainian history to us; when going with us to Korsun, he would show us the Rizanyi ravine and the graves in the environs of Korsun where Bohdan Khmelnytsky fought with the Poles; he would indicate Nalyvaiko's road, which leads from the Korsun road to the village of Petrushky....
>
> Father had *Ukrainian History* [*sic*] by Markevych and Bantysh-Kamensky and the *Eyewitness Chronicle*, which I would read when I came home on vacation.[73]

Nechui's father's stories and books, of course, sharply contrasted with his school textbook. But once again, like most other Ukrainian teachers, Nechui tells us *nothing* about his own experience as a teacher of Russian history.

A possible explanation of this silence is that resistance to the official interpretation of the Ukrainian past was channeled into other spheres, such as collecting historical songs and creative writing. This form of resistance remained indirect not only because of fear of administrative and police action, but also because, until the early twentieth century, there was no scholarly alternative to the well-developed "traditional scheme" of Russian/East Slavic history. The non-conformist vision of the Ukrainian past existed in the form of critical comments on this scheme; based on the idea of nationality, this vision found its best expression in topics and themes that were absent by definition from the school curriculum.

The next generation of Ukrainian patriots was born in the 1860s. Perhaps the two most famous and, at the same time, contrasting

73. I. Nechui-Levyts'kyi, "Zhyttiepys," in Luts'kyi, ed., *Sami pro sebe*, pp. 229–30.

representatives of this generation were Ievhen Chykalenko (1861–1929) and Mykhailo Hrushevsky (1866–1934).

Like Nechui-Levytsky, Chykalenko was of non-noble background and in his early childhood lived a life close to that of the peasantry. (He came from a wealthy free peasant family with Cossack roots.) When he started school, the other students ridiculed his inability to speak Russian. He was, however, exceptionally lucky, for three of his teachers at the Odesa private gymnasium were outstanding Ukrainian activists: the teacher of the Russian language, Oleksii Andriievsky; the teacher of geography (and Ukrainian composer and translator), Petro Nishchynsky; and, most beloved and respected of all, the teacher of *history*, Leonid Smolensky.[74] This exceptionally bold teacher's method of lecturing on the beginnings of the Moscow principality provides an insight into his view of Russian history: "According to the chronicles, Moscow ("turbid water" in Finnish) was founded on territory settled by a Finnish tribe, the *Mer'*, so that the Muscovite people who emerged from this cross-breeding are *merzkii* [loathsome], and a single Muscovite should be called *merin* [gelding], as in Gogol's expression 'stupid as a gelding.'"[75] No less forthright was his comment on the accession of Nicholas II to the throne in 1895: "I was born under one rod [Nicholas I], studied under two rods [Alexander II], and thought that I would die under three [Alexander III], but suddenly there came a relief—two rods."[76] Chykalenko testifies that even though Smolensky taught in Russian in the mainly Russian-speaking city of Odesa, many his students became nationally conscious Ukrainians. He noticed Chykalenko, a shy boy who was afraid to speak his mother tongue, and encouraged him to read Gogol, Shevchenko, and Marko Vovchok and to sing Ukrainian songs. As the result of this encouragement, recalls Chykalenko,

> [F]or days at a time I was not able to think about anything but Zaporozhian Cossacks in red jerkins with forelocks on their heads; I could not fall asleep at night and dreamt constantly of finding, like Columbus, a new land and establishing there the Zaporozhian Host, or of encircling the old Zaporizhzhia, *of which I had read in our textbook but somehow did not pay attention*, with a huge Chinese wall. I felt somehow subconsciously that B[ohdan] Khmelnytsky also was not a *katsap*, but ours....[77]

---

74. Ievhen Chykalenko, *Spohady (1861–1907)*, 2d ed. (New York, 1955), p. 74.

75. Ibid., p. 77.

76. Ibid.

77. Ibid., pp. 79–80. Emphasis added. *Katsap* is a derogatory Ukrainian term for a person of Russian nationality.

Mykhailo Hrushevsky, who came from the Russian-speaking family of a wealthy educator, did not experience any linguistic difficulties at school. In his reminiscences, this great historian of Ukraine is highly critical of the Tiflis gymnasium in the 1880s: "The most important subjects in the humanities—the history of literature and history—were staffed in such a way that they gave us very little. The hours of history were empty; the history teacher [was] phlegmatic, a person without temperament or any interests whatsoever; he might have dispelled any interest in his subject."[78] Elsewhere he adds, "The history teacher gave us nothing—it all amounted to the notorious textbooks by Ilovaisky."[79] Hrushevsky claims that he also was not impressed by Mykola Markevych's *History of Little Russia* and, even as a teenager, doubted the authenticity of the historical songs cited in *The History of New Sich* by Apolon Skalkovsky.[80] What, then, was the emotional or intellectual impulse that prompted him to become a historian of Ukraine? It was the Ukrainian scholarly and literary journal *Kievskaia starina* (Kyivan Antiquity, 1882–1906), to which his father began to subscribe at the end of its first year of publication, 1882. Hrushevsky recalls his enthusiasm for this journal, a true encyclopedia of Ukrainian studies and the only medium of Ukrainian cultural life and scholarship in the empire:

> As a matter of fact, I spent the year 1883 engaged in this kind of civic, national and political self-education on the basis of the contents and according to the directions of *Kievskaia starina*. When I realize just how much I owe to its first two years of issues, my feeling of gratitude and thankfulness to its founders and managers for their public service becomes stronger. How many generations of Ukrainians did it serve as such a school during the first two decades of its existence?[81]

Hrushevsky goes on to say that the program of *Kievskaia starina* was limited and apolitical, but another point should be stressed. Throughout the nineteenth century, the intelligentsia of the Russian Empire created and cultivated an entire subculture of "thick journals" with an encyclopedic range of subjects. During an era when there was no national political life as such, these journals served as a public forum.

---

78. Mykhailo Hrushevs'kyi, "Spomyny," *Kyïv*, 1988, no. 11: 132.

79. Hrushevs'kyi, "Spomyny," *Kyïv*, 1988, no. 12: 137.

80. Ibid., pp. 117–18.

81. Ibid., p. 121. On *Kievskaia starina*, see V. M. Matiakh, "Bilia vytokiv 'Kievskoi stariny,'" *Ukraïns'kyi istorychnyi zhurnal*, 1992, no. 1: 142–50.

And it was through this habitual medium of the "thick journal" that the Russian or Russified intelligentsia was prepared to accept Ukrainian scholarship and literature. Hrushevsky, in fact, mentions that before the appearance of *Kievskaia starina* he had already been an attentive and appreciative reader of such Russian thick journals as *Vestnik Evropy* and *Russkoe slovo*.[82]

The last Ukrainian patriots in this discussion are those born in the 1880s and early 1890s. More than any earlier generation, the students of the 1890s and 1900s stood on the shoulders of their predecessors, who had created a network of Ukrainian cultural and political organizations, supplemented by journals and scholarly works by Kostomarov and Antonovych. Social background and family traditions became less significant in this generation's rejection of Russian history. For example, in 1893–94, Iurii Kollard (1875–1951), the son of a Belgian engineer, joined both the Ukrainian self-education circle and the Ukrainian political circle at the Poltava non-classical secondary school (*real'noe uchilishche*).[83] Dmytro Doroshenko (1882–1951), the scion of a famous Cossack family, while isolated in the 1890s as the only Ukrainian in the far-off Vilnius gymnasium, subscribed to a Galician Ukrainian newspaper, *Zoria,* and after its demise to the journal *Literaturno-naukovyi visnyk*. He writes that these journals "became for me, so to speak, a school of Ukrainian national consciousness."[84] Around 1905, Mykola Kovalevsky (1892–1957) first heard the slogan of Ukrainian autonomy from a young local gymnasium teacher in Chernihiv gubernia. The young Kovalevsky subscribed to the leading (and only daily) Ukrainian newspaper in the Russian empire, *Rada,* and for that reason was obliged to quit the Chernihiv gymnasium at the time of the post-1905 reaction.[85]

An episode from his memoirs connected with an excursion to the Tarnovsky Museum in Chernihiv presents a direct confrontation between the textbook view of the Ukrainian past and an alternative Ukrainian vision. Sometime around 1905, a group of students visited the museum:

> A picture of the old times in Ukraine was presented to us, and historical personalities we knew from our textbooks of history or literature appeared in our imagination as if in the flesh. During

---

82. Hrushevs'kyi, "Spomyny," pp. 121–22.

83. Iurii Kollard, *Spomyny iunats'kykh dniv* (Toronto, 1972), pp. 24–25.

84. Dmytro Doroshenko, *Moï spomyny pro davnie-mynule, 1901–1914* (Winnipeg, 1949), p. 7.

85. Mykola Kovalevs'kyi, *Pry dzherelakh borot'by: Spomyny, vrazhennia, refleksiï* (Innsbruck, 1960), pp. 22–23, 75.

> our visit to the museum, an interesting discussion sprang up between our tutor, Grozdov, and the director of the museum, Shelukhin, the brother of the Shelukhin who subsequently became a senator. Shelukhin was giving explanations in Ukrainian, and our tutor, after listening to him for some time, began to explain various exhibits as well, speaking in Russian and from the viewpoint of Russian history. Incidentally, an argument began on the basis of Shelukhin's assertion that Hetman Mazepa had played an important role in the development of culture in Ukraine; [that he had] built many schools and churches. Our tutor considered it necessary to explain that Mazepa was a traitor and that his role in the cultural life of Ukraine was not so important. Shelukhin flared up and began giving examples of Mazepa's activities, all from the Chernihiv region, and remarked that he was not concerned with the political tendencies of this or that personality, since the task of his historical museum was to preserve the relics of the past, which were monuments of Ukrainian culture and history. Accordingly, he could not call anyone a traitor and sling mud at the Ukrainian hetmans. After that our tutor became silent and began trying to put our visit to the Tarnovsky Museum to an end as quickly as possible.[86]

Later on Kovalevsky adds, "I remember that the tour of the Tarnovsky Museum made a great impression on us."[87]

Perhaps the most detailed and revealing account of the initial acceptance and subsequent rejection of the ideas of school history textbooks was written by Mykola Halahan (1882–?), a student of the 3rd Kyiv gymnasium and then the Galagan (no relation) College in the 1890s and early 1900s. Halahan came from a clerical family of modest means with some indistinct memories of its noble origin and the Cossack past. Like many people of similar origin, he did not speak Russian before starting school. Nevertheless, as Halahan writes frankly in his memoirs, after a year in the gymnasium, the nine-year-old boy knew that "we all are Russians" and loyal subjects of the tsar. He was still interested in Bohdan Khmelnytsky and Cossack times,

---

86. Ibid., p. 73. Elsewhere in the text the name of Tarnovsky is misspelled "Taranavsky." The Tarnovsky Museum of Ukrainian Antiquities was formally opened in Chernihiv in 1901, but for several decades before that Vasyl Tarnovsky's private collection of articles and documents of Cossack times, Shevchenko memorabilia, etc. had functioned as a de facto private museum. For a scholarly treatment of the question of Mazepa's "treason," see Orest Subtelny, "Mazepa, Peter I, and the Question of Treason," *Harvard Ukrainian Studies* 2, no. 2 (June 1978): 158–83.

87. Kovalevs'kyi, *Pry dzherelakh borot'by*, p. 73.

but, he writes, "Ilovaisky's *History* threw much light upon my 'sore' question. It explained clearly and understandably everything about 'Little Russia,' the 'Little Russian' Cossacks, and Bohdan Khmelnytsky."[88] Like other students, Halahan teased a classmate from Belarus (whom they called "Lytvyn") by quoting various unpleasant comments about the *lytvyns* from Ilovaisky's *History*.[89]

He even tried to persuade his parents' housemaid Khrystia that "we all are Russians" and was surprised at her objections. The Russians wear different dress and use different words, argued the housemaid, unwittingly evoking the modern idea of nationality. Confused, the boy addressed the question to a new teacher at the village school, himself a self-educated Ukrainian peasant. The teacher did not give him any definite answer, but brought to his attention several historical facts that perhaps could not be easily reconciled with the textbook's "all-Russian" history.[90] Soon Halahan came under the influence of an older member of the informal circle of his fellow-countrymen, Hryts Chuprynka, who himself came from a well-off and nationally conscious Cossack family. After some discussion and reading of Nikolai Gogol (Mykola Hohol) and Danylo Mordovets (Daniil Mordovtsev), the members of the circle "came to the conclusion that we were not Russians but 'Little Russians,' or the 'Little Russian' Cossacks whom Hetman Khmelnytsky brought under Moscow to their detriment and ours."[91] Only after repeatedly frequenting the *Kievskaia starina* bookshop and reading Shevchenko's *Kobzar* and forbidden poetry did Halahan realize that "there is no Little Russia, but there is Ukraine."[92]

* * *

We now are approaching the roots of the apparent contradiction that prompted this discussion. The Russian history textbooks were indeed

88. Mykola Halahan, *Z moïkh spomyniv (80–ti roky do svitovoï viiny)*, 4 vols. (Lviv, 1930), 1: 52.

89. Ibid., pp. 59–60. Although "Lytvyn" literally means "Lithuanian," in Ukraine it was also traditionally applied to Belarusians.

90. Ibid., pp. 54–56.

91. Ibid., pp. 64–65.

92. Ibid., pp. 67, 80. In 1900–1905, while still a student at the Galagan College, Halahan was an active member of the Ukrainian *hromada* of secondary-school students (Ukraïns'ka hromada seredn'oshkil'nykiv). It united several secret political circles and was ideologically close to the Revolutionary Ukrainian Party (ibid., p. 80).

loyalist and followed the officially approved scheme of "Russian" history, but their interpretation of the Ukrainian past suffered from a major flaw: in their discussion of non-Russian Eastern Slavs, the textbooks did not satisfactorily accommodate the modern idea of nationality. The "official nationality" of imperial Russia united all Eastern Slavs into a single "Russian" nationality that ignored a principal factor in the modern idea of nationhood—the distinctive ethnic traits of peasant culture. The failure of the textbooks to discuss and appropriate the new "ethnographic" understanding of nationality and their reliance on the old dynastic and territorial schemes resulted in significant silences and blind spots in the narrative of imperial history. This "imperfection" of the Grand Narrative provided the intellectual space for and the key to recovering the separate identities and pasts of its subjects. Such substantial omissions opened up the possibility of an alternative narrative suppressed within the dominant discourse of "Russian history."

On the other hand, students did not learn about the Ukrainian past only from textbooks. Family influence, folklore studies (which acquainted pupils with the new notion of nationhood), liberal and/or patriotic teachers, and, in the course of time, Ukrainian scholarship and literature, journals and newspapers, cultural and political circles—all these sources undermined the official scheme and provided an alternative, if not very coherent, patriotic vision of the Ukrainian past. This vision, which defended the silenced and oppressed minorities against the progress of the imperial universal narrative, was necessarily fragmented and unsystematic. For the time being, it was not interested in creating totalizing master narratives or appropriating others as the objects of its story.

The grand narrative of the rise of the Russian Empire and the fragmented discourse of national resistance, made up of songs, legends, and journalistic articles, coexisted without acknowledging each other. The textbooks were silent about the students' nationality; the students' memoirs were silent about the textbooks. A lesson on the reign of Peter I did not erase the impressions made by a song about Hetman Mazepa, and no amount of textbook cramming made the language of the local peasants sound like Russian.

In other words, the imperial school could not and did not prevent thousands of young Ukrainians from heeding Shevchenko's famous dictum:

> Only look well, only read
> That glory through once more,
> From the first word to the last,
> Read; do not ignore

Even the last apostrophe,
Not one comma even,
Search out the meaning of it all,
Then ask yourself the question:
"Who are we? Whose sons? Of what sires?
By whom and why enchained?"[93]

The outgrowth of this inquiry was an academic tradition of Ukrainian history that produced an elaborate scholarly alternative to the Russian Grand Narrative at the beginning of the twentieth century. The efforts of the two pillars of nineteenth-century Ukrainian historical writing, Mykola Kostomarov and Volodymyr Antonovych, to undermine the official view of East Slavic history found their intellectual culmination in Mykhailo Hrushevsky's historical scheme. In his famous article of 1904, "The Traditional Scheme of 'Russian' History and the Problem of a Rational Organization of the History of the Eastern Slavs," Hrushevsky first established the continuity of the Ukrainian historical process.[94] His monumental ten-volume *Istoriia Ukraïny-Rusy* (History of Ukraine-Rus'), which began to appear in 1898, furnished a solid academic basis for Ukrainian history. At the same time, Hrushevsky produced several best-selling one-volume surveys of Ukrainian history in Russian and Ukrainian.[95] Thus a coherent interpretation of Ukrainian national history was expressed for the first time in textbook form. From this point, Ukrainian historical thought proceeded to develop its own grand narrative.

---

93. Taras Shevchenko, "To My Fellow-Countrymen, in Ukraine and Not in Ukraine, Living, Dead and As Yet Unborn, My Friendly Epistle," in his *Song out of Darkness: Selected Poems*, translated from the Ukrainian by Vera Rich (London, 1961), pp. 77–78.

94. Mykhailo Hrushevsky, "The Traditional Scheme of 'Russian' History and the Problem of a Rational Organization of the History of East Slavs," in Lubomyr R. Wynar, *Mykhailo Hrushevsky: Ukrainian-Russian Confrontation in Historiography* (Toronto, 1988), pp. 35–42. Originally published in Ukrainian as M. Hrushevs'kyi, "Zvychaina skhema 'Rosiis'koï' istoriï i sprava ratsional'noho ukladu istoriï skhidnoho slovianstva," in *Sbornik statei po slavianovedeniiu* (St. Petersburg, 1904), pp. 298–304.

95. M. Grushevskii [Hrushevs'kyi], *Ocherk istorii ukrainskogo naroda* (St. Petersburg, 1904); M. Hrushevs'kyi, *Iliustrovana istoriia Ukraïny* (Kyiv, 1911).

Christine D. Worobec

Conceptual Observations on the Russian and Ukrainian Peasantries

At the turn of the twentieth century a vast array of villages and hamlets stretched across the diverse landscape of the fifty provinces of European Russia. These settlements differed not only in size but also in ethnic composition. Russians and Ukrainians comprised the largest ethnic groups, accounting for approximately sixty million and twenty million rural inhabitants respectively. Russians predominated in the north, central industrial, and central agricultural provinces, as well as in the Ural and Volga regions, while Ukrainians dominated Left-Bank and Right-Bank Ukraine and New Russia. Ukrainian and Russian peasants lived cheek by jowl in some areas, such as the New Russian provinces of Katerynoslav (Ekaterinoslav), Tavriia (Tavrida), and Kherson and the southern black-earth provinces of Voronezh, Kursk, and Tambov. While they retained cultural and linguistic differences, they influenced each other as they adapted to similar ecological conditions and responded to the market and other external forces. Yet even distinctive ethnic enclaves varied tremendously in terms of land management, inheritance practices, and the degree to which peasants pursued non-agricultural economic activities. Customs, dress, and dialects also changed from village to village. At the same time, the commonality of subsistence agriculture, suspicion of strangers, collective practices, and various types of passive and active resistance characterized these diverse settlements.

Ethnicity presents a conundrum in the study of the Ukrainian peasantry. While historians of Russia have not always been sensitive to ethnicity, scholars of pre-nationalist or pre-modern Ukraine have gone to the other extreme in assuming that ethnicity is the determinant factor in post-emancipation Ukrainian society. Peasant societies, however, naturally share similarities because their economic activities are rooted in subsistence agriculture. Even in areas where agricultural and non-agricultural wage labor supplements farm income, peasants are rooted to the land. Their concerns tend to be insular as they strive to feed their families, pay taxes, and fulfill obligations to community and state. At the same time, peasants react both positively and negatively to market pressures, government exactions, and the inroads that outsiders—teachers, clerics, doctors, feldshers, and statisticians—make into the local community. They have their own sense of justice and shape their communities through a panoply of customs and a worldview that do not always correspond neatly to those of elite society. A historian of any peasant group must be cognizant of the complexities of that society, its regular patterns and diversity, as well as its similarities with and differences from other peasant cultures. Given the common religious identity, political experience, and patriarchal culture of the Russian and Ukrainian peasants in the post-emancipation period, comparative analyses are in order. In a sophisticated historiographical and methodological analysis, ethnicity will perforce not always be the dominant factor.

The two peasantries accounted for more than eighty and ninety percent of the Russian Empire's Russian and Ukrainian populations respectively, and their social, economic, and cultural activities and interactions are a fundamental part of late imperial history. Yet only in the last three decades have historians begun the study of these peasant groups. Other agendas, largely political in nature, have preoccupied and, in many cases, still preoccupy the attention of historians of both Russia and Ukraine.

In the West, the political systems of the pre-revolutionary and post-revolutionary periods have received greatest attention. After the October Revolution of 1917 and the collapse of the Provisional Government, Russian émigrés were stunned by the rapid demise of the fledgling experiment in liberalism and the Bolshevik victory. The characterization of communism as evil increased with the development of the Cold War as the West, including historians, built a wall of defenses against this system and touted the superiority of democracy and capitalism to socialism. In the late 1960s and early 1970s, as Cold War sentiments waned and the new social history took hold, a few brave souls abandoned the political middle ground of Russian history to investigate other aspects of Russian society. Influenced by the work of the *Annalistes* and American social historians, these revisionists posited that history was much more than the chronicling of political events and the manipulation of power by individuals, oligarchies, or elites. That claim forced them to dig below the surface to examine less fortunate and sometimes politically voiceless social groups, be they peasants, workers, or women.

Historians of Russia turned their attention initially to workers. If the revolutions of 1905 and 1917 had been such cataclysmic events, it stood to reason that perhaps more than revolutionary ideologies and political parties were involved. Given socialism's stress on the need for a politically conscious working class, historians asked questions about the origins, makeup, and self-identity of workers within the Russian Empire, as well as about their roles in the revolutions.[1] Studies of this type are still continuing and providing an ever richer picture of the revolutionary period that is challenging the traditional view of the October 1917 Revolution as a simple coup d'état. That revolution, it now is apparent, was as much a worker, soldier, and peasant victory as a Bolshevik one.

Inspired by this new social history, scholars and graduate students in North America and Great Britain finally tackled the study of the Russian peasantry in the late 1970s and early 1980s. Working independently of one another for the most part, they were somewhat fearful of pioneering in an immense field. Two conferences in the summer of 1986, one in London, England, and the other in Boston, Massachusetts, broke that isolation. For the first time, scholars shared the fruits of their research on the nineteenth- and early twentieth-century Russian peasantry. Since then, two volumes of these conference papers have appeared in print, as have numerous monographs and essays on the Russian peasantry.[2] They tackle such diverse topics as land management, peasant resistance, family and household

---

1. See, for example, Victoria Bonnell, *Roots of Rebellion: Workers' Politics and Organizations in St. Petersburg and Moscow, 1900–1914* (Berkeley, 1983); Robert Eugene Johnson, *Peasant and Proletarian: The Working Class of Moscow in the Late Nineteenth Century* (New Brunswick, N.J., 1979); Diane Koenker, *Moscow Workers and the 1917 Revolution* (Princeton, N.J., 1981); Allan K. Wildman, *The Making of a Workers' Revolution* (Chicago, 1967); and Reginald E. Zelnik, *Labor and Society in Tsarist Russia: The Factory Workers of St. Petersburg, 1855–1870* (Stanford, 1971).

2. The two conference volumes are Roger Bartlett, ed., *Land Commune and Peasant Community in Russia: Communal Forms in Imperial and Early Soviet Society* (Houndmills, UK, 1990); and Esther Kingston-Mann and Timothy Mixter, ed., *Peasant Economy, Culture, and Politics of European Russia, 1800–1921* (Princeton, N.J., 1991). Other selected works include Jeffrey Burds, *Peasant Dreams and Market Politics: Labor Migration and the Russian Village, 1861–1905* (Pittsburgh, Pa., 1998); Ben Eklof and Stephen P. Frank, eds., *The World of the Russian Peasant: Post-Emancipation Culture and Society* (Boston, 1990); Barbara Alpern Engel, *Between the Fields and the City: Women, Work, and Family in Russia, 1861–1914* (New York, 1994); Beatrice Farnsworth and Lynne Viola, eds., *Russian Peasant Women* (New York, 1992); Stephen P. Frank, *Crime, Cultural Conflict, and Justice in Rural Russia, 1856-1914* (Berkeley, 1999); Cathy A. Frierson, *Peasant Icons: Representations of Rural People in Late Nineteenth-Century Russia* (New York, 1993); Steven L. Hoch, *Serfdom and Social Control in Russia: Petrovskoe, a Village in Tambov* (Chicago, 1986); David Ransel, *Mothers of Misery: Child Abandonment in Russia* (Princeton, N.J., 1988); and Christine D. Worobec, *Peasant Russia: Family and Community in the Post-Emancipation Period* (Princeton, N.J., 1991). Other works are cited in the article.

structure, the status of women, out-migration, domestic industries, crime, customs, and *mentalités*. Some historians have adopted a macro approach, preferring to investigate the broad social, cultural, and economic patterns of the Russian peasantry, while others have favored local or microcosmic studies that emphasize both the distinctiveness and the typicality of an area. In the end, these two methodological approaches enrich each other as historians gain a deeper understanding of Russian peasant society.

While traditional historians of Russia were preoccupied with political questions, Western scholars of Ukraine focused their attention on nationalism and statehood. They found themselves beset by a stateless people who by the end of the eighteenth century were under the domination of the Austrian Habsburgs and Polish lords in the west and the Russian Romanov dynasty in the east, and yet in 1917–18 enjoyed a short-lived independence. Using independence as a starting point, much as the revolutions of 1917 have preoccupied historians of Russia, scholars of the Ukrainian experience grappled with the rise of a Ukrainian national consciousness and the obstacles to development in the multinational empires of Russia and Austria-Hungary. Studies concentrated on the formation of a small intelligentsia within whose ranks could be found activists dedicated to the creation of a Ukrainian national identity. Despite the nineteenth-century Ukrainian intelligentsia's passionate interest in peasant culture and language as the defining traits of Ukrainian identity, scholars, ironically, have by and large ignored the bulk of the Ukrainian population. Given their extremely low literacy rate and economic and social backwardness, Ukrainian peasants in the Russian Empire were largely irrelevant to the Ukrainian national struggle before 1917. After 1917 they were not loyal supporters of the ill-fated bourgeois Ukrainian state that the Central Rada established. Accordingly, they did not merit attention in the eyes of scholars intent upon proving that Ukraine deserved independence. Ukrainian scholars in the diaspora have been kinder to the Galician Ukrainian peasantry of Austria-Hungary because of that group's nascent national consciousness. Thanks to a higher literacy rate, as well as a strong network of cooperatives and a better-developed intelligentsia-led national movement on the eve of World War I, Galicians working within the Austrian parliamentary system were able to secure tangible benefits for Ukrainians in the Habsburg Monarchy.[3] The fact that Galicians

---

3. See the pioneering work by John-Paul Himka, *Galician Villagers and the Ukrainian National Movement in the Nineteenth Century* (Edmonton, 1988); and

dominated Ukrainian émigré life in North America until after World War II also guaranteed greater scholarly attention to this area.

In order to discuss the relations that Ukrainian peasants had with Russians in the post-emancipation Russian Empire, scholars need to ask new questions of and apply new methodologies to the bountiful primary materials available for the post-emancipation period.[4] While illiterate peasants did not keep records of their thoughts and experiences, government and church officials, ethnographers, and other observers of the peasantry did so. Naturally, there are problems with such sources as population and tax censuses, parish and court records, household budget studies, accounts of peasant disturbances, and records of oral culture, but careful and critical readings of these documentary records reveal vital information.[5] The path-breaking work of historians of the post-emancipation Russian peasantry can aid historians of the Ukrainian peasantry in the critical use of sources and new methodologies.

At the same time, historians of the Russian peasantry are not without fault in their treatment of Ukrainian peasants. While not entirely neglectful of Ukrainian peasants in their studies, they have fallen into the trap of Russian imperial policy, which ignored the ethnicity of Ukrainian peasants. Using the designation "Little Russians" to refer to Ukrainians of any class, Russian officials denied the existence of a distinct Ukrainian nationality. They argued instead that Ukrainians comprised a subgroup of the Great Russians and that the Ukrainian language constituted a Russian dialect, two beliefs that are still elements of the Russian national myth. Historians of the Russian Empire's peasantries, while careful to identify their subjects' geographical location by district and province, for example, are not always attuned to their ethnic identities.[6] Those who are more

---

Stella Hryniuk, *Peasants with Promise: Ukrainians in Southeastern Galicia, 1880–1900* (Edmonton, 1991).

4. Two historians of Ukraine, Andreas Kappeler and Orest Subtelny, have recognized the need to apply the methods of social history to the study of Ukraine, especially with regard to the peasantry. See Andreas Kappeler, "The German Perspective," *Slavic Review* 54, no. 3 (Fall 1995): 699; and Orest Subtelny, "The Current State of Ukrainian Historiography," *Journal of Ukrainian Studies* 18, nos. 1–2 (Summer–Winter 1993): 43.

5. For a discussion of sources, see Worobec, *Peasant Russia*, pp. 225–31; and idem, "Temptress or Virgin? The Precarious Sexual Position of Women in Postemancipation Ukrainian Peasant Society," *Slavic Review* 49, no. 2 (1990): 227–29.

6. An example of this may be found in Judith Pallot, "The Commune in the 1870s," in *Landscape and Settlement in Romanov Russia, 1613–1917* (Oxford,

sensitive to ethnicity do not always know what to do with that designation once they have recognized it. This latter problem raises the issue of the relative importance of ethnicity in creating distinctive features among peasant groups.

The study of any peasant society cannot be conducted in a vacuum. Given the agricultural nature of much peasant economic activity around the world, contemporary and historical peasant societies share a variety of characteristics that anthropologists, rural sociologists, and political economists have identified.[7] For example, reluctance to experiment with new agricultural technologies in subsistence systems of agriculture, creative adaptation to change, suspicion of outsiders, subaltern strategies of resistance, and a penchant for collective action typify peasant societies the world over. This internationalism is mitigated, however, by ecological, cultural (including religious), economic, ethnic, historical, and political distinctions. Indeed, regional differences within individual ethnoses in pre-modern, largely agrarian societies are natural, given inadequate communications systems, low literacy rates, and the absence of a systematic state policy meant to instill respective populations with a particular national consciousness.

The internationalism of peasant societies and the seemingly contradictory distinctions among villages within a single ethnic group are no doubt most troubling to Ukrainian historians caught in the web of persecution history and nationalism. Professor George G. Grabowicz, a prominent scholar of Ukrainian literature and culture, has recently criticized what he considers a devaluation of the Russification policies of the tsarist government after 1861:

> The counterargument that the imperial policy of cultural suppression was not directed at a single group, e.g., Ukrainians, but was "universal" and "egalitarian," so to speak, that "Russification" ... was also directed at the Russians themselves (the

---

1990), pp. 136–63. In discussing the differences in the communal systems of Kharkiv and Archangel provinces in the 1870s, Pallot does not mention that the peasants of Kharkiv province were overwhelmingly Ukrainian.

7. Some of the more influential works in this respect include George M. Foster, "Peasant Society and the Image of Limited Good," *American Anthropologist* 67, no. 2 (1965): 292–315; Robert Redfield, *Peasant Society and Culture: An Anthropological Approach to Civilization* (Chicago, 1956); James C. Scott, *Domination and the Arts of Resistance: Hidden Transcripts* (New Haven, Conn., 1990); idem, *The Moral Economy of the Peasant: Rebellion and Subsistence in Southeast Asia* (New Haven, Conn., 1976); idem, *Weapons of the Weak: Everyday Forms of Peasant Resistance* (New Haven, Conn., 1985); and Eric R. Wolf, *Peasants* (Englewood Cliffs, N.J., 1966).

> favorite analogue here was the French policy of turning peasants into Frenchmen) is not persuasive.[8]

Grabowicz is here referring to the influence of Eugen Weber's brilliant study, *Peasants into Frenchmen* (1976), on revisionist scholars.[9] These researchers accordingly emphasize the diversity of the Ukrainian peasantry and the fact that the city's colonization of the countryside through education, railroads, a national market, and a conscript army brings with it new ways of thinking that attack peasant culture, be that culture Russian or Ukrainian.

Social historians are not denying that the tsarist government banned the publication of materials in the Ukrainian language with successive acts in 1863 and 1876. In calling attention to Ukrainian and Russian peasant societies, however, rather than to the Ukrainian intelligentsia, whose work was adversely affected by the Valuev and Ems decrees, they are questioning the primacy of nationality issues among pre-modern groups. They ask instead that greater attention be paid to the ways in which the state affected peasants, the manner in which peasants reacted to the demands placed upon them and in turn affected government policy, and the role of peasants as actors in their own society.[10] A brief examination of Russian government policy on primary education and its treatment of Ukrainian peasants, as well as Ukrainian peasants' sense of identity, suggests that Russian and Ukrainian peasant experiences and notions of self were similar.

At the time the Ems and Valuev decrees were announced, primary education for the peasantry was in its infancy in European Russia and Ukraine; consequently, illiteracy was almost universal among Russian and Ukrainian peasants. The imperial Russian government had been wary about the potential of an educated population to undermine the

---

8. Professor Grabowicz was reacting to opinions voiced at the second workshop, "Peoples, Nations, Identities: The Russian-Ukrainian Encounter," 13–15 November 1994, Columbia University, New York. See George G. Grabowicz, "Ukrainian Studies: Framing the Contexts," *Slavic Review* 54, no. 3 (Fall 1995): 677–78.

9. Eugen Weber, *Peasants into Frenchmen: The Modernization of Rural France, 1870–1917* (Stanford, 1976).

10. Reacting to the Polish insurrection of 1863 and the potential threat of the Ukrainophile movement to the integrity of the Russian Empire, Minister of the Interior Petr Valuev banned the publication of all scholarly, religious, and pedagogical materials in the Ukrainian language, exempting only belles lettres. The 1876 Ems decree supplemented the earlier ban by prohibiting the import and publication of Ukrainian books, the use of Ukrainian in theatrical productions, and the teaching of Ukrainian in elementary schools.

autocracy. Consequently, it had resisted education for the peasantry until the crushing military defeat of the Crimean War in 1855 and the necessity of economic modernization forced its hand. The zemstvos, local administrative units created by the reforms of 1874 (which did not extend to Right-Bank Ukraine because of the Polish uprising of 1863 and fear of further Polish agitation), began to establish primary schools in the countryside. Their results were mixed. According to the historian Ben Eklof, Russian peasants who spoke hundreds of different dialects generally reverted to their local patois after studying Old Church Slavonic and Russian at the elementary level for an average of three years.[11] Ukrainian peasant children must have found the purely liturgical Old Church Slavonic just as mystifying as did their Russian counterparts. They may have been at a greater disadvantage in learning Russian, a question that surely needs study, yet there is no denying that many similarities between the two languages do exist.

Ultimately, the relatively late concern for primary education meant that prior to 1914 European Russia remained the least literate European state, with three-quarters of its rural population illiterate. With the exception of the figures for Right-Bank Ukraine, the 1911 statistics concerning educational attainment in Russian and Ukrainian areas do not show significant discrepancies. The percentage of students in primary schools and per 1,000 inhabitants in the Russian Central Agricultural Region and Left-Bank Ukraine are comparable, as are those in New Russia and the Central Industrial Region. Clearly, Right-Bank Ukraine was at some disadvantage, as it had no zemstvo schools until 1911.[12] As regards literacy rates, once again figures for the Central Agricultural Region (35 percent for rural men and 6 percent for rural women), this time for 1897, are comparable to the predominantly agricultural Left Bank (34 percent and 6 percent) and Right Bank (30 percent and 9 percent) of Ukraine. Literacy in the Central Industrial region (48 percent and 14 percent) and New Russia (42 percent and 13 percent) was notably higher. In the former area, higher literacy may have been associated with the peasants' economic need to pursue non-agricultural work away from the village for substantial periods of time in order to supplement their meager

---

11. Ben Eklof, *Russian Peasant Schools: Officialdom, Village Culture, and Popular Pedagogy, 1861–1914* (Berkeley, 1986), pp. 403–7; also noted in Robert J. Kaiser, *The Geography of Nationalism in Russia and the USSR* (Princeton, N.J., 1994), pp. 70–71.

12. Unfortunately, no study of church schools in Right-Bank Ukraine (or elsewhere in Ukraine or in Russia, for that matter) has yet been conducted.

agricultural income. The attraction of urban and rural industry raised peasant awareness of the economic advantage of literacy. Substantial Russian peasant migration from the land-poor Central Industrial Region to the fertile lands and newly established heavy industries of New Russia accounts in part for the higher literacy rates there.[13]

While literacy rates do not testify to any specific suppression of literacy among Ukrainian peasants, did the Russian government have a colonial mentality that led it to treat the Ukrainian peasantry as second-class subjects? According to Professor Grabowicz, a definite colonial mentality existed in imperial Russia. He writes: "... membership in the dominant nation transcended class distinctions: a Russian laborer could feel superior to a Ukrainian intellectual simply because the latter was a "*khokhol*" [a pejorative term alluding to the Cossacks' penchant for wearing a lock of hair on an otherwise clean-shaven head]; by itself this is racial discrimination without actually invoking color of skin ..."[14]

How systematic was the use of the term *khokhol*? A perusal of government documents of the 1890s concerning various forms of peasant resistance, from poaching wood to refusing to pay taxes to threatening violence against nobles, did not produce evidence that government officials described peasants as *khokhol*s. In fact, there is rarely anything to distinguish these government reports from those chronicling Russian peasant resistance.[15] The general silence on the part of officials about the Ukrainian question confirms the historian Theodore Weeks's careful reading of other types of government reports.[16] Educated society generally viewed all peasants, regardless of ethnicity, as ignorant and lazy children who needed guardianship and discipline. In fact, they tended to blame outside agitators for stirring up the peasants, believing that peasants could not possibly act on their own.

---

13. Kaiser, *Geography of Nationalism*, pp. 67, 69.

14. Grabowicz, "Ukrainian Studies," p. 678.

15. A. V. Shapkarin, ed., *Krest'ianskoe dvizhenie v Rossii v 1890–1900 gg.* (Moscow, 1959).

16. Theodore Weeks, "Ukrainians and Official Russia: A Deafening Silence," paper delivered at the second workshop, "Peoples, Nations, Identities: The Russian-Ukrainian Encounter," 13–15 November 1994, Columbia University, New York.

TABLE 1. **LEVEL OF EDUCATIONAL ATTAINMENT IN 1911 (PERCENTAGE OF STUDENTS AND PER 1,000 POPULATION)**

Region	% in secondary schools	% in trade schools	% in primary schools	per 1,000 total population	per 1,000 aged 10–19
Central Ind.	7.2	4.9	88.2	50.7	290.2
Central Agr.	5.5	2.7	91.7	46.1	211.1
New Russia	7.4	3.8	88.9	62.7	297.4
Left-Bank Ukr.	6.3	2.2	91.5	46.4	210.6
Right-Bank Ukr.	5.4	3.7	90.9	42.5	188.4

SOURCE: Tsentral'nyi statisticheskii komitet, *Statisticheskii ezhegodnik Rossii 1911* (St. Petersburg, 1912), part 1; cited in Robert J. Kaiser, *The Geography of Nationalism in Russia and the USSR* (Princeton, N.J., 1994), p. 74.

In a much earlier case of peasant resistance in the fall of 1862, Major General Chertkov made a rare assessment of peasant behavior on the basis of ethnicity. In this episode, which took place on a large estate of 3,000 souls in Voronezh province, an area with a mixed Russian and Ukrainian population, peasants denounced the emancipation provisions and the imposition of a land charter by refusing to prepare their assigned fields for winter crops. When the peasants continued their defiance, the governor ordered troops to surround the crowd and administer corporal punishment to individuals until the peasants agreed en masse to desist from further protest. In his report to the minister of the interior, Chertkov attributed the peasants' behavior to the area's steppe traditions and the "particularly stubborn character of 'Little Russians.'"[17] Sentiments such as these need to be studied systematically within the context of accounts of Russian peasant disturbances in order to make valid comparisons and assessments of racial intent. How frequent were such designations, and when did officials invoke traditions of other regions and the stubbornness of other peasant groups? By evoking the steppe traditions of the Cossacks, is it not possible that Major Chertkov was alluding to Cossack rather than peasant leadership of this protest?

Interestingly, the term *khokhol* was not the preserve of non-Ukrainians. In fact, Ukrainian peasants used it to refer to themselves.[18] Masters of subterfuge and dissimulation, the peasants might have used the epithet to describe themselves to government officials. By exploiting the myth of the peasant as a poor and ignorant country bumpkin who needed the guidance of his educated superiors, they could negotiate terms that were more favorable to them. In cases of rural disturbances, the peasants' professed loyalty to the tsar and claims of ignorance sometimes resulted in lesser punishments.[19]

In defining themselves, Ukrainian peasants countered the Russians' use of *khokhol* with their own pejorative epithet, *katsap* (bearded like a billygoat), for Russians.[20] At other times, they used the more

17. Allan K. Wildman, "The Defining Moment: Land Charters and Post-Emancipation Agrarian Settlement in Russia, 1861–1863," *The Carl Beck Papers in Russian and East European Studies*, no. 1205, p. 31.

18. Orest Subtelny, *Ukraine: A History* (Toronto, 1988), pp. 275, 526.

19. For a superb discussion of the myths of tsar and peasant, including a substantial analysis of the peasant rebellion of the 1870s in Kyiv province, known as the Chyhyryn (Chigirin) Affair, see Daniel Field, *Rebels in the Name of the Tsar* (Boston, 1989).

20. Subtelny, *Ukraine*, p. 275.

innocuous but all-encompassing noun *moskal* (Muscovite) when speaking of Russians. This designation was particularly apt for government officials and soldiers who represented the "other," individuals who were not part of village culture and therefore hostile to it. After all, these outsiders collected taxes, recorded information that could be used against the peasants, and carried out punitive expeditions against rebellious villages.

Like other peasants, Ukrainians had a strong sense of place. They did not think in national terms but in regional ones, often referring to themselves as *tuteshni* (from around here). Indeed, in 1898 an observer of migrant agricultural workers who left various parts of Ukraine and central Russia in summer to work on estates in Kherson province noted that these laborers identified one another by colorful nicknames that corresponded to specific provinces. Thus they referred to people from Poltava as "dumpling eaters," from Chernihiv as "wearers of bast shoes," from Kharkiv as "trunk/valise carriers," from Kyiv as "chimney fliers" (a reference to witches on their way to the sabbath atop Bald Mountain), from Podilia as "*tropak* dancers," from Kherson as "unmarried," from Vladimir as "icon painters," and from Moscow as "sugar eaters."[21] As workers from different areas competed for the same jobs, solidarity with individuals from the home village or region offered a degree of comfort.

Ethnic cleavages were more pronounced in areas of mixed economy such as the industrializing Donbas-Dnipro Bend at the turn of the twentieth century. The historian Charters Wynn has noted the tensions between the Ukrainian countryside and the industrial cities and towns that attracted mainly Russian and Jewish migrants. In contrast to peasants from Central Russia, Ukrainians farmed relatively large tracts of land in the rich steppe region. Enjoying a healthier economic status, they generally did not have to pursue artisanal trades, domestic industry, or migrant work to supplement their agricultural earnings. Ukrainian peasants also profited from the opening of mines, renting

---

21. P. Nazorov, "Lechebno-prodovol'stvennyi punkt v s. Golte-Bogopole," in *Deiatel'nost' lechebno-prodovol'stvennykh punktov dlia prishlykh rabochikh v Khersonskoi gubernii za 1898 g.: Otchety zaveduiushchikh punktami* (Kherson, 1899), p. 48n, quoted in Timothy Mixter, "The Hiring Market as Workers' Turf: Migrant Agricultural Laborers and the Mobilization of Collective Action in the Steppe Grainbelt of European Russia, 1853–1913," in *Peasant Economy*, p. 313. Russian peasants also distinguished outsiders from local villagers by means of nicknames. For example, they might call villagers from Perm "white-eyed fools" and those from Iaroslavl "big-ears." See Esther Kingston-Mann, "Breaking the Silence: An Introduction," in *Peasant Economy*, p. 15.

or selling communal land and rights of use to mine owners. They were particularly contemptuous of mine workers, whom they continued to regard as convict laborers, even after emancipation. Ethnic antagonisms sometimes erupted in weekend brawls in which migrant Russian laborers joined forces against Tatar or Ukrainian workers or peasants in the neighboring countryside; these same workers often split into groups defined by province and attacked workers from other provinces (meaning that Russians brawled with other Russians). However, as Wynn points out, "these regional divisions within the Donbass-Dnepr Bend working class paled before the demarcation based on ethnicity that separated industrial workers from [Jewish] artisans." Both Ukrainians and Russians joined forces in violent pogroms against Jews of all classes.[22]

While this discussion has demonstrated that a delineation between "us" and "them" pervaded Ukrainian and Russian peasant consciousness in similar ways, it has not dealt with the question of whether Ukrainian peasants were second-class subjects within the post-emancipation Russian Empire. Ukrainian peasants were indeed second-class subjects, but shared this inferior status with their Russian counterparts. The imperial Russian government was far more concerned with the social status and service obligations of all its inhabitants than with ethnic identity. Indeed, it chose to ignore the issue of ethnicity altogether when non-Russian ethnic groups, including substantial numbers of Ukrainians, shared the same religious confession as Russians—Orthodoxy.[23] Since the eighteenth century the autocracy had divided society into various estates, each with its own duties and responsibilities to the state. Under serfdom it classified peasants in terms of their owners, that is, nobles, monasteries (until Catherine the Great), the state, or the crown. After emancipation all peasants, regardless of ethnic origin, were grouped together as a single estate.

The drafters of the emancipation legislation were concerned with maintaining law and order, as well as with compensating nobles for the loss of their property and unpaid labor force. They hoped to secure a smooth transition to freedom through a gradual easing of

---

22. In 1897, 79 percent of laborers in the iron and steel mills of the Donbas-Dnipro Bend were Russians and Poles, while 74 percent of the coal miners were Russians. See Charters Wynn, *Workers, Strikes, and Pogroms: The Donbass-Dnepr Bend in Late Imperial Russia, 1870–1905* (Princeton, N.J., 1992), pp. 42, 45, 47, 93, 262.

23. A campaign to convert Uniate Ukrainians in Right-Bank Ukraine to Orthodoxy began under Catherine II and was renewed in 1839.

peasant obligations to their lords. This same concern, as well as Slavophile sentiments, prompted them to ensure that the Emancipation Statutes respected local customs with regard to land management, peasant administration, and daily village life. On the one hand, this meant that once land surveys had been carried out and land reapportioned, Ukrainian and Russian peasants were allowed to live their lives largely as they pleased. On the other hand, both peasantries differed in legal status from the remainder of society: *volost'* or cantonal courts, which ruled on the basis of customary and written law, were specifically designed for peasants perceived by educated society to be too simple, ignorant, and childlike to be regulated by written law. The intent of some jurists had been to allow the dual legal system to exist temporarily until they could incorporate elements of customary law into the legal codes. Although jurists began to study customary law and debate numerous reform proposals from the 1870s, the dual legal system existed until 1917. Consequently, in their daily affairs peasants were governed by different legal principles than the rest of society, and they were the only estate in the realm subject to corporal punishment. The penal code that guided the higher courts after emancipation had removed punishment by whipping, whereas cantonal court judges were allowed to sentence peasants to the birch rod until 1904. Even after 1904, however, peasants, regardless of ethnicity, could be subject to the birch in the pacification campaigns against agrarian disturbances. As the historian Stephen Frank points out, "The state had created a modern judicial system while simultaneously codifying juridical *apartheid* among ... [its] rural population ..."[24]

Given the fact that post-emancipation Ukrainian and Russian peasants arbitrated their day-to-day problems according to their customary laws and traditions, it is incumbent on historians to uncover those laws and customs, paying close attention to differences as well as similarities between and within the two ethnic groups. At times this means that ethnicity may have to take a back seat to religion, ecology, and economic circumstances. In my own work on popular religion, for example, I have made a conscious decision to investigate the beliefs of nineteenth-century Russian and Ukrainian Orthodox peasants in a comparative framework.[25] For

---

24. Stephen P. Frank, "Emancipation and the Birch: The Perpetuation of Corporal Punishment in Rural Russia, 1861–1907," *Jahrbücher für Geschichte Osteuropas*, n.s. 45, no. 3 (1997): 416.

25. By popular religion, I mean religion as practiced in contradistinction to the ideal of prescribed religion. See Christine D. Worobec, "Death Ritual

reasons pertaining to the peasant economy and environment, as well as the commonality of Orthodoxy, substantial differences in the two peasantries' beliefs and practices regarding death and witchcraft are not apparent, with the exception of the phenomenon of *klikushestvo*. A form of devil possession causing shrieking and convulsions among women, *klikushestvo* appears to have been largely absent from the Ukrainian provinces. That discovery has led me to investigate demon possession and to chart the cultural, religious, economic, and social causes of the phenomenon in the Russian provinces, as well as to speculate on its relative non-existence in Ukraine. Despite the absence of *klikushestvo* from Ukrainian areas, there were multiple similarities in the beliefs of Ukrainian and Russian peasants in witches and demons. Those similarities warrant as much study as the differences.

While scholars have begun to address the issue of popular Orthodoxy in Russian villages, they have by and large ignored Orthodoxy among Ukrainian peasants.[26] Pilgrimages to monasteries and religious shrines for religious communion, healings, and fairs were an integral part of daily life among nineteenth- and early twentieth-century Ukrainian and Russian peasants, and as such deserve systematic study. Ethnicity may figure in such a project when Russian and Ukrainian peasants visited the same shrines, or when, as in 1896, a canonization of a Ukrainian bishop took place.[27] It is also relevant in the much-needed exploration of relations between Russian-speaking priests and monks and the Ukrainian-speaking faithful.

---

among Russian and Ukrainian Peasants: Linkages between the Living and the Dead," in *Cultures in Flux: Lower-Class Values, Practices, and Resistance in Late Imperial Russia*, ed. Stephen P. Frank and Mark D. Steinberg (Princeton, N.J., 1994), pp. 11–33; idem, "Witchcraft Beliefs and Practices in Prerevolutionary Russian and Ukrainian Villages," *Russian Review* 54, no. 2 (April 1995): 165–87; and idem, *Possessed: Women, Witches, and Demons in Imperial Russia* (DeKalb, Ill., 2001).

26. See, for example, Chris Chulos, "Myths of the Pious or Pagan Peasant in Post-Emancipation Central Russia (Voronezh Province)," *Russian History* 52, no. 2 (Summer 1995): 181–216; Gregory Freeze, "Counter-reformation in Russian Orthodoxy: Popular Response to Religious Innovation, 1922–1925," *Slavic Review* 54, no. 2 (Summer 1995): 305–39; Vera Shevzov, "Chapels and the Ecclesial World of Prerevolutionary Russian Peasants," *Slavic Review* 55, no. 3 (Fall 1996): 585–613; and idem, "Miracle-Working Icons, Laity, and Authority in the Russian Orthodox Church, 1861–1917," *Russian Review* 58, no. 1 (January 1999): 26–48.

27. The Russian Orthodox Church canonized Bishop Feodosii of Chernihiv (Chernigov) in 1896.

Otherwise, ethnicity may not be a significant variable in discussing belief structures.

In their study of marriage patterns in the Russian Empire, Ansley Coale, Barbara Anderson, and Erna Härm discount ethnicity as an overriding factor in determining those patterns. They identify the populations of the Ukrainian provinces, like those in the Russian provinces, as belonging to the East European variant of almost universal marriage and early mean ages at first marriage for women. In carrying out various manipulations so as to identify the influences pertaining to age at marriage, they conclude:

> ... the customary behavior of other groups (that is, the marriage patterns of other nationalities combined) is a more important determinant of nuptiality than the average education or social status of a particular nationality. Each geographical area appears to have evolved a normative environment that prescribes the proper age at marriage, and the distinctive characteristics of a nationality group act only as marginal disturbing factors, moving the group's pattern of marriage only slightly from the prescribed behavior.[28]

Such a conclusion does not mean that historians cannot examine specific marriage customs in Ukrainian provinces and the rich variations that occurred from village to village. While marriage patterns may not have distinguished Ukrainian peasants from Russian ones, other patterns such as household size and structure, inheritance, and child care may have done so. Moreover, as in the case of Russian peasants, tremendous variation may be charted within specific regions. Like Central Russia, the Ukrainian provinces of the Russian Empire consisted of distinct regions: the Left Bank, the Right Bank, and New Russia. All were predominantly agricultural areas with extremely rich soils and estates owned by Russian and Polish noblemen. Of these three areas, New Russia was the last to be colonized, and consequently the most diverse in ethnicity. In the two overwhelmingly Ukrainian-populated regions, the Left Bank and the Right Bank, historical differences guaranteed distinctions within their populations. It is only by studying such differences and bearing a comparative perspective in mind that the historian can create a nuanced picture of peasant life. As the historian Allan Wildman has suggested, regional history also provides a window onto the ways in which the state affected the periphery, and the Ukrainian provinces were certainly part of the frontier:

---

28. Ansley J. Coale, Barbara Anderson, and Erna Härm, *Human Fertility since the Nineteenth Century* (Princeton, N.J., 1979).

> Regional history overthrows the prejudice that what the state decrees, or what is initiated in the metropolitan center, automatically ramifies to the periphery. Not only are many impulses lost or transformed in transmission, it is also a two-way street; and what occurs in the periphery, such as peasant disturbances or the migration of upwardly or outwardly mobile elements to the center, greatly affects the overall shape of things.[29]

Robert Edelman's investigation of peasant disturbances in Right-Bank Ukraine in 1905, a rare regional study, shows how the Right Bank developed distinctive characteristics because of the high concentration of commercialized sugar-beet estates that employed significant numbers of poor Ukrainian peasants as wage laborers. Since village land allotments were too meager to sustain their families, women worked on the plantations, leaving men in the village to farm household plots (a reversal of the pattern in Central Industrial Russia, where men abandoned the village for non-agricultural jobs, leaving their wives and daughters behind on the land). While the nobles' estates provided a stopgap solution to the peasantry's perennial land hunger, the factors of surplus labor, depressed wages, and wartime inflation made for an explosive confrontation between peasants and landowners. In documenting active female participation in the strike movements of 1905 on sugar-beet estates, Edelman argues that wages provided women with a new-found independence that challenged traditional patriarchal authority, a pattern not found elsewhere in Ukraine and European Russia.[30] More studies of this kind are needed not only to test Edelman's conclusions, but also to uncover other variations in labor experiences, land management, proletarianization, resistance, and patriarchal relations.

In conclusion, I would like to give a sense of how two Ukrainian provinces, Kyiv province on the right bank of the Dnipro River and Kharkiv province on the left bank, offer interesting contrasts that merit further inquiry.[31] Kyiv province came under the suzerainty of

---

29. Allan K. Wildman, "Retrospect," in *Politics and Society in Provincial Russia: Saratov, 1590–1917*, ed. Rex A. Wade and Scott J. Seregny (Columbus, Oh., 1989), p. 327.

30. Robert Edelman, *Proletarian Peasants: The Revolution of 1905 in Russia's Southwest* (Ithaca, N.Y., 1987). Unfortunately, Edelman does not investigate the workings of either the institutional peasant community (*hromada*) or the *podvornoe* system of land management.

31. The discussion of the differences between Kyiv and Kharkiv provinces is based on Christine D. Worobec, "Patterns of Property Devolution among

the Russian autocrat in the last decade of the eighteenth century as a result of the partitions of Poland. Its Ukrainian peasants had long been reduced to the status of serfs by the Polish and Polonized Ukrainian nobility. Kharkiv province, on the other hand, had been settled relatively late. It was only after the Khmelnytsky Uprising of 1648 and the defeat of Khmelnytsky's armies in the Polish-dominated Ukrainian lands that Ukrainian peasants and Cossacks fled political, religious, and social oppression for the virgin lands of what later became known as Kharkiv province. They were joined by Russian serfs who gravitated to the frontiers to escape Muscovite serfdom. Freedom, however, especially in the north-western regions of Sloboda Ukraine (later Kharkiv province), was short-lived. In the eighteenth century Ukrainian and Russian landowners, in their search for a stable labor force to work their newly acquired lands, began to limit the movement of peasants and Cossack yeomen and levy corvée obligations on them. Restrictions on mobility, the extension of Russian taxation and census-taking to Sloboda Ukraine, and peasant indebtedness combined to ensure the gradual enserfment of peasants living on gentry, Cossack, and monastic lands. This process culminated in Catherine II's ukase of 3 May 1783 that bound the peasants of all Little Russia (Poltava and Chernihiv provinces) and Sloboda Ukraine to their landowners on the basis of the 1782 revision or census.[32]

In addition to differences in the historical development of settlement and serfdom, Kyiv and Kharkiv provinces were distinguished by the composition of their respective peasant populations. According to the 1858 revision, state peasants—that is, peasants and Cossack farmers who had settled on lands claimed by the Russian state as its patrimony, former serfs on secularized monastic and ecclesiastical lands, and military inhabitants of low rank—accounted for 45.46 percent of the population of Kharkiv province and only 11.79 percent of the population of Kyiv province.[33] Like serfs, state peasants of

---

Ukrainian Peasants in Kyiv and Kharkiv Provinces, 1861–1900," *Kennan Institute for Advanced Russian Studies Occasional Paper*, no. 206, pp. 5–7.

32. For a discussion of the enserfment process in Left-Bank and Sloboda Ukraine, see A. K. Kasymenko et al., ed., *Istoriia Ukraïns'koï SSR*, 2 vols. (Kyiv, 1953), 1: 311ff; V. A. Diadychenko, "Posylennia pokripacheniia i vyzysku selianstva na Livoberezhzhi i Slobozhanshchyni v pershii polovyni XVIII st.," in *Istoriia selianstva Ukraïns'koï RSR*, ed. V. A. Diadychenko et al., 2 vols. (Kyiv, 1967), 1: 213ff; and I. M. Sheker, "Ostatochne zakripachennia selian Livoberezhnoï, Slobids'koï ta Pivdennoï Ukraïny v druhii polovyni XVIII st.," in *Istoriia selianstva Ukraïns'koï RSR*, 1: 243ff.

33. Jerome Blum, *Lord and Peasant in Russia from the Ninth to the Nineteenth Century* (Princeton, N.J., 1961), p. 477n. The serf populations of Kharkiv and

Kharkiv province paid a soul tax to the state and were subject to military recruitment. They differed from serfs, however, in having independent economies and paying quitrent directly to the state. The state peasants of Right-Bank Ukraine, on the other hand, did not enjoy the relative independence of their Kharkiv and Russian counterparts, but rather worked on properties that the state leased until 1853 mainly to the Polish gentry.[34]

Despite the greater representation of state peasants in Kharkiv province, land in both Kyiv and Kharkiv provinces in the immediate pre-emancipation period was heavily concentrated in the hands of the nobility. The latter held 67.9 percent and more than 75 percent of the land in Kharkiv and Kyiv provinces respectively. Large latifundia predominated in Kyiv, while small estates characterized Kharkiv province.[35] In the decades immediately following emancipation, privately owned land diminished by approximately 50 percent in both provinces.[36]

The Russian repartitional commune, in which land passed from household to household over specified periods of time according to changes in the composition of households, had been alien to Kyiv and parts of Kharkiv provinces. Consequently, the Emancipation Decree of 19 February 1861 and the Local Statutes for Left- and Right-Bank Ukraine recognized the indigenous *podvornoe* system of landholding, whereby land had been apportioned to households in hereditary tenure, not on the basis of souls (i.e., taxable units within households), but according to their labor capacities and number of draft animals.[37]

Kyiv provinces amounted to 29.77 and 57.66 percent of their respective total populations. See A. Troinitskii, comp., *Krepostnoe naselenie v Rossii, po 10-i narodnoi perepisi* (St. Petersburg, 1861), p. 49.

34. V. P. Teplyts'kyi, *Reforma 1861 roku i ahrarni vidnosyny na Ukraïni (60–90-ti roky XIX st.)* (Kyiv, 1959), p. 124; and Blum, *Lord and Peasant*, pp. 480–81.

35. Figures for Kharkiv province apply to 1846 and for Kyiv to 1845. See N. N. Leshchenko, "Izmeneniia v agrarnykh otnosheniiakh na Ukraine v rezul'tate provedeniia reformy 1861 g.," *Ezhegodnik po agrarnoi istorii vostochnoi Evropy 1958 g.* (Tallinn, 1959), pp. 186–87.

36. Between 1845 and 1877 nobiliary landownership in Kyiv province decreased by 50 percent, and by 1885 it had decreased in Kharkiv province by almost 50 percent. N. N. Leshchenko, *Klasova borot'ba v ukraïns'komu seli v epokhu domonopolistychnoho kapitalizmu (60–90–ti roky XIX st.)* (Kyiv, 1970), p. 37; and [n.a.], "Estestvennye i proizvoditel'nye sily Khar'kovskoi gubernii i ekonomicheskaia deiatel'nost' ee naseleniia za 1885 god," *Khar'kovskii sbornik* 1 (1887): 87.

37. Leshchenko, "Izmeneniia," p. 188; and P. A. Zaionchkovskii, *Provedenie v zhizn' krest'ianskoi reformy 1861 g.* (Moscow, 1958), p. 240.

As in the case of the repartitional commune, land ultimately belonged to the commune (*hromada*). When a household had no lineal or lateral heirs, its so-called "escheated" property reverted to the commune.[38] Redemption dues were levied on individual households rather than entire communes. The mutual responsibility of commune members for taxes and obligations pertained only to hayfields that had not been divided among individual households.[39]

Despite the hereditary nature of land tenure, the *podvornoe* system shared some characteristics with the Russian commune. Land was not consolidated, but rather dispersed among three fields in small strips as a result of decades of subdivision among heirs and sale of parcels. Often these strips were interspersed with land belonging to individual landowners and other communes. The three-field system and its dependence on fallow also demanded that sowing, harvesting, and pasturing be conducted on a collective basis.

The substantial areas of Kharkiv province in which the repartitional commune prevailed among Ukrainian serfs and state peasants came under the general emancipation provisions.[40] Here only the *usad'ba* or farmstead came into the hereditary possession of the household. The commune had control over the arable and other lands that it periodically repartitioned among its members. It also enforced the mutual responsibility of commune members for taxes, dues, and obligations.

The differences in land management in Kharkiv and Kyiv provinces may have arisen not only for historical reasons, but also as a result of ecological conditions. Those conditions need exploration, as do these different systems' effects on such matters as inheritance practices, as well as household size and structure. The existence of the repartitional commune in Kharkiv province also raises the question of the ostensible "Russianness" of the repartitional commune.

The Ukrainian peasantry awaits its historians. I encourage historians to seize the opportunity to explore diverse and common patterns among Ukrainian peasants of different regions, as well as differences and similarities between Ukrainian and Russian peasants. Only

---

38. *Polnoe sobranie zakonov Rossiiskoi imperii*, 2d series, no. 36663, art. 97. Cited henceforth as *PSZ*.

39. *PSZ*, no. 36663, arts. 97, 99; and Teplyts'kyi, *Reforma 1861 roku*, pp. 95–97.

40. In the immediate pre-emancipation period, 65.9 percent of the lands belonging to state peasants in Kharkiv province were located in the southern steppe counties. Zack J. Deal, III, *Serf and State Peasant Agriculture: Kharkov Province, 1842–1861* (New York, 1981), p. 119.

through a synthetic discussion of all the variables (including ethnicity, but not limited to it) that influenced and framed the Ukrainian and Russian peasantries can a genuine picture of agrarian life in late imperial Russia emerge.

Dieter Pohl

Russians, Ukrainians, and German Occupation Policy, 1941–43

The following thoughts do not concern the Russian-Ukrainian encounter, but rather German occupation policy in the Second World War. I do not concentrate, therefore, on the mutual perception and interaction of the two nationalities, but rather on the conceptions, plans, and political aspects of National Socialist (NS) rule over Russians and Ukrainians in the occupied territories of the Soviet Union from 1941 to 1943, with some attention to developments in 1944. I have chosen four focal points: (1) anti-Slavism as a component of the racism of the NS leadership; (2) the NS ideological war against Russians and Ukrainians; (3) the contours of occupation policy in Ukraine and the RSFSR; and (4) occupation policy in an area of mixed nationality. In the fourth section of this article, I have chosen to examine eastern Ukraine, including the Donets Basin and the Kharkiv region, as only there did Russians and Ukrainians live together under NS rule for an extended period. Comparable regions would be Transnistria, which, however, was under Romanian rule;[1] the Crimea, where a third nationality, the Crimean Tatars, was significant;[2] and the regions around Voronezh and the Kuban, which were under German rule for less than a year and, in the latter case, were complicated by the Cossack question.[3]

NS Racism in Relation to Russians and Ukrainians

The question of the extent to which NS racism differentiated between Russians and Ukrainians can only be answered by examining the

---

1. See Arkadii Zhukovs'kyi, "Ukraïns'ki zemli pid rumuns'koiu okupatsieiu v chasi druhoï svitovoï viiny," *Ukraïns'kyi istoryk* 24, nos. 1–4 (1987): 83–96; and Alexander Dallin, *Odessa, 1941–1944: A Case Study of Soviet Territory under Foreign Rule* (Santa Monica, Cal., 1957).

2. The standard work is still Martin Luther, "Die Krim unter deutscher Besetzung im Zweiten Weltkrieg," *Forschungen zur osteuropäischen Geschichte*, 1956, no. 3: 28–98.

3. See the tendentious work of Joachim Hoffmann, *Kaukasien 1942/43: Das deutsche Heer und die Orientvölker in der Sowjetunion* (Freiburg i. Br., 1991).

various attitudes of individual NS elite functionaries. This problem has been studied quite thoroughly.[4] Hitler, apparently, made hardly any distinction.[5] He assumed a uniform Slavic mass that he regarded as "racially inferior" and ruled by a "Jewish Bolshevik" system. Occasionally he did draw certain distinctions, noting, for example, that the western Ukrainian intelligentsia under Jewish leadership had been wiped out.[6] Of greater immediate significance for occupation policy were the views of the leader of the SS, Heinrich Himmler, and the head of the Security Police (*Sicherheitspolizei* or Sipo) and Security Service (*Sicherheitsdienst* or SD), Reinhard Heydrich. In the "General Plan for the East" (*Generalplan Ost*), which detailed their racist schemes for reorganization, Ukraine occupied an intermediate position. While the Baltic region and most of Poland and eastern Galicia were to be Germanized in the long run, German "islands of settlement" were to be established in the regions of Zhytomyr, Kamianets-Podilskyi, and Vinnytsia. These plans entailed deporting a large part of the population—up to 65 percent of the western Ukrainians—to Siberia. Plans for the Russian areas, on the other hand, were strangely vague. Initially, a policy of total destruction was envisaged: there were proposals for the complete extermination of the Russians. Northern Russia and western Siberia were designated as receiving areas for the racially undesirable Jews and Slavs.[7] Only in the spring of 1942 were the Crimea and the region around Leningrad (Ingermanland) earmarked as areas of settlement.[8] While the course of the war ensured that Himmler's and Heydrich's

---

4. See Alexander Dallin, *Deutsche Herrschaft in Rußland 1941–1945: Eine Studie über Besatzungspolitik* (Düsseldorf, 1958), p. 19ff.

5. Volodymyr Kosyk, *Ukraïna i Nimechchyna u Druhii svitovii viini* (Paris, New York, and Lviv, 1993), p. 38. See also Jerzy W. Borejsza, *Antyslawizm Adolfa Hitlera* (Warsaw, 1988), pp. 37–44.

6. Remark at a meeting with the Bulgarian ambassador on 3 December 1940: see Andreas Hillgruber, ed., *Staatsmänner und Diplomaten bei Hitler*, vol. 1 (Frankfurt am Main, 1967), p. 345. In the autumn of 1942, Hitler suspected that there were descendants of Germanic tribes among the Ukrainians. See Ulrich Herbert, *Fremdarbeiter: Politik und Praxis des "Ausländer-Einsatzes" in der Kriegswirtschaft des Dritten Reiches* (Berlin, 1985), p. 176.

7. See Karl Heinz Roth, "'Generalplan Ost' — 'Gesamtplan Ost'" in Mechthild Rössler and Sabine Schleiermacher, ed., *Der 'Generalplan Ost': Hauptlinien der nationalsozialistischen Planungs- und Vernichtungspolitik* (Berlin, 1993), pp. 25–95, here 40.

8. For details, see the documentary collection edited by Czesław Madajczyk, *Vom Generalplan Ost zum Generalsiedlungsplan* (Munich and New Providence, 1994), p. 20ff.

ideas were only partially realized, Himmler immediately put into practice a specific policy regarding collaboration. This initially involved Ukrainians in the form of the Ukrainian Auxiliary Police and later the Waffen SS Galizien Division,[9] and subsequently Russians as well. Apparently, the head of the SS did not have consistent backing from Hitler for this policy.

Lesser influence on policy-making was exerted by NS functionaries who advocated a more constructive policy toward the Ukrainians in particular. They have received special attention from historians. Alfred Rosenberg and his Reich Ministry for the Occupied Eastern Territories must of course be mentioned in this context. Rosenberg planned the establishment of dependent puppet regimes by the Reich in the occupied Soviet Union, with a nationalities policy specifically favoring the Balts and Ukrainians. This conception did not prevail against Hitler's ideas and Erich Koch's more radical policy.[10] Only in eastern Galicia, which had been annexed to the *Generalgouvernement* of Poland, were Governor Otto Wächter and several of his officials able to pursue such a policy.[11]

A small group of officers in the Military Counter-Intelligence Section (*Amt Ausland/Abwehr*) of the Armed Forces (*Wehrmacht*), notably Hans Koch and Theodor Oberländer, had ideas that went even further in this direction. They were in close contact with representatives of the Organization of Ukrainian Nationalists (Orhanizatsiia ukraïns'kykh natsionalistiv or OUN) outside Ukraine and pleaded for a more constructive policy toward the Ukrainians. Oberländer's well-known memoranda became more pro-Ukrainian, however, only when it became clear that the Eastern campaign could not be won. In the crucial years of 1941–42 their influence was minimal, and the experiment with Ukrainian soldiers in the Nightingale (*Nachtigall*) and Roland units of the *Abwehr* proved a failure.

In the supreme army command (*Oberkommando des Heeres*), too, it was widely assumed that the Ukrainians were "culturally superior to the Great Russians."[12] We do not know much about the attitude

---

9. See Himmler's speech to the Galizien SS Volunteer Infantry Division on 16 May 1944, National Archives, T-175, roll 94, fr. 4657–80.

10. This has been extensively treated in Dallin, *Deutsche Herrschaft*; and Timothy P. Mulligan, *The Politics of Illusion and Empire: German Occupation Policy in the Soviet Union, 1942–1943* (New York, 1988).

11. Włodzimierz Bonusiak, *Małopolska Wschodnia pod rządami Trzeciej Rzeszy* (Rzeszów, 1990), p. 105ff.

12. Memorandum entitled "Kriegswehrmacht der Sowjetunion" from Abteilung Fremde Heere Ost, December 1941, cited in Hans-Erich Volkmann,

within the military administration toward Russians and Ukrainians, although Russia and a large part of Ukraine never came under civilian administration. Apparently, many officers and officials in the military administration had differing attitudes toward the occupied population. Many high-ranking officers had been in Ukraine before the war, including, for example, the commander of the 213th Security Division (*Sicherungsdivision*), with responsibilities for occupation policy, who had served in Ukraine in 1918.[13] Little is known about the attitudes of ordinary German soldiers and officials on the subject.[14]

In general, there were only two views in the NS state concerning occupation policy in the Soviet Union: either unbridled repression or a type of patriarchal rule that envisaged cooperation with the subordinate peoples while suppressing any political aspirations on their part. There was a predominant view that the Ukrainians were "racially" somewhat superior to the Russians and generally also more amicably disposed to the Germans. In the final analysis, however, most NS functionaries regarded both nationalities as "inferior." The crucial dividing line for the occupiers was not the one between Russians and Ukrainians, but between Jews and non-Jews and between Communists and non-Communists.

The NS Ideological War against Russians and Ukrainians

In analyzing the ideological war, it must be taken into consideration first and foremost that regions settled by Ukrainians were taken over completely at an early stage of the Eastern campaign, whereas the Russian-dominated areas were occupied only later and to a small extent. Initially, the racial war of destruction in the Soviet Union was directed primarily against the so-called "Jewish-Bolshevik" intelligentsia. Accordingly, the principal victims of the NS murder campaigns were male Jews from the intelligentsia and party and higher state functionaries. From August 1941 on, Jews were killed en masse, then the mentally ill, some Gypsies and, above all, "suspected partisans"

---

ed., *Das Rußland-Bild im Dritten Reich* (Cologne, Weimar, and Vienna, 1994), p. 157. This was a modified version of a memorandum dating from January 1941.

13. Sicherungsdivision 213 to Befehlshaber rückwärtiges Heeresgebiet [Befh. HGeb.] Süd, 9 March 1942, Bundesarchiv, Abt. Militärarchiv Freiburg i. Br. [BA-MA] RH 22/204.

14. On this, see Klaus Latzel, "Tourismus und Gewalt: Kriegswahrnehmungen in Feldpostbriefen," in Hannes Heer and Klaus Naumann, ed., *Vernichtungskrieg: Verbrechen der Wehrmacht 1941–1944* (Hamburg, 1995), pp. 447–59.

(*Bandenverdächtige*). During the initial phase, then, Ukrainian and Russian party and higher state functionaries were at risk of being killed by the National Socialists. Based on current knowledge, Russians made up a disproportionately large part of this stratum in the non-Russian regions. It may therefore be assumed that in 1941 many of them were killed in the areas of the Soviet Union annexed in 1939–40. Further east, the evacuation of the functionaries was largely successful.[15] For western Ukraine, there are some indications that the anti-Jewish pogroms of June and July 1941 were sometimes directed against Russians as well.[16]

The search for activists of the Soviet regime was taken up periodically. To some degree, the life of every captured Communist Party member and every Komsomol functionary was in danger.[17] When hostages were executed in Ukraine, Jews were generally selected first, then Russians, and then Ukrainians: "Acts of sabotage are ... to be blamed not on Ukrainians but on Jews and Russians."[18] In numerical terms, victims of "campaigns against partisans" (i.e., partisans and their supporters) became more prominent from 1942 on. These were mainly individuals who had become involved in the partisan war only by chance.[19] Ukrainians were victims of these mass murders mainly in northern Volhynia, Polisia, and in the area of Chernihiv and Sumy, while Russians accounted for most of the victims in the areas of Elnia and Briansk and in the Crimea.[20] In

---

15. According to A. L. Perkovs'kyi and S. I. Pirozhkov, "Demohrafichni vtraty narodonaselennia Ukraïns'koï RSR u 40–kh rr.," *Ukraïns'kyi istorychnyi zhurnal*, 1990, no. 2: 15–25, here 17. A total of 115,000 people were evacuated from western Ukraine.

16. As in Lviv, for example: see Kriegstagebuch (KTB) 1. Gebirgsdivision, 1 July 1941, BA-MA RH 28–1/20, p. 35. This pogrom apparently began even before the Germans entered: see the report of the 100. Infanteriedivision/Ic re interrogations of Red Army deserters, 28 June 1941, BA-MA RH 26–100/36, p. 111.

17. Helmut Krausnick and Hans-Heinrich Wilhelm, *Die Truppe des Weltanschauungskrieges: Die Einsatzgruppen der Sicherheitspolizei und des SD 1938–1942* (Stuttgart, 1981), p. 157.

18. Order of Befh. HGeb. Süd, 16 August 1941, cited in Krausnick and Wilhelm, *Truppe des Weltanschauungskrieges*, p. 219.

19. See Bettina Birn, "Zweierlei Wirklichkeit? Fallbeispiele zur Partisanenbekämpfung im Osten," in Bernd Wegner, ed., *Zwei Wege nach Moskau: Vom Hitler-Stalin-Pakt zum "Unternehmen Barbarossa"* (Munich and Zurich, 1991), pp. 275–90.

20. For a list of "operations against guerrillas," see Erich Hesse, *Der sowjetrussische Partisanenkrieg 1941 bis 1944 im Spiegel deutscher Kampfanweisungen und Befehle*, 2d ed. (Göttingen, 1993), pp. 319–21.

addition to these groups of civilians, Red Army prisoners of war became victims of the ideological onslaught. For calculating the proportion of Ukrainians and Russians among the dead in the POW camps, the initial composition of the Red Army is important. A total of 4.5 million inhabitants of Ukraine served in the Red Army.[21] It must be assumed that Ukrainians were generally recruited only during the first months of the war, although recruitment was broader after July 1941. Consequently, a disproportionately large number of Ukrainians became German POWs in 1941 and died in huge numbers shortly after being taken prisoner. Rough estimates show that by the end of 1941, 1.3 million of the 3.8 million Soviet prisoners of war were Ukrainians.[22] In killing operations, Jewish prisoners of war were certainly sought out first, then a disproportionately large number of Asians and (usually Russian) political commissars.

In the camps, prisoners were quickly segregated according to nationality.[23] Early on, the German military leadership envisaged the release of non-Russian prisoners of war, primarily Ukrainians and Balts. This began in the summer of 1941: volunteers for the auxiliary units (*Hilfsmannschaften*), local Ukrainian POWs, and those unfit for work could be freed.[24] Here, too, there were considerable regional differences. The commander of the Rear Army Southern District (*rückwärtiges Heeresgebiet Süd*), for example, gave an order on 13 August 1941 to release all Ukrainian prisoners of war in his area of command whose homes were no more than three or four days' march from their camp. After the initial releases, though, this order

---

21. Bohdan Krawchenko, *Social Change and National Consciousness in Twentieth-Century Ukraine* (Basingstoke, UK, 1985), p. 169.

22. Orest Subtelny, *Ukraine: A History*, 2d ed. (Toronto, 1994), p. 460, without source reference. This number is apparently identical to the one on p. 468, which refers to the number of dead POWs on Ukrainian territory. See also T. S. Pershina, *Fashistskii genotsid na Ukraine, 1941–1944* (Kyiv, 1985), p. 151.

23. Christian Streit, *Keine Kameraden: Die Wehrmacht und die sowjetischen Kriegsgefangenen 1941–1945* (Stuttgart, 1978), p. 75.

24. On the order of the quartermaster general, dated 25 July 1941. See *Grif sekretnosti sniat: Poteri Vooruzhennykh Sil SSSR v voinakh, boevykh deistviiakh i voennykh konfliktakh* (Moscow, 1993), p. 333. See also records of a meeting of the Wirtschaftsführungsstab Ost, 31 July 1941, BA-MA RW 31/11, p. 109. A telegram from the OKW/KrGef to the Militärbefehlshaber im Generalgouvernement, 26 September 1941, Institut für Zeitgeschichte, Munich (IfZ) MA 679/9, fr. 192f., mentions a similar order of the OKW dated 7 August 1941. The whole matter is only superficially dealt with in Kosyk, *Ukraïna i Nimechchyna*, p. 161ff.

was withdrawn.[25] Hitler himself approved releases only on 29 September 1941. Owing to the spread of typhus by freed POWs beginning in October 1941, releases from camps in the *Generalgouvernement* were drastically reduced, and in November they were forbidden by the NS leadership.[26] By the end of 1941, about 319,000 POWs had apparently been freed, including 278,000 Ukrainians.[27] Apparently, Russian POWs were freed in 1941–42 only if they became unable to work on Russian territory, that is to say, if they were half-starved.[28] A total of 530,000 Red Army soldiers were released from imprisonment, only a fraction of them Russians.[29] Moreover, scattered Ukrainian Red Army soldiers who had not been captured and had made their own way home found themselves in an anomalous situation. They had to be registered, but usually were not interned.[30] After the war, the Soviet repatriations commissar ascertained that of the 1.37 million repatriated Soviet POWs, 48 percent were Russians and 28 percent Ukrainians.[31]

Until now it has been difficult to determine the scale of the NS war of destruction in Ukraine and Russia. In all probability, older estimates of 5.5 million civilians and POWs killed in Ukraine, and 1.8 million in Russia,[32] can no longer be sustained. These numbers are

---

25. KTB 454. Sicherungsdivision, 19 August 1941, BA-MA RH 26–454/5.

26. Dallin, *Deutsche Herrschaft*, p. 426ff.

27. *Grif sekretnosti sniat*, p. 334. An unsigned exposé from the Health Department of Lviv dating from late 1941 mentions 170,000 released Ukrainian POWs: Archiwum Akt Nowych, Warsaw, Stadthauptmann Lemberg/4, pp. 82–84. In the *Generalgouvernement* some 24,000 POWs were freed, almost all of them Ukrainians: cf. a note of the Militärbefehlshaber im Generalgouvernement (2 December 1941), IfZ MA 679/10, fr. 967.

28. Cf. Streit, *Keine Kameraden*, p. 184ff.; Theo J. Schulte, *The German Army and Nazi Policies in Occupied Russia* (Oxford and New York, 1989), p. 199ff.

29. Hans-Adolf Jacobsen, "Kommissarbefehl und Massenexekutionen sowjetischer Kriegsgefangener," in *Anatomie des SS-Staates*, vol. 2 (Munich, 1979), pp. 135–232, here 232.

30. Cf. order of 444. Sicherungsdivision/Ic, 14 January 1942, BA-MA RH 26–444/18, p. 11.

31. Report of the repatriation commission, 3 October 1945 (*Grif sekretnosti sniat*, p. 339). Apparently these numbers do not include all survivors, since they do not tally with German calculations, and many survivors were not repatriated.

32. Kosyk, *Ukraïna i Nimechchyna*, pp. 453–56, 626. However, Kosyk does not explain that his calculations were made by territory and not by nationality, i.e., they also include foreigners who came to Ukraine. Cf. O. I. Kruhlov,

based largely on the findings of the Extraordinary State Commission for the Investigation of NS Crimes, which was active until 1947. The numbers of dead POWs and victims of killing operations in large cities may be particularly subject to exaggeration.[33]

Basic Principles of Occupation Policy in the RSFSR and in Ukraine

It should be remembered that Ukraine was mainly under civilian administration, while Russia was exclusively under military administration. The basic instructions of the NS leadership regarding both types of occupation were the same, but the occupation personnel varied considerably. In the Reich Commissariat Ukraine (*Reichskommissariat Ukraine*), for example, the top administrative posts (particularly those of acting regional commissars) were occupied to a large degree by career party members from East Prussia under the leadership of Erich Koch. In regions administered by the military, occupation duties were carried out by Department VII of the commanders of the *Armeegebiete* or commanders of the rear *Heeresgebiete*.[34] Civil service recruits or elderly officers with extremely diverse views made up most of the personnel there.[35]

"Znyshchennia fashystamy inozemnykh hromadian na okupovanii terytorii Ukraïny (1941–1944 rr.)," *Ukraïns'kyi istorychnyi zhurnal*, 1989, no. 5: 82–87. Detailed numbers for Ukraine are to be found in Pershina, *Fashistskii genotsid*, pp. 87, 151.

33. I have been able to establish a number of 650,000–700,000 victims on this territory, as opposed to the State Commission's findings of 1.3 million killed (Dieter Pohl, *Nationalsozialistische Judenverfolgung in Ostgalizien 1941–1944* [Munich, 1996]). For a critique of the Belarusian data, see Jerzy Turonek, *Białoruś pod okupacją niemiecką* (Warsaw, 1993), p. 236 (750,000 instead of 1.4 million civilians killed). However, recent research on Belarus by Christian Gerlach (Berlin) has again produced estimates of greater losses.

34. The *Armeegebiet* (rear army area) was the most easterly area to the rear of each army; the *Heeresgebiet*, which encompassed a much larger territory, was west of the *Armeegebiet* and was administered by the *Heeresgruppe*, a level of command superior to that of individual armies.

35. This also applies to the subordinate Security Divisions and Field Commander Units (*Feldkommandanturen*): see Schulte, *German Army*, pp. 55ff, 66ff.; and Norbert Müller, *Wehrmacht und Okkupation, 1941–1944: Zur Rolle der Wehrmacht und ihrer Führungsorgane im Okkupationsregime des faschistischen deutschen Imperialismus auf sowjetischem Territorium* (Berlin, 1971), p. 76ff.

A central question of German occupation policy was the recruitment of Russians and Ukrainians for military and police duties. Initially, army units immediately set up Ukrainian militias, often recruited from the OUN. When these militias were subordinated to the German regular police (*Ordnungspolizei*), their membership was purged and they were renamed "Auxiliary Police" (*Hilfspolizei*).[36] This process was later repeated in the occupied RSFSR. After the summer of 1942, paramilitary auxiliary police units known as Escort Battalions (*Schutzmannschafts-Bataillone*) were recruited from the Ukrainian but not the Russian population.[37] The local auxiliary police force was significantly involved in NS crimes, while the Schuma battalions mainly fought partisans and guarded forced laborers. In a few cases, Schuma battalions were deployed on Russian territory, especially in the Crimea.[38]

The German Army used Ukrainians and Russians primarily as volunteers for auxiliary purposes or as auxiliary guards for military sites. After the autumn of 1941, the recruitment of non-German, primarily Cossack, units was discussed. Freed Ukrainian POWs were also recruited into the mounted squadrons of the Security Divisions (*Sicherungsdivisionen*).[39] Ukrainian units were later added at the company level.[40] Only in 1943 were large non-German units formed, such as the 14th Waffen SS Galizien Division or the Vlasov troops, which will not be examined here. Generally speaking, the same policy, albeit with a time lag, was pursued toward both Russians and Ukrainians.

Finally, I would like to examine two special cases: occupation policy vis-à-vis the Ukrainians in the *Generalgouvernement* and the so-called Lokot autonomous district. After 1939, the administration of the *Generalgouvernement* already favored the Ukrainian minority over the

---

36. The military administration included the Schuma (auxiliary police) and Gema (policemen and non-German auxiliaries): cf. order of Befh. HGeb. B, 3 October 1942, BA-MA RH 22/67.

37. Approximately 74 Ukrainian Schuma battalions are listed in Hans-Joachim Neufeldt, Jürgen Huck, and Georg Tessin, *Zur Geschichte der Ordnungspolizei 1936–1945* (Koblenz, 1957), pt. 2, pp. 103–6. Such units were also recruited among the Balts, Belarusians, Cossacks, and Caucasians.

38. Also in Orel, e.g., Schuma Battalion 146 (Neufeldt, Huck, and Tessin, *Zur Geschichte der Ordnungspolizei*, p. 106).

39. Order of Generalstab des Heeres/Org II, 16 November 1941, BA-MA RH 22/32.

40. See Befh. HGeb. B to Sicherungsregiment 57, 18 December 1942, regarding the establishment of Ukrainian rifle companies (*Schützenkompanien*), BA-MA RH 22/88, p. 65.

Polish population to a certain degree, particularly in the local administration.[41] With the annexation of eastern Galicia to the *Generalgouvernement* on 1 August 1941, this policy was continued, in contrast to the repressive measures taken against Ukrainians in the Reich Commissariat. Worthy of special mention is the role of the OUN in organizing the administration and the Ukrainian Senior or National Council (*Senioren-* or *Nationalrat*) by February 1942;[42] the Ukrainian Central Committee as a central welfare institution; the establishment of the Lviv technical courses;[43] the limits on the use of terror against Ukrainians until September 1943; and, finally, particular agreements between the Germans and the Ukrainian Insurgent Army (*Ukraïns'ka povstans'ka armiia* or UPA) in 1944. This case reveals the extent to which the German occupation authorities could accommodate the Ukrainian population. While this exception affected about 5 million of the 35–40 million people living under German occupation in Ukraine, only a little more than 40,000 Russians lived in the "Lokot autonomous district" south of Briansk. This local experiment by the commandant of Rear Army Area 532 (*Rückwärtiges Armeegebiet 532*) offered the population a certain degree of autonomy—with the primary goal of anti-partisan warfare—under the radical Bronislav Kaminsky.[44]

In addition to the ideological war of destruction, the aim of National Socialist rule in the "occupied Eastern territories" was economic exploitation. While it was intended that Soviet industry be completely destroyed and cannibalized, the agrarian sector was expected to accomplish miracles in feeding the Reich. It was tersely stated that "Without doubt, umpteen millions of people will starve in this process."[45] In actual fact, Soviet industry had been largely

---

41. See Volodymyr Kubiiovych, *Ukraïntsi v Heneral'nii hubernii, 1939–1941* (Chicago, 1975).

42. See Stephan M. Horak, "Ukraïntsi i Druha svitova viina," in *Ukraïns'kyi istoryk*, 1979, no. 16: 23–40; 17 (1980): 58–70; and Roman Ilnytzkyj, *Deutschland und die Ukraine, 1934–1945*, vol. 2 (Munich, 1956), pp. 208–56.

43. See Marian Walczak, "Ukrainer und Polen als Studenten in Lemberg, 1942–1944 (Lemberger Fachkurse)," *Nordost-Archiv*, 1992, no. 1: 577–92. In the rest of Ukraine, courses were temporarily permitted for physicians only (Volkmann, *Rußland-Bild im Dritten Reich*, p. 444ff.).

44. Schulte, *German Army*, pp. 172–79; Alexander Dallin, "The Kaminsky Brigade," in *Revolution and Politics in Russia*, ed. Alexander and Janet Rabinowitch (Bloomington, Ind., 1973), pp. 243–80.

45. Rolf-Dieter Müller, "Von der Wirtschaftsallianz zum kolonialen Ausbeutungskrieg," in *Das Deutsche Reich und der Zweite Weltkrieg*, vol. 4 (Stuttgart, 1983), pp. 89–189, citation on 147.

dismantled by the time the German Army arrived. Grain deliveries fell far short of German expectations. Consequently, the occupation authorities implemented a selective strategy of starving urban populations not working for German ends, especially POWs.[46] The demographic structure of Ukraine meant that its large cities suffered most from this policy. As a result of evacuation, flight, deportation and death, the population of Kyiv decreased from 850,000 (1939) to 350,000 (1942) and then 180,000 (1943); that of Kharkiv from 830,000 to 300,000; that of Dnipropetrovsk from 500,000 to 234,000; and that of Staline from 462,000 to 120,000.[47] According to Soviet estimates, 110,000–120,000 people died of malnutrition and disease in Kharkiv alone.[48] In the RSFSR, the only comparable occupied city was Smolensk, whose population decreased from 157,000 to 17,000 inhabitants (1943).[49] The military administration in particular realized very quickly that the depopulation of large cities, as propagandized by Hitler, was counterproductive for German rule, and tried, with no great success, to correct it. Industrial policy was also reconsidered. Once the Russian industrial centers were found to be as good as unconquerable, German efforts concentrated on Ukraine, especially on the Donets Basin and the manganese ore mines at Nikopol. Oil production was successful only in the area of Drohobych, while the Maikop fields were completely destroyed.[50] The expected yield from

---

46. Rolf-Dieter Müller, "Das Scheitern der wirtschaftlichen 'Blitzkriegsstrategie,'" in *Das Deutsche Reich*, 4: 936–1029, esp. 1002ff.

47. John A. Armstrong, *Ukrainian Nationalism*, 3d rev. ed. (Englewood, Colo., 1990), p. 243; report of Propaganda-Abteilung U, 11 September 1942, BA-MA RH 22/174, p. 13 (the figure for Kharkiv differs from Armstrong's); *Entsyklopediia ukraïnoznavstva*, vol. 2 (repr. Lviv, 1993), p. 572. For detailed statistics on Kyiv, see Nicholas G. Bohatiuk, "The Economy of Kiev under Foreign Conquerors, 1941–1944," *Ukrainian Quarterly* 42, nos. 1–2 (1986): 35–58.

48. Pershina, *Fashistskii genotsid*, p. 92; Krawchenko, *Social Change*, p. 166, mentions 70,000–80,000 victims.

49. Paul Kohl, *"Ich wundere mich, daß ich noch lebe": Sowjetische Augenzeugen berichten* (Gütersloh, 1990), p. 138. The cities of Rostov on the Don and Voronezh came under occupation for only a short period, and the tragedy of Leningrad was not the result of direct occupation.

50. For more on this, see Rolf-Dieter Müller, ed., *Die deutsche Wirtschaftspolitik in den besetzten sowjetischen Gebieten 1941–1943: Der Abschlußbericht des Wirtschaftsstabes Ost und Aufzeichnungen eines Angehörigen des Wirtschaftskommandos Kiew* (Boppard, 1991); and Josef Werpup, "Ziele und Praxis der deutschen Kriegswirtschaft in der Sowjetunion, dargestellt an einzelnen Industriezweigen" (diss. phil., Bremen, 1992).

agriculture failed to materialize, at least in 1941–42. The "New Agrarian Order" of 1942 did not entail the dissolution of collective farms in most of Ukraine or the occupied Russian regions. Western Ukraine was the only region where agriculture had not been completely collectivized by the time of the German invasion; in eastern Galicia and the regions under Romanian rule, collectivization was reversed. In the RSFSR, especially in the north Caucasus, as well as in the easternmost part of Ukraine, state farms were transformed into so-called "agricultural associations" (*Landbaugenossenschaften*), which stood halfway between collective and private agriculture. This policy affected only about ten percent of the Ukrainian state farms. As a rule, the occupation powers granted land to individuals only in regions of partisan activity as a reward for participation in so-called "anti-guerilla campaigns."[51]

As a result of the disappointing agricultural output and the failed industrial policy, economic policy from 1942 on focused on the recruitment of manpower. Hitler initially refused to use Soviet manpower in the Reich because of the apparent risk of "Bolshevik infection." After this viewpoint changed, efforts were made to recruit mainly Russians, as their language was more familiar to the German supervisors; moreover, Ukrainians were to serve the Germans in their own country. Ultimately, however, Ukrainians made up the majority of "eastern workers" (*Ostarbeiter*). The very first contingent of workers, which consisted of Russian and Ukrainian miners from Kryvyi Rih, came from Ukraine.[52] In addition to skilled workers, Ukrainian farm laborers (more precisely, female farm laborers) soon became the focus of foreign-worker policy, once "individual assignment" to German farms was permitted. In all, of the 2.8 million deported foreign workers (according to Soviet estimates), 2.3 million came from Ukraine; in view of the geographic distribution of their regions of origin, this means that more than 90 percent of them were Ukrainians.[53] These figures do not include Ukrainians deported from Belarus

---

51. See Wacław Długoborski, "Die Landwirtschaft in der Sowjetunion 1941–1944," in *Agriculture and Food Supply in the Second World War*, ed. Bernd Martin and Alan S. Milward (Ostfildern, 1985), pp. 143–60, here 153; Włodzimierz Bonusiak, "Die Landwirtschaft in den besetzten Gebieten der Sowjetunion (1941–1944)," *Studia Historiae Oeconomicae*, 1982, no. 17: 217–32, 221ff.; most recent and most important is Christian Gerlach, "Die deutsche Agrarreform und die Bevölkerungspolitik in den besetzten sowjetischen Gebieten," in *Besatzung und Bündnis: Deutsche Herrschaftsstrategien in Ost- und Südosteuropa* (Berlin, 1995): 9–60.

52. Herbert, *Fremdarbeiter*, p. 144ff.

53. Pershina, *Fashistskii genotsid*, p. 104. This figure also includes Poles from eastern Galicia. According to one source, in the autumn of 1944, 2.8 million

and the RSFSR, nor do they include those evacuated during the German retreat of 1943–44 for forced labor in Germany. As a rule, the treatment of Ukrainians and Russians did not differ, but depended rather on specific working and living conditions in the Reich. The question of whether Ukrainians should be given special status was discussed at the end of 1941. Ultimately, however, no such status was accorded them.[54] There was only some initial uncertainty about Ukrainians from eastern Galicia—whether to treat them like the somewhat better-off Poles or like *Ostarbeiter* in general.[55]

The Effect of German Occupation Policy in Eastern Ukraine

Three basic facts must be taken into consideration here: (1) From 1941 to 1943, areas east of the Dnipro were exclusively under military administration, not civilian rule; (2) Until 1941, all in all, Ukrainians made up about 60 percent of the population in this region, while in the cities Russians comprised about 50 percent of the population; (3) These regions were very useful for German war aims: the coal deposits in the Donets Basin were expected to yield raw materials and, later, qualified mining personnel for the Reich. The commandants of Rear Army Areas 550 (Army High Command 17) and 585 (Army High Command 6) and, later, the commander of the Southern Rear Army District (later B or Don) were responsible for the administration of this area. This is important inasmuch as, first, the initial wave of mass destruction always took place under military administration and, second, the military administration did not always pursue the brutal policy of exploitation implemented by Erich Koch in the Reich Commissariat. Two factors were significant here: far fewer people fell victim to NS mass murder in eastern than in western Ukraine because many members of threatened groups, such as Jews, were able to flee, and the supply situation in the eastern Ukrainian cities was catastrophic.

Two methodological problems make an investigation difficult: German occupation policy—with the exception of industrial policy[56]—has not been examined, and only fragmentary records have

---

people, including POWs, from the Soviet Union were working in the Reich, including 2.17 million *Ostarbeiter* (Herbert, *Fremdarbeiter*, p. 258). For different statistics, see Włodzimierz Bonusiak, *Polityka ludnościowa III Rzeszy na okupowanych obszarach ZSRR (1941–1944)* (Rzeszów, 1992), p. 92ff.

54. Herbert, *Fremdarbeiter*, p. 155ff.

55. Ibid., 189.

56. Dietrich Eichholtz, "Wirtschaftspolitik und Strategie des faschistischen deutschen Imperialismus im Dnepr-Donez-Industriegebiet 1941–1943,"

survived.[57] Moreover, the term "Russians" is used indiscriminately in German occupation records, usually as a synonym for all inhabitants of the Soviet Union, including soldiers of the Red Army in general and inhabitants of eastern Ukraine. "Ukrainians" are usually identified as such only in western Ukraine, or generally in auxiliary units or the civil administration. It is also difficult to reconstruct the ethnic situation in eastern Ukraine under German occupation. The proportion of Russians must have dropped significantly, as the urban population in particular had been evacuated in good time. Even in the large cities, the proportion of Russians dropped.[58] Women, children, and the elderly remained.

As far as can be reconstructed, the population of eastern Ukraine cautiously welcomed the German invasion, but there were few public displays of jubilation such as had taken place in western Ukraine.[59] Differences in the behavior of ethnic groups are rarely noted in military records. In a few cases, greater compliance was perceived among the Russians: during the first annual celebration of the conquest of Staline (now Donetsk), for example, more Russians than Ukrainians made a public appearance.[60]

The military administration warned units proceeding into eastern Ukraine and beyond primarily about the Russians, who were regarded as racially more dangerous than the Ukrainians and of whom the troops were to beware:[61]

> The fundamental character of the inhabitants of the region settled by Great Russians or dominated by the Russian language differs

---

Militärgeschichte 18 (1979): 281–96; and Matthias Riedel, "Bergbau und Eisenhüttenindustrie in der Ukraine unter deutscher Besatzung (1941–1944)," *Vierteljahrshefte für Zeitgeschichte* 21, no. 3 (1973): 245–84.

57. Cf. Bernd Boll and Hans Safrian, "Auf dem Weg nach Stalingrad: Die 6. Armee 1941/42," in Heer and Naumann, *Vernichtungskrieg*, pp. 260–96. Important source material on the military occupation can be found in the Bundesarchiv-Militärarchiv, Freiburg, and in the Kharkiv State Oblast Archives. For an extensive survey of sources on Ukraine under Nazi rule, see Karel C. Berkhoff, "Ukraine under Nazi Rule (1941–1944): Sources and Finding Aids. Part 1," *Jahrbücher für Geschichte Osteuropas* 45, no. 1 (1997): 85–103.

58. Armstrong, *Ukrainian Nationalism*, p. 243.

59. General observation in German military files, which are certainly biased.

60. Situation report of Oberfeldkommandantur (OFK) Donez/Ic, 13 November 1942, BA-MA RH 22/206.

61. On the attitude toward the "Great Russian population," see the instruction of Befh. HGeb. B, 15 August 1942, BA-MA RH 22/60.

> strongly from the Ukrainian character. While the Ukrainian's rustic outlook on life reveals a cheerful disposition, an appreciation of nature, and pleasure in play and dance, the Great Russian is reticent to the point of mistrust, sparing in inner and outer appreciation, and less attuned to nature than to intellectual problems, becoming lost in skepticism, pessimism and fatalism. The Ukrainian, thanks to the infusion of German blood and the course of his history, has always had an awareness of the tasks of Central European culture and a receptivity to them. The Great Russian, on the other hand, suffused with Mongolian blood, had no understanding at all of Central European, especially German, culture even in the pre-Bolshevik period. His rejection of it often amounted to hatred. Moreover, his instincts seduced him into surrendering to the leveling influence of Asia.

Many officers shared this view. Many, however, realized after some time that Ukrainians behaved no differently than Russians:

> Field Commander (*Feldkommandantur*) region inhabited approximately equally by Russians and Ukrainians. No significant difference in behavior. Overall, Ukrainians are a little more open and lively in temperament. In Ukraine, isolated traces of nationalist ambition; in the Russian region, from our experience, there is a complete absence of political aims.[62]

In the recruitment of personnel for the civil administration and auxiliary police, Ukrainians were clearly favored, this being to a certain degree logical in western and central Ukraine, and coming into question only with the conquest of the eastern Ukrainian regions: "The question has arisen whether objections should be raised if Russian nationals serve in Ukrainian institutions."[63] The lack of qualified personnel was most significant here: hardly any representatives of the Ukrainian or Russian intelligentsia remained. The appointment of Russian raion (district) heads, which occurred in a few cases, was, however, generally forbidden.[64] The sole exception to the favoring of Ukrainians was the appointment of ethnic German (*Volksdeutsche*) raion heads or auxiliary police chiefs. Even among auxiliary personnel for the German Army and the police, Ukrainians

---

62. Situation report of Feldkommandantur (FK) 754 Obojan, 15 October 1942, BA-MA RH 22/206.

63. Activity report of Befh. HGeb. Süd/Abt. VII, 15 December 1941, BA-MA RH 22/203.

64. Instruction No. 40, Befh. HGeb. Süd/Abt. VII, 8 April 1942, BA-MA RH 22/205, p. 34.

must have predominated.[65] Apparently, more volunteers came forward from their ranks.[66] Throughout the civil administration, Ukrainians were able to conduct a nationalities policy on a small scale. Some Ukrainian civil officials proposed the introduction of Ukrainian as the only non-German official language:

> Among the Ukrainians, repeated efforts are being made to introduce Ukrainian as the official language. The raion chief of Avdiivka, for example, has made such a proposal. The heavy penetration of industrial sites by Russian elements, however, would present obstacles to the introduction of Ukrainian as the sole official language.[67]

In Voroshylovhrad, a gathering of Ukrainian teachers demanded the use of Ukrainian as the sole language of instruction.[68]

In the Russian-dominated areas east of Ukraine, as in the Crimea, the military administration usually employed Russians or Cossacks in the civil administration and the auxiliary police force. Beyond personnel policy, German functionaries only rarely made distinctions in their policies toward Ukrainians and Russians. Food rations were differentiated not according to ethnicity (Russian or Ukrainian), but according to productivity. It must generally be assumed, however, that the Russians were worse off than the Ukrainians, as they were concentrated mainly in the large cities, which suffered from constant hunger in 1941–42. Moreover, only Ukrainian welfare committees, whose main task was to care for freed POWs, were permitted to a limited degree.[69]

The Army report (*Wehrmachtbericht*) was published in three languages in eastern Ukraine; newspapers were printed in Ukrainian and in Russian. Further cultural encouragement, however, was given only to the Ukrainians through the approval of Prosvita (Enlighten-

---

65. For example, a survey of local volunteers at OFK 399, dated after August 1942, BA-MA RH 22/98, pp. 257–70.

66. For example, during the inspection trip of Befh. HGeb. B., 6–15 September 1942, BA-MA RH 22/98, pp. 257–270.

67. Situation report of OFK Donez, 24 September 1942, BA-MA RH 22/206.

68. Bohdan Krawchenko, "Soviet Ukraine under Nazi Occupation, 1941–4," in *Ukraine during World War II: History and Its Aftermath. A Symposium*, ed. Yury Boshyk (Edmonton, 1986), pp. 15–37. Further west, in Kremenchuk, the use of Russian in theater performances was to be forbidden: see Monthly Report FK 239, 24 November 1941, BA-MA RH 22/201.

69. Order of Kommandant rückwärtiges Armeegebiet 583, 17 March 1942, BA-MA RH 23/319.

ment Society) activity or the formation of theater groups.[70] As is generally known, educational policy vis-à-vis the Ukrainians engendered protracted debate, which concluded with the restriction of instruction to elementary and technical schools,[71] as had been the practice in the occupied Russian areas from the beginning. The revival of the Ukrainian Autocephalous Orthodox Church invigorated Ukrainian religious life, but led to fierce confrontations over church buildings. Such conflicts generally took place among Ukrainians, and only to a very limited extent between Ukrainians and Russians. As a rule, the occupation administration did not intervene.[72]

The extent of national consciousness is difficult to determine, German reports describing it as rather weak in eastern Ukraine. Ukrainian nationalism, which had great political significance in western Ukraine, was sporadic here. An expeditionary group (*pokhidna hrupa*) of the OUN set out for Kharkiv, but its members were arrested and shot in Myrhorod. A local group was established in Kharkiv.[73] When German troops took the Donets Basin, the OUN was already considered a political enemy and was mercilessly suppressed. In Sumy, Nizhyn, and Kozelets in particular, OUN groups were uncovered.[74] Eastern Ukrainian OUN groups pursued integral

---

70. Cf. Krawchenko, *Social Change*, p. 158ff.

71. See Blanka Jerabek, *Das Schulwesen und die Schulpolitik im Reichskommissariat Ukraine 1941–1944 im Lichte deutscher Dokumente* (Munich, 1991). Despite its title, the book includes the military occupation area. For a critical view, see Volodymyr Kosyk, "Nimets'ka shkil'na polityka v Raikhskomisariiati Ukraïna (1941–1944)," *Vyzvol'nyi shliakh* 47, no. 3 (1994): 351–59.

72. See Harvey Fireside, *Icon and Swastika: The Russian Orthodox Church under Nazi and Soviet Control* (Cambridge, Mass., 1971), p. 153ff.; Hans-Heinrich Wilhelm, "Der SD und die Kirchen in den besetzten Ostgebieten 1941/42," *Militärgeschichtliche Mitteilungen*, no. 29 (1981): 55–99, here 81ff.; Friedrich Heyer, *Die orthodoxe Kirche in der Ukraine, 1917–1945* (Cologne and Braunsfeld, 1953); and Blanka Jerabek, "National Socialist Religious Policy in Ukraine, 1941–1944," *Ukrainian Quarterly* 42, nos. 1–2 (1986): 25–34.

73. See Lev Shankovs'kyi, *Pokhidni hrupy OUN* (Munich, 1958); and *Na zov Kyieva: ukraïns'kyi natsionalizm u II svitovii viini: Zbirnyk statei, spohadiv i dokumentiv* (Kyiv, 1993), pp. 301ff., 309ff.

74. Activity report by Befh. HGeb. Süd/VII, 15 January 1942, BA-MA RH 22/203; situation report FK 197/VII Njeshin, 23 March 1942, BA-MA RH 22/204; and telegram from Befh. HGeb. B to HGr. B/OQu, 20 December 1942, BA-MA RH 22/69, p. 85. Krawchenko, however, claims that there was a OUN network of 500 members in several towns (*Social Change*, p. 168). Cf. Evhen Stakhiv, "Pokhidni hrupy OUN na Skhidnii Ukraïni v 1941–1943 rokakh," in

nationalism less radically than their counterparts in exile and in Galicia; about half of the underground propaganda in the Donets Basin was distributed in Russian.[75] The occupation authorities recorded the presence of armed OUN units in Sumy.[76] There was virtually no evidence of a Russian national movement in eastern Ukraine. In the Konotop area, the "Russian National Socialist Combat Troop" (*Russische Nationalsozialistische Kampftruppe*) was active intermittently.[77] In the region of Melitopil, national stirrings were observed among the Russians; traces could also be found further east, for instance, in Kursk.[78]

Russian nationalism in these regions was supported almost exclusively by the Soviet partisan movement. According to statistics in Soviet historiography, which should be treated with caution, Ukrainians made up approximately 46 percent and Russians approximately 37 percent of the personnel of the large partisan units operating mainly in the Chernihiv-Sumy area.[79] More significant than ethnic composition, though, were the origins of the units. After the groups of dispersed Red Army soldiers, it was mainly underground CP and NKVD units that unconditionally followed the Russian nationalist line of the party leadership. This attitude was expressed in the systematic killing of Ukrainian village leaders and auxiliary policemen (often with their families) in the partisan regions until the autumn of 1942.[80] According to German reports, the mostly Ukraini-

---

Natsional'no-vyzvol'na borot'ba 20–50–kh rokiv XX st. v Ukraïni (Kyiv and Lviv, 1993), pp. 145–59, here 147, 156ff.

75. See especially Armstrong, *Ukrainian Nationalism*, p. 197ff.; Krawchenko, *Social Change*, p. 158; and Stakhiv, "Pokhidni hrupy," p. 157.

76. Befh. HGeb. B.: Nachrichten über den Feind Nr. 21, 29 October 1942, BA-MA RH 22/175.

77. Gerhart Hass, "Deutsche Okkupationsziele und die Kollaboration in den besetzten Gebieten der Russischen Föderativen Sowjetrepublik 1941–1944," in Werner Röhr, ed., *Okkupation und Kollaboration (1938–1945): Beiträge zu Konzepten und Praxis der Kollaboration in der deutschen Okkupationspolitik* (Heidelberg and Berlin, 1994), pp. 273–91, here 282.

78. Situation report 444, Sicherungsdivision/Abt. VII for May/June 1942, 22 June 1942, BA-MA RH 22/202; Stimmungsbericht Propaganda-Abt. Ukraine, December 1942, 1 January 1943, BA-MA RH 22/177.

79. Nikolai V. Starozhilov, *Partizanskie soedineniia Ukrainy v Velikoi Otechestvennoi voine* (Kyiv, 1983), p. 67.

80. A. Chaikovs'kyi, *Nevidoma viina (Partyzans'kyi rukh v Ukraïni 1941–1944 rr. movoiu dokumentiv, ochyma istoryka)* (Kyiv, 1994), pp. 59–62. In the autumn of 1942, these activities apparently ceased: see Befh. HGeb. B: Nachrichten über den Feind Nr. 21, 29 October 1942, BA-MA RH 22/175.

an rural population was quite intimidated by the partisan attacks and expected protection from the occupation authorities. In the Donets Basin itself, the partisan movement was quite weak, however, since there were no forests to serve as bases for their activities.[81] In general, partisans tried to maintain a semblance of Soviet rule in the occupied regions as well. Wherever they had contacts on unoccupied Soviet territory, they reported in detail on the behavior of the Ukrainian national movement, as is apparent from NKVD reports on occupied Ukraine.[82] This was intended to prepare the ground for the reconquest of Ukraine, which was an ever-present fear of the eastern Ukrainian population in particular.

Summary and Prospects

What effect did the German occupation have on Russians and Ukrainians and on relations between them? I argue that in general the crucial factor was not the distinction between Ukrainians and Russians, but rather the early and complete occupation of Ukraine in 1941. "Racial" and functional differentiations were made later in only a few areas. This accounts for the paradox that while parts of the NS elite and occupation administration considered Ukrainians "racially" superior to Russians, many more Ukrainians than Russians became victims of the occupation. Only the sporadic release of Ukrainian POWs was substantially based on racial motivations.

In 1943–44, Ukraine was in a tenuous position. Many Ukrainians tried to save themselves by fleeing or were evacuated, especially members of Ukrainian auxiliary bodies, civil officials, and their families. Their fears were well-founded. Ukrainians were especially hard hit by Stalinist repression against real and alleged collaborators. According to a rather unreliable source, when Kharkiv was first retaken, 4 percent of the population was shot for collaboration.[83] As

---

81. Krawchenko, *Social Change*, p. 302. He mentions a total of two communist leaflets distributed in Stalino.

82. Surveillance report (*razvedsvodka*) No. 32/67 Opergrupa NKVD USSR to Khrushchev, 19 September 1942, on Ukrainian nationalism, Central State Archive of Civic Associations of Ukraine, Kyiv (TsDAHOU) P-1/23/115, pp. 1–63; NKVD reports, 15 August to 7 November 1943, TsDAHOU P-1/23/523; and additional examples in Ivan Bilas, *Represyvno-karal'na systema v Ukraïni, 1917–1953*, vol. 2 (Kyiv, 1994), pp. 328ff.

83. According to a German investigation report following the reoccupation: see Joachim Hoffmann, "Die Kriegführung aus der Sicht der Sowjetunion," in *Das Deutsche Reich und der Zweite Weltkrieg*, 4: 713–809, here 782. In his recent and highly tendentious book, Joachim Hoffman claims, without source

the reoccupation proceeded from 1943 on, more formalized procedures were introduced. By September 1943, the NKVD in Staline oblast had imprisoned 515 alleged collaborators,[84] while at the same time the NKVD tribunal for eastern Ukraine investigated 633 cases of treason.[85] In the following years, the numbers rose to tens of thousands, probably totaling well over 100,000.[86] Repatriated foreign workers, most of whom came from Ukraine, now had to undergo screening procedures.[87] The virulence of the national movement in western Ukraine persisted, and the Soviet Ministry of Internal Affairs (MVD) conducted an underground war there against the UPA until the early 1950s.

The break in continuity in Ukraine was therefore much deeper than in the RSFSR. While in 1941 the Bandera wing of the OUN wanted to exploit the new power relations for the purpose of nation-building, the Germans never considered restoring the conditions of the 1920s. Russian influence was indeed completely eliminated, but Ukrainians were not granted even limited self-determination or a reversal of collectivization policies. Rather, the readiness of the population to cooperate was exploited exclusively for National Socialist ends. As a result, the German occupation accelerated the process of Russification

---

references, that the NKVD shot without trial hundreds of thousands of alleged collaborators after the reoccupation (*Stalins Vernichtungskrieg, 1941–1945* [Munich, 1995], p. 151ff.).

84. Among those arrested were 211 auxiliary policemen: see a report from UNKVD Staline to UNKVD Kharkiv, 24 September 1943, Donetsk Oblast State Archive, R-1838/1/1, pp. 2–8 (my thanks to Nadezhda Borisovna Metalnikova of Donetsk for this information).

85. Report of the NKVD Military Tribunal for the Ukrainian District for July–September 1943 (22 October 1943), TsDAHOU P-1/23/684, pp. 6–15.

86. Werner Brockdorff, *Kollaboration oder Widerstand: Die Zusammenarbeit mit den Deutschen in den besetzten Ländern während des zweiten Weltkrieges und deren schreckliche Folgen* (Munich and Wels, 1968), p. 230. The author mentions, without source references, that 50,000 former auxiliary policemen were sentenced in Ukraine and that 30,000 of them were executed. In Chernivtsi oblast alone, 8,500 trial records were reviewed by the summer of 1992 and 4,500 defendants unjustly sentenced for collaboration or OUN membership were rehabilitated. See *Litopys neskorenoï Ukraïny: Dokumenty, materialy, spohady*, vol. 1 (Lviv, 1993), p. 417ff.

87. See Bernd Bonwetsch, "Sowjetische Zwangsarbeiter vor und nach 1945: Ein doppelter Leidensweg," *Jahrbücher für Geschichte Osteuropas* 41, no. 4 (1993): 532–46. For a detailed source-based study of the fate of repatriated *Ostarbeiter*, see Pavel Markovich Polian, *Zhertvy dvukh diktatur: Ostarbaitery i voennoplennye v Tret'em Raikhe i ikh repatriatsiia* (Moscow, 1996).

that had begun in the 1930s by incapacitating the Ukrainians; the Soviet reoccupation reinstated the policy of Russification from 1944 on.[88] It would be inappropriate, therefore, to mythologize the years 1941 to 1944.

---

88. See Gerhard Simon, *Nationalismus und Nationalitätenpolitik in der Sowjetunion von der totalitären Diktatur zur nachstalinschen Gesellschaft* (Baden-Baden, 1986), p. 234. For a different interpretation of the 1944–46 period, claiming that there was a brief Ukrainianization, see Krawchenko, "Soviet Ukraine," p. 31.

Oleh S. Ilnytzkyj

Modeling Culture in the Empire: Ukrainian Modernism and the Death of the All-Russian Idea

> *Russia must be and cannot not be a Russian national state.*
> *Russian culture is, of course, intimately tied to the state and its history, but at the present time it [Russian culture] is a fact even more important and fundamental than the state itself.*
> *These facts contain part of the answer to the question: What is Russia?*
> *Petr Struve (1911)*[1]

Introduction

Since the disintegration of the Soviet Union, one of many problems vexing scholars and laymen, Russians and non-Russians alike, has been: "What is Russia?" In the West, much of this discussion has had a political dimension, as in Zbigniew Brzezinski's question: "Is Russia primarily a nation-state or … a multinational empire?"[2] Most scholars tend to endorse the latter as a rejoinder, which then raises the less frequently posed but equally intriguing query: "If Russia is an empire, what is 'Russian' culture and identity?" Is it "national" or "imperial" (multinational)? What function does the national component play in relation to the "imperial" one and vice versa? Should one distinguish between a narrow "Russian" culture and a more broadly defined "imperial" one?

One reason to ponder such issues is that, clearly, much more took place in 1991 than just the geopolitical disintegration of a state: the end of the Russian Empire marks the closure of an imagined universe, of metanarratives (to borrow a term from Jean-François Lyotard) that governed, among other things, the very idea of "Russianness." With the demise of the Soviet Union, there is every indication that Russians face much more than economic and political uncertainty: they must come to terms with the dislocation of a symbolic order and reevaluate

1. Petr Struve, "Na raznyia temy," *Russkaia mysl'*, 1911, no. 1: 184, 185.

2. "The Premature Partnership," *Foreign Affairs* 73, no. 2 (March–April 1994): 72.

the cultural mythology that hitherto determined their very sense of self.

Nowhere is this problem more apparent than in Russia's relationship to Ukraine. As one newspaper headline put it, Ukraine, by exiting (and destroying) the Soviet Union, appears to have taken the "Russians' identity with it."[3] Even if one is prone to disagree with such a sweeping generalization, it is certainly true that the "loss" of Ukraine represents a very special dilemma for Russia that goes well beyond the loss of prime real estate. Certainly, no other "secessionist" part of the Soviet Union has had as much symbolic and psychological meaning for Russians as Ukraine—the repository of much of what Russians regard as their own history and culture, inhabited by people traditionally considered junior partners of the Great Russians, but acknowledged as co-creators of Russian (or is it "imperial"?) culture. To put it briefly: while an independent Ukraine poses a variety of strategic problems for the Russian Federation, these pale in comparison with the archetypal challenge it poses to Russia's national identity. After all, Russia's long presence on the historical stage as an empire, both tsarist and Soviet, was largely motivated and sustained by a belief in East Slavic unity, best typified by the notion of a common "all-Russian" culture. Over the last two centuries, the Russian cultural canon (and the modern Russian identity) was constructed on the premise of this historical thinking, which accounts for the relatively few distinctions it made between, say, the Gogols and Kostomarovs on the one hand and the Dostoevskys and Tolstoys on the other, or between "Southwest Russian [i.e., Western Ukrainian] literature" and Muscovite writings: all were equally "Russian."[4] As late as the 1980s, the Ukrainian-Russian relationship was couched in the rhetoric of "unity" and "oneness," even by so prominent a figure as Dmitrii Likhachev. For Likhachev, Russia represented an "incredible variety and yet some kind of higher unity. All Russian. Even after division into three eastern Slavic peoples..."[5] Likhachev literally could not fathom Russia without Ukraine:

---

3. Mary Mycio, "Ukraine Takes Russians' Identity with It," *The European*, 30 August 1992. Cf. also *Nationalities Papers* 20, no. 2 (1992): 8, 86, 88, 112, and passim.

4. See, for example, D. S. Mirsky, *A History of Russian Literature from the Earliest Times to the Death of Dostoyevsky (1881)* (New York, 1937).

5. Dmitrii S. Likhachev, *Reflections on Russia*, ed. Nicolai N. Petro, trans. Christina Sever (Boulder, Colo., 1991), p. 160.

> Dissected by blows of Tatar swords and by a clever policy of partition, Rus' remained united even after its split into the Ukraine and Great Russia, just as the celestial bodies remain united as they revolve around an invisible center and around each other.
>
> The culture of northern Rus' was always drawn to the culture of southern Rus', not only to the ancient, common one, but also the contemporary one. Ukrainian baroque penetrated northern Rus' from the south—in architecture, poetry and music. Ukrainian cultural figures visited northern Rus', and Ukrainians occupied important posts in the Russian government and church ...
>
> Over the course of the centuries following their division into two entities, *Russia and the Ukraine have formed not only a political, but also a culturally dualistic unity. Russian culture is meaningless without Ukrainian, as Ukrainian is without Russian.*
>
> Artists Dmitrii Levitskii, Vladimir Borovikovskii, Anton Losenko and Arkhip Kuindzhi came from the Ukraine, but is the history of Russian painting conceivable without them?...
>
> *Russian culture of the seventeenth century would have been impossible without the Ukraine ...*
>
> Could anyone have written the history of Russian poetry of the nineteenth century without taking into account Shevchenko? Would Gogol's works have been possible without the Ukraine...?
>
> *But it is also true that there is no Ukraine without Russia!...*
>
> Kiev has always evoked a feeling of nostalgia in Russians, as the ancient capital of Russia, as the "mother of the cities of Rus'," and as the center of the most important Russian holy places, which were never considered separate from Ukrainian ones.[6]

Leaving aside the question of whether Ukrainians would agree with Likhachev's narrative reconstruction of history (on the whole, an unlikely proposition), his words certainly reveal the extent to which the idea of "Ukrainian-Russian" (i.e., "all-Russian") unity serves as a major epistemological premise of the Russian polity, motivating its cultural and political agenda in equal measure. The vitality of this explanatory paradigm for the construction of Russia's identity is evidenced not only in Likhachev's use of it in reference to the distant past, but in a more recent instance (1992) as well, when a Moscow publication claimed several Ukrainian painters as members of the "unknown Russian avant-garde" and included the Ukrainian Futurist journal *Nova generatsiia* (Kharkiv, 1927–30) in a chronology of Russian art history.[7] From such examples one might deduce a characteristic

---

6. Ibid., pp. 73–76. Emphasis added.

7. Cf. A. D. Sarab'ianov, *Neizvestnyi russkii avangard v muzeiakh i chastnykh sobraniiakh* (Moscow, 1992). The painters in question were: O. A. Bohomazov

dynamic of Russia's cultural formation: the ability to assimilate and subordinate imperial (East Slavic; all-Russian; Soviet) cultural phenomena to the notion of some integral "Russian" *national* process. The question is, now that Ukraine is no longer part of Russia, can ideas such as Likhachev's (and cultural arrogation of the type represented by the Moscow publication) be sustained for long, either in theory or in practice?

Outwardly, the current crisis created for Russians by Ukrainians may not seem unique. For a good part of their modern history, Ukrainians have been challenging—in one form or another and with varying degrees of success—Russia's manner of national self-imaging and self-legitimization. However, the truth is that until 1991, none of these counter-narratives made any deep or lasting impression on the Russian psyche, inasmuch as the empire had been quite adept at managing the public discourse on East Slavic history, carefully orchestrating Ukrainian voices so as to harmonize with the imperial chorus. In other words, the totalizing power of the Russian historical metanarrative—supported by the full power of the state's institutions—has hitherto managed to shunt aside or neutralize specifically Ukrainian narratives, either construing them as illegitimate (e.g., "nationalist") or relegating them to minor and manageable subplots of the all-Russian master narrative (e.g., official Russian imperial and Soviet historiography has always portrayed Ukraine as expressing a desire for "union" or "reunification" with Russia).

What is unique at present, then, is not only the clear-cut political sovereignty of Ukraine, but also the disappearance of "all-Russian" and "Soviet" bridging structures (the idea of a "commonwealth" [the Commonwealth of Independent States or CIS], with respect to Ukraine, remains essentially stillborn). Previously, such structures bestowed figurative as well as actual unity on the Ukrainian-Russian relationship, helping to patch over the more obvious logical cracks in the imperial metanarrative. For Russians, moreover, the crisis is exacerbated by the fact that, unlike the Russian Empire, the present-day Russian Federation is not in a position to pattern the East Slavic historical/cultural discourse for the benefit of the Russian nationality. In a decentered post-Soviet world in which a Ukrainian Kyiv exercises political and cultural sovereignty, arguments about culture and history that Moscow could (and did) previously control, for better or worse, have acquired a self-justifying autonomy that neither needs nor seeks

---

(A. K. Bogomazov), O. V. Hryshchenko (A. V. Grishchenko), V. D. Ermilov, and V. N. Palmov.

Russia's imprimatur. Ukraine's new status effectively deconstructs East Slavic history, unsettling "Russian" culture as hitherto conceived and undermining the authority it previously enjoyed among Russians. In fact, current irredentist sentiments in Russia might be seen as evidence of this anxiety, a desire to avoid a difficult national soul-searching. The imperialist revival (especially on the rhetorical plane) is a form of admission that political/territorial control was a major factor in maintaining the Russian symbolic universe, i.e., a traditional understanding of what "Russia" and "Russian" mean. Thus it is easy to understand why the idea of a Russian-dominated CIS, a Greater Russia or reconstituted Soviet Union—goals of many Russian political factions—serves as an attractive palliative. Clearly, while the physical empire has crumbled, the empire of the mind survives, struggling either to cope with the contradictions or to recreate the world in the old image.

Russia's current national predicament might be better appreciated if we recall something written more than eighty years ago by Petr Struve, who even then tried to imagine the possible consequences for Russia of the loss of Ukraine:

> Should the *intelligentsia['s] "Ukrainian" idea* ... strike the *national* soil and set it on fire ... [the result will be] a gigantic and *unprecedented schism* of the *Russian nation*, which, such is my deepest conviction, will result in a veritable disaster for the state and for the people. All our "borderland" problems will pale into mere bagatelles compared to such a prospect of bifurcation and—should the "Belorussians" follow the "Ukrainians"—the "trifurcation" of *Russian culture*.[8]

Struve wrote these words in 1911. In retrospect, it could be said that Ukraine's independence in 1991 has become for many Russians the "veritable disaster" Struve so feared. In view of what continues to be said, one might conclude that Russians—having averted permanent trifurcation by means of reunification with Belarus on 2 April 1996—nevertheless see themselves as a bifurcated nation, the casualty of nothing less than the "Ukrainian idea." With Ukraine no longer a constituent of the so-called "Russian nation," Russians by their own admission are confronted with an unusual personal and national problem. The Russian philosopher and nationalist Aleksandr Tsipko, for example, has voiced the opinion that without Kyiv

8. Quoted in Richard Pipes, *Struve: Liberal on the Right, 1905–1944* (Cambridge, Mass., 1980), pp. 211–12 (emphasis added). For the original, see Petr Struve, "Obshcherusskaia kul'tura i ukrainskii partikuliarizm," *Russkaia mysl'*, 1912, no. 1: 85.

"there can be no Russia in the old, *real* [N.B.] sense of the word."[9] A feeling of unreality and national diminution certainly haunts Solzhenitsyn, who has expressed these feelings in the apocalyptic language of Struve: "This *tearing off* of Belorussia and Ukraine from *us* [N.B.]," he is quoted as saying, "is just the *same* [*sic*] as the division of Germany after the war .... *Historically, it must not endure.*"[10] Such emotion and dubious historical analogies are not uncommon. Intellectuals as well as politicians seem to suggest that Ukraine remains the key to Russian cultural and political wholeness. Nevertheless, as often in the past, this southern neighbor is ascribed an ambivalent role: on the one hand, Ukraine is felt to be essential, even indispensable to the Russian psyche and state; on the other, when recognized for what it is, i.e., the apotheosis of a competing nationality, Ukraine immediately becomes a source of anxiety and an object of loathing.[11]

While many explanations are being offered for the sudden collapse of the Soviet Union, I am not aware of any discussion that has sought to interpret this epochal event from a cultural perspective, more specifically, as a consequence of the death of the "all-Russian" idea, i.e., the growing irrelevance of the notion that Ukraine is part of a "Russian" nation. This paper will try to posit the disintegration of the Russian Empire (including the Soviet Union) as the failure of a *cultural*

---

9. "The Post-Cold-War War," *Economist*, 19 June 1993, p. 49. Emphasis added.

10. Cf. "Solzhenitsyn Says Slavic Division Must Not Last," Reuters, 6 August 1994. Emphasis added. In 1911, Struve, too, drew analogies between Germany and Russia, arguing that the Ukrainian language was to Russian as Plattdeutsch was to German. Cf. "Obshcherusskaia kul'tura i ukrainskii partikuliarizm," pp. 69–71. For a discussion of Solzhenitsyn's views on Ukraine, see John-Paul Himka, "Ukrainians, Russians, and Alexander Solzhenitsyn," *Cross Currents: A Yearbook of Central European Culture*, no. 11 (1992): 193–204. In contrast, it is interesting to note Solzhenitsyn's reaction to Chechnya. The Associated Press (11 January 1995) reported the following: "Solzhenitsyn said it was not too late to end the conflict by recognizing Chechnya's independence. 'It is not too late to offer Chechnya a choice even now,' he said. 'Let it be independent if it wants to be.' Solzhenitsyn said Russia would be better off without Chechnya. 'When an organ is affected by gangrene, it should be cut off to save the body,' he said. 'The integrity of Russia is more important.'"

11. Russian historiography and political rhetoric is rich in sobriquets for those Ukrainians who, presumably owing to immaturity or mental disorder, "betrayed" the Russian idea in favor of some misguided independence. They have been known to Russians as Mazepites, Khvylovites, Petliurites, Banderites, and bourgeois nationalists, to cite but a few epithets.

paradigm; as the institutional collapse of an inherently untenable *cultural* model that over the past century has rapidly been losing its power to effect (and legitimize) social, political, and cultural practices of the state, let alone fashion a common identity or culture. More generally, I shall postulate the Ukrainian-Russian relationship as an extended contest between *two* ideas of culture, both of which vied to establish distinct *national* institutions. It will be my argument that recent events mark the endgame of a protracted historical process whereby the "Ukrainian idea" has sought to undermine, in theory and in practice, the notion of East Slavic (i.e., "all-Russian") unity. For the sake of argument, Ukraine's independence will be taken as the triumph of this once marginalized cultural paradigm; in turn, pronouncements by present-day Russians will be interpreted as last-ditch attempts to resuscitate an archetype of Russia and Russian culture that has sustained their national formation up to this time. My working hypothesis will be that over the last two centuries, behind the facade of empire, two nations were being constructed on the basis of radically different ideologies of culture. The goal here will be to trace the interaction of the "Ukrainian" and the "all-Russian" ideas as expressed in the discourse of the Ukrainian and Russian imperial intelligentsia. The emphasis on the intelligentsia (largely literary or academic) is based on the premise that it is this stratum that endowed these respective ideas with authority and helped transform them into social and political instruments.

Among Ukrainians, the death of the all-Russian idea, *as an idea*, occurred long before 1991. I would submit that, as far as social thought is concerned, Ukraine's post-colonial period began not with independence (that being already a consequence of the idea), but at the point when Ukrainian intellectuals ceased to conceptualize their culture in relation to Russia and embraced an alternate model for explicating their nation's cultural existence. That fateful transformation, as I shall show below, occurred around the turn of the century, during what is generally termed the modernist period—i.e., the years 1890–1930, especially the 1910s—a crucial interval when Ukrainian and Russian cultural ideologies drifted completely and irrevocably apart, prefiguring today's political realities on the symbolic level by nearly a century. If this hypothesis is correct, then it clearly means that Struve's alarm of 1911 was probably at least a decade too late. His articles on the Ukrainian question were in fact symptoms of the beginning of the end of the "all-Russian" idea—for Ukrainians. The replies to Struve from the Ukrainian intelligentsia, especially in the modernist journal *Ukraïns'ka khata* (Kyiv, 1909–14), which I shall highlight here, presented an uncompromising rejection of "all-Russian" culture, i.e., the foundation on which men like Struve still believed "Russia" could be built.

But even as the all-Russian idea, as a factor of social and national mobilization, was steadily waning among Ukrainians (becoming increasingly synonymous with "Russification" and assimilation), it continued to enthrall Russians like Struve, showing that Russian society had no mechanism for coping with, or adjusting to, the Ukrainian transformation without doing violence to its own identity. The reanimation of the "all-Russian" idea continued during the Civil War[12] and the 1920s (e.g., Dmytro Lebid's notion of "The Struggle of Two Cultures"),[13] only to be decisively rebuffed by the intelligentsia of Ukraine. By then the elite was aggressively promoting hegemony for Ukrainian culture in Ukraine: it struggled to wrest control of cultural production from the center and dissociated itself as never before from all-Russian (i.e., all-Soviet) social structures, chiefly by founding entirely independent cultural, literary and artistic organizations. The basic message of the 1920s was that Russian culture was destined to retreat from Ukraine into its own ethnic borders. So complete was the ideological defeat of the all-Russian concept among Ukrainians by end of the decade that the state—always on the side of the Russian idea—had to resort to extreme (some would say genocidal) methods to "convince" Ukrainians of their ideological errors. Coercion, of course, was a traditional tool in this "debate" between Ukrainians and Russians, dating back to the various repressive measures against Ukrainian activities in the nineteenth century. This was, in some sense, the ultimate "argument" employed by that segment of imperial society which was bent on fashioning the "all-Russian" man and later, of course, Homo Sovieticus. Struve personally rejected the use of police methods (*politseiskoe nasilie*) in this debate, but he was of the opinion that "Russian progressive social thought must, without any ambiguity and indulgence, enter energetically into an ideological struggle with 'Ukrainianness' [*ukrainstvom*]—a

---

12. Cf. Anna Procyk, *Russian Nationalism and Ukraine: The Nationality Policy of the Volunteer Army during the Civil War* (Edmonton, 1995).

13. There is a rich literature on this period. See, for example, George S. N. Luckyj, *Literary Politics in the Soviet Ukraine, 1917–1934* (New York, 1956); Myroslav Shkandrij, *Modernists, Marxists and the Nation: The Ukrainian Literary Discussion of the 1920s* (Edmonton, 1992); James E. Mace, *Communism and the Dilemmas of National Liberation: National Communism in Soviet Ukraine, 1918–1933* (Cambridge, Mass., 1983); and George O. Liber, *Soviet Nationality Policy, Urban Growth, and Identity Change in the Ukrainian SSR, 1923–1934* (Cambridge, 1992).

tendency," he said, designed to "weaken and, to some extent, even to abolish the great achievement of our history, i.e., all-Russian culture."[14] Struve viewed this as a struggle against the "huge, indeed, titanic plan of bifurcating ... Russian culture across its entire length—from the primer to 'general pathology' and 'crystallography,' from the folk song to translations of Ovid, Goethe, Verlaine, or Verhaeren."[15] Since this was in fact the strategy of the Ukrainian intelligentsia, Struve's opposition made him virtually indistinguishable from Russia's chauvinists and reactionaries.

I

From S. S. Uvarov's "official nationality" to Solzhenitsyn's cries of dismemberment, the Russian conception of how to organize the cultural space of the Eastern Slavs has remained fairly uniform, its constancy no doubt betokening its centrality for Russian cultural identity, nation- and empire-building.[16] The Ukrainian idea, on the other hand, has been anything but constant, having gone through several important iterations, i.e., from being roughly compatible with the all-Russian idea to rejecting it outright. When Struve tackled the Ukrainian question, the debate between Ukrainians and Russians was already a century old.

The origins of this "debate," which initially had a largely implicit character, can be traced to the end of the eighteenth century. This was the moment when Russian centralism triumphed, doing away with the last vestiges of Ukrainian autonomy and dissolving Ukraine's old Slavonic culture in imperial institutions. Indeed, this period may well have been the apogee of a true "all-Russian" culture, the closest Ukraine and Russia came to achieving a dualistic unity. Ironically, this very moment also marked the start for Ukraine of an entirely new cultural cycle, the logic of which would lead to ever-increasing differentiation from imperial civilization and a strengthening of its distinct local features. Language became a major, though not exclusive, focus in this effort, with the vernacular adopted by fits and starts as the basis for a new secular Ukrainian literature. Folklore, Cossack history, and the Ukrainian peasant class, with its characteristic customs and mores, came into play as national markers for distin-

14. "Obshcherusskaia kul'tura i ukrainskii partikuliarizm," p. 86.

15. "Na raznyia temy," p. 185.

16. For an interesting and concise summary of Russian historical thinking about Ukraine, see Stephen Velychenko, *National History as Cultural Process* (Edmonton, 1992), pp. 79–140.

guishing and delineating Ukrainian existence in the empire. Clearly, the forces that were shaping Russia in the late eighteenth and early nineteenth centuries, namely, secularization, Romanticism, and nationalism—Russifying, so to speak, the "all-Russian," Slavonic-based culture of the empire—also had a huge impact on Ukraine. That effect, however, was more equivocal, given the lack of state support and the serious competition encountered by this emergent culture from the vigorous imperial one. An extremely significant consequence of Ukraine's new cultural cycle was that it inaugurated in Ukrainian society an extended condition of liminality, i.e., an existence caught between local and imperial imperatives, most obviously manifested as bilingualism and biculturalism, vestiges of which survive to this day.

Soon after the appearance of Ivan Kotliarevsky's *Eneïda* (1798), culture became the most frequent, as well as the most contentious, subject of debate between Ukrainians and Russians for nearly two centuries. Disagreements centered on how to define and demarcate *nationally* the history, people, and artifacts produced in the empire. For a century, the two sides argued whether Ukrainian was a dialect or an independent language, and even in 1905, when the Russian Academy of Sciences declared it the latter, the state saw no reason to give up the prerogatives of the Russian language in areas of the empire inhabited by Ukrainians. In short, Struve's attempt at a cultural explication of Russia was certainly nothing unusual; some form of tacit or overt cultural "engineering" had been under way in the empire since the beginning of the nineteenth century.

A central premise of the all-Russian idea, predating Vissarion Belinsky's negative reaction to the works of Taras Shevchenko, was that Ukrainian literature/language/culture could not and should not perform "high" functions in the empire, and that the Ukrainian intelligentsia must make its cultural contribution through imperial/all-Russian media and institutions. As Belinsky put it in 1841 with reference to Shevchenko: "The literary language of Little Russians must be the language of their educated society, namely the Russian language. Even if a great poet should appear in Little Russia, this could only be subject to the condition of his being a *Russian* poet."[17] This position was buttressed by the assumption that Ukrainians and Russians were one nationality, and that, local differences notwithstanding, they shared a common culture and language. At the beginning of the twentieth century, Struve embraced this view

17. Victor Swoboda, "Shevchenko and Belinsky," in *Shevchenko and the Critics*, 1861–1980 ed. George S. N. Luckyj (Toronto, 1980), p. 311.

unconditionally as something that could be taken for granted.[18] He was quite adamant about the existence of "a [single] Russian nation [*natsiia*] and Russian culture," distinct from such "ethnographic" notions as "Great Russian," "Little Russian," and "White Russian." "The term 'Russian' [*russkii*]...," he wrote, "is not some kind of abstract 'average' of the three 'terms' (with the prefixes 'great,' 'little,' [and] 'white'), but a living cultural strength, a grand, developing, and growing national force [*natsional'naia stikhiia*] ... a 'nation in the making,' as the Americans say about themselves." Elsewhere he voiced this opinion: "I start with the conviction that there is an all-Russian culture and its organ, the all-Russian language."[19] Clearly, Struve never regarded Ukrainians as *other* Eastern Slavs; for him, they were provincial Russians with an underdeveloped sense of their own nationality: "The Little Russian," Struve said, "... is simply illiterate in the national and state sense, he has not yet read the national and state primer [*national'no-gosudarstvennogo bukvaria*]."[20] At best, therefore, Ukrainians could aspire to a "humble regional development" of their local—essentially, peasant and rural—culture. Struve anticipated no role for the Ukrainian language in higher education, in urban life, or in the new capitalist economy.[21] He understood this situation to represent the natural order, a consequence of Russia's historical development that "could only be changed with the complete destruction of ... the state [and] Russian society."[22] His special concern was therefore to avoid the creation of "parallel cultures"[23] and avert a conflict between the "the 'all-ethnic' [*obshchenarodnoi*]" or "national [*natsional'noi*]" culture on the one hand and the "local [*mestnoi*] element" on the other.[24] In opposing the "Ukrainian idea," he stressed the need to preserve the "cultural unity of *Russian* Russia [*russkoi Rossii*]."[25] He was especially apprehensive about the possible development, out of a "local 'way of life' [*byt*] and 'dialect,' of a new

---

18. Struve's "Russian nation" is made up of three "Russian tribes": Great Russians, Little Russians, and White Russians. Cf. "Na raznyia temy," p. 186, note 2.

19. "Obshcherusskaia kul'tura i ukrainskii partikuliarizm," p. 67.

20. "Na raznyia temy," p. 187.

21. "Obshcherusskaia kul'tura i ukrainskii partikuliarizm," pp. 71–72, 81.

22. Ibid., p. 66.

23. "Na raznyia temy," p. 185.

24. "Obshcherusskaia kul'tura i ukrainskii partikuliarizm," p. 84.

25. Ibid., pp. 85–86.

national and all-embracing culture" that might "compete with all-Russian culture and force it out of the territory of 'ethnographic' Ukraine" (84). Ironically, as indicated above, in little more than a decade this became the ultimate and openly espoused objective of the Ukrainian intelligentsia, for which the raison d'être of "Ukrainization" lay precisely in attaining hegemony for Ukrainian culture across its whole "ethnographic" span. Not surprisingly, the writer who expressed these thoughts most directly, Mykola Khvylovy (see especially his "Ukraïna chy Malorosiia?"),[26] was severely criticized by the party, which also banned his writings; their rehabilitation, tellingly, came only on the eve of the Soviet Union's demise.

Given the events of the 1920s, it is rather ironic that one of the most candid and vituperative articulations of the all-Russian idea should have been produced in 1927—i.e., at the height of the Ukrainization process—by no less a figure than Nikolai Trubetskoi (1890–1938). Writing in Paris and acutely aware of developments in Soviet Ukraine, Trubetskoi saw fit to argue even at that late date for the vitality of the "all-Russian" cultural idea, while accentuating the unproductiveness of its Ukrainian counterpart.[27]

Much like Struve before him, Trubetskoi declared that Russian culture was composed of a Great Russian and a Ukrainian "variant" (the Belarusian, he admitted, existed too, but was "less well developed" [253] and hence did not play a prominent role in his argument). Alluding to the influence of Ukrainian learning on Russia in the seventeenth and eighteenth centuries, Trubetskoi argued "that at the turn of the eighteenth century the intellectual and spiritual culture of Great Russia was Ukrainized. The differences between the West Russian [his synonym for "Ukrainian"] and the Muscovite variants of Russian culture were eliminated through the eradication of the latter. Now there was only one culture ... [T]his culture lost over time any specific Great Russian or Ukrainian identification and became all-Russian" (251). He continued: "The cultural Ukrainianization of Great Russia and the transformation of Ukrainian culture into the all-Russian culture led quite naturally to the loss of its specifically Ukrainian provincial character. But it could not become specifically

26. *Slovo i chas*, 1990, no. 1: 7–31, and *Vitchyzna*, 1990, nos. 1 and 2: 179–88, 168–78, respectively. Cf. Oleh S. Ilnytzkyj, "The Modernist Ideology and Mykola Khvyl'ovyi," *Harvard Ukrainian Studies* 15, nos. 3–4 (December 1991): 257–62.

27. "The Ukrainian Problem" in Nikolai Sergeevich Trubetzkoy, *The Legacy of Genghis Khan and Other Essays on Russia's Identity* (Ann Arbor, 1991), pp. 245–67.

Russian, because … the continuity of the Great Russian cultural tradition had been finally and irretrievably broken." (252). At this point of history, Trubetskoi continued, "groups appeared in Russian society" (252) that reacted against "the generalized character of all-Russian culture and strove to replace it with the specific and concrete" (252–53), which led them "to select one of the individualizations of the Russian people [*sic*]—[that is] the Great Russians, Ukrainians or Belorussians—since only [they] exist in fact, while 'all-Russians' are mere abstractions" (253). Trubetskoi saw this individualization along "tribal" lines as a desire to bridge the gap between "higher strata" of society and "the people." While he accepted this as a necessary and desirable goal, his primary interest was focused on what he called the "top story" of culture, that is, high culture, the culture of the intelligentsia, which he contrasted with the "bottom story" or the culture of the people. High culture, he argued, could not be individualized, could not be tribe-specific or national; it could only be "all-Russian." He wrote: "[A] regional and tribal differentiation of Russian culture should not extend to the very top of the cultural edifice, to cultural assets of a higher order. There must be no tribal or regional boundaries on the top story of Russian culture in the future." (263)

Trubetskoi then set out a series of reasons why Ukrainians should avoid creating their own high culture. First, he said, it would be an entirely superfluous creation, because Ukrainians already had a high culture in the so-called "all-Russian" culture. He elaborated:

> Several partisans of Ukrainian cultural separatism [*sic*] have tried to argue that the culture which has existed in Russia up to the present is not all-Russian, but simply Great Russian. This is factually incorrect…. It is obvious that Ukrainians participated actively and on an equal footing with the Great Russians not only in the genesis but in the development of this all-Russian culture; and they did so as Ukrainians, without abandoning their ethnic identity. On the contrary, they affirmed it. No one would exclude Gogol from Russian literature, Kostomarov from Russian historiography, Potebnia from Russian philology, and so on. It is simply impossible to deny the fact that Russian culture during the post-Petrine era is all-Russian and that it is not foreign to Ukrainians. If this native culture is viewed by some Ukrainians as not fully their own, and if the incompatibility between the cultural elite and the masses is obvious when this culture is juxtaposed with the thought patterns and life style of common Ukrainian people, the same phenomenon can be observed in Great Russia. Consequently, it has causes altogether different from the mistaken belief that this culture is Great Russian. (255–56)

Trubetskoi's second argument against creating a separate high Ukrainian culture amounted to the proposition that such a goal was simply unattainable:

> [H]owever likely it is that a new Ukrainian culture would resolve the problem of conforming the bottom story of its edifice to its foundations in the people, it will never resolve even partially the other problem: creating a new top story that could satisfy the needs of the intelligentsia more fully than the top story of the old all-Russian culture did. A new Ukrainian culture would be in no position to compete successfully with the old culture in meeting these spiritual and intellectual needs. (257)

According to Trubetskoi, one reason the new Ukrainian culture would fail was that "talented people," "given completely free choice ... will quite naturally opt for the culture of the ethnological whole [all-Russian culture] and not for the culture of a part of that whole [Ukrainian culture]. *It follows that the only people who could opt for Ukrainian culture are those biased in some way or limited in their freedom of choice*" (258).

At this juncture of his argument, Trubetskoi paints a scurrilous portrait of those who might choose to align themselves with Ukrainian culture. They are described as "talentless or mediocre creators," "narrow, fanatical regional chauvinists who have never learned to evaluate high culture impartially," people with an "imprint of petty provincial vanity, of triumphant mediocrity, banality, and obscurantism," who "will try to deny [other] Ukrainians the opportunity to learn the Russian literary language, to read Russian books, to absorb Russian culture ...." These people will foster hatred of everything Russian, writes Trubetskoi, "[b]ecause if Ukrainians do not begin to hate everything Russian, the possibility will always remain that they will opt for the all-Russian culture" (259). He concludes: "Such are the unsightly vistas that await Ukrainian culture *if it decides to replace all-Russian culture, to repudiate it, if it enters into competition with it*" (260). "To escape this lamentable future, *Ukrainian culture must be built so that it supplements all-Russian culture, and is not in competition with it*; in other words, Ukrainian culture must become an individualized variant of all-Russian culture" (261; emphasis added).

Leaving aside the accuracy of Trubetskoi's "history" (e.g., his notion of the "eradication" of Great Russian culture, etc.), it is clear that, as an apologia for "all-Russian" culture, this essay was completely out of step with Ukrainian thinking and cultural achievements. There can be no doubt that by 1927 Ukrainian society was well on its way to completing almost every cultural task that Trubetskoi insisted was impossible: (a) its best representatives were no longer preoccupied with adapting themselves to society's lower strata or modeling culture on the "bottom story" (more on this below); (b) Ukrainian intellectuals were determined to have "cultural assets of a higher order" that were simultaneously (to use Trubetskoi's phrase) "tribe-specific or national" and satisfied them "more fully than the top story of the old all-Russian culture did"; (c) by the end of the 1920s several generations of "talented people" had already opted freely for a Ukrainian national culture, often at great political cost to themselves; finally, and, most importantly, (d) the twenties offered clear proof that, given the chance, Ukrainian culture could compete successfully with all-Russian culture "over its entire length."

For all its incongruity, Trubetskoi's intervention in the Ukrainian cultural debate of the twenties was remarkable in that it underscored the unbridgeable gap between the Ukrainian and Russian intelligentsias and showed to what degree Russian thinking was a prisoner of the "all-Russian" idea. Although Trubetskoi's reasoning stood absolutely no chance of striking a chord with Ukraine's elite of the twenties, it did nevertheless resonate strangely with views that had held sway in Ukrainian society between the 1860s and 1880s. His was, in some respects, the language of Panteleimon Kulish, Mykola (Nikolai) Kostomarov, and Mykhailo Drahomanov (Struve, incidentally, cited the latter's ideas with approbation). Although the social and political views of these three men were far from identical, they did share one propensity—a willingness to describe Ukrainian culture in relation to, and in terms of, all-Russian culture.[28] Drahomanov, for example, framed his particular vision as a tripartite system, mapping out a "Ukrainian," "Great Russian," and "Imperial" (*rosiis'ka*) literary culture. He ascribed to the "national" cultures (Ukrainian and Great Russian) limited, parochial functions that, with some exceptions, were duty-bound to address the peasantry. The "common" imperial culture (a distillation of the best features of the two national cultures, irrespective of language) was credited with transcendent universal values typical of the empire's educated classes. In its most optimistic guise, the vision of men like Drahomanov posited Ukraine and Great Russia as equal regional societies within a

28. For a representative sample of their ideas, see: Panteleimon Kulish, "Ob otnoshenii malorossiiskoi slovesnosti k obshcherusskoi: Ėpilog k 'Chernoi rade,'" in his *Tvory v dvokh tomakh* (Kyiv, 1989), 2: 458–76; Mykhailo Hrushevs'kyi, ed., *Naukovo-publitsystychni i polemichni pysannia Kostomarova* (Kharkiv, 1928); and Mykhailo Drahomanov, "Literatura rosiis'ka, velykorus'ka, ukraïns'ka i halyts'ka," in his *Literaturno-publitsystychni pratsi u dvokh tomakh* (Kyiv, 1970), 1: 80–220.

bicultural Slavic state, sharing a third, i.e., all-Russian, culture. Although the intricacies of such theories cannot be explored here, one aspect deserves to be emphasized: as late as the third quarter of the nineteenth century, Ukrainian culture was not yet systematically imagined as something wholly independent and self-sufficient. Trubetskoi would probably have found an important segment of the Ukrainian intelligentsia of this period identifying itself with at least some of his views, especially with the admission that Ukrainians were important contributors to an all-Russian culture. To be sure, few would have agreed even then that Ukrainian culture was just a "variant" of Russian culture or that it was destined forever to inhabit the "lower story." Nevertheless, that generation was not uncomfortable in regarding Ukrainian culture as a *complementary* and *auxiliary* subsystem *within* a larger, i.e., imperial (all-Russian) construct; these individuals were still capable of considering imperial culture "their own," "not foreign," and at least partly "native." For men like Kulish and Kostomarov (and before them, obviously, Gogol), this accorded with their experience as participants in both Ukrainian and all-Russian (imperial) society. If at that moment of history the Ukrainian idea was, more or less, still compatible with the all-Russian, it was certainly not because the intelligentsia was prepared to accept the notion of Ukrainians as a tribal or ethnic variant of generic "Russians," but because it continued to feel a certain allegiance to an overarching imperial culture and was prepared to restrict its own national cultural ambitions to a regional configuration, essentially to propaedeutic and pragmatic purposes.

As Trubetskoi and Struve demonstrated, the all-Russian discourse considered Ukrainian culture inherently "low," incapable of performing the functions of all-Russian culture. Trubetskoi portrayed it as a locus of incompetence and benightedness, the refuge of "talentless or mediocre creators"—not an infrequent Russian stereotype over the last two centuries. To be sure, Ukraine's culture, as an underdeveloped institution, paled in comparison with the imperial construct. Nevertheless, even in the nineteenth century, members of Ukrainian society made remarkable achievements in many areas (esthetic and otherwise), both in the new vernacular and in the lingua franca of the empire, Russian. Significantly, only Russian-language accomplishments—or those attained through sanctioned imperial cultural institutions (the press, universities, etc.)—won validation in the empire, and then primarily by being embraced as "Russian" culture (cf. Trubetskoi's reference to Gogol, Kostomarov, and Potebnia, as well as Likhachev's mention of Ukrainian artists above). Clearly, there was a lesson in this for Ukrainian society, especially in the person of

Gogol, who became a highly ambivalent figure for Ukrainians. For many, his prominent position in Russian/imperial letters and the visibility he brought to Ukrainian themes was unquestionably a source of pride. At the same time, he became a cautionary example, an omen of what must inevitably happen to Ukrainian cultural contributions in an imperial context. Even if an individual preserved his national identity (and Gogol certainly had more than a rudimentary sense of himself as a Ukrainian), his objective sociocultural role was still that of a builder of an imperial (all-Russian) cultural institution with which every successive generation of Ukrainians had more and more difficulty identifying itself, both because it was assuming ever more obvious Great Russian characteristics and because it had room only for the most stereotypical (Little Russian, "low") Ukrainian features.

By the 1890s it was becoming obvious to the Ukrainian intelligentsia that the so-called "lowliness" of Ukrainian culture was neither an objective assessment of its prevailing condition nor a reliable prognosis of its future. The issue, increasingly, was not the intrinsic quality of the Ukrainian creative mind or of the cultural artifacts it produced, but their contemptuous valuation by imperial society. By this point, the relative "highness" or "lowliness" of Ukrainian society's cultural praxis had little to do with actual merit and virtually everything to do with the prevailing cultural paradigm, i.e., the empire's generally low regard for anything that did not conform to imperial institutions. By the end of the nineteenth century, the intelligentsia began to recognize that Ukrainian culture was in a structural or systemic trap. Discrepancies between the maturation of Ukrainian society, with its broadening cultural sophistication, and its lack of approbation and limited room for growth in the imperial system made the overthrow of the all-Russian paradigm an urgent social imperative.

II

Ukrainian culture first broke free of its all-Russian complement, i.e., from the imperial cultural system, through a process that might be described as the discovery of "Europe." This gradual and initially almost imperceptible intrusion of the West as a model into Ukrainian cultural consciousness displaced the ubiquitous, defining presence of the empire. The imagining of Ukraine in a European framework—and the corresponding rejection of the all-Russian/imperial context—was a profound paradigm shift that allowed Ukrainian culture to view itself not as a subsystem or a complement, but as a complete world in its own right, equivalent (if not in fact, at least potentially) to all other self-contained European national cultural systems. By embracing Europe as a point of reference, Ukraine symbolically transformed itself from a dependent *provincial* culture in an empire to an independent *national* culture within a European framework. Ukrainian culture could now be imagined as accommodating both the "high" and the "low" *within itself.* Whereas the empire had distributed culture's social function between a (high) all-Russian society and a (low) Ukrainian one, this "European" vision integrated all functions within a single "Ukrainian" domain. The effect on cultural activity was particularly empowering: it not only "gentrified" the pursuit of culture *within* the Ukrainian context, but also eliminated the "all-Russian" option as the sole recourse for those Ukrainians who sought to escape provincialism. This essentially modernist consciousness ended any possibility of Ukrainian-Russian cultural rapprochement on an imperial foundation and was the central premise on which Ukraine's political and social life entered the twentieth century.

Naturally, the modernist revolution to which I am alluding was the culmination of a lengthy process that had several discrete phases, none of which can be elaborated here. The first obvious evidence of a break with Russian/imperial culture was already apparent in much of Shevchenko's poetry, which played a crucial role in establishing the dignity of its subject matter and medium, while simultaneously giving birth to a highly ironic and distanced attitude with respect to things imperial. A later articulation, which had the semblance of a manifesto, belonged to the realist and populist writer Ivan Nechui-Levytsky. The very first sentence of his lengthy essay "Contemporary Literary Directions" (1878) postulated the essential hopelessness of pursuing a common literature (and, by extension, culture) for "Ukraine and Great Russia."[29] By the 1890s, this was a fairly ordinary idea even for such a radical populist as Pavlo Hrabovsky (1864–1902), who promoted "Europeanism on a Ukrainian foundation" in 1894 and cautioned against the "all-Russian" and "integrationist" sentiments of Russian revolutionaries.[30] However, the final step in this transformation was taken at the turn of the century by the modernists, who were the first to espouse, with total premeditation, a literature for and of the intelligentsia. By finally severing all links between "culture" and "the people," by appointing the well-educated class as the

29. Ivan Nechui-Levyts'kyi, "S'ohochasne literaturne priamuvannia," *Pravda*, pt. 1, 1878, no. 2: 1–41; pt. 2, 1884 (supplement): 195–231. See also his (under the pseudonym I. Bashtovyi) *Ukraïnstvo na literaturnykh pozvakh z Moskovshchynoiu* (Lviv, 1891).

30. Cf. his "Lyst do molodi ukraïns'koï," in Pavlo Hrabov'skyi, *Tvory v dvokh tomakh* (Kyiv, 1964), 2: 144–48.

custodian of cultural taste, this generation helped explicate Ukraine's national purpose not in terms of social or class issues ("serving the people"), but in terms of an elitist culture. The previous modeling of Ukraine on ethnographic and populist criteria, the embrace of the "bottom story" as a cultural and national cause (a legacy of Romanticism reinforced by realism and populism), was emphatically cast aside: indeed, the modernists actually encouraged social polarization in the name of a high national art and culture. This is not to suggest that questions of mass education, literacy, and social justice were absent from their agenda. However, none of these pragmatic issues was now entangled with high culture, which became a conscious and separate cause to which European (rather than populist) standards and fashions were applied. The intelligentsia, in effect, embarked on nothing less than a complete redefinition of the Ukrainian nation through the idea of high culture. The very concept of "Ukrainianness" (*ukraïnstvo*) assumed an essentially cultural rather than a social (class/peasant) meaning. Not surprisingly, it was the modernists who uncovered a new foe, lowbrow "culture," in their national midst. In their ensuing zeal to eradicate it, they invented a hypercritical rhetoric that was reminiscent of Russia's worst detractors of Ukrainian culture. Of course, the difference between Ukrainian modernists and a man like Trubetskoi was that they understood Ukraine's impoverishment as an effect of colonialism, not as a consequence of rejecting all-Russian culture; they despised Ukraine's cultural poverty, not the culture itself. Moreover, rather than using this poverty as an excuse for associating themselves with all-Russian/imperial institutions, they treated it as an inducement to create their own exemplary counterparts.

From the 1890s, attitudes such as these not only set the stage for the literary and artistic practice of the modernists, but also became a prominent component of their polemical and theoretical arsenal. As early as 1902, they were already being berated for their cultural snobbery and disdain for the people.[31] By 1909 the Kyiv monthly *Ukraïns'ka khata*, which was thoroughly steeped in the modernist esthetic, had become the chief exemplar of this new cultural elitism.[32] The journal, essentially, had two ideological adversaries: Russian chauvinism, with its notion of an all-Russian culture, and Ukrainian

31. Cf. Serhii Iefremov, "V poiskakh novoi krasoty," *Kievskaia starina*, 1902, no. 10: 100–30; no. 11: 235–82; no. 12: 394–419.

32. Oleh S. Ilnytzkyj, "*Ukraïns'ka khata* and the Paradoxes of Ukrainian Modernism," *Journal of Ukrainian Studies* 19, no. 2 (1994): 5–30.

cultural provincialism (called Ukrainophilism or populism). On the latter issue, one of the journal's leading critics, Mykola Sribliansky (i.e., Mykyta Shapoval, 1882–1932), took the position that "popular Ukrainian culture"[33] was unfit for the intelligentsia and condemned "trade in populist-artistic goods ... [as] a serious problem for high culture" (356). This type of culture, he argued, "might satisfy people with a primitive psyche and low expectations, [but] it is definitely insufficient for others" (357). He called the culture of the masses "a sterile field, on which no living being can survive" (361). Yet despite this pessimistic and deliberately polemical assessment of his own milieu, Sribliansky invited "everyone who desires to live and create ... [to] come out into the fresh air of action, movement, work and individual creativity in the name of complexity and broad ambition; [to struggle] at the hearth of ambiguity in the name of a mysterious, deep blue *superiority*" (361). Although his words were fashionably nebulous, the expectations behind them were clear enough: the new intelligentsia was determined to pursue a culture that would end Ukraine's dependence on the culture of imperial Russia. "The governing form [of Ukrainian culture] does not satisfy a Ukrainian. Ukrainian culture [*ukraïnstvo*] itself ... excludes the possibility of a cultural existence within it. Because of this Ukrainians do not love their own culture [*ukraïnstvo*], and quietly graze on foreign fields."[34] Sribliansky was aware that continued cultural provincialism would compel Ukrainians to embrace Russian culture, which in turn would undermine Ukraine's nationhood. As a corollary, he also understood that a sophisticated culture would act as a barrier to Russification and contribute to national independence.[35]

Ukraïns'ka khata had carried disparaging remarks about Struve as early as 1909,[36] but a full-blown analysis of his positions did not appear until 1912. The author of the critique was another young critic

---

33. M. Sribliansʹkyi, "Apoteoza prymityvnii kul'turi," *Ukraïns'ka khata*, 1912, no. 6: 354. In another article, he states that the "culture of the simple folk (*prostonaroddia*)" is "useless (*nepotribna*)" to the "intelligentsia." Cf. "Z hromads'koho zhyttia," *Ukraïns'ka khata*, 1913, no. 9: 564. A few years earlier he criticized the idea that "the concept of nation has been completely equated with the Ukrainian folk, without restrictions or limitations." Cf. "Nova era," *Ukraïns'ka khata*, 1911, no. 10: 491. See also A. Tovkachevs'kyi, "Literatura i nashi 'narodnyky,'" *Ukraïns'ka khata*, 1911, no. 9: 417.

34. "Apoteoza prymityvnii kul'turi," p. 351.

35. M. Sribliansʹkyi, "Borot'ba za indyvidual'nist'," *Ukraïns'ka khata*, 1912, no. 2: 104.

36. Cf. *Ukraïns'ka khata*, 1909, no. 2: 98–100.

associated with the journal, Andrii Tovkachevsky (b. 1886), who systematically dismantled the notion of an all-Russian nationality, language, and culture in a lengthy and witty two-part article entitled "A Building on Sand, or the 'Gathering of Rus'' by Petr Struve." Tovkachevsky considered Struve's concept a farce, either "the fruit of a sick imagination or a malicious invention."[37] "A Russian [i.e., all-Russian] nation not only does not exist, but now will never exist,"[38] declared Tovkachevsky.

> In order to make the Ukrainian people part of the 'Russian nation,' the 'local characteristics' [*mestnyia osobennosti*] that Struve discovered among us must be devalued in the eyes of the people themselves as they are devalued in the eyes of those who forsake their nationality. However, the point is that this kind of devaluation is now impossible. The intelligentsia has placed before the Ukrainian nation a common goal—Ukrainian culture [*ukraïnstvo*]—and thereby has stirred to life an entire people, giving them an existence as a nation. The intelligentsia, by its own example, has taught the nation to love its own cultural values and thereby made it impossible to reject them. The [Ukrainian] intelligentsia may not have anything more in common with the people; its culture and ideals may run counter to the ideals of the masses, but it has achieved one thing: it has placed forever before the Ukrainian nation Moses's copper rod, at which [the nation] now gazes with faith, hence it cannot die.[39]

On a different occasion Tovkachevsky would elaborate: "There is something greater than the Ukrainian people, namely, Ukrainian culture [*ukraïnstvo*]... [We must] preserve our existence as a cultural and national complex. We can only be a modern nation through culture, not through ... ethnographic characteristics; not through our common roots; not through our common traditions."[40] To the argument that only all-Russian culture could satisfy the intelligentsia, Tovkachevsky had a ready response: "For me, a higher culture can only be my culture, raised to a higher level."[41] Specifically in response to Struve,

---

37. A. Tovkachevs'kyi, "Budynok na pisku, abo 'sobiraniie Rusi' Petrom Struve," *Ukraïns'ka khata*, 1912, no. 2: 126. For the development of his arguments, see pp. 124–26.

38. Ibid., p. 120.

39. Ibid., p. 120.

40. A. Tovkachevs'kyi, "Pryiateli i vorohy naroda," *Ukraïns'ka khata*, 1913, no. 2: 129, 130. See also his "Literatura i nashi 'narodnyky,'" *Ukraïns'ka khata*, 1911, no. 9: 417.

41. A. Tovkachev'skyi, "Problema kul'tury," *Ukraïns'ka khata*, 1912, no. 1: 52. Cf. also Sribliansky's words: "It is our goal; it is a joy to our soul when all of

Tovkachevsky wrote: "The desire for a higher level of culture should not necessarily go hand in hand with assimilation" (229). He noted that the Russian intelligentsia's orientation on Western Europe did not make it German or French. Similarly, when the Ukrainian intelligentsia turned to Russian culture, it would "remain the intelligentsia of its own nation; it will not become 'Russian.'" As if anticipating Trubetskoi's arguments, Tovkachevsky concluded: "To be a nationally conscious Ukrainian does not mean renouncing higher culture in general or Russian culture in particular" (230).

While Struve had portrayed the hegemony of all-Russian culture as a result of natural processes ("history has established, continues to establish, and will establish the cultural unity of the Russian tribe"),[42] Tovkachevsky depicted it as the unnatural, immoral and coercive consequence of assimilation unleashed by the power of the state.[43] Indicating the empire's history of persecuting Ukrainian cultural activities, he writes: "When 'history' is made with the hands of a butcher, we must not only *not* continue it, but are morally obliged to 'turn back that wheel of history'" (228). "What kind of culture can the Russian gendarme spread?" (231), he asks rhetorically. "You hold a living being chained hand and foot and say that he cannot walk.... Unchain him, give him freedom, and you will then see that he can not only walk, but also run" (229). Tovkachevsky was rather taken by the irony that a purportedly low and ill-fated culture like that of Ukraine should be the object of the state's harassment and Struve's ideological offensive. Tovkachevsky maintained that, contrary to Struve's fears,

---

us as a family gather around our house [i.e., Ukraine] and begin work to improve it, to catch up culturally to people who have far, far outdistanced us." Cf. "Z hromads'koho zhyttia," *Ukraïns'ka khata*, 1913, no. 9: 568.

42. Struve never allows for the possibility that his conception of Russia might be a consequence of a particular imperial sociocultural and political context. Struve's reply to his Ukrainian opponent, Bohdan Kistiakovsky (pseud. Ukrainets), who initiated the debate with the article "K voprosu o samostoiatel'noi ukrainskoi kulture" (*Russkaia mysl'*, 1911, no. 5), contained this telling passage: "I now turn to that strange statement of my opponent which affirms that the existence of the Russian nation and Russian culture, in my sense, is a product of the imagination ... of the Russsian intelligentsiia and that my view—[i.e.,] 'the hegemony of Russian culture in Russia is the fruit of our entire historical development and an entirely natural fact'—that *that* view 'arose under the influence of official Russian historical scholarship.' *I do not know what my opponent understands under that term, but it does not disturb or even interest me, for such a statement, as a matter of fact, cannot have any meaning*" ("Obshcherusskaia kul'tura i ukrainskii partikuliarizm," p. 68; emphasis added).

43. Tovkachevs'kyi, "Budynok na pisku," pp. 226–27.

Ukrainian culture could not destroy Russian culture; all it could destroy was "Mr. Struve's chimerical culture" (232).

> Struve imagines that culture is a sum of objective values used in common by Great Russians, Ukrainians and Belarusians, and hence believes that when Ukrainians walk away from the Great Russians, they will take with them their portion of culture and divide it up, as brothers divide a family inheritance when they want to live separately. But culture cannot be divided; it is within us, not outside us.... Therefore the separation of the Ukrainians from the Great Russians (if we were to assume that they now compose a single whole) cannot result in the division of culture; cannot in any way do any harm to the Great Russians; it means that Great Russian culture will remain as it was before.
>
> A new culture can emerge next to an existing culture, but this cannot do any harm to anyone.... Did Ukrainians affect the appearance of geniuses in Great Russian literature and art so strongly that without them "the Russian nation will fall into decline"? If so, then this is a promise of a great future for the Ukrainians. (232–33)

Finally, to Struve's desire that Ukrainians maintain a provincial existence, Tovkachevsky had this rejoinder:

> We Ukrainians wish to be a nation; we want to have everything our own—"from the primer to 'general pathology' and 'crystallography,' from the folk song to translations of Ovid, Goethe, Verlaine or Verhaeren"—and we will leave it to Struve and his ilk to nurture in their imagination "local characteristics" and "local culture." (235).

One could doubtless argue that in some respects this brave cultural vision is still waiting to be fully realized by the new Ukrainian state. But whatever the gaps in its implementation, there can be no doubt that, for Ukraine's elite, this vision has constituted a major agenda since the 1890s and that, as such, its results have been extremely successful.

Conclusion

I have tried to show the process whereby Russia's "grand narrative" about the Eastern Slavs as a "Russian nation" lost its power over Ukrainians and failed as a legitimizing ideology for maintaining the empire. The narrative's end came after nearly a century of Ukrainian differentiation from the imperial cultural mainstream, an evolution that, while successful in its own right, nevertheless left Ukrainian culture occupying a subordinate position in the imperial (all-Russian) system. Final emancipation from this status occurred during the modernist period, when Ukraine rediscovered itself as a distinct

European national polity, entered into conscious competition with the official culture of the empire, and set its sights on becoming an equal in esthetic and intellectual matters, as well as in social resources, functions, and rights. Ukrainian political behavior during the twentieth century has largely constituted an effort to strengthen and preserve this new cultural identity and paradigm.

I have also suggested that no similar deliverance from the all-Russian "grand narrative" occurred among the Russians, largely because it was an essential element in the construction of their identity. In fact, this unitary *cultural* conception of the Eastern Slavs allowed the Russians to sublimate, so to speak, the reality of the empire (especially with respect to Ukraine) and think of themselves as a nation-state: this explains why the disappearance of the empire has been so painful for Russians. As long as Ukrainians and Russians were conceived as one "culture," "people," "nation," or "nationality" (as opposed to, say, some kind of *political* coalition of two separate peoples), as long as it could be said that they were primordially destined for unity,[44] and as long as theirs was understood to be a single semiotic space that always signified "Russianness," the Russian identity was free to see *itself* reflected in all of eastern Slavdom and roam freely through a thousand years of history. Ukrainians were admitted to this experience primarily as members of the "Russian tribe." Obviously, the collapse of the "one nation" theory—which Ukrainian independence makes manifest—not only carries negative implications for any further political "union," but also spells problems for the old concept of a "Russian" *national* culture and identity that purportedly originated in the tenth century and took as symbols of its nationality everything from Kyiv to places such as Lviv and Ostrih. After all, it is clear that Russians have treated most of the East Slavic legacy not as a culture that *influenced* them but as a culture that they themselves authored and created.

When the Ukrainian-Russian relationship is examined as a dialogue of cultural paradigms, it reveals that the sociology and ideology of culture in the empire was far more complex than the totalizing term "Russian" admits. For Russians, the cultural experience was, generally speaking, monolithic and monolingual, inasmuch as their development was integrated into, and constituted a function of, imperial institutions. As a result, most cultural activities that occurred by way

---

44. Likhachev posits the existence of an "eastern Slavic *national* group which existed up to about the thirteenth century" (cf. *Reflections on Russia*, p. 62, n. 51).

of those institutions could be assimilated as "Russian," whether they were Great Russian or not. The aforementioned statements by Trubetskoi and Likhachev (to wit, that "the history of *Russian* painting" was inconceivable without *Ukrainian* artists, and that "no one would exclude Gogol from *Russian* literature, Kostomarov from *Russian* historiography, Potebnia from *Russian* philology ...") are thus symptomatic of this experience. The reason Trubetskoi and Likhachev do not use *imperial* (as in "the history of *imperial* painting") when writing about culture is that, unlike Ukrainians, they fail to distinguish between "Russia" and the "Russian Empire."

Russian perceptions notwithstanding, it is clear that the reading offered by these two scholars is just one way of conceiving the cultural space, communities, and processes of the empire. The conflation of "Ukrainian," "Great Russian," and "all-Russian" under the term "Russian" (and the absence of any *cultural* sense of empire) misrepresents a nationally pluralistic, diverse, and contentious (high) cultural process as a single homogeneous (Russian) one in which the Ukrainian component is denied all independent functionality or identity, except, of course, as a variant of the "(all-)Russian" or as a signifier of the "low." This approach leaves unexplained by what logic "Ukrainian painters" must become only "Russian"; why they might not, perhaps, be conceived as part of a "history of *Ukrainian* painting," or why such figures as Gogol, Kostomarov, and Potebnia might not be "included" in respective *Ukrainian* disciplines.

In short, the assimilation of imperial phenomena by Russian society as its own *national* process does not alter their social complexity in general or their significance for the Ukrainian cultural process in particular. The notion that such individuals as Gogol, Kostomarov, and Potebnia have only one, primarily "Russian," signification is patently untenable, unless, of course, one is prepared (as many were) to deny the existence of Ukrainians and a Ukrainian society, arguing instead for some single undifferentiated "Russian" cultural process for the empire. To argue thus is to ignore the fact that these individuals were products of a cross-cultural experience generally unfamiliar to ethnic Russians, but typical for members of Ukrainian society. This Ukrainian experience, as I have argued, was essentially liminal (i.e., dualistic in terms of language and institutions). Therefore, when discussing culture in the empire, it is not irrelevant to maintain, for example, that, while Karamzin, Pogodin, and Kostomarov were indeed *imperial* historians, they were hardly all "Russian" (the first two never wrote Ukrainian plays and poems, whereas the latter did, to cite just one distinguishing feature). Certainly, Gogol's "Russianness" (if that is what we wish to call it) and that of, say, Pushkin or

Dostoevsky were qualitatively different phenomena, a fact clearly obvious from, among other things, Gogol's letter of 24 December 1844 to Aleksandra Smirnova-Rosset. In response to her query about his national filiation, Gogol replies with something quite unimaginable in a letter of a (Great) Russian writer:

> Let me say a word on the issue of what kind of soul I have, Ukrainian [*khokhlatskaia*] or Russian [*russkaia*], because, as I see from your letter, this was at one time a subject of discussion and argument with others. In answer, I will tell you that *I myself do not know* what kind of soul I have, Ukrainian [*khokhlatskaia*] or Russian [*russkaia*]. I only know that in no way would I give preference [*preimushchestvo*] either to a Ukrainian [*malorossiianinu*] over a Russian [*russkomu*] or to a Russian over a Ukrainian. Both their temperaments [*prirody*] are too generously endowed by God, and, as if deliberately, each of them individually contains that which is missing in the other—a clear sign that they are meant to complement [*popolnit'*] each other. For this reason the very history of their past existence was different, so that they might cultivate the separate strengths of their character in order that, later, having merged into one, they might form something most perfect in humanity. Do not base yourself on my works and do not make use of them to come to any conclusions about me.[45]

This letter is remarkable for several reasons, not the least of which is the year of its composition. By 1844 Gogol had produced practically everything by which Russian literature would judge him great (*The Inspector General, Dead Souls,* the Petersburg tales) and on the basis of which he had been hailed by Belinsky and others as the greatest living Russian writer. Given his stature in the empire, it is noteworthy, first of all, that Gogol felt unable to declare himself a *Russian*. In fact, he seems to confess to having no identity at all, and is obviously still far from having achieved that "all-Russian" "perfection" at which he hints. It is also striking that Gogol's Ukrainian "soul"—despite all the social disadvantages under which it labored—still commanded such strong allegiance and acted as an exact counterweight to the Russian "soul" within him. Ten years earlier (December 1833), writing to Mykhailo Maksymovych and dreaming of coming to Kyiv, Gogol had displayed a keen sense of the difference between "them" (the Russians) and "us" (Ukrainians):

> Imagine, I was also thinking: go, go to Kyiv, to ancient, beautiful Kyiv. It is ours, it is not theirs, is that not so? [*On nash, on ne*

45. N. V. Gogol', *Polnoe sobranie sochinenii: Pis'ma, 1842–1845,* vol. 12 (Moscow, 1952), pp. 418–19.

> *ikh—ne pravda li?*] There, around [Kyiv], the events of our ancient history took place.... There one can recuperate one's strength.... But I am disturbed by the thought that this [trip to Ukraine] may not take place ... Not to have someone to talk to in the language of one's soul—that is frightening.[46]

Gogol's words and professional career reasonably reflect the problematic nature of identity among Ukrainians in the first half of the nineteenth century, not only with respect to its "Ukrainian" character, but, surely, also with respect to the "Russian." The construction of Gogol and other Ukrainians as "Russians" in the course of the last two centuries therefore corresponds to a unitary conception of "high" culture in the empire as exclusively "(all-) Russian." As Gogol's case attests, however, a single system of national classification, such as "Russian," is unlikely to do justice either to a person's socio-cultural identity or to explain the origins and function of creative work in such a complex society. Gogol's case shows that participation in the social structures of the empire did not automatically turn individuals into "Russians." This gives grounds not only to recognize other national processes in the empire, but also to embrace the notion of the "imperial" as a special type of cultural community and space therein.

1995, revised 1996

---

46. V. I. Shenrok, ed., *Pis'ma N. V. Gogolia,* vol. 1 (St. Petersburg, 1901), p. 268.

Yuri Shapoval

The GPU-NKVD as an Instrument of Counter-Ukrainization in the 1920s and 1930s

The incorporation of Ukraine into the Union of Soviet Socialist Republics (USSR) following its defeat in the national-liberation struggle of 1917–20 created the conditions required to reduce the country to an object of sustained terror—a terror with a well-defined direction, a certain internal logic, a set of distinct stages, and a number of consequences.

Soon after the formation of the USSR, in April 1923, the Twelfth Congress of the Russian Communist Party (Bolshevik) (RCP[B]) proclaimed a policy of indigenization (*korenizatsiia*) in the union republics. It entailed the selection, training, and promotion of cadres from the native population, consideration of the ethnic factor in the formation of the party and state apparatus, and the establishment of schools of all levels and cultural institutions employing the languages of the titular ethnic groups, as well as the publication of newspapers, journals, and books in those languages. In Ukraine, this policy came to be known as Ukrainization (*ukrainizatsiia*).

For Lenin, a sophisticated pragmatic politician, independent Ukrainian statehood was not acceptable in essence, but only in form, as a forced compromise, since Bolshevik rule in Ukraine was in practice anti-Ukrainian. Pursuant to this compromise, Lenin advocated cooperation with those political forces that seriously supported the ideals of Ukrainization. A more straightforward attitude toward the policy of indigenization in general and Ukrainization in particular was adopted by Stalin, although at the Tenth Congress of the RCP(B) in 1921 he had spoken about the future Ukrainization of Ukrainian cities and even compared them to Prague, which had been predominantly German-speaking until the 1870s, when Czech became the dominant language. Stalin's directness was dictated not only by the features of his personality as a political leader (on which researchers have usually focused), but also by the growth of Bolshevik power. As he set about creating a regime of personal dictatorship, Stalin developed an original and universally applicable political instrument that, given prevailing conditions, helped justify the inhuman policies directed against particular union republics, their leaders, their intelligentsia, and broad strata of the population. This instrument consisted in accusations of "nationalism" or "nationalist inclinations." In this connection, Mykola Skrypnyk, then Ukraine's commissar of justice, noted in his speech at the Twelfth Congress of the RCP(B): "It is considered necessary to balance any complaint about great-power chauvinism with an opposite one about the chauvinism of non-state-forming ethnic groups, and such double-entry bookkeeping is always in operation."[1]

Historians have cited numerous facts to show that Ukraine was destined to become one of the first proving grounds for Stalin's "double-entry bookkeeping." This was no accident, as it was well understood in Moscow that there could be no USSR without Ukraine. The Fourth Meeting of the RCP(B) Central Committee with "responsible workers" (*otvetstvennye rabotniki* or executive officials) from the republics and the regions, which took place in Moscow from 9 to 12 June 1923, made this clearly apparent. Its agenda included a report by the Central Control Commission on the case of a former member of the People's Commissariat for Nationality Affairs, Mirsaid Sultan-Galiev, and the content and destiny of the policy of indigenization were essentially determined there. It was on this occasion that Stalin referred to Ukraine as the "second weak spot of Soviet power" (i.e., after Turkestan), and called for turning it into a "showcase republic."[2] At the same time, he criticized Skrypnyk for "obscuring" the danger of local nationalism and characterized the chairman of the Council of People's Commissars of Ukraine, Khristian Rakovsky, as a proponent of confederacy.[3]

Stalin simultaneously expressed his support for the secretary of the Communist Party (Bolshevik) of Ukraine (CP[B]U), Dmytro Manuilsky, who proclaimed that the decisions of the Twelfth Congress on the national question had "unleashed the national element" and become "something of a Magna Carta of liberties for communists of the nationalities oppressed by the former Russian Empire…."[4] He called upon communists from the borderlands of the USSR to "combat their own nationalisms," leaving it "to the Russian comrades to fight Russian nationalism."[5]

---

1. *XII s"ezd RKP(b)—17–25 aprelia 1923 g.: Stenograficheskii otchet* (Moscow, 1968), p. 528.

2. *IV soveshchanie TsK RKP s otvetstvennymi rabotnikami natsional'nykh respublik i oblastei v Moskve, 9–12 iiunia 1923 g.: Stenograficheskii otchet* (Moscow, 1923), p. 224.

3. Ibid., pp. 227, 233–34.

4. Ibid., p. 43.

5. Ibid., pp. 44–45.

It was precisely those "Russian comrades" from the Main Political Administration (GPU) of the USSR, however, who fabricated the "case of Sultan-Galiev" in the spring of 1923. He was accused of having created a nationalist organization that spoke out against the party and state leadership with regard to the national question.[6] In pressing for a denunciation of Sultan-Galiev, Stalin sent a signal to the local leaders concerning his attitude to the policy of indigenization, which in practice could mean nothing other than "de-Russification," and thus a strengthening of the tendency toward decentralization.

By sending this signal, Stalin basically gave local GPU units complete freedom of action in their efforts to counteract the policy of indigenization. Understandably enough, Skrypnyk expressed alarm on this occasion, since he had long been associated with the Central Committee and was aware of its vast experience in fighting "nationalist counterrevolution." He regarded the very placement of Sultan-Galiev's case on the agenda of the Fourth Council as foreshadowing a change in party policy.[7] On the basis of previously inaccessible documents and materials, it can now be shown that the GPU played an active and specific role in bringing about such a change in nationalities policy and in creating an unattractive image of indigenization (and hence of Ukrainization).

Describing the events of the 1920s, Andreas Kappeler remarks that "national-communist tendencies within the Ukrainian party were bound to generate suspicion in Moscow sooner or later."[8] That was indeed the case, and we may add that this suspicion was gradually and deliberately planted by the Cheka and the GPU. They zealously investigated all prominent members of the CP(B)U who had been active in civic affairs or had belonged to other political parties or movements. This applied particularly to former Borotbists (members of the left-wing faction of the Ukrainian Party of Socialist Revolutionaries), who accounted for a large number of cadres in the cultural sphere and through whose efforts the policy of Ukrainization was being implemented.

One of the Borotbists, Oleksander Shumsky, served in 1924–27 as people's commissar of education of the Ukrainian SSR. With the concurrence of the then general secretary of the CP(B)U, Lazar Kaganovich, Shumsky was identified as the leader of the "nationally

---

6. "O tak nazyvaemoi 'sultan-galievskoi kontrrevoliutsionnoi organizatsii,'" *Izvestiia TsK KPSS*, 1990, no. 10: 79.

7. *IV soveshchanie*, p. 71.

8. A. Kappeler, *Kleine Geschichte der Ukraine* (Munich, 1994), p. 196.

inclined" cadres. To be sure, there was a personality conflict between Kaganovich and Shumsky, but let us also recall that in the autumn of 1925 Shumsky had a meeting with Stalin. Thanks to the previously unknown testimony of a participant in that conversation, we are now aware that in the course of it, Shumsky stated that "the Central Committee of the CP(B)U is supposed to control and oversee the national and cultural processes ... in Ukraine, but Moscow kept sending cadres that did not understand Ukraine's national issues."[9] Another key remark was that "the Ukrainian communists are mature and capable of electing their party and government leaders themselves."[10] These were the very demands—not to send bureaucrats from the "center" who had no knowledge of conditions in Ukraine and to allow Ukrainian politicians to choose their own leaders—that the Stalin regime was not prepared to grant.

In my opinion, several stages may be distinguished in the growth of GPU-NKVD resistance to Ukrainization. The first stage is associated with the return of several prominent Ukrainian émigrés following the proclamation of the policy of indigenization (Mykhailo Hrushevsky, the former chairman of the Central Rada and a leading historian, returned to Ukraine in March 1924). This stage was also marked by a large-scale campaign of brutal criticism launched in the mid-1920s against the above-mentioned Oleksander Shumsky, the writer Mykola Khvylovy, and the economist Mykhailo Volobuiev. Gradually the campaign against them grew into a wave of terror against the intelligentsia—but that would come later. At this time, the GPU of Ukraine was dutifully collecting all the necessary information (including informers' reports) about those who were soon to be persecuted.

On 26 June 1925, at a closed meeting of the Politburo of the Central Committee of the CP(B)U, the Chairman of the GPU of Ukraine, Vsevolod Balitsky,[11] reported on the work of his organization. Following his report, a resolution was adopted calling for the material strengthening of the GPU and the provision of additional funds for "informational and anti-sabotage activity."[12] Balitsky

---

9. State Archives of the Security Service of Ukraine (henceforth SBU State Archives), case 59881 FP, t. 118, l. 30.

10. Ibid.

11. The first biographical sketch of Balitsky was prepared by the present author, together with Vadym Zolotariov. See V. A. Zolotar'ov and Yu. I. Shapoval, "V. A. Balyts'kyi: Na shliakhu do pravdy pro n'oho," *Ukraïns'kyi istorychnyi zhurnal*, 1993, no. 3: 50–63; no. 7–8: 53–69.

12. Central State Archive of Civic Organizations of Ukraine (TsDAHOU), f. op. 16, case 1, l. 178.

exploited the situation to draw the leader's attention once again to the question of the Ukrainian intelligentsia. The reaction was exactly the one that the GPU had hoped for: "To create a commission consisting of Kaganovich, [Vlas] Chubar, Shumsky, [Hryhorii] Hrynko, and Balitsky to study the question of the Ukrainian intelligentsia, our tactics concerning it, especially the Academy and Hrushevsky, for drawing them into our work, and so forth."[13]

On 22 February 1926, the Politburo returned to the question of the "attitudes of the Ukrainian intelligentsia." Balitsky was among the speakers, and it was the materials he provided that decided the nature of the resolution adopted: "To consider it necessary to embark upon a course of decisive struggle against right-wing groupings in the midst of the Ukrainian intelligentsia. To assign Comrade Balitsky to report in a month on further initiatives for subverting right-wing groupings within the Ukrainian intelligentsia."[14]

Stalin became personally involved in these events; notably, on 22 April 1926, he wrote a letter "To Comrade Kaganovich and Other Members of the Central Committee of the CP(B)U" in which he effectively gave his blessing for a merciless struggle against the "nationally inclined" cadres. In essence, this was another signal meant to intensify measures against the policy of Ukrainization.

It was precisely in 1926, deep inside the GPU, that there appeared several extremely important and strictly classified documents that throw light on the true meaning of this institution's actions with regard to Ukrainization. Let us first examine two letters: "About the Ukrainian Citizenry," dated 30 March 1926, and "On Ukrainian Separatism," dated 4 September 1926. Both were prepared in the Secret Division of the GPU, which played a key role in that body's attempts to provide the party and state leadership with information concerning tendencies in the sphere of nationality relations.[15] The GPU leadership made use of such documents to instruct its local units concerning the "essence, history, and tactics of Ukrainian separatism" and to give them concrete assignments. Noting that the "new course of nationalities policy" after the Twelfth Congress of the RCP(B) had rendered impossible the continuation of armed resistance to Bolshevik

13. Ibid., case 14, l. 121^{v}.

14. Ibid., case 2, l. 136.

15. It is worth noting that there was not a single ethnic Ukrainian among the heads of the Secret Division (*sekretnyi viddil*), which was known from 1932 as the Secret Political Division (*sekretno-politychnyi viddil*). Of the nine individuals who occupied that post, seven were Jews, one a Russian, and one an Armenian.

power, these documents focused on assertions that the Ukrainian nationalists had shifted their efforts to the "cultural front," exploiting legally sanctioned means of resisting Bolshevik power. These documents noted in straightforward fashion that Ukrainization was "being used to rally supporters of nationalist ideas in all vital parts of the state organism."[16]

They also singled out the principal agents of Ukrainian nationalism: the Ukrainian Autocephalous Orthodox Church, the All-Ukrainian Academy of Sciences and, generally speaking, the whole cultural sphere, especially literature. These and other documents offer compelling evidence that from the very beginning, contrary to all official declarations, the GPU viewed Ukrainization with suspicion and hostility and set about collecting material to be used against its active supporters. Among the key tasks of the GPU organs, particular attention was given to the following:

"the identification of right-wing groupings, their activities and ties with other circles of the Ukrainian citizenry";

"not limiting oneself to mere observation of all strata of Ukrainian citizenry, but carrying on active intelligence work among prominent representatives of anti-Soviet Ukrainian trends";

"linking work on the Ukrainian intelligentsia with work in the countryside";

"the identification of current attitudes among the Ukrainian citizenry with regard to our internal and international political life."[17]

I have had the opportunity to familiarize myself in detail with many documents that testify to the consistent execution of these tasks. For instance, there is a unique series of GPU materials that throw light on the surveillance of Mykhailo Hrushevsky. The very fact that the famous scholar was registered as "subversive" as early as 20 July 1924, soon after his return to Ukraine, and subjected to close surveillance from the very moment of his return, is noteworthy. From that time on, for the whole decade up to his death, he was under constant surveillance, and the circle of his close acquaintances was infiltrated by a large number of secret informers who reported in detail about his attitudes, conversations, intentions, political sympathies and antipathies, as well as his personal relationships with other prominent persons. On 6 November 1926, the Secret Division of the GPU, noting the decisions of the GPU leadership, suggested that those in charge of

---

16. SBU State Archives, collection of directive documents.
17. Ibid.

intelligence take Hrushevsky under "external supervision."[18] This was done, and the academician was then referred to in the surveillance reports as "the Elder" (*Starets'*).

The *Chekisty* stressed in particular the reasons for Hrushevsky's return to Ukraine. They scrupulously recorded his critical remarks concerning the Bolshevik regime and his plans for promoting the development of scholarship and culture in Ukraine. These reports concluded that the academician was playing a "double game," hoping to exploit Ukrainization for the execution of his own "nationalist" plans. For example, on 1 November 1926, the secret informer who used the pseudonym "Tychyna" reported: "I met Hrushevsky at his home, where we had the following conversation. I asked Hrushevsky about Ukraine's future. 'Ukraine,' Hrushevsky replied, 'is more precious to me than anything else, and perhaps this is why I, an old man, can survey the life of Ukraine from a historical viewpoint. This is where I differ from the communists.... We would be able to combat Russia once all Ukrainian forces were united.'"[19]

As early as January 1927, there was a report alleging that Hrushevsky had created a "hostile political organization" at the Historical Section of the All-Ukrainian Academy of Sciences, gathering around himself the "active 'lads' from Ukrainian counterrevolutionary circles."[20]

In similar fashion, the GPU investigated and gradually articulated the "counterrevolutionary nature" of other prominent figures who were hoping to exploit Ukrainization in order to strengthen Ukraine's scholarly and cultural potential. In particular, the reports about Hrushevsky mention a great many individuals whom the GPU would soon begin to "organize" into the "Union for the Liberation of Ukraine" (SVU) and the "Ukrainian National Center" (UNTs) and involve in other cases brought forward in the late 1920s and early 1930s.

It was at this point, as George Liber has emphasized, that the communist regime truly sensed the undesirable consequences of Ukrainization for its nationalities policy and began the second stage of GPU action.[21] This is supported, inter alia, by statistical data from those years concerning the number of educational institutions with instruction in Ukrainian, Ukrainian-language book publishing, and

---

18. SBU State Archives; M. S. Hrushevsky documentary collection (vol. 2, 1. 212).

19. Ibid. (vol. 2, 1. 200).

20. Ibid. (vol. 2, 1. 312).

21. George O. Liber, *Soviet Nationality Policy, Urban Growth, and Identity Change in the Ukrainian SSR, 1923–1934* (Cambridge, 1992), p. 133.

even the increase in the numbers of Ukrainians within the party and state apparatuses.

Other factors should also be taken into account. Stalin's "great turn" (*bol'shoi perelom*, meaning accelerated industrialization and forced collectivization) constituted such an abrupt change of course that it could not help but arouse dissatisfaction and resistance among the broadest social strata. Such opposition arose within the Bolshevik Party itself, even among its leaders. Documents and facts attest that the retreat from the New Economic Policy, which had been proclaimed in 1921, brought about a situation comparable to civil war in the countryside. Let us illustrate this thesis with some excerpts from GPU reports on the course of collectivization in Ukraine in early 1930.

In his report on the political status of the Ukrainian peasantry in connection with the "liquidation of the kulaks as a class" for the period from 20 January to 12 February 1930, Balitsky reported that in January 1930 there were 37 cases of mass unrest among the peasants, in which 12,000 people had participated. By 9 February 1930, 11,865 persons had been arrested, and 40 terrorist acts had been committed by peasants in response to the policy of "dekulakization."[22]

Balitsky personally headed the "operational headquarters" in charge of combating peasant resistance. On 16 March 1930, he reported to Stanislav Kosior, Genrikh Iagoda, and Efim Evdokimov:

> Arrived in Tulchyn *okruha*[23] yesterday. The entire *okruha* is overcome with unrest and uprisings.
>
> Of the *okruha*'s 17 districts, 15 are stricken. At present there is unrest in 153 villages. Soviet power has been completely driven out of 50 villages.
>
> In some villages they come out under SVU slogans, making statements to the effect that "Iefremov is on trial, but [illegible] lives...."
>
> In some villages there has been armed unrest. Trenches have been dug and occupied by armed men who do not let anyone into the villages.
>
> In some villages they sing "Ukraine Has Not Yet Died," and one hears the slogans "Down with Soviet power. Long live independent Ukraine ..."
>
> The entire *okruha* is divided into operational sectors; each of them has been assigned armed detachments of communists and

---

22. Andrea Graziosi, "Collectivisation, révoltes paysannes et politiques gouvernementales," *Cahiers du monde russe*, 1994, no. 3: 480–81.

23. *Okruha* (Russ. *okrug*), district. In 1927, Ukraine had 26 *okruhy*; their number fluctuated in subsequent years.

> mounted armed groups from the GPU. Orders have been given resolutely to suppress the unrest.
>
> I am also staying to perform operational leadership duties.[24]

These are only a few sample descriptions of the war waged by the regime against the peasantry. It comes as no surprise, then, that Stalin's line was criticized not only by Nikolai Bukharin and his followers, but also by numerous rank-and-file party members, creating an unstable situation for the regime. In Moscow, the opinion was gaining ground that these internal difficulties, together with a series of crises in foreign relations, were weakening the position of the USSR and favoring the activization of "counterrevolutionary," "wrecking" (*vreditel'skie*), and, in particular, "nationalist" forces. The GPU leaders considered that the policy of indigenization (and hence Ukrainization) was largely responsible for these sinister developments. Not surprisingly, a decision was made in the late 1920s to conduct a series of open political trials with the goal of condemning the "nationalists." These were to involve individuals who were already under clandestine surveillance, some of whom found themselves in the dock at the Kharkiv opera house, where the SVU trial was held from 19 April to 19 September 1930. There were forty-five defendants, among them two members of the All-Ukrainian Academy of Sciences, fifteen university professors, two university students, a secondary-school principal, ten schoolteachers, a theologian, a priest of the Ukrainian Autocephalous Orthodox Church, three writers, five editors, two cooperative members, two proofreaders, and a librarian. Fifteen of the accused worked in the All-Ukrainian Academy of Sciences, 31 were former members of various Ukrainian political parties, one of them was the prime minister of the Ukrainian People's Republic (UNR), two had been ministers of the UNR, and six had been members of the Ukrainian Central Rada. There were two Jews and three women among the accused.

The trial became something of an appeal for an offensive against the forces of the Ukrainian national renaissance, personified by representatives of the older intelligentsia, especially from academe, as well as activists of the Ukrainian Autocephalous Orthodox Church. By no coincidence, the words repeated during the interrogations by the investigator Solomon Bruk, as recalled by one of those on trial, were: "We must bring the Ukrainian intelligentsia to its knees; this is our task and it shall be fulfilled; those whom we cannot bring to their

24. Graziosi, "Collectivisation, révoltes paysannes et politiques gouvernementales," pp. 549–50.

knees we will shoot!"[25] The SVU trial thus became the tragic inception of not only the physical but also the moral destruction of those intellectual strata through whose efforts the policy of Ukrainization could potentially have advanced the self-assertion of Ukrainians as a people and Ukraine as a state. This is evidenced by an editorial in an issue of the journal *Bil'shovyk Ukraïny* for 1930, which read: "At the SVU trial the Ukrainian proletarian government is not only considering the case of the counterrevolutionary aspirations of the Petliurites, but also making a retrospective historical judgment on Ukrainian nationalism as a whole, the nationalist parties, their policy of treason, and their unworthy ideas of bourgeois independence and sovereignty for Ukraine."[26]

Indeed, the organizers had conceived this trial less as an indictment of specific persons than of a whole period of the Ukrainian people's struggle for national liberation. The individuals selected by the GPU were meant to symbolize this period, its philosophy and outlook.

The above-mentioned 45 individuals were the main dramatis personae at the SVU trial. However, 700 more (not 400, as was believed earlier) were soon arrested in connection with the trial.[27] Altogether, according to some estimates, in the course of the SVU trial and soon thereafter, more than 30,000 individuals were arrested, killed, or exiled.

It all began with the arrest between 18 May and 18 June 1929, in Kyiv, of a number of young people charged with participating in an illegal organization. Some of them had been collaborating with the GPU since 1928, entering into contact with "nationalistically inclined" persons and reporting on them. The testimony of these individuals was used to break down the students Mykola Pavlushkov and Borys Matushevsky and force them to testify against the vice-president of the All-Ukrainian Academy of Sciences, the prominent literary scholar Serhii Iefremov, and other future participants in the SVU trial.

In December 1929 the preparation of the SVU trial under joint party and Cheka supervision entered a decisive phase. The GPU produced a series of documents covering all matters associated with the SVU in

---

25. H. Sniehir'ov, *Naboï dlia rozstrilu (Nen'ko moia, nen'ko...): Liryko-publitsystychna rozvidka* (Kyiv, 1990), p. 110.

26. "Ukraïns'ka kontrrevoliutsiia pered proletars'kym sudom," *Bil'shovyk Ukraïny*, 1930, nos. 5–6: 9.

27. SBU State Archives, case 67098 FP, t. 238, "Dokladnaia zapiska o rezul'tatakh raboty po vskrytiiu ukrainskogo kontrrevoliutsionnogo podpol'ia v sviazi s delom SVU," l. 1.

great detail. These documents (to be discussed below) were sent to the Central Committee of the CP(B)U, the Central Committee of the All-Union Communist Party (Bolshevik) (VKP[B]), and the United State Political Directorate (OGPU) of the USSR. Stalin acquainted himself with them and sent the following coded telegram (*shyfrohrama*) to Stanislav Kosior and Vlas Chubar: "When is the trial of Iefremov and others supposed to take place? Here we think that the trial should concentrate not only on the medical tricks intended to kill responsible officials.... Our request is that the plan of carrying the case through trial be coordinated with Moscow."[28]

All the details of the SVU trial were duly coordinated with the Moscow leadership, even though the Ukrainian GPU proposed its own "dramaturgy" of the trial. This "dramaturgy" was contained in the above-mentioned documents, most of them signed by the head of the Secret Division of the Ukrainian GPU, Valerii Gorozhanin, and the head of the Second Department of the Secret Division, Boris Kozelsky, who may be considered the "principal conductors" of the SVU trial and many other cases.[29]

---

28. Quoted from T. Zamiatina, "Iosif Stalin: 'Vinovnykh sudit' uskorenno. Prigovor—rasstrel'. Rassekrechen lichnyi arkhiv vozhdia narodov," *Izvestiia*, 11 June 1992.

29. Since historical studies do not contain information about these persons, I offer the following brief biographical sketches:

Valerii Mikhailovich Gorozhanin (actual surname Kudelsky), born in 1889 into a Jewish family in the town of Akkerman, Bessarabia gubernia (now Bilhorod-Dnistrovskyi, Odesa oblast). He enrolled in the Law Faculty of Novorossiisk University in Odesa in 1909, but was expelled in 1912 for being a member of the Socialist Revolutionary Party. After the February 1917 revolution he sought to reenter the university, but was barred because of his political activities. By then he was a member of the Borotbist Party, and in 1919 he joined the CP(B)U. From 1907 to 1914 he was engaged in underground political activities in Odesa and Bessarabia. He made a trip to France, where he wrote a pamphlet entitled *Anatole France and the Vatican.* October 1917 found him in Odesa as a contributor to the newspaper *Golos revoliutsii,* using the pen name Gorozhanin ("city dweller"). In May 1919 he began working for the Cheka and served as a special investigator for particularly important cases in the Odesa gubernia Cheka. He served in 1920–21 as head of the investigative and operations division and a member of the collegium of the Mykolaiv gubernia Cheka, in 1921–22 as head of the Secret Division of the GPU of the Ukrainian SSR, in 1923 as head of the secret-operations section of the Right-Bank Ukraine division of the GPU, and in 1923–24 as an assistant to the head of the Kyiv gubernia division of the GPU. At that time he was directly involved in the fabrication of the "Kyiv Regional Action Center." On 23 May 1924, he was appointed head of the Secret Division of the GPU of the Ukrainian SSR, and in 1930, after conducting the SVU trial, he was sent to serve in the Moscow apparatus of the GPU. Until 21 May

The most important documents are a lengthy "Report on the Results of Work on Uncovering the Ukrainian Counterrevolutionary Underground throughout Ukraine in Conjunction with the SVU Case," a "Memorandum on the Case of the Odesa Branch of the SVU," a "Report on the Activities of the Medical Line of the SVU," and a "Tentative List of Those Arrested in Kyiv to Be Presented at the Trial." I have also managed to locate several other documents never before analyzed by researchers. In these documents we find a systematic presentation of a number of "lines" of "SVU activity" that were later mentioned at the trial, as well as those discarded because the Cheka was unable to make them appear truly dangerous. In this regard, the above-mentioned "Tentative List" is of particular interest, as is a document entitled "Candidates for Trial from the Periphery." He we find not only the surnames of individuals who later found themselves among the accused at the trial, but also those "circumstantially involved" who were being "prepared for trial." The handwritten corrections on these documents deserve particular attention. For instance, the "Tentative List" includes among the members of the "Presidium of the SVU" the writer Liudmyla Starytska-Cherniakhivska and the academician Mykhailo Slabchenko, who would later be accorded the more modest role of leader of the Odesa branch.[30] Next to the names of the four candidates for the "church line," there is an addition in a firm hand: "A number of

---

1935 he was an assistant to the head of the Foreign Division of the Chief Administration of State Security of the all-Union People's Commissariat of Internal Affairs (NKVD), then a second deputy head of the same department. From November 1935 he was a major (senior grade) of state security, then deputy head of the Special Bureau of the all-Union NKVD. Dismissed from the state security organs on 21 November 1937, he was shot in the same year.

Boris Vladimirovich Kozelsky (actual name Bernard Volfovich Golovanievsky), born in May 1902 into a Jewish family in the town of Proskuriv (now Khmelnytskyi). Graduated in 1919 from the School of Commerce in Kyiv, working for some time as a proofreader. At the end of 1919 he became a member of the Bolshevik Party, but as early as 1921 he was dismissed by the purge commission as a "passive member." Admitted in 1928 to a party cell of the GPU of the Ukrainian SSR as a candidate for party membership. Began working in the Cheka apparatus in 1921; head of the Second Department, Secret Division, GPU of the Ukrainian SSR from 1927; assistant to the head of the Secret Division, GPU of the Ukrainian SSR, from 1930; head of the Secret Political Division, State Security Division, NKVD of the Ukrainian SSR from 1934. Shot himself on 2 January 1936; charged posthumously with having created a "Trotskyite organization" within the NKVD.

30. SBU State Archives, case 67098 FP, t. 238, "Orientirovochnyi spisok arestovannykh po Kievu, podlezhashchikh predstavleniiu na protsess," l. 1.

persons from the periphery will be taken."[31] The list of "Candidates for Trial from the Periphery" includes plus signs next to some names and minus signs next to others. In the case of the schoolteacher Z. M. Hudz-Zasulsky, for example, the plus sign is changed to a minus. I believe that these notes were made by Balitsky himself, who read these documents carefully and made notes on others.

What are the most striking features of these documents? First of all, they do not contain a single mention of a specific criminal act committed by the persons accused of participating in the SVU. Paradoxical though it may seem, this is nevertheless the case. The documents mention certain "criminal" intentions, conversations, and some strange plans for "mutiny," but not a single specific act.

Another characteristic feature of the documents prepared at the GPU of Ukraine at the end of 1929 is their relentless anti-Ukrainianism. These documents lead one to conclude that the fabrication of the SVU case and the preparation of the public trial of those involved in it constituted a decisive step toward the implementation not only of physical but also of moral terror against everything Ukrainian, and toward the active discrediting of the policy of Ukrainization. Anything and everything Ukrainian appears in these documents as "Petliurite," "nationalistic," "wrecking," and so on.

The above-mentioned report ("Dokladnaia zapiska") is telling in this respect. This lengthy document describes the results of the GPU's work in the *okruha* centers of Ukraine and shows convincingly that the organizers of the SVU case directed their attack mainly against the Ukrainian intelligentsia, and not only its older generation at that.

Thus, in the Vinnytsia area, all unofficial circles and organizations, such as Ukrainian language-study groups, were classified as "nationalistic."[32] Even in the Luhansk area the GPU uncovered a "counterrevolutionary chauvinistic group" consisting, naturally, of teachers of the Ukrainian language who had organized a "circle of Ukrainizers." The report notes that "the group's goal was to organize Ukrainian chauvinists and influence schoolteachers and students."[33]

Academician Slabchenko was charged with organizing a group of "future young Ukrainian professors" who, once again, were accused of "chauvinistic work."[34]

---

31. Ibid., l. 2.

32. See n. 27 above. "Dokladnaia zapiska," l. 57.

33. Ibid., l. 60.

34. Ibid., l. 4.

The question arises: who exactly was determining the levels of "chauvinism" and "nationalism"? Was it the poorly educated GPU investigators, to whom the Ukrainian environment and Ukrainian culture were alien in principle? For them, anything Ukrainian automatically became "nationalistic," and they knew beyond a doubt that they were making no mistake, since this was precisely what their bosses expected of them.

A reading of these and many other documents related to the SVU case leads one to conclude that this trial was designed as the decisive step toward discrediting the policy of Ukrainization, which, notably, the personnel of the GPU of the Ukrainian SSR never considered serious or lasting. Thus, in preparing the SVU case, the Cheka was laying the foundations, as it were, for the subsequent utterly pogromist anti-Ukrainian actions initiated on a mass scale in 1932–33.

Another characteristic feature of these documents is the attempt to discredit completely the Ukrainian Autocephalous Orthodox Church (UAPTs) and prepare the ground for its destruction. Indeed, one of the above-mentioned documents detailed the exact charges that were to be laid against the UAPTs clergy. The principal charge was the "atheism of most of the autocephalous clergy," although this again raises the question: who was to decide the extent of that atheism, using what criteria? This was followed by charges of the "Petliurite past of most autocephalous believers," the SVU's use of the UAPTs as a "tool of anti-Soviet influence for the purpose of conducting underground work among the broad masses," and "the Ukrainization of the church and of religion as a means of carrying out the SVU's goals."[35]

The GPU personnel made a tremendous effort to "decipher" all these goals. In his article "The Case of the Ukrainian Autocephalous Orthodox Church at the Trial of the Union for the Liberation of Ukraine and Its Liquidation in 1930," Osyp Zinkevych advances the hypothesis that as the GPU investigators were unable to obtain concessions during the pre-trial investigation from two UAPTs activists, the brothers Volodymyr and Mykola Chekhivsky, they decided to convoke an "extraordinary council" of the UAPTs on 28–29 January 1930.[36] Let us remember that this "council," called on the eve of the SVU trial, passed a resolution on the ties of the UAPTs with the SVU, on the "counterrevolutionary nature" of the UAPTs and,

35. Ibid., "Dokladnaia zapiska GPU USSR V. A. Balitskomu," l. 8.

36. O. Zinkevych, "Sprava Ukraïns'koï Avtokefal'noï Pravoslavnoï Tserkvy na protsesi Spilky vyzvolennia Ukraïny i ïi likvidatsiia u 1930 r.," *Suchasnist'*, 1988, nos. 7–8: 219.

naturally, on its liquidation. However, documents previously inaccessible to Zinkevych and other researchers show that as early as 1929, prior to the convocation of the "council," the Chekhivsky brothers had already begun providing testimony required by the GPU after they had been "worked on." The "council" itself was thus an event planned by the GPU of Ukraine in order to document the "bankruptcy" of the UAPTs.

In his analysis of the political goals of the SVU trial, Gerhard Simon notes that it is very difficult to tell which elements of the accusations "corresponded to reality and what existed only in the minds of the GPU personnel."[37] On the basis of the GPU documents with which I have had the opportunity to work, I can assert that the SVU as described in 1929–30 did not exist. This phantom "organization" was fabricated and ably exploited for counter-Ukrainization purposes, as was the "Ukrainian National Center" (the verdict on which was pronounced at a closed trial in February 1932), into which, among others, the academicians Mykhailo Hrushevsky and Matvii Iavorsky were dragged, and which turned into a veritable witch hunt against persons born in Galicia.

The third and decisive stage of these measures was begun by the GPU in late 1932 and early 1933, when Stalin made the final decision to put an end to Ukrainization. The removal of Oleksander Shumsky in February 1927 from the post of people's commissar of education (effectively in charge of the spheres of culture, ideology and inter-ethnic relations) had not led to complete Russification. Mykola Skrypnyk, a firm believer in the possibility of a synthesis of communist internationalism with a national revival, served as people's commissar of education from 1927 to 1933 and actively defended Ukrainian culture. The forced collectivization of agriculture and the suppression of critical thinking among communists, the crystallization of the structures of power and repression against the background of the deteriorating socio-economic situation and the outbreak of the famine—all these were linked by the Stalinist leadership with a new offensive against "nationalism."

On 14 December 1932, together with Viacheslav Molotov, Stalin signed a resolution of the Central Committee of the VKP(B) and the Council of People's Commissars of the USSR on the conduct of the bread-requisitioning campaign. Along with other issues, this document stressed the need for the "correct conduct of Ukrainization"

37. G. Simon, *Nationalismus und Nationalpolitik in der Sowjetunion: Von der totalitären Diktatur zur nachstalinschen Gesellschaft* (Baden-Baden, 1986), p. 99.

within Ukraine and beyond its borders (in regions of compact Ukrainian settlement), which essentially signified the termination of the policy. On 15 December 1932, Stalin and Molotov signed a directive telegram similar in content.[38] A resolution of the Central Committee of the VKP(B) adopted on 24 January provided for the replacement of cadres in Ukraine. In accordance with it, Postyshev returned to Ukraine as second secretary of the Central Committee of the CP(B)U: it was he whom Stalin had entrusted with the mission of destroying the Ukrainian national renaissance. The suicides of Khvylovy in May and of Skrypnyk in June 1933 symbolized the end of that renaissance. At a joint plenary session of the Central Committee and the Central Control Commission of the CP(B)U in November 1933, a resolution was adopted stating unequivocally that "at the present moment the principal danger is local Ukrainian nationalism, which is uniting with imperialist interventionists" (i.e., with the West).[39] This "present moment," which continued for several years, meant the destruction of Ukraine's intellectual resources; of its writers, artists, and politicians who had believed in "Ukrainization," as well as a pogrom of the educational and scholarly research system. The political and ideological supervision of this process was in the hands of Postyshev (as well as Stanislav Kosior, Nikolai Popov, Andrii Khvylia, and others), and its material base, so to speak, was provided by the boss of the GPU-NKVD, Vsevolod Balitsky. The cases that were fabricated included those of the "Ukrainian Military Organization" (UVO), the "Union of Ukrainian Nationalists" (OUN), the "Counterrevolutionary Borotbist Organization," the "Bloc of Ukrainian Nationalist Parties," the "Polish Military Organization" (POW), and so on.

At this time, the "explosive material" accumulated for years by the GPU and later by the NKVD was most effectively employed against many individuals, above all the Ukrainian intellectuals who began actively "Ukrainizing" the Solovets Islands, Siberia, and Central Asia in 1933–34. The fates of the "nationalistically inclined" Oleksander Shumsky and Mykhailo Volobuiev, among others, proved dramatic,[40] as did those of many others who had striven to implement the policy of Ukrainization. Postyshev reported that between January and November 1933, "more than 2,000 nationalist elements [were driven

---

38. TsDAHOU, f. 1, op. 1, case 2038, l. 6.

39. *Chervonyi shliakh*, 1933, nos. 8–9: 267–68.

40. See my book *Liudyna i systema: Shtrykhy do portretu totalitarnoï doby v Ukraïni* (Kyiv, 1994), pp. 134–67.

out] of the system of the People's Commissariat of Education, as were more than 200 persons occupying scholarly and editorial posts. Within eight central Soviet institutions alone, we have expelled more than 200 nationalists and White Guardists who occupied the posts of department and sector heads, etc."[41]

During 1933 alone, 100 percent of the leadership of the oblast boards of people's education and 90 percent of that of the district boards was replaced, and all were subjected to some form of repression. Four thousand schoolteachers were dismissed from secondary schools throughout Ukraine as "hostile class elements," even as Russian schools and classes increased in number. Of the 29 directors of pedagogical institutes, 18 were dismissed, as were 210 lecturers.[42]

The new people's commissar of education, Volodymyr Zatonsky, noted in November 1933: "Next year as well, we shall have to train no less than 9,000 schoolteachers in short-term courses, since cultural needs are increasing at such a rate, especially in the schools, that institutes and technical schools cannot supply us with sufficient teacher cadres. Thus we are forced to use surrogates. Moreover, in addition to the need to increase the cadres of schoolteachers at a swift rate, the cadres that we do have are deteriorating. Some of them die, others we expel ourselves, and some are taken by the GPU."[43]

According to the new people's commissar of education, "hostile class elements" among the schoolteachers constituted 9.5 percent of their total number.[44] And these were "teachers who themselves write in questionnaires that they are children of kulaks, or kulaks themselves, or priests, or Petliurites.... The shortage of pedagogical cadres does not allow us to frame the questions in such terms that if you are descended either from the kulaks or from the clergy, we shall dismiss you."[45]

The campaign was not limited to the educational sphere. In 1933, a new Ukrainian orthography was adopted (replacing the one approved in 1928); this was accompanied by a purge of nationalists at the Institute of Scholarly Terminology of the All-Ukrainian Academy of Sciences. In general, the Academy suffered greatly, for Skrypnyk was the secretary of its communist faction, as did the All-Ukrainian

---

41. Ibid., p. 188.
42. Ibid., p. 189.
43. Ibid.
44. Ibid.
45. Ibid.

Association of Marxist-Leninist Institutes (VUAMLIN), which he headed for a time. On 14 January 1934, Postyshev made a speech at a gathering of the VUAMLIN party organization in which he called for the "cleansing" of all scholarly "fronts" (i.e., philosophy, economics, etc.) of representatives of "Ukrainian national-fascism." And that "cleansing" was actively carried out.

At that time, for purposes of "uncovering" "Ukrainian nationalists," the GPU of Ukraine employed a number of provocateurs, of whom the most notable were the director of the Rukh publishing house and chairman of the board of the Ukrainian Soviet Encyclopedia, Antin Bilenky-Berezynsky, and the well-known philosopher Volodymyr Iurynets. They were recruited as informants, and their reports led to the destruction of many Ukrainian intellectuals, among them Mykola Kulish, Hryhorii Epik, Iuliian Bachynsky, and Oleksa Slisarenko.

The work of the GPU-NKVD had its consequences: through a series of special political resolutions adopted between 1933 and 1940, Ukrainization and indigenization were completely eliminated. From January 1938, the person in charge of this process was Nikita Khrushchev, who became head of the Central Committee of the CP(B)U on Stalin's recommendation. This new campaign of Russification was the final step in the reduction of Ukrainian culture to the status of "folklore, *hopak* and *varenyky*," as George Liber has put it.

The sequence of events in the 1920s and 1930s makes it apparent that the principal "co-author" of the GPU-NKVD in carrying out the campaign of terror was the Ukrainian party organization. In obliterating the Ukrainian national renaissance of the 1920s, the partocracy also doomed to destruction those communists whose activities were actually or hypothetically associated with that renaissance.

It should be noted that as in the punitive organs, where the executioners turned into victims once they had done their duty, so in the party hierarchy the principle "the Moor has done his job, and now the Moor may depart"[46] was in effect. At the end of the 1930s, the "great terror" turned against those who in the 1920s and early 1930s had been fervent adherents of the "general line," crushing a variety of "oppositions" and "inclinations" only to be swallowed up themselves by the Moloch of totalitarianism. This was a logical consequence of class-based "morality" and the theory of the "intensification of the class struggle" that had been unwaveringly supported in both the prewar and the postwar eras. Ukraine's communist officials of the

---

46. A line from Friedrich Schiller's tragedy *The Fiesco Conspiracy in Genoa* that has become proverbial in Russia and Eastern Europe.

period under consideration here, as well as thousands of rank-and-file party members, were hostages to the system they had built with their own hands—a system that invariably turned out to be completely merciless not only to its enemies but also to its adherents.

It is striking that the attack on the older generation of the Ukrainian cultural elite was conducted in tandem with the one against members of the communist intelligentsia who displayed "nationalist inclinations." A typical instance was the sequence of events associated with the destruction of the former Borotbists, particularly in the case of the "Bourgeois Nationalist Anti-Soviet Organization of Former Borotbists" (1937). At the very beginning of 1937, the campaign of terror was revived by a resolution of the Central Committee of the VKP(B) "on the unsatisfactory party work of the Kyiv oblast committee of the CP(B)U and shortcomings in the work of the CP(B)U." The targets of this critique were Postyshev and his team, who were soon destroyed. The Ezhov campaign of 1936–38 finished what had remained undone in the preceding years, destroying the remnants of opposition groups, army cadres, and NKVD personnel. According to incomplete calculations, between 1930 and 1941, a total of 110 "counter-revolutionary organizations" were uncovered in Ukraine. Like a stone cast into a pond, each "case" rippled throughout Ukraine in ever-widening circles.

In conclusion, it may be said that, as evidenced by documents and events during the period under consideration here, the organs of the GPU-NKVD played a significant and specific role in the process of counter-Ukrainization, turning Ukraine into a political and spiritual backwater of the Moscow-based Bolshevik empire. At the same time, it is clear that questions pertaining to the interrelations and actual role of the party organs and those of the GPU-NKVD in counteracting Ukrainization require further attention and particular effort on the part of researchers. Another point is equally clear: this research must be based on solid documentary material and a thorough analysis of the historical sources.

Translated by Vitaly Chernetsky and Myroslav Yurkevich

Stanislav Kulchytsky

The Phenomenon of Soviet Statehood

With the proclamation of Ukraine's independence on 24 August 1991, the Supreme Rada of the Ukrainian SSR renounced Soviet statehood and began a new chapter in the thousand-year-old tradition of Ukrainian state-building. This initiative was undertaken by a political elite that had been brought up and educated by the Communist Party. Despite zigzags in policy during the crisis of the socio-economic system that this party created, the principal guideline for this experiment in state-building was the experience of the Ukrainian People's Republic (Ukraïns'ka Narodna Respublika, UNR).

With the assent of the communist majority of deputies, the Ukrainian parliament gave official approval to a set of national symbols. Thus, post-Soviet Ukraine adopted a flag, coat of arms, and anthem as a legacy from the UNR, which the Bolsheviks had destroyed. In a solemn ceremony the last president of the UNR, Mykola Plaviuk, transferred his powers to President Leonid Kravchuk of Ukraine, who had been elected by popular vote. The official residences of representatives of the state administration began to display portraits of leaders of the national-liberation movement. In school curricula the history of the USSR was replaced by the history of Ukraine, with significant attention to the liberation struggle of 1917-21.

The sole legacy of the UNR to Ukrainian state-building was its historical tradition. The material foundation of post-Soviet Ukraine was the Ukrainian SSR (known before 1936 as the Ukrainian Socialist Soviet Republic and afterwards as the Ukrainian Soviet Socialist Republic). One might ask why political leaders who personified Soviet power chose to accept an anti-Soviet legacy. An answer to this question calls for an examination of the phenomenon of Soviet statehood.

* * *

On the eve of the October Revolution, the party of Vladimir Lenin renounced slogans that derived from communist doctrine and advanced slogans of a populist character. In particular, it acknowledged the utility of a federal structure instead of a centralized state.

This was done in order to impede the growth of the national-liberation movement and, indeed, to exploit its potential for the party's own interests.

After coming to power, the Bolshevik Party destroyed the political opposition, transformed itself into a state structure, and set about building a communist system. The old slogans implicit in party doctrine were restored. However, the party oligarchy remained faithful to the pledge it had made in the autumn of 1917 to reconstruct the former empire as a federation. As it turned out, that pledge was not incompatible with dictatorship.

Lenin called the party that he founded the "mind, honor, and conscience" of the age. This definition made a claim to intellectual and moral leadership, but no direct demand for power. As the Communist Party did not intend to acknowledge its governing role in the constitution, it referred to its power as "Soviet." In the first Soviet constitutions the functions and prerogatives of the soviets were defined in detail, but the party was not mentioned at all. Thus the real center of power, which was concentrated in the party committees, was not constitutionally defined.

Under these conditions subordinate centers of Soviet power, which enjoyed a number of real prerogatives, could be established to the party's advantage. Among such centers were national republics endowed with attributes of statehood, including a territory with fixed boundaries and governing institutions situated in their capital cities. These Soviet institutions by no means encroached on the constitutionally anonymous and therefore unlimited prerogatives of the governing party. Thus, the very presence of two unequal centers of power made it possible to conduct certain experiments in nation- and state-building without placing any limits on the party dictatorship.

In investigating the nature of Soviet statehood, one needs to pay attention to the peculiarities of the formation of party and state centers in Ukraine. The key question was that of the party center.

For the Bolsheviks, this became a practical issue only after the UNR came into being. Two regional branches of the Russian Social Democratic Workers Party (of Bolsheviks) (RSDWP[B])—those of the Donetsk-Kryvyi Rih oblast and the southwestern region—operated within the borders of Ukraine designated by the Central Rada. The former branch also included the party organizations of the Kharkiv region, while the latter included those of the Chernihiv, Poltava, and Kherson regions. The ethnic composition of the Bolshevik organizations of Ukraine was predominantly Russian and Jewish. Their leaders meant to consider the nationality factor in their work, but their view of Ukraine was similar to that of the Provisional Government, which did not recognize the Ukrainian character of the western and southern gubernias. Consequently, only the obkom (oblast committee) of the RSDWP(B) of the southwestern region reacted to the formation of the UNR. In November 1917, it turned to the Central Committee (CC) of the RSDWP(B) with a proposal to establish a party center in Ukraine. The secretary of the CC, Iakov Sverdlov, did not object, but found it necessary to warn the obkom against taking steps toward the creation of "a separate Ukrainian party under whatever name, and no matter what program it adopted," that would be distinct from the RSDLP(B).[1]

Shortly thereafter, the CC RSDWP(B) initiated the establishment of a territorial branch of the party in Ukraine. At a meeting on 29 November, the CC considered the question of creating a Ukrainian Social Democratic Workers' Party and instructed Lenin to do so.[2] Within a few days one of Lenin's closest associates, Grigorii Zinoviev, arrived in Kyiv, where a party conference was taking place, and pushed through a resolution on the establishment of a regional organization to be called "RSDWP(B)-Social Democracy of Ukraine." At a conference of Bolshevik organizations of the Donetsk-Kryvyi Rih region that took place in Kharkiv at the time, the issue of a Ukrainian party center was not raised.

The creation of a Soviet government center in Ukraine also began in November 1917. On 16 November the Central Rada issued a law on elections to the Ukrainian Constituent Assembly. The next day the People's Commissar for Nationalities, Joseph Stalin, wired Sergei Bakinsky, a representative of the southwestern regional obkom, and proposed advancing the convocation of an All-Ukrainian Congress of Soviets in Kyiv in order to create a Central Executive Committee capable of replacing the Central Rada.

The most important point of the instructions issued by the people's commissar was published by the newspaper *Pravda* at the time and consisted of the following declaration: "We all expect you—residents of Kyiv, Odesa, Kharkiv, Katerynoslav, and other cities—immediately to start working toward the convocation of such a congress." This identification of Bolsheviks by regional affiliation was a clear sign that the central party leadership had significantly shifted

---

1. *Bol'shevistskie organizatsii Ukrainy v period ustanovleniia i ukrepleniia sovetskoi vlasti (noiabr' 1917–aprel' 1918): Sbornik dokumentov i materialov* (Kyiv, 1962), p. 419.

2. *Protokoly Tsentral'nogo Komiteta RSDRP(B): Avgust 1917–fevral' 1918* (Moscow, 1958), pp. 155, 157.

its position concerning the borders of Ukraine. There can be no doubt about the practical meaning of such a step: while the Bolsheviks enjoyed substantial influence in the western and southern gubernias, for the first time their governing center had recognized the borders of the UNR. Sooner or later the Council of People's Commissars and the Rada would leave the historical stage, but a Ukraine in the form of nine provinces of the former empire would remain.

On 12 December 1917, in the city of Kharkiv, which had been taken by the Soviet troops of Volodymyr Antonov-Ovsiienko, the Congress of Soviets proclaimed the creation of Soviet Ukraine. In so doing, the Bolsheviks did not change the name that the Central Rada had given the Ukrainian state, and they named the government the People's Secretariat, following the Kyiv model rather than the Petrograd one. Such mimicry made it possible to legitimize the armed invasion of Ukraine by the Red Guard.

The first period of Soviet rule was short: under the terms of the Treaty of Brest-Litovsk, concluded in March 1918, the Council of People's Commissars agreed to recognize the independence of the UNR and withdraw its armed forces from Ukraine. However, Lenin did not intend to accept the loss of Ukraine and awaited the imminent defeat of Germany in the war with the Entente. On the eve of a new invasion he thought it expedient to push for the unification of Bolshevik organizations in Ukraine under the aegis of a party with a distinct name. It was not so much a matter of acknowledging the national feelings of the few Bolsheviks of Ukrainian ethnic origin as it was of making the party appear indigenous to the local population.

The name already existed: the Communist Party (of Bolsheviks) of Ukraine, abbreviated as CP(B)U. It was ratified by a conference of leading party officials who met in April 1918 in Taganrog after their evacuation from Ukraine. As Lenin saw it, the CP(B)U was to constitute a regional branch of the Bolshevik Party with the status of a provincial party organization. He firmly rejected the decision taken by a majority of participants in the Taganrog conference to establish the CP(B)U as an independent party associated with the Russian Communist Party, like the communist parties of other states, through an international commission. (This was a reference to the future Communist International, whose first congress took place in Moscow in March 1919.) At the First Congress of the CP(B)U in Moscow in early July 1918, the Ukrainian Bolshevik center was organized according to Lenin's instructions.

Paradoxically, the First Congress of the CP(B)U opposed the creation of a national government center. In the course of the debate on relations between Ukraine and Russia, the CP(B)U was assigned the task of "fighting for a revolutionary union of Ukraine and Russia based on the principles of proletarian centralism within the boundaries of the Russian Soviet Socialist Republic."[3] In one of the resolutions adopted at the congress, union with Russia was proposed quite openly, with no mention of the term "federation" in the official name of Soviet Russia. During the voting on this resolution no one spoke against it, although seven delegates abstained. They were asked to state their reasons, "so that it would be clear to those who elected these delegates why they had voted that way and not differently."[4]

Soon, however, it became clear that the Bolsheviks of Ukraine wanted to be holier than the pope. The leaders of the RSDWP(B) took measures to restore the Ukrainian government center as soon as conditions were deemed favorable for invasion. On 28 November the Provisional Workers' and Peasants' Government of Ukraine was formed, with Georgii Piatakov as its head. The next day, in a letter to the Soviet supreme commander, Ioakim Vatsetis, Lenin gave a detailed explanation of the situation: "As our troops advance westward into Ukraine, provisional Soviet governments are being created in the provinces to reinforce the local soviets. The advantage of this procedure is that it deprives the chauvinists of Ukraine, Lithuania, Latvia, and Estonia of the opportunity to treat the advance of our units as an occupation and creates a favorable atmosphere for the further advance of our troops."[5]

When the head of the UNR government, Volodymyr Chekhivsky, sent a telegram to the people's commissar of foreign affairs asking why troops from Russia were advancing on Kharkiv when there had been no declaration of war, Georgii Chicherin replied that there were no Russian armed forces in Ukraine, and that hostilities were taking place between the troops of the Directory and the Soviet government of Ukraine, which was completely independent. At the same time the people's commissar sent Piatakov a coded warning: "Inasmuch as we have declared our non-intervention in Ukrainian affairs, there is absolutely nothing to prevent your further success."[6]

---

3. *Komunistychna partiia Ukraïny v rezoliutsiiakh z'ïzdiv, konferentsii i plenumiv TsK,* vol. 1 (Kyiv, 1976), p. 20.

4. *Pervyi s"ezd KP(B)U: 5–12 iiulia 1918* (Kyiv, 1988), p. 130.

5. V. I. Lenin, *Povne zibrannia tvoriv*, 55 vols. (Kyiv, 1969–75), 37: 224.

6. Tsentral'nyi derzhavnyi arkhiv vyshchykh orhaniv vlady ta upravlinnia Ukraïny (Central State Archive of Supreme Government and Administrative Institutions of Ukraine), f. 1, op. 13, spr. 11, ark. 2.

By January 1919, the Red Army controlled virtually all of Ukraine. Khristian Rakovsky was dispatched from Moscow to become the head of government, which in Lenin's time was considered the most important office in the power hierarchy. Addressing local leaders, Rakovsky stated openly: "The Provisional Workers' and Peasants' Government of Ukraine, which was created in agreement with the CC of the Russian Communist Party (of Bolsheviks), is its organ, and carries out all the instructions and orders of the CC RCP(B) unconditionally."[7] There was no longer any need for pretense, and the state was given a name modeled on that of Soviet Russia (Ukrainian SSR), as was the government (Council of People's Commissars).

The state apparatus of Soviet Ukraine was formed in the first months of 1919. The central Moscow agencies regarded it as an inalienable part of their own administrative system. Characteristically, on 3 March the presidium of the All-Russian Council of the National Economy (VSNKh) declared itself in favor of the direct management of the national economy of the Soviet republics according to the principles of "democratic centralism." The Ukrainian Council of the National Economy, which was run by "comrades from the center," reacted to this almost immediately: on 7 March it adopted a resolution on the merger of the USNKh and the VSNKh into a single system and on the extension of the operations of the Russian People's Bank onto Ukrainian territory.[8]

The gradually expanding practice of placing enterprises and institutions under the authority of agencies in Moscow raised doubts about the practicality of retaining people's commissars in the national republics and even about those republics' very existence. The Bolshevik leaders regarded existing arrangements as provisional in nature. This is confirmed by both the content and the wording of a resolution of the CC RCP Politburo adopted on 8 April 1919, which was distributed to the national republics in a circular bearing the signatures of Stalin, Nikolai Krestinsky, and Lenin: "If in the form of a concession to independent tendencies it is politically necessary for the immediate future to retain independent commissariats of military and naval affairs and transport in the fraternal Soviet republics, as well as supply agencies, then it is necessary to issue the strictest instructions to the appropriate administrative organs, with the understanding that these independent commissariats should work exclusively and in strictest conformity with instructions issued by the

---

7. Ibid., f. 2, op. 1, spr. 1, ark. 17.
8. Ibid., spr. 18, ark. 47; spr. 49, ark. 15.

corresponding commissariats of the RSFSR, inasmuch as this is the only possible way to attain the requisite unity, speed, and accuracy in the implementation of all instructions and actions."[9]

In this lengthy quotation the word "independent" appears three times, initially as a Ukrainianism (*samostiinye tendentsii*) that had entered the Russian language long before in order to convey the haughty and disdainful attitude of the empire's upper echelons to manifestations of independence in the provinces. The content of the resolution testified strikingly to the fact that the leaders of the Communist Party were not inclined to tolerate the formal independence of the national republics for long. The frank tone employed in communicating with the leaders of the republics on such a delicate matter is easily explained: they were members of the same order, their rapport consolidated by similarity of views and long years of underground struggle.

It was decided that the "strictest instructions" mentioned in the quoted circular were to be implemented through resolutions of Soviet administrative bodies in the national republics. The CC RCP(B) sent appropriate instructions to the party center of the Ukrainian SSR. Again one must pay attention to the wording of the protocol resolution adopted by CC of the Politburo on 23 April, which was not meant for publication: "We propose to the CC CP(B)U that it place on the agenda the question under what terms, when, and in what form the merger of Ukraine with Soviet Russia is to be carried out."[10]

On the same day Lenin ordered the Revolutionary Military Council "to prepare the text of a directive from the Central Committee to all 'nationals' on unity (merger) of the armed forces."[11] It is not known who exactly composed the "draft directive of the CC on military unity," but it entered history under the signatures of Lenin and Stalin. The directive deemed absolutely necessary "for the duration of the socialist defensive war" the merger not only of the armies of the Soviet republics but also of the supply agencies of the Red Army. Given the militarization of industry, this meant uniting the management agencies as well. The need to unify the railway system was also recognized.[12]

---

9. Ibid., f. 1, op. 6, spr. 1, ark. 4. RSFSR = Russian Soviet Federated Socialist Republic.

10. Rossiiskii gosudarstvennyi arkhiv sotsial'no-politicheskoi istorii (Russian State Archive of Socio-Political History), f. 17, op. 3, spr. 3, ark. 1.

11. Lenin, *Povne zibrannia tvoriv*, 50: 287.

12. Ibid., 38: 388–89.

The directive of Lenin and Stalin was approved in Kyiv on 19 May at a conference of members of the CC CP(B)U with representatives of the CC RCP(B) and higher officials from the central offices of the Ukrainian SSR. On the same day, with the support of the Bolshevik deputies, the Central Executive Committee (TsIK) of the soviets of Ukraine adopted a resolution "On the unification of the armed forces of the Soviet republics." On 1 June the All-Russian Central Executive Committee (VTsIK) issued a decree later referred to as a decree on the military and political union of Soviet republics. In accordance with it, the administration of five agencies—the military commissariat and the councils of national economy, railways, finance, and labor—was centralized in Moscow. The post of "People's Commissar of the Ukrainian SSR" was maintained in the newly centralized departments, with the exception of the military, but these figureheads became plenipotentiaries of the people's commissariats of the RSFSR.

On two occasions, after the Twentieth Congress of the Communist Party of the Soviet Union (CPSU) and again during Gorbachev's perestroika, historians took their magnifying glasses in hand and searched for differences in the approaches taken by Lenin and Stalin to the problem of the formation of the USSR. But the internal structure of the Soviet state always entailed the centralized management of the military-industrial complex and the "commanding heights" of the economy, the outlines of which were first sketched in the joint directive on unity of the armed forces.

The leadership of the CC RCP(B) concluded that it was not necessary for Ukraine to have the facade of an independent state. In a conversation with a *Pravda* correspondent published on 24 May 1919, Lev Kamenev indicated that it was not enough to unify the basic administrative branches. "As a matter of principle, Ukraine must be merged with Russia," he declared. The idea of a merger soon took on organizational form: a committee was formed at the VTsIK consisting of Kamenev (head), Rakovsky, and the people's commissar of justice of the RSFSR, Dmitrii Kursky. It was to examine the question of the incorporation of the national republics into Soviet Russia with rights of autonomy.[13] But in the summer of 1919, when Anton Denikin occupied Ukraine and advanced on Moscow, Kamenev's commission dissolved itself.

In the winter of 1919-20 the advance of Leon Trotsky's three Soviet armies again brought Ukraine under Moscow's control. The

---

13. V. M. Volkovyns'kyi and S. V. Kul'chyts'kyi, *Khrystyian Rakovs'kyi: Politychnyi portret* (Kyiv, 1990), p. 187.

question of whether the Ukrainian SSR should exist was once more on the agenda.

On 19 November 1919, Rakovsky sent Lenin a document titled "Theses on the Ukrainian Question." At issue was the practicality of the continuing existence of the Ukrainian SSR as a formally independent state, with its defense capacities and the "commanding heights" of the national economy centralized in Moscow. Lenin submitted these theses for discussion at the Politburo of the CC RCP(B) and then presented them as his own for debate at a conference of the central party leadership with senior Ukrainian officials. In early December these same theses were presented, this time on behalf of the Politburo, to the Eighth All-Russian Party Conference. The latter approved the idea contained in them: to retain centralized management of defense and the economy, but recognize the independence of the Ukrainian SSR. The conference presented RCP(B) members in Ukraine with a demand "to implement in practice the right of the working masses to study and speak their native language in all Soviet institutions, counteracting any attempt to relegate Ukrainian artificially to subordinate status."[14]

Thus the resolution of the party conference "On Soviet Power in Ukraine" contained declarations that promised much. It was quoted in full by Volodymyr Vynnychenko in his journalistic memoir *Vidrodzhennia natsiï* (The Rebirth of the Nation). Vynnychenko commented: "The flesh and blood of a living conviction is apparent here, as well as a desire to put these convictions into practice by means of real, concrete, active measures."[15] In February 1920 the CC of the Ukrainian Socialist Revolutionary Party declared that it was ceasing its active struggle against Soviet Russia, withdrawing its recognition of the Directory, and condemning the parallel existence of the UNR and an independent Ukrainian SSR. The declaration contained the following basis for this radical change of attitude toward the Ukrainian SSR: "Having assumed political power, the communists have declared a new course of national and social policy in Ukraine."[16]

---

14. *KPRS v rezoliutsiiakh i rishenniakh z'ïzdiv, konferentsii i plenumiv TsK,* vol. 2 (Kyiv, 1979), p. 120.

15. V. Vynnychenko, *Vidrodzhennia natsiï,* vol. 3 (Kyiv and Vienna, 1920; repr. Kyiv, 1990), pp. 486–87.

16. Tsentral'nyi derzhavnyi arkhiv hromads'kykh orhanizatsii Ukraïny (Central State Archive of Civic Organizations of Ukraine, hereafter TsDAHO), f. 1, op. 6, spr. 18, ark. 68.

Kamenev and other advocates of the "autonomization" of the national republics feared that forces desiring true independence would consolidate under the red flag of the Ukrainian SSR. Lenin, on the other hand, was convinced that his party would manage to control the situation.

Archival documents related to the discussion of the resolution "On Soviet Power in Ukraine" have always been (and remain to this day) inaccessible to scholars. The Bolshevik leader delivered a major speech in which he probably gave a candid assessment of relations between the RSFSR and the Ukrainian SSR. According to assurances given by the compilers of the complete edition of Lenin's works at the Institute of Marxism-Leninism, that speech "has not been preserved in stenographic transcript." Judging by the words of Rakovsky and Zatonsky, who quoted Lenin's address in their own speeches, he stressed the need for concessions to the Ukrainians. Lenin won those concessions in a debate with those who wanted simply to attach the Ukrainian provinces to Russia and thereby put an end to the Ukrainian question.

Discussions similar to the one that took place at the Eighth Party Conference were also going on within the CP of Ukraine. This was particularly the case at a meeting of the Poltava provincial party committee on 26 December 1919. Its chairman, Ian Drobnis, emphasized the need for attention to relations between Russia and Ukraine, taking as his premise that a Ukrainian state was unthinkable. A senior staff member of the committee, Panas Butsenko, declared the following: "If the policy of the CC RCP(B) on the nationality question does not change, it may be said for certain that we shall have to leave Ukraine once again. The CC RCP(B) should recognize the CC CP(B)U and allow it to work."[17]

The Politburo of the CC RCP(B) returned to deliberations on the Ukrainian question at its sessions on 17 and 18 January 1920, with the participation of the leading members of the CC CP(B)U.[18] The main result of these deliberations was a decision to preserve for the postwar period the centralized management of the "commanding heights" of the national economy, as stipulated in the VTsIK decree of 1 June 1919, and to ratify the formal independence of the Ukrainian SSR that had been declared at the Eighth All-Russian Party Conference. These decisions were to be published in a document that would be attributed to the CP(B)U.

---

17. Ibid., op. 20, spr. 6, ark. 18.

18. V. A. Chirko, *Kommunisticheskaia partiia—organizator bratskogo sotrudnichestva narodov Ukrainy i Rossii v 1917–22 gg.* (Moscow, 1967), p. 178.

Even the leading activists of the CP(B)U, who had been used to "Marxist dialectics," had trouble in understanding how to reconcile a military and political alliance that amounted to the merger of the governing structures of Russia and Ukraine with the slogan of the Ukrainian SSR's independence. This is apparent from the reaction of two members of the Politburo of the CC CP(B)U, Georgii Piatakov and A. S. Bubnov. On 7 February 1920, they wrote to the leadership of the RCP in a condemnatory tone: "From October to December of last year the CC RCP(B) accepted in fact and implemented two fundamental principles: (1) Ukraine should not have a single communist center, either a Soviet one or a government one; (2) the more or less independent communists who are associated with the revolutionary movement in Ukraine and are capable of carrying out the political directives of the CC RCP(B), considering all the complicated circumstances of time and place, should not be allowed to go to Ukraine."[19]

As is apparent from the cited passage, Piatakov and Bubnov did not question Moscow's right to the last word in everything that concerned Ukraine, but demanded a certain freedom of action for the regional political elites. But their worry was for naught. The CC RCP(B) soon reviewed and approved Rakovsky's proposal concerning the reorganization of the All-Ukrainian Revolutionary Committee (*revkom*) as the Council of People's Commissars of the Ukrainian SSR and the restoration of the presidium of the All-Ukrainian Central Executive Committee (VUTsIK). On 21 February 1920, the Kharkiv newspaper *Komunist* published a document entitled "State Relations between Soviet Ukraine and Soviet Russia," which was based on the results of the January discussion on the Ukrainian question in the CC RCP(B). It was presented in the form of theses of the CC CP(B)U for the Fourth All-Ukrainian Party Conference. That conference, which took place from 17 to 23 March, approved the theses without change by an overwhelming majority of votes. It is worth noting that on other matters the Fourth Party Conference made decisions that had not been sanctioned by the center, and it went down in party history as the only instance of open insubordination vis-à-vis the leadership by a party organization of a national republic.

The resolution on "State Relations between Soviet Ukraine and Soviet Russia" was full of angry invective against the UNR, which allegedly had turned Ukraine into a colony of the great powers and its workers and peasants into slaves of international capital. But the most important message of the document was contained in the

19. TsDAHO, f. 1, op. 20, spr. 130, ark. 72.

penultimate of its two dozen points, leaving no doubt as to the limits of the Kharkiv government center's prerogatives: "The following commissariats, which serve the specific interests of the Ukrainian masses, remain under the authority of the All-Ukrainian Central Executive Committee: the people's commissariats of education, internal affairs, agriculture, justice, health care, and social security."[20]

The Ukrainian emigration reacted bitterly to this document. The leaders of the Ukrainian Party of Socialist Revolutionaries, Mykhailo Hrushevsky and Arkadii Zhyvotko, wrote to Volodymyr Zatonsky from Prague in July 1920, terming the resolution a great error. In their view, this resolution dashed the hopes of those who were prepared to reconcile themselves to any government, as long as the sovereignty of the Ukrainian people was secured.[21]

Meanwhile, Lenin took advantage of the Polish-Soviet War to take full control of conquered Ukraine. Feliks Dzerzhinsky, who was dispatched to Ukraine for several months to "secure the rear," unleashed a wide-ranging purge of politically active elements. These repressive measures were directed first and foremost against "the party's own," Bolsheviks and Borotbist communists alike, through whose efforts the Soviet Ukrainian administration was being established at the time. The goal was obvious: to purge the "party of power" of any intention whatever of turning the declared independence of the Ukrainian SRR into genuine independence.

Under pressure from the Bolsheviks, the Borbist and Borotbist parties dissolved themselves. Most of their members, including those who dared to join the ranks of the CP(B)U, were gradually eliminated by the organs of state security. After the "rebellion" at the Fourth Party Conference, the newly elected CC CP(B)U was dissolved. The CC RCP(B) dispatched almost a thousand leading party workers to Ukraine from Russia. Together with local activists who remained loyal to the center, they purged the membership of the Ukrainian party organizations and refused to readmit more than one-third of the membership of the CP(B)U.

The creation and purge of the official apparatus took place simultaneously with the establishment of Soviet armed forces in Ukraine. By the end of 1920, six armies were already stationed in the republic (the fourth, sixth, twelfth, thirteenth, fourteenth and the First Cavalry). They consisted of thirty-five divisions, eight separate brigades, and special units, totaling 1,200,000 men.[22] Owing to its

---

20. *Komunistychna partiia Ukraïny v rezoliutsiiakh,* 1: 71.

21. TsDAHO, f. 1, op. 20, spr. 327, ark. 33.

22. Rossiiskii gosudarstvennyi voennyi arkhiv (Russian State Military

vast numerical superiority over the troops of the Whites, Petliura, and the Poles, Soviet Russia succeeded in maintaining control of Ukraine.

On 9 December 1920, the plenum of the CC RCP(B) approved the "Political Directives of the CC RCP(B) to the CC CP(B)U." The VUTsIK and the people's commissar of foreign affairs of the Ukrainian SSR were instructed, together with the Presidium of the VTsIK and the commissariat of foreign affairs of the RSFSR, to determine the form of inter-state relations in the postwar period.[23] As before, they first sought a formula for uniting Russia and Ukraine, and then extended it to include other national republics.

The leaders of the central and regional branches of the Communist Party, which was characterized by its iron discipline, did not come up with any new formula, nor did they even attempt to do so. The form of relations between Russia and Ukraine (i.e., inter-state relations) had been determined in advance, and their essence was defined in the above-mentioned resolution of the Fourth All-Ukrainian Party Conference. During the Eighth All-Russian Congress of Soviets, the head of the Russian government, Lenin, and the people's commissar of foreign affairs, Georgii Chicherin, signed a "worker-peasant treaty of union" with Rakovsky, who held both these posts in the Ukrainian SSR. On the day of the signing, 28 December 1920, the agreement was solemnly ratified by the All-Russian Congress of Soviets and, on 2 March 1921, by the Fifth All-Ukrainian Congress of Soviets. Thus, after the "military and political union," there emerged a second form of organization of territories of the former Russian Empire now conquered by the Bolsheviks—the "treaty-based federation." Its actual content did not differ at all from the former one.

The preamble and opening articles of the union treaty between Russia and Ukraine contained phrases about the independence and sovereignty of both states. It was even stressed that the Ukrainian SSR had no obligations toward Soviet Russia arising from the fact that the territory of Ukraine had formerly belonged to the Russian Empire. At the same time, the treaty ratified the subordination of key sectors of the Ukrainian government to Russian people's commissariats.[24]

Taking advantage of the right of direct administration throughout the territory of the "treaty-based federation," the central institutions paid no attention to the Kharkiv government and maintained direct

---

Archive), f. 15, op. 2, spr. 61, ark. 50.

23. V. M. Babii, *Soiuz RSR i rol' Ukraïny v ioho utvorenni* (Kyiv, 1972), p. 100.

24. *Istoriia Radians'koï Konstytutsiï v dekretakh i postanovakh Radians'koho uriadu, 1917–1936* (Kyiv, 1937), pp. 152–53.

contact with their respective enterprises and organizations in the Ukrainian provinces. There were countless instances in which the government of the Ukrainian SSR was openly disregarded, including cases involving matters of principle. The CC CP(B)U was obliged to direct its protests against such arbitrary actions to the CC RCP(B), which was the highest authority of all. In March 1921 the Council of People's Commissars of the Ukrainian SSR declared itself in favor of creating a federal constitution that would define the rights of the national republics in the sphere of government.[25] The CC CP(B)U submitted this proposal to the party center and won its approval. However, the RSFSR delegated second-rank figures to the constitutional commission (the Ukrainian SSR was represented by Mykola Skrypnyk), which did very little work. On 10 December 1921, in his report on the activity of the CC CP(B)U to the Sixth All-Ukrainian Party Conference, Rakovsky ironically expressed the hope that the preparation of the Soviet constitution would not take 200 to 300 years.[26]

At Rakovsky's initiative, the Politburo of the CC CP(B)U adopted a resolution on 11 March 1922 on the "need to clarify the mutual relations of the RSFSR and the Ukrainian SSR by defining and making more precise the rights and duties of the Ukrainian SSR."[27] This work was to be done by a special commission of members of the CC RCP(B) and the CC CP(B)U. In Soviet historiography this resolution has been regarded as the starting point of the creation of a single Soviet state. But the text of the resolution speaks only of making inter-state relations more precise. The leaders of the Ukrainian SSR did not propose to liquidate the regime of the "treaty-based federation."

The formation of the USSR gained momentum in Moscow after the initial onset of Lenin's fatal illness, which deprived him of influence on events for several months. Stalin's new position as secretary general of the CC RCP(B), to which he was appointed in April 1922, made him a more influential figure. Encountering no resistance in the central party leadership, Stalin made it his aim to consolidate Moscow's legal control over the national republics. He thought that under postwar conditions the independent status of these republics would lose its propaganda value, and that they should therefore be turned into autonomous republics of the RSFSR.

---

25. Chirko, *Kommunisticheskaia partiia*, p. 230.

26. TsDAHO, f. 1, op. 1, spr. 59, ark. 21.

27. Rossiiskii gosudarstvennyi arkhiv sotsial'no-politicheskoi istorii, f. 17, op. 14, spr. 874, ark. 34.

* * *

The formation of the USSR has always been described on the basis of certain well-known facts whose authenticity is not subject to doubt. However, these facts represent no more than elements of a scenario carefully worked out in the Orgburo of the CC RCP(B). That scenario predetermined the content and sequence of events that were to take place; the nature of pronouncements by political leaders, who were assigned beforehand to act out certain roles; the forms and locations in which the "people's will" would be expressed; the content of the Union's constitution, and so forth.

A certain departure from this scenario occurred when a majority of leaders of the national republics, especially the most influential one, Rakovsky, opposed "autonomization." The attitude of Stalin's opponents objectively corresponded to the national interests of the republics, but was determined above all by their position in the administrative apparatus. Lenin became the arbiter in this conflict, the scope of which should not be exaggerated. Up to a point, Lenin had no reason to refuse to satisfy the ambitions of the provincial leaders of his own party in the government sphere. What was of fundamental importance was that in the party sphere the subordination of the republics to the Moscow center was absolute. That is why the idea of a "two-tier federation" was proposed: Russia, together with Ukraine, the republics of the Transcaucasus, and Belarus would create a "second-tier" federation, the Soviet Union.

Russia had been called a federation since 1918, but in truth it did not constitute one. A federal system endows its constituent members with constitutional prerogatives that cannot be challenged by the center. That is to say, such a system provides for the separation of powers between the center and the periphery. In a dictatorship there is no such separation of powers; hence no federation exists. It is no accident that in the text of the constitution of the Russian Federation this term was employed only in the name of the state.

Similarly, the proclamation of the Soviet Union as a federation could not affect its unitary essence. Even the constitutional provision for the free secession of Soviet republics from the USSR was no more than a declaration. That is why members of the central party leadership, including even Stalin, had no objection to Lenin's concept of a "two-tier federation."

Nevertheless, in the long run the concession that Lenin made to regional leaders proved fateful for Ukraine. Stalin tied the independent republics to the Russian state. Lenin, on the other hand, gave them a status legally identical to that of Russia within the newly established state. The republics were tied to the Communist Party as the guarantor of the existence of a single multinational state. With the disappearance of that party, the USSR lost its political basis. Ukraine would not have attained sovereignty after the liquidation of the CPSU in 1991 if it had only enjoyed autonomous status within Russia.

The facts cited above indisputably attest that the statehood of the national republics rendered them puppets of the center. It would nevertheless be a mistake to refer to the Ukrainian SSR, whether independent or a member the Union, as a pseudo-state. It was created by the Russian Communist Party with a single aim: to weaken the national-liberation movement and facilitate the destruction of the UNR. But it is also true that behind the scenes of the Soviet state there stood a people that had not forgotten its thousand-year-old history and culture, respected the customs and traditions of its ancestors, and had a vision of its own future. The life of the nation endowed the statehood of Soviet Ukraine with actual content.

The party oligarchy regarded the national states—especially the largest of them, Soviet Ukraine—with mistrust and fear. Having imposed Soviet power on Ukrainian society by military force, it expended a great deal of effort to implant the party and state apparatus there. The program of Ukrainization justified itself in the sense that it made easier for the central authorities to control events in Ukraine. At the same time, however, Ukrainization promoted a rapid national revival in culture and politics. In order to overcome this unanticipated side effect, the Stalin regime subjected the peasantry and intelligentsia of Ukraine to cruel and unrelenting repression. During Stalin's rule, the Ukrainian people suffered from repression incomparably more than any other nationality, with the exception of those peoples that were deported. More often than not, repression served as a preventive measure intended to nip all possible opposition in the bud.

The combination of terror and propaganda made possible the long duration of Soviet statehood. The political regime created by the Communist Party exhausted itself only with the emergence of a systemic crisis resembling a cancerous growth within the social-economic order. As this crisis intensified, government institutions in the republics and the party institutions associated with them became less dependent on the center and strengthened their ties with their own societies. When the totalitarian system collapsed under the cumulative weight of its unsolved problems, the transformation of the Soviet state into a number of democratic national republics became possible.

Mark von Hagen

States, Nations, and Identities: The Russian-Ukrainian Encounter in the First Half of the Twentieth Century

Whatever may have been the character of the relationships between Russia and Ukraine or Russians and Ukrainians in the nineteenth century, those relationships were transformed dramatically in the process of major structural and conjunctural changes of the early twentieth century, notably the 1905 Revolution, the Great War and subsequent revolutions and civil war that followed upon the collapse of the Old Regime, and the Stalin revolution from above at the end of the 1920s. My narrower aim is to suggest how the Ukrainian and Russian national/imperial movements evolved in close, dynamic relations with one another and how those who identified themselves with the Russian or Ukrainian causes defined themselves and each other in the process of confrontation and encounter. My broader aim is to situate this particular set of relations in the general transformation of political life brought about by the structural and conjunctural changes mentioned above, changes fundamentally linked to a prolonged crisis of legitimacy of the Old Regime. That crisis was not resolved by the coming to power in 1917 of the Bolshevik leadership, but persisted and evolved at least until the mid-1930s (and probably until after World War II).[1]

The crisis of legitimacy was above all a political crisis (but more than that as well) that revolved around the relocation of sovereignty from the autocrat to the body politic. Later, with the consolidation of Soviet power, a further relocation of legitimacy to an authoritarian party-state coopted the rhetoric and institutions of popular sovereignty. In the course of the crisis of legitimacy, there occurred a longer-term shift in the way imperial society was structured, from traditional dynastic, confessional, and estate principles and categories to ones of class and nationality, which emerged in the interstices of

---

1. On Stalinism as *démesure*, a constant condition of state-induced crisis in which the response to crisis only leads to new crises, see Moshe Lewin, *The Making of the Soviet System: Essays in the Social History of Interwar Russia* (New York, 1994), pp. 26–29.

the Old Regime and were significantly influenced by ideologies and social movements abroad, especially in Europe (both socialism and nationalism).[2] In the post-reform period, a modernizing bureaucracy began to see itself as the repository of legitimacy within the regime, a view that entailed an ever-diminishing role for the autocrat himself. This view of the state was adapted and transformed by liberal politicians and theorists, who began serious discussions about the need for and means to construct a political nation.

The 1905 Revolution marked the beginnings of the formation of a political nation in which sovereignty was to be relocated. Those beginnings entailed the formation of political parties, including ones that claimed mass membership and situated themselves primarily in relation to the more "modern" organizing principles of class and nationality, even when pretending to stand above them, as did the Kadets.[3] The period from 1905 to the war saw the flowering of imagined alternatives to the Old Regime, structured along the new principles of class and nationality, federalism, and various pan-movements (Pan-Slavism, Pan-Turkism, Pan-Islamism, Zionism). At the same time, the relatively belated advent of mass politics and the peculiar features of nationalism in the multinational Russian Empire contributed to what Leopold Haimson has characterized—albeit in a different context and not treating ethnic politics as such—as a profound crisis of the political parties themselves, which were unable to establish a stable social base within the context of highly indeterminate social and national identities.[4]

Nevertheless, these developments did not significantly change the character of late imperial politics of identity, which allowed (with

---

2. See the discussion of estate, class, and social identities in Gregory L. Freeze, "The Soslovie (Estate) Paradigm and Russian Social History," *American Historical Review* 91, no. 1 (February 1986): 11–36; and Leopold Haimson, "The Problem of Social Identities in Early Twentieth Century Russia," *Slavic Review* 47, no. 1 (Spring 1988): 1–21.

3. See Terence Emmons, *The Formation of Political Parties and the First National Elections in Russia* (Cambridge, Mass., 1983); and William G. Rosenberg, *Liberals in the Russian Revolution: The Constitutional Democratic Party, 1917–1921* (Princeton, N.J., 1974).

4. Haimson, "The Problem." To Haimson's emphasis on estate and class categories, I have added confessional and national/ethnic ones. Of course, class and ethnicity function in various ways, sometimes undercutting and sometimes reinforcing each other. On these matters, see R. Grigor Suny, "Rethinking Social Identities: Class and Nationality," chapter 1 of his book *The Revenge of the Past: Nationalism, Revolution, and the Collapse of the Soviet Union* (Stanford, 1993).

important qualifications) minority communities to combine adherence to local languages, cultures, and even institutions with an overarching loyalty to the tsar and the imperial state. Baltic German bureaucrats, Jewish merchants, Tatar mullahs, and even Russophile Ukrainian publicists comprised a cosmopolitan elite whose loyalties focused on the transnational autocrat and the state. The imperial administration very resolutely ignored ethnic categories in its public documents in favor of traditional ones of confession and estate.[5] Curiously, more "modern" ethnic categories were delineated by the military statisticians who drew the security maps used in the schools of the General Staff, but these were exceptions and, notably, remained classified.[6] Despite the tendency of the last two tsars (Alexander III and Nicholas II) to cultivate a more "Russian" image of the autocracy[7] and despite the various policies in education, religious administration, and local government that have been called Russification,[8] Hans Rogger is correct to identify Russian nationalism as a dilemma for state bureaucrats, who perceived all forms of Pan-Slavism and Russian nationalism as challenges to the dynastic principle of the cosmopolitan state and as obstacles to their pursuit of a cautious foreign policy in the interests of the Russian state.[9]

The deliberate, or perhaps inadvertent, efforts of the state bureaucracy to maintain a distance from such nation-based politics and identities survived the 1905 Revolution and the elections to the first two Dumas, but with the shift of political course under Prime Minister Petr Stolypin in June 1907, interests that were perceived as

---

5. See, for example, government employment documents (*formuliarnye spiski*).

6. See A. M. Zolotarev, *Zapiski voennoi statistiki Rossii*, vol. 1, *Teoriia statistiki. Obshchee obozrenie Rossii. Vooruzhennye sily* (St. Petersburg, 1885).

7. Richard Wortman, "Moscow and Petersburg: The Problem of Political Center in Tsarist Russia, 1881–1914," in *Rites of Power: Symbolism, Ritual and Politics since the Middle Ages*, ed. Sean Wilentz (Philadelphia, 1985).

8. See the debate over these policies in Edward Thaden, ed., *Russification in the Baltic Provinces and Finland, 1855–1914* (Princeton, N.J., 1981), pt. 1; and Andreas Kappeler, *Rußland als Vielvölkerreich: Entstehung, Geschichte, Zerfall* (Munich, 1992), chapter 6.

9. Hans Rogger, "Nationalism and the State: A Russian Dilemma," *Comparative Studies in Society and History*, no. 4 (1961/1962), 253–64. See also Dietrich Geyer, *Russian Imperialism: The Interaction of Domestic and Foreign Policy, 1860–1914*, trans. Bruce Little (New Haven, Conn., 1987), pt. 1, on the "radicalizing" impact of Russian nationalists, especially Katkov and Pobedonostsev, during, for example, the Russo-Turkish War of 1877–78.

more and more national came to play a shaping role in imperial politics. In other words, an influential part of the imperial state chose to reconsolidate its authority by appealing, above all, to the principle of nationality.[10] Parts of the bureaucracy and of the Orthodox ecclesiastical hierarchy lent their support to Russian nationalist organizations,[11] the most prominent being the Nationalist Party and the Union of the Russian People, whose membership, in turn, was largest in the southwestern provinces of the empire,[12] which the Ukrainian national movement would claim as its own.

And yet, for all its gains, the Russian nationalist right was still constrained by the emerging rules of "civil society" and the more legalistic proprieties of the quasi-constitutional monarchy. Paul Bushkovitch has argued that Russian national politics at the end of the Old Regime remained backward vis-à-vis its Western and Central European variants, where greater militancy and chauvinism were becoming the norm before the outbreak of the Great War.[13] Jeffrey Brooks argues that Russian popular literature suggested a similarly more tolerant and cosmopolitan attitude toward non-Russians, especially when contrasted to contemporary fiction in America and Britain.[14] I take a somewhat less benevolent view of inter-ethnic relations in the empire on the eve of the war (policies of Russification in religion, education, and culture dating from the reign of Alexander III provoked protest movements that expressed themselves in national and religious language; more seriously, after the initial concessions of 1905–6, the Stolypin reforms once again disadvantaged many vocal

---

10. Roberta Manning has identified a "gentry reaction" that crystallized during this period and blocked significant reform of the state bureaucracy, but these defenders of Old Regime estate privileges were able to find much more common ground with the regime when their "Russian" and "Orthodox" estate interests overlapped with Stolypin's nationalist agenda in the western borderlands. See Manning, *The Crisis of the Old Order in Russia: Gentry and Government, 1861–1914* (Princeton, N.J., 1972). For other aspects of late imperial politics, see Geoffrey Hosking, *The Russian Constitutional Experiment: Government and Duma, 1907–1914* (Cambridge, 1973).

11. See the memoirs of Archbishop Evlogii, *Put' moei zhizni: Vospominaniia Mitropolita Evlogiia, izlozhennye po ego rasskazam T. Manukhinoi* (Paris, 1947), for example, on his campaign for the partition of Kholm province.

12. Robert Edelman, *Gentry Politics on the Eve of the Russian Revolution: The Nationalist Party, 1907–1914* (New Brunswick, N.J., 1980).

13. See his article "What Is Russia? Russian National Identity and the State, 1500–1917" in the present volume.

14. See his *When Russia Learned to Read* (Princeton, N.J., 1985), chapter 6.

non-Russian communities) and therefore argue that the war certainly exacerbated many existing tensions in prewar imperial society and politics, but nonetheless contributed to a qualitative change in relations among the peoples of the empire.

The Great War was a watershed in relations between Russians and non-Russians and among non-Russians. By this I mean not just war per se, but the character of the regimes waging it (especially the Austro-Hungarian and Russian multinational empires), the character of the war itself, and the wartime policies pursued by those regimes (military manpower policy, wartime propaganda, occupation and evacuation policy, and even refugee aid). As far as the character of the war is concerned, with Russia facing its three powerful neighbors to the west and south, no war in recent memory (since the Napoleonic invasion, in fact) had directly involved such large populations and territories or so much transfer, destruction, and occupation of the densely populated European provinces of the empire.[15]

The Great War transformed the political environment. The consequence of the war was the internationalization and militarization of the Russian Empire's ethnic politics (as it was, in different ways, for the Habsburg and Ottoman empires as well). Wartime policies had as their consequence a narrowing of the choices available to many communities and a raising of stakes for having or choosing the "wrong" national identity. Within the imperial elites themselves, wartime policies and the war's impact on other political conflicts led to polarization along national lines. The result of these changes and of the policies that shaped them was the politicization of ethnic differences and the superimposition of an ethnic or national element on many otherwise non-national political, economic, and social conflicts. Advocates of a more militant and chauvinist Russian nationalism came to set the tone of political discussion and to implement wartime policy, most clearly in the martial-law regime that held for all occupied territory and a large zone behind the front lines of combat.[16] Wartime occupation and evacuation policies targeted

---

15. Leonid Heretz reminds us that the war was also the "most massive intrusion of the modern, outside world into the traditional peasant culture" ("Russian Apocalypse 1891–1917: Popular Perceptions of Events from the Year of Famine and Cholera to the Fall of the Tsar," Ph.D. dissertation, Harvard University, 1993).

16. Daniel Graf, "Military Rule behind the Russian Front, 1914–1917: The Political Ramifications," *Jahrbücher für Geschichte Osteuropas*, n.s. 22, no. 3 (1974): 390ff. See also A. Iu. Bakhturina, *Politika Rossiiskoi imperii v Vostochnoi Galitsii v gody Pervoi mirovoi voiny* (Moscow, 2000).

ethnic communities in the name of national security and the longer-term war aims of liberation of territories that were claimed rightfully to belong to the Russian Empire. It was the regime's policies that inadvertently introduced the politics of national liberation into the imperial army: its manpower, propaganda, and deployment policies all served to heighten the national principle of social organization. The regime's occupation policies broke down the boundaries between the civilian and military worlds, as well as between the Austrian and Russian empires. Occupation authorities sent hundreds of thousands of citizens from the western borderlands—those regions that had the most experience with modern national politics—into the interior provinces of the empire, bringing Poles, Jews, and Galician Ukrainians into close contact with Ukrainians of the Russian Empire. Ultimately, and paradoxically, it was the Russian regime and Russian nationalist organizations, far more than the Austrians and Germans who were blamed for this, that made radical nationalism possible in 1917, yet this lesson was not learned by the new elite that assumed power as the Provisional Government in 1917.

Furthermore, wartime policies had economic and social consequences that amounted to a dramatic undermining of the position of many traditional elites, especially those most closely linked to the social and political structures of the Old Regime, namely, the gentry. I propose here that the war had an impact equivalent to a rapid drive for economic modernization, even more devastating than Witte's industrialization program and Stolypin's agrarian reforms in sweeping aside elements of the social and political structure that, however undermined since Emancipation, had held on tenaciously to their declining power. Most scholars, for example, agree that the heavy losses in the army during the first two years of the war contributed to a democratization of the officer corps that had its parallels elsewhere, resulting in a sharp decline in the significance and power of the gentry and other traditional elites. When the Provisional Government abolished estates and ranks in February 1917, it was acknowledging a *fait déjà accompli*.[17]

But the war did more than achieve a demographic turnover. As the focus of national attention, the war became a testing ground for social privilege, especially Old Regime social privilege. The war was waged with patriotic appeals to national sacrifice; exemption from

---

17. In his study of Russian involvement in World War I, *The Eastern Front, 1914–1917* (London and Sydney, 1975), Norman Stone also makes the argument that the war contributed to the administrative and economic modernization of the Old Regime.

wartime service became a source of resentment among those who were serving or who had relatives on the fronts. The autocracy's performance in the war itself became a test of its legitimacy, as when the liberal spokesman Pavel Miliukov accused the tsar and his entourage of treason or stupidity after military losses. This conflation of notions of patriotism, national security, and national communities contributed to a veritable obsession with treason and enemies; all sides in the national discussions found "agents" and "spies" in the service of the German or Turkish enemies to blame for every calamity that beset the regime.[18]

With traditional anchors of identity such as estate no longer effective and the legitimacy of the autocracy and its ruling dynasty repudiated even by its most conservative and loyal servitors, the political arena witnessed heightened emphasis on national and ethnic components of identity on the one hand and class components on the other. And what Ernest Gellner argues is the necessary condition for a successful revolution, namely, the conflation of social and national politics,[19] occurred during 1917 as the emergent elites abandoned the Old Regime. Although those elites were somewhat prepared for the rise of the "social question" to the top of society's political agenda, they were quite taken aback by the rapid parallel rise of the "national question."[20] Confident in its own liberal and socialist agendas, the new government expected the national question to be provisionally "solved" after it abolished all discrimination based on nationality and religion and proclaimed the full equality of all citizens regardless of religion, race, or nationality.[21]

As part of the exit from the Old Regime, the Provisional Government and the Petrograd Soviet called for "society" to organize itself

---

18. On the empire's Germans during the war, see Ingeborg Fleischhauer, *Die Deutschen im Zarenreich: Zwei Jahrhunderte deutsch-russische Kulturgemeinschaft* (Hamburg, 1986), pp. 479–522. On the Jews, see Heinz-Dietrich Loewe, *Antisemitismus und reaktionäre Utopie: Russischer Konservatismus im Kampf gegen den Wandel von Staat und Gesellschaft, 1890–1917* (Hamburg, 1978).

19. Gellner develops this theme in his perceptive critique of Miroslav Hroch's work in "An Alternative Vision" in his *Encounters with Nationalism* (Oxford, 1994), esp. pp. 196–98.

20. See, for example, the memoirs of I. G. Tsereteli, *Vospominaniia o Fevral'skoi revoliutsii*, vol. 2 (Paris and The Hague, 1963), pp. 69–161; and L. D. Trotskii, *Moia zhizn'* (Berlin, 1930), p. 63.

21. For the key documents on the Provisional Government's politics of nationality, see R. P. Browder and A. F. Kerensky, eds., *The Russian Provisional Government, 1917*, vol. 1 (Stanford, Cal., 1961), pp. 317–472; and S. M. Dimanshtein, ed., *Revoliutsiia i natsional'nyi vopros* (Moscow, 1930), vol. 3.

in defense of the revolution and began immediately to appoint their "own" people as commissars to local governments, effectively establishing alternative power bases against the local and municipal administrations of the Old Regime.[22] "Society" responded by forming councils and executive committees to coordinate the activities of already existing and newly founded organizations. But once the common enemy of autocracy was removed from the scene, a bewildering diversity of political interests began to compete for the loyalty of various constituencies. The Ukrainian Central Rada competed, for example, with a multinational Committee of Social Organizations and the Kyiv Soviet of Workers' and Soldiers' Deputies. Each of these organizations took upon itself the sanctioning of several more congresses that brought their various politics to the localities.

Thus the struggle that emerged between the Central Rada in Kyiv and the Dual Authority in Petrograd was replicated at nearly every subordinate level of the new authority. Those struggles revolved around the delineation and timing of the introduction of autonomy in post-autocratic Russia. They were also replicated in the imperial army, where the slogan of Ukrainization was one of many appeals by war-weary soldiers to form military units based on territorial and national principles (from Ukrainians to Siberians and Jews). Despite the opposition of an influential part of the Imperial High Command and the officer corps, the politics of military "nationalization" swept across the empire and provoked conflicts with the "Russian" majority everywhere.[23]

Those conflicts in turn both shaped and were shaped by the transformation of national and nationalist politics throughout the empire. The war with the Central Powers had become a key focus of political struggle and transformed notions of patriotism—especially Russian national identity—among former imperial elites and, to a largely unexplored degree, among non-elite social groups, especially soldiers. The theme of treason, which had already mobilized much patriotic sentiment during the first years of the war, especially the fear of German influence at the imperial court, shifted its focus to fears of a separate peace to be negotiated by the new "revolutionary"

---

22. Daniel T. Orlovsky, "Reform during Revolution: Governing the Provinces in 1917," in *Reform in Russia and the U.S.S.R.: Past and Prospects*, ed. Robert Crummey (Urbana, Ill., 1989).

23. I am currently working on the politics of nationality in the imperial army, but M. S. Frenkin, *Russkaia armiia i revoliutsiia 1917–1918* (Munich, 1978), and Allan Wildman, *The End of the Russian Imperial Army* (Princeton, N.J., 1980 and 1987), have treated many of the key issues for 1917.

government and the dissolution of the empire. Apprehensions of treason shaped much of the worldview of the movements that would come to be known as the Whites, who established their proto-states on the peripheries of the former empire in opposition not only to the Bolshevik but also to other "un-Russian" proto-states, most prominently the succession of Ukrainian states that claimed authority over "historically Ukrainian lands," beginning with the Central Rada.[24]

In the meantime, national self-determination had been given international sanction by the competition between Soviet (largely Leninist) ideas of national self-determination with liberal-democratic Wilsonian ideals and the often desperate efforts of post-Russian proto-states (including the Ukrainian ones) to win official recognition of their claims of sovereignty at the Versailles Peace Conference. The postwar "opening" made possible by the defeat of several multinational dynastic empires saw a wave of state formation across the Eurasian continent (and elsewhere).[25]

The Evolution of Ukrainian and Russian Politics after 1917

The proclamation of new states, however, including the Soviet one, did not "solve" the crisis of the Old Regime, certainly not in 1917 or during the Civil War. Of course, the elites at the very top changed and new political principles were announced and enacted, but the legitimacy of the new regimes everywhere remained as acute a political problem as did the persistence of other aspects of the structural crisis. In its confrontation with state power during the Civil War, the Bolshevik regime was forced to adjust its theoretical tenets, as well as to learn unfamiliar techniques of governance. The soviet itself evolved almost imperceptibly from an institution of popular politics and anti-statism into a new form of statist ideology, the first expression of which was the dictatorship of the proletariat, with ever-present "vestiges" of popular sovereignty (*narodovlastie*).[26]

---

24. Anna Procyk, *Russian Nationalism and Ukraine: The Nationality Policy of the Volunteer Army during the Civil War* (Edmonton and Toronto, 1995).

25. See Geoffrey Eley, "Remapping the Nation: War, Revolutionary Upheaval and State Formation in Eastern Europe, 1914–1923," in Peter J. Potichnyj and Howard Aster, eds., *Ukrainian-Jewish Relations in Historical Perspective*, 2d ed. (Edmonton, 1988); and his "War and the Twentieth-Century State," *Daedalus* 124, no. 2 (Spring 1995): 155–74.

26. Neil Harding traces the transformation of the Bolshevik political vision from that of the Paris Commune to what he calls the "organic-labor state" of the

The Civil War, which certainly can be alternately viewed as a Russo-Ukrainian war, a Russo-Polish war, and a Ukrainian-Polish war, saw a continuation of the patriotic testing of social and political privilege for emergent regimes. Everywhere the "fatherland" was declared to be in danger,[27] and those who failed to rise to the call to defend it were cast into the ranks of mortal enemies, while those who served were promised status and authority in the new post-victory order. In the peripheries, the Bolsheviks portrayed their military and political ambitions as "national liberations" from foreign puppet regimes, whether the Entente-backed White movements or the German-backed Central Rada or Hetman government. Although on occasion Lenin (and not only Lenin) reprimanded some of his closest comrades and broader groups in the Bolshevik Party for their Great Russian chauvinism, the relationship between Russian nationalist ideology and movements, including the extremist parties that emerged before and during 1917, and the Bolshevik Party has remained largely unexplored.[28] Many a non-Russian Bolshevik, not without justification, accused his comrades of masking their Russian or imperial attitudes behind the rhetoric of internationalism. Certainly it is not unreasonable to assume that ethnically Russian working-class or agricultural colonist communities in Turkestan or Ukraine, for example, might have perceived political conflict in ethnic and national terms; indeed, many of them did just that.[29]

---

proletarian dictatorship. See his "Socialism, Society and the Organic Labour State" in Harding, ed., *The State in Socialist Society* (Albany, N.Y., 1984), pp. 1–50. On the vestiges of "popular sovereignty" and the never quite suppressed conflict between the bureaucratic principle and *narodovlastie*, see the provocative essay-memoir by Aleksandr Zinov'ev, "Nashei iunosti polet," *Kontinent*, no. 35 (1983), 176–206.

27. See Lenin's decree "Sotsialisticheskoe otechestvo v opasnosti!" (21 February 1918), in *Dekrety Sovetskoi vlasti*, vol. 1 (Moscow, 1957), pp. 490–91. Similar proclamations were issued by Petliura, Skoropadsky, and the Whites.

28. One author whose working assumptions and scholarly methods have probably alienated more readers than they have attracted is the émigré Mikhail Agursky: see his book *The Third Rome: National Bolshevism in the USSR* (Boulder, Colo., 1987). Still, Agursky brings together a great deal of disparate information that warrants greater scrutiny. Elsewhere, Robert Tucker and Moshe Lewin have made passing references to the admixture of Russian nationalism and Bolshevism in Stalinist political culture. See their contributions to Tucker, ed., *Stalinism: Essays in Interpretation* (New York, 1977).

29. On the evolution of Bolshevik ideas during the Civil War and after, see the stimulating essay by Andrea Graziosi, "G. L. Piatakov (1890–1937): A Mirror of Soviet History," *Harvard Ukrainian Studies* 16, nos. 1–2 (June 1992): 102–66.

Provisionally, class and nationality remained fundamental principles of the new order, but these principles were often perceived to be in conflict, and class was most certainly favored by a party-state that took its Marxist heritage seriously, however it interpreted that heritage. Class was enshrined in the new proto-state's proto-ideology of proletarian dictatorship and in the nomenclature of state institutions as worker-peasant (e.g., Worker-Peasant Red Army), as well as in constitutive documents on citizenship, which operated with discriminatory provisions against members of the former elites of imperial society and in favor of the formerly disfranchised.[30] Nationality was enshrined in the self-proclaimed federal structure, but with considerable qualifications and a great deal of apparent ambivalence. For example, the USSR was conceived as a distinctly and consciously non-ethnic formation, while the early administrative divisions (the Russian SFSR, the Belarusian and Ukrainian SSRs, and the Transcaucasian SFR) operated in an ideological tension between the territorial and ethnic understandings of politics. Of course, nationality was institutionalized in the nation-building policies of the 1920s (*korenizatsiia*), again not for Russians (although one might make an argument that the Russians were also undeveloped as a true political nation), but, importantly and primarily, for the Ukrainians. The 1926 census categories also institutionalized this acceptance of nationality as a tool of governance. Significantly, with the introduction of the passport system during the First Five-Year Plan, both class and nationality were officially proclaimed constituent elements of identity for all Soviet citizens.[31]

Simultaneously with these processes, other contrary trends were working to change the place and functioning of class and nationality in Soviet society. As state institutions and elites became more confident of their legitimacy and power, new loyalties and identities began to squeeze out class and nationality. "Soviet" identity and party loyalties were reinforced by the NKVD, by the Soviet ideological apparatus (hegemony), and by the emerging systems of rewards and advancement available to the new elites to consolidate their authority. Class and nationality were not removed from the panoply of concepts

---

30. Elise Kimerling, "Civil Rights and Social Policy in Soviet Russia, 1918–1936," *Russian Review* 41, no. 1 (1982): 24–46.

31. See Yuri Slezkine, "The USSR as a Communal Apartment, or How a Socialist State Promoted Ethnic Particularism," *Slavic Review* 53, no. 2 (Summer 1994): 414–52; R. Grigor Suny, "State-Building and Nation-Making: The Soviet Experience," chapter 3 of *The Revenge of the Past*; and Terry Martin, *The Affirmative Action Empire: Nations and Nationalism in the Soviet Union, 1923–1939* (Ithaca and London, 2001).

that formed identities, but they were certainly rearranged in what appears superficially to have been an effort to replicate the complicated loyalties of prewar late imperial society, including a self-consciously cosmopolitan (or internationalist) elite and the continued cultivation of local and regional identities and loyalties. As one example that perhaps illustrates the general tendencies, I offer the campaign to gain a measure of legitimacy for the Red Army in the 1920s. The commissars who served as representatives of the new regime and especially as watchdogs over the loyalties of the officer corps were characteristic of early Bolshevik distrust of the state and entrenched elites. By the mid-1920s, the Red Army leadership felt secure enough to demote the commissar and raise the status of the officers, thereby acknowledging that a measure of professionalism was needed to run a modern state.[32] The "cultural revolution" unleashed against various bureaucracies appeared temporarily to reverse that process of gradual accretion of legitimacy and authority, but the concurrent First Five-Year Plan nonetheless produced a tremendously expanded state apparatus that continued to grow during the 1930s. Further measures to entrench the new elites (or "new class") were introduced in the mid-1930s, only to be set back once again by the Great Terror and its precursors and aftershocks.

The new and expanded central institutions usurped more and more power for themselves from the republican and lower-level administrative units, often in violent (and murderous) fashion. The expansion of the bureaucracies was accompanied by a brutal assault on the countryside with collectivization and famine, whose demographic results left several "emerging nations," especially Ukraine and Kazakhstan, in a catastrophically debilitated state. Ideological and administrative harassment of non-Russian cultural and intellectual elites during the late 1920s and early 1930s was part of a realignment of "patriotic" values, reversing the trend toward greater cultural autonomy that had been the hallmark of, say, Ukrainization. Finally, these campaigns coincided with a renewed assault on popular and institutional religion and especially with mass arrests and limitations on the clergy, thereby eliminating yet another pool of community leadership and maintenance of ethnic and national identities.[33] There also seems to have been some overlap between those of the new elites who resented the NEP compromise of

---

32. See my *Soldiers in the Proletarian Dictatorship* (Ithaca, N.Y., 1990).

33. See Gerhard Simon, *Nationalism and Policy toward the Nationalities in the Soviet Union: From Totalitarian Dictatorship to Post-Stalinist Society* (Boulder, Colo., 1991), chapters 2–6.

a mixed economy and those who opposed the Ukrainization policies; in any event, the end of the NEP clearly brought changes that limited the capacities of non-Russian national elites to control political processes in their republics. Because so many of the non-Russian nations remained overwhelmingly peasant and rural in the 1920s (the Ukrainians being a good example of this), Bolshevik attitudes and policies toward peasants often had the (conscious or unconscious) consequence of (at least provisional) denationalization.[34]

The promulgation of the Soviet constitution of 1936 tacitly acknowledged the gradually diminishing importance of class markers after the Great Break with its suspension of class quotas and its acceptance of a leading role for the Soviet intelligentsia (a term that served to cover the growing managerial strata of the bureacracy).[35] The disappearance of published statistics on nationality at the beginning of the 1930s, despite the persistence of the nationality entry in Soviet passports, similarly marked the end of the nation-building experiment without any formal or public repudiation of the principle. Once again, the primary acceptable identities (in terms of political power) for Soviet citizens were bound to a political leadership that had become more conscious of itself as a multinational elite with great-power ambitions. This reconfiguration evolved in the course of the 1930s with the official recovery of a positive reevaluation of the imperial past. It was perhaps challenged by the first years of the war, but then in the postwar period the results of the war were employed to consolidate the national reconfiguration of Russian and Ukrainian identities within a Soviet context of Russian cultural domination.[36]

---

34. Alvin W. Gouldner, in discussing the agrarian policies of the Soviet state, labels the regime "internal colonialism." He does not touch, however, on ethnic communities, although he well might have. See his "Stalinism: A Study of Internal Colonialism," *Telos*, no. 34 (Winter 1977–78): 5–48.

35. Sheila Fitzpatrick has traced the origins of the "decline of class" to the decisions of the First Five-Year Plan regarding the promotion of workers from the bench to managerial positions and preferential access to educational opportunities. See her *Education and Social Mobility in the Soviet Union, 1921–1934* (New York, 1979).

36. See Amir Weiner's book on postwar Vinnytsia for a description of the working out of a new Soviet Ukrainian patriotism and the realignment of Russian and Ukrainian loyalties: *Making Sense of War: The Second World War and the Fate of the Bolshevik Revolution* (Princeton, N.J., 2001); Lowell Tillett, *The Great Friendship: Soviet Historians on the Non-Russian Nationalities* (Chapel Hill, N.C., 1969); Erwin Oberländer, *Sowjetpatriotismus und Geschichte: Dokumentation* (Köln, 1967); and Konstantin Shteppa, *Russian Historians and the Soviet State* (New Brunswick, N.J., 1962).

As the Stalinist state consolidated its ever-expanding hold over broader swaths of society, the elites embarked on the restoration of authoritarian models and rhetoric, vigorously repudiating the decade of officially tolerated (and often encouraged) anti-establishmentarianism and youth and proletarian "counter-cultures," with their radical egalitarianism.[37] The 1930s may be seen as a period of fixing new hierarchies and boundaries, often in the language and symbolic representation of the Old Regime (but mixed with elements of the revolutionary "canon"). Leon Trotsky lamented and Nicholas Timasheff embraced what both understood to be a "great retreat";[38] what that meant in concrete terms was the general establishment of clearer boundaries. In class terms, the 1930s enforced the dominance of the bureaucratic managerial classes in politics, economic life, and cultural affairs, with a panoply of privileges and special access to material goods and high social status; in terms of gender, elements of the traditional patriarchal family and male-female roles were "restored" with restrictive laws on abortion, divorce, and homosexuality, as well as the abolition of coeducation. Finally, in nationality policy, the primacy of Russian culture over all other Soviet cultures and peoples was introduced in education, cultural policy, cadre practice, and other areas. Everywhere, the anti-hierarchical spirit of the 1920s was supplanted with attempts to put people back in their "proper places," especially in relation to the state institutions.

As far as the specific Russian-Ukrainian dynamic is concerned, the policies of the Stalin regime may appear discontinuous and contradictory. On the one hand, the terror-famine and official coercion against Ukrainian elites weakened any Ukrainian initiatives or autonomy in shaping republican policies; on the other hand, at the end of the decade, the annexation of eastern Poland/western Ukraine was carried out in the name of Ukrainian reunification and the fulfillment of "ancient popular aspirations," with barely concealed irredentist rhetoric—a rhetoric that had been part of the Comintern's official agenda since its Fifth Congress in July 1924. How the annexed region and its populations were integrated into the existing Soviet Ukrainian nation has barely been investigated, but the brief period before the German invasion did not permit any continuous development of new

---

37. See Richard Stites, *Revolutionary Dreams: Utopian Vision and Experimental Life in the Russian Revolution* (New York, 1989), esp. chapters 3 and 6.

38. Trotsky, *The Revolution Betrayed* (New York, 1972), esp. chapters 6–8; and Timasheff, *The Great Retreat: The Growth and Decline of Communism in Russia* (New York, 1946), chapters 7–9.

identities in the Soviet context. Amir Weiner has given a fascinating picture of the working out of a Soviet Ukrainian identity in the course of the "liberation struggle" and the settling of post-collaboration scores in Ukraine.[39] After a brief wartime (and even briefer postwar) expansion of the permissible expressions of Ukrainian identity and patriotism, the Stalinist state reinforced anew the relationship of subordination and a more or less strictly regional identity, a Soviet version of Little Russian loyalty toward imperial Russia.

By way of conclusion, the relationship between Russian and Ukrainian identities, as well as that between Russians and Ukrainians—leaving aside the question of how to identify the populations in the Soviet context—stood at the heart of larger processes of state formation and deformation, inter-state competition, late imperial and Stalinist politics and economic development, and important transformations of imperial and Soviet ideology. These processes offer very revealing glimpses of the larger adjustments of state and society that took place during the first half of the twentieth century.

Nationality/ethnicity and class identities came to the fore whenever the state was in crisis, with reinforcement from international ideologies, particularly the several varieties of Marxism and the doctrines of national self-determination and nationalism generally, and from conscious state policies and their often unintended consequences. With the reassertion of the centralized state, boundaries of identities were more rigidly realigned and hierarchies of nation, class, and gender reconstructed.

---

39. Amir, *Making Sense of War*.

Marc Raeff

Afterword

In October 1981 a conference convened in Hamilton, Ontario, to examine a number of issues that were a point of contention between Ukrainian and Russian scholars (similarly focused conferences considered Ukrainian-Polish and Ukrainian-Jewish "encounters"). The only conclusion that could be, and was, reasonably reached at the end of the session was that a dialogue had been initiated and should be continued. And obviously it was, witness the quickening of pace in Ukrainian studies and the publication of many works (of various length and merit) on history and culture on the territory of Ukraine. With the dissolution of the Soviet Union it became apparent that there was a need to clarify the terms of scholarly discourse, especially to come to grips with the notion of national identity as a constituent element of historical and socio-cultural reality. The conference of 1994—and subsequent ones—in both the United States and Germany endeavored to address the issue.

As evidenced by the papers collected in the present volume, the search for or identification of a Russian national identity or consciousness occupied but a subordinate place in the proceedings. In fact, only Professor Bushkovitch addresses the issue directly (and Professor Kappeler by implication). His findings, reinforced by Professor Yekelchyk, make it clear that Russia's identity was essentially statist and dynastic, that is, it identified nationality with a political system—whether traditional monarchist or a modernist Soviet and ideocratic one (the latter well described by Stanislav Kulchytsky). Fair enough, but the question then arises as to what is meant by statist and dynastic. Loyalty to a dynasty (or monarchic state) may occur in a unitary polity (witness ancien-régime France) as well as in a confederacy based on personal union (Austria-Hungary, Spain). In other terms, it may imply "national" uniformity and centralization or multicultural autonomy and federalism. In the case of Russia, both imperial and Soviet, one thinks of Isaiah Berlin's description of Leo Tolstoy wishing to be a pluralist "fox," while in actuality he was a "hedgehog" knowing only one thing. Similarly, the Russian elites (cultural and political) fancied themselves "foxes" supporting cultural pluralism, when in fact they were "hedgehogs" firmly defending integration into a uniform "all-Russian" political culture. As the dominant ethnic and political nation, the Russians felt little need to pay much attention to other peoples in their state—although, on occasion, some recognition was given to the special cases presented by Poland and Finland.

Quite clearly, this state of affairs not only created tensions and conflicts with other nations, both within and beyond the borders of the empire/Soviet Union, but also denied the importance of regional differences among the Great Russians themselves. Indeed, Russian historiography practically ignores regional history and local peculiarities. While much work has gone into identifying, collecting, and publishing local sources (both medieval and modern), these have not been analyzed and synthesized into regional histories. A prime task for historians, sociologists and scholars of literature, the arts, and culture is to create a body of writing that will enable us to study and understand the many elements that constituted Russia. Siberia's *oblastnichestvo* (regional loyalty), rudely interrupted by the Soviets, could be both a model and an inspiration in this regard.

Among the benefits that such a development may bring is the elimination of "negative definitions" of national identity on the part of Ukrainians and others—i.e., identification in terms of stark opposition to and rejection of "Russia" (defined in global and essentialist terms). What is needed is an energetic effort to define actual individual traits that make up the identity of a nation or ethnic group. I mention this because most of the contributions concerned with Ukrainian identity in this volume deal with it in terms of an opposition to (if not outright enmity or hatred of) an assumed imperial and colonial Russian essence. As a first step on the way to self-definition, this is perfectly natural, but one would hope that it will quickly lead to serious exploration and identification of those elements that go into the making of Ukraine's national personality, so that we may speak of "Ukrainianness" as we do apropos the notions of Frenchness, Englishness, and the like. Only such a development would contribute to a "reconciliation" and elimination of angry confrontational stances between Ukrainians and Russians, or any other nationality in the former empire and Soviet Union.

No doubt the task is fraught with many difficulties. The first arises from the question as to whether or not we can see Ukrainian identity as a single and uniform entity in time and space. Several contributions to the present collection allude, without going into specifics, to important differences between the eastern and western regions of Ukraine. This should not come as a surprise after reading the chapters dealing with the seventeenth century. Ukraine has forever been torn between the pull of the northeast (Moscow) and the northwest (Poland-Lithuania), not to speak of the powerful impact of a European-type "modernization" carried out through Russia's agency, although the latter was fostered by impulses originating in seventeenth-century Ukrainian political, ecclesiastical, and cultural circumstances. We thus have here another scholarly agenda: to identify and analyze the dynamic cultural elements that have gone into the making of "a" or "the" Ukrainian identity.

Quite clearly, then, in order to tease out a Ukrainian identity and its mutations through time and space, it is necessary to investigate closely the relations between Ukrainians (however defined) to the many "others" that contributed to this identity. In the first place, we have their historical neighbors: Muscovy/Russia, Poland, Lithuania, Austria, Hungary, Crimea, and Turkey. But of course we should not forget the several "others" in their midst—Jews, Gypsies, Germans, and the numerous "immigrants" from within the empire (Russian service nobles and peasants, Caucasian and European entrepreneurs and traders, etc.). Nor should the various religious groups and sects be forgotten, even though their separateness may owe nothing to ethnic, linguistic, or social distinctiveness. In the process of this research, too, the regional differentiations, not to speak of socio-cultural diversities, may become more apparent and contribute to a sophisticated understanding and accurate image of Ukrainian reality, past and present.

Professor Worobec suggests a novel approach to that end: namely, comparative anthropological studies of the peasantry and their culture on Russian and Ukrainian territories. One can only welcome the suggestion, while avoiding several possible pitfalls: the first, and most obvious, is to ascribe *essential* differences to superficial and accidental features of peasant behavior and equipment that are the fortuitous results of historical and geographical accidents. More serious, and harder to come to grips with, is the ability or willingness of peasants to identify themselves in terms of concepts and categories alien to their normal experience, whatever their ethnic make-up. Last, but not least, is the ever-present fact of interethnic and intercultural mixing. This was particularly true of imperial Russian society, whose "porousness" (E. K. Wirtschafter) gave rise not only to shifting boundaries between social and juridical categories, but also to a great deal of geographic mobility (and hence familial and ethno-racial mixing). In Soviet times this porousness was enhanced by the brutality of an ideology-driven government's efforts at social engineering. That our categories or concepts of national identity may not be helpful, perhaps not even applicable, is underscored by Professor Ilnytzkyj when he writes that at the turn of the century Ukrainian intellectuals deliberately embraced modernism for the sake of a nationalist agenda in order to counteract the uniformist, Russificatory tendency of populism.

One last point, already adumbrated in the proceedings of the previous conference: it is not only people and their circumstances that change over time, but also their mental equipment, their ways of thinking. Nationalism in its "original" meaning is a phenomenon of the nineteenth century, usually—albeit far from always—arising in conjunction with individualism and political liberalism. In the course of the twentieth century, the notion acquired a new content and "valence" through the inclusion of biological (racist) concepts; it also became more aggressive and intolerant. Whether this evolution may be reversed or negated is more than doubtful. In any case, it imposes upon us the obligation, when we speak of national identity, to make it unambiguously clear with what content we endow the term. This should not only help to prevent the drawing of deplorable conclusions, but also impart greater realism to our search for as accurate a picture of the past as possible, as well as a better understanding of the present. And let us guard against the siren call and hubris of wanting to predict and shape the future. Scholarship deals with what has happened and what is: prophecy is quite beyond its ken.

Contributors

OLGA ANDRIEWSKY is an associate professor of history at Trent University. She is the author of a forthcoming book, "The Politics of National Identity: The Ukrainian Question in Russia, 1900–1914."

PAUL BUSHKOVITCH is a professor of history at Yale University. He is the author of *Religion and Society in Russia: The Sixteenth and Seventeenth Centuries* (1992) and *Peter the Great: The Struggle for Power, 1671–1725* (2001).

DAVID A. FRICK is a professor of Slavic Languages and Literatures at the University of California, Berkeley. He is the author of *Polish Sacred Philology in the Reformation and the Counter-Reformation* (1989) and *Meletij Smotryc'kyj* (1995). He is currently at work on a study of peoples and confessions in seventeenth-century Vilnius.

GEORGE G. GRABOWICZ is the Dmytro Čyževs'kyj Professor of Ukrainian Literature at Harvard University and editor in chief of *Krytyka* (Kyiv). His publications include *The Poet as Mythmaker: A Study of Symbolic Meaning in Taras Ševčenko* (1982), *Do istoriï ukraïns'koï literatury* (Toward a History of Ukrainian Literature, 1997), and *Shevchenko, iakoho ne znaiemo* (The Shevchenko We Do Not Know, 2000).

OLEH S. ILNYTZKYJ is a professor in the Department of Modern Languages and Cultural Studies at the University of Alberta, where he teaches Ukrainian language and literature. His publications include *Ukrainian Futurism, 1914–1930: An Historical and Critical Study* (1997) and a four-volume *Concordance to the Poetic Works of Taras Shevchenko* (2001), compiled and edited with George Hawrysch.

ANDREAS KAPPELER is a professor of East European history at the University of Vienna. His publications include *The Russian Empire: A Multiethnic History* (2001; German ed. 1992), *Kleine Geschichte der Ukraine* (2d ed., 2000), and *Russische Geschichte* (2d ed., 2000).

ZENON E. KOHUT is director of the Canadian Institute of Ukrainian Studies, University of Alberta. He is the author of numerous works on early modern Ukraine, Ukrainian historiography, and the development of Ukrainian identity, including *Russian Centralism and Ukrainian Autonomy: Imperial Absorption of the Hetmanate* (1988; revised Ukrainian version, 1996).

STANISLAV KULCHYTSKY is deputy director of the Institute of the History of Ukraine, National Academy of Sciences of Ukraine in Kyiv. He is the author of numerous monographs, textbooks, articles, and chapters in edited collections on the twentieth-century history of Ukraine. His books include *Tsina "Velykoho perelomu"* (The Cost of the "Great Break," 1991); *Komunizm v Ukraïni: Pershe desiatyrichchia (1919–1928)* (Communism in Ukraine: The First Decade, 1919–1928, 1996); and *Ukraïna mizh dvoma viinamy (1921–1939 rr.)* (Ukraine between the Wars, 1921–1939, 1999).

DIETER POHL is a research fellow at the Institut für Zeitgeschichte in Munich. He has published studies of Nazi crimes and occupation policy, the postwar legal system in East Germany, and Ukrainian history of the 1930s and 1940s.

MARC RAEFF, Bakhmeteff Professor Emeritus of Russian Studies at Columbia University, has published widely in the field of Russian and European history from the seventeenth to the twentieth century.

YURI SHAPOVAL is head of the Historical Political Studies Center at the Institute of Political and Ethnonational Studies, National Academy of Sciences of Ukraine in Kyiv. He is the author or editor of more than a dozen books and documentary collections on the Stalin period in Ukraine, including *Ukraïna 20–50-kh rokiv: Storinky nenapysanoï istoriï* (Ukraine, 1920s–1950s: Pages of an Unwritten History, 1993); *Liudyna i systema* (Man and System, 1994); (with Volodymyr Prystaiko and Vadym Zolotar'ov) *ChK-GPU-NKVD v Ukraïni* (The Cheka-GPU-NKVD in Ukraine, 1997) and *Ukraïna XX stolittia: Osoby ta podiï v konteksti vazhkoï istoriï* (Twentieth-Century Ukraine: People and Events in the Context of a Difficult History, 2001).

FRANK E. SYSYN is director of the Peter Jacyk Centre for Ukrainian Historical Research at the Canadian Institute of Ukrainian Studies, University of Alberta, and editor in chief of the Hrushevsky Translation Project. A specialist in Ukrainian and Polish history, he is the author of *Between Poland and the Ukraine: The Dilemma of Adam Kysil,*

1600–1653 (1985) and studies on the Khmelnytsky Uprising and the Hetmanate, Ukrainian historiography, and early modern Ukrainian political culture.

HANS-JOACHIM TORKE (1938–2000) was a professor of Russian and East European history at the Free University of Berlin. His publications include books on the Russian bureaucracy in the first half of the nineteenth century and on state and society in seventeenth-century Muscovy, as well as articles on Russian absolutism and on Russian and Soviet historiography. He was a coeditor of *Ukraine and Russia in Their Historical Encounter* (1992).

MARK VON HAGEN is an associate professor of Russian, Ukrainian, and Eurasian history at Columbia University. He is the author of *Soldiers in the Proletarian Dictatorship: The Red Army and the Soviet Socialist State, 1917–1930* (1990) and coeditor (with Karen Barkey) of *After Empire: Multiethnic Societies and Nation-Building. The Soviet Union and the Russian, Ottoman, and Habsburg Empires* (1997).

CHRISTINE D. WOROBEC is a professor of Russian history at Northern Illinois University and author of *Peasant Russia: Family and Community in the Post-Emancipation Period* (1991) and *Possessed: Women, Witches, and Demons in Imperial Russia* (2001).

SERHY YEKELCHYK, is an assistant professor of history and Slavonic studies at the University of Victoria. He is the author of several studies of Ukrainian nation building and Russo-Ukrainian relations during the late nineteenth and twentieth centuries and of a forthcoming book, *Stalin's Empire of Memory: Russian-Ukrainian Relations in Soviet Historical Imagination.*

VIKTOR M. ZHIVOV is a professor in the Department of Slavic Languages and Literatures, University of California at Berkeley, and deputy director of the Institute of the Russian Language, Russian Academy of Sciences. His publications include *Sviatost': Kratkii slovar' agiograficheskikh terminov* (Holiness: A Compact Dictionary of Hagiographic Terms, 1994), *Iazyk i kul'tura v Rossii XVIII veka* (Language and Culture in Eighteenth-Century Russia, 1996), and *Razyskaniia v oblasti istorii i predystorii russkoi kul'tury* (Studies in the History and Prehistory of Russian Culture, 2002).